Language Processing and Grammars

Studies in Language Companion Series (SLCS)

This series has been established as a companion series to the periodical *Studies in Language.*

For an overview of all books published in this series, please see *http://benjamins.com/catalog/slcs*

Volume 150

Language Processing and Grammars. The role of functionally oriented computational models
Edited by Brian Nolan and Carlos Periñán-Pascual

Language Processing and Grammars

The role of functionally oriented computational models

Edited by

Brian Nolan
Institute of Technology Blanchardstown Dublin

Carlos Periñán-Pascual
Universidad Politécnica de Valencia

John Benjamins Publishing Company
Amsterdam / Philadelphia

Library of Congress Cataloging-in-Publication Data

Language processing and grammars : the role of functionally oriented computational models / Edited by Brian Nolan, Carlos Periñán-Pascual.

p. cm. (Studies in Language Companion Series, ISSN 0165-7763 ; v. 150)

Includes bibliographical references.

1. Natural language processing (Computer science) 2. Functionalism (Linguistics) 3. Generative grammar. 4. Computational linguistics. I. Nolan, Brian, 1952- II. Periñán Pascual, Carlos.

P98.L357 2014

006.3'5--dc23 2013047822

ISBN 978 90 272 5915 8 (Hb ; alk. paper)

ISBN 978 90 272 7064 1 (Eb)

John Benjamins Publishing Co. · P.O. Box 36224 · 1020 ME Amsterdam · The Netherlands

John Benjamins North America · P.O. Box 27519 · Philadelphia PA 19118-0519 · USA

Table of contents

Introduction 1
Brian Nolan and Carlos Periñán-Pascual

From the extraction of continuous features in parallel texts to visual analytics of heterogeneous areal-typological datasets 13
Thomas Mayer, Bernhard Wälchli, Christian Rohrdantz and Michael Hund

Lexical-syntactic analysis model of Spanish multi-word expressions 39
Jorge Antonio Leoni de León

Three-place predicates in RRG: A computational approach 79
Judith Gottschalk

A Role and Reference Grammar parser for German 105
Elke Diedrichsen

Extending a lexicalist functional grammar through speech acts, constructions and conversational software agents 143
Brian Nolan

The implementation of the CLS constructor in ARTEMIS 165
Carlos Periñán-Pascual and Francisco Arcas-Túnez

FrameNet and FunGramKB: A comparison of two computational resources for semantic knowledge representation 197
Alba Luzondo-Oyón and Rocío Jiménez-Briones

Exploring the thematic-frame mapping in FunGramKB 233
Fátima Guerra García and Elena Sacramento Lechado

FunGramKB term extractor: A tool for building terminological ontologies from specialised corpora 251
Ángel Felices-Lago and Pedro Ureña Gómez-Moreno

Deep semantic representation in a domain-specific ontology:
Linking EcoLexicon to FunGramKB 271
Antonio San Martín and Pamela Faber

A functional and constructional approach for specialized knowledge resources 297
Beatriz Sánchez-Cárdenas and Pamela Faber

Applying the lexical constructional model to ontology building 313
Elena Montiel-Ponsoda and Guadalupe Aguado de Cea

The interaction of non-linguistic and linguistic knowledge in FunGramKB 339
Fátima Guerra García

Low-level situational cognitive models within the Lexical Constructional
Model and their computational implementation in FunGramKB 367
Francisco José Ruiz de Mendoza Ibáñez

Index 391

Introduction

Brian Nolan and Carlos Periñán-Pascual

This book examines recent and current work in the use of functional, cognitive and constructional approaches to the computational modelling of language and grammars. We examine in particular computational models that are linguistically motivated and that deal with problems at the interfaces between concept, semantics, lexicon, syntax and morphology, including language processing and grammar.

The editors are part of a European group of linguists, computational linguists and computer scientists who, since the 2004 Role and Reference Grammar (RRG) International Conference (Nolan 2004) in Dublin (and more recently since hosting the Societas Linguistica Europaea (SLE) workshops on *Functionally motivated computational approaches to models of language and grammar* in Logroño, Spain 2011 and Stockholm, Sweden 2012) have formulated computational proposals in different areas concerned with the lexicon and ontologies, and the computational processing of the syntax, morphology and semantics of a variety of languages. Functionally oriented models of grammar have been applied to computational linguistic **projects** that are quite diverse as we can see from the chapters in this volume.

The main **topics and research issues** of the present work include the following:

- Computational applications (information mining and complex data visualisation) to support typological linguistic analysis
- The architecture of the lexicon
- Motivating the linking system between semantics, lexicon and morphosyntax
- The deployment of functional models in parse and generation across the interfaces
- Interpretation of the linguistic model into an algorithm specification
- Issues for the layered structure of the clause, NP and word
- Devising an architecture for integrating speech acts, agents and dialogue systems
- Complexity issues, language processing and computational adequacy
- Concept formation and the role of ontologies in meaning construction

In sum, the **aim** of this book is to present current research on functionally oriented computational models of grammar, language processing and linguistics, and thereby to offer a forum for discussion and critical evaluation of the full gamut of research projects concerned with a broadly functional computational linguistics and that also contributes to our understanding of languages in a functionally oriented way. We would like to present a functional and cognitive linguistic, computational research agenda.

To us, the need for a book that foregrounds the role of role of functionally oriented computational models and approaches to linguistic analysis is very clear. Indeed, today, a professional linguist can be found working in many areas of knowledge and skills using strategies and techniques that, frankly, did not exist a generation ago. These include such linguistically relevant areas as

- Data, text and internet mining for linguistic purposes
- Building and searching of online digital corpora
- Information visualisation of complex linguistic data
- Machine translation and construction of lexicon-based interlingua
- Implementing constructions as grammatical objects in software
- Dialogue systems, conversational agents and avatars.
- Meaning construction, digital ontologies and computational semantics
- The discovery and deployment of design patterns in ontologies across specialised domains
- Cognitive modelling using software testbeds
- Ontological and knowledge engineering

Additionally, with the rise of the Semantic Web and the realisation that we live in a globalised, multicultural and multilingual world, the need for language aware software applications that are grounded in a robust linguistic model, with a robust model of semantics, is important and critical to our society. Added to this is the ubiquity of the Internet as a global phenomenon. It is the primary communications channel across the world that facilitates the immediate flow of multilingual information, this essential need is even more pressing. Therefore, there is an immediate need for real-time access to many languages. The multicultural and multilingual communities in Europe, plus the migration of peoples and communities in today's world, has re-enforced the urgent need for a shared understanding of linguistic information relevant and important to different peoples, especially in a multicultural and diversity rich Europe and beyond. The integration of peoples and communities with common access to information is not available to the extent that is desirable. This represents an information gap that can be addressed by the strategic application of functionally oriented computational linguistics, Information Technology, the Internet and language aware applications.

Linguistic research is concerned with the many dimensions of language (ontological, lexicon and grammatical) including what it is that constitutes knowledge of language and the architecture of the language system. This will include language as a cognitive system, the computational and logical modelling of this system, and the study of the interfaces between its components. Linguists are also interested in the manner in which language is acquired and along with the definition of the cognitive processes of language acquisition. Linguists are additionally concerned with the linguistic processes underlying language production, perception and interpretation under varying circumstances and situations.

In our work we look for the generalisations that are applicable across all natural languages. That is, we look to identify the nature of the computational system of human language in all its richness and complexity. In other words, as linguists we aim at explicating that deeper understanding of the constraints and forces that shape human languages. To achieve this we need to go beyond descriptive, explanatory and typological adequacy to examining the dimensions of computational adequacy, within our functional perspective, to arrive at an understanding of the architecture of the language system and knowledge of its main components and interfaces, for example between lexicon, semantics and syntax.

There are very many **approaches to the study of language** as a complex human system. Some linguists view language as an independent system with a particular architecture and illustrate the relationships between the various parts of that system and its interfaces across ontological concept formation, semantics and the lexicon, morphology, syntax, and pragmatics. Other scholars are interested in the processes of language acquisition and cognition. What is beyond dispute is that language is a window into the cognitive abilities of people and, as such, is often studied in order to understand the nature of the mind that produces it.

As functional linguists, we use testable models to help us make sense of this. We model language by providing an abstract representation of its central characteristics, a functional grammar. Linguists cannot make any progress without using models that are testable. Of course, given the richness of opinion about linguistic adequacy, there are many diverging ideas about which models are appropriate and relevant.

We have constrained the **scope of this work** to models within a broad functional perspective. Nonetheless, we need a more thorough understanding of the architecture of the language subsystems and how the different components of grammar and the systems of use interact. That is, we need more information on the computational dimension. Such understanding cannot be achieved without robust in-depth study of concept formation, lexicon, morphology, syntax, semantics and pragmatics.

Computational modelling has also been used to simulate how the brain processes language when it produces concepts that are syntactically realised in well-formed clauses. Computer models have been used to address several questions in parsing as well as how speech information is used for higher-level processes, such as word recognition (Nolan 2004; Ayres & Nolan 2006; Nolan & Salem 2011; Nolan 2011, Nolan, Mairal & Perniñan 2009) As a useful metaphor, the conception of human beings as information processing systems underlies the cognitive sciences. This metaphor allows researchers to study natural and artificial intelligence, including the interactions between the two, from a coherent theoretical perspective. This has changed the outlook of linguistics by establishing close connections with the computer sciences, leading to computational linguistics, and cognitive science.

The recent efforts to link linguistics and other cognitive domains hold considerable promise for the understanding of the cognitive faculties involved in language and it does not entail a reduction of linguistics to other disciplines. It depends on one's position on the question whether mental entities like concepts are reducible to the algorithm or system that produces them. There is viable research for linguistics in connecting linguistic theory with psychology, mathematics and computer science. Many studies, including a number of contributions to this volume, are examples of that fact.

Many would agree that our linguistic behaviour can be described in terms of rules and principle But, as one looks at the significant details of what this actually means we fins a number of important questions and considerations. What does it mean, for example, for ones mind to be engaged in a specific cognitive function when forming a concept? Does the (module for a particular) cognitive function have to be domain specific, mandatory, fast and informationally encapsulated? How do we parse language when we hear it and how do we unpack the clause so quickly? What about parsing of visual-gestural sign languages? When we use language naturally, do we deploy knowledge from outside the direct linguistic input? This question has been the topic of much debate in recent linguistic inquiry and has a hidden additional question embedded within it: Is language informationally encapsulated? If it is, we must assume that ontological knowledge of our world (possibly, as constrained by our cultural considerations), hearer's expectations, speaker's intentions etc. do not play a role in the processing and production of language. Can we assume that only particular aspects of language, for example, grammatical processing, are informationally encapsulated. Is language just a part of a unified cognitive system?

These questions have a particular relevance when, as in this book, we describe the nature of the linguistic system with respect to its computational dimensions from a functional perspective. We will also find that by employing computational linguistic applications, for example, for visualisation of complex linguistic information that we gain new knowledge about the spread and interrelationships between languages, with an immediate benefit to those scholars working within functional models of grammar and functional typology.

The **theoretical framework** that the majority (but not all) of the book's authors work in is Role and Reference Grammar (RRG), a model of grammar (Van Valin 2005; Nolan 2012, 2013; Nolan & Diedrichsen 2013) that posits a direct mapping between the semantic representation of a sentence and its syntactic representation. The theory allows a sentence in a specific language to be described in terms of its logical structure and grammatical procedures. RRG creates a linking relationship between syntax and semantics, and can account for how semantic representations are mapped into syntactic representations. The languages that have undergone a computational treatment in RRG have included English, Arabic (Nolan & Salem 2009, 2011) and Spanish, and others. Sign Languages (Murtagh 2011ab), as visual gestural languages, pose interesting problems for both functional models of grammar (Leeson & Nolan 2008) and computational models of these languages. A consequence of this computational work has been the enrichment of the theoretical elements of the RRG theory, as a functional model, especially in its semantics and lexical underpinnings where they connect with concepts, and the building of frame based applications in software that demonstrate its viability in natural language processing. Furthermore, this computational work provides compelling evidence that functional approaches to grammar have a positive and crucial role to play in natural language processing. We claim that a functional approach to grammar delivers a credible and realistic linguistic model to underpin these kinds of NLP applications, and also in applications within functional typology. RRG is a monostratal theory, positing only one level of syntactic representation, the actual form of the sentence and its linking algorithm can work in both directions from syntactic representation to semantic representation, or vice versa. In RRG, semantic decomposition of predicates and their semantic argument structures are represented as logical structures. The lexicon in RRG takes the position that lexical entries for verbs should contain unique information only, with as much information as possible derived from general lexical rules. The main features of RRG are the use of lexical decomposition, based upon predicate semantics, an analysis of clause structure and the use of a set of thematic roles organized into a hierarchy in which the highest-ranking roles are 'Actor' (for the most active participant) and 'Undergoer'. The RRG model creates a relationship between syntax and semantics and can account for how semantic representations are mapped into syntactic representations. RRG also accounts for the very different process of mapping syntactic representations to semantic representations. Of the two directions, syntactic representation to semantic representation is the more difficult since it involves interpreting the morphosyntactic form of a sentence and inferring the semantic functions of the sentence from it. Accordingly, the linking rules must refer to the morphosyntactic features of the sentence.

One question however remains; why should a grammar deal with linking from syntax to semantics at all. Should not simply specifying the possible realizations of a particular semantic representation suffice? The answer of course is 'no'. Functional linguists of all persuasions refute this using the argument that theories of linguistic structure should be directly relatable to testable theories of language production and comprehension. Computational models assist in this process. Based on our experience to date with functionally oriented computational models of grammar, we can verify that functional models of grammar, and RRG in particular, are very suitable as a basis for computational implementation in software in this regard. Functionally oriented computational models of grammar serve as a rich testing ground for the linguistic theories.

This book is a collection of papers, characterising current research at the intersection of leading edge computer science and linguistics with an interesting collection of languages by scholars across the world, that place emphasis on a functional linguistic perspective within their work. The **challenges of the book** are to place functionally oriented computational models into a more prominent perspective and to integrate current thinking regarding the role that computational thinking and applications can play into the functional framework. RRG as a functional grammar is strongly lexicalist with a robust linking algorithm mediating the interface between semantics, lexicon and syntax. RRG makes strong claims regarding descriptive and typological adequacy (Van Valin & LaPolla 1997, Van Valin 2005, Butler 2003a and 2003b, Butler 2009: 24; Butler & Arista 2009).

The book will serve the scholarly community as a reference work. As we indicated earlier, there is a growing awareness of the significance of functionally oriented computational models in grammar in assisting our understanding of the world's languages. Because of this, there is a need for a scholarly book that creates a well-motivated connection between the work in computer science, computational linguistics and functional linguistics. This edited volume will contribute to this awareness, offering a collection of papers dealing with different aspects of functionally oriented computational models in grammar in a range of related and unrelated topics. As a result, this volume represents the first instance of these important discourse, concept formation, meaning construction and various syntax-related phenomena are characterised through the use of information technology and computing science within a functional linguistic perspective. Further, this volume will contribute towards providing a comprehensive overview of these urgent and increasingly important domains.

Uniquely, the book serves to motivate a structured connection between research in computer science, computational linguistics and functional linguistics. Each chapter provides an analysis of elements of a grammar of the language under study with an emphasis on the interfaces between syntax, semantics, lexicon and constructions, including speech act constructions. Accordingly, the book provides a context for an integrated view of the role of computational strategies, techniques, models and approaches within the functionalist linguistic theory and in the grammars of several of the worlds languages. The book raises and addresses important challenges for functional, constructional and computational approaches to understanding language within the broad functionalist framework. This work will serve to create a bridge between the world of the various functional linguistics models, computer science, computational linguistics, such that present day researchers can have a principled and motivated position within a theory of a modern functional grammar, and be grounded in robust real analyses of real languages by scholars who are experts in these languages. The work will be of interest to scholars of linguistics, computer scientists, computational linguist, researchers and postgraduate students internationally who work at the interfaces between syntax, semantics and the lexicon and computing.

The **structure of the book** is as follows:

The first chapter, by Mayer et al, shows that functionally motivated procedural approaches may help to automatically extract typological features from texts. They demonstrate that using strategies and techniques from visual analytics allows for detecting patterns or regularities in automatically extracted features. At the heart of their approach lies an extended sunburst visualization and an advantage of this computational technique is that it enables a cross-comparison of a very large number of features within the context of language genealogy and areal information. This is an approach that is of immediate benefit to those scholars working in functional typology, where the visualizations of the extracted features reveal interesting insights. In the second chapter, De Leon analyses the lexical status and the syntactic phenomena of multi-word expressions by first proposing a typology of phraseological units and employing a formal system in the description of their characteristics, and allows for their collection and identification.

The computational adequacy of a functional model of grammar, RRG, is the concern of Gottschalk, in our second chapter. In her view, the standard linking algorithm of RRG cannot adequately account for variable undergoer linking in English three-place predicates and cannot therefore be said to be computationally adequate. Her proposal is to use an alternative approach based on constructional schemas. In Gottschalk's approach semantic macroroles are epiphenomenal and are replaced by thematic relations to develop a computable account to RRG.

Diedrichsen also works with RRG. In the fourth chapter she describes a java based sentence parser for German that implements the linking system of RRG from syntax to semantics. RRG includes a strong theory of the lexicon and also provides a bidirectional-linking algorithm for the linking of syntactic arguments with semantic functions. This RRG parser for German employs the concept of a CONSTRUCTION as a language-specific structural pattern to guide its operation over the 'Bracket Structure' of the German clause. In this, one component of the predicate, mostly the finite verb, is realised in an early position in the sentence and therefore forms the "left bracket", whereas the more meaningful part of the predicate, mostly the infinite predicate, appears at the end of the sentence and forms the "right bracket". Inside these brackets, the main information of the sentence is placed in an order that reflects the information structure. The software will accept an input sentence in German from the user through a Java Swing graphical user interface and parses that sentence into its respective tokens using the Java native string processing capability. Each token is checked to determine its lexical category and the morphological marking of each token is unpacked for its feature set. The result of the parse displays the structural representation of the clause and some grammatical features like tense in an RRG notation. The parser is able to recognise and parse the eight construction types of the Standard German clause.

This paper by Nolan in the fifth chapter advances a model of conversational agents in a computational framework that builds on the notion of speech act performatives from discourse based on a computational implementation of RRG. The language specific elements of the intelligent conversational agents paradigm is described. A view is proposed in which a conversational agent has 'internal' and 'external' models to support the speech acts. The internal model of the agent is concerned with the internal state of the agent, based upon the intersection at any given time on the agent's internal <u>b</u>eliefs, <u>d</u>esires, and <u>i</u>ntentions, known as BDI states. The external model of the agent is composed of an interaction model with its world (human and other agent). The software agent has a language model related to its interaction model to support bi-directional communication in human language through speech acts in an RRG perspective.

The benefits of interlingua-based systems in multilingual settings is highlighted by Periñán-Pascual and Arcas-Túnez in the sixth chapter. As we have seen in other chapters, this work is also based on an implementation of RRG in software. The authors' goal is to describe the various stages in the development of one of the first computational systems to employ a lexico-conceptual knowledge base to generate the logical structure of sentences. In their software model, they convert the logical structure of a clause into an ontology-grounded representation of sentential meaning. Through this work, they convincingly demonstrate that constructional schemata should become the cornerstone of the syntax-semantics interface in a computationally adequate model of Role and Reference Grammar.

FrameNet is a lexical resource for English whose objective is to document the range of semantic and syntactic combinatory possibilities of each sense of a word. This seventh chapter compares FrameNet with a Functional Grammar Knowledge Base knowledge base called FunGramKB, a multipurpose lexico-conceptual base for Natural Language Processing (NLP) systems. The authors address their similarities and differences by focusing on the following issues: (1) methodology; (2) information at the lexical and conceptual levels; (3) relations between frames and concepts; (4) information management; and (5) multilingualism. As an important case study, they analyze how the verb *dry* is represented in each knowledge base as a suite of inter-related frames and concepts.

The objective of the 8th chapter, by Guerra García and Sacramento Lechado, is to analyse how the interaction of deep and shallow semantics takes place within a full-fledged called FunGramKB. FunGramKB has three levels of knowledge representation (conceptual, lexical, and grammatical) such that conceptual modelling takes place within the Ontology. They discuss how the implementation of both the semantic and the constructional information of lexical units belong to the lexical level. While these processes are completely independent within the knowledge base, concept encoding and representation at the level of deep semantics and the semantic definitions of the predicates belonging to the lexicons of different languages are clearly intertwined. They analyse the relationship between ontology, lexicon, thematic frame and meaning postulate.

Ontological engineering, a new discipline, is the topic of the ninth chapter by Felices-Lago and Ureña Gómez-Moreno. This area is interesting as it intersects Artificial Intelligence, Machine Translation, and the Semantic Web. A key focus is the building of specialised ontologies, and concept hierarchies to formalise knowledge from expert areas of human activity such as medicine or law. This chapter focuses on the methodological aspects of the construction of specialised taxonomies in the framework of the FunGramKB knowledge base and discusses a corpus-based tool for the semi-automatic extraction of terms.

This chapter is one of two that operate with EcoLexicon, a frame-based visual thesaurus on the environment that is gradually evolving towards the status of a formal ontology. Here, San Martín and Faber discuss in the tenth chapter how information in a relational database is in the process of being linked to the ontological system of FunGramKB, a multipurpose knowledge base to facilitate the explication of specialized knowledge as an extension of general knowledge. This is represented within a domain-specific satellite ontology of a main general ontology. This chapter describes the linking process and how the general concepts in FunGramKB can be extended and reused in deep semantic representations in a domain-specific ontology. The second chapter concerning EcoLexicon, by Sánchez-Cárdenas and Faber in Chapter 11, describes how verbs are represented in EcoLexicon, Based on the hypothesis that human cognition organizes concepts in semantic categories, verbs can be said to be conceptually structured in lexical domains, Once the members of a lexical domain are established, the conceptual structure of the domain is mapped. While semantic categories are organized in a tangled hierarchy, the semantic relation of troponymy determines the hierarchical structure of verbal lexical domains. The authors' support their argumentation through an analysis of French and English verbs of movement in the field of Volcanology.

Knowledge acquisition strategies based on lexico-syntactic patterns are known to significantly contribute to the automatic identification of concepts and relations from texts. However, they have not yet been investigated as a strategy to represent that information in ontologies. In the 12th chapter, Montiel-Ponsoda and Aguado de Cea claim that this is one of the most critical steps in ontology building and propose to establish a correspondence between lexico-syntactic patterns, specifically verbal patterns representing taxonomic and meronymic relations, and their corresponding ontological structures represented by Ontology Design Patterns. An advantage of this is that it would lead to the automatic transformation of linguistic expressions into ontological structures. Additionally, it support domain experts in the development of ontologies. The authors' demonstrate how such a model permits the identification of an ontological structure(s) that better capture the meaning of predicates in an ontological resource. A key component in this is the use of Ontology Design Patterns.

This 13th chapter, by Guerra García, investigates how the non-linguistic knowledge stored in the conceptual level of FunGramKB interacts with the idiosyncratic linguistic knowledge stored in the lexical and the grammatical levels. Guerra García argues that the central module of this knowledge base, the Ontology, and the conceptual information stored for the concepts building its taxonomy may be a good source to predict certain aspects of the different lexicalization patterns of the lexical units that lexicalize those concepts and the constructions in which they are subsumed. This work critically explores how a verb-framed language like Spanish and a satellite-framed language like English draw different information from the same conceptual base.

The 14th and final chapter, by Ruiz de Mendoza Ibáñez, examines the assumption that word meaning cannot be understood independently of the vast repository of encyclopaedic knowledge to which it is linked, building on research in artificial intelligence (AI) and theoretical linguistics on schemata, schemas, scripts and scenarios. A frame, for example, is construed as a memory structure that people select when faced with a new situation. A frame is a kind of a data-structure for representing a stereotyped situation. Connected to each frame, one finds several kinds of information. Some of this information is about how to use the frame, some about what one can expect to happen next and some about what to do if these expectations are not confirmed. These constructs, which were originally created in order to organize and encapsulate world knowledge into a computer-readable format, went beyond the domain of AI and Natural Language Processing (NLP) into linguistics through discourse studies and Frame Semantics. Cognitive linguistic models extended many of these ideas into domains and Idealized Cognitive Models (ICMs). This paper argues for a revision of the notion of ICMs by drawing on the explanatory potential of the Lexical Constructional Model (LCM), a meaning construction model with a functional-cognitive grounding. The LCM provides a far-reaching typology of coherent schematizations of our experience based on two basic taxonomic criteria: (i) the situational versus non-situational nature of knowledge; and (ii) the degree of genericity of their elements. This paper provides a classification of the typology of cognitive models within the framework of the LCM and directly deals with the formal nature of low-level situational cognitive models while offering different parameters to enrich former descriptions (like scripts), In particular, this paper is concerned the representation of low-level situational cognitive models in the *cognicon* of FunGramKB.

References

Ayres, Anthony & Nolan, Brian. 2006. Voice activated command and control with Java-enabled speech recognition over Wifi. *Science of Computer Programming* 59(1–2): 109–126. <http://www.sciencedirect.com/science/article/pii/S0167642305000882>

Butler, Christopher, S. 2003a. *Structure and Function: A Guide to Three major Structural-Functional Theories*, Part-1 [Studies in Language Companion Series 63]. Amsterdam: John Benjamins.

Butler, Christopher, S. 2003b. *Structure and Function: A Guide to Three major Structural-Functional Theories*, Part-2 [Studies in Language Companion Series 64]. Amsterdam: John Benjamins.

Butler, Christopher, S. 2009. Criteria of adequacy in functional linguistics. *Folia Linguistia: Acta Societatis Linguisticae Europaeae* 42(1): 1–66.

Butler, Christopher S. & Arista, Javier Martín (eds). 2009. *Deconstructing Constructions* [Studies in Language Companion Series 107]. Amsterdam: John Benjamins.

Leeson, Lorraine & Nolan, Brian. 2008. Digital Deployment of the signs of Ireland corpus in elearning. Language Resources and Evaluation LREC2008 – 3rd Workshop on the Representation and Processing of Sign Languages: Construction and Exploitation of Sign Language Corpora, Marrakech, Morocco.

Murtagh, Irene. 2011a. Developing a linguistically motivated avatar for Irish Sign Language visualisation. Paper presented at the International Workshop on Sign Language Translation and Avatar Technology (SLTAT 2011), Dundee, Scotland. <http://vhg.cmp.uea.ac.uk/demo/SLTAT2011Dundee/7.pdf>

Murtagh, Irene. 2011b. Towards an RRG-enabled Sign Language Avatar. Paper presented at the International Conference on Role and Reference Grammar on 'Functional Linguistics: Grammar, Communication & Cognition'. Facultad de Letras, at the Pontificia Universidad Católica de Chile, Santiago de Chile.

Nolan, Brian (ed.). 2004. Linguistic theory and Practice: Description, implementation and processing. In *Proceedings of the RRG 2004 Dublin Conference.* <http://linguistics.buffalo.edu/people/faculty/vanvalin/rrg/RRG2004%20Book%20of%20Proceedings.pdf>

Nolan, Brian. 2011. Meaning construction and grammatical inflection in the layered structure of the Irish word: An RRG account of morphological constructions. In *New Perspectives in Role and Reference Grammar,* Wataru Nakamura (ed.), 64–103. Newcastle upon Tyne: Cambridge Scholars.

Nolan, Brian. 2012. *The Syntax of Irish: A Functional Account.* Sheffield: Equinox.

Nolan, Brian. 2013. Constructional polysemy and argument realisation with the Irish GET verb. In *Argument Structures in Flux: The Naples/Capri papers* [Studies in Language Companion Series 131], Johanna Barðdal, Michaela Cennamo & Elly van Gelderen (eds). Amsterdam: John Benjamins.

Nolan, Brian & Diedrichsen, Elke. 2013. *Linking Constructions into Functional Linguistics* [Studies in Language Companion Series 145]. Amsterdam: John Benjamins.

Nolan, Brian, Mairal-Uson, Ricardo & Periñán, Carlos. 2009. Natural language processing applications in an RRG framework. In *Proceedings of the 10th International Role and Reference Grammar Conference, University of California, Berkeley.*

Nolan, Brian & Salem, Yasser. 2011. UniArab: RRG Arabic-to-English machine translation. In *New perspectives in Role and Reference Grammar,* Wataru Nakamura (ed.), 312–346. Newcastle upon Tyne: Cambridge Scholars.

Van Valin, Jr., Robert. 2005. *Exploring the Syntax-Semantic Interface.* Cambridge: CUP.

Van Valin, Jr., Robert & LaPolla, Randy. 1997. *Syntax: Structure, Meaning, and Function.* Cambridge: CUP.

From the extraction of continuous features in parallel texts to visual analytics of heterogeneous areal-typological datasets

Thomas Mayer[†], Bernhard Wälchli[††], Christian Rohrdantz[†††] and Michael Hund[†††]
Philipps University Marburg, [††]Stockholm University and [†††]University of Konstanz

The aim of this paper is twofold. First, we show that functionally motivated procedural approaches may help to automatically extract typological features from texts. This idea is illustrated with measuring cross-linguistic variation in the domain of morphological typology based on parallel texts. Second, we demonstrate that the methodology developed in the field of visual analytics allows for detecting patterns or regularities in the automatically extracted features. At the heart of our approach lies an extended sunburst visualization, which enables a cross-comparison of a large number of features within the context of language genealogy and areal information. We provide evidence of the usefulness of the present approach with case studies where the visualizations of the extracted features reveal interesting insights.

1. Introduction

Typology in the sense of massive cross-linguistic comparison plays a major role in developing functional models of language (Croft 2003: 2). A major desideratum for functionally motivated computational approaches is to develop algorithmic approaches to typology, and this both for practical and theoretical reasons. Manual data extraction and analysis in typology is very costly. If some typological work can be automated or semi-automated, much more typological work can be done in shorter time, and if it can be automated, this also means that it can be replicated. However, algorithmic approaches to typology are also important from a theoretical perspective, since they presuppose a procedural text-to-structure modeling of language that is close to an acquisition perspective and treats material from all languages in exactly the same manner.

Basic elements of typologically oriented models to language and grammar are universals and hierarchies. In algorithmic terms, universals and hierarchies can be viewed procedurally rather than structurally and hence be turned into algorithms which may serve both for the acquisition of linguistic categories from corpora (learning) and for measuring cross-linguistic variation in texts (typology). This is well in line with emergent models of language structure (see, e.g., Hopper 1998; MacWhinney 1999). In particular, it is also compatible with findings from language acquisition research that categorization is guided by focusing attention on different semantic dimensions through the different formal distinctions made in a language, i.e., a tradeoff between formal distributional cues and semantic hypotheses (Bowerman 2007).

The compilation of manually edited typological databases is a laborious and time-consuming task, which has many drawbacks with respect to the comparability of the language data. It necessarily entails many gaps and forces typologists to consider only a subset of the available data. Most importantly, however, it does not guarantee that the typological features for cross-linguistic comparison have been analyzed in the same way for each language in the database. The automatic extraction of typological features from massively parallel texts (translations of the same text into a large number of languages; cf. Cysouw & Wälchli 2007) with the help of universally applicable procedures offers an alternative way to compile typological databases. The advantage of such an approach is that languages can be compared directly on the level of language use, with each language being analyzed by the same procedure, thus instantiating the postulate of some philosophers of language such as Fritz Mauthner and Ludwig von Wittgenstein that language is the same thing as language use. A further advantage is that a larger number of languages can be processed in a short period of time and with less data reduction. While it is common in typology to classify languages into a small number of discrete types as if language was parametric ("data reduction typology", see Wälchli 2009), algorithmic approaches based on texts allow for more precise measurements where features can be viewed as continuous scales rather than discrete types. This is particularly important for morphological typology where it is well known at least since Greenberg (1960) that features are continuous rather than discrete.

The availability of automatically extracted structural features for many languages allows for an extensive investigation of the relationship and areal distribution of features. Traditionally, linguistic typology explores the unity and diversity of language in terms of structural features and tries to explain their distribution on the basis of other structural features. More recently, however, cross-linguistic research has shown that linguistic diversity is not randomly distributed but that there are areal patterns. This reunited the three disciplines of linguistic typology, historical-comparative and areal linguistics in areal typology, whose aim is to investigate the typological, genealogical and areal properties in their interplay. This includes, among other things, the genealogical stability of features and their propensity for areal diffusion.

The sheer mass of language data and possible interactions that can be studied, however, calls for an additional component that renders potential patterns or regularities more easily accessible. The emerging field of visual analytics offers methods and techniques to employ our visual ability to understand complex interactions that might otherwise go unnoticed. Although linguists have successfully employed visualizations in some areas, e.g., spectrograms in phonetic research or brain imaging in neurolinguistics, there is enormous potential for more sophisticated graphical representations that make it possible to gain insights through an at-a-glance overview of large amounts of data. At the same time, an interactive visualization allows for a closer inspection of individual aspects of the data at several levels of detail. The basic idea is that an adequate mapping of relevant features to visual variables enhances the detection of potentially interesting patterns. In the realm of areal typology, this means the integration of information from the areal data space into the hierarchical (genealogical) data space in a single visualization.

In this paper, we present a two-step procedure for the cross-linguistic study of language features, with special reference to their areal and genealogical distribution. Its two main components are, in principle, totally independent of one another. The first component deals with the automatic extraction of structural features on the basis of parallel texts whereas the second component is about the visual representation of language features in their genealogical and geographical context. The visualization component can be used with any kinds of features, both automatically extracted or manually compiled. However, one reason why automatic extraction of features is particularly challenging for visual representation is its propensity to supply continuous rather than discrete data, which is more difficult to visualize.

We will exemplify the automatic extraction approach in the domain of morphological typology on the basis of parallel texts. Parallel texts have the advantage that they are an indirect key to semantics by way of distribution. Categories with highly similar distributions across parallel texts are most likely to be equivalent even though the huge cross-linguistic differences in morphological complexity are a challenge to statistical approaches of category identification. Parallel texts are thus an environment where it is possible to operationalize the notion of functional domain that has played a major role in many functional approaches to typology. According to Miestamo (2005: 293), a functional domain is "any domain of related (semantic or pragmatic) functions that (one or more) language(s) encode with the formal means they possess." Functional-domain typology examines the ways in which languages morpho-syntactically encode functional domains (see Givón 1981; Stassen 1985: 1–23; and Miestamo 2005: 26–50).

The visualization component contains several contributions to the visual analysis of language data. Most importantly, we propose to display the language genealogy as a so-called sunburst visualization (Stasko & Zhang 2000). The sunburst is a radial space-filling hierarchy visualization where the top-node of the hierarchy is represented in the center while nested rings and segments indicate the layers of the hierarchy. We complement this sunburst display with feature rings, which allow for the cross-comparison of several features at once, within the context of the language genealogy. These feature rings are plotted differently, depending on their data type (nominal, ordinal, quantitative). We also propose different ways to integrate areal information into the hierarchical data space.

The paper is structured as follows. Section 2 describes the automatic extraction of structural features based on parallel texts and how they compare to manually compiled features. In Section 3, we give a brief overview of the methodology developed in the field of visual analytics and how it can be applied to language data in general. After that, we focus on how genealogical and geo-spatial information can be integrated in a single visualization that allows for a cross-comparison of several language features at once (Section 4). The usefulness of the approach is illustrated with two case studies where the visualization of the automatically extracted features reveals interesting insights and suggests new hypotheses about the data (Section 5). Finally, Section 6 concludes the paper and suggests some avenues for future research.

2. Algorithmic typology

Linguistic universals can be understood as structures or as processes. Whereas a structural universal claims that there are constant structures attested in all languages (e.g., all languages have vowels), procedural universals refer to a universally applicable procedure that extracts different structures from different corpora in different languages. The result of such a procedure is both a typology (a measurement of features) and an analysis (e.g., the extraction of affixes from word forms).

A number of simple typological features can be extracted from parallel texts on the basis of procedural universals. This is especially true for morphological typology, the subfield of linguistic typology that deals with the degree of cross-linguistic variation in the internal structure of words (Greenberg 1960). A simple example of a universal in morphological typology is that any language with non-concatenative morphology (e.g., infixes, ablaut) also has concatenative morphology (stems, prefixes and suffixes only).[1] In procedural terms, this means that we first have to identify stems, prefixes and suffixes. If there are any such structures, we may proceed to look for internal inflection, infixes, stem alternations etc. (see also Wälchli 2012). In what follows, we will briefly discuss four families of values and how they can be automatically extracted on the basis of parallel texts, such as the New Testament: (1) degree of synthesis, (2) amount of prefixing and suffixing, (3) case and (4) synthetic vs. analytic negation marking. The extraction methods are all implemented in the programming language Python 2.

2.1 Degree of synthesis

Languages differ in the amount of information that is contained in their word forms. This variation is traditionally measured as the degree of synthesis of a language. Degree of synthesis can be extracted from parallel texts by indirect measurement (Juola

1. See, for instance, Greenberg's (1963) Universal 26: If a language has discontinuous affixes, it always has either prefixing or suffixing or both.

2008; Wälchli 2012). In parallel texts, languages with more complex morphology show more types of word forms with lower token frequency than languages with less complex morphology. That is, the same (parallel) text in an analytic language has more tokens (the total number of all words) and fewer types (the number of unique word forms). A simple measure for synthesis in parallel texts is thus the type-token ratio. An alternative is to use trigonometry in type-token diagrams (Popescu et al. 2009).

2.2 Amount of prefixing and suffixing

The simplest distinction in morphological markers is between prefixes and suffixes. With the help of parallel texts such a distinction can be inferred from the forms that belong to one lemma. Given the distribution of lexical elements is known for one language (by taking a lemmatized text), all corresponding parallel forms of a lemma can be extracted for the other languages with considerable accuracy. The extracted forms then can be split into an invariant part, which constitutes the stem or stems of the lemma, and variable parts, which in most cases mark prefixes and suffixes (depending on their position).

By way of illustration, consider the Koine Greek lemma *ἄνθρωπος* [*ánthrōpos*] 'human being', which occurs in its various inflected forms 553 times in the New Testament. The distributional approach yields the following corresponding "stems" (to the left of the colon) together with their word forms in the English, Hungarian, Zulu and Maori texts (to the right of the colon):[2]

English (American Standard translation)
man: man 336 man*'s* 9
men: men 186 men*'s* 3

Hungarian
ember: ember 170 ember*nek* 104 ember*ek* 85 ember*eknek* 36 ember*t* 40 ember*ektől* 16 ember*eket* 15 ember*i* 10 ember*ekkel* 5 ember*eknél* 5 ember*ből* 6 ember*ben* 5 ember*e* 4 ember*nél* 3 ember*ekhez* 3 ember*ekért* 2 ember*ekre* 2 ember*rel* 3 ember*re* 3 ember*t-é* 2 ember*ünk* 2 ember*en* 2 ember*hez* 3 ember*től* 2 ember*ért* 1 ember*ré* 1 ember*eken* 1 ember*be* 1 ember*eit* 1 ember*-é* 1 *gazda*ember*hez* 1 ember*em* 1 ember*ei* 1 ember*é* 1 *pásztor*ember*ek* 1 ember*ről* 1

Zulu
ntu: *umu*ntu 114 *yomu*ntu 89 *mu*ntu 64 *aba*ntu 62 *kuba*ntu 38 *kwaba*ntu 20 *baba*ntu 11 *yaba*ntu 9 *ngaba*ntu 12 *kumu*ntu 11 *nomu*ntu 9 *ba*ntu 7 *okwaba*ntu 4 *kunaba*ntu 5 *zaba*ntu 8 *ngokwaba*ntu 3 *ngumu*ntu 5 *ungumu*ntu 3 *naba*ntu 6 *komu*ntu 4 *laba*ntu 2

2. All word forms sharing the same invariant part are listed, together with their frequencies in the text, after the invariant element. The variable parts are written in italics.

*ngomu*ntu 4 *waba*ntu 3 *lomu*ntu 3 *ngingumu*ntu 3 *kunjengomu*ntu 2 *somu*ntu 2 *mu*ntu*ndini* 2 *okomu*ntu 2

Maori
tangata: tangata 532

With this method, it is possible to measure the degree of prefixing and suffixing in different languages. The results above suggest that English is weakly and Hungarian strongly suffixing, while Zulu is strongly prefixing and Maori shows no affixation at all in the lexical domain considered. An index over a set of one or two hundred lexeme domains can then be compiled as a measure of prefixation and suffixation and the results can be compared to a manual assessment based on reference grammars (Dryer 2005), which reveals that the automatic approach yields quite similar results, but with less data reduction.[3]

2.3 Amount of case marking

Another indirect measurement of a typological feature deals with the amount of case marking in a language. The basic idea is that case markers can be effectively extracted if the same method as above considers only the forms of proper names. This is because proper names do not usually vary in any other grammatical category except case (Wälchli 2012: 84). Any variable grammatical element in proper names is thus taken to be a case marker. The results of the extraction procedure for Hungarian, Swahili, Zulu, Tepehuan Norte and Zoque (Francisco León) with Koine Greek as trigger are as follows:

Hungarian: jános 14 jános*t* 5 jános*nak* 3 jános*tól* 1 jános*sal* 1 jános*ról* 1 jános*ra* 1
Swahili: yohane 26
Zulu: *u*johane 10 *no*johane 9 *lika*johane 2 *kuka*johane 2 *baka*johane 2 *ngu*johane 1
Tepehuan Norte: ʌvuaana 21 vuaana 2 *ʌrʌ*vuaana 1 *siʌ*vuaana 1 *ʌr*vuaana 1
Zoque (Francisco León): jua*n* 18 jua'*nis* 6 jua*nete* 2

Again, (case) suffixes and (case) prefixes – the latter being very rare cross-linguistically – can be distinguished. Swahili and Tepehuan Norte are instances of arguably incorrect extraction. Swahili has very special marginal local case marking, which occurs only on attributes, not on the head noun. The extraction method catches only case marking on head nouns, not anywhere else in the noun phrase. Tepehuan Norte has prefixed complementizers, which are clause initial (e.g. <si>) and which sometimes occur prefixed to nouns, and a definiteness marker (<ʌ>), which can but need not occur on proper nouns. Tepehuan Norte is one of very few languages where the heuristic procedure for case extraction is overgenerating. Again, the results of the automatic approach can be compared to a manual count of the number of cases in 261 languages

3. See Wälchli (2012: 83) for the details of how the index is compiled.

by Iggesen (2005), which shows that the extraction method, despite the indirect measurement, produces similar results.

2.4 Synthetic vs. analytic negation marking

Finally, the amount of synthetic vs. analytic marking of negation is measured with two different methods (Wälchli 2014). The first method works exactly like the extraction procedure discussed above and looks recursively for all word forms for a given input domain. The second method extracts recurrent continuous sequences of word forms ("morphemes"), which are overrepresented in the search domain. The starting point for the method is a trigger distribution for the input domain for which markers (be it stand-alone items such as English *not* or affixes as in Czech *ne-*) are extracted. Polish is a good candidate to provide a trigger distribution for negation because it has only a single marker (*nie*) for negation whereas other languages such as English show a range of markers (e.g., *not, no, never, nobody, nothing*), in some cases univerbated with modals (e.g., *cannot*). With the 237 tokens of Polish *nie* in the Gospel according to Mark, the method extracts the following results for English and Koine Greek, in both cases word forms rather than morphemes:

English:
not 135, *nothing* 13, *no* 43, *cannot* 5, *neither* 6, *lest* 4, *except* 4, *none* 3 (24 tokens without correspondence)

Koine Greek:
ouk 69, *mē* 67, *ou* 38, *oude* 10, *oukh* 6, *mēketi* 4 (43 tokens without correspondence)

All the extracted features presented above represent continuous values. In comparison to manually compiled typological features, which are typically grouped into various categories, they have the advantage that languages can be compared with less data reduction. All features are functional in the sense that meaning is taken into account as much as form even though meaning is accessed indirectly by means of distribution across parallel texts. The features serve as the input for the visualization that will be presented in Section 4 and discussed in Section 5. Before that, however, we give some background on the usefulness of visual representations for the exploration of language data.

3. Visual analytics

With the availability of large amounts of manually or automatically compiled language data, the computational analysis of languages allows for the search of linguistic patterns and interdependencies in a broad range of data. Yet the enormous amounts of data make the detection of patterns and potential interactions a laborious and time-consuming task. The need to analyze a multitude of factors at the same time calls for an additional component that makes the patterns more readily accessible to human perception. The emerging field of visual analytics, whose aim is to graphically represent information so that interesting patterns and relations become visible, provides the required methodology to perform this task.

Pictures have always been an appropriate means to communicate information, even before the invention of written language. Pictures can convey a wealth of information and are processed much more quickly than text. Vision research has shown that there is "a limited set of visual properties that are detected very rapidly and accurately by the low-level visual system" (Ward et al. 2010: 89). The task of visualization design is thus to adequately map relevant features to visual variables in order to provide the user with "the greatest number of ideas in the shortest time with the least ink in the smallest space" (Tufte 1983: 51).

The application of visual representations to convey information requires a basic understanding of graphic primitives. In total, there are eight visual variables to which input features can be mapped: position, shape, size, brightness, color, orientation, texture and motion (cf. Ward et al. 2010: 137). When designing a visualization, these eight variables can be adjusted and intermingled so as to maximize the effectiveness of communicating information. Yet at the same time, it is important to stick to some general principles of visualization, that is, to adhere to conventional uses of visual variables (e.g., blue to represent water in cartography), not to overload the visualization and to make clear what is left out (Culy 2012). Complex ideas are at best communicated with clarity, precision and efficiency (Tufte 1983: 51).

Visual analytics shares with information visualization its three major goals: (1) to present one's analysis to an audience, (2) to confirm or reject existing hypotheses about the data, (3) to explore the data space in order to generate new hypotheses. The main emphasis in this paper will be on exploratory data analysis and especially the generation of informed hypotheses. In particular, visual data exploration lends itself very well for linguistic research as it can easily deal with highly non-homogeneous and noisy data while at the same time providing a qualitative overview of the data. The data visualized in this paper is noisy in various respects. First, it derives directly from language use and not from idealized descriptions. Second, since the features are extracted automatically with indirect measurement, we have to expect some inconsistencies due to unusual orthographic representation of the data or other cases where indirect measurement goes astray.

Visual analytics is more than just information visualization. The field is inherently interdisciplinary, combining methods and techniques from data mining, statistics and computer graphics (among others). An integral part of any visual analytics approach is the interactive component that enables the user to directly interact with the information, to refine input parameters or focus on different parts of the data. The basic idea of including humans in the analysis process is to complement the enormous storage capacity and computational power of computers with the flexibility, creativity and background knowledge of the human analyst. To include human experts in the analysis process is particularly important when the data visualized has been extracted automatically. Whereas in some areas of data analysis the human component has already become obsolete, "the transformation of data into meaningful visualizations is not a trivial task that will automatically improve through steadily growing computational resources" (Keim et al. 2008: 78).

Visual analytics has most successfully been applied to data exploration tasks in business applications, physics and astronomy, software and engineering analytics or biology and medicine. Early approaches to the visualization of language data are mostly related to the field of information retrieval and the extraction of the topical content of text data, but recently first approaches for the visual comparison of language features have been published (e.g., Mayer et al. 2010). Despite the ubiquity and indispensability of graphical methods in linguistics, there is enormous potential for more sophisticated visualization techniques. The present paper is a first step to employ visual methods in studies of areal typology.

4. Combining genealogical and areal information in a single visualization

The field of areal typology seeks to investigate the geographical distribution of structural features within the context of genealogical relationships. In principle, there are four reasons why two languages can share a certain feature (cf. Comrie 1989: 201). Beyond the trivial cases where (1) the feature is a universal property of human languages and (2) the similarity is at least partly coincidence, areal typologists are mainly interested in (3) whether the shared feature is a result of language contact among neighboring languages or (4) whether it reflects a genealogical relationship where the feature has been inherited from a common ancestor. It has been shown that there are macro-areal patterns of continental or even hemispheric size (Dryer 1992; Nichols 1992; Dryer & Haspelmath WALS Online), which cannot be explained with standard historical methods. In order to better describe these patterns, Dryer (1992) divides the world into six regions (macro areas) where language contacts are most likely to have occurred. Whenever features in genera are not distributed the same way across all macro areas, this is taken as evidence for a non-random distribution.

Despite the increasing availability of manually or automatically generated language features, researchers have only marginally employed interactive visual interfaces for cross-linguistic comparison and exploration. The World Atlas of Language Structures (http://wals.info) provides a variety of structural features of languages, which have been collected mostly on the basis of descriptive material and which can be mapped to the geo-positions where the languages are spoken. Although the database also contains genealogical information for each language, this cannot be included in the visual representation. In contrast, the Multitree Tool <http://multitree.org> allows the user to visually access information about language relationships without providing any geo-spatial information in the visualization. To our knowledge, no work exists that attempts to combine both geo-spatial and hierarchical information in a single visualization.

In what follows, we will present a visualization that aims at combining areal and genealogical information in order to be able to distinguish between language contact (borrowing) and genealogical inheritance. The combination of both types of information can be approached from two different angles. The first approach focuses on a given geographical distribution to find out whether the languages in that area all belong to the same family and thus lead to a clustering of the inherited feature at a certain region of the world or whether there is a real contact situation with unrelated or distantly related languages sharing the feature through borrowing. The second approach concentrates on a given language family to check whether the feature values are the same or similar for all members of the family or whether a divergent feature value can be attributed to the fact that the language is spoken in a different region and might have borrowed the divergent feature from a neighboring language. We propose graphical solutions for both approaches, yet in this paper we focus on the second approach, as it is more interesting from the perspective of visual analytics.

The entire visualization consists of three panels that present different views on the language data and that are interactively linked.[4] First, a tree representation shows the genealogical hierarchy for the selected language family. The hierarchy is depicted as a horizontally growing tree, with the root node on the left and all children extending to the right. In this way, it is easier to inspect larger subtrees. Second, a world map displays the geo-spatial location of the languages. The map is complemented with a different coloring for each macro area. Finally, a sunburst visualization shows the genealogical hierarchy. The visual analytics software is implemented in Java and makes use of some external open source Java libraries for visualization: the Prefuse Visualization Toolkit[5], Christopher Collins' RSF-Tree library[6], SwingX 1.6.1[7] and Swingx-ws 1.0[8].

4.1 The extended sunburst display

The core of the visualization is an extended sunburst display, which depicts the family hierarchy as nested rings in a circle with the top node of the hierarchy as its center. Each ring is thereby divided on the basis of the number of nodes at that level so that the number of terminal nodes in a subtree determines the space that is allocated for it (cf. Ward et al. 2010: 272–274). For the visualization of language genealogies this means that families with a large number of languages are displayed with larger segments

4. For a more detailed description of the technical aspects of the visualization, the reader is referred to Rohrdantz et al. (2012).

5. <http://prefuse.org>

6. <http://vialab.science.uoit.ca/find/software>

7. <https://swingx.java.net>

8. <https://java.net/projects/swingx-ws/>

in the sunburst. We complement the genealogical information with feature rings, that is, the outer rings of the circle are reserved to display feature values for the individual languages in the hierarchy. Segments belonging to the same feature dimension are aligned in one ring around the circle and thus allow for a comparison of feature values across languages.

Feature rings have different graphical representations depending on their data type. Research in visual analytics has shown that some visual variables are more appropriate for displaying certain data types than others (Mackinlay 1986). Since the most valuable visual variable, namely position, is already used to display the genealogy, we pick the next best choice for the language features. For nominal features we use different color hues to distinguish between different categories, for ordinal data different color saturation values are employed. Finally, the quantitative features rings, which are most relevant for our language features, depict their values in a histogram, where the height of the bar corresponds to the feature value. This is because the visual variable 'size' is most appropriate to reveal relevant differences among quantitative feature values. The interactive visualization allows the user to change the pre-configured mapping in case a different representation might seem more suitable in a given context (e.g., the user can pick color saturation to represent quantitative features). Using different visual variables for the different data types also has the advantage that the user can immediately recognize the data type of a feature ring.

So far, the visualization includes a mapping of feature values to the rings of the sunburst display within the context of the language genealogy. On top of that, we also integrate geographical information into the sunburst. To this end, we make use of Dryer's (1992) macro areas. As mentioned before, Dryer divides the world into six regions within which language contact is most likely to have happened and across which language contact has been traditionally rare: North America, South America, Eurasia, Africa, Australia/New Guinea, South East Asia. These macro areas are shown on a world map, with each macro area dyed in a different color hue. Hence, world regions are readily distinguishable if they belong to different macro areas. In order to get a more fine-grained distinction within macro areas, the user has the option to pick a color gradient (east-west or north-south) so that different saturation values of one color hue give more detailed information about the location of a language.

The user can include the information about macro areas in two different ways in the sunburst display. First, the macro areas can be directly included as sisters at the top level in the language hierarchy. This means that all language families are grouped under the respective macro areas where they are spoken. Since macro areas are defined in such a way that language families do not spread across area borders, this leaves only a few exceptional cases where languages due to their family membership are not grouped under the correct macro area (see, for instance, the case of Afrikaans discussed in one of the case studies below). Second, the macro areas can be included as the innermost ring in the sunburst. In this case, the areal information is treated as a nominal data dimension, just like other language features. The coloring of the segment, however, corresponds to the coloring of the respective macro area on the world map. In that way, the user can immediately recognize if two languages are spoken in a similar region.

4.2 User interaction

The use of colors to represent macro areas is not the only way how areal information is integrated in the visualization. To further enhance the exploration of geographical information, the sunburst display is interactively linked to the world map. When hovering over a certain segment in the sunburst display, the location of the language(s) belonging to a selected branch in the genealogy is shown on the world map. Each language is thereby represented by one point on the world map. The user can also choose to select one of the language features to be displayed as different color hues of the point. In this way, the geographical distribution of a certain feature can be directly read off the world map through the coloring of the points. At the same time, the user is able to select an arbitrary rectangular region on the world map and create a sunburst display showing only those languages that are located in the selected area. The selected area can also be attributed its own bipolar color gradient while ignoring the coloring of the macro areas in order to enable an even more fine-grained distinction of language locations. In all cases, the world map and the sunburst display are linked and thus enable the user to highlight certain languages or language families in the visualization.

The linking of the world map and the sunburst display is only one of the interactive functionalities of the visualization. Both the sunburst and the world map allow for panning and zooming interaction by the user. It is thus possible to focus on different aspects and at the same time to get an overview of the data. Furthermore, the user can choose to sort the languages (resp. features) in the sunburst display according to their similarity. The order of presentation may have a strong impact on the detection of visual patterns and is thus a crucial part of the visualization. When experimenting with the sorting function, it turned out that both maximizing and minimizing the sum of pairwise similarities are useful options, with either highly homogeneous or heterogeneous subtrees sticking out, which can be identified at a glance. However, the sorting is a computationally complex problem despite the fact that the hierarchical structure already precludes certain possibilities and therefore reduces the number of permutations. Hence, it is recommendable to run the sorting algorithm as a batch process before the actual analysis and save the result to be reloaded later. Apart from that, all other interactive functionalities can be directly used in the visual analytics process.

4.3 Design decisions

The design of the visualization was developed in close cooperation between linguists and experts in visual analytics and with a clear analysis task in mind. The idea was to combine geo-spatial and genealogical information and to use insights from typological research to enhance the graphical representation. The greatest challenge is thereby to adequately integrate the geographical information in the visualization. On the one hand, the areal spread of languages can be fairly large, with some areas, such as the Pacific or Atlantic, being sparsely populated. On the other hand, there are densely populated areas where many different languages are spoken in the same region. A meaningful visualization must therefore allow for different resolutions in the display. On top of that, some regions, namely Dryer's macro areas, are known to be more prone to language contact than others. In order to reduce the search space in the visualization, we include this knowledge by reserving different color hues for the macro areas. Further, earlier research has shown that populations, together with their languages, tend to spread within the same climate zone, and not across climate zones (cf. Güldemann 2010 inter alia). This behavior is accounted for in our visualization by the one-dimensional gradient (either north-south or east-west, depending on whether the user wants to concentrate or ignore likely candidates for borrowing). Moreover, in the standard configuration, the Pacific Ocean is located in the center of the world map display. This is because, historically, the Atlantic Ocean has been a real diffusion border until the early days of colonization whereas the Pacific has always been an area of language spread. All design decisions are thus directly attuned to insights from (areal) typological research.

In addition, the user has the option to change many pre-configured settings concerning the genealogical and areal information. The visualization tool only serves to display the data and links the information from various sources through the ISO code of the language. The center of the world map can be shifted to any location to fit the number of languages that are currently displayed. Users are also able to modify the number and delimitation of macro areas. Furthermore, researchers can input their own family hierarchies and thereby adjust the genealogical information to their wishes. Hence, the input features and languages as well as the meta-information for all languages can be changed according to the analysis task. This is especially needed for the genealogical classification in less well-studied language families where opinions about the proper classification diverge.

4.4 Meta-information

The default genealogical and areal information for all languages in the visualizations is taken from different sources. The hierarchical structure of language families is given as an input xml or csv file when starting the visualization. The standard genealogy is taken from the online version of the Ethnologue <http://www.ethnologue.com>, which contains a comprehensive listing of 6,909 living languages together with their genealogical relationships.[9] The standard configuration can easily be changed if the user wishes to employ a different family tree for individual groups of languages.

The geographical information for all languages is collected from two different sources, namely the database of the Automated Similarity Judgment Program (ASJP)

9. Accessed on October 11th, 2012.

and the database of the World Atlas of Language Structures (WALS). The ASJP database is a collection of Swadesh list items in over 5,700 ASJP doculects (languages, dialects, variants in different documentations) together with their single point longitude/latitude geo-coordinates (Wichmann et al. 2012). The WALS database, mentioned above, is a collection of structural features of languages that have been compiled by various authors on the basis of descriptive material. It currently contains 76,492 data points for 2,678 languages and 192 language features.[10] Each language in the database is complemented with genealogical and areal information. As in the ASJP database, the areal information is provided in the form of single point longitude/latitude geo-coordinates.

5. Case studies

As mentioned before, the study of language contact and its influence on language features can be approached from two different angles. This is reflected in our visualization approach where the user has the possibility to concentrate either on a given language family (through the sunburst display) or on a given geographical region (through the world map). In the first case, the user can check for the homogeneity of feature values within a family and connect exceptional values to the location where the languages are spoken. In the latter case, researchers can focus on a given geographical distribution of feature values in order to get more insight into the genealogical classification of the languages involved. Both approaches can be directly combined by selecting a particular area on the world map to create a sunburst displaying only those languages that are spoken in the selected region. Beyond that, all parts of the visualization are interactively linked so that the user can, in principle, start an investigation from both angles at the same time in order to arrive at new conclusions.

In what follows, we concentrate on the sunburst display with two application case studies that demonstrate the usefulness of the visualization approach. The case studies show the visualizations of the automatically extracted language features that were discussed in Section 2. As mentioned before, these features give a good approximation to the manual analysis of structural properties of languages and also prove relevant for contact situations. In our experiments, we inspected a number of language families. The following case studies present some interesting findings that could be inferred from the visual representation of the features.

5.1 Case study 1: Indo-European languages

In our first case study, we focus on the Indo-European family. Figure 1 (left) shows the sunburst display for all Indo-European languages in our sample of languages and

10. Accessed on June 19th, 2013.

Figure 1. Sunburst display of all Indo-European languages in the sample (left). The rings show (from inside to outside) type-token ratio, amount of prefixing, amount of suffixing and amount of case marking. The world map display (bottom right) is linked to the sunburst and shows the location of all Indo-European languages. The sunburst display of all Germanic languages in the sample (top right) shows only the prefixation and suffixation (outermost) feature rings.

features together with their hierarchical structure of subfamilies (genera). The innermost ring of the sunburst represents the macro areas where the languages are spoken. The coloring immediately shows that all but one language are located in the same macro area (Eurasia), with the sole exception of Afrikaans, which is spoken on the African continent. However, the sunburst display not only reveals the special status of Afrikaans with respect to its macro-area but it can easily be detected that Afrikaans has some feature values that deviate strongly from those of the other Indo-European languages in the display.[11] The graphical representation readily exposes Afrikaans as an outlier in comparison to its sister languages.

For a closer inspection of the visualization we select only the subfamily of Germanic languages and restrict the rings to just two features in the display: the synthesis parameters of prefixation and suffixation (cf. Section 2.2). The sunburst in Figure 1 (top right) has both features as its outer rings, with the suffixation feature as the outermost ring and the prefixation feature next to it. The visual representation clearly shows that Afrikaans is special regarding both its areal ring as well as its feature values. In comparison to the other (West) Germanic languages, Afrikaans has a higher prefixation and a lower suffixation value. Note that the feature rings display a relative scale. Thus,

11. This effect is partly due to the fact that some features are correlated and thus show a similar distribution across all languages. Yet Afrikaans is visually salient independent from that.

Afrikaans does not have as much prefixing as Icelandic has suffixing. Rather Afrikaans has most prefixing and Icelandic most suffixing in the selected subset of languages.

The world map visualization also reveals that Afrikaans is in a contact situation with the neighboring Bantu languages Zulu and Xhosa, which are also contained in our sample. Including the Bantu languages in the visualization reveals that they also show a high prefixation value.

This example illustrates that the tool has mainly a heuristic function. It does not give definitive linguistic answers, but rather serves to come up with hypotheses about areal relationships, which can be confirmed or rejected on closer inspection of the data. Whenever a visualization suggests a certain hypothesis, the next step is to look more closely into the data to see whether a visible pattern is due to mere coincidence or reflects a true areal pattern. On closer inspection, it turns out that the relatively high prefixation value is largely due to the fact that Afrikaans makes extensive use of the perfect construction involving the prefix *ge-* in the past participle (similar to Dutch and German). Donaldson (1993: 222) notes that the synthetic past tense forms (the so-called *imperfect tense*) have disappeared except for a few vestigial cases. In the Bible texts from which the feature values have been extracted, the perfect construction is the dominant way when referring to past events. The relatively low suffixation value is caused by the fact that the past participle does not show much variation at the end of the word. This is different from the synthetic past tense forms, which are no longer dominant in Afrikaans but which are (still) used in the other Germanic languages, except for Swiss German, which also has a higher prefixation value. In the synthetic forms a further distinction for person and number is made. Hence, the different feature values are a direct result of a difference in language use. The visualization, however, readily enables the researcher to detect such suspicious patterns, which can later be inspected in more detail.

5.2 Case study 2: Languages of Papua New Guinea

While in the case of Afrikaans and the Germanic languages in particular there have been many studies regarding the genealogical and areal status, for other language families the available knowledge can be very limited. One of the most under-resourced language areas in the world is Papua New Guinea with its enormous number of indigenous languages, only a few of which are described and documented in reference grammars.[12] By contrast, translations of Bible texts are available for a large number of them <http://www.pngscriptures.org>. We thus decided to automatically extract the features from Section 2 for a sample of 125 languages of Papua New Guinea and

12. The languages of Papua New Guinea can be divided into Papuan and Austronesian languages. While Austronesian languages constitute a proper family of related languages in the sense that they all descend from a common ancestor, Papuan languages are not all genealogically related (cf. Foley 1986).

visualize them. Unlike with Afrikaans and the Germanic languages, where the genealogical classification is well established, some of the language families in Papua New Guinea are less well documented and family relationships are still a matter of current research. It is especially in such cases that a visualization approach might lead to potentially interesting hypotheses about the relationship between the genealogical structure and the extracted features.

Although the linguists among us are not experts in the languages of Papua New Guinea, we can see structural features reflecting existing hypotheses about the broader families simply by looking at the sunburst display in Figure 2. The visualization clearly shows that Austronesian languages are more homogeneous in their feature values than Papuan languages and thus represent a structurally coherent language family.[13] This is well in line with the general assumption that Papuan is not an actual language family but only a cover term for those languages of New Guinea that do not belong to the Austronesian phylum.

Further interesting aspects that confirm some of the established genealogical subgroupings can be seen in the visualization. The Huon-Finisterre subfamily (Wurm

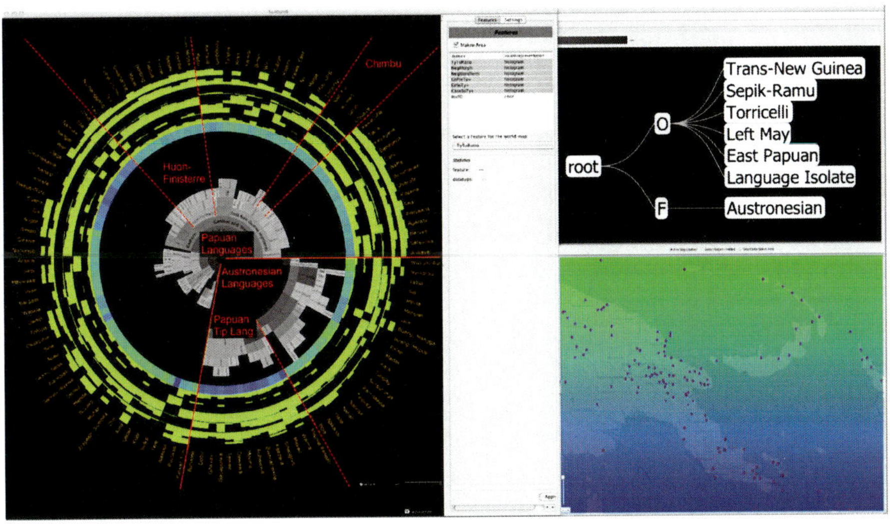

Figure 2. The visualization tool with all three panels for the sample of 125 Papua New Guinea languages. The left panel shows the sunburst display together with the feature selection menu. The language hierarchy is displayed as a tree in the upper right corner, while the world map visualization (bottom right) shows the locations of all languages in the selection.

13. From the inside to the outside of the sunburst, the feature rings mark the macro area (blue-greenish color), type-token ratio, amount of negation morphemes, amount of negation word forms, amount of prefixation, amount of suffixation, amount of case suffixation (green histograms).

1982: 108–116) is characterized by a very homogeneous distribution of its feature values across languages (high synthesis, no morphological negation, very little prefixing, much suffixation with case marking). The display thus shows that the assumption that the Huon and Finisterre languages are related (McElhanon 1975, cited in Foley 1986: 244) and can be subsumed under one super-stock is paralleled with a strong structural similarity of those languages. It is important to note that the tool cannot serve to prove or disprove assumed genealogical relationships. Rather, its purpose is to display how a given genealogical classification with a given areal configuration of languages relates to a given typological dataset.

The Chimbu subgroup (Foley 1986: 237) shows up as clearly distinct in the sunburst display with high morphological negation, lack of case marking and a rather low degree of synthesis. Overall, there is much heterogeneity in East Papuan, which is well in line with the fact that East Papuan is not established at all as a language family. Within the Austronesian language family, the subgroup of Papuan Tip languages can be distinguished, both with respect to certain of their feature values and to their geographical locations, from the other Austronesian languages. The higher degree of synthesis of the Papuan Tip languages, for instance, may suggest a hypothesis that these languages have undergone stronger language contacts with Papuan languages than other Austronesian languages.

A few interesting findings can be obtained simply by looking at the sunburst display. Figure 3 shows a sorted sunburst visualization for a subset of the Papuan languages in detail. The display reveals that Abau is somewhat different from the other Sepik languages with respect to its prefixation and suffixation values. Wurm (1982: 210) notes that suffixation predominates in Sepik languages, which can be seen in the relatively higher bars in the suffixation ring in Figure 3 (second ring from the outside). The high prefixation and low suffixation value for Abau is therefore surprising for a Sepik language. When looking at reference grammars, it seems that the difference between Abau and the other Sepik languages, which the visualization has pointed to, is supported by the structure of the languages. Abau is the westernmost member of the Sepik language family and "is located in an area of extreme linguistic diversity" (Lock 2011: 9). The languages bordering it are unrelated to it. Lock (2011: 9) states that Abau "[v]erbs do not inflect for tense, aspect, mood or person" but that "the verb takes a number of prefixes encoding manner and direction" (Lock 2011: 126). There is a set of frequent manner prefixes, such as *nuw-* 'intensity', *saw-* 'quickly', *kiy-* 'actuality', *ma-* 'again' etc., which contribute to the relatively higher prefix scores. Thus, Abau prefixes are of a very special kind. Nouns are not marked "for number and gender nor do they carry any information on noun classes or semantic or syntactic function" (Lock 2011: 42). Affixation on nouns is very limited, there are many noun phrase markers following nouns but they are not suffixes and do not figure therefore in the suffix index. What looks like suffixes (and as "cases" to proper names) are in fact often second parts of compounds (*-uwr* 'man', *-om* 'group'). From what we read in the grammar, it is not surprising that Abau shows a comparatively high prefixation value. Degree of synthesis

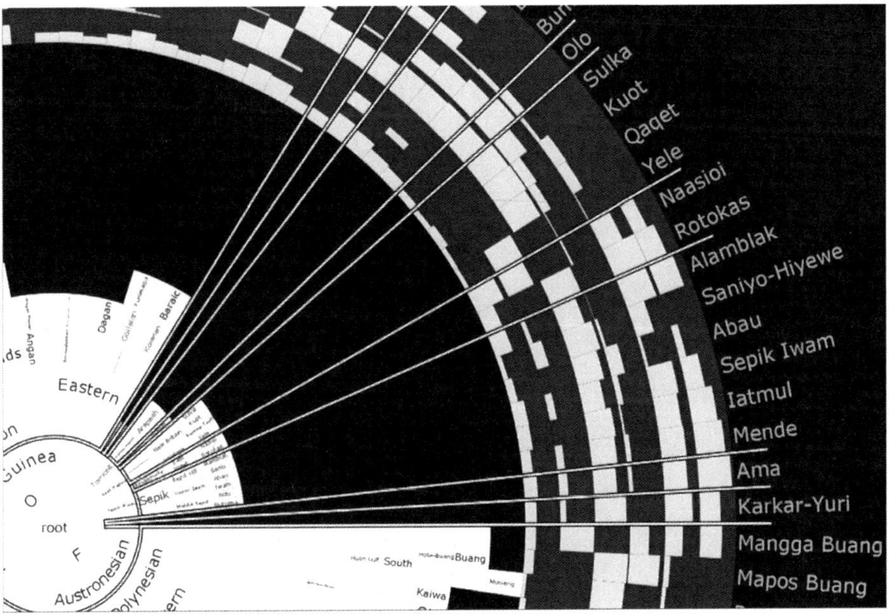

Figure 3. Sunburst of the Sepik languages. The feature rings show (from the inside to the outside of the sunburst) type-token ratio, amount of negation morphemes, amount of negation word forms, amount of prefixation, amount of suffixation, amount of case suffixation.

is generally rather low, negation is analytic. In the related language Mende, on the other hand, nouns are inflected for accusative and genitive case and verbs for tense, aspect and mood by suffixes, with no prefixation for verbs (Hoel et al. 1994: 19, 61–68). The sunburst display in Figure 3 has thus attracted our attention to an interesting discrepancy between Abau and its sister languages, which is paralleled with a particular geographical position of Abau.

The non-Sepik languages Karkar-Yuri and especially Ama, on the other hand, look very similar to the other Sepik languages in their feature values (among others, high suffixation, low prefixation) even though they are not grouped under the Sepik language family.[14] The visualization thus indicates that the structural features relate Karkar-Yuri and Ama to the languages in the Sepik family (except Abau). At the same time, the world map display reveals that all Sepik languages (except Abau) are spoken in the East Sepik Province and that both Karkar-Yuri (in the Sandaun Province like Abau) and Ama (in the East Sepik Province) are located close to them. A preliminary hypothesis on the basis of the visualization would thus suggest that intense language

14. Hammarström (2010: 196) reports that Karkar-Yuri was formerly considered a language isolate but that Timothy Usher identified a close similarity in word lists between Karkar-Yuri and the Eastern Pauwasi languages Emem and Zorop. Ama is a language of the Left-May family and not related to Karkar-Yuri or Abau and the other Sepik languages.

contact has taken place that made Karkar-Yuri and Ama similar to the neighboring languages. But note that this is only a hypothesis, which needs further investigation.

A similar observation can be made for other languages and subfamilies as well. Figure 4 (left) shows that Mangga Buang is an outlier within the Western Oceanic branch of Austronesian languages. Its case value is much higher than for the other languages in the family (outermost ring) and it seems to have bound negation marking (second ring to the center). Both feature values are fairly different from the other Western Oceanic languages. For this reason, the automatic sorting algorithm has placed Mangga Buang at the margin of the family segment in the sunburst. On closer inspection, the high negation and case marking scores are due to the orthographic conventions in the New Testament. There, the negation marker *(-)me-* is directly attached to the verb stem like in some descriptive material on the language (Healey 1984: 14):

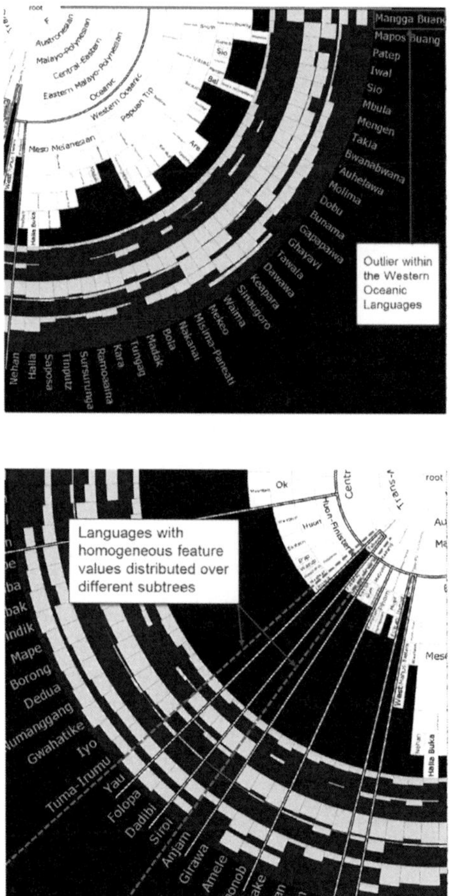

Figure 4. Sunburst of the Western Oceanic languages with Mangga Buang as an outlier (*top*) and sunburst of languages with homogeneous features that are distributed over different subtrees (*bottom*). The feature values are in the same order as in Figure 3.

(1) *ham na-wiing dakaa-jo me-lohvu le*
you continuous-did little-this not-equalled not
'(That) you are doing this little (thing) is not right'

However, Hardwick and Healey (1967: 7) write the negation marker as a separate word (e.g., *Sa me haahe re* 'I didn't see it'). Likewise, the high case marking score is caused by the genitive clitic *-a(to)* and some other clitics including the relative pronoun clitic *-(a)to*, which is placed at the end of the relative clause in Mangga Buang (Healey 1984: 6). In the New Testament, from which the feature values are extracted, the clitic is directly attached to the preceding word, which happens to be a proper name in some cases. In that way, it is interpreted as a case marker and therefore leads to a high case marking score. In other descriptions, the relative pronoun clitic is written as a separate word (e.g., *Sen yahe geen ato?* 'That which we saw today?' in Hardwick and Healey 1967: 8). The special status of Mangga Buang within the Western Oceanic language family in the sunburst display in Figure 4 can thus be explained in terms of the orthographic conventions in the Bible text.

In contrast to the example of the presumed outlier above, Figure 4 (right) shows a number of languages with homogeneous feature values that are distributed over several subtrees. In this case, the automatic sorting of the values in the sunburst display would suggest that all languages are structurally related. At the same time, the world map display reveals that two of these languages, Yau and Siroi, are located close to one another on different sides of the border between the provinces of Madang and Morobe. Siroi is known to be a local trade language (cf. Lewis 2009) and thus might be in contact with Yau. Hence, an informed hypothesis is that the similar feature values for both languages are due to language contact. A more detailed examination of the data, however, is needed to answer the question whether the visualization results are only an artifact of the extraction methods or the visualization approach.

6. Conclusions and outlook

In this paper, we have presented a two-step procedure for the cross-linguistic comparison of language features. The first part of the procedure deals with the automatic extraction of typologically relevant structural features from parallel texts. In corpus-based approaches to typological research, parallel texts are the most straightforward way to operationalize the notion of functional domain, which is highly relevant in functional approaches to typology. We have seen that the results of the extraction method are similar to manually compiled feature values and thus can be employed for a typological comparison of languages. The second part of the procedure is concerned with the graphical representation of language features. It is, in principle, independent of the first part, as all sorts of structural features (e.g., manually compiled features from the WALS database) can serve as the input for the visualization component. We have focused on the representation of continuous rather than discrete values because they are more challenging to visualize and more characteristic of a functional approach.

Unlike traditional simple visualization tools in typology such as maps the visualization method used in this paper has the advantage of representing both genealogical and areal information rather than only areal information and multiple features and their interrelations rather than just a single feature. The core part of our visualization is an extended sunburst display. It is complemented with feature rings that allow for the comparison of several language features at the same time, within the context of the language genealogy. These feature rings are represented differently, depending on their data type (see also Rohrdantz et al. 2012). We have proposed several ways to integrate areal information in the sunburst display. One solution is to link the hierarchical display to a geo-spatial visualization where the macro-areas are plotted with different colors. The coloring can then also be included as a feature ring in the sunburst display. The resulting visualization thus combines genealogical and areal information in a single graphical representation.

The visualization examples in the two case studies in our paper have revealed several potentially new insights into the relationships between the languages considered. At the same time, they also confirmed previous research results as to the relationship between the genealogical structure of the languages and the homogeneity of their features. It should be kept in mind that the aim of the visualization is not to replace linguistic research but to assist and guide it. After examining the graphic displays, which reflect a large amount of data, the next step is to look into a small segment of particularly intriguing data in order to decide to what extent the patterns emerging in the visualizations reflect relevant areal-typological patterns. The emergent patterns discussed in Section 5.2 can be due to different reasons associated with the automatic extraction procedure from parallel texts, such as particular orthographic conventions. It is also important to note that the choice of visual variables and their arrangement can play an important role. Thus, at-a-glance patterns in the visual display will not necessarily lead directly to new insights regarding genealogical relationships and areal contacts of the languages considered. However, the advantage of the present approach with its extended procedure ranging from primary data to a full-fledged areal-typological survey is that the user can intervene on every level of the procedure where closer inspection is required in order to check why certain patterns emerge in the visualizations.

The main advantage of the present approach is that well-grounded hypotheses can be generated with little knowledge about the data and languages at hand. Whereas it is common practice to only look at a manageable but relatively small number of examples or languages and to generalize from the observed facts, the visualization approach, together with the automatic feature extraction method, enables the researcher to inspect a larger number of features and languages at the same time. This in turn allows us to make more informed hypotheses about the languages and features involved.

The sunburst display is particularly useful when comparing the structure of languages (in the form of structural feature values) with their genealogical relationships. We have seen in the case studies above that the visualization clearly reveals if languages in a family do not show the same features as their sister tongues. One possible explanation for this, in fact, the one we envisioned in the discussion of the case studies, is that language contact might have led to a borrowing of features from neighboring (but more distantly related) languages. However, the comparison of structural and genealogical information is also interesting from a typological point of view. It makes a typological survey less dependent on the genealogical structure of the languages. Note also that it is possible to replace a genealogical classification at any point of the investigation with another one. A structurally informed approach such as ours might suggest different hierarchies of languages that are more interesting for sampling methods (cf., e.g., Rijkhoff & Bakker 1998). However, we do not claim that the visualization as such, when showing the homogeneity or heterogeneity of members of a family, can prove or disprove assumed genealogical relationships. Rather, the aim of the tool is to display how members of a given language family behave with respect to certain typologically relevant features and thereby to guide research in areal typology.

In this paper, we have focused on the hierarchically structured genealogical information and its graphical representation in a sunburst. The integration of geo-spatial information in the form of the world map is still on a fairly basic level. We have identified several potential improvements for the future. First, distorted maps might be useful to grant more space for those regions that are more densely populated in terms of data points. One problem is that current map distortion algorithms do not allow a constant re-calculation according to the current selection of languages in interactive time. Such an additional component will thus be deferred to future research in this direction. Second, the likelihood of language spread is not only dependent on climate zones but also involves a more complex interaction of natural, cultural and political borders. While it is difficult to assess the existence and strength of political and cultural borders, it would be comparatively easy to integrate natural borders (such as mountain ranges, deserts and seas) in the visualization. This would involve, among other things, a color map that somehow encodes a "spread" distance between languages. We also aim to experiment with further interaction techniques that allow the user to combine the geographical and genealogical information in a more effective way. At the same time, it will be important to keep the visualization tool as simple as possible and not to overload the graphical information on the screen.

We hope that future studies will further explore the potential of more advanced possibilities of visualization in areal typology beyond simple map displays. Like many other disciplines where visual analytics is already a more accepted research tool, linguistics, and in particular functionally oriented computational approaches to language structure, can benefit immensely from well-designed visual methods.

Acknowledgments

We would like to thank Östen Dahl for his help in pre-processing some of the N.T. data and Ljuba Veselinova for her help with the language data. We are also grateful to Michael Cysouw, Miriam Butt and two anonymous reviewers for valuable suggestions and comments. This work was partially funded by the German Research Foundation (DFG) under grant BU 1806/7-1 "Visual Analysis of Language Change and Use Patterns" and the project "Algorithmic corpus-based approaches to typological comparison" at the LMU Munich and the Philipps University of Marburg.

References

Bowerman, Melissa. 2007. Containment, support, and beyond: Constructing topological spatial categories in first language acquisition. *The Categorization of Spatial Entities in Language and Cognition* [Human Cognitve Processing 20], Michel Aurnague, Maya Hickmann & Laure Vieu (eds.), 177–203. Amsterdam: John Benjamins.

Comrie, Bernard. 1989. *Language Universals and Linguistic Typology,* 2nd edn. Oxford: Blackwell.

Croft, William. 2003. *Typology and Universals,* 2nd edn. Cambridge: CUP.

Culy, Christopher. 2012. Some challenges and directions for the visualization of language and linguistic data. Paper presented at the AVML 2012 conference in York.

Cysouw, Michael & Wälchli, Bernhard. 2007. Parallel texts: Using translational equivalents in linguistic typology. *Sprachtypologie und Universalienforschung STUF 60*(2): 95–99.

Donaldson, Bruce C. 1993. *A Grammar of Afrikaans.* Berlin: Mouton de Gruyter.

Dryer, Matthew S. 1992. The Greenbergian word order correlation. *Language* 68(1): 80–138.

Dryer, Matthew S. 2005. Prefixing vs. suffixing in inflectional morphology. In *The World Atlas of Language Structures,* Martin Haspelmath, Matthews S. Dryer, David Gil & Bernard Comrie (eds), Ch. 26. Oxford: OUP.

Dryer, Matthew S. & Haspelmath, Martin (eds). *The World Atlas of Language Structures Online.* Munich: Max Planck Digital Library. <http://wals.info/>

Foley, William A. 1986. *The Papuan Languages of New Guinea.* Cambridge: CUP.

Givón, Talmy. 1981. Typology and functional domains. *Studies in Language* 5: 163–193.

Greenberg, Joseph H. 1960. A quantitative approach to the morphological typology of languages. *International Journal of American Linguistics* 26: 178–194. First published in Spencer, Robert. 1954. *Festschrift for Wilson D. Wallis. Method and Perspective in Anthropology.* University of Minnesota Press.

Greenberg, Joseph H. 1963. Some universals of grammar with particular reference to the order of meaningful elements. In *Universals of Language,* Joseph H. Greenberg (ed.), 110–113. Cambridge MA: The MIT Press.

Güldemann, Tom. 2010. 'Sprachraum' and geography: Linguistic macro-areas in Africa. In *The Handbook of Language Mapping,* Alfred Lameli, Roland Kehrein & Stefan Rabanus. Berlin: Mouton de Gruyter.

Hammarström, Harald. 2010. The status of the least documented language families in the world. *Language Documentation & Conservation* 4: 177–212.

Hardwick, Roma & Healey, Joan. 1967. *Manga Buang Language Lessons,* First Draft. Brisbane: SIL Publications.

Healey, Joan. 1984. *Some Aspects of Topic Continuity in Mangga Buang Discourse.* Ukarumpa, Papua New Guinea: SIL Publications.

Hoel, Hanna Marie, Ikaheimonen, Tarja & Nozawa, Michiyo. 1994. *Mende Grammar Essentials.* <http://www.sil.org/pacific/png/pubs/928474531144/Mende_Grammar_Essentials.pdf>

Hopper, Paul J. 1998. Emergent grammar. In *The New Psychology of Language. Cognitive and Functional Approaches to Language Structure,* Michael Tomasello (ed.), 155–175. Mahwah NJ: Lawrence Erlbaum Associates.

Iggesen, Oliver. 2005. Number of cases. In *The World Atlas of Language Structures,* Martin Haspelmath, Matthews S. Dryer, David Gil & Bernard Comrie (eds), Ch. 49. Oxford: OUP.

Juola, Patrick. 2008. Assessing linguistic complexity. In *Language Complexity, Typology, Contact, Change* [Studies in Language Companion Series 94], Matti Miestamo, Kaius Sinnemäki & Fred Karlsson (eds.), 89–108. Amsterdam: John Benjamins.

Keim, Daniel A., Mansmann, Florian, Schneidewind, Jörn, Thomas, Jim & Ziegler, Hartmut. 2008. Visual analytics: Scope and challenges. In *Visual Data Mining: Theory, Techniques and Tools for Visual Analytics,* Simeon Simoff, Michael H. Böhlen & Arturas Mazeika (eds), 76–91. Berlin: Springer.

Lewis, M. Paul. 2009. *Ethnologue: Languages of the World,* 16th edn. Dallas TX: SIL International.

Lock, Arnold Hugo. 2011. *Abau Grammar. Data Papers on Papua New Guinea Languages.* Ukarumpa, Papua New Guinea: SIL-PNG Academic Publications.

Mackinlay, Jock. 1986. Automating the design of graphical presentations of relational information. *ACM Trans. Graph.* 5(2): 110–141.

Mayer, Thomas, Rohrdantz, Christian, Butt, Miriam, Plank, Frans & Keim, Daniel A. 2010. Visualizing vowel harmony. *Journal of Linguistic Issues in Language Technology (LiLT)* 4(2):1–33.

McElhanon, Kenneth A. 1975. North-eastern Trans-New Guinea Phylum languages. In *New Guinea Area Languages and Language Study,* Vol. 1: *Papuan Languages and the New Guinea Linguistic Scene* [PL, C-38], Stephen A. Wurm (ed.), 527–567.

MacWhinney, Brian (ed.). 1999. *The Emergence of Language.* Mahwah NJ: Lawrence Erlbaum Associates.

Miestamo, Matti. 2005. *Standard Negation: The Negation of Declarative Verbal Main Clauses in a Typological Perspective* [Empirical Approaches to Language Typology 31]. Berlin: Mouton de Gruyter.

Multitree: A Digital Library of Language Relationships. Ypsilanti MI: Institute for Language Information and Technology (LINGUIST List), Eastern Michigan University. <http://multitree.org/>

Nichols, Johanna. 1992. *Linguistic Diversity in Space and Time.* Chicago IL: The University of Chicago Press.

Popescu, Ioan-Iovitz, Mačutek, Ján & Altmann, Gabriel. 2009. *Aspects of Word Frequencies.* Lüdenscheidt: RAM.

Rijkhoff, Jan & Bakker, Dik. 1998. Language sampling. *Linguistic Typology* 2(3): 263–314.

Rohrdantz, Christian, Hund, Michael, Mayer, Thomas, Wälchli, Bernhard & Keim, Daniel A. 2012. The World's Languages Explorer: Visual analysis of language features in genealogical and areal contexts. *Computer Graphics Forum* 31(3): 935–944.

Stasko, John & Zhang, Eugene. 2000. Focus+context display and navigation techniques for enhancing radial, space-filling hierarchy visualizations. In *Proceedings of the IEEE Symposium on Information Visualization,* 57–65. Los Alamitos CA: IEEE Computer Society.

Stassen, Leon. 1985. *Comparison and Universal Grammar*. Oxford: Blackwell.
Tufte, Edward R. 1983. *The Visual Display of Quantitative Information*. Cheshire CT: Graphics Press.
Wälchli, Bernhard. 2009. Data reduction typology and the bimodal distribution bias. *Linguistic Typology* 13(1): 77–94.
Wälchli, Bernhard. 2012. Indirect measurement in morphological typology. In *Methods in Contemporary Linguistics* [Trends in Linguistics. Studies and Monographs TiLSM 247], Andrea Ender, Adrian Leemann & Bernhard Wälchli (eds), 69–92. Berlin: de Gruyter.
Wälchli, Bernhard. 2014. Algorithmic typology and going from known to similar unknown categories within and across languages. In *Aggregating Dialectology, Typology, and Register Analysis: Linguistic Variation in Text and Speech, Within and Across Languages*, Benedikt Szmrecsanyi & Bernhard Wälchli (eds), 355–393. Berlin: de Gruyter.
Ward, Matthew, Grinstein, Georges & Keim, Daniel A. 2010. *Interactive Data Visualization: Foundations, Techniques, and Applications*. Natick MA: A.K. Peters.
Wichmann, Søren, Müller, André, Velupillai, Viveka, Wett, Annkathrin, Brown, Cecil H., Molochieva, Zarina, Bishoffberger, Julia, Holman, Eric W., Sauppe, Sebastian, Brown, Pamela, Bakker, Dik, List, Johann-Mattis, Egorov, Dmitry, Belyaev, Oleg, Urban, Matthias, Hammarström, Harald, Carrizo, Agustina, Mailhammer, Robert, Geyer, Helen, Beck, David, Korovina, Evgenia, Epps, Pattie, Valenzuela, Pilar & Grant, Anthony. 2012. The ASJP Database (version 15).
Wurm, Stephen A. 1982. *Papuan Languages of Oceania*. Tübingen: Gunter Narr.

Lexical-syntactic analysis model of Spanish multi-word expressions*

Jorge Antonio Leoni de León
University of Costa Rica

In this article we analyze the lexical status and the syntactic phenomena of multi-word expressions. We propose a typology of phraseological units based on our findings and we describe a formal system, called Tsool, which preserves these characteristics and allows their collection and identification (even after complex operations). Tsool was implemented in a prototype called Mulkin.

1. Introduction

Multi-word expressions constitute one of the most important linguistic issues in recent years due to their frequency, their manner to mediate meanings, and the complexity of relations that they entangle in the phrase. In this latter regard, it is worth noting the morphosyntactic behavior of multi-word expressions. For instance, in Spanish, we have:

(1) cama elástica
trampoline

(2) abrelatas
can opener

(3) El cliente siempre tiene la razón.
The client is always right

(4) pedir cacao
Ask forgiveness to a boyfriend or girlfriend (Literal: ask for cocoa).

(5) meter la pata
make a blunder

* I want to express my deep gratitude to Daniela Sánchez Sánchez, Ericka Vargas Castro, and Constanza Enciso Bahler because of their help during the preparation of this document, and also to the Vicerrectoría de Investigación and the Instituto de Investigaciones Lingüísticas of the University of Costa Rica for the support provided to the research Project N° 745-B1-001.

(6) cometer una falta
make a mistake

(7) hacer un cambio de oficina
change office

The examples (1–7) show that these expressions can be associated with certain type of lexical nominal units, as in (1) and (2), or they may correspond to verbal expressions, of which examples (3–7) have different degrees of cohesion ranging from a complete sentence sequence (4), to a collocation (6) that allows alternations, more or less free, of its constituent elements. In (7) we have a structure with a light verb whose idiomaticity is not always easy to establish.

Probably, translation constitutes the best source of examples about the general problem that multi-word expressions produce. Their generation requires using the same type of resources than in interpretation, but in reverse meaning and put on a different linguistic structure. Multi-word units present, therefore, a particular difficulty, since the correspondence of the elements of an expression is often not univocal from one language to another. For example, the literal translation of the French term *pomme de terre* makes no sense in English (8):

(8) pomme de terre (*potato*) → * apple of ground

An additional difficulty is the representation of these expressions, because if we treat them as simple lexical units, procedures as common as pluralization can lead to new paradigms and heuristic interventions, as we can see in (9) and (10) for French, and in (11) and (12) for Spanish:

(9) maison (*house*) → maisons
(10) pomme de terre (*potato*) → *pomme de terres
(11) casa (*house*) → casas
(12) ojo de agua (*spring, water source*) → *ojo de aguas

The correct form in French for (10) is *pommes de terre* and, similarly, in Spanish, (12) would be *ojos de agua*. Following our reasoning, if compound nouns belong to the lexicon, plural would be a morphosyntactic exception because in nouns (French and Spanish) the number morpheme is placed at the end of the morphological sequence with phonologically determined variations, such as we saw in examples (9) and (11). In other words, the inclusion of compound nouns in the lexicon leads to an adaptation of the treatment of plural to the specific characteristics of the complex lexical units. The interest in maintaining multi-word units in the lexicon is great, because their meaning does not often come from their constituent elements necessarily. Moreover, the property of becoming passive, that some expressions have, among other options, increases the difficulty of the task of representing, generating, and interpreting multi-word expressions, as we shall see later. In any case, the phenomenology of multi-word units highlights the need to solve a number of fundamental linguistic issues such as idiosyncrasies, compositionality, and lexicon's discursive value (Grossman and Tutin 2003). For our part, we are required to account for the structure and the combinatory of multi-word units focused on natural language processing (NLP) from a lexicographic perspective.

The concept of multi-word units encompasses diverse phenomena, linked by the coincidence of lexical units that have a common denotative (or stylistic) effect. Among them, we find the compound words, locutions, proverbs, and collocations. Given this diversity, and based on our computational decisions[1], we chose a syntactic point of view that allows us to establish a particular profile for such idiomatic phenomena. This profile takes the form of a typology that helps us establish the basic criteria to identify multi-word units. Hence, we must answer two enquiries: the role of syntax in the multi-word unit formation mechanisms, and the retrieval of information from syntactically interpretable data (recount of possible operations). Thus, it is necessary to reach an operational definition of multi-word units that allows proposing a set of computational procedures for their processing.

Our model must allow two operations: identification and recognition of multi-word units. The first one is the full validation of an expression in the model, while the second one refers to a set of syntactic criteria on the idiomaticity of a given expression. Consequently, our problem can be summarized as: *which is the most adequate computational representation of multi-word expressions, taking into account their syntactic behavior?*

Our goal is to create a computational phraseological model of Spanish based on the lexical-syntactic phenomenology of multi-word units. The model that emerged from this research involves two operations. The first one is the identification, which expresses the validation of the expression at all levels of the model. The second one is the recognition that marks the introduction of a sequence of words as a possible multi-word unit from lexical and syntactic criteria.

In Section 2 we discuss the lexicological and syntactical theoretical basis we develop. Section 3, devoted to the syntactic particularities of multi-word units, leads to a typology of such expressions. Section 4 presents a system for representing phraseological units able to reproduce the syntactic features of idiomatic units through the transposition of linguistic structures, in terms of configuration relations and automatically processable data description. Section 5 brings together the contributions made to the research, work constraints, and fields open for future developments.

2. Lexicon and syntactic phenomena

The starting point of our research is lexicon and its *combinatory*. By the term combinatory we refer to the co-occurrence of lexical items necessary to evoke a precise

1. We refer to FIPS parser (Wehrli 2004). Both our formalization and multi-word processing units are favored with FIPS Parser. FIPS is a deep parser, inspired by Chomskyan generative grammar (Wehrli 1997, 2004, 2007). FIPS is a lexicon tagger, FIPSTG, a lexical database, FIPS-DB, and a parser, FIPFSYN. In addition, FIPS has a web interface, FIPSWEB, that we draw on our computational model.

meaning, with some autonomy in relation to syntactic or semantic processing. The science specialized in this area is lexicology, which is an applied sub-discipline that takes part in the base definition of lexical units and their meanings.

It is worth noting the similarity of our research with the *FrameNet project* (Fillmore et al. 2003) and *Sens-Texte model* (Mel'čuk 1993), although there are different objectives and goals. FrameNet is a computational lexicography project aimed at extracting linked information on the semantic and syntactic properties, within very large electronic corpora with manual and automated processes (Fillmore et al. 2003). The theoretical basis is related to the *Frame Semantics*[2]. According to this approach, the lexical meaning must be described in relation to semantic frames or scenarios, which are schematic representations of conceptual structures (models of beliefs, practices, institutions, etc.) that provide the basis for an interaction that produces meaning within a speech community. FrameNet identifies and describes semantic frames present in a syntactic form. The lexical unit is defined as the joining of a word and a meaning. The meanings of a word correspond to the lexical frames in which it can participate.

Moreover, Sens-Texte model (Mel'čuk 1993: 41–133) seeks to replicate the behavior of language. This model is based on two fundamental concepts: the meaning understood as the invariable of the paraphrases of the language, and the text that refers to all materiality of language (morphemes, sentences, paragraphs, etc.). To refer to the representation of the sound, the term phonetic representation is used (RPhon), while semantic representation (RSém)[3] is the representation of the meaning. In order to ensure passage between a meaning and the texts that express it (or, conversely, between a text and the meanings it can express), Sens-Texte model first uses a system of linguistic rules that specifies correspondence {RSémi} ↔ {RPhonj} for a given language in an esthetic (synchronic) way and, then, to a system of procedures that specify the process of moving between meanings and texts. One of the most outstanding benefits of Sens-Texte is the lexicographic production, especially to the production of a series of dictionaries called combinatorial and explanatory (Mel'čuk 1984) in harmony with the objectives of the model[4].

Furthermore, in our research, language tasks related to multi-word units are divided into three groups: identification, interpretation, and register. Interpretation, as an encyclopedic or pragmatic operation, is based on the use of knowledge, while the register depends on the criteria for the selection and use. Computational linguistics, as a discipline aimed to allow automatic systems to understand and use natural language, must face a different challenge for each of these activities.

---

2. For full references on frame semantics mentioned in Fillmore et al. (2003), it is important to see Fontenelle (2003).

3. Abbreviations RPhon and RSém come from the French *phonétique représentation* and *representation* sémantique respectively.

4. Under the frame of Sens-Texte model, a dictionary of Spanish collocations is in the process of drafting (Alonso Ramos 2003 and 2004)

Word-Forms are the basis that computational linguistics explodes at work. They are formed by smaller units, graphemes, with no semantic meaning: the characters. In automatic processing of language, we can distinguish two positions according to the strategy taken for processing texts: stochastic methods that use statistical methodologies to find linguistic units and assign them a place in a conceptual system, and syntactic (or linguistic) methods that use linguistic theories for language processing. We will apply the second method.

In the Laboratory of Analysis and Language Processing (LATL, due to its initials in French) at the University of Geneva, various methods are used (Balanescu 2000). Idiomatic expression recognition is done either at the lexical level or in syntax, which is important because the meaning of a co-occurrence can eventually be cancelled (*estirar la pata* -idiom equivalent to *kick the bucket* can actually mean *estirar la pata -stretch the leg*, which is a literal translation). Being FIPS a robust parser, it allows exploring various possibilities of language processing, which were very useful in this investigation. A parallel work to this one, but from a different theoretical perspective, was developed also in the LATL by Nerima et al. (2006) and Seretan (2011) on the extraction of collocations (in the broad sense) from large corpus or from the web. Seretan created a method that combines syntactic and statistical approaches. The syntax is used to determine the characteristics of the identified units; the statistics are intended to evaluate the chances that a sequence is a collocation.

2.1 The Lexicon

Behind the concept of multi-word units, a set of distinct phenomena, whose relation is the coincidence of several lexical units with a single unit of meaning, is outlined. However, their behavior at the level of the sentence can vary. One consequence of this is the need for a definition of multi-word units that takes into account their syntactic diversity for automatic processing. Due to the abundance of definitions of these units[5], we must draw the boundaries of the phenomenon we are working with. Therefore, in the following part, we present the basic notions concerning the phenomenology and the representation of locutions.

The contemporary syntax is based, generally, on the concept of compositionality, which states that the meaning of the sentence is the sum of the combinatory of its words. Nevertheless, it is not difficult to find examples where the meaning does not necessarily come from this type of processing, for certain words in the sentence do not have the semantic values expected. In this case, we talk about non-compositional[6] meaning of certain lexical sets, which would be words grouped into other words, i.e., multi-word expressions. However, this term is insufficient because it is general and tautological: it is built from a vague notion (word) that is part, simultaneously, of the

5. Leoni de León (2011), for more details on this aspect.

6. That means that it is not calculable from the component elements.

definition (word grouped in other words) and the signifier to specify, both by a synonym (expression) and by the signifier itself (word). Consequently, it is necessary to choose between delimiting the meaning of words or using other more useful operational concepts to have a typological filter to establish difference between the various phenomena which are grouped under the term multi-word expressions, so that we can raise well oriented analysis and treatment strategies.

According to the formal linguistic theory of Principles and Parameters (Chomsky 1981), the phenomena of language are product of a series of operations, triggered by the need to satisfy conditions that balance the components of the phrase from an abstract level (deep) to the level of the sentence realization (surface). Analogously, we can say that, for the lexicon, there are also two levels: the deep one that reckons the lexical units with idiosyncratic information, and the surface one, which constitutes the realization of these units, provided that all conditions were met. Units that are subject to the rules of grammar are lexemes (Moreno de Alba 1992: 31); the units subject to these rules (and thus expressed in speech) are word-forms[7] or morpholexemes[8]. The discourse, as linguistic substance, is ambiguous because it consists on word-forms that are units identified with morpholexemes. In this research we consider the following classification, where we provide a definition of locution:[9]

1. *Word-Form*. Grapheme sequence between white spaces (orthographic form). A statement is a sequence of word-forms (which implies that the statement belongs to speech).
2. *Morpholexeme*. Smallest unit of speech, bearing a grammatical category, with unit of meaning, in which the meaning is the result of the ideas given by the morphemes that compose it. It can also be defined in terms of the morphemic string that produces an inflected form; in other words, a morpholexeme is the realization of a lexeme (see the concept of word-form in Mel'čuk (1993, 1997 and 2003) and Polguère (2003).
3. *Lexia*. Lexical unit with sense, composed either by a lexeme, or by a locution. In here:
    a. *Lexeme* is a set of phonological, morphological, syntactic, and semantic features common to several morpholexemes whose morphological features are neutralized, representing a single meaning.
    b. *Locution* is a grouping of lexemes with simultaneous presence relations, whose meaning is not necessarily compositional.[10]

7. Contrary to Polguère (2003: 50–51), we do not use the term *vocable* to refer to the set of meaningful units associated with the same signifier.

8. The notion of morpholexeme has to do with the word-form of Mel'čuk (1993).

9. This research has also been inspired by other grammar frameworks, among them we cannot avoid to mention Culicover and Jackendoff (2005) and Tomasello (2003).

10. Locution should be understood as idiom.

As can be deduced from the above definitions, the locutions depend on lexemes without establishing a sub-set relation between them. We understand locutions as sets of lexemes with structural links among them; these links can occasionally escape the semantic processing. Although we have outlined the levels of lexical representation according to the condition of realization or abstraction of the lexias, we have to refine the concept of locution. The characterization of this concept in terms of relation between lexemes is not enough because we must still clarify two points: the first one concerns the term locution denoting the representation of a set of lexemes with arbitrary meaning, and the second point concerns the realization of this set.

Regarding the first point, we should return to the discussion of the term word because, analogical to this one, the term *locution* is extensively used, while expressions with multiple words has the disadvantage of being built with inaccurate terms. Therefore, the locution is at risk of being interpreted loosely. As a consequence, we must turn to another term, that of *phraseme*, already used by Mel'čuk et al. (1995), to refer to the meaning of locution mentioned below. It is interesting to compare the term phraseme with phraseolexeme. The latter comes from German lexicography and designates idiomatic units of various elements with denominative function. The components of phraseolexemes show the explicit syntactic relations between them. They also need external components to the unit in order to create a structure of the statement (Larreta Zulátegui 2002: 7)[11]. From this concept, we retain both the syntactic and denominative character of the units as well as their need to be realized as part of the statement.

Regarding the second point, which concerns the realization of phrasemes, there are no specialized terms. Given the parallelism with the lexemes and, due to the fact that for this case we talk about the form of the phrasemes, we propose the term *morphophraseme* for any manifestation of a phraseme. Hence, phrasemes are to morphophrasemes what lexemes are to morpholexemes. Based on Ruiz Gurillo (1996: 14), we affirm that phrasemes are fixed syntagmas with lexeme behavior. Then, a lexia is either a lexeme or a phraseme. Accordingly, the set of lexias composes the lexicon[12] (Leoni de León 2011).

2.2 Lexical and syntactic phenomena

The notion of fixedness is an axiomatic fact in the definition of locutions and idiomatic expressions. Because of its importance, we express it through the following condition:

---

11. The examples cited by Larreta Zulátegui (2002) come from various authors; we take up the German expressions attributed to Fleischer (1982), "die Flucht ergreifen" (where the verb has a metaphorical sense) and "in Misskredit bringen", which can be translated as "escape" and "discredit someone" respectively.

12. See Polguère (2003: 50).

(13) Condition of co-occurrence
$\Gamma(\Lambda)$ is a multi-member lexical unit if and only if the following three conditions are met:
a. $\Gamma(\Lambda)$ comprises a sequence of lexemes $[\Lambda_i ... \Lambda_{i+n}]$.
b. At least two constituent elements of $\Gamma(\Lambda)$ come from open lexical categories.
c. The meaning denoted by $\Gamma(\Lambda)$ vanishes in the absence of any component from $\Gamma(\Lambda)$ (compulsory co-occurrence).

About the notation in (13), we point out that Γ is the symbol for group and that the capital letters indicate lexemes, while the lower case refer to realizations. So, for all $\Gamma(\Lambda)$, which is a lexeme, there is at least one $\Gamma(\lambda)$ representing all its units (i.e. morpholexemes), realized by a $\Gamma(\beta)$ (a set of word-forms). For generation, we have $\Gamma(\Lambda) \rightarrow \Gamma(\lambda) \rightarrow \Gamma(\beta)$; while $\Gamma(\beta) \rightarrow \Gamma(\lambda) \rightarrow \Gamma(\Lambda)$ corresponds to the reverse sense. $\Gamma(\beta)$ is a set belonging to a sequence of a character string. If $\Gamma(\Lambda)$ is realized by a group $\Gamma(\beta)$, then there are two possible realizations:

(14) *Clustering and sequence of word-form relations*
Let $\Gamma(\beta)$ be an identity of at least two $\underline{\beta_n}$, then $\Gamma(\beta)$ can be:
a. Continuous: $[\beta_1\ \underline{\beta_2\ \beta_3}\ \beta_4]$; or
b. Discontinuous or disintegrated: $[\underline{\beta_2}\ \beta_1\ \underline{\beta_3}\ \beta_4]$.

A locution such as *saco de dormir* (*sleeping bag*) is of type (14a), since it is impossible to introduce modifiers within the sequence, while en *señal de protesta* (*in protest*) is of type (14b), as an adjective can interrupt the sequence, en *evidente* señal de protesta (*in evident protest*).

The continuity of the expressions is complemented by the substitution. This corresponds to our concept of commutation. Substitution is a paradigmatic characteristic related to the identity of the expressions. Accordingly, it does not operate on the syntax. As the name implies, it refers to the ability to find an element instead of another, without changing the meaning. Table 1 presents these two binary features.

With the help of these conceptual tools, we can now propose an economic lexical scheme. In order to do this, it is necessary to consider that a set of lexemes corresponding to a unit of meaning can have one of the following two properties: it either accepts

Table 1. Basic typological features of multi-member units

Type	Substitution	Continuity
A	+	+
B	–	+
C	+	–
D	–	–

syntagmatic-level modifiers within its boundaries (i.e., is [–continuous]),[13] or is refractory ([+ continuous]). Regarding the lexicon, the implications of the presence of this feature are important. The continuous sequences are an integral part of the lexicon, whereas discontinuous sequences are the result of systemic relations. These latter ones are made possible because of the inter-lexical links. Leoni de León (2011) proposes a lexical representation in two levels consisting on well-defined units, each corresponding to a lexeme. All lexeme, by definition, is [+ continuous], either monomial – *caja* (*box*), *saco* (*sack*), or polynomial – *caja de música (music box)*, *saco de dormir* (*sleeping bag*). Since lexical units carry the feature [–continuous] – *estirar la pata* (*kick the bucket*), *romper un récord* (*break a record*), they are seen as ties or links between lexemes, such as bridges connected with other lexical items which do not belong to the same expression. This information is provided with the idiosyncratic lexical dataset.

The continuity is directly reflected in the distribution of word-forms. The operation of recovering lexemes from word-forms requires three stages for the continuous units and the lexemes (Leoni de Leon 2011). We can consider this process as relations (16) between sets, the latter defined in (15):

(15) a. V = {x| x = any sequence of characters separated by a space in a character string}.
b. M = {x| x is an n-tuple, where each member belongs to V}
c. L = set of lexical units in a language.

Let us recall that an n-tuple in mathematics is a collection of n objects such that it is possible to say exactly which the first element is, the second one, ..., the n-th, with the condition that n is a nonzero natural whole number. The elements are also called components. Then, the transition from one stage to another is the implementation of a different function for each stage:

(16) Let f be a function of V in M and g a function of M in L, it is composed in the function of V in L (g[f (x)]): g ° f

In our view, the members of phrasemes (P) would constitute, from this fact, a subset of L:

(17) $\forall x \in P, x \in L$. Then $P \subset L$.
Where: $P = \{x \mid x = < y_1 ... y_n >$; such that $y_1 ... y_n \in L, n > 1 \}$[14]

Thus, the continuity is a relation of M in V, where V is considered a list whose distribution of elements is also the result of applying a function, denoted projection, annotated as p(x). Also, the feature [± continuous] comes into play with the possibilities of projection of an expression, being the structure of the tuples in M the result of applying a function on selected elements of L. These definitions allow us to identify the area of

13. As "evidente" (*evident*) in the example "en evidente señal de protesta" (*in evident protest*).

14. That is, the members of P are tuples.

influence of the phenomena related to expressions and, at the same time, to exploit these concepts as valid criteria for classification. This conception of the lexicon establishes three levels (word-forms, morpholexemes and lexicon, V, M, and L, respectively). V is the raw lexical material; the relations between the members of V are set in M, where long distance grammatical relations can be found. The discontinuity is best exemplified in French, where it is possible to insert adverbs between the auxiliary verb avoir and the past participle:

(18) Il a toujours neigé en Tlön
It has always snowed in Tlön

In (18) the auxiliary verb *avoir*, realized as the third person singular, and the lexeme (*snow*), form a single unit of meaning. Once the relation between the two has been established, it has to be linked to a lexeme in L. The morpholexemes are conceived as links between word-forms that point to a lexeme in the lexicon (see Leoni de León 2011 for details).

3. Combinatorial interdependencies

The display of expressions on the sentence requires taking into account its syntax to retrieve the information they contain. Thus, we establish two axes, one of vertical relations that we call paradigmatic, another of horizontal relations that we call syntagmatic. Locutions can vary paradigmatically without having their meaning affected. These facts lead us to divide the combinatorial possibilities of phraseological units into two classes. The first one (syntagmatic) directly concerns their ability of permutation that, although low, requires significant analysis resources. The second one (paradigmatic) has to do with commutation of elements without altering the meaning. The lack of freedom of action of the phraseological unit members in relation to the lexemes is a distinguishing feature that should be considered at all times. It is clear that the syntagmatic axis is the one that defines the characteristic of continuity, whereas the paradigmatic axis represents substitution options. Numerous dependency and commutation phenomena were addressed in the specialized literature (Makkai 1972; Gross 1996; Fernando 1996; Ruiz Gurillo 1996), from where we have gotten some of our examples.

3.1 Syntagmatic relations

Syntagmatic relations are relations of horizontality in the sentence, that is, among syntagmas. These involve a hierarchy and a set of interdependencies between components. Consequently, if we consider V a list, the position of elements in this list is necessarily significant. When a phraseological unit is realized within a sequence of word-forms, syntagmatic relations typical of the sentence can hide another order that affects its interpretation:

(19) Intervention of phraseological units in syntagmatic relations
$\Gamma(\beta) = (a\ \underline{b}_1\ c\ \underline{d}_2 ...)$

For example, in (19), each element of Γ(β) is interpreted according to its position, dictated by the rules of syntax, the processing ends in a meaning given to the whole sentence. However, noticing the contextual phraseological values of bγ and dγ can produce a second meaning, far from the first one, which constitutes an alternative. The scheme in (19) also represents phraseological discontinuity relations. Following we will mention the main operations on the syntagmatic axis. We do not omit to point out that this relation of syntactic phenomena was inspired originally from Fernando (1996), which was further developed by Leoni de León (2011).

Addition

Addition is the possibility of adding the modifiers, both around the expression and in the expression itself. Fernando (1996: 47) considers addition a rare option in English:

(20) English:
a. ivory towers → *carpeted* ivory towers
b. tongue-in-cheek → tongue *only partly* in cheek

(21) Spanish
a. saco de dormir → *gran* saco de dormir
sleeping bag *big sleeping bag*
b. en señal de [protesta] → en *evidente* señal de [protesta]
in protest *in evident protest*

Examples (20a) and (21a) are product of a normal operation of a nominal locution being qualified by an adjective. By contrast, in (20b) and (21b), the same operation is performed within multiple-member units. Obviously, the internal cohesion is not the same in both cases, and neither is the scope of the adjectives. The addition is made possible by an internal flexibility of the multi-member unit. In other words, (20a) and (21a) do not come from the data of their respective members in L, but from the functions responsible for the distribution of morpholexemes[15]. In contrast, the flexibility of (20b) and (21b) is encoded in the L level as P[16] units.

Ellipsis

Some expressions allow the omission of some of their components, often with a pause in the place of the elided element, without altering the meaning:

15. Regardless of the sequence belonging to L or P.

16. These phenomena are similar to those of the paradigmatic axis to the extent that their processing is very similar, as is explained in Section 3.2.

(22) a. A buen entendedor, pocas palabras.
A word to the wise

b. A buen entendedor...
A word...

However, it is not possible to remove segments arbitrarily; often only the components at the end of the expression can be suppressed. Further study should allow confirmation of this hypothesis. For now, we must remember that the information on the elements that can be omitted is encoded at the level of L. Later, we will discuss a type of ellipsis in which obligatorily the omitted element belongs to a functional category.

Permutation

Permutation is the adjustment of the components of the multi-member lexical units in the sentence. That is, it is the syntactic choices. This characteristic, offered to the any phraseological unit that has the feature [–continuous], is the result of applying p(x). It is generally described in negative terms, seeking the restriction of operations of a unit more than its available options. On our account, we will try to put more weight on the options than on restrictions. The most important permutation possibilities described here are the clitization, nominalization, adjectivization, wh-movement, and versification.

The permutation phenomenon demonstrates the relevance of a syntactic analysis for the recognition of idioms, because, even if you have stored phraseological sequences, one must consider the many forms in which it can manifest.

Pronominalization test. The clitization is allowed only by a small number of expressions. When it happens, the meaning of the sentence is particularly dark for automatic processing systems. Often pronominalization also implies some other form of insertion:

(23) Clitizable Phrasemes:
a. meter la pata
make a blunder (literal: to put the foot)

b. meterla hasta el fondo
make a big blunder (literal: to put it all the way to the bottom)

(24) Non-clitizable Phrasemes:
a. ponerle el cascabel al gato
undertake a difficult or dangerous task (literal: "put a bell on the cat")

b. ponérselo al gato*
(literal: "put it on the cat")

Clitization can also be activated when taking parts of speech back, e.g. repetition of the expression with a different subject (Mendívil Giró 1999: 517):

(25) Juan abrió la boca y también la abrió Pedro.
John opened his mouth, and Pedro opened it too.

This phenomenon is not unique to Spanish. In French, the clitization is also possible, but it is more restricted:

Paul a parlé: Paul a ouvert la bouche. → Paul l'a toujours ouverte.
Paul spoke: *Paul opened his mouth.* *Paul always opened it.*

Let us stress here the insertion of an adverbial syntagma in French toujours. In comparison with the Spanish example in (23b), where clitization is accompanied by the sum of a circumstantial complement – *hasta el fondo* (*all the way to the bottom*), this example illustrates the complexity of the operation undergone by an internal argument of a phraseological unit. The emptiness of the argument, taken up by the clitic in a position next to the verb, is offset necessarily by a syntagma with circumstantial value (either an adverb or a phrase). The example (25) seems to confirm this hypothesis – the adverb present is *también* (*too*).

For automatic processing, there are two possibilities. The first one is to consider the forms with clitics as synonyms of a main or base expression. The data recovery work would be enormous, and would always be incomplete. By contrast, the second option would be to enrich the system with the required knowledge just described. This strategy would give the system flexibility in the idiomatic processing. Moreover, nothing prevents from naming the versions with clitics and considering them as synonyms of the expression. We will return to this idea later.

Nominalization. Nominalization acts on the main verb of an expression, without loss of argument structure:

(26) a. blanquear dinero
launder money

b. blanqueo de dinero
Money laundering

(27) a. ponerse el Sol
get dark

b. puesta del Sol
sunset

(28) a. meter la pata
make a blunder (literal: put the foot)

b. metida de pata
a blunder

(29) a. untar la mano
grease someone's hand

b. untada de mano
hand greasing

The fact that the arguments are saturated with the components of the original expression allows nominalization, as the *Co-occurrence Condition* (13) is respected. Again, the data recovery is a possibility to identify nominalized phrasemes, but the establishment of trans-categorical links among the members L should facilitate the search for nominalizations of phrasemes already recovered. Other than this, the choice of prepositions when there is a nominalization is often calculable. Leoni de León (2011) shows an overview of these possibilities according to the nominal type, based on a more restricted version of D'Introno (2002) classification. The proposed scheme establishes a relation between the nominal type and the prepositions selected. Thus, there is a link between the predicative nominal and the preposition added. Extended to the set of nominals, we found a phraseological sensitivity zone (bottom of figure). The boundaries of a syntactic approximate are reached quickly since the moment in which the need for lexical-syntactic criteria is imposed, particularly for predicative nominals.

Adjectivation and Passivization. The adjectivation and passivization are closely linked, since the first operation needs the adjective form of the verb (the participle) to be made. However, the passive form is rare in expressions:

(30) a. Pedro estiró la pata.
Pedro kicked the bucket.

b. *La pata fue estirada por Pedro.
**The bucket was kicked by Pedro.*

c. Carlos agarró de maje a Luis.
Carlos fooled Luis.

d. Luis fue agarrado de maje por Carlos.
Luis was fooled by Carlos.

The example (30d) shows the only expression we found that can undergo the passive structure in Spanish. However, it is not completely opaque. It is also more common that the direct object of the expression be put before, under the condition of finding an adjective associated with the verb or of using the participle of the verb as an adjective.

If there is an adjective form concurrent to the participle, we prefer the adjective, as shown in Table 3. This data supports the hypothesis of links between the members of L. Such links are used to select the best candidates belonging to an expression (in case one would have to choose between a participle and an adjective). Phenomena in Tables 2 and 3 can be classified into the nominalization, but we prefer to consider them adjectivations of the past passive participle, as its processing requires a prior knowledge of the expression in its transitive form in order to recognize the participle as a derivative of the verb, thanks to the analysis.

Interrogatives and relativizations. Phraseological units are greedy in terms of wh-movement[17]. In any case, in Spanish we do not find convincing facts in this regard, as shown in the following examples:

17. With the exception of collocations.

Table 2. Deverbal Adjectivation

Spanish		French
Cerrar el pico		Fermer le bec
↓	Passivization	↓
El pico <SER> cerrado		Le bec <ÊTRE> fermé
↓	Ellipsis	↓
(con) el pico cerrado		(avec) le bec fermé

Table 3. Deverbal adjectivation with lexical alternation

Spanish		French
Bajar la guardia		Baisser la garde
↓	Passivization	↓
La guardia <SER> bajada/baja	Alternative adjective	La garde <ÊTRE> baissé/basse
↓	Ellipsis	↓
(con) la guardia baja		(avec) la garde basse

(31) a. Une mouche l'a piqué.
b. Quelle mouche l'a piqué?

(32) a. (A él) lo ha picado una mosca.
He's acting weird. Literal: He has been bitten by a bug.

b. ¿Cuál mosca lo ha picado?
What bug has bitten him?

Our first example (31), in French, seems to contradict our claim on wh-movement sensitivity. However, in Spanish, the equivalent sentences differ in terms of their connotation. For example, (32a) expresses a feeling of uneasiness, while (32b) is about the cause of an illness considered inappropriate by the speaker. In fact, the idea of untimeliness changes everything between these two examples in Spanish and leads us to consider them as different units. Obviously, there is a link between these sentences, but at the moment we can only say that it goes beyond syntax. The sentences in (33) and (34) illustrate the difficulties to produce relativizations and topicalizations from the internal arguments of idiomatic expressions:

(33) Relativizations and interrogatives:
a. Dar en el clavo.
Hit the nail on the head

b. *El clavo en el que has dado [me pertenece].
The nail you have hit (belongs to me)

c. Ponerle el cascabel al gato.
Literal: put a bell on the cat.

d. ¿Qué le puso al gato? El cascabel.
Literal: what did you put to the cat? The bell.

(34) Topicalization:

a. Buscarle tres pies al gato.
Split hairs. Literal: look for three legs on the cat.

b. *Al gato, le buscas tres pies.
Literal: on the cat you look for three legs.

These phenomena involve shifting the arguments of the phraseological verb outside its area. Furthermore, phraseological units need their internal arguments to remain in the domain of the verb or of the predicative nominal to preserve its idiomatic sense. Thus, the *condition of co-occurrence* (13) must be read together with the domain of the verb or of the predicative nominal. In the case of clitization, the *co-occurrence condition* is respected because the clitic occurs next to the verb. Now, we can understand more easily why the passivization is rare, but it plays an important role in adjectivation: it is possible as long as the elements transformed remain in the same domain. However, Mendivil Giró (1999: 539) notes that some expressions allow interrogatives phrases and relativizations; such as the phraseological unit *tomar el pelo a alguien* (*to tease someone*):

(35) a. Guillermo le tomó el pelo a Lidia.
Guillermo teased Lidia (Literal: Guillermo pulled Lidia's hair)

b. ¿A quién le tomaron el pelo?
Who was teased? (Literal: Whose hair was pulled?)

The interrogation is possible because the dative (a Lidia) is an argument of the expression itself and not part of the internal structure. Stated another way, the phraseological unit functions here as a verb. This finding leads to differentiate the internal structure of the units, expression of its surroundings[18].

Versification

The musicality, through rhyme, is important in certain expressions[19]:

(36) a. Quien tiene boca, se equivoca.
He who has a mouth, makes mistake

b. Prometer el oro y el moro.
To promise the earth or the moon

18. In the definition of our formalism, *Tsool*, we go deeper on this topic.

19. The concept of collocation of Firth also contained meaning pairs linked by rhyme (Firth, 1957: 197–198).

c. A lo hecho, pecho.
It's no use crying over spilt milk

d. A ciencia y paciencia.
With full knowledge and consent.

Rhyme, in these cases, serves to highlight the cohesion of an idiomatic set as to help in its interpretation. Noticing the versification can be useful for retrieval tactics. It should be noted, also, that the substitution of components here is hardly possible. In our case, taking into account the diversification adds an additional criterion to calculate idiomaticity; its presence in a phraseme is a good phraseological indication.

3.2 Paradigmatic relations

Paradigmatic relations are relations of substitution without altering the meaning. They are called vertical because the syntagmatic sequence is not altered. In Table 1, paradigmatic relations are marked by the feature [± substitution]. This feature implies preservation of the form and meaning. No feature is modified in the substitution. We consider three possibilities for substitution: either it can be done with previously known elements (commutation), with an element spontaneously introduced (deautomatization), or it is entirely impossible (invariability).

Commutation

Commutation refers to the simple substitution of a lexical item for another without altering the meaning of the expression:

(37) Non-commutable Components
a. pagar el pato
get the blame (Literal: to pay the duck)

b. *pagar el conejo
get the blame (Literal: to pay the rabbit)

(38) Commutable Components
a. importarle un pito (a alguien)
Someone could not care less (Literal: care (give) a whistle)

b. importarle un [bledo, pepino, comino, rábano, pimiento] (a alguien)
Someone could not care less (Literal: care (give) a pepper, a cucumber, cumin, a radish)

(39) Commutable Components
a. meter la pata
Make a blunder. (Literal: to put the foot)

b. meter [la pata, las de andar]
To put (the foot, those to walk)

We must take into account many aspects. First, the substitution belongs to a finite set of possibilities. Then, only a part of the expression can be substituted. For example, in (38) and (39), *importarle* (*care*) and *meter* (*put*) cannot be replaced. Changes are often limited by the semantic (or phonetic) characteristics of the item to be replaced: in (38) it is related to small edible objects ending with the vowel [o][20], while (39) has a paraphrase of the original nominal. This knowledge will be encoded in our model.

Deautomatization

Deautomatization[21] designates a lot of sentence operations. Essentially, it denotes the creative alteration of an expression (Mena Martínez 2003):

(40) a. dar gato por liebre
deceive someone (Literal: to give cat instead of hare)

b. [que a los europeos no les] den gato por euro
that Europeans don't get deceived (Literal: that Europeans don't get cat instead of Euro)

Sentence (40a) becomes (40b) by a process of deautomatization, i.e., due to the replacement of the word LIEBRE (*hare*) by EURO (the latter is not part of the list of possibilities to substitute *liebre* (*hare*). Mena Martínez (2003) postulated volition or intentionality of the speaker to accept this type of construction. However, it is difficult, almost impossible, to determine the intention behind changing a phraseme. It seems that the difference with the commutation lies in the spontaneity and frequency, in relation to a famous expression. Nevertheless, it is clear that part that undergoes change, like in commutation, is usually found at the end of the expression, and it is also likely to have relevant phonetic and semantic features. Prior knowledge of the expression is mandatory in order not to fail in the act of language. Consequently, this operation must be applied to very famous expressions.

Morpho-syntactic invariability features

So far we have shown the diversity of the combinatorial possibilities of expressions and how they can be of many types, like with clitization or adjectivization. The opposite, that is the lack of variety, is also possible. The morpho-syntactic features (such as gender, person, or time) or semantic-syntactic features (as the feature [± definite] of the article) are true indicators of invariability:[22]

20. Other phonological similarities are predictable, such as the presence of consonants (bi)labial
21. The French term for deautomatization is *réformulation* (*reformulation*).
22. Examples (42) and (43) were discussed in Ruiz Gurillo (1996).

(41) Number

a. No hay moros en la costa.
Nobody is around (Literal: There are no Moors in the cost)

b. No hay moro en la costa.*
Nobody is around (Literal: There is no Moor in the cost)

(42) Time

a. El que a buen árbol se arrima, buena sombra lo cobija.
No investment pays larger dividends than friendship. (Literal: The one that goes near a good tree, gets good shadow)

b. *El que a buen árbol se arrimó, buena sombra lo cobijó.
No investment pays larger dividends than friendship. (Literal: The one that went closer to a good tree, got good shadow)

(43) [±definite]

a. Guillermo le tomó el pelo a Lidia.
Guillermo teased Lidia (Literal: Guillermo pulled Lidia's hair)

b. Guillermo le tomó un pelo a Lidia.*
Guillermo teased Lidia (Literal: Guillermo pulled a hair of Lidia)

These examples show that the idiomaticity may depend on a single element (though, obviously, other factors may also come into play).

3.3 Inflectional morphology of complex lexical units

The morphology of phraseological expressions has a long list of possibilities in terms of paradigmatic diversity[23]. However, each unit's options are often very limited, almost nonexistent. For example, let us take a combined lexeme whose internal sequence is $[_{VP}\, V^0\, [_{DP} \ldots]]$. In Spanish this type of lexemes has no blank spaces separating the nuclei that form them. This phenomenology is illustrated in Table 4. Furthermore, in Spanish morphology, resulting lexemes have {ø} for singular and {-s} for plural. Table 5 corresponds to this situation.

Table 4. Combined lexemes formation

[VPguardia[DPmeta]]	→	{guarda}{meta}	→	[guardameta] *goalkeeper*
[VPgarde[DPbut]]	→	gardien de but		
[VPguarda[DPbosque]]	→	{guarda}{bosque}	→	[guardabosque] *ranger*
[VPgarde[DPforêt]]	→	{gardien}{forestier}	→	gardeforestier *ranger*

23. Savary (2000) partially discussed the problem of multi-word units' morphology in French.

Table 5. Combined lexemes' inflexional morphology

GUARDAMETA				
goalkeeper	$\rightarrow_{sing}$	[guardameta]	$\rightarrow_{plur}$	[guardametas]
GUARDABOSQUE				
ranger	$\rightarrow_{sing}$	[guardabosque]	$\rightarrow_{plur}$	[guardabosques]

Table 6. Nominal decomposition

Features	Morphemes	Scheme*	Example
sing	{ø}	[NP{...}_[AP{...}]]	cielo raso *ceiling*
		[NP{...}[AP{...}]]	cielorraso
plur	{-s}	[NP{...}{-s}_[AP{...}{-s}]]	cielos rasos
		{[NP{...}_[AP{...}]]}{-s}	cielorrasos

*We use the symbol "_" to mark a typographic mandatory space.

We consider combined lexemes whole lexemes as long as their components are always together. If this is not so, we classify them as compound lexemes in what is known as decomposition, a phenomenon illustrated in the following table.

The double writing of the term *cielo raso* (*ceiling*) in Table 6 can make us think that this is just a spelling variation. However, this hypothesis is refuted easily by the double plural form, which can only be explained if, in one case, it is a combined lexeme (*cielorrasos*), and in the other case (*cielo rasos*), we are facing a poly-lexemic lexeme (i.e., composed by several lexemes). Anyway, we should not forget that this is a single term. Other cases are also possible, such as *mal humor* (*bad mood*), which has an alternate form in singular, *malhumor*, and two plurals, *malos humores* and *malhumores* (rare).

Previously, we showed the limits and possibilities of syntactic phrasemes (as passivization and clitization). These may be defective (les, *them, indirect object*, is impossible to be in all moods, times and persons), or they can occur only with a single grammatical accident. Multi-member lexemes are not far behind in terms of lexical-syntactic possibilities, which also give us indication about their lexical status. Nominal sequences containing a PP have the characteristic of receiving the feature of nominal in the nucleus of the group, as shown in Table 7. The plural is called *inner*, as it occurs inside the expression. In other cases, it is impossible to put it in plural without changing the meaning denoted by the unit, phenomenon illustrated in Table 8.

Furthermore, there are cases in which singular is characteristic of a phraseological sequence and plural is interpreted literally (Table 9). However, the agreement of all elements of the unit is not always mandatory. Thus, in the sequences [NP [N [N ...]]] only the first element pluralizes, the contrary would produce an ungrammatical sequence (Table 10). Derivational morphology is often applicable in Spanish. It can be within certain phraseological units. Particularly, this is the case of the diminutive:

SACO DE DORMIR $\rightarrow_{dim}$ saquito de dormir $\rightarrow_{plur}$ saquitos de dormir
Sleeping bag
METIDA DE PATA $\rightarrow_{dim}$ metidita de pata $\rightarrow_{plur}$ metiditas de pata
A blunder
SALTO MORTAL $\rightarrow_{dim}$ saltito mortal $\rightarrow_{plur}$ saltitos mortales
Somersault

The morphological derivations are experienced, then, in the nucleus of the unit. Nevertheless, derivational morphology also has its limits:

CIELO RASO $\rightarrow_{dim}$?cielito raso $\rightarrow_{plur}$?cielitos rasos
ceiling $\rightarrow_{dim}$?cielorasito $\rightarrow_{plur}$?cielorrasitos

All morphosyntactic and lexical characteristics studied in this section outline the contours of our research topic. In the next section, they will help us to differentiate between the types of expressions, fundamental distinction for our model.

Table 7. Inner plural

Features	Morphemes	Scheme	Examples
Singular	{ø}	[NP {...} [PP ...]]	saco de dormir *(sleeping bag)*
Plural	{-s}	[NP {. . .}{–s} [PP . . .]]	sacos de dormir *(sleeping bags)*

Table 8. Mandatory singular, non-existent plural

Sub-type	Features	Morphemes	Scheme	Examples
I	Singular	{ø}	[NP{...}_[ConjP y_[DP...]]]	Crema y nata *The best of the best*
	Plural	–	–	–
II	Singular	{ø}	[NP[AP{...}]_{...}]	Buena gente *Nice people*
	Plural	–	–	–

Table 9. Mandatory Plural, non- existent singular

Morphemes	Scheme	Example
{-s}	[NP{...}_[AP{...}]]	Patas vueltas *Dopey*

Table 10. Partial Pluralization

Features	Morphemes	Scheme	Examples
Singular	{ø}	[NP{...}_[NP{...}]]	Buque insignia (Flagship)
Plural	{-s}	[NP{...}{-s}_[NP{...}]]	Buques insignia (Flagships)

3.4 Formal definitions

So far, we mentioned the main features that characterize multi-member lexical units, in order to outline the basic units of our knowledge model. Throughout the discussion, certain terms such as phraseme, polylexical unit, multi-member unit, or phraseological unit were used indifferently. These terms refer, in general, to the phenomenon of lexical co-occurrence in a set that produces a unique meaning. This set should be involved in syntactic changes in the same level as the syntagmas represented by a single lexical unit. From now on, for this conception of lexical co-occurrence, we reserve the synonyms *phraseological unit, complex unit, multi-member unit, and expression.* Now, it is time to exploit these criteria, which we define below, to identify the units that make up our system. These definitions deal with multi-member lexemes, phrasemes, collocations, and thematic fusions that form the higher types of our classification, as well as some of its sub-classes, such as poly-lexemic lexemes and combined lexemes.

3.4.1 *Multi-member lexemes*

Multi-member lexemes are units belonging to the lexicon (L), formed from at least two *lexical morphemes*, where one is the nucleus of the unit: it is the one containing either the primary meaning, or the features that characterize the poly-lexemic construction. At least two of the lexemes that make up the unit must belong to one of the open lexical classes: nouns (N), adjectives (A), preposition (P), or adverbs (Adv). They do not belong, then, to the category verb (V). The expressions created this way are carriers of one of the following lexical categories: {N, A, P, Adv}.

The other members of the unit may belong to any lexical or functional class open or closed; their distribution responds to syntactic constraints. In (44) we have a Spanish sample for this type of construction:

(44) a. palabra de honor
word of honour

b. cuerpo técnico-administrativo
technical and administrative staff

c. hispanoárabe
Hispanic-Arabic

d. luso-japonés
Luso-Japanese

e. nomeolvides
forget-me-not

In order to have a formal definition of lexemes, we must first tune the idea of lexemes in relation to L, with the aim of determining the composition of the multi-member lexemes:

(45) Lexicon and lexeme
Let L be the lexicon in language G, and let S be the set of meanings represented by L.
Λ_α is a lexeme if and only if:
a. $\Lambda_\alpha \subset L$.
b. Λ_α receives one and only one of the following lexical categories: {N, A, P, Adv}
c. Λ_α is assigned at least one of the meanings of S.

(46) Multi-member lexemes
A lexeme Λ_n of G is called multi-member if and only if all the following conditions are met simultaneously:
a. Λ_n is the result of the union of at least one Λ_α and one Λ_β
b. $[\Lambda_\alpha \Lambda_\beta] \subset L$ and preexist to $\not\subset_n$ in L
c. Λ_n receives one and only one of the following lexical categories: {N, A, P, Adv}
d. Λ_n denotes a meaning $S_n \subset S$

In (46a) and (46b), multi-member lexemes are defined in terms of other members of the lexicon. They transform into the result of the combination of lexemes to create a new lexeme. A more general consequence of (46) is the conception of multi-member lexemes as the result of a process of lexicalization that we might call *catachresis*, figure of speech that is a lexicalized metaphor representing an idea devoid of its own sign in the lexicon. We consider multi-member lexemes a solution provided by the language to grant an entry in the lexicon with a meaning to be expressed. For this reason, as it is clear from the lexical representation of Leoni de León (2011), and just as it results from (46c) and (46d), multi-member lexemes belong to the level of lexemes. Another consequence appears in the composition of our lexicon, which consists of two types of lexemes: simple lexemes, whose morphological division has no trace of another lexeme, and multi-member lexemes formed from simple lexemes that still respect the paradigms of declension and conjugation.

In Spanish, as the apostrophe is archaic, multi-member lexemes can only be written in one of three ways: with no hyphen (44a), with hyphen (44b), or fused (44e). The agrammaticality of multi-member lexemes that are modified by other syntagmas is the consequence of the insertion of a lexeme (a segment of reference) within the lexical unit. The spelling reflects this possibility[24]. With this point made, we provide with (47) a definition of *poly-lexemic lexeme*:

(47) Poly-lexemic Lexemes
A lexeme Λ_n is poly-lexemic if and only if all the following conditions are met simultaneously:
a. all members of Λ_n are separated by a space in writing, and
b. the lexical category of Λ_n is endocentric.

Thus, the lexeme in (44a)[25] is an example for Spanish. The relevance of spelling comes from the fact that we chose the text as the substance to be analyzed in our research. We can express the definition (47) in another way:

(48) Poly-lexemic Lexemes
A lexeme Λ_n is poly-lexemic if and only if all the following conditions are met simultaneously:
a. Λ_n is [+continuous]; and
b. the lexical category of Λ_n is endocentric.

Accordingly, a sequence of word-forms may correspond to a lexical entry. The spaces are then spelling signs of the same level as the hyphens and apostrophes. A frequent access to the memory will be needed to verify a possible correspondence between these sequences and a lexeme, different from the combined lexemes, which contain no spaces:

(49) Combined Lexemes
A multi- member lexeme Λ_n is called *combined* if and only if:
a. Λ_n is [+continuous];
b. the members of Λ_n are fused or separated by punctuation (hyphen or apostrophe);
c. the lexical category of Λ_n can be exocentric or endocentric.

Examples (44b), (44c), (44d), and (44e) are Spanish combined lexemes. The relevance of this sub-category comes from the fact that, given the differences between the two sub-groups, for each kind of polylexical phenomenon, it is necessary to have an analysis and processing adapted to the characteristics of the polylexical class concerned, especially for the case of plural. Then, a question arises: how to recognize the multi-member lexemes? One possibility is to apply a series of tests that demonstrate the status of the multi- member lexeme. Bouvier (1999) is a good example. He proposes a

24. Gross (1989: 35–38) and Silberztein (1989) wrote about the particularities of the French spelling in TALN. The processing of multi-member lexemes is described in Wehrli (1997).

25. We leave in suspense other ambiguous cases such as *adjective-adjective*.

sequence of procedures to recognize them. We quote (and adapt) the most relevant ones to our research[26]:

(50) $D^0_{[-\text{definite, +plural}]}$ **Test:**

Be

$\Psi = D^0_{[-\text{definite, +plural}]}$; and

$\Phi = [_{NP}\, \alpha\, [_{AP}\, \beta]]$

Where Ψ precedes a sequence Φ, such that $[_{DP}\, \Psi\Phi]$:

a. If Ψ cannot take the plural mark and preserve the idiomatic meaning, then the sequence Φ is not a multi- member lexeme; inversely

b. If Ψ precedes a sequence Φ and must take a plural mark, then, this sequence Φ is a multi- member lexeme.

Examples (51a) and (51b), quoted by Bouvier, have their equivalent in Spanish in (51c) and (51d):

(51) a. J'ai eu des bons points.

b. *J'ai eu de bons points.

c. Obtuve buenas notas.
I got good grades.

d. Obtuve unas buenas notas.*
I got some good grades.

In opposition to French, in Spanish, the absence of the article is a marker of idiomaticity in these constructions, taking the preposition *de* (*of*) and the indefinite *un* (*a*) (in French) a different behavior in this context. Accordingly, we reformulate (50) to fit it into Spanish:

(52) D^0 **elided:**

Let ξ be a verification feature in syntax in a sequence Γ of the form:

a.

$$\Gamma = \left[NP \left\{ \begin{matrix} N_{[\xi]} \left[AP\, \gamma_{[\xi]} \right] \\ \left[AP\, \gamma_{[\xi]} \right] N_{[\xi]} \end{matrix} \right\} \right]$$

and Δ a syntagmatic sequence that may contain Γ, such that:

$\Delta = [_{DP}\, [_{D}{}^{0}\, ø]\, \Gamma]$

and let Y be a syntagmatic sequence that may also contain Γ, such that:

b.

$$\Delta = \left[DP \left[D^0 \theta \right] \Gamma \right]$$

26. We omit non-interruptibility, unmodifiability, and unique concept (denotation) tests.

In this case, the meaning of a sequence Y differs in the content from which the result is the processing of the set of its elements. Furthermore, the plural and gender, which are not always compositional in multi-member lexemes, are useful to determine the fixedness (Bouvier 1999):

(53) If a sequence Mod[ifier] + N or N + Mod[ifier] that carries plural marking on at least one of the two elements can be attached to a $D^0_{[-\text{plural}]}$, then this sequence forms a compound.

The examples in Spanish (54), which belong to the oral register, show that this type of structure is possible in this language:

(54) a. un patas vueltas
a dopey guy

b. unos patas vueltas
some dopey guys

c. Ellos son unos patas vueltas.
They are some dopey guys

(55) Idiosyncratic features:

a.
$$\Delta = \left[DP\alpha_{[+\mu]} \left\{ \begin{array}{l} NP\,\beta_{[+\mu]}\left[AP\,\gamma_{[+\mu]}\right]\Big] \\ NP\left[AP\,\gamma_{[+\mu]}\beta_{[+\mu]}\right]\Big] \end{array} \right\} \right]$$

Let μ be an inflectional feature (for syntax verification) and be the agreement sequences the following:

and

b.
$$\Gamma = \left[DP\alpha_{[+\mu]} \left\{ \begin{array}{l} NP\,\beta_{[-\mu]}\left[AP\,\gamma_{[-\mu]}\right]\Big] \\ NP\left[AP\,\gamma_{[-\mu]}\beta_{[-\mu]}\right]\Big] \end{array} \right\} \right]$$

Where μ is an agreement feature for syntax verification.

In this case, the full syntagma is compositional, if the agreement configuration is Δ, but if the agreement configuration is Γ, then the DP in Γ contains a poly-lexemic lexeme. For example, (55) allows to recognize a syntagma with a poly-lexemic lexeme like (54c), where the features you need to check are the *feminine* and *plural.*

Other tests are possible, for example, a verification of phonological features (ligatures, elided vowels, etc.), or the possibilities of combining polylexical constructions with other maximum projections. The main difficulty with these suggestions resides in the fact that they require prior knowledge of the characteristics of the complex lexical construction, in order to be able to classify them. Consequently, one must know *beforehand* that a sequence is a multi-member construction, while we seek criteria to recognize them without knowing about their nature. For now, although (52) and (55) are about nominal projections forming poly-lexemic lexemes, they show our heuristic tactic. For combined lexemes, we show some spelling and lexical features that will be of great use.

3.4.2 *Phrasemes*

A phraseme is a unit of meaning formed from at least two open-class lexical morphemes, one of which constitutes the nucleus of the unit and bears the category V. The denotative value of the unit is associated with the co-occurrence of lexemes that it contains and not with the result of the syntagmatic processing and semantic values of the elements of the set; this quality is often pointed out with the epithets tropic and *opaque*. Mel'čuk (2003) defines them in following terms.

(56) Complete phraseme (= fixed locution, Engl. *idiom*)
The expression AB with meaning "S" is called complete phraseme if and only if one of the following two conditions is met:
a. "S" $\not\subset$ "A" y "S" $\not\subset$ "B"
b. "S" $\supset$ "A" pero "S" $\not\subset$ "B" y "A" is not in the communicatively dominant position in (S).

This definition, not based on a selection criteria, supports the inclusion, among phrasemes, of units of all lexical features. Thus, in the examples quoted by Mel'čuk, we find lexemes (poly-lexemic or combined) and phrasemes themselves. For condition (56a), the author quotes the examples in French pas question, *être dans les choux, battre son plein, graisser la patte, pied-noir, coq de village, traîner N dans la boue*[27] where none of the elements that make them up are part of the original signifier of the expression as modifier (in a communicatively non-dominant position). We consider many of these examples multi-member lexemes. Only *être dans les choux, battre son plein*, and *graisser la patte* can be considered, from our definition, phrasemes.

Our position regarding poly-lexemic verbal units as a separate class is rooted in the nature of the verb. Indeed, since this category is the center of the complex syntactic operations (e.g., passivization and clitization), the situation of phrasemes in the lexicon can be easily reconsidered. On one hand, if we admit that the phrasemes belong to the lexicon, we must anticipate the possibility that such operations occur in the lexicon, in which highly complex structures would be stored. On the other hand, if we consider that the lexicon contains only lexemes (simple or multi-member), two questions must

27. Literally in English, *without question, be in the cabbages, Fighting your field, grease the leg, black feet, rooster of the people, drag in the mud*, respectively. Figuratively in English, *say no more, fail, being in the peak intensity stage, bribe, French who lived in Algeria and returned to France because of the Algerian War, the Don Juan of the town, public slander to someone* respectively.

be answered by computing: how is it that idiomatic knowledge operates on syntax? Is it proper to each kind of unit? These questions are discussed in Leoni de León (2011), when describing the syntactic processing of phrasemes. But first, we must make a more formal definition of phraseme, in which the conditions of (45) are still valid:

(57) Concomitant Phrasemic Conditions:
Let the conditions be as in (45),
then, the appropriate conditions to consider a sequence Π as a phraseme are:
a. Π is the result of the union of at least a Λ_α and a Λ_β;
b. $[\Lambda_\alpha \Lambda_\beta] \subset L$;
c. one of the members of Π is of category V and one of the remaining members belongs to one of the following categories: {N, A, Adv}.
In other terms: $\Pi = VP \cup XP$[28]

(58) Binary conditions of phrasemes:
Let Π be a phraseme that represents a meaning S_δ comprising, at least, a Λ_α and a Λ_β; then one of the following three conditions must be met:
a. $S_\delta \not\subset S_\alpha$ and $S_\delta \not\subset S_\beta$
b. $S_\delta \subset S_\alpha$ and $S_\delta \not\subset S_\beta$
c. $S_\delta \not\subset S_\alpha$ and $S_\delta \subset S_\beta$

Therefore, we can define the phrasemes as follows:

(59) Phrasemes
Let S_i be a set of meanings of a lexeme Λ_i or of a phraseme Π_i.
A sense unit Π_δ that denotes a meaning S_δ of the language L is a phraseme if and only if all the conditions in (57) are simultaneously met, and if at least one of the conditions in (58) is met.

This definition is valid for all sequences whose nucleus is a verb. However, we still need to establish the limits of the action of the members of a phraseme, which we will do in the next chapter. We still have to refer to the last two classes of our typology.

3.4.3 *Collocations*

We have referred to collocations many times[29]. It is worth adding that in *Natural Language Processing* (NLP), collocations do not cause particular problems when parsing. For example, the verbal syntagma *cometer una falta* (*make a mistake*) has (almost) the same expectations of success and the same general difficulties in the analysis than its synonym *hacer una falta* (*make a mistake*). These deeds are the result of the status of collocations in relation to the lexicon and syntax: they are not part of the syntax, but of the discourse and the cultural and encyclopedic knowledge necessary in certain contexts. Collocations are a *style* of speech problem and not of the actual content of the

28. Where XP represents a syntagma.

29. Table 11 and Figure 1 summarize our views.

speech. Knowledge on collocations is needed to generate a correct and socially acceptable text.

Thus, the value of collocations is related to what they communicate about the speaker, the target of the information, and the best way to present it, and not with the information itself, or with the sequences of the elements that carry them. In this sense, they tend to give additional cultural and social information on the communicative situation: they connote. Hence, and with an operational definition, a collocation is, above all, a change of selection in the possible choices of a lexical item that belongs to the (communicative) context by another lexical element that acts as the nucleus. The alternative should be understood as the possibility to replace one of the elements of the collocation in the given context, by another element with the same meaning, without compromising the meaning of the sentence or the syntactic structure. In (60), we define the relation of lexical alternation:

(60) Lexical alternation
Two elements α and β are in a relation of lexical alternation if and only if, for a syntagma ZP:
a. α and β belong to the same category;
b. α and β have the same structure of arguments (i.e., the same features of selection);
c. α and β are interchangeable, such that sequences $[_{ZP}\, Z^0\alpha]$ and $[_{ZP}\, Z^0\beta]$ are equivalent from the point of view of meaning and the substitution of one by the other retains all lexical features and respects the same syntactic order.

According to (60), the Spanish verbs *amar* (*love*) and *gustar* (*like*) are not in lexical alternation. This is because the sentences *amo las manzanas* (*I love apples*) and *me gustan las manzanas* (I like apples) do not have the same structure of arguments, contrary to *hacer* (*do*) and *cometer* (*commit*) in *hicimos un error* (*we made a fault*) and *cometimos un error* (*we made a mistake – literal: we committed a mistake*). Now, we can define collocations as follows:

(61) Collocation
A collocation is syntactic relation such that, for a sequence $[_{XP}\, X^0\alpha]$ or $[_{XP}\, \alpha X^0]$:
a. X^0 selects α for the discursive context;
b. X^0 constitutes the nucleus of the collocation;
c. α is in lexical alternation with, at least, a β;
d. α belongs to an open lexical category.

In this form, the French verb *exploiter* in *exploiter un mythe* is a collocation, since there exists an alternation relationship with *utiliser*, which has the same meaning in *utiliser un mythe*.[30] Thus, the definition (61) requires, that for every α in collocation, there exists a lexeme in the lexicon in lexical alternation situation accompanying the nucleus. Therefore, in a defined lexicon, alternation relation is a necessary condition to identify collocations.

3.4.4 *Thematic fusion*

Thematic fusions are the result of the combination of a *supporting verb* and a *predicative nominal* (Leoni de León 2011). A supporting verb is a verb that serves as support to a predicative nominal, allowing the latter to distribute its structure of arguments in sentence. In Spanish, we can mention *hacer* (*make*), *poner* (*put*), and *tener* (*have*) as examples of supporting verbs; *oferta* (*offer*) and *traducción* (*translation*) are predicative nominals in that language. The combination of these elements gives us sequences with a value equivalent to a verb, but the structure of arguments is inherited from the nominal: *hacer una oferta de dinero* (*make a money offer*).

Put another way, if α and β are arguments selected by a predicative nucleus N^0, a thematic fusion occurs when a supporting verb has this nucleus as argument that produces a fusion of the predicates. For example, in *hacer una oferta de dinero*, the nominal *oferta* has two thematic roles, both Agent and Theme, which are assimilated by the verb *hacer*. We consider *light verb constructions* a phenomenon explicable in syntactic terms. Thematic fusions show that the thematic structure is highly relevant to analyze poly-lexicality. The relations between the verb and the predicative nominal are also of interest in our research.

3.5 Typology of multi-member lexical units

Fixedness (or fossilization), which we redefined in terms of continuity, is certainly the most used concept to identify and classify poly-lexemic units; it is a first indication of any process of lexicalization of expressions. Thus, from fixedness, we can establish two groups. The first one consists of *multi-member lexemes and phrasemes*, since both are units of meaning without necessarily being lexical units; the second one covers *collocations* that are a lexical choice probably motivated by communication style, with no semantic implications. Thematic fusions are grouped in the first major class because of the unclear boundaries of its own definition and due to the fact that they are most likely found in the root of many syntagmatic expressions. Consequently, our classification (Figure 1) has two large classes. It is useful to examine other characteristics that play an important role in it. For example, lexicalization, as a result of the inclusion of units of meaning in the lexicon, does not cause problems for multi-member lexemes, apart from pluralization and other morphological phenomena that won't be taken into account at the moment. However, phrasemes are not lexicalized. They are product of

30. In English, "exploit a myth" and "use a myth" respectively.

the relation between lexical units. In the next chapter, we will approach to their representation in our model.

On the contrary, multi-member lexemes engage in the sentence with values directly recoverable from the lexicon, without undergoing remarkable transformations. Thus, multi-member lexemes and phrasemes form two separate sub-groups. Also, multi-member lexemes are, in turn, divided into two sub-classes (poly-lexemic lexemes and combined lexemes) according to the procedures (whether morphological or syntactic) used to create them. The phrasemes are divided into *complete phrasemes,*[31] continuous expressions that extend across a sentence, and syntagmatic phrasemes, discontinuous expressions that can be replaced by a verb. Both syntagmatic phrasemes and any other element of the classification can be either tropics, or referential. These characteristics, not being syntactic themselves, are not reflected in our classification.

Figure 1 reproduces, in a tree form, our general classification of poly-lexicality phenomena. Table 11 summarizes the distinctive features. The first column makes a list of the types and sub-types. In the second column, ***Cat*** indicates only if the polylexical unit has a grammatical category (e.g., phrasemes assimilate into verbs). Columns Tra, ***Sub***, and **Con** relate with Table 11. Lexicalization, understood as incorporating a sequence of lexemes as a single unit in L, is marked in the **Lex** column. Poly-lexemic multi-member lexemes differ from combined lexemes by the existence of spaces in spelling and by inflectional morphology. The last column, **Lie**, marks this distinction according to the existence of links with its constituting elements (intra-lexical links), where the first ones respect the morphological paradigm.

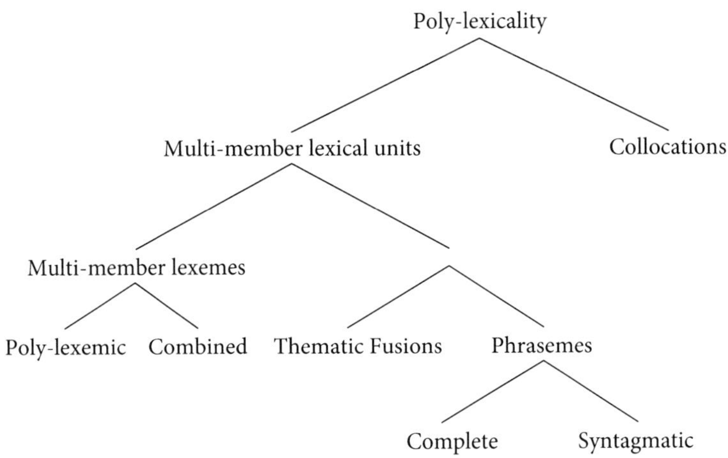

Figure 1. Poly-lexicality Phenomena

31. For example *a buen entendedor, pocas palabras* (a good listener needs few words).

Table 11. General features of poly-lexicality phenomena[32]

Type	Cat	Tra	Sub	Con	Lex	Lie
Multi-member poly-lexemic lexemes	+	B	-	+	+	+
Multi-member combined lexemes	+	B	-	+	+	-
Phrasemes	+	C	+	-	-	+
Collocations	-	C	+	-	-	+
Thematic fusions	+	D	-	-	-	+

Abbreviation:
Cat: category **Con:** continuity **Lex:** lexicalization
Lie: intra-lexical links **Tra:** typological features **Sub:** substitution

The creation of a phraseological knowledge system requires formal conceptions of the expressions, from which it is expected that this system supply relevant information. This fact led us to take a position in relation to the definition of complex units as objects of study. First, a reinterpretation of the traditional concepts of fixedness and co-occurrence was established, as they are the most general properties that characterize phraseological units. Then, we distinguished between two types of relations present in the expressions: syntagmatic relations (or continuity) and paradigmatic relations (substitution). Such distinctions allowed us to examine the scope of the underlying relations in phraseological units, either within themselves, or in the sentence. This conceptual work concluded in a classification of poly-lexemic units.

We did not think essential to create sub-classes based on tropes. This decision was taken by the fact that tropes are not syntactically relevant. In addition, the top level of our typology considers collocations, given their importance in the genesis of phraseological units, aspect that was also mentioned in relation to thematic fusions. However, they won't be part of our analysis in the next part of this work. Two reasons justify this position. First, collocations, as we define them, have little interest in the syntactic level and the lexical alternation that characterizes them demands a semantic-lexical approach that is beyond the scope of this investigation. Second, thematic fusions that belong to all phenomena of syntax are not true phraseological units. The meaning and construction of these units are syntactically measurable and identifiable. From the examples (1) – (7) at the beginning of this section, we obtain the classification in Table 12.

The term cama *elástica* (*trampoline, Literal: elastic bed*) is a *multi-lexemic multi-member lexeme* because it consists of two lexemes, whose nucleus, cama (bed), determines gender and plural features. Instead, *abrelatas* (*can opener*) is combined because its forming elements have been fused. In relation to phrases, we have *El cliente siempre tiene la razón* (*The customer is always right*) as complete because it constitutes a complete sentence unit, whereas *meter la pata* (*blunder, Literal: put the foot*) is syntagmatic

32. Abbreviations were taken from French; therefore, **Lie** comes from "liens intralexicaux" and **Tra** from "traits typologiques."

Table 12. Polylexical phenomena with examples

	Polylexical phenomena	
	Multi-member lexical units	
Multi-member lexemes	Multi-lexemic	*cama elástica*
	Combined	*abrelatas*
Phrases	Complete	*El cliente siempre tiene la razón*
	Syntagmatic	*meter la pata*
Thematic fusions		*hacer un cambio de oficina*
	Collocations	
		cometer una falta

because of the morphosyntactic changes that it can undergo. Thematic fusions are part of multi-member lexical units because the boundary that separates them from the other types of expressions in this typology is unclear. Finally, collocations are a type apart since, as we have shown, they are not idiomatic units.

4. Formal representation

The typology allows us to characterize the main lexical-syntactic phenomena. However, it was necessary to define a formal basis to describe, identify, and reproduce previously explained phenomena. This was done through Tsool[33] formalism. Tsool is inspired by Lexical Functional Grammar (Bresnan 2001); its basic unit is the phraseological unit (UP). Tsool is a formalism based on correlations. It is composed of five parts:

Canonic form: FC.
Labeling: BS.
Features: Φ.
Transformations: AXE.
Lexicographic data: LEX.

Each label, which is actually an array of features, can contain other arrays of features. Thus, for example, in Φ, ARG (for arguments) and CTG (by category) are contained; the latter refers to any grammatical category of any phraseological unit (UP). Additionally, there is also SCT[34] containing the set of sub-categorization of the

33. In Peninsular Maya (or Yucatec), *tsool* means *to declare, describe, sort out,* and also *order, rank, serial, correlation* (Bastarrachea *et al.* 1992). *Tsool* has its own notation, but in this study we only used it in the description of the abbreviations (Leoni de León 2011).

34. Our equivalent of PRD in Lexical Functional Grammar (Bresnan 2001).

expression described (see Figure 2). Nuclei are carriers of their own structures. The sub-categorization of the members of the UP is specified in MOR, while the sub--categorization of the UP is expressed in ARG, as just noted. There are no need relations between the arguments of any UP and the inner arguments ruled by the nucleus, but it can be expected that, once one of the nucleus arguments of the UP is saturated, the arguments of the latter are restructured from remaining arguments. Operations that could be done within the UP (modification, commutation) must be specified. Tsool is described in detail in Leoni de León (2011).

The computational processing of any phenomenon requires a view about its operation and action limits provided by the researcher. The formalism Tsool summarizes our view on idiomatic expressions. It relates the morphological (FipsTg), lexical (FipsDB), and syntactic functions (FipsSyn) of Fips with a restraining description of phraseological units, in order to describe better their behavior.

The fact that phraseological structures dependencies do not adapt themselves to a correct tree representation and that the phraseological continuum does not have linear order justifies our use of a representation based on independent feature sets. The features of the elements of the UP are separated from those from the UP itself, since the configuration of the arguments of the expression tends, for example, to differ from their nucleus structure. Consequently, *Tsool* pretends to gather, in a single structure, the UP that share the same meaning with the proviso that form differences are representable in syntagmatic and paradigmatic terms, without loss of identity of the UP.

Tsool formalism should facilitate the processing of expressions in our model, as it makes explicit the data sources and their relation to the other elements involved in the description of the UP. Strictly speaking, Tsool itself is not the model, but it helps not only to understand how it works, but also to specify, in the model, the function of pieces of information that constitute a UP.

The definition of Tsool in computing terms, in the form of an electronic dictionary of phraseology, was conducted in the form of a concept test, in the implementation Mulkin. This computing model has a framework for the database KaxanBD, a data

$$
{}^{\text{UP}}\begin{bmatrix} \text{FC} & [\textit{hacer pistola}] \\ \text{BS} & [\text{hacer}]_{\boxed{1}}\#[\text{pistola}]_{\boxed{2}} \\ \Phi & \begin{bmatrix} \text{ARG} & {}_{1}\begin{bmatrix} \text{CTG} & \text{V} \\ \text{SCT} & {}_{1}\begin{bmatrix} \langle x\_y \rangle \\ x_{suj} \leftarrow \theta^{agent}, \text{cas}^{nom}, \text{sel}^{0} \\ y_{obj} \leftarrow \theta^{thème}, \text{cas}^{acu}, \text{sel}^{0} \end{bmatrix} \end{bmatrix} \end{bmatrix} \end{bmatrix}
$$

Figure 2. Partial analysis of a phraseological unit in Tsool

description language, LanXTsool, a web application that allows filling a database of the dictionaries, Kaxan. In addition, we also have a content management system, Kwebmin, for creating web applications. In Mulkin we made a partial implementation of some phenomena: commutation, versification, pseudo-affixations (see Leoni de León 2011). The morpho-syntactic information necessary was given by Fips. Mulkin was programmed in XML and Perl.

5. Conclusions

In our research we showed that phraseological units have a syntactic nature, whose singularities deserve to be taken into account in order to use the information they carry. Thus, we arrived to a lexical-syntactic typology which allows us to specify lexical-syntactic formalization which can be the basis for an automatic processing of phraseological units, term that we prefer over multi-word units.

The study of the syntax of phraseological units is characterized, on the whole, for the loan of lexicographic notions unsuitable for describing a rich phenomenology, based on criteria that are not always clear (as fixedness) and often with lexical-semantic base (as tropes). Thus, we demonstrated the need for a more accurate terminology, which is able to denote the treated phenomena. Hence, first, we defined a conception of lexicon that takes into account the levels of realization of lexemes from the abstract (*lexemes*) to the concrete (*word-forms*), with an intermediate level (*morpho-lexemes*) corresponding to the relation of *lexemes* with the *word-forms*. This conception of the lexicon allows representing *phraseological units* as either belonging to the lexicon, or according to the relations they establish with lexemes. Our representation of the lexicon is a response to the theoretical gaps in generative syntactic theory regarding the relation between the lexicon and syntax, which helps to understand the general phenomenology of idiomatic expressions.

We emphasized that the grammaticality of expressions, from a theoretical point of view, was always out of the question, because their validity is sanctioned by usage. Instead, what can be discussed is the theoretical framework and its explanatory capacity. It is equally likely that our ability to process *phraseological units* says more about the state of our theoretical approach or of our methodology than about the expressions themselves. Moreover, we pointed out the importance of considering lexicographic and syntactic research in automatic processing of *phraseological units*.

Thus, we developed a conception of the lexicon more favorable to the good understanding of the syntactic phenomenology of *phraseological units*. This allowed us, mainly, to characterize better syntactic phenomenology of these expressions from the affected axis (paradigmatic, syntagmatic), which required formal clarification as to the types of phraseological units. We showed how these types are the result of the relation between these units with the lexicon and syntactic operations where they are possible. Then, our typology was based on lexical-syntactic formal definitions. We identified several syntactic phenomena affecting *phraseological units*, such as the addition, the clitization, commutation, nominalization, and versification.

Our typology resulted in a classification of poly-lexemic units into two great classes: *collocations* and *multi-member lexical units*. The creation of sub-classes based on tropes proved useless in the framework of our work, because tropes are not relevant syntactically. *Collocations* did not keep our attention, for, as we define them, they are not of great interest in the syntactic level, and the lexical alternation, which characterizes them, requires a lexical-semantic approach that is beyond the scope of our research. In addition, *thematic fusions*, which belong to the set of phenomena of syntax, are not real *phraseological units* because the meaning and construction of these units are syntactically measurable and identifiable. Then, we focused on *multi-member lexical units*, excluding thematic fusions because their values are syntactically calculable.

Anyway, a typology is only a starting point in the study of a phenomenon; it is only a generalization of knowledge. A typology does not respond to the questions of the representation of the components of *phraseological units* and of the interactions between different levels of the lexicon. Consequently, we focused on the definition of a formal system of phraseological description that allows the reproduction and the identification of the phenomena described. The formalism *Tsool* that we developed summarizes our understanding of idiomatic expressions. It links the morphological, lexical, and syntactic features of FIPS with a restraining description of phraseological units, in order to describe and identify better their behavior.

We showed that the dependencies of phraseological structures are not suitable for an arborescent representation and that the phraseological continuum does not have linear order. Consequently, *Tsool* follows a representation based on sets of interdependent features. Furthermore, *Tsool* separates the features of the elements of the UP from those of the UP itself, since the configuration of the arguments of the expression tends, for example, to differ from their nucleus structure. *Tsool* joins, in the same structure, the UP that share the same meaning provided that such form differences are representable in syntagmatic and paradigmatic terms, without loss of identity of the UP. *Tsool* formalism facilitates processing expressions that make explicit the relations between data sources and the other elements involved in the description of the UP.

This work also leaves many questions, such as phono-semantic processing of plausibility in commutation. This is certainly linked to the processing of the arguments in the nominal structure, which is an important source of new expressions. Furthermore, although Mulkin is in the stage of proof of concept, this does not prevent us from affirming that it can be very useful as a filter in conjunction with statistical systems of expression extractions. Similarly, although we were only on the surface with the requirements for translation of *phraseological units*, we offered some clues for inter-linguistic phraseology. Also, although we stuck to the Spanish language, we should analyze and test the relevance of our model to another language or language family. Adaptations, undoubtedly necessary in the new contexts of application, shall not cease to give us answers to the problems of *phraseological units*, but, perhaps, even more importantly, will force us to make us more questions.

References

Alonso Ramos, Margarita. 2003. La nature des collocatifs: Leur statut en tant qu'unités lexicales. In *Les collocations: Analyse et traitement* [Série E – Lexicologie et lexicographie], Francis Grossman & Agnès Tutin (eds), 45–60, Amsterdam: Revue Française de Linguistique Appliquée, Editions De Werelt.

Alonso Ramos, Margarita. 2004. Diccionario de colocaciones del español. <http://www.dicesp.com/content/view/full/232> (6 June 2005).

Balanescu, M. 2000. L'analyse des collocations pour le traitement automatique du langage naturel. Mémoire de DES en linguistique, Département de Linguistique Informatique, Université de Genève.

Bastarrachea, Juan R., Yah Pech, Ermilo & Briceño Chel, Fidencio. 1992. *Diccionario Básico Español/Maya/Español.* <http://www.mayas.uady.mx/diccionario/index.html> (18 May 2006).

Bouvier, Yves-Ferdinand. 1999. Comment reconnaître & classifier les mots composés. Mémoire de licence en linguistique générale, Département de Linguistique Générale, Faculté de Lettres, Université de Genève.

Bresnan, Joan. 2001. *Lexical-Functional Syntax* [Blackwell Textbooks in Linguistics]. Oxford: Blackwell.

Chomsky, Noam. 1981. *Lectures on Government and Binding* [Studies in Generative Grammar]. Dordrecht: Foris.

Culicover, Peter W. & Jackendoff, Ray. 2005. *Simpler Syntax.* Oxford: OUP.

D'Introno, F. 2002. Niveles de complementación. Ms, Caracas, Venezuela.

Fernando, Chirtra. 1996. *Idioms and Idiomaticity. Describing English Language.* Oxford: OUP.

Fillmore, Charles J., Johnson, Christopher R. & Petruck, Miriam R. 2003. Background to Framenet. *International Journal of Lexicography* 16(3): 235–250.

Firth, John R. 1957. Modes of meaning. Essays and studies (The English Association). In *Papers in Linguistics 1934–1951*, 190–215. Oxford: OUP.

Fleischer, Wolfgang. 1982. *Phraseologie der deutschen Gegenwartssprache.* Leipzig: VEB Bibliogr. Institut.

Fontenelle, Thierry. 2003. References. *International Journal of Lexicography* 16(3): 363–366.

Gross, Maurice. 1989. The use of finite automata in the lexical representation of natural language. In *Electronic Dictionaries and Automata in Computational Linguistics: LITP Spring School on Theoretical Computer Science, Saint-Pierre d'Oléron, France, May 1987*, Maurice Gross & Dominque Perrin (eds), 34–50, Berlin: Springer.

Gross, Gaston. 1996. Les expressions figées en français: Noms composés et autres locutions. In *Collection L'Essentiel Français.* Paris: Ophrys.

Grossman, Francis & Tutin, Agnès. 2003. Quelques pistes pour le traitement des collocations. In *Les collocations: Analyse et traitement* [Lexicologie et lexicographie Série E, 1], Francis Grossman & Agnès Tutin (eds), 5–22, Amsterdam: Revue Française de Linguistique Appliquée, Editions De Werelt.

Larreta Zulátegui, Juan Pablo 2002. En torno a la semántica de las colocaciones fraseológicas. *Estudios de Lingüística* 16: 5–41.

Leoni de León, Jorge Antonio. 2011. *Modèle phraséologique léxico-syntaxique: Une analyse sur les locutions de l'espagnol*. Éditions Universitaires Européennes.

Makkai, Adam. 1972. *Idiom Structure in English*. The Hague: Mouton.

Mel'čuk, Igor. 1984. Un nouveau type de dictionnaire: Le dictionnaire explicatif et combinatoire du français contemporai. In *Dictionnaire explicatif et combinatoire du français contemporain: Recherches lexico sémantiques* I, Igor Mel'čuk, Nadia Arbatchewsky-Jumarie, André Clas, Suzanne Mantha & Alain Polguère (eds), 3–16. Montréal: Université de Montréal, Presses de l'Université de Montréal.

Mel'čuk, Igor. 1993. Cours de morphologie générale. In *Cours de morphologie générale*, Vol. 1, Ch: Mot-forme et lexème: Étude préliminaire, 97–107. Montréal: Les Presses de l'Université de Montréal/CNRS Éditions.

Mel'čuk, Igor. 1997. *Vers une linguistique Sens-Texte*. Paris: Collège de France.

Mel'čuk, Igor. 2003. Les collocations: Définition, rôle et utilité. In *Les collocations: Analyse et traitement* [Lexicologie et lexicographie, Serie E, 1], Francis Grossman & Agnés Tutin (eds), 23–32, Amsterdam: Revue Française de Linguistique Appliquée, Editions De Werelt.

Mel'čuk, Igor, Clas, André & Polguère, Alain 1995. *Introduction à la lexicologie explicative et combinatoire*. Louvain-la-Neuve: Editions Duculot.

Mena Martínez, Florentina. 2003. En torno al concepto de desautomatización fraseológica: Aspectos básicos. *Revista Electrónica de Estudios Filológicos* 5. <http://www.um.es/tonosdigital/znum5/estudios/H-Edesautomatizacion.htm>

Mendívil Giró, José. Luis. 1999. *Las palabras disgregadas: Sintaxis de las expresiones idiomáticas y los predicados complejos* [Colección Humanidades 34]. Zaragoza: Prensas Universitarias de Zaragoza.

Moreno de Alba, José G. 1992. *Diferencias léxicas entre España y América*. Madrid: MAPFRE.

Nerima, Luka, Seretan, Violeta & Wehrli, Éric. 2006. Le problème des collocations en TAL. *Nouveaux Cahiers de Linguistique Française* (27): 95–115.

Polguère, Alain. 2003. *Lexicologie et sémantique lexicale*. Montréal: Les Presses de l'Université de Montréal.

Ruiz Gurillo, Leonor. 1996. Una clasificación no discreta de las unidades fraseológicas del español. In *Estudios de fraseología y fraseografía del español actual* [Lingüística Iberoamericana], Gerd Wotjak (ed.), 13–38, Madrid: Iberoamericana.

Savary, Agata. 2000. Recensement et description des mot composés. Méthodes et applications. PhD dissertation, Laboratoire d'Automatique Documentaire et Linguistique, Université Paris 7, Université de Marne-la-Vallée.

Seretan, Violeta. 2011. *Syntax-Based Collocation Extraction* [Text, Speech and Language Technology 44]. Berlin: Springer.

Silberztein, Max. 1989. The lexical analysis of French. In *Electronic Dictionaries and Automata in Computational Linguistics: LITP Spring School on Theoretical Computer Science, Saint-Pierre d'Oléron, France, May 1987*, Maurice Gross & Dominique Perrin (eds), 93–110, Berlin: Springer.

Tomasello, Michael. 2003. *Constructing a Language: A Usage-Based Theory of Language Acquisition*. Cambridge MA: Harvard University Press.

Wehrli, Éric. 1997. *l'Analyse syntaxique des langues naturelles: Problèmes et méthodes*. Paris: Masson.

Wehrli, Éric. 2004. Un modèle multilingue d'analyse syntaxique. In *Structures et discours: Mélanges offferts à Eddy Roulet. Langue et pratiques discursives*, Antoine Auchlin, Marcel Burger, Laurent Filliettaz, Anne Grobet et al. (eds), 311–329, Montréal: Éditions Nota Bene.

Wehrli, Éric. 2007. Fips, a 'deep' linguistic multilingual parser. In *ACL 2007 Workshop on Deep Linguistic Processing*, 120–127, Prague: Association for Computational Linguistics.

Three-place predicates in RRG

A computational approach

Judith Gottschalk
Aalborg University, Denmark[1]

This book chapter presents a computational linguistics analysis of Role and Reference Grammar [RRG] (cf. Van Valin 2005). RRG, formulated as a pseudo-code program is not executable on a random access machine since the linking algorithm cannot account for variable undergoer linking in English three-place predicates. Consequently RRG is not computationally adequate. Therefore a new approach to RRG is developed using Nolan's (2011) constructional schemas; the RRG semantics-to-syntax linking algorithm is revised, using the lexicon, information structure and constructional schemas to account for variable undergoer linking. A revised approach to the mental lexicon based on Gottschalk (2010) is developed, accounting for three-place predicates. In this approach macroroles are epiphenomenal and replaced by thematic relations to develop a computable account to RRG.

1. Introduction

From a computational linguistics perspective, Role and Reference Grammar [RRG] (cf. Van Valin 2005) is a rather informally described linguistic theory. If one seeks to use RRG within a computational implementation it would first be necessary to specify the formal meaning of RRG. This is an approach this book chapter follows for the purpose of using RRG as linguistic engine for an intelligent tutoring system (cf. Gottschalk 2012b). With such a formal framework of RRG it is possible for the theory to be interpreted by an ordinary computer program (cf. Gottschalk 2012a). It turned out, however, that the attempt of developing a formal approach to RRG causes various problems, leading to the following research questions: 1) How must RRG be

1. I would like to thank Hagen Langer, Brian Nolan, Nicolai Winther-Nielsen and two anonymous readers for helpful comments on earlier drafts and fruitful discussions in the development of this book chapter. Many thanks to Kim Hülsewede for proofreading the book chapter.

modified to work in a computational implementation of the theory, 2) How should a computational linguistics processing model of RRG formally look like?

The motivation for using RRG as linguistic engine for an intelligent tutoring system lies in the specific architecture of RRG, which uses the term 'linking algorithm'. This use naturally results in associations of implementability on a computational device in terms of a procedurally executable processing model. The linking algorithm is bidirectional and it links the semantic representation of a clause with the syntactic representation and vice versa. Van Valin (2005: 129) writes about the linking algorithm:

> Viewed in terms of a processing model, the semantics-to-syntax linking is an aspect of the production process, while the syntax-to-semantics linking is an aspect of the comprehension process. In the comprehension process, the parser would take the input and produce a structured syntactic representation of it, identifying the elements of the layered structure of the clause and the cases, adpositions and other grammatically relevant elements. It is then the task of the grammar to map this structure into a semantic representation, as the first steps in interpreting it, and this is where the syntax-to-semantics linking algorithm is required. The same syntactic and semantic representation are used in both algorithms. (Van Valin 2005: 129).

It is this strong claim by Van Valin, that the linking algorithm in RRG is naturally tied to being a linguistic processing model, which led to a first attempt in the development of a formal framework of RRG: The direct translation of the linking algorithm into a program in pseudo-code, which could be executed on an abstract machine model like a Random Access Machine [RAM]. The aim was to derive a formal model from it and a) to see whether the linking algorithm when translated directly into machine code can be used to derive a semantic structure from the syntactic representation of the clause and to use this approach for a later implementation and b) to develop a formalizable approach to RRG which can answer the question whether RRG as a linguistic theory is tractable or whether it is Turing complete, because the the intelligent tutoring system should be used as a testbed for a direct implementation of RRG as a linguistic theory.

However, as Section 3 shows, using a direct pseudo-code implementation of RRG to formalize the linking algorithm for later implementation results in the undecidability of assigning the undergoer in three-place predicate constructions in English, as the algorithm cannot be used to decide which argument is to be assigned undergoer in these constructions. In a first step, this results in the conclusion that the linking algorithm in RRG should better be understood as a coarsely grained guidance principle rather than a formal linguistic theory, which is in its whole not computational in linguistics applications. RRG therefore is not a computationally adequate linguistic theory which can be used for implementing a linguistic processing model. This however is unsatisfactory, as parts of RRG have already been implemented in a few computational linguistic applications.

Guest (2008) developed an RRG-based parser, which uses extensions of a chart parser to parse languages with different degrees of word order. In this approach, parsing is executed via syntactic templates as used in RRG instead of rules. Winther-Nielsen (2009) and Wilson (2009) describe a software tool called Role-Lexicon Module, which is database driven and can be used for the parsing of Biblical Hebrew. This system uses an EMDROS database and contains an active chart parser, which generates the layered structure of the clause. Nolan and Salem (2009) and Salem (2009) on the other hand have developed a machine translation program called UniArab, which uses a rule-based lexical framework to process Arabic based on RRG. In Murtagh (2011), a linguistically motivated Irish Sign Language conversational agent is introduced, which uses RRG as the linguistic engine in the development of a conversational agent for sign languages. Also, within FunGramKB aspects of RRG – especially the semantic representation of RRG – are used to create a knowledge base for natural language processing (cf. Periñán-Pascual & Arcas-Túnez 2010). Most of these implementations focus on the software developed, but they do not focus on the specific computational problems caused by the architecture of RRG (cf. Gottschalk 2012a: 125). An exception to this is found in "The implementation of the CLS constructor in ARTEMIS" (this monograph) by Periñán-Pascual and Arcas-Túnez, who have described the various stages in the development of a computational system which employs a lexico-semantical knowledge-base to generate the logical structure of sentences and demonstrate that for a computerized model of the RRG syntax-semantics interface, constructional schemas should be the cornerstone.

At least parts of RRG seem to be implementable, or, as shown in the ARTEMIS project, the whole theory of RRG seems to be implementable, if it is consequently adjusted to the formal needs of a computational processing model. These observations result in the attempt to develop a computationally adequate model of RRG which can be used as a formal blueprint for intelligent computational systems using RRG as linguistic engine.

By computational adequacy I mean that a theory should refer to formal systems which are computationally tractable, in order to support the level of explanatory adequacy within a Chomskyan framework. This is because a theory which is not tractable and has a Turing complete generative power, as pointed out in Carpenter (1991) with respect to HPSG, is less explanatory than a theory which is tractable and has less generative power, in the sense of not being Turing complete (cf. Gottschalk 2012a: 130). Computational adequacy means to process language with low storage demands without mistakes. One crucial assumption with respect to computational adequacy is that it is based on the Church-Turing-thesis, which assumes that everything which is computable on a machine is intuitively computable. The Church-Turing thesis is bidirectional. This means that since natural language is intuitively computable, it should also be computable on a machine (cf. Blass & Gurevitch 2001). This way, a computer can be used as a test bed for linguistic theories in order to show that a linguistic theory actually works.

The book chapter is organized as follows: In Section 2, two approaches to three-place predicates in RRG are presented. First Van Valin's (2007) account to this phenomenon is presented and then Haspelmath's (2008) approach with four macroroles is introduced. Both accounts fail in different ways and cannot properly deal with variable undergoer linking in English within a computational processing model. This critique is discussed in some detail. Section three presents a new computational linguistics account to RRG which is lexically based and which uses constructional schemas developed by Nolan (2011). A conclusion follows in Section 4.

2. RRG accounts to three-place predicates

Van Valin (2007) accounts for three-place predicates by using a modified version of the Actor-Undergoer-Hierarchy [AUH] – developed in Van Valin (2005) – in terms of identifying three different patterns for variable undergoer assignment in verbs with three argument positions. Van Valin (2007) notes that abstract predicates in the lexical decomposition system employed in RRG can only have zero, one or two arguments. From these findings, Van Valin (2007: 43) concludes that three-place predicates must have complex LSs, which are made of at least two abstract predicates (cf. Gottschalk 2012a: 147). Examples of the semantic representation of English three-place predicates are given in (1):

(1) [**do′**(x, Ø)] CAUSE [PROC & INGR **predicate′**(y, z)]

a.	give, present	[**do′**(x, Ø)] CAUSE [PROC & INGR **have′**(y, z)]
b.	show	[**do′**(x, Ø)] CAUSE [PROC & INGR **see′**(y, z)]
c.	teach	[**do′**(x, Ø)] CAUSE [PROC & INGR **know′**(y, z)]
d.	load	[**do′**(x, Ø)] CAUSE [PROC & INGR **be-on′**(y, z)]
e.	put	[**do′**(x, Ø)] CAUSE [PROC & INGR **be-LOC′**(y, z)]

(cf. Van Valin 2007: 43)

Van Valin (2007: 44) interprets the logical structures in (1), based on Larson (1988) and others, as embedded predications in sentences involving verbs like *give, present, show, teach, load* and *put*. In RRG the rightmost argument in LSs in (2) is the default choice for undergoer. In principle it is possible for the *y* argument to be selected as undergoer. How this works is illustrated for English in (2), which may be termed 'transfer alternation' (cf. Van Valin 2007: 44; Gottschalk 2012a: 148).

(2) a. [**do′**(Abby, Ø)] CAUSE [PROC & INGR **have′**(McGee, security key)]
b. Abby [Actor] gave the security key [Undergoer] to McGee
Unmarked choice
c. Abby [Actor] gave McGee [Undergoer] the security key
Marked choice (cf. Van Valin 2007: 44)

In (2b), the leftmost argument in the LS (Abby) is selected as actor, while the rightmost argument is selected as undergoer (the security key). Because the sentence is in active voice, the actor appears as core-initial PSA, which is similar to 'subject' in traditional grammatical theories, while the undergoer occurs in the immediate post-nuclear position, which in traditional grammatical theories is the 'direct object'. In this sentence, the third argument *McGee* is a non-macrorole and therefore a preposition assignment rule applies, which assigns *to* to it (cf. Van Valin 2007: 44). In (2b) this is the situation where the following rule applies:

(3) Preposition assignment rules for English
  a. Assign *to* to non-MR x argument in LS segment:
     PROC & INGR/INGR **pred'** (x, y)
  b. Assign *from* to non-MR x argument in LS segment:
     ... PROC & INGR/INGR NOT **pred'** (x, y)
  c. Assign *with* to non-MR y argument if, given two arguments,
     x and y, in a logical structure, with x
     lower or equal to y on the AUH, y is not selected a macrorole.
(cf. Van Valin 2007: 42)

In (2b), the rule in (3a) applies and, as shown in (2c) *McGee* is marked by the '*to-rule*', since here the verb is *give*. Examples like these are often referred to as 'dative-shif constructions' while the example in (2c) is a ditransitive construction (cf. Gottschalk 2012a: 148).

In Van Valin (2007) the AUH has been modified and the three principles given in Figure 1 have been identified based on cross-linguistic evidence:

This means that in three place predicates in English, based on the evidence from (3b) and (3c), principle C applies in that either the lowest ranking argument in the LS can be undergoer, in this case the z-Argument, or the second highest ranking argument in LS can be undergoer. The question is how this can be captured in a semi-formalization in a computational meta-language which will be used in Section 3.

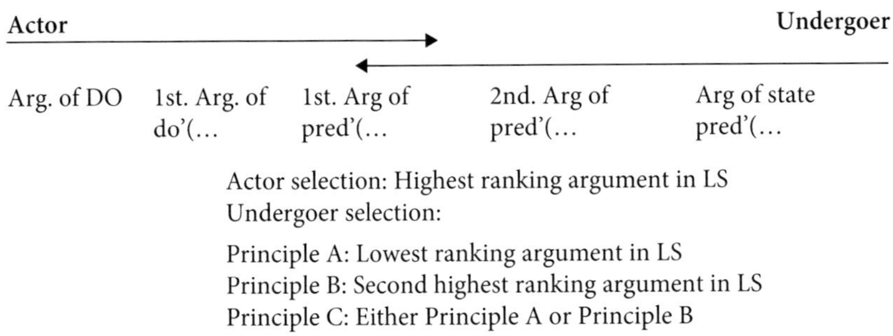

Figure 1. Modified Actor-undergoer hierarchy (Van Valin 2007: 55)

What is crucial with respect to the analysis of three-place predicates in Van Valin (2007) is that RRG uses a configurational approach to the assignment of semantic macroroles based on the AUH. As pointed out above, the basic idea of the AUH is that the left-most argument in the LS is assigned Actor and the right-most argument is assigned Undergoer. However, Van Valin (2005) and Van Valin (2007), assume that the situation in (2b) is the unmarked choice for undergoer assignment, since this construction is in accordance with the AUH (cf. Haspelmath 2008). In fact Van Valin's (2007) analysis runs into difficulties, since, as pointed out in Erteschik-Shir (1979) and Diedrichsen (2011), the unmarked word order pattern in English is as in (2c) rather than in (2b). Variable undergoer linking is found in 10% of the languages (cf. Haspelmath 2008: 85). Following Siewierska (1998) and Haspelmath (2005) it is not the case that the pattern given in (2b) is the more frequent pattern (cf. Gottschalk 2012a: 149). This means that the unequal treatment of the patterns given in (2) in Van Valin's (2007) analysis and in RRG in general seems to be a feature inherited from transformational approaches where one alternating pattern is regarded as the underlying pattern from which the other pattern is derived (cf. Haspelmath 2008: 86). However, RRG is a monostratal linguistic theory. No intrinsic reason can be found why one alternation pattern has a privileged status over another pattern (cf. Haspelmath 2008: 86). Therefore, this book chapter provides a different analysis for these patterns based on the inclusion of information structure considerations and a detailed computational linguistics analysis of the linking algorithm from semantics to syntax in Van Valin (2005) (cf. Gottschalk 2012a: 149).

Haspelmath (2008) develops a new sketch for a radically new account of RRG. In his approach Haspelmath suggests the use of four macroroles to avoid several problems with Van Valin's approach with only two macroroles. The four macroroles are given in (4):

(4) Four semantic macroroles and their definitions
A = actor, defined as before
U = undergoer of monotransitive sentences
R = macro-recipient, corresponding to Primus's (1999) proto-recipient
T = (macro-)theme (Haspelmath 2008: 91)

These macroroles are defined on a purely semantic basis and no 'non-default' or 'marked' choice of macroroles is found. In fact, the macroroles provided by Haspelmath are defined on an extensive analysis of ditransitive constructions and the concept of undergoer (Van Valin 2007) is decomposed into macro-recipient and macro-theme. Haspelmath (2008: 91) points out that no criterion for grouping macroroles is given an inherent priority.

Haspelmath's main point is the advantage of the use of four macroroles, since non-actor arguments of monotransitive and ditransitive sentence have different macroroles. So the question whether the ditransitive non-actor argument is the undergoer does not arise (cf. Haspelmath 2008: 91). Based on this argumentation, Haspelmath develops a macrorole hierarchy with four macroroles which is given in (5)

(5) Macrorole hierarchy:
A > R, U > T

The idea is to put the actor in the highest and the ditranstitive theme in the lowest role of the hierarchy. In this approach, ditransitive recipient and monotranstive undergoer are both intermediate and have no rank relative to each other (cf. Haspelmath 2008: 93).

Although Haspelmath succeeds in developing an approach in which the third argument in three-place predicates receives a proper semantic status, his approach has specific problems. Van Valin (2005) argues that adding a third macrorole has the disadvantage that it is not universal across languages in that it would receive a different status from actor and undergoer. This is not in accordance with his purely semantical definition of the macroroles actor and undergoer.

Actually, the same argumentation is true for Haspelmath's approach with four macroroles. This new approach decomposes the monotransitive undergoer into two separate macroroles for ditransitives. This results in an under-representation of either the undergoer in three-place predicate constructions, in that it is decomposed into macro-theme and macro-recipient and does not occur in ditranstive constructions; or in an under-representation of macro-theme and macro-recipient in transitive constructions.

It is the case that there is an under-representation of macro-theme and macro-recipient, since these two macroroles are fused into the undergoer in this predicate setting. The reasons for this mismatch lie in the fact that Van Valin's two macroroles are generalizations of the continuum of thematic relations. Actually, theme and recipient are thematic relations with a narrower semantic status than undergoer. They are finer grained than undergoer, which is the coverage term for thematic relations in the continuum which cannot be subsumed as actor because of being opposed to it in transitive and ditranstive constructions.

Also, the status of actor becomes unclear in Haspelmath's approach as it is the only macrorole referring to an entity which displays some agency-hood. Its focus is much wider than the focus of the three macroroles denoting entities exhibiting patient-hood.

So the conclusion from this argumentation is that in Haspelmath's approach the four macroroles all have a different semantic load which excludes an equal and universal treatment as demanded by RRG. Its architecture seeks for universal constructs as can be concluded from Van Valin's (2005) discussion of a third macrorole.

3. A new computational model to RRG

The semantic representation of the clause in terms of logical structures [LSs] is linked to the syntactic representation of the clause via the Linking Algorithm in RRG. The syntactic structure is called the layered structure of the clause [LSC] (cf. Van Valin 2005). Rather than focusing on the whole linking algorithm, I will concentrate on one particular step in the semantics to syntax linking which causes problems from a computational linguistics point of view, as it results in unexecutability on a RAM. This particular step is given in below (6):

(6) 2. Determine the actor and undergoer assignments, following the actor-undergoer hierarchy [...] (Van Valin 2005: 136)

In Gottschalk (2012a), this step was semi-formalized as the following program snipped in pseudo-code:

(7)
```
algorithm step2
if number_argument_slots = = 1 in logical structure do
    if lexical_entry_verb = = takes_undergoer do
    undergoer = referring_expression_x;
    else
    actor = referring_expression_x;
    end if.
if number_argument_slots = = 2 in logical structure do
    actor = leftmost_argument;
    undergoer = rightmost_argument;
end if.
if number_argument_slots = = 3 in logical structure do
    actor = leftmost_argument:
    undergoer = new.choice();
    non_macrorole = new.choice();
end if.
```

What is shown in the algorithm in (7) is, that if the number of argument slots in the logical structure equals 1, it is necessary to have access to the lexicon in order to determine whether the lexical entry of the verb suggests that it can only be satisfied by an undergoer, or whether it can be satisfied by an actor. However, the situation in which the verb takes an actor is the default situation.

The only situation where the AUH can apply as sole basis for the determination of macroroles, is a situation in which two argument slots occur in the logical structure (cf. (7)). This suggests that, from an RRG-perspective, being transitive is the default situation for verbs. However, this results from theory internal considerations, in which the application of the AUH is an essential part of the theory, since the assignment of macroroles in the lexicon is the marked situation (cf. Van Valin 2005: 66).

If three argument slots in the LS occur, RRG runs into a difficult problem, RRG cannot account for three-place predicates solely based on its procedural approach and on the AUH (cf. (7)). What is crucial in this part of the linking algorithm is, that it is not possible to determine the macroroles of the sentence solely on the basis of the AUH in case the verb has three argument-slots. In cases with variable undergoer linking the algorithm cannot determine to which of the possible candidates for the undergoer, the corresponding macrorole should be assigned. This is because based on Van Valin's principle C in the AUH it is not possible to decide which argument should be assigned undergoer as it leaves choice between using principle A or B without giving any indication on which basis it is to be decided when which principle applies. Therefore the function 'choice' is used in the pseudo-code. This function simply states that it is the speaker's choice of assigning undergoer to one of the arguments in the LS. As pointed out in Section 2, Van Valin (2007) deals with this situation and describes how it is possible to account for three-place predicates in the semantics to syntax linking. However, the preposition assignment rules as proposed in Van Valin (2007) cannot apply to this part of the algorithm, since the assignment of prepositions takes place in step 3 of the linking algorithm in Van Valin (2005: 136). In addition, the AUH developed in Van Valin (2007) leaves a choice with respect to the assignment of three-place predicates.

The question is: On what basis can a variable undergoer be assigned and how is it possible to not depend on a function like *choice*, which in an implementation of RRG does not give clue, how a software like an intelligent teaching agent could decide in which situations it is supposed to use the ditransitive construction and when it should use the dative shift alternation.

It is actually possible to account for variable undergoer linking in English three-place predicates on a purely lexical basis. Therefore, the hypothesis is, that variable undergoer linking is rather a lexical process than a process in the grammar as argued in Van Valin (2007). By using this approach it is possible to show that Van Valin's or Haspelmath's (2008) macroroles are epiphenomenal in that they are set on top of a hierarchy of thematic relations.

Drawing on a revised version of Gottschalk's (2010) lexicon, in which multi-layered inheritance networks are used to account for lexical processes like verb alternations, different inheritance networks storing *Aktionsarten* and semantic clusters for verbs are used. Thus, lexical entries constitute a lexical semantic structure, which contains a linguistically relevant subset of inheritance relations among elements in a semantic neighborhood cluster (cf. Figure 2).

The inheritance network given in Figure 2 is based on a decompositional analysis of transfer verbs. Davis (2001: 113) explains that transfer in verbs is based on abstract motion. There are two transfer directions: x → y or y → x (cf. Gottschalk 2012a: 169). Therefore, the two main branches in the inheritance network in Figure 2 are grouped under two main binary features which are: [+ moving direction x → y] and [– moving direction x → y]. These features of transfer verbs are ontological feature nodes (cf. Gottschalk 2010). A neighborhood cluster of transfer verbs is given in Figure 2 below.

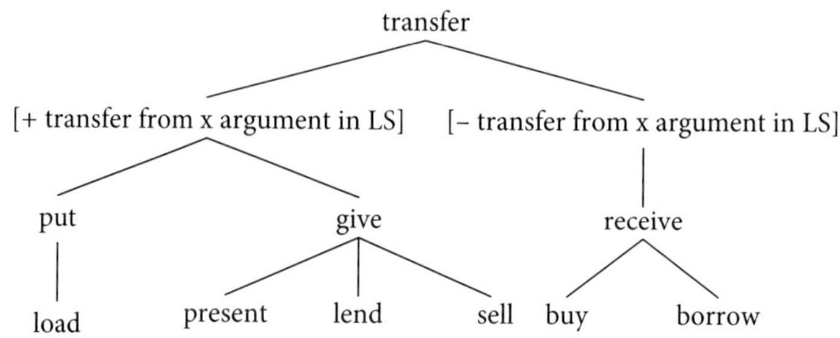

Figure 2. Neighborhood cluster of transfer verbs

Since there is no neutral way of transfer as in these motion verbs (cf. Gottschalk 2010), the neighborhood cluster does not have a neutral node.

The neighborhood cluster of transfer verbs has an upper inheritance network, which defines a broader class of verbs and which is needed to cluster different kinds of neighborhood clusters together by their general logical structure [GLS], which is the root node of the selectional property network.

It is possible for transfer verbs to have a GLS, because transfer is encoded as an abstract form of motion, so that different, more specific neighborhood clusters, can use this GLS. So verbs belonging to the class of knowledge acquisition, like learn or teach, can inherit from this GLS, too.

This idea is based on a remark made in Van Valin and LaPolla (1997: 117) in which they point out that it is possible to unite all verbs of a specific lexical domain in a single logical structure. Specific semantic differences in verbs belonging to a specific neighborhood cluster can be captured by using internal variables which are empty in the GLS and which are filled by inheritance within the neighborhood cluster of the specific verb domain (cf. Gottschalk 2010). A possible GLS for two- and three-place transfer verbs is given in (8):

(8) a. [**do'**(x, [**movement.direction(α).in(β).manner'**(x, (y))]
b. [**do'**(x, [**movement.direction(α).in(β).manner** (x, (y))]
CAUSE [PROC & INGR **truth.value.of.have'**(x, z)]

It has been accounted for the encoding of abstract motion in transfer verbs by using **movement.direction(α)** to refer either to the x → y or y → x movement direction. The **(β).manner** variable on the other hand refers to the manner in which the transfer takes place (cf. Gottschalk 2012a). With the use of a GLS, it is assumed that no verb under investigation is lexically transitive or intransitive. Rather, based on an inheritance process within the lexicon, input from internal or external states and input from information structure which is sent to the lexicon, it is possible to determine whether a verb is intransitive, transitive or ditransitive in language processing.

The inheritance network of lexical semantic relations contains typed feature structures with information on the possible thematic relations. Lexical semantic relations contain information on the semantic argument structure of verbs and they semantically define the semantic relations realized in a specific verb (cf. Davis 2001; cf. Gottschalk 2012a: 48).

In RRG it is generally assumed that macroroles are a generalization of thematic relations and part of the grammar. However, it is also possible to assume that semantic roles, which are items of lexical semantic structures, are stored as typed feature structures in the lexicon and that macroroles are actually epiphenomenal and set on top of thematic relations. The advantage of this perspective is, that variable undergoer linking does not occur randomly based on the AUH as proposed in Van Valin (2007). This way, one is dealing with a lexical process which is pragmatically motivated.

In Davis (2001), a cross-linguistically valid inheritance network of several lexical semantic relations was developed, (cf. Figure 3). This network shows how lexical semantic relations are stored lexically. The different lexical semantic relations inherit information from each other via non-monotonic multiple inheritance. The root node of this network is *rel* and it is an abstract node. The most basic lexical semantic relations *soa-rel, act-rel* and *und-rel* inherit from *rel.* A typical *act-rel* would refer to an intransitive activity verb like *sing*, a prototypical *und-rel* refers to a typical intransitive verb. This relation encodes a verb like *die* in which, within the theory of RRG (cf. Van Valin 2005), the macrorole would be an undergoer. The other lexical semantic relations referred to in this network are special kinds of the three lexical semantic relations *soa-rel, act-rel* and *und-rel.*

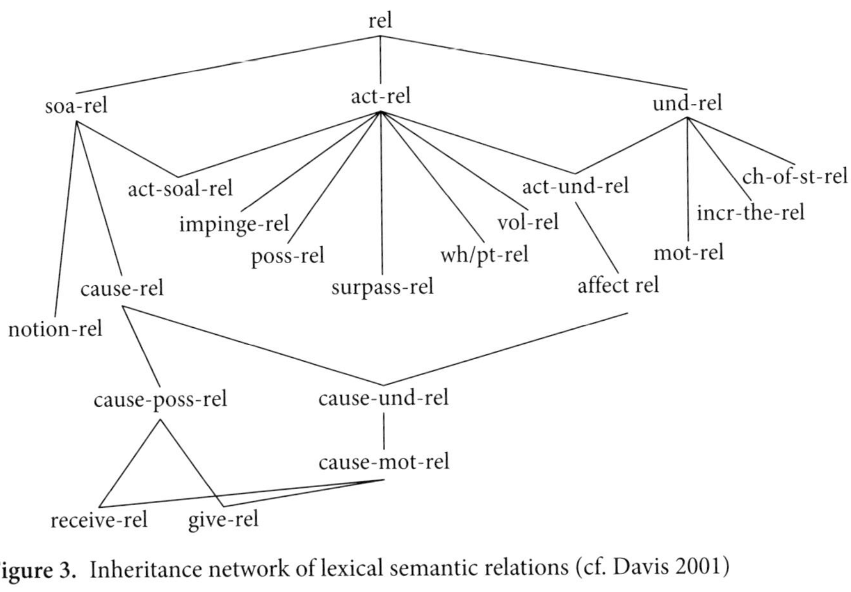

Figure 3. Inheritance network of lexical semantic relations (cf. Davis 2001)

This book chapter has its focus on the two lexical semantic relations *give-rel* and *receive-rel*. The assumption is that all lexical semantic relations are stored in a data structure, called attribute value matrix [AVM]. These AVMs form the nodes representing lexical semantic relations within the inheritance network of lexical semantic relations. The matrix consists of a column for feature names and one in which the corresponding values are stored. This means that an AVM is a list of key-values pairs. Formally it is possible to represent such an AVM as directed acyclic graph, which for a future formalization of RRG is highly important. The two AVMs for the *give-rel* and the receive-relation are given in (9) below:

(9) a.

receive-rel
AGNT 1
THM 2
(POSSE 3) // Activated by logical structure
MEANS [*mot-rel*
THM 2
GRND [*path*
ENDPT]]

b.

give-rel
AGNT 1
REIC 2 3 //Choice activated by IS
THM 3 2
MEANS [*mot-rel*
THM 2
GRND 3 [*path*
ENDPT 2]]

The AVMs in (9) are organized as follows: In (9a), a constraint is found, referred to by the *receive-rel*. This constraint marks the lexical semantic relations by means of the attributes AGNT, THM and POSSE which refer to agent, theme and possessor. In difference to the macroroles in Van Valin (2005) and Van Valin (2007), it assigns a thematic relation, which has a specific semantic structure (cf. Gottschalk 2012a: 49f). The second attribute used in the lexical semantic relation refers to THM, referring to the thematic relation theme in the thematic relations continuum in Van Valin (2005: 58). The third attribute in this AVM is POSSE, which is also contained in Van Valin's (2005) thematic relations continuum. This last attribute is optional, since the same AVM is used to describe transitive and ditransitive transfer verbs. The reason for this is that, in this approach to the mental lexicon, verbs are stored underspecified and are therefore neither lexically transitive nor lexically ditransitive. All attributes in the AVM are co-indexed. Coindices refer to tokens in constructional schemas for transfer verbs, these are discussed later. The general idea is that tokens can be activated in the signatures contained in constructional schemas as introduced in Nolan (2011). The approach used here is that tokens in the constructional schema co-index within the AVMs for lexical semantic relations and with variables in LSs for verbs; this way they unify and finally result in an argument in the semantic representation of the clause. In the AVM in (9a), co-indexation is determined because no case of variable undergoer linking occurs in verbs which inherit from receive. The AVM in (9a) has an embedded AVM, referring to the abstract motion event which is described by transfer verbs. This is indicated by constraint *motion-rel*. Like the *receive-rel*, in which the *motion-rel* is embedded, the *motion-rel* has attributes. These attributes are THM for theme and GRND. The latter refers to the attribute *ground* and describes a path which is transversed by another participant in an event (cf. Davis 2001). The thematic relation is not co-indexed because it is an internal thematic relation which is not overtly marked.

Also, the *motion-rel* hosts a further embedded AVM, which is called path. It refers to the endpoint, marked with ENDPT, which in the morphosyntactic realization of clauses refers to the endpoint of a transfer. ENDPT is co-indexed by 1. This means that it refers to the argument, which is coded as token 1 in the constructional schema. In fact the *motion-rel* is a feature of the internal thematic relation MEANS and refers to the manner in which the transfer takes place. It is similar to the manner concept in the GLS (cf. Gottschalk 2012a: 50).

The architecture of the *give-rel* is parallel to the *receive-rel* and also hosts a *mot-rel*, hosting a path which is a feature of the thematic relation MEANS. What is different in the *give-rel* is that it has the thematic relation recipient REIC, which is indicated by REIC and THM. In Van Valin's (2005) thematic relations continuum, REIC is not found. It has already been noted by Diedrichsen (2012) and Nolan (2011) that there are good reasons to assume that there is a need for the thematic relation theme in RRG. REIC as well as THM can either be co-indexed with the tokens 2 or 3 in the signature of the constructional schema. This co-indexation is undetermined, since in the *give-rel* cases of variable undergoer linking occur. Later, I show that here information structure regulates the proper assignment of the undergoer or patient as it is called in this new framework. Actually, this means that the lexicon needs to account for this by some sort of lexical indeterminism and underspecification rather than hosting two different types of thematic relations of the same kind.

The binary features defining the thematic relations used in this framework are given in (10). The approach is that the attributes used in AVMs, which define the nodes in the inheritance network of lexical thematic relations, can be defined by using the operators '+' and '-'. This way the semantic features of lexical semantic relations are defined on a two-value basis, as in approaches to classical logics, which also use truth-values such as 'true' or 'false'.

(10) a. Agent
[+ effecting influencing participants]
[+ volitional]
[+ notion perception of participants]
[+ forceful contact on]
[+ includes another participant in state or event]
[+ possesses another participant in state or event]

b. Patient
[– effecting influencing participants]
[± volitional]
[+ undergoes a change of state in event]
[+ incremental theme in event]
[+ moves with respect to another participant]

c. SOA:
[+ conceived perceived by one or the other participant in event or state]
[+ resulting event or state caused by event]
[+ event or state necessarily accompanying another event]

d. THM:
[+ entity which undergoes a change of state in terms of moving]

e. REIC:
[+ undergoes a transfer process as receiving entity]
[+ acts as receiving entity in a transfer process]

f. MEANS:
[+ abstract instrument used to achieve a state or activity]

g. GRND
[+ path transversed by another participant in event]

h. IMP-ON
[+ forcefully impinged in an event]

i. PART:
[+ included in part of another participant in state event]

j. INF:
[+ inferior compared to another participant]

k. POSSD:
[+ possessed by another participant in state event]

l. ENDPT
[+ state of affairs coding the goal of an activity]

m. POSSE
[+ acts as possessing entity]
[+ undergoes a transfer as possessing entity]

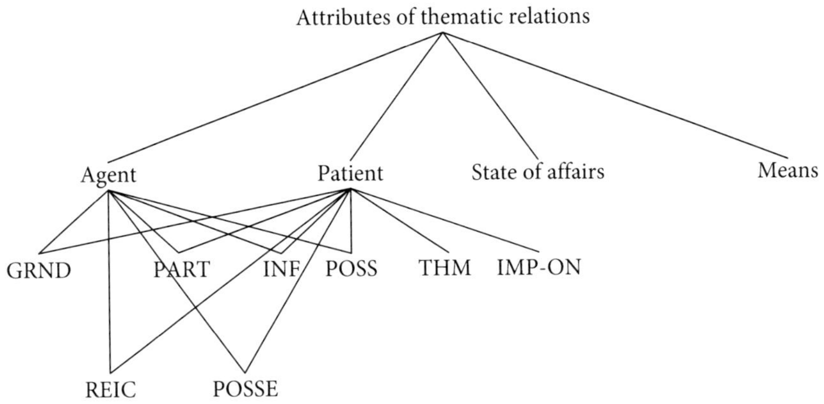

Figure 4. Inheritance network of attributes of lexical semantic relations

It is possible to represent the attributes defining lexical semantic relations also in an entailment-based inheritance network. This inheritance network is given in Figure 4.

This hierarchical inheritance network of attributes in thematic relations describes, based on an entailment hierarchy, the attributes used in AVMs, which finally make up lexical semantic relations. The network has an abstract node called attributes of thematic relations, which is the root node. From this root node four basic attributes, agent, patient, state of affairs and means are inherited. These attributes form a superset of attributes lower in the hierarchy. Attributes like GRND, PART, INF, REIC, POSS and POSSE all inherit features from agent and patient. The latter two are entailed in these attributes. On the other hand, the attribute PART inherits from agent, since it entails features of this attribute. THM and IMP-ON only inherit from patient. This is because in these two attributes only features of patient are entailed and inherited.

The idea is that the network of attributes in lexical semantic relations inherits from the hierarchical inheritance network of attributes in thematic relations since this way, attributes in AVMS in the first network are semantically defined via inheritance.

The lexical entries for transfer verbs are nodes in the neighborhood cluster in Figure 2 developed in this section. They are AVMs which make use of unification and contain attributes and constraints. The neighborhood cluster has an abstract root node, functioning as assemblage point for information inherited from the SPN, which spreads information to be inherited from the ontological feature nodes. Via these nodes, information is inherited from the primitive in the SPN as well as the ontological feature node to the neighborhood cluster. This is the reason why the assemblage point has no manner qualities. The assemblage point in this network has the following manner of transfer qualities <manner of transfer> = = assemblage point β = Ø. What is important is that the assemblage point in this neighborhood cluster inherits all relevant qualities from the non-abstract entity node in the SPN. This node on the other hand inherits everything from its mother node of the SPN, which is the abstract primitive of the domain of transfer verbs (cf. Gottschalk 2012a: 175).

If a verb inherits all qualities of its predecessor node, this is represented by the expression < > == predecessor. The assemblage point is a root node and it contains all the basic information about the selectional properties of a neighborhood cluster in its AVM. Selectional properties in an AVM indicate the content of the variables determined by the GLS. For the verb domain examined here, the selectional properties look like this: <selectional properties> $y = \alpha$ & non-abstract entity β <manner of transfer> (cf. Gottschalk 2012: 176). Consequently, this is a kind of variable, or, it forms a reference point within the particular lexical entires. Another possibility is to refer to this behavior as local inheritance within a node, or rather within an lexical entry.

Also, lexical entries in this framework contain the following node: <thematic relation>. Because the root node of the neighborhood cluster is an assemblage point, this attribute marks which thematic relation is specified in an inheritance network and it marks which properties are inherited from this node. Via this node, the assemblage point inherits all properties from the AVM of the specific thematic relation. Nodes which are lower in the neighborhood cluster of transfer verbs.

Verbs which are direct daughter nodes of the assemblage point are basic verbs. These verbs inherit from the superior ontological feature node. This node is connected to a world ontology which describes the features of this node in detail. Like all other nodes, ontological feature nodes have semantic features, which are represented as AVMs. The ontology is based on binary features and in case of transfer verbs, the most relevant binary feature is [± transfer from x argument in LS].

Usually basic verbs inherit all qualities from ontological feature nodes. A second characteristic of basic verbs is that they inherit the selectional properties from the root node, which is regarded as assemblage point. However, the semantic qualities of the assemblage point are not passed on to the ontological description node. Rather, the inheritance quality inside the specific network is expressed by the reference point <selectional properties> == transfer. This is a case of global inheritance; it can skip nodes. Also, basic verbs have a reference point <manner of transfer>, which stores their idiosyncratic qualities.

Lexical entries have an additional attribute, which is called <pointer to constructional schema>. This attribute operates as pointer to a signature in a construction repository as developed in Nolan (2011). Because this attribute is only a pointer, signatures are not stored in the lexical entries, but rather the pointer is used as bookmark, which points to the referring signature in the construction repository. Also, this attribute inherits from verbs higher in the hierarchy to verbs lower in the hierarchy via default. This is the reason why only basic verbs contain this attribute. A lexical entry for the English three-place predicate receive is given in example 11:

(11)

receive:
<> = = [- transfer from x argument in LS]
<selectional properties> = = transfer
<manner of transfer> = = Transfer of a non-abstract entity realized as y argument to x argument. Transfer f a non-abstract entity realized as z from y argument to x argument. Describes a neutral way of transfer to x argument.
<thematic relation> = = *give-rel*
<pointer to constructional repository> = = ^[RP$_{Agent}$ V[RP | PN]Recipient RP$_{Theme}$];
^[RP$_{Agent}$ V RP$_{Theme}$ [PREPPN | RP]$_{Recipient}$];
^[RP$_{Agent}$ V RPTheme[PREP indef det N]$_{Recipient}$]

What causes variable undergoer linking in three-place predicates in English are information structure considerations. Van Valin (2005: 72) notes that one can distinguish two focus types: narrow focus and marked focus. The difference between them is where narrow focus falls. In English, unmarked narrow focus falls on the final constituent. Marked focus is found when it falls to the left or right of the final constituent. A common example of narrow focus is WH-questions. An example for this is *Whom did Gibbs shoot?* The corresponding answer is *He shot _*, here the WH-word and the RP filling its slot in a reply are both marked as narrow foci (cf. Van Valin 2005: 72). Narrow focus also occurs in yes-no questions.

It is possible to formally capture the interaction of focus as well as of proposition and assertion by using DRSs, which Van Valin introduces as follows:

> In Section 3.1 above, Lambrecht's (1994) definition of 'focus' is 'the semantic component of pragmatically structured proposition whereby the assertion differs from the presupposition'. This yields the actual focus domain, and, in order to derive it, it is necessary to have representations of both the pragmatic assertion and the pragmatic presupposition. This can be done in terms of a simplified version of Discourse Representation Theory [...] These is a discourse representation structure for each sentence, and it contains the referent and the proposition expressed in the sentence. Co-reference relations between pronominals and established referents are explicitly represented. In order to derive the different focus structures, it is necessary to have a representation of the presupposition and the assertion (Van Valin 2005: 171).

How DRSs interact with focus assignment in three-place predicates in English is exemplified in (12) below:

(12) a. Speaker A: What did McGee give to Gibbs?
b. Speaker B: McGee gave a/the book to Gibbs.
c. Speaker A: Who did McGee give the book to?
d. Speaker B: McGee gave Gibbs the book. (Gottschalk 2012: 182)

In speaker A's utterance in (12a), *what* is the focus and in speaker A's utterance in (12c),*who* is the focus; both utterances are examples of narrow focus. The interesting question is which focus structure types are found in speaker B's responses in (12). Since speaker B's responses are used in order to respond narrow focus questions, these sentences are narrow focus, too. This is because the focus domain is a single constituent, in this case an RP (cf. Van Valin 2005: 72; Gottschalk 2012a: 183). It is possible to represent (12) in the following DRSs in Figure 5.

The question is *What did McGee give to Gibbs?* and the presupposition of the speaker uttering this sentence is '*x was given to Gibbs by McGee*'. The assertion uttered in response is that the book was given to Gibbs by McGee. What is new in this assertion – and this way a possible candidate for focus – is *the book*. The second question in Figure 5 is *Who did McGee give the book to?* Here, the presupposition of the speaker is '*X was given a book by McGee*'. In the response *McGee gave Gibbs the boo*k, the RP *Gibbs* is not in the presupposition, however, it is in the assertion and this means it is focus. This can clearly be seen in the DRSs used. Based on the native speaker interviews introduced in Erteschik-Shir (1979) and also shown in the example in 12, it is also possible to conclude that in cases of predicate focus and sentence focus, the order is *McGee gave Gibbs the book*. This conclusion is possible since this is the unmarked situation. The unmarked situation in these examples does not mean that this word order is the basic one, since in this approach both constructions, the ditransitive and the dative-shift, are treated alike. This is in contrast to Van Valin's (2007) analysis (cf. Gottschalk 2012a: 183).

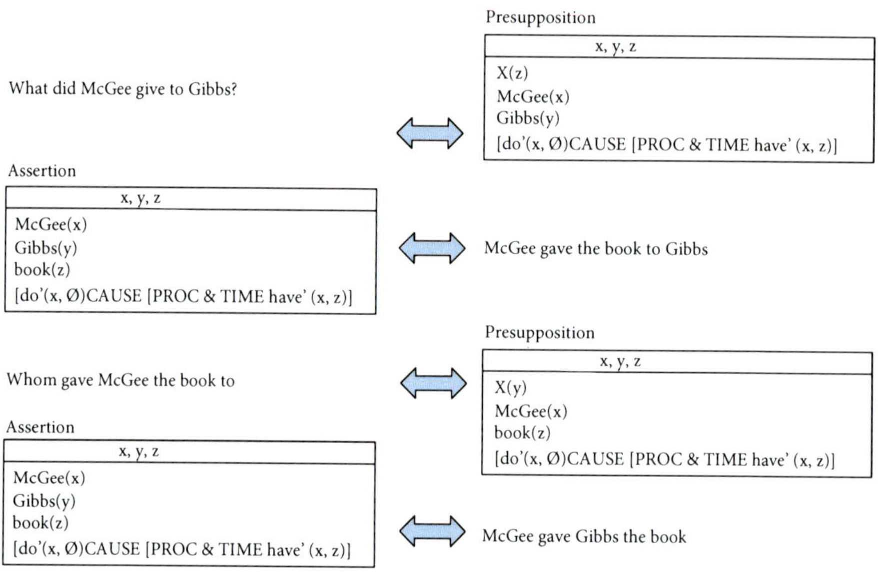

Figure 5. Discourse representation structures for ditransitive and dative-shift constructions

As assumed in Erteschik-Shir (1979) information structure governs variable undergoer linking in three-place predicates in English DRSs can be used in order to determine the focus of a sentence. However, it is important to note that the post-verbal element in three-place predicate constructions is not always focus, since, following Lambrecht (1994: 217), focus usually is a pragmatically relation of an element to a proposition (cf. Gottschalk 2012a: 184).

The architecture of the constructional schema as a grammatical object for three-place predicates in English is based on Nolan (2011). The constructional schema has a signature which uniquely identifies it. The object represented by the constructional schema refers to transfer situation in English and it can be used to represent both the semantics to syntax linking and the syntax to semantics linking. This approach to linking in RRG is computationally adequate and it can be executed on a RAM. In the constructional schema, three signatures are possible which can be used to identify the construction and activate it. In the first signature, the first RP is actor while the third token can either be an RP or a pronoun. In this case, both are treated as recipient. In this signature, the last RP is the theme. In the second signature, the first token is an RP, too, and it is actor. The third token is an RP which is a theme and the fourth token can either be a pronoun or an RP, which are both marked by a preposition. This token is a recipient. The third signature has an actor RP as first token, while the third token is a theme RP. The last token is an indefinite RP which is a recipient and marked by a preposition (cf. Gottschalk 2012: 185). In all three signatures the verb is in V2-position; they consist of four tokens with an optional preposition.

This construction can either receive as input a clause consisting of the tokens [1], [2] or [3] or an LS. Furthermore, grammatical patterns for sentences, which are identified after the parsing took place, are stored in constructional schemas. Verbs in the V2-position are inflected. Because this construction is activated by a signature, also semantic roles are assigned. A second possibility is that the constructional schema receives an LS as input which is generated within the lexicon in advance and sent to the constructional schema as a grammatical object. The corresponding constructional schema is given in (13)

(13)

Signature

[1] = [RP_{Agent} V [Recipient | $_{Recipient}$] RP_{Theme}] OR

[2] = [RP_{Agent} V RP_{Theme} [PREP PN | RP]$_{Recipient}$] OR

[3] = [RP_{Agent} V RP_{Theme} [PREP indef det N]$_{Recipient}$]

as tokens [1 2 3 (PREP) 4]

Input

RP_{Agent} [_] **and** V = **pred.** [TNS: _] **and** [$_{\textbf{Recipient}}$ [_] | $_{Recipient}$ [_]] **and** RP_{Theme} [_] = [4]

elseif

RP_{Agent} [_] **and** V = **pred.** [TNS: _] **and** RP_{Theme} [_] **and** [[PREP] PN_{Rec} [_] | RP_{Rec} [_]] = [5]

elseif

RP_{Agent} [_] **and** V = **pred.** [TNS: _] **and** RP_{Theme} **and** [[PREP] PN_{Rec} [_] | RP_{Rec} [_]] = [6]

or

LS = [**do**′(x, <) CAUSE [PROC & INGR **have**′ (x, y)]]

Method body

if semantics to syntax linking = = true **do**

syntactic pattern = semantics.to.syntax.linking(LS)

else

LS = syntax.to.semantics.linking([4] **or** [5] **or** [6], **tokes**[1, 2, 3, prep 4])

Output

[**do**′(x, <) CAUSE [PROC & INGR **have**′ (x, y)]] = LS

or

Well formed three-place predicate construction = LS

for semantics to syntax linking

or

RP_{Agent} [_] **and** V = **pred.** [TNS: _] **and** [$_{\textbf{Recipient}}$ [_] | $_{Recipient}$ [_]] **and** RP_{Theme} [_] = syntactic pattern

elseif

RP_{Agent} [_] **and** V = **pred.** [TNS: _] **and** RP_{Theme} [_] **and** [[PREP] PN_{Rec} [_] | RP_{Rec} [_]] = syntactic pattern

elseif

RP_{Agent} [_] **and** V = **pred.** [TNS: _] **and** RP_{Theme} **and** [[PREP] PN_{Rec} [_] | RP_{Rec} [_]] = syntactic pattern

The construction consists of two methods and the workspace which is contained in the constructional schemas developed in Nolan (2011) is part of the methods which describe the linking direction. In the method body it is tested whether the semantics to syntax linking takes place or whether the syntax to semantics linking takes place. In the first case a semantics to syntax linking method is called. This method receives an LS as input. In the latter case, the syntax to semantics linking takes place. In this case, the method receives a clause as input (cf. Gottschalk 2012a: 186). After a method is executed within a constructional schema, which is a sub constructional schema, the result is stored either in a variable called LS or in a variable called syntactic patterns which in the output section of the constructional schema assign the proper output to this variable. The output represents a grammatical object, either the LS [**do**′(x, Ø) CAUSE [PROC & INGR **have**′(x, y)]] or the information *Well-formed three-place predicate construction*. The output of this information should be realized by the assignment of the method for the syntax to semantics linking to the syntax to semantics linking method. Basically, the representation in this case is a bit fuzzy from a computational linguistics point of view, but it is clear from an illustrative point of view. This is because generally, the output is realized by the variable LS and it can either be an LS or the information that the sentence is well-formed (cf. Gottschalk 2012: 186). By realizing the constructional schema using one of these methods, it is possible to have a close set of language specific constructions. These are treated as objects and they can properly account for the b-directional linking in RRG using methods which represent the two linking directions. By using constructional schemas, the linking algorithm developed in Van Valin (2005) becomes computationally adequate in this revised version. It can be executed on a RAM. A possible method for the semantics to syntax linking for three-place predicates in English, which exhibit variable. The continuation of the constructional schema is given in (14).

(14)

English three-place predicate construction 'give-rel' Semantics to Syntax Linking
Workspace: input [1], [2] **or** [3]
Construction Body
[SEM to SYN]
Retrieve the logical structure from linking algorithm
Inherit information of lexical semantic relations from lexicon
Assign LS(x) argument with actor according inherited information from lexical semantic relations from lexicon
if predicate focus structure = = true **or** sentence focus = = true **or** token 3 = = narrow focus **do**
co-index token [3] with recipient in logical structure
co-index toked [4] with theme in logical structure

```
generate syntactic pattern = [1]
elseif signature [3] = = true do
co-index token[3] with theme in logical structure
co-index token [4] with recipient in logical structure
generate syntactic pattern = [2]
elseif
co-index token[3] with theme in logical structure
co-index token [4] with recipient in logical structure
generate syntactic pattern = [3]
end if
Morphology: none
Pragmatics: topic = PSA
```

Arguments in the LS are assigned actor, which is defined based on the signature, which was activated based on typed feature structures stored in the lexicon. If an example of predicate focus structure is found or sentence focus is true, or token 3 is in narrow focus, then token 2 is co-indexed with recipient in the logical structure, and token 4 is co-indexed with theme in the logical structure, and syntactic pattern [1] is generated and stored in the variable 'syntactic pattern'. If, however, signature [3] is true because it is activated based on the interaction of the construction repository and the lexicon, then token [3] is co indexed with theme in the logical structure, and token [4] is co indexed with recipient, and syntactic pattern [2] is generated. In all other cases, token [3] is co indexed with theme in the logical structure and token [4] is co indexed with recipient in the logical structure, and syntactic pattern [3] is generated. As noted in the constructional schema, morphology does not play any role, while the PSA is always topic in this construction. Of course the method cannot only retrieve values by the object of which it is part, but it can also retrieve information from the general linking algorithm. This is what takes place in the construction body. After the constructional schema was applied as a kind of method in the pseudo-code meta-language, the populated logical structure is sent to the algorithm again and the usual linking process can start. For a revision of the semantics to syntax linking algorithm, this means that in the first step DRSs, which are automatically filled in a discourse situation, are analyzed and focus structure is determined algorithmically.

For the development of a computationally adequate semantics to syntax linking algorithm, a more rigorous inclusion of information structure is necessary, resulting in a revised linking algorithm which in a first step can be used to determine topic and focus. This algorithm is given in (15):

(15)

access information from DRS for presupposition;
access information form DRS for assertion;
if RP in presupposition **and** assertion **do**
    topic = RP;
if (NUC **and** $RP_1 ... RP_n$ in assertion == **true)**
and (NUC **and** $RP_1 ... RP_n$ in presupposition == **false**) **do**
    predicate focus = (NUC **and** RP_1 ... RP_n);
if DRS for presupposition = = **false and** DRS for assertion = = **true do**
    focus = assertion;
if (RP **or** PP **or** NUC **not in** presupposition) **and** (RP **or** PP **or** NUC **in** assertion) **do**
    narrow focus = RP **or** PP **or** NUC;

In this pseudo-code representation of the focus structure determination, algorithm information is accessed from both the DRS for the presupposition and the DRS for the assertion. First, it is checked whether an RP is contained in both the presupposition and the assertion, and if such an element exists, it is assigned topic. If NUC and RP1 are contained in the assertion and not in the presupposition, the elements are assigned predicate focus. In cases where no presupposition exists, but the statement 'DRS for assertion == true' is valid, the whole assertion is assigned focus. In situations where RPs, PPs, or NUCs are not contained in the presupposition, but occur in the assertion, either the RP, PP or NUC is assigned narrow focus.

In the second step, the logical structure is accessed from the lexicon via unification of the logical structure, information from the lexicon and a database containing world knowledge. Afterwards a logical structure is accessed from the lexicon.

In the third step, a populated logical structure is accessed from the lexicon. The next step in the new version of the linking algorithm takes place after the fully populated logical structure is sent from the lexicon to the linking algorithm; as a result of this step in the new linking algorithm is a fully constructed logical structure with attached operators and a notion of the discourse status of the referents in the logical structures. Such a logical structure is given in (16) below:

(16) <IF DEC <TNS PAST < [[**do**′(McGeeACT,)] CAUSE [PROC & INGR **have**′ (SivaACS, USB-stickACT)]] >>>

The activation level of referents of RPs filling argument positions is coded in logical structures (cf. Van Valin 2005: 79). Since in the new version of the linking algorithm topic and focus are determined in the first step rather than later in the algorithm, topic and focus are assigned in the lexicon within a logical structure construction process. This is possible since the arguments in the logical structure are matched with information from DRSs. Also, the activation levels are assigned in this step of the linking algorithm. Besides information on the activation level – topic and focus as well as the attachment of operators to the logical structure – also pointers to possible signatures in the construction repository are contained in the logical structure. The logical structure is sent from the lexicon to the algorithm. These pointers to the construction repository occur in situations where the necessity of a construction is coded in the lexicon (cf. Gottschalk 2012: 189). This LS is given in (17):

(17) <IF DEC <TNS PAST < [[**do**′(McGeeACT --> Topic agent,)] CAUSE [PROC & INGR **have**'(SivaACS --> Focus recipient, USB-stickACT theme)]] >>> **and** ^ [RPActor V [Recipient | Recipient] RPTheme]; ^[RPActor V RPTheme [PREP PN | RP]Recipient]; ^[RPActor V RPTheme [PREP indef det N]Recipient]

The next step in the linking algorithm therefore looks as follows and is given in (18) below.

(18)

access full-fledged logical structure from the lexicon
if pointer to signature in construction repository = = **true do**
new constructional schema **in** construction repository;
else
determine morphosyntactic coding properties in one-place predicates **or** determine morphosyntactic coding properties in two-place predicates.

This part of the algorithm accesses populated logical structures from the lexicon and checks whether a pointer to a signature in the construction repository exists. If this is the case, a new constructional schema is called. Otherwise, the morphosyntactic coding properties of the logical structures with assigned thematic relations are determined. In cases where a constructional schema is called, the assignment of thematic relations within the constructional schema takes place. Afterwards a logical structure with assigned thematic relations is sent to the linking algorithm, where the other linking steps take place. Constructional schemas are flexible with respect to what part of the linking takes place within them. It is possible, as in the case of three-place predicates of the give-rel structure in this section, that they only take place to a certain degree. However, it is also possible that the whole linking takes place in the constructional schema. Since in this book chapter I focus on the generation of three-place predicates, I will not go on to describe how the linking should precede in more detail.

4. Conclusion

A direct implementation of the RRG-linking algorithm is not possible as this results in undecidability problems with respect to three-place predicates. A first conclusion for that is that the semantics to syntax linking algorithm, in Van Valin's version, is too coarsely grained and fuzzy to account for three-place predicates with variable undergoer linking. This resulted in the development of a computational linguistics processing model for RRG. Therefore, the answer to the two research questions in the introduction is as follows: Based on a lexical approach to transfer verbs, which uses various inheritance networks and typed feature structures for the give- and receive-relation, a unification-based approach to RRG has been developed, which is computable and can be used as a computational processing model for RRG.

This resulted in a version of RRG where macroroles are epiphenomenal and where the AUH is superfluous. The first step in the linking algorithm should be on the discourse level in terms of using DRSs, rather than starting with accessing the semantics structure. This way, it is possible to account for variable undergoer linking in English via information structure. Actually, this approach is very fruitful in that accessing information structure first naturally results in a processing model envisioned by Van Valin (2005: 129). In general, in a new version of the linking algorithm from semantics to syntax, it is necessary to first analyze DRSs by parsing and to send this information to the lexicon. If one assigns topic and focus to the logical structure in the mental lexicon and uses a pointer to the signatures in the constructional schemas stored in the construction repository, as developed in Nolan (2011), it is possible to connect logical structures in the mental lexicon.

References

Blass, Andreas & Gurevitch, Yuri. 2001. *Algorithms: A Quest for Absolute Definitions*. <http://www.math.lsa.umich.edu/~ablass/abs.pdf>

Carpenter, Bob. 1991. The generative power of categorial grammars and head-driven phrase structure grammars with lexical rules. *Computational Linguistics* 17(3): 301–314.

Davis, Anthony R. 2001. *Linking Types in the Hierarchical Lexicon*. Stanford CA: CSLI.

Diedrichsen, Elke. 2011. The influence of person hierarchies on preferences with word order in German ditransitive constructions. Paper presented at the International Workshop on Referential Hierarchies in three- participant constructions. The University of Lancaster, England.

Diedrichsen, Elke. 2012. The theoretical importance of constructional schemas in RRG. In *New perspectives in Role and Reference Grammar,* Wataru Nakamura (ed.), 64–103. Newcastle upon Tyne: Cambridge Scholars.

Erteschik-Shir, Nomi. 1979. Discourse constraints on dative movement. In *Syntax and Semantics,* Vol. XII: *Discourse and Syntax,* Talmy Givón (ed.), 441–467. New York NY: Academic Press.

Gottschalk, Judith. 2010. Storage of linguistic knowledge in the mental lexicon: An approach within Role and Reference Grammar. *ITB Journal* 19: 20 – 45. <http://www.itb.ie/files/journal/issue-19.pdf>

Gottschalk, Judith. 2012a. On the computability of Role and Reference Grammar: A new approach to the analysis of three-place predicates and the hierarchical lexicon. *ITB-Journal* 22: 124 – 192. <http://www.itb.ie/files/journal/issue-22.pdf>

Gottschalk, Judith. 2012b. The persuasive tutor: A BDI teaching agent with Role and Reference Grammar Language Interface. *ITB Journal* 23: 31–51. <http://www.itb.ie/files/journal/issue-23.pdf>

Guest, Elizabeth. 2008. Parsing for Role and Reference Grammar. In *Investigations of the Syntax-Semantics-Pragmatics Interface* [Studies in Language Companion Series 105], Robert D. Van Valin Jr. (ed.), 435–453. Amsterdam: John Benjamins.

Güting, Ralf H. & Dieker, Stefan. 2004. Datenstrukturen I. Kurseinheit 1: Einführung Programmiersprachliche Konzepte für Datenstrukturen. Ms, Fern Universität Hagen.

Haspelmath, Martin. 2005. Argument marking in ditransitive alignment types. *Linguistic Discovery* 3(1): 1 – 21. <http://linguistic-discouvery.dartmouth.edu/>

Haspelmath, Martin. 2008. Ditransitive constructions – Towards a new Role and Reference Grammar account? In *Investigations of the Syntax-Semantics-Pragmatics Interface* [Studies in Language Companion Series 105], Robert D. Van Valin, Jr. (ed.), 75–100. Amsterdam: John Benjamins.

Lambrecht, Knud. 1994. *Information Structure and Sentence Form*. Cambridge: CUP.

Larson, Richard. 1988. On double object construction. *Linguistic Inquiry* 19: 335–392.

Murtagh, Irene. 2011. Towards a linguistically motivated Irish Sign Language conversational avatar. *ITB Journal* 19: 72 – 101.

Nolan, Brian. 2011. Constructions as grammatical objects: A new perspective on constructions in RRG. Paper presented at the International Conference on Role and Reference Grammar on "Functional Linguistics: Grammar, Communication & Cognition". Facultad de Letras, at the Pontificia Universidad Católica de Chile, in Santiago de Chile.

Nolan, Brian & Salem, Yasser. 2009. UNIARAB: A universal machine translator system for Arabic based on Role and Reference Grammar. <http://linguistics.buffalo.edu/people/faculty/vanvalin/rrg.html>

Periñán-Pascual, Carlos & Arcas-Túnez, Francisco. 2010. The architecture of FunGramKB. In *Proceedings of the 7th International Conference on Language Resources and Evaluation*, 2, 667–2674. Malta: European Language Resources Association.

Salem, Yasser. 2009. A generic framework for Arabic to English machine translation of Simplex sentences using the Role and Reference Grammar linguistic model. <http://linguistics.buffalo.edu/people/faculty/vanvalin/rrg.html>

Siewierska, Anna. 1998. Languages without objects. *Languages in Contrast* 1(2): 173 –190.

Van Valin, Jr., Robert D. 2005. *Exploring the Syntax-Semantics Interface*. Cambridge: CUP.

Van Valin, Jr. Robert D. 2007. The Role and Reference Grammar analysis of three-place predicates. *Suvremena Lingvistika* 33.1(63): 31 – 64.

Van Valin, Jr., Robert D. & LaPolla, Randy J. 1997. *Syntax: Structure, Meaning and Function*. Cambridge: CUP.

Wilson, Chris. 2009. Lex: A software project for linguists [Technical Report SEE-J Hiphil 6]. <http://www.see-j.net/index.php/hiphil/article/view/60>

Winther-Nielsen, Nicolai. 2009. Biblical Hebrew parsing on display: The Role Lexical Module (RLM) as a tool for Role and Reference Grammar. SEE-J Hiphil 6: 1– 51. <http://www.see-j.net/index.php/hiphil/article/view/78>

A Role and Reference Grammar parser for German

Elke Diedrichsen
Google EU HQ Dublin

This paper[1] describes the development of a sentence parser for German based on Role and Reference Grammar (RRG). German has a number of characteristics which are very challenging to a computational approach to syntactic processing that is semantically motivated. These include the German sentence structure, which is organised as a "bracket structure", in which one component of the predicate, mostly the finite verb, is realised in an early position in the sentence and therefore forms the "left bracket", whereas the more meaningful part of the predicate, mostly the infinite predicate, appears at the end of the sentence and forms the "right bracket". Inside these brackets, the main information of the sentence is placed in an order that reflects information structure, i.e. the given information precedes the new information inside the bracket. The bracket structure has recurrent formal elements. It therefore provides a formal structuring principle for sentences that is particular for German and serves functions for sentence processing, information structure and turn taking. German has a three-way gender system for nouns. Gender is marked on the article. Tense is marked on the verb. There is an aspectual system in the realisation of perfect in that telic verbs select sein in the perfect, while atelic verbs select haben. The software is developed using Java and will accept an input sentence in German from the user through a Java Swing graphical user interface. The software parses an input sentence into its respective tokens using the Java native string processing capability. Each token is checked against the respective German lexicons (noun, verb, etc.) to determine its lexical category. The morphological markings of the tokens are unpacked for their feature sets. These features are recorded for each token. The lexical entry for the verb is determined and its logical structure is retrieved from the lexicon. The result of the parse displays the populated RRG logical structure and its operators, i.e. tense, aspect etc. A trace of the application of the linking system, in mapping from syntactic clause to semantic representation, is presented.

1. "I thank Brian Nolan for valuable suggestions and discussion. Any errors are mine."

1. Introduction

The parser presented here is designed to process German. German has several characteristics which are very challenging to a computational approach to syntactic processing that is semantically motivated.

1.1 Grammatical features of German

The German sentence structure is organised as a "bracket structure", in which one component of the predicate, mostly the finite verb, is realised in an early position in the sentence and therefore forms the "left bracket", whereas the more meaningful part of the predicate, mostly the infinite predicate, appears at the end of the sentence and forms the "right bracket". Inside these brackets, the main information of the sentence is placed in an order that reflects the information structure, i.e. the given information precedes the new information inside the bracket. The bracket structure has recurrent formal elements, and it also has a recognisable intonation contour. It therefore provides a formal structuring principle for sentences that is particular for German and serves functions for sentence processing, information structure and turn taking.

Further grammatical features of German have to be considered for the parser:

- German has a three-way gender system for nouns. Gender is marked on the article.
- Tense is marked on the verb. There is an aspectual system in the realisation of perfect in that telic verbs select *sein* in the perfect, while atelic verbs select *haben* (Diedrichsen 2013a).
- There are several passive forms in German, of which the most commonly described ones are the *werden*-passive (plain passive) and the *bekommen*-passive (recipient passive). Like the perfect, the formation of the passive requires an auxiliary and a past participle form of a full verb. In periphrastic tense forms and passives, the finite auxiliary always forms the left brace and the past participle forms the right brace in every main declarative sentence.

1.2 The grammar model

RRG organises the structure of the clause in layers. The Core holds the elements of the simple clause, which means the arguments and the predicate. "Clause" is a super-Core level which holds extra Core elements. The prefield position in German is argued to correlate with the PreCore slot position in RRG. The Core, then, is structurally embedded in the two braces. The left brace (finite verb) is assumed to belong to the Core, if it is not an auxiliary. The right brace, which holds the full verb in a periphrastic construction, is considered to belong to the Core. Thus, the Core holds the full verbal information and the arguments in the middle field. Auxiliaries do not belong to the

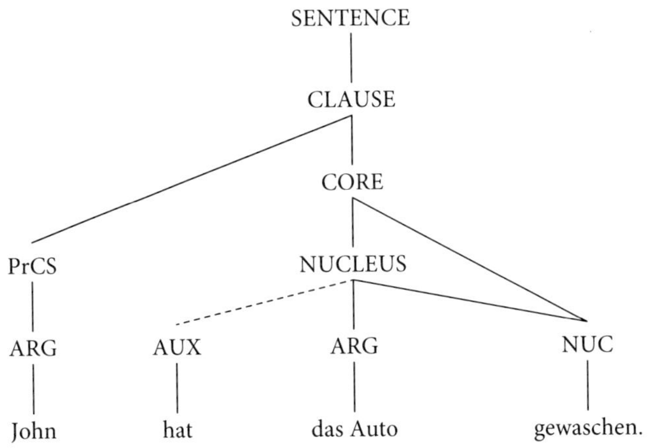

Figure 1. Constituent projection for a periphrastic construction in a main declarative clause[2]

Core in terms of the constituent projection (Van Valin 2005; Diedrichsen 2008; Van Valin & Diedrichsen 2006).

For the description of sentence structure, RRG formulates a set of general rules, which includes the view that on the basis of Aktionsart classes, the semantics of the verb can be translated into a logical structure for the syntax of the sentence including this verb. Grammatical relations like subject and object are assigned on the basis of Generalised Semantic Roles and language specific PSA selection rules. The word order is allocated by using pre-formulated syntactic templates that save basic syntactic structures of the language, and language-specific word order rules that assign the actual words to positions in these syntactic templates (Van Valin 2005).

2. German sentence structure in a RRG construction representation

I will argue that the bracket structure, given its continuous appearance across German syntax, is adequately described by a construction-based model. The bracket construction will be represented as a sentence structure pattern that is part of the linguistic knowledge of an individual. Its formal and functional properties will be represented in a Constructional Schema, as it is applied for constructions in Role and Reference Grammar (Van Valin 2005, Diedrichsen 2010, 2011, 2013b, Nolan 2012).

2. Note that the auxiliary is not part of the constituent projection. The dotted line is there to express its relation with the full verb, which counts as the Nucleus and is part of the core.

The bracket structure is formed by the strict V2 word order rule that holds for main declarative sentences, but it appears in V1 structures as well. The finite verb and another part of a discontinuous verbal expression form a bracket in the formal appearance of the sentence. It potentially includes all the information of a simple clause (a Core in RRG terms), even though it is possible to place arguments outside the right bracket. The word order in the middlefield, which is the field between the two brackets, has a strong tendency to reflect topic-comment structure. The bracket puts a frame around this important part of the utterance and therefore supports the processing of the utterance, as well.

Note that these word order rules only apply to main declarative clauses. Subordinated clauses have verb-final order, and the verbal elements stand adjacent to each other. Thus, the prefield only exists in main declarative clauses.

In (2), the use of the bracket structure is illustrated for different types of sentences (see e.g. Eisenberg 2006; Grewendorf et al. 1994; Wöllstein-Leisten et al. 1997). The basic sentences exemplified in (2a–b) are represented with glossings in (1a–b). (2c–k) are variations of this sentence with different word order.

(1) a. John wäscht heute das Auto
John wash.PRES3SG today DEFNSGACC car.SG
John washes the car today.

b. John hat heute das Auto gewaschen.
John have.PRES3SG today DEFNSGACC car.SG wash.PSTP
John has washed the car today.

(2) **German sentence topology**

	VVF	VF	lSk	MF	rSk	NF
a.		John	wäscht	heute das Auto		
b.		John	hat	heute das Auto	gewaschen	
c.	John,	der	hat	heute das Auto	gewaschen	
d.		John	hat	das Auto	gew.	heute
e.			weil	J. heute das A. gew.	hat	
f.		Das Auto	hat	John heute	gewaschen	
h.		Gewaschen	hat	John das Auto heute		
i.		Das A. gew.	hat	John heute		
j.			Hat	John heute das Auto	gewaschen?	
k.			Wasch	das Auto!		

In all kinds of clauses, the left brace has to be occupied, while the right brace may remain free (2h,i). In main declarative clauses, there has to be a constituent in the prefield.

Table 1. The German bracket structure construction

CONSTRUCTION:	German bracket structure construction
SIGNATURE:	V_{FIN} [$_{ARG1...ARG2....ADJ1....PARTICLE}$] PART.OF.VERBAL.EXPRESSION Space between brackets may be empty (if clause is intransitive)
CONSTRAINT:	No constraints or restrictions.
WORKSPACE:	*Real-time processing according to the following construction-specific rules*

SYNTAX:
"Bracket Structure" (cf. Drach 1937 [[4]1963]):
Bracket is ALWAYS opened by the finite verb. The right bracket is filled according to the following rules:

1. If V_{FIN} =AUX
   { PART.OF.VERBAL.EXPRESSION = full verb (PSTP)};
2. If V_{FIN} =full verb
   { PART.OF.VERBAL.EXPRESSION = separable prefix};
3. If V_{FIN} =light verb
   { PART.OF.VERBAL.EXPRESSION = rest of collocation};

(Ronneberger-Siebold 1991, Nübling 2008, Hentschel and Weydt 2003).
Order of arguments within brackets follows topic comment structure and principle of end weight
(Hawkins 1994, 2004).
The following rules apply (Van Valin and Diedrichsen 2006, Diedrichsen 2008):

1. **General constraints: pronoun > other, RP > PP**
2. **Case-based argument ordering constraint: NOM > DAT > ACC (default)**
3. **If ACC = pronoun, then ACC > DAT (default)**

MORPHOLOGY:
AUX: May be any auxiliary or modal verb
V_{FIN} may be any verb.

PHONOLOGY: Not specified.

SEMANTICS:
[+telic], where telicity may be only invoked for conversational purposes: adds intensity, expression

PRAGMATICS:
Turn taking: Signal for dimension of Turn Constructional unit; right brace marks end of TCU (Uhmann 1997)
Illocutionary force: not specified
Focus structure inside braces: TOP>FOC

3. Functional and technical requirements

It is proposed that this application will have the following functionality to successfully parse sentences of German according to the rules and constraints of the Role and Reference Grammar linguistic model.

- The software will accept an input sentence from the user through an appropriate graphical user interface.
- The software will parse the input sentence into its respective tokens using the Java native string processing capability.
- The software will parse active and passive sentences.
- Each token will be checked against the lexicon (noun, verb, etc.) to determine its lexical category. The morphological marking of the token will be unpacked for its feature set. These features will be recorded for each token.
- The result of the parse will display the representation of the Layered Structure of the Clause according to RRG, and its operators, i.e. tense, aspect etc.

The parser is developed in Java Version 7 (Deitel & Deitel 2012; Horton 2011). The graphical user interface is developed using Java Swing. Therefore it is platform neutral and will run on MacOSX, Windows and Linux, as long as these platforms have a Java virtual machine available.

4. The constructions used for the parser

The parser developed here will give an RRG syntactic description of eight constructions. In the examples provided here, a constructional variation of a proposition will be given. The lexemes used in these constructions can be varied according to the contents of the lexicon. This will be explained in more detail below.

The constructions include conventional sentences using active transitive and intransitive structures with V2 and V1 structures. The word order is varied, such that the direct object may appear in sentence initial position. One of the constructions is more complex in that it involves a prepositional element. One of the constructions is a passive structure, and one has marked word order in that the main verb appears in sentence initial position. The structures will be parsed in terms of the Layered Structure of the Clause, which involves a Nucleus, a Core with arguments, a PreCore slot and a Clause layer, which subsumes the other elements. It will be shown that the Layered Structure of the Clause accounts for the varieties in structure that are common in German sentence formation. With the sentences introduced here, there is variety in tense as well. Note that in the parsed representation, capitalisation and punctuation will not be applied.

4.1 Construction 1: Die Katze trinkt die Milch

(3)

Die	Katze	trinkt	die	Milch
The-FSGNOM	cat-SG	drink-3SGPRES	the-FACC	milk

The cat drinks the milk.

This sentence has a regular V2 structure, where the subject precedes the finite verb and the direct object is placed after the verb. It is a transitive sentence. The finite verb is the Nucleus of the sentence. This is always the case in simple tenses like present and preterite. The subject noun is in the PreCoreSlot, which is the position before the finite verb in all V2 structures. The Nucleus opens the Core, which also contains the object argument *die Milch*. The subject noun phrase appears with a determiner and the head noun. The head noun is only marked for number. The determiner is generally the locus of gender, number and case information. Note, however, that there is case and number syncretism with feminine determiners, such that neither nominative nor singular is actually unequivocally marked on the determiner. These categories are merely given here for orientation. *Trinkt* is the finite main verb in present tense. It is the Nucleus, which carries the main verbal information and also the valence information. As *trinken* is a verb that requires two arguments, there is both a subject and an object in the sentence. The finite Nucleus is marked for person, number and tense. These are operators in the RRG operator projection. The object NP, *die Milch*, is recognisable as an object only by semantic knowledge. The determiner *die* does not provide a distinction between singular and plural for feminine nouns, and it does not provide a case distinction between nominative and accusative, either. *Milch* is a feminine noun. The gender is a lexical feature that is aligned with the noun and cannot be changed. *Milch* is also a mass noun and therefore does not have a plural form.

4.2 Construction 2: Die Katze trank die Milch

This construction has basically the same structure as the one in 4.1, example (3), but the verb is in past tense. Like present, past is a simple tense which does not require the support by an auxiliary. Therefore, the finite verb *trank* is the Nucleus of the sentence. The subject noun *Die Katze* is in the PreCore slot, and *trank* opens the Core. The object noun *die Milch* is a Core argument.

4.3 Construction 3: Die Katze ist auf dem Tisch

(4)

Die	Katze	ist	auf	dem	Tisch
The-FSGNOM	cat-SG	be-3SGNOM	on	the-MSGDAT	table-SG

The cat is on the table.

In this sentence, the Nucleus is a copula verb. It gives the location of the cat. The arguments of this Nucleus are *die Katze* and *auf dem Tisch*. The sentence structure itself works according to the RRG principles introduced above: *Die Katze* appears in the PreCore slot, which is the position before the finite verb. It is functionally part of the Core, but placed in the PreCore slot for a structural interpretation. The finite Nucleus opens the Core for the linear structure of the sentence. The Core thus includes the location predicate *ist* and the locative prepositional phrase *auf dem Tisch*.

4.4 Construction 4: Trinkt die Katze die Milch

(5)	Trinkt	die	Katze	die	Milch
	drink-3SGPRES	the-FSGNOM	cat-SG	the-FACC	milk

lit.:Drinks the cat the milk
Possible translation: Does the cat drink the milk?

This construction can be used in yes/no questions: The finite verb is in initial position. For the representation of the sentence in terms of RRG, this means that the PreCore slot position is empty. The finite Nucleus, as it appears in a simple tense like present, opens the Core. The Core also contains two arguments, which are the subject argument *die Katze* and the object argument *die Milch*. Note again that with these feminine nouns, there is no distinctive marking for either subject or object. The distinction is drawn on the basis of common world knowledge, which lets the reader assume that it is the animate being that consumes the substance, and not the other way around.

4.5 Construction 5: Die Katze hat die Milch getrunken

(6)	Die	Katze	hat	die	Milch	getrunken
	The-FSGNOM	cat-SG	have-3SGPRES	the-FACC	milk	drink-PSTP

The cat drank the milk.

This is a perfect construction which is formed by a periphrastic tense form that requires an auxiliary. The full verb that carries the main semantic content and the valence appears in the form of a past participle. German has two perfect auxiliaries, *sein* ('be') and *haben* ('have'). All transitive verbs form their perfect with *haben*. *Sein* as a perfect auxiliary is used for telic intransitive verbs (Diedrichsen 2013a). The strict V2 word order rule that holds in German declarative clauses demands that the finite verb appear in the second position in the sentence. The two parts of the periphrastic verb form thus appear discontinuously, which has led to the assumption of the bracket structure model for German sentence topology that has been extensively discussed in Section 2. The finite auxiliary opens up a bracket that is closed with the infinite (past participle) full verb.

In the RRG-based layer model, this is represented as follows: The first constituent in the sentence is in the PreCoreSlot position. The finite auxiliary, which is NOT the Nucleus, as it does not carry any semantics, has no position in the constituent projection. It is only connected to the operator projection, as it carries the information about grammatical categories like tense. After the finite auxiliary lies the Core, and in a periphrastic construction, the infinite Nucleus is the last element in the Core. The noun phrase *die Milch* is inside the Core. It is the direct object in this sentence. The subject argument, *die Katze,* is in the PreCoreSlot.

4.6 Construction 6: Getrunken hat die Katze die Milch

(7) Getrunken hat die Katze die Milch
drink-PSTP have-3SGPRES the-FSGNOM cat-SG the-FACC milk
The cat DRANK the milk.

This construction represents a marked, but perfectly acceptable variation in word order. In order to emphasize the fact that the cat DRANK the milk (instead of spilling it or bathing in it, for example), the Nucleus, which is the full verb with the main semantic information, may be fronted. Note that this only works if the Nucleus is non- finite. This is because the word order rule for declarative clauses demands the finite verb in the second position of the sentence. Therefore, if there is a finite auxiliary that can be placed in the second position, the first position (the PreCore slot in RRG terms) is free for any other constituent, including the Nucleus. The structural restriction of V2 (finite verb in 2nd position) therefore gives way to a number of word order variants, which have pragmatic function in that they change the emphasis on constituents of the sentence. Thus, it is perfectly fine to utter (8), if it is to be emphasized that it is the MILK that the cat drank and not the water.

For the fronted Nucleus, the condition is that there be a finite auxiliary that can be placed in the second position, see above. This requires that sentences with fronted Nucleus be expressed in a periphrastic tense like perfect. What if a speaker wanted to place the emphasis on an activity that is going on in the present? For this case, a substandard dummy auxiliary, *tun* ('do') is used (9), and the infinitive form of the verb, *trinken*, appears in the PreCoreSlot (cf. Diedrichsen 2008 for a more elaborate discussion of the functionality of the German word order rules and their alignment with the RRG system).

(8) Die Milch hat die Katze getrunken
the-FSGACC milk have-3SGPRES the-FSGNOM cat-SG drink-PSTP
It is the milk that the cat drank.

(9) Trinken tut die Katze die Milch.
Drink-INF do-3SGPRES the-FSGNOM the-FACC milk
The cat is DRINKING the milk.

4.7 Construction 7: Die Milch wird von der Katze getrunken

(10) Die Milch wird von der Katze getrunken
The-FSG NOM become-3SGPRES by the-FSGDAT cat-SG drink-PSTP
The milk is drunk by the cat.

This is a passive construction with the auxiliary *werden* ('become'). In a *werden*-passive, also called plain passive, the allocation of agent and patient roles with subject and object functions is reversed, such that the patient argument of a sentence can become subject. This is useful in situations in which the speaker wants to emphasize the role of the patient in a scene, or if the patient is the thing that is being talked about. In passive sentences, the agent is less important and can be left out altogether. It may, however, be mentioned in a prepositional phrase with *von*. In the RRG model, the *von*-phrase with the agent is placed in the Periphery of the sentence. The passive subject, *die Milch*, appears in the PreCore slot, as usual in V2 structures. The finite auxiliary in this case is the passive auxiliary *wird*, which occupies the 2nd position in the sentence. As auxiliary, it is not part of the constituent projection, and therefore not part of the Core. The Core includes only the Nucleus, *getrunken*, whereas *von der Katze* appears in the Periphery, which is an extra Core position. In the prepositional phrase, the noun appears in the dative. This has to be accounted for by the parser.

4.8 Construction 8: Die Katze hat die Milch auf dem Tisch getrunken

(11) Die Katze hat die Milch
The-FSGNOM cat have-3SGPRES the-FACC milk
auf dem Tisch getrunken
on the-MSGDAT table drink.PSTP
The cat drank the milk on the table.

This sentence represents a V2 transitive structure with two Core arguments and one peripheral element. The prepositional phrase *auf dem Tisch* locates the cat's activity. Again, this is a structure with a complex verb that forms perfect tense. The finite auxiliary is placed in second position, the position before it is the PreCore slot. The nonfinite part of the verb, which is the main verb, called Nucleus in RRG, appears at the end of the sentence. The Core starts with the position after the finite verb. *Die Milch* is a Core argument. The peripheral element is not part of the Core, according to the RRG model. It is an extra-Core position that is, however, still included in the Clause layer. In the German sentence structure, it is still placed before the nonfinite verb form that closes the sentence bracket. The Periphery has to be conceived of as a position that lies outside the Core functionally, as it holds adjuncts as opposed to arguments. In English, it is indeed placed at the end of the sentence (cf. the translation in (11)), and is therefore optically and functionally detached from the Nucleus and its arguments. One specialty of German word order, however, is that the bracket structure overwrites these functional specifications, such that the linear structure does not reflect the functional differences between Core and Periphery.

5. Functional requirements of the parser

Role and Reference Grammar has three projections, which are constituent projection, operator projection and focus projection. We will not be concerned with the focus projection, as it is beyond the scope of this paper. The operator projection has relevance for the Layered Structure of the Clause and the Layered Structure of the noun phrase. In this regard, we are concerned with only two operators in the Layered Structure of the Clause: the ones of tense and aspect. Tense is recorded on the matrix verb or the auxiliary. Aspect is realised in syntax as the choice of auxiliary in the perfect. The operators on the Layered Structure of the noun phrase, which are of interest for this parser, are to do with definiteness and the mass/count noun distinction.

5.1 Sentence structure

The parser is able to recognise and parse the significant major sentence constructions of German. These are the following constructions

Note that the parser will only recognise capitalisation on a nominal, but not on any clause initial word. This is intentional to simplify the coding. A future enhancement of the parser will facilitate sentence initial capitalisation.

Table 2. The 8 clausal constructions to be recognised by the parser

1. die Katze trinkt die Milch	Active transitive present, V2
2. die Katze trank die Milch	Active transitive past, V2
3. die Katze ist auf dem Tisch	Active intransitive with copula, present, V2
4. trinkt die Katze die Milch	Active transitive present, V1
5. die Katze hat die Milch getrunken	Active transitive perfect, V2, perfect auxiliary = *haben*
6. getrunken hat die Katze die Milch	Active transitive perfect with *haben*, V2, Nucleus in the PrCs
7. die Milch wird von der Katze getrunken	Passive present, V2, agent appears in a *von*-Phrase
8. die Katze hat die Milch auf dem Tisch getrunken	Active transitive perfect with *haben*, prepositional locative phrase

5.2 The lexicon

In this section, the content of the lexicon is discussed. The lexicon is loosely designed on the basis of the Role and Reference Grammar lexicon. However, features of lexemes are also recorded for matrix verbs, nominals, the copula verb, determiners, auxiliary verbs and prepositions.

5.2.1 *The nominal lexicon*

For nominals, we will need to record the following features in each lexical entry, in order to enable the parser to work (note: 'd.n.a' (---) means 'does not apply'):

Table 3. Noun feature structures in the lexical entry for the noun Katze

Katze	Lexical word: Katze
	Lexical part of speech type: n
	Lexical feature definiteness: def+/-
	Lexical feature person: 3
	Lexical feature gender: F
	Lexical feature number: sg
	Lexical feature case: NOM/GEN/DAT/ACC
	Lexical feature noun type: COUNT
	Lexical feature verb type: d.n.a. (---)
	Lexical feature animacy: ANIM+
	Lexical feature humanness: HUM-
	Lexical verb tense: d.n.a. (---)
	Lexical logical structure: d.n.a. (---)

Table 4. Noun feature structures in the lexical entry for the noun Mann

Mann	Lexical word: Mann
	Lexical part of speech type: n
	Lexical feature definiteness: def+/-
	Lexical feature person: 3
	Lexical feature gender: M
	Lexical feature number: sg
	Lexical feature case: NOM/DAT/ACC
	Lexical feature noun type: COUNT
	Lexical feature verb type: d.n.a. (---)
	Lexical feature animacy: ANIM+
	Lexical feature humanness: HUM+
	Lexical verb tense: d.n.a. (---)
	Lexical logical structure: d.n.a. (---)

Table 5. Noun feature structures in the lexical entry for the noun Milch

Milch	Lexical word: Milch
	Lexical part of speech type: n
	Lexical feature definiteness: def+/-
	Lexical feature person: 3
	Lexical feature gender: F
	Lexical feature number: d.n.a. (---)
	Lexical feature case: NOM/GEN/DAT/ACC
	Lexical feature noun type: MASS
	Lexical feature verb type: d.n.a. (---)
	Lexical feature animacy: ANIM-
	Lexical feature humanness: HUM-
	Lexical verb tense: d.n.a. (---)
	Lexical logical structure: d.n.a. (---)

Table 6. Noun feature structures in the lexical entry for the noun Hund

Hund	Lexical word: Hund
	Lexical part of speech type: n
	Lexical feature definiteness: def+/-
	Lexical feature person: 3
	Lexical feature gender: M
	Lexical feature number: sg
	Lexical feature case: NOM/DAT/ACC
	Lexical feature noun type: COUNT
	Lexical feature verb type: d.n.a. (---)
	Lexical feature animacy: ANIM+
	Lexical feature humanness: HUM-
	Lexical verb tense: d.n.a. (---)
	Lexical logical structure: d.n.a. (---)

Table 7. Noun feature structures in the lexical entry for the noun Tisch

Tisch	Lexical word: Tisch
	Lexical part of speech type: n
	Lexical feature definiteness: def+/-
	Lexical feature person: 3
	Lexical feature gender: M
	Lexical feature number: sg
	Lexical feature case: NOM/DAT/ACC
	Lexical feature noun type: COUNT
	Lexical feature verb type: d.n.a. (---)
	Lexical feature animacy: ANIM-
	Lexical feature humanness: HUM-
	Lexical verb tense: d.n.a. (---)
	Lexical logical structure: d.n.a. (---)

Table 8. Noun feature structures in the lexical entry for the noun Matte

Matte	Lexical word: Matte
	Lexical part of speech type: n
	Lexical feature definiteness: def+/-
	Lexical feature person: 3
	Lexical feature gender: F
	Lexical feature number: sg
	Lexical feature case: NOM/GEN/DAT/ACC
	Lexical feature noun type: COUNT
	Lexical feature verb type: d.n.a. (---)
	Lexical feature animacy: ANIM-
	Lexical feature humanness: HUM-
	Lexical verb tense: d.n.a. (---)
	Lexical logical structure: d.n.a. (---)

Table 9. Noun feature structures in the lexical entry for the noun Wasser

Wasser	Lexical word: Wasser
	Lexical part of speech type: n
	Lexical feature definiteness: def+/-
	Lexical feature person: 3
	Lexical feature gender: N
	Lexical feature number: sg
	Lexical feature case: NOM/DAT/ACC
	Lexical feature noun type: MASS
	Lexical feature verb type: d.n.a. (---)
	Lexical feature animacy: ANIM-
	Lexical feature humanness: HUM-
	Lexical verb tense: d.n.a. (---)
	Lexical logical structure: d.n.a. (---)

5.2.2 *The determiner lexicon*

For determiners, we will need to record the following features in each lexical entry, in order to enable the parser to work:

Table 10. Determiner feature structures in the lexical entry for the determiner der

der	Lexical word: der
	Lexical part of speech type: det
	Lexical feature definiteness: def+
	Lexical feature person: 3
	Lexical feature gender: M/F
	Lexical feature number: sg
	Lexical feature case: NOM/DAT
	Lexical feature noun type: d.n.a. (---)
	Lexical feature verb type: d.n.a. (---)
	Lexical feature animacy: d.n.a. (---)
	Lexical feature humanness: d.n.a. (---)
	Lexical verb tense: d.n.a. (---)
	Lexical logical structure: d.n.a. (---)

Table 11. Determiner feature structures in the lexical entry for the determiner die

die	Lexical word: die Lexical part of speech type: det Lexical feature definiteness: def+ Lexical feature person: 3 Lexical feature gender: F Lexical feature number: sg/pl Lexical feature case: NOM/ACC Lexical feature noun type: d.n.a. (---) Lexical feature verb type: d.n.a. (---) Lexical feature animacy: d.n.a. (---) Lexical feature humanness: d.n.a. (---) Lexical verb tense: d.n.a. (---) Lexical logical structure: d.n.a. (---)

Table 12. Determiner feature structures in the lexical entry for the determiner das

das	Lexical word: das Lexical part of speech type: det Lexical feature definiteness: def+ Lexical feature person: 3 Lexical feature gender: N Lexical feature number: sg Lexical feature case: NOM/ACC Lexical feature noun type: d.n.a. (---) Lexical feature verb type: d.n.a. (---) Lexical feature animacy: d.n.a. (---) Lexical feature humanness: d.n.a. (---) Lexical verb tense: d.n.a. (---) Lexical logical structure: d.n.a. (---)

Table 13. Determiner feature structures in the lexical entry for the determiner dem

dem	Lexical word: dem
	Lexical part of speech type: det
	Lexical feature definiteness: def+
	Lexical feature person: 3
	Lexical feature gender: M
	Lexical feature number: sg
	Lexical feature case: DAT
	Lexical feature noun type: d.n.a. (---)
	Lexical feature verb type: d.n.a. (---)
	Lexical feature animacy: d.n.a. (---)
	Lexical feature humanness: d.n.a. (---)
	Lexical verb tense: d.n.a. (---)
	Lexical logical structure: d.n.a. (---)

Table 14. Determiner feature structures in the lexical entry for the determiner ein

ein	Lexical word: ein
	Lexical part of speech type: det
	Lexical feature definiteness: def-
	Lexical feature person: 3
	Lexical feature gender: M/N
	Lexical feature number: sg
	Lexical feature case: NOM/ACC
	Lexical feature noun type: d.n.a. (---)
	Lexical feature verb type: d.n.a. (---)
	Lexical feature animacy: d.n.a. (---)
	Lexical feature humanness: d.n.a. (---)
	Lexical verb tense: d.n.a. (---)
	Lexical logical structure: d.n.a. (---)

Table 15. Determiner feature structures in the lexical entry for the determiner eine

eine	Lexical word: eine
	Lexical part of speech type: det
	Lexical feature definiteness: def-
	Lexical feature person: 3
	Lexical feature gender: F
	Lexical feature number: sg
	Lexical feature case: NOM/ACC
	Lexical feature noun type: d.n.a. (---)
	Lexical feature verb type: d.n.a. (---)
	Lexical feature animacy: d.n.a. (---)
	Lexical feature humanness: d.n.a. (---)
	Lexical verb tense: d.n.a. (---)
	Lexical logical structure: d.n.a. (---)

5.2.3 *The matrix verb lexicon*

For verbs, we will need to record the following features in each lexical entry, in order to enable the parser to work:

Table 16. Matrix verb feature structures in the lexical entry for the matrix verb trank

trank	Lexical word: trank
	Lexical part of speech type: v
	Lexical feature definiteness: d.n.a. (---)
	Lexical feature person: 3
	Lexical feature gender: d.n.a. (---)
	Lexical feature number: sg
	Lexical feature case: d.n.a. (---)
	Lexical feature noun type: d.n.a. (---)
	Lexical feature verb type: fin+
	Lexical feature animacy: d.n.a. (---)
	Lexical feature humanness: d.n.a. (---)
	Lexical verb tense: past
	Lexical logical structure: "do' [(x), drink' (y)] & CAUSE [BECOME consumed' (x, y)]"

Table 17. Matrix verb feature structures in the lexical entry for the matrix verb trinkt

trinkt	Lexical word: trinkt
	Lexical part of speech type: v
	Lexical feature definiteness: d.n.a. (---)
	Lexical feature person: 3
	Lexical feature gender: d.n.a. (---)
	Lexical feature number: sg
	Lexical feature case: d.n.a. (---)
	Lexical feature noun type: d.n.a. (---)
	Lexical feature verb type: fin+
	Lexical feature animacy: d.n.a. (---)
	Lexical feature humanness: d.n.a. (---)
	Lexical verb tense: present
	Lexical logical structure:
	"do' [(x), drink' (y)] & CAUSE [BECOME consumed' (x, y)]"

Table 18. Matrix verb feature structures in the lexical entry for the matrix verb trinken

trinken	Lexical word: trinken
	Lexical part of speech type: v
	Lexical feature definiteness: d.n.a. (---)
	Lexical feature person: d.n.a. (---)
	Lexical feature gender: d.n.a. (---)
	Lexical feature number: d.n.a. (---)
	Lexical feature case: d.n.a. (---)
	Lexical feature noun type: d.n.a. (---)
	Lexical feature verb type: fin-
	Lexical feature animacy: d.n.a. (---)
	Lexical feature humanness: d.n.a. (---)
	Lexical verb tense: d.n.a. (---)
	Lexical logical structure:
	"do' [(x), drink' (y)] & CAUSE [BECOME consumed' (x, y)]"

Table 19. Matrix verb feature structures in the lexical entry for the matrix verb getrunken

getrunken	Lexical word: getrunken
	Lexical part of speech type: v
	Lexical feature definiteness: d.n.a. (---)
	Lexical feature person: d.n.a. (---)
	Lexical feature gender: d.n.a. (---)
	Lexical feature number: d.n.a. (---)
	Lexical feature case: d.n.a. (---)
	Lexical feature noun type: d.n.a. (---)
	Lexical feature verb type: fin-
	Lexical feature animacy: d.n.a. (---)
	Lexical feature humanness: d.n.a. (---)
	Lexical verb tense: d.n.a. (---)
	Lexical logical structure: "do' [(x), drink' (y)] & CAUSE [BECOME consumed' (x, y)]"

Table 20. Matrix verb feature structures in the lexical entry for the matrix verb isst

isst	Lexical word: isst
	Lexical part of speech type: v
	Lexical feature definiteness: d.n.a. (---)
	Lexical feature person: 3
	Lexical feature gender: d.n.a. (---)
	Lexical feature number: sg
	Lexical feature case: d.n.a. (---)
	Lexical feature noun type: d.n.a. (---)
	Lexical feature verb type: fin+
	Lexical feature animacy: d.n.a. (---)
	Lexical feature humanness: d.n.a. (---)
	Lexical verb tense: present
	Lexical logical structure: "do' [(x), eat' (y)] & CAUSE [BECOME consumed' (x, y)]"

Table 21. Matrix verb feature structures in the lexical entry for the matrix verb aß

aß	Lexical word: aß
	Lexical part of speech type: v
	Lexical feature definiteness: d.n.a. (---)
	Lexical feature person: 3
	Lexical feature gender: d.n.a. (---)
	Lexical feature number: sg
	Lexical feature case: d.n.a. (---)
	Lexical feature noun type: d.n.a. (---)
	Lexical feature verb type: fin+
	Lexical feature animacy: d.n.a. (---)
	Lexical feature humanness: d.n.a. (---)
	Lexical verb tense: past
	Lexical logical structure:
	"do' [(x), eat' (y)] & CAUSE [BECOME consumed' (x, y)]"

Table 22. Matrix verb feature structures in the lexical entry for the matrix verb fraß

fraß	Lexical word: fraß
	Lexical part of speech type: v
	Lexical feature definiteness: d.n.a. (---)
	Lexical feature person: 3
	Lexical feature gender: d.n.a. (---)
	Lexical feature number: sg
	Lexical feature case: d.n.a. (---)
	Lexical feature noun type: d.n.a. (---)
	Lexical feature verb type: fin+
	Lexical feature animacy: d.n.a. (---)
	Lexical feature humanness: d.n.a. (---)
	Lexical verb tense: past
	Lexical logical structure:
	"do' [(x), eat' (y)] & CAUSE [BECOME consumed' (x, y)]"

Table 23. Matrix verb feature structures in the lexical entry for the matrix verb frisst

frisst	Lexical word: frisst
	Lexical part of speech type: v
	Lexical feature definiteness: d.n.a. (---)
	Lexical feature person: 3
	Lexical feature gender: d.n.a. (---)
	Lexical feature number: sg
	Lexical feature case: d.n.a. (---)
	Lexical feature noun type: d.n.a. (---)
	Lexical feature verb type: fin+
	Lexical feature animacy: d.n.a. (---)
	Lexical feature humanness: d.n.a. (---)
	Lexical verb tense: present
	Lexical logical structure:
	"do' [(x), eat' (y)] & CAUSE [BECOME consumed' (x, y)]"

5.2.4 *The copula verb lexicon*

For copula verbs, we will need to record the following features in each lexical entry, in order to enable the parser to work:

Table 24. Copula verb feature structures in the lexical entry for the copula verb ist

ist	Lexical word: ist
	Lexical part of speech type: cop
	Lexical feature definiteness: d.n.a. (---)
	Lexical feature person: 3
	Lexical feature gender: d.n.a. (---)
	Lexical feature number: sg
	Lexical feature case: d.n.a. (---)
	Lexical feature noun type: d.n.a. (---)
	Lexical feature verb type: fin+
	Lexical feature animacy: d.n.a. (---)
	Lexical feature humanness: d.n.a. (---)
	Lexical verb tense: present
	Lexical logical structure: "be' (x, y)"

Table 25. Copula verb feature structures in the lexical entry for the copula verb war

war	Lexical word: war Lexical part of speech type: cop Lexical feature definiteness: d.n.a. (---) Lexical feature person: 3 Lexical feature gender: d.n.a. (---) Lexical feature number: sg Lexical feature case: d.n.a. (---) Lexical feature noun type: d.n.a. (---) Lexical feature verb type: fin+ Lexical feature animacy: d.n.a. (---) Lexical feature humanness: d.n.a. (---) Lexical verb tense: past Lexical logical structure: "be' (x, y)"

5.2.5 *The auxiliary verb lexicon*

For auxiliary verbs, we will need to record the following features in each lexical entry, in order to enable the parser to work:

Table 26. Auxiliary verb feature structures in the lexical entry for the auxiliary verb wird

wird	Lexical word: wird Lexical part of speech type: AUX Lexical feature definiteness: d.n.a. (---) Lexical feature person: 3 Lexical feature gender: d.n.a. (---) Lexical feature number: sg Lexical feature case: d.n.a. (---) Lexical feature noun type: d.n.a. (---) Lexical feature verb type: fin+ Lexical feature animacy: d.n.a. (---) Lexical feature humanness: d.n.a. (---) Lexical verb tense: present Lexical logical structure: "become' (x, y)"

Table 27. Auxiliary verb feature structures in the lexical entry for the auxiliary verb hat

hat	Lexical word: hat
	Lexical part of speech type: AUX
	Lexical feature definiteness: d.n.a. (---)
	Lexical feature person: 3
	Lexical feature gender: d.n.a. (---)
	Lexical feature number: sg
	Lexical feature case: d.n.a. (---)
	Lexical feature noun type: d.n.a. (---)
	Lexical feature verb type: fin+
	Lexical feature animacy: d.n.a. (---)
	Lexical feature humanness: d.n.a. (---)
	Lexical verb tense: present
	Lexical logical structure: "have' (x, y)"

5.2.6 *The preposition lexicon*

For prepositions, we will need to record the following features in each lexical entry in order to enable the parser to work:

Table 28. Preposition feature structures in the lexical entry for the preposition auf

auf	Lexical word: auf
	Lexical part of speech type: prep
	Lexical feature definiteness: d.n.a. (---)
	Lexical feature person: d.n.a. (---)
	Lexical feature gender: d.n.a. (---)
	Lexical feature number: d.n.a. (---)
	Lexical feature case: d.n.a. (---)
	Lexical feature noun type: d.n.a. (---)
	Lexical feature verb type: d.n.a. (---)
	Lexical feature animacy: d.n.a. (---)
	Lexical feature humanness: d.n.a. (---)
	Lexical verb tense: d.n.a. (---)
	Lexical logical structure: "be_ON'(x)"

Table 29. Preposition feature structures in the lexical entry for the preposition von

von	Lexical word: von
	Lexical part of speech type: prep
	Lexical feature definiteness: d.n.a. (---)
	Lexical feature person: d.n.a. (---)
	Lexical feature gender: d.n.a. (---)
	Lexical feature number: d.n.a. (---)
	Lexical feature case: d.n.a. (---)
	Lexical feature noun type: d.n.a. (---)
	Lexical feature verb type: d.n.a. (---)
	Lexical feature animacy: d.n.a. (---)
	Lexical feature humanness: d.n.a. (---)
	Lexical verb tense: d.n.a. (---)
	Lexical logical structure: "by' (x)"

Table 30. Preposition feature structures in the lexical entry for the preposition in

in	Lexical word: in
	Lexical part of speech type: prep
	Lexical feature definiteness: d.n.a. (---)
	Lexical feature person: d.n.a. (---)
	Lexical feature gender: d.n.a. (---)
	Lexical feature number: d.n.a. (---)
	Lexical feature case: d.n.a. (---)
	Lexical feature noun type: d.n.a. (---)
	Lexical feature verb type: d.n.a. (---)
	Lexical feature animacy: d.n.a. (---)
	Lexical feature humanness: d.n.a. (---)
	Lexical verb tense: d.n.a. (---)
	Lexical logical structure: "be_IN'(x)"

5.3 The layout of the Role and Reference Grammar structure representation

The Role and Reference Grammar structure representation is ordered according to the principles of the Layered Structure of the Clause. Rather than present the structure hierarchically, as a tree structure, in this presentation, we present the sentence structures as a series of embedded frame structures according to the style of attribute value matrices (AVMs).

This style of representation has the format of [FEATURE: VALUE]. Value can contain nested AVMs such as [FEATURE: [FEATURE: VALUE]]. An example of this for the simple German transitive clause *Die Katze trinkt die Milch* ('The cat drinks the milk') is indicated following in Figure 2.

Should a token not exist in the lexicon, this is flagged by the parser and then, on the graphical user interface, this token is appended to the screen with an appropriate error message that says "Word not found". If the unknown word is part of an otherwise complete and valid clause, the parse information and lexical entries for the other known tokens is displayed on the parse trace on the Java system console, but a Role and Reference Grammar structure representation is not presented in the text area, as technically, the clause is incomplete.

```
[SENTENCE [ die Katze trinkt die Milch ]
[CONSTRUCTION type 1: active transitive present V2 construction ]
[         CLAUSE [
                   [PRCS         [ die ]            [ Katze ]
                                 [ det ]            [ n ]
                                 [ def+ ]
                                 [ 3 ]              [ 3 ]
                                 [ sg/pl ]          [ sg ]
                                 [ F ]              [ F ]
                                 [ NOM/ACC ] [ NOM/GEN/DAT/ACC ]
             ]
                   [CORE [
                          [NUC  [ trinkt ]
                                [ v ]
                                [ fin+ ]
                                [ 3 ]
                                [ sg ]
                                [ PRS ]
                                [ do' [(x), drink' (y)] & CAUSE [BECOME consumed' (x, y)] ]
                          ] NUC ]
                          [ARG-NP       [ die ]            [ Milch ]
                                        [ det ]            [ n ]
                                        [ def+ ]
                                        [ 3 ]              [ 3 ]
                                        [ sg/pl ]          [ --- ]
                                        [ F ]              [ F ]
                                        [ NOM/ACC ] [ NOM/GEN/DAT/ACC ]
                          ] ARG-NP ]
                   ] CORE ]
                   [ PERIPHERY [
                   ] PERIPHERY  ]
          ] CLAUSE ]
] SENTENCE ]
```

Figure 2. The RRG representation of a simple transitive clause in present tense

6. Testing and results

In this section, we are concerned with testing and evaluation of the Java application to parse the eight major constructions of German within the Role and Reference Grammar model.

These constructions are:

(1)	Die	Katze	trinkt	die	Milch	
	The-FSGNOM	cat-SG	drink-3SGPRES	the-FACC	milk	
	The cat drinks the milk.					

(2)	Die	Katze	trank	die	Milch	
	The-FSGNOM	cat-SG	drink-3SGPST	the-FACC	milk	
	The cat drank the milk.					

(3)	Die	Katze	ist	auf	dem	Tisch
	The-FSGNOM	cat-SG	be-3SGNOM	on	the-MSGDAT	table-SG
	The cat is on the table.					

(4)	Trinkt	die	Katze	die	Milch
	drink-3SGPRES	the-FSGNOM	cat-SG	the-FACC	milk
	lit.:Drinks the cat the milk				
	Possible translation: Does the cat drink the milk?				

(5)	Die	Katze	hat	die	Milch	getrunken
	The-FSGNOM	cat-SG	have-3SGPRES	the-FACC	milk	drink-PSTP
	The cat drank the milk.					

(6)	Getrunken	hat	die	Katze	die	Milch
	drink-PSTP	have-3SGPRES	the-FSGNOM	cat-SG	the-FACC	milk
	The cat DRANK the milk.					

(7)	Die	Milch	wird	von	der	Katze	getrunken
	The-FSGNOM	milk	be-3SGPRES	by	the-FSGDAT	cat-SG	drink-PSTP
	The milk is drunk by the cat.						

(8)	Die	Katze	hat	die	Milch
	The-FSGNOM	cat	have-3SGPRES	the-FACC	milk
	auf	dem	Tisch	getrunken	
	on	the-MSGDAT	table	drink.PSTP	
	The cat drank the milk on the table.				

In the next sections, we test the parser for each of these constructions in turn and comment on whether the parse output, that is, the RRG structure representation, is correct and appropriate and displays well.

6.1 Testing of construction 1

Test: Parse of construction 1
Result: Sentence parsed
Evaluation: Parsed into correct structure representation

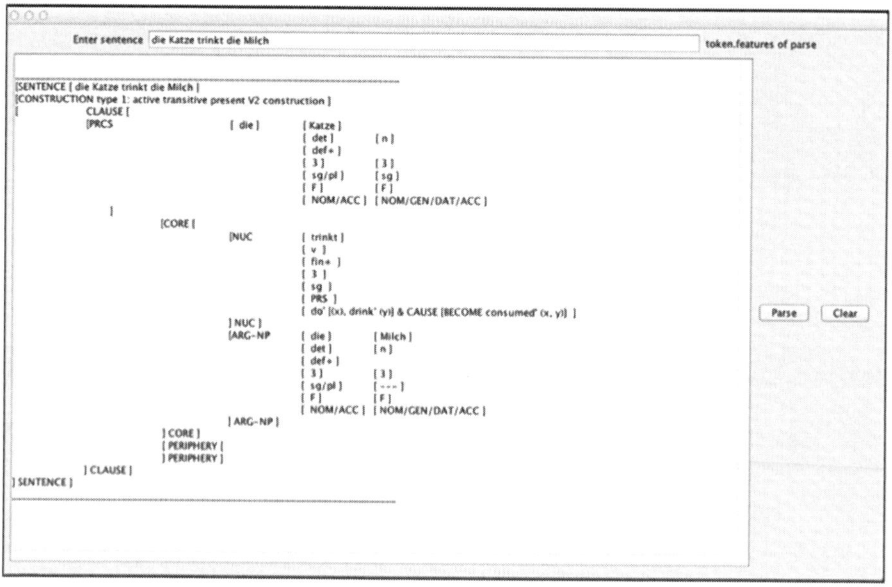

Figure 3. Parse of construction 1

6.2 Testing of construction 2

Test: Parse of construction 2
Result: Sentence parsed
Evaluation: Parsed into correct structure representation

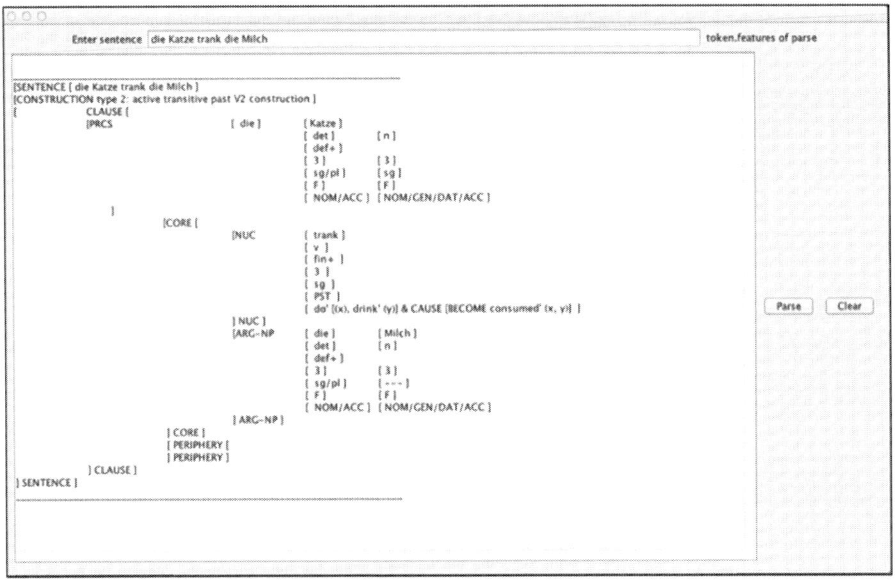

Figure 4. Parse of construction 2

6.3 Testing of construction 3

Test: Parse of construction 3
Result: Sentence parsed
Evaluation: Parsed into correct structure representation

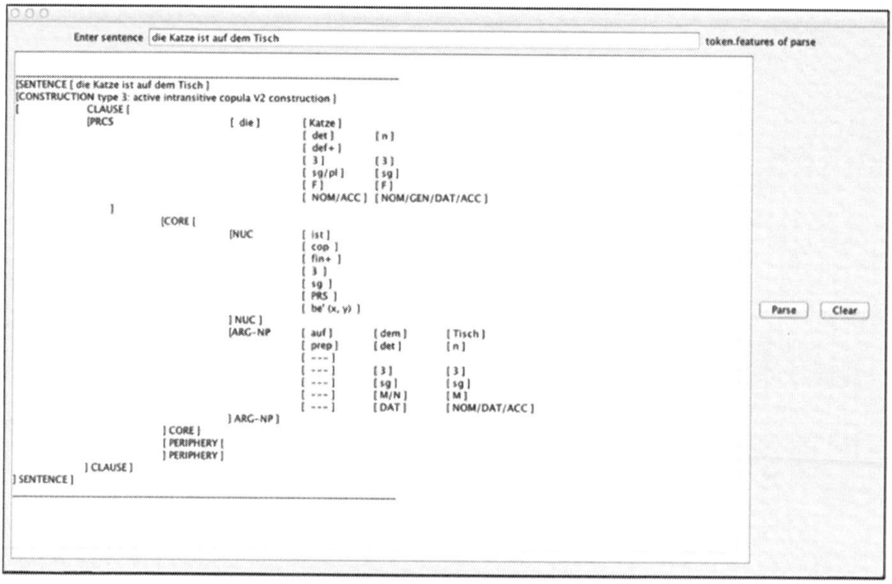

Figure 5. Parse of construction 3

6.4 Testing of construction 4

Test: Parse of construction 4
Result: Sentence parsed
Evaluation: Parsed into correct structure representation

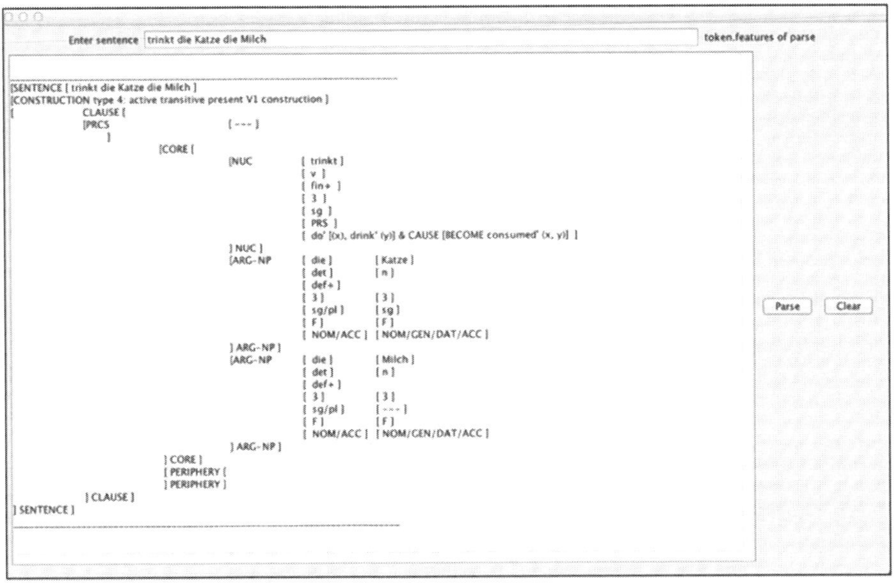

Figure 6. Parse of construction 4

6.5 Testing of construction 5

Test: Parse of construction 5
Result: Sentence parsed
Evaluation: Parsed into correct structure representation

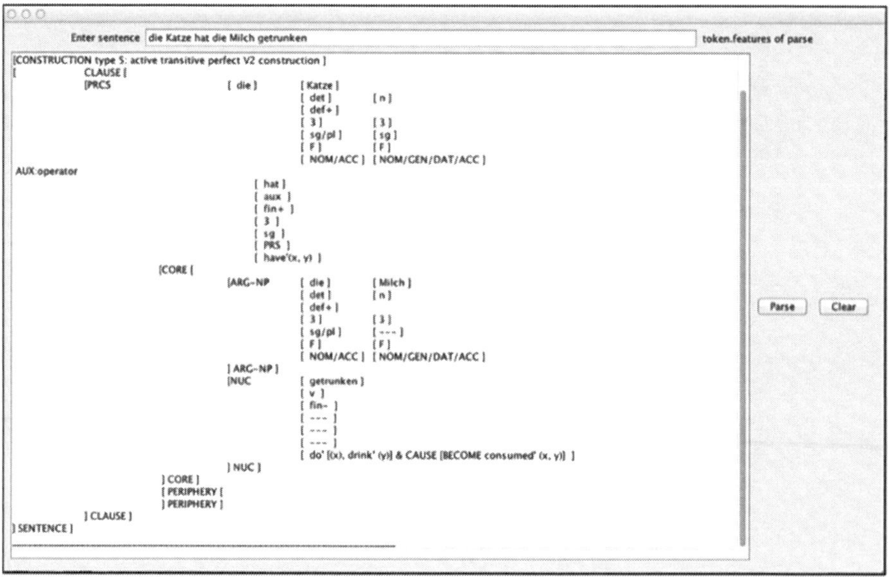

Figure 7. Parse of construction 5

6.6 Testing of construction 6

Test: Parse of construction 6
Result: Sentence parsed
Evaluation: Parsed into correct structure representation

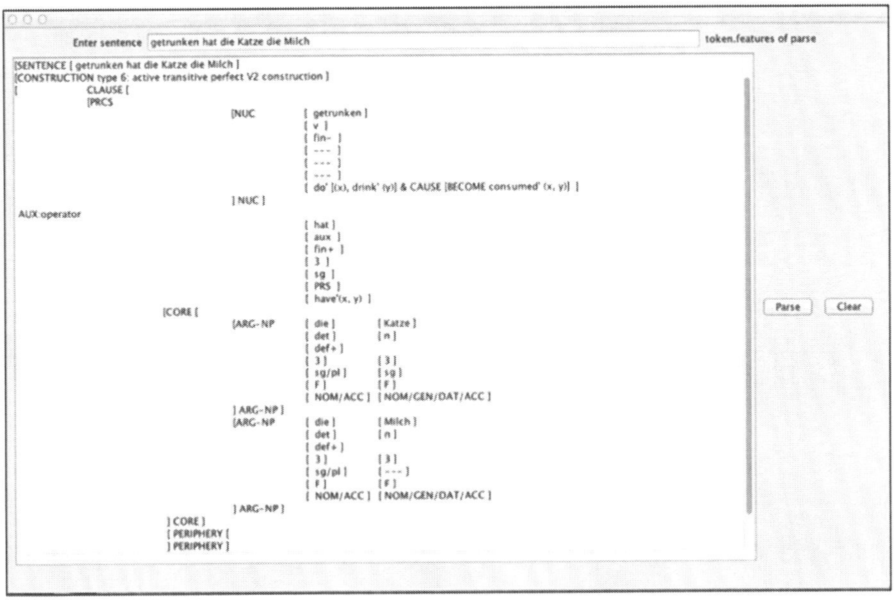

Figure 8. Parse of construction 6

Note that the bottom part of the structure representation is below the scroll bar, which is visible in this figure.

6.7 Testing of construction 7

Test: Parse of construction 7
Result: Sentence parsed
Evaluation: Parsed into correct structure representation

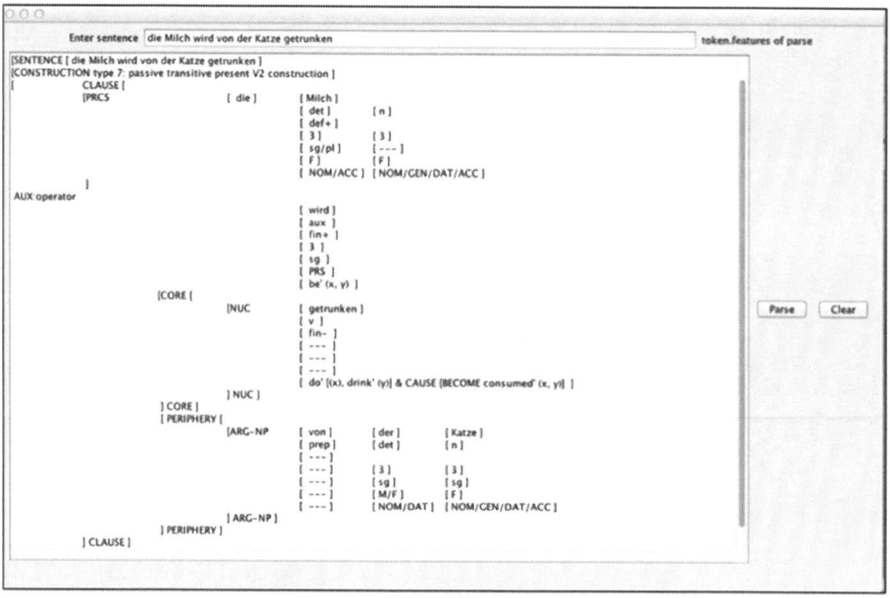

Figure 9. Parse of construction 7

Note that, here again, the bottom part of the structure representation is below the scroll bar, which is visible in this figure.

6.8 Testing of construction 8

Test: Parse of construction 8
Result: Sentence parsed
Evaluation: Parsed into correct structure representation

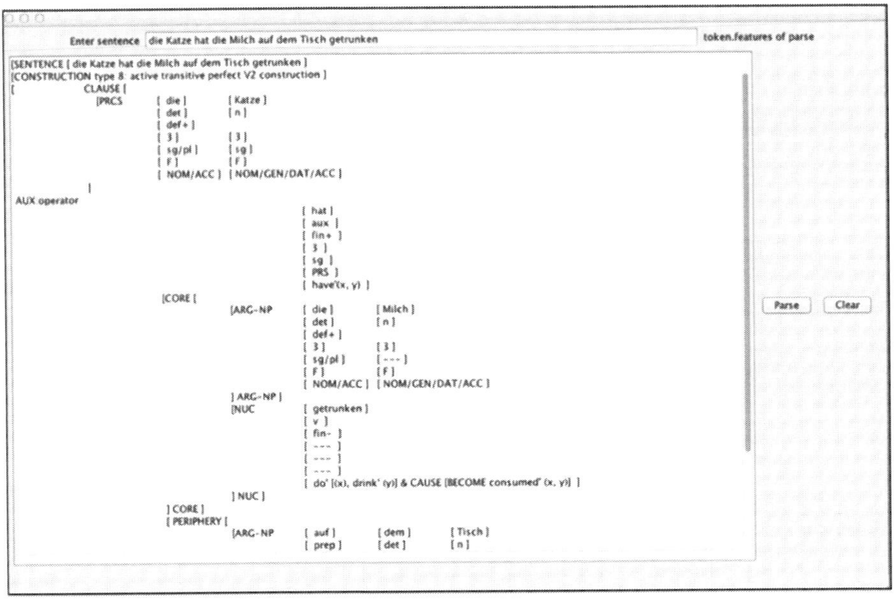

Figure 10a. Parse of construction 8, upper part of the screen

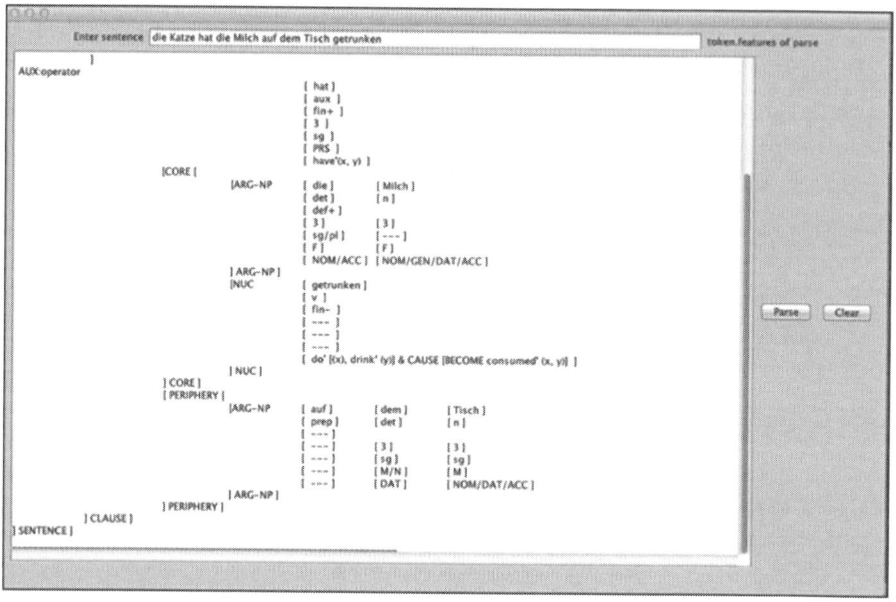

Figure 10b. Parse of construction 8, lower part of the screen, showing the Periphery

7. Discussion

7.1 Purpose

This paper discussed a RRG linguistic parser for German. It was designed to parse a selected set of constructions by accepting an input sentence and tokenising the words into the respective lexical items. The lexical features of each lexical item were retrieved from the lexicon. The parse also provides a full set of features for each of the lexical items. Furthermore, this parser was intended to be able to parse the sentence structure of each of the eight constructions according to the grammatical model of Role and Reference Grammar, which involves layers of presentation with sentences. The layers are called Nucleus, Core, PreCore slot, Periphery, clause and Sentence. We have designed this parser such that it provides a user-friendly graphical user interface and clear, readable parse results which may be copied out of the GUI for further use.

7.2 Significance of this work

The parser presented here is the first of its kind within the Role and Reference Grammar model. It is the first application that is able to parse German sentence constructions according to RRG rules and thereby to provide an elaborate set of features with each of the tokens from the constructions.

It is particularly valuable as German grammar is notoriously difficult for computational applications, as it has a variety of forms in its lexicon set, due to the three genders and its rich morphology, and it also has great freedom in word order, of which the only regularity is that with declarative clauses, the finite verb has to appear in the second position within the order of constituents. This parser therefore is an approach to a full computational representation of German, which can by no means claim full coverage. It may, however, serve as a robust proof of concept. This parser demonstrates also that the RRG linguistic model is amenable to computational implementation.

7.3 Future enhancements

While this model is a working proof of concept, it would benefit from a number of technical and structural enhancements. It is planned to provide these in the next phase of this application. The first enhancement will be to make extensive use of xml to hold and store the lexicon as a persistent data storage object across multiple uses of the application. The use of xml will provide for a scalable resource that can hold more language information without particular concern for storage requirements. The second enhancement will be to allow for the lexicon to be populated with new lexical items and their distinctive features online through a graphical user interface based application. This will enable the parser user to enter a new word in the lexicon when the parser informs the user that a word is not found. The third enhancement will be to extend the use of constructions in more detail, such that they may be fully used as grammatical objects. They may therefore be useful in the modelling of supra-lexical processes and subsequent argument realisation consequences, whereby a verb with a valence of 2 may have 3 arguments in syntax, due to constructional considerations. A fourth enhancement could be to add a parse capability for additional languages, for example Spanish, English, Irish, and Icelandic etc. A fifth enhancement will be to extend the functional range to model the semantics to syntax mapping, thereby allowing for the development of a machine translation system with translation from source language 1 to target language 2, according to the RRG model.

References

Deitel, Paul J. & Deitel, Harvey. 2012. *Java – How to Program*, 9th edn. Upper Saddle River NJ: Pearson Education International.

Diedrichsen, Elke. 2008. Where is the PreCore slot? Mapping the layered structure of the clause and German sentence topology. In *Investigations of the Syntax-Semantics-Pragmatics Interface* [Studies in Language Companion Series 105], Robert D. Van Valin Jr. (ed.), 203–224. Amsterdam: John Benjamins.

Diedrichsen, Elke. 2010. Towards a reconsideration of Constructional Schemas in RRG: Are all constructions driven by "constructions"? In Proceedings of the 10th International RRG

Conference (RRG 2009), Wataru Nakamura (ed.), 52–79. <http://linguistics.buffalo.edu/people/faculty/vanvalin/rrg/ProceedingsofRRG2009_02.pdf>

Diedrichsen, Elke. 2011. The theoretical importance of constructional schemas in RRG. *In New perspectives in Role and Reference Grammar*, Wataru Nakamura (ed.), 168–198. Newcastle upon Tyne: Cambridge Scholars.

Diedrichsen, Elke. 2013a. Auxiliary selection in German: Constructional gradience with perfect formation. In *Argument Structure in Flux: The Naples/Capri Papers* [Studies in Language Companion Series 131], Elly van Gelderen, Jóhanna Barðdal & Michela Cennamo (eds), 405–434. Amsterdam: John Benjamins.

Diedrichsen, Elke. 2013b. From idioms to sentence structures and beyond: The theoretical scope of the concept "Construction". In *Linking Constructions into Functional Linguistics. The Role of Constructions in Grammars* [Studies in Language Companion Series 145], Brian Nolan & Elke Diedrichsen (eds), 295–330.

Drach, Erich. 1937 [[4]1963]. *Grundgedanken der deutschen Satzlehre.* Frankfurt: Diesterweg.

Eisenberg, Peter. 2006. *Grundriss der deutschen Grammatik: Der Satz.* Stuttgart: Metzler.

Grewendorf, Günther, Hamm, Fritz & Sternefeld, Wolfgang. 1994. *Sprachliches Wissen.* Frankfurt: Suhrkamp

Hawkins, John. 1994. *A Performance Theory of Order and Constituency.* Cambridge: CUP.

Hawkins, John. 2004. *Efficiency and Complexity in Grammars.* Oxford: OUP.

Hentschel, Elke & Weydt, Harald. 2003. *Handbuch der deutschen Grammatik.* Berlin: De Gruyter.

Horton, Ivor. 2011. *Beginning Java. Java 7 edition.* Indianapolis IN: John Wiley and Sons.

Nolan, Brian. 2012. *The Structure of Modern Irish. A Functional Account.* Sheffield: Equinox.

Nübling, Damaris. 2008. *Historische Sprachwissenschaft des Deutschen,* 2nd edn. Tübingen: Narr.

Ronneberger-Siebold, Elke. 1991. Funktionale Betrachtungen zu Diskontinuität und Klammerbildung im Deutschen. In *Beiträge zum 8. Bochum-Essener Kolloquium über 'Sprachwandel und seine Prinzipien',* Norbert Boretzky, Werner Enninger, Benedikt Jeßing, Thomas Stolz (eds). Bochum: Universitätsverlag Dr. N. Brockmeyer.

Uhmann, Susanne. 1997. Grammatische Regeln und konversationelle Strategien. Fallstudien aus Syntax und Phonologie. Tübingen: Niemeyer.

Van Valin, Jr., Robert D. 2005. *Exploring the Syntax-semantics Interface.* Cambridge: CUP.

Van Valin, Jr., Robert D. & Diedrichsen, Elke. 2006. *A Bonsai Grammar for German.* <http://linguistics.buffalo.edu/people/faculty/vanvalin/rrg/BonsaiGrammarGerman.pdf>

Wöllstein-Leisten, Angelika, Heilmann, Axel, Stepan, Peter, Vikner, Sten. 1997. *Deutsche Satzstruktur. Grundlagen der syntaktischen Analyse.* Tübingen: Stauffenburg.

Extending a lexicalist functional grammar through speech acts, constructions and conversational software agents

Brian Nolan
Institute of Technology Blanchardstown Dublin

This paper advances a model of conversational agents in a computational framework that builds on the notion of speech act performatives from discourse within a functional model of grammar. We describe the language specific elements of the intelligent conversational agents paradigm and how it can be usefully employed in the modelling of human language in software through use of agent-embedded speech acts. The linguistic model employed is Role and Reference Grammar (RRG). We propose a view in which a conversational agent has 'internal' and 'external' models to support the speech acts. The internal model of the agent is concerned with the internal state of the agent, based upon the intersection at any given time on the agent's internal beliefs, desires, and intentions, known as BDI states. The external model of the agent is composed of an interaction model with its world (human and other agent). Importantly, the conversational agent also has a language model in software that is related to its interaction model to support bi-directional communication in human language through speech acts. For this, we employ the RRG model to motivate the design of the language model and use the RRG bi-directional linking system. We present a framework that connects the intelligent conversational agents paradigm to the RRG model of language. This has significance in that it has potential for use with linguistically oriented ontological semantics modelling and as a framework for testing of hypotheses on languages to support claims of adequacy within a functional approach. It also extends the breadth of computational work within RRG.

1. Introduction

In this paper, a model of conversational agents in a computational framework is advanced that builds on the notion of speech act performatives from discourse within a functional model of grammar. We describe the language specific elements of the intelligent conversational agents paradigm and how it can be usefully employed in modelling of human language in software through use of agent-embedded speech acts. This work builds on earlier research (Nolan & Salem 2011) on an RRG Interlingua-based machine translation engine. It also builds on recent work (Nolan 2011abcd, 2012ab, 2013; Diedrichsen 2010, 2012; Nolan & Diedrichsen 2013) on understanding constructions as grammatical objects within RRG and the role of computational approaches to functional grammars (Nolan & Periñán 'to appear').

Models of language make strong claims about the levels of descriptive, typological, psychological and explanatory adequacy required in a viable model of language (Butler 2009). Another level of adequacy is also required, that of computational adequacy, to do with how the person actually computes the link between the concept-semantics-syntax interfaces. Frequently, this is also used to describe the behaviour of a model of grammar implemented in software. While these levels of adequacy are essential, one implication of attention to computational adequacy is that one must address the appropriate levels of granularity required for software specifications to actually model a grammar. This poses significant challenges, particularly for a functionally oriented model where syntax is not viewed as autonomous but semantically motivated. In functionally motivated models of language a grammar-lexicon-construction continuum exists and the interfaces between these need to be rigorously expressed. Additionally, the architecture of the lexicon must also be strictly defined.

One software paradigm that offers huge potential in the expression of functionally motivated models of language with a grammar-lexicon-construction continuum is that of intelligent conversational agents (ICA). We describe elements of the intelligent conversational agents paradigm and how it can be usefully employed in modelling of human language in software through use of agent-embedded speech acts. We present a framework with the potential to connect the intelligent conversational agents paradigm to the Role and Reference Grammar (RRG) model of language and onwards to FunGramKB (Nolan, Mairal-Uson & Periñán 2009; Periñán-Pascual & Mairal Usón 2009; Periñán-Pascual & Arcas Túnez 2007, 2010; Mairal Usón & Ruiz de Mendoza 2009) and the Lexical Constructional Model.

To advance this discussion, we first present a brief overview of previous work on computational models involving RRG and then present the core ideas with an intelligent conversational agent framework. This is followed with proposals whereby the RRG model, the intelligent conversational agents framework, and FunGramKB, can unify in a common functionally motivated computationally adequate model of language. This can then be used to benchmark the claims of descriptive, typological, psychological and explanatory adequacy that are present in, for example, RRG. It will also allow us to make assessments on computational adequacy and linguistic complexity as well.

2. Intelligent conversational agents

What are intelligent conversational agents? Intelligent conversational agents are a software paradigm that can be used to exploit the possibilities presented by human knowledge, human language and human/agent spoken and written communications, possibly over massive open distributed systems such as the Internet.

A software agent, as envisioned here, has an internal state model, an external interaction model plus a model of language. The internal model of the agent is concerned with the internal state of the agent, based upon the intersection at any given time of the agent's internal beliefs, desires, and intentions. The external model of the agent is composed of an interaction model with its world (human and other agent). The agent's language model is related to its interaction model to support bi-directional communication in human language through speech acts. To build an intelligent conversational agent in software we need to be able to represent a number of important aspects of a conversational agent-based system (1).

(1) Important aspects of a conversational agent-based system
  a. The set of *beliefs* that the agent has at any given time
  b. The *goals* that agent will try to achieve;
  c. The *actions* that agent performs and
  d. The knowledge of the *effects* of these actions;
  e. The *environment information* the agent has (which may be incomplete or incorrect);
  f. The *ongoing discourse interaction* that agent has with other (human) agents and their environment over time;
  g. Human *language understanding* and *conversation tracking* over a discourse.

In order to meet the standards of adequacy required to model, test and benchmark the levels of adequacy required in a functional model of language, we need to ensure a motivated conversational agent architecture that builds on a robust natural language parse/generation system, for example, the bi-directional linking system such as is found in RRG. We need this in order to incorporate an agent's conversational behaviours. Additionally, for conversational realism and to address issues of psychological adequacy in our model of language we need to allow for elements of language that are dependent upon the agent's personality, the agent's current emotional state and the agent's beliefs about the social relationship between the disparate conversational actors (agent and human), and social and cultural norms that impact use of language in real time.

Of course, it is also possible to develop conversational agents that incorporate models of emotion and personality to produce virtual characters and which exhibit believable conversational behaviour. Indeed, much work has been undertaken with these avatars for Deaf Sign Language research (Murtagh 2011).

We next introduce the functional model at the heart of this architecture, Role and Reference Grammar and then proceed to discuss recent work on the role of constructions as grammatical objects. After this, we discuss the dialogue management framework for a language understanding system supporting conversational agents.

3. Role and reference grammar as the linguistic engine

We situate this research work within the lexical-functionalist theory of Role and Reference Grammar (RRG) (Van Valin 2005), a theory of grammar concerned with the interaction of syntax, semantics and pragmatics in grammatical systems. It is a mono-stratum theory that posits a single syntactic representation for a sentence, linked directly to a semantic representation by means of a bi-directional linking algorithm.

There is a direct mapping link between the semantic representation of a sentence and its syntactic representation. The semantic representation is based on a system of lexical representation and semantic roles. The relationship between the macroroles and the various argument positions in the logical structures is captured in the Actor-Undergoer Hierarchy in Figure 1. The system of lexical representation employed in RRG uses an aktionsarten classification of verbs into states, activities, achievements and accomplishments, with an additional class, called active accomplishments, for telic uses of activity verbs. Examples of the formal representation of verb classes with a logical structure are given in (2). See Van Valin (2005) and Nolan (2012a) for more information on RRG.

(2) Formal representation of verb classes with a logical structure

– State	**predicate'**(x)or (x,y)
– Activity	**do'** (x, [**predicate'**(x)or (x, y)]}
– Achievement	INGR(ESSIVE) **predicate'**(x)or (x, y), or INGR **do'** (x, [**predicate'**(x)or (x, y)]}
– Accomplishment	BECOME **predicate'**(x)or (x, y), or BECOME **do'** (x, [**predicate'**(x)or (x, y)]}
– Active accomplishment	**do'** (x,[**predicate;'**(x,(y))]) & BECOME **predicate;** (z, x) or (y)
– Causative	*a* CAUSE *b* where *a*, *b* are representations of any type

RRG recognizes the importance of constructions by positing constructional schemas (Van Valin 2005: 132) (See Figure 2). Constructional schemas permit the capturing of cross-linguistic generalizations while expressing the language-particular properties of grammars. Each constructional schema contains detailed syntactic, morphological, semantic and pragmatic information on the construction under examination, as appropriate (Nolan 2011bc, 2012a, Nolan and Diedrichsen 2013).

Actor → Undergoer

Argument of DO	1st Argument of **do'**(x...	1st argument of **pred'**(x,y)	2nd argument of **pred'**(x,y)	Argument of state **pred'**(x)
AGENT	EFFECTOR	LOCATION	THEME	PATIENT
	MOVER	PERCEIVER	STIMULUS	ENTITY
	EMITTER	COGNISER	CONTENT	
	PERFORMER	WANTER	DESIRE	
	CONSUMER	JUDGER	JUDGEMENT	
	CREATOR	POSSESSOR	POSSESSED	
	SPEAKER	EXPERIENCER	SENSATION	
	OBSERVER	EMOTER	TARGET	
	USER	ARIBUTANT	ATTRIBUTE	
			PERFORMANCE	
			CONSUMED	
			CREATION	
			LOCUS	
			IMPLEMENT	

Figure 1. The Actor-Undergoer Hierarchy (Van Valin 2005:58)

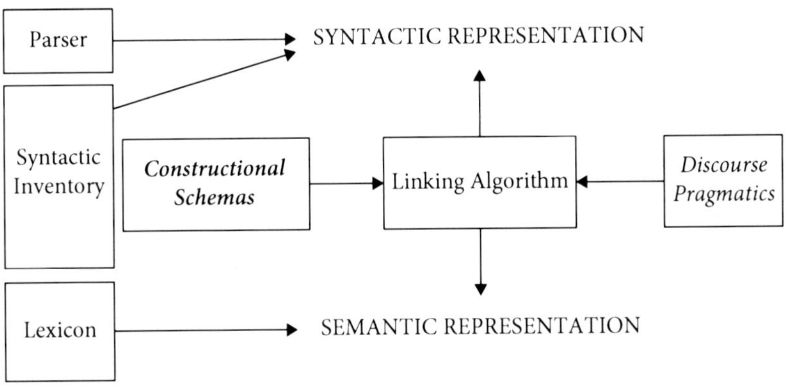

Figure 2. The generalised organisation of Role and Reference Grammar

4. Constructions as grammatical objects in RRG

To-date, the RRG approach has provided a descriptive approach to constructions without having in depth consideration of how to formalise aspects of the processing of actual constructions. Recent work in RRG (Nolan 2013, Nolan and Diedrichsen 2013), FunGramKB and the Lexical Constructional Model, along with work in Construction

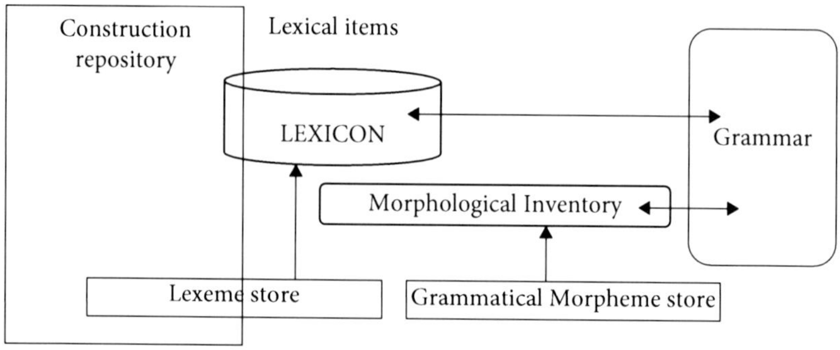

Figure 3. The construction repository and the lexicon in grammar

Grammar, has made constructions more central in accounts of the grammar of real language use, whether the construction is at word or clausal level.

In Nolan (2012b) (see Figure 3), we apply a model of constructions as grammatical objects in a construction repository in a view of RRG that is computationally and cognitively plausible, in an approach that gives a general acceptance to an increased centrality of constructions while retaining the importance of the lexicon. Our position allows for a continuum between the lexicon and the construction repository.

4.1 Construction internal architecture

We construe a construction within RRG schematically (3), as a structured grammatical object. We consider the construction as having an internal structure consisting of: a) a unique **SIGNATURE**, b), a set of **CONSTRAINTS** on the signature, c) an **INPUT** string that is processed in the activated schema, and d) an **OUTPUT** of a particular kind (the exact nature of these outputs depends on the direction of execution of the activated schema from, for example, syntax→ semantics or semantics→ syntax), and e) a **CONSTRUCTION BODY** (cx-body) that appropriately encodes the relationship between morphosyntax, semantics and pragmatics within f) a **WORKSPACE** local to the construction. Within this perspective, we can usefully consider the construction as a grammatical object that can be uniquely identified, has internal structure, accepts an input and produces an output.

(3) Schema of the construction as a grammatical object

SIGNATURE: some pattern of [...x_1 y_2 z_3....] CONSTRAINTS: C_1 C_2...C_n
INPUT: clause (token$_1$, token$_2$, token$_n$)
WORKSPACE: input [1], [2], [3] and output [1]
CONSTRUCTION BODY SYNTAX: PSA SEMANTICS: Linking MORPHOLOGY: PROSODY: PRAGMATICS:
OUTPUT: [LS]$_1$

The activation of the construction schema instance is sensitive to the direction of application. The workspace can be considered as a construction internal processing area for the application of construction specific linking rules. This internal linking within the construction is activated to map between syntax-morphology-semantics-pragmatics etc., according to the internal specification of the particular construction.

It can be argued that, from lexicon to grammar, the notion of construction is a basic unit of analysis and representation. In this view, constructions are considered to be conceptual entities out of which speakers build complex expressions. This is what we find in FunGramKB and the Lexical Constructional Model, which now have within their models the notions of *construct* and *construction*. It is also a similar view that we argue for here to support the computational framework for agents using speech acts within an RRG perspective. Utterances therefore are the product of the interaction between grammatical constructions and lexical constructions.

4.2 Construction internal processing workspace

In relation to the nature of constructions as grammatical objects and the linking rules that apply, we need to consider: *where do lexical and/or grammatical rules reside*? Additionally, as we will need to achieve with conversational agents, if one takes the online computation of the various constructions in real-time at speech act production as something that needs to be accounted for, the question is where do the processing rules that are applied in real-time online computation reside. Obviously, of course, these reside in human memory and have real-time access to a processing workspace. This leads one to consider that an account of real time online computation of the speech act could be motivated as residing within the construction instance that is retrieved from the construction repository and activated each time as a 'live' grammatical object, for each construction.

The lexicon is still, of course, accessed within the construction and a logical structure retrieved and populated based on the input data string. In this view, the lexicon is an information provider to the construction (see Figure 4). This is computed online in real-time in the construction instance and the lexicon is simply projected into the construction. The lexical information including the logical structures can be overridden by the constraints identified within the constructional schema. This manipulation of variables occurs within the local workspace within the construction.

By way of illustrating this point we can say that a ditransitive construction will have a workspace with capacity to store the abstract information requirements of the three arguments and all language specific relevant features, such that these can be accessed and processed within the construction as part of the mapping between, firstly, form and meaning for the computation of meaning and, secondly, the computation of form and function in particular for information structure or other functional needs, as may be required.

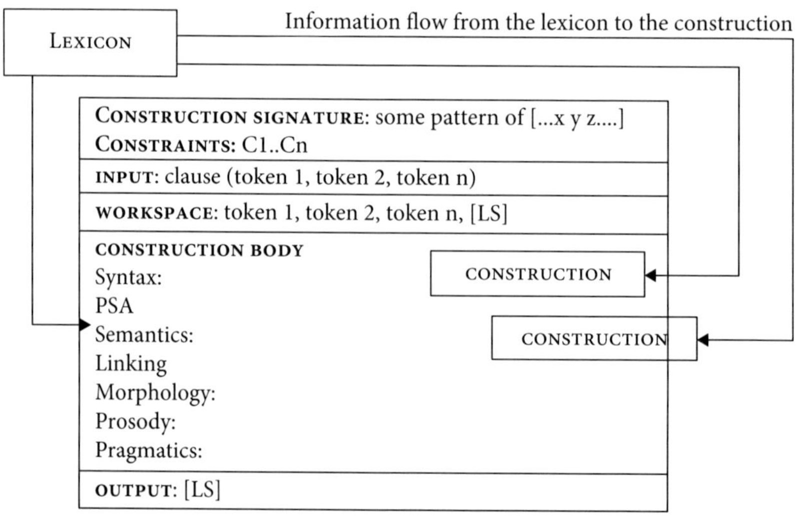

Figure 4. Constructional object in the RRG grammar inheriting from the lexicon

5. Motivations for use of RRG in the agent framework

Is RRG a suitable paradigm for computational linguistic research and development? The answer to this is 'yes' – it has been demonstrated that RRG is a suitable paradigm for computational models of language (Nolan, Mairal Usón & Perinan 2009). We briefly discuss two instances where this has been achieved.

5.1 The UniArab machine translation system

In Nolan and Salem (2011), a machine translation system called UniArab supporting the fundamental aspects of Arabic is presented. UniArab is based on the linking algorithm of RRG (syntax to semantics and vice versa). UniArab takes MSA Arabic as input in the native orthography, parses the sentence(s) into a logical meta-representation based on the fully expanded RRG logical structures and, using this, generates perfectly grammatical English output with full agreement and morphological resolution.

In UniArab, the lexical properties of the Arabic words are extracted. From this parse, it then creates a computer-based representation for the logical structure of the Arabic sentence(s). The RRG theory is used to motivate the computational implementation of the architecture of the lexicon in software. UniArab also implements in software the RRG bidirectional linking system to build the parse and generate functions between the syntax-semantic interfaces. Through seven input phases, including the morphological and syntactic unpacking, UniArab extracts the logical structure of an Arabic sentence. Using XML-based metadata representing the RRG logical structure, UniArab then accurately generates an equivalent grammatical sentence in the target language of English through four output phases.

The UniArab system has been tested and evaluated generating equivalent grammatical sentences, in English, via the logical structure of Arabic sentences, based on MSA Arabic input with very significant and accurate results. Research on UniArab has demonstrated that RRG is a viable linguistic model for building accurate rule-based semantically oriented machine translation software. This supports our claim that RRG is very suitable for machine translation of Arabic and that demonstrates that RRG can be implemented in software as the rule-based kernel of an Interlingua bridge MT engine. We briefly discuss the FunGramKB system next.

5.2 Computing FunGramKB

FunGramKB (Periñán-Pascual & Arcas-Túnez 2007, 2010; Periñán-Pascual & Mairal Usón 2009, 2010) is a multifunctional, multilingual and multipurpose lexical-conceptual knowledge base for natural language processing and natural language understanding. FunGramKB has a knowledge base comprised of three knowledge levels and consisting of several independent but interrelated modules. These are indicated in (4).

(4) FunGramKB model and its three knowledge levels

Conceptual level:

- The *Ontology* is presented as a hierarchical catalogue of the concepts in a human mind, such that semantic knowledge is stored as meaning postulates.
- The *Cognicon* stores procedural knowledge as scripts, i.e. conceptual schemata in which a sequence of stereotypical actions is organised on the basis of temporal continuity.
- The *Onomasticon* stores information about instances of real world entities and events.

Lexical level:

- The *Lexicon* stores morphosyntactic, pragmatic and collocational information about lexical units.
- The *Morphicon* manages the requirements of inflectional morphology.

Grammatical level:

- The *Grammaticon* stores the constructional schemata that help Role and Reference Grammar to construct the semantics-to-syntax linking algorithm

As the *Ontology* is the primary module for the whole architecture, FunGramKB adopts a conceptualist approach to the construction of meaning. Additionally, the FunGramKB lexical and grammatical levels are based on RRG (Van Valin, 2005) and the Lexical Constructional Model (Mairal Usón & Ruiz de Mendoza Ibáñez 2009; Ruiz de Mendoza Ibáñez & Mairal Usón 2011). Every lexical or grammatical module is language-dependent in FunGramKB but each conceptual module is shared across all languages.

Based on this work with UniArab, and our awareness of the computational work on FunGramKB, also based on RRG in part, we justify our use of RRG for the computational implementation of a model of conversational agents and speech acts.

5.3 Supporting the grammar-lexicon-construction continuum

Functionalist theories regard lexicon and grammar as separate and postulate that information from lexical semantics is projected onto morphosyntax via the linking system. Cognitive constructionist theories (Butler & Arista 2009; Goldberg 1995, 2006; Michaelis 2006, 2010) hold that a continuum exists between lexicon and grammar and, as such, linking rules are not needed. Instead, constructions are considered to be a pairing of form and meaning.

A disadvantage of constructivist accounts is that they do not pay sufficient attention to how lexical elements are combined into particular language-specific constructions, and to how the constraints that operate over these constructions are resolved. The model proposed here resolves this.

In our model proposed here, supporting the grammar-lexicon-construction continuum, the lexicon both projects into the construction or the construction inherits from the lexicon depending in the direction of operation from syntax-to-semantics or semantics-to-syntax. In our view of the construction, no information is obligatory and there is no minimum number of features that a construction must specify other than, perhaps its SIGNATURE (so as to be recognised as a construction), and its constructional OUTPUT. Grammatical and lexical constructions interact and integrate in complex and non-trivial ways.

6. The dialogue management framework for conversational agents

I will now proceed to propose the dialogue management framework needed to support conversational agents that use natural language, and in which is situated an implementation of the RRG model as the linguistic engine. To produce the required conversational behaviour we require an architecture that builds upon and integrates with a generic natural language parse/generation system and which incorporate sub-models of conversational agent personality and agent awareness of social context.

6.1 Generic conversational architecture for language aware software agents

The dialogue management framework for a language understanding system supporting conversational agents is seen in Figure 5. Here, the natural language processing system is at the heart of the architecture. By design, the system needs to be flexible enough to allow for creative choices in language use to be determined from the contribution of the personality, emotion, social role and conversational partner dimensions in the overall architecture. Therefore, for naturalistic agent behaviour over a conversation, the determination of the agent parameters covering emotional status, personality etc. and use of these as in conversational behaviour is important.

The key component of this architecture is a DIALOGUE MANAGER, which determines the relationship between the emotional status and personality type of the agent's 'character' and the behavioural choices made in generating natural language. Specifically, the DIALOGUE MANAGER determines the choices in conversational behaviour such as turn taking, word choice and sentence structure based on the grammar of the particular language. This consults the personality/emotion/social role and conversational partner model to decide the exact choices to be made, based on rules and constraints. The determining parameters for the conversational agent range over the several important areas (5).

(5) Parameters for the conversational agent
  a. Personality and emotional Status
  b. Social Context
  c. Conversational Partner Model (= OTHER conversational actor)
  d. Dialogue tracking
  e. Agent dialogue-turn tracking
  f. Linguistic information concerning language specific grammar and clause structure and speech acts.

In the architecture outlined here, the relationship between agent parameters and behavioural choices made during the parse/generation of natural language conversation is governed by the Agent Dialogue Manager. This would typically be a rule-based system that consults other elements of the architecture to maintain the Belief, Desire and Intention (BDI) state of the conversational agent, its personality and emotional status etc. to control a generalised natural language conversation system and supply the appropriate parameters for conversational behaviour.

We suggest that at least the following sub-models may be applicable, along with the language model based on RRG (see Figure 5). A personality model will be needed in order to maintain a model of personality for the conversational agent. The relevant dimensions of personality need to include those personality factors that have marked, or specific, effects upon conversational behaviour and most relevant to language use. It incorporates a model of emotion to maintain simple interaction with conversational behaviour. The emotional model will be modified in response to conversational actions to reflect the emotional impact of the current conversation upon the agent. This also determines the specific emotional change caused by a given conversational action. It ideally should cover personality factors such as tolerance, grumpiness, etc. and interacts with the agent's 'temperament' to determine these personality factors. Temperament is used to specify relevant and appropriate personality parameters that modulate the agent's reaction and response to conversational utterances. It will assist in guiding the emotional model in conjunction with the underlying natural language system.

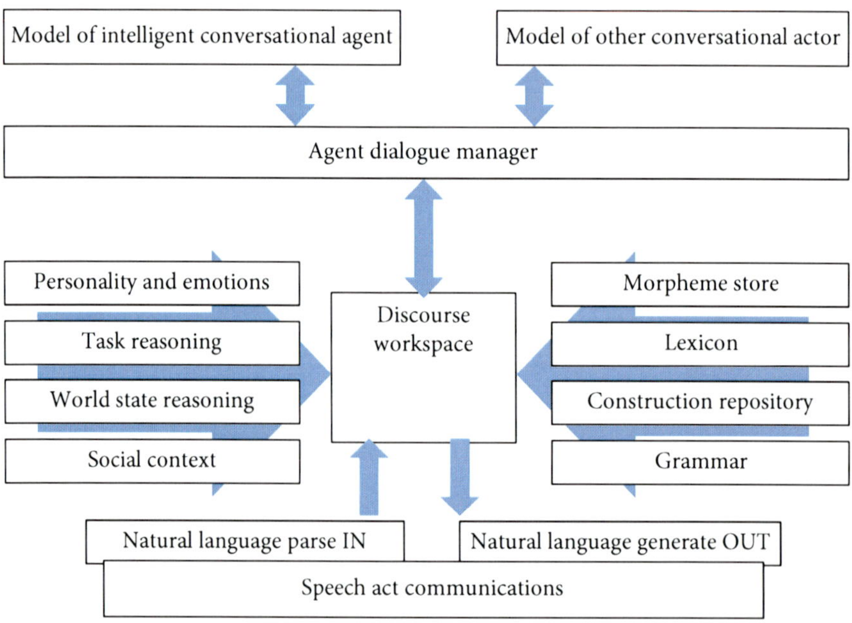

Figure 5. Dialogue management framework for a language understanding system w conversational agents

The SOCIAL CONTEXT Model specifies the conversational agents belief about the social status of the two conversational actors, as well as the social relationship between them to the extent that it is known. Using concepts such as age, social position and level of authority, this module can be used to modulate scalar considerations such as the degree of confidence displayed by the agent in its language use. A CONVERSATIONAL PARTNER MODEL is needed to maintain the BELIEF, DESIRE and INTENTION statuses of the other conversational partner within a dialogue.

The important issues for the intelligent conversational agent architect to resolve are therefore (6):

(6) Issues for the intelligent conversational agent architect
  a. What exactly does my agent know?
  b. How can the agent access and use the knowledge in human language discourse?
  c. How best can this knowledge be represented in an agent?
  d. How will I build a conversation in natural language that uses this knowledge?

One way of resolving these issues is to use a model of speech acts situated in an implementation of RRG within the framework for agent communication. This is, of course, an excellent choice as we know from linguistic research that all discourse interaction consists of speech acts. Natural language consists of actions, e.g., when a judge in a court of law declares a defendant to be guilty, this action changes the social status of the defendant. Speech act theory is a high level theoretical framework developed to account for human communication and it is concerned with the role of language as action (Labrou and Finin 1994). The three aspects of a speech act include locution, illocution and perlocution, as shown in (7).

In a speech act, the intent of the message in isolation may be unclear. e.g., 'I am cold', or 'the window is wide open' could be an assertion or a request to increase the room temperature. For agent communication, there should never be any doubt about the type of message. Therefore, to provide clarity and remove ambiguity where it may exist we employ a model of speech act performatives. A PERFORMATIVE explicitly identifies illocutionary force. Performative verbs in English include *promise, report, convince, insist, tell, request, demand*, and these are classified into the categories of performatives in (8).

(7) The three aspects of a speech act
  1. LOCUTION: the actual physical utterance with a certain context and reference;
  2. ILLOCUTION: the conveying of the speakers intentions to the hearer; an illocution is usually considered to have two parts: an illocutionary force and a proposition
  3. PERLOCUTION: the action that results from the locution.

(8) Categories of performatives
  a. Assertive: statements of fact
  b. Directive: commands (imposing obligations on the addressee)
  c. Commissive: imposing obligations on the speaker (e.g., promises)
  d. Declarative: establishing social facts (e.g., "I hereby declare ...")
  e. Expressive: expressions of emotion, feelings and attitudes

Following Labrou and Finin (1994), we adopt Searle's (1969) approach to speech acts where a speech act may be described more formally as illocutionary_force(Prepositional content), or simply F(P), recognising that P can actually be prepositional content plus some syntactic features encoding a construction pattern, and an utterance context. The components in (9) are suggested to hold of the illocutionary force.

(9) a. The **illocutionary force** is a fundamental primitive. The illocutionary points are *assertive, directive, commissive, declarative* and *expressive.* The illocutionary point of the type of illocutionary act is achieved if the act is successful.
  b. The **degree of strength of the illocutionary point** is a scalar between, for example, command ("shut the door") and plea ("could you close the door").
  c. The **mode of achievement** suggests the special ways or sets of conditions under which the illocutionary point has to be achieved in the performance of the speech act, including the appropriate level of authority of the speaker.
  d. The **propositional content conditions** impose what can be in the prepositional content P for a specific illocutionary force F.
  e. The **preconditions** that hold for the successful performance of an illocutionary act. We can view these as preconditions for on the cognitive state of the agent.
  f. The **sincerity conditions** that relate to the cognitive state of the agent with respect to Belief, Desire and Intention.
  g. The **degree of strength of the sincerity conditions.**

In order to define the cognitive states for an agent and use them to describe the various performatives, preconditions, post-conditions and satisfaction conditions, we can employ several predicates that have a reserved meaning (10).

(10) a. **Believe′** (A, P), has the meaning that A believes that P is true for A, where P is an expression in a human natural language.
  b. **Know′** (A, P) expresses a state of knowledge of the agent A with respect to P

c. **Want′** (A, P) means that agent A desires the event or state coded by P to occur.

d. **Intend′** (A, P) means that A intends to do P.

The concept of illocutionary force lets us define the type of message. Illocutionary force constrains the semantics of the communication act itself and this constraint will help simplify the design of intelligent conversational agents. We can relate this to an RRG logical structure representation, with modal and other operators, within a speech act construction for a speech act within an agent.

6.2 The structure of a speech act for a conversational agent

The basic schema for a speech act is defined by the structure in (11), with an example in (12). It is important to note that the <expression> associated with:CONTENT may be a named CONSTRUCTION with a particular signature (13). Such a construction will encapsulate its own workspace and linking requirements and will reside in the construction repository.

(11) Basic schema for a speech act

(<***PERFORMATIVE***>

:SENDER	<word>
:RECEIVER	<word>
:LANGUAGE	<word>
:ONTOLOGY	<word>
:CONTENT	<expression>

...)

(12) Simple example of a speech act

(<**Assertive: TELL**>

:SENDER	<Brian>
:RECEIVER	<Agent-1>
:LANGUAGE	<English>
:ONTOLOGY	<FunGramKB>
:CONTENT	< **do'** (Aifric, [**eat'** (Aifric, pizza)]) & INGR **consumed'** (pizza)]>

...)

(13) The model structure of a speech act construction

(<*PERFORMATIVE*>
:SENDER <word>
:RECEIVER <word>
:LANGUAGE <word>
:ONTOLOGY <word>
:CONTENT <
SIGNATURE: some pattern of [...x_1 y_2 z_3....] CONSTRAINTS: C_1 C_2...C_n
INPUT: clause ($token_1$, $token_2$, $token_n$)
WORKSPACE: input [1], [2], [3] and output [1]
CONSTRUCTION BODY SYNTAX: PSA SEMANTICS: Linking MORPHOLOGY: PROSODY: PRAGMATICS:
OUTPUT: $[LS]_1$
>

7. Conversational agent – Human actor: Dialogue steps as pseudo code

We have already indicated that we extend the RRG linking system to include speech acts within a system of conversational agents. As we mentioned earlier, there is a direct mapping link between the semantic representation of a sentence and its syntactic representation. The semantic representation is based on a system of lexical representation and semantic roles. Here we link the agent dialogue to the RRG model of the grammar via the particular speech act construction in the dialogue model. The steps in (14) and (15) are indicative outline stages in the agent – human dialogue. In (14), the linking from the speech act is shown for the dialogue direction of human to software conversational agent whereas in (15) we indicate the steps in linking from the software agent to the human.

This approach to modelling the paradigm provides a way to express functionally motivated models of language with a grammar-lexicon-construction continuum, using intelligent conversational agents (ICA), at the appropriate level of granularity that is required in computer software. These levels of granularity are essential to address the issue of computational adequacy of the model. There are complex challenges within this, as we mentioned earlier, for a functionally oriented model with a semantically motivated syntax with a continuum across grammar-lexicon-construction and a robust bi-directional linking system.

In this regard, we have described elements of the intelligent conversational agents paradigm and how it can be usefully employed in modelling of human language in software through the use of agent-embedded speech acts within a framework based on the RRG model of language.

(14) Dialogue direction: Human → Software conversational agent

1. Agent accepts input text via GUI from human language user.
2. Parse input text string into tokens
3. Determine POS/lexical category of tokens [as features]
4. Determine type of speech act
   - Assume ASSERTATIVE speech act for this example
5. Identify signature of construction underlying speech act
6. Invoke construction object
7. Pass tokens + features in speech act to construction object
8. Activate construction workspace
9. Activate linking system and lexicon in the construction object [SYN→SEM]
10. Unpack tokens as *input 1 – n*.
11. Build LS
12. Identify propositional content in the speech act within the construction
13. Reason with propositional content and adjust Agent and Other conversational actor states using:

1. THIS.conversational actor

a. This.Agent-BELIEF-DESIRE-INTENTION
b. This.Agent-PERSONALITY AND EMOTION
c. This.Agent-SOCIAL CONTEXT

2. OTHER.conversational actor

a. Other.conversational actor-B-D-I
b. Other.conversational actor-PERSONALITY AND EMOTION
c. Other.conversational actor-SOCIAL CONTEXT

(15) Dialogue direction: Software conversational agent → Human

1. Build response in the agent
2. Identify the appropriate N, V etc. from the lexicon
3. Populate the LS for the V as per the lexical entry
4. Retrieve the appropriate construction for the speech act of the response.
5. Build the construction for the speech act
   - Assume QUESTION speech act for this example
6. Pass the LS and NPs etc. to the construction as *inputs 1 – n.*
7. Activate the construction workspace
8. Activate the linking system [SEM→SYN]
9. Map LS to syntax and apply morphosyntactic marking to the clause, adjust word order as necessary as an output of the construction
10. The constructional object delivers the appropriate output to the agent
11. Agent delivers the grammatical clause as a response to the user.

8. Discussion

Social interactions are highly complex activities requiring from those who are involved in them the ability to possess a huge amount of lexical, grammatical, semantic and pragmatic linguistic knowledge, world knowledge, cultural norms and conversational practices. Conversations are structured linguistic entities which occur in a coherent way in virtue of the coordinated contributions of the participants in a speech community, notwithstanding that they may have different knowledge sets and conversational goals.

A framework for modelling conversational agents requires that we recognise conversations as a cooperative activity between agents with multichannel communication taking place between each agent where each monitors and updates in real time several levels of interaction. We also require in our framework that the agents can reason about mental states and perform speech acts to transmit their mental states to other agents. In order to achieve this, speech acts are considered as structured objects which correspond to mental states of the respective conversational agents.

The agent intentional structure consists of the beliefs, desires and intentions as expressed in discourse elements, as well as the relations linking these. The goals, and related beliefs, desires and intentions, are linked to the global discourse goals of each conversational agent. Additionally, the most salient objects, properties and relations of each discourse element compose the attentional state of the agent and this is maintained in a WORKSPACE for each agent. Mental states composed of beliefs, desires and intentions constitute the agents plans. Successful communication is accomplished if a listening agent recognises the felicity conditions from the speaker's speech acts. Default rules within the agent enable it to draw inferences with incomplete situational knowledge, based on the speech act construction, its constraints and world and cultural knowledge.

This framework proposed will provide an implementable model of conversational agents with conversation management based on speech acts and a robust functional linguistic model. Conversation is a co-operative activity is which conversational agents try to influence the other agent's mental states, including those of beliefs, desires, intentions, emotions and expectations. Agents interacting in a dialogue can be considered as constituting a system of agents. As a system this has structure that can be modelled in software. Human agents communicate using several modal channels including verbal utterances, gesture (for example in Deaf Sign Languages), facial expression and body language.

A communicative act is composed of the various spoken and non-uttered acts performed by the agent in a turn taking move, i.e., framed within a speech act construction. Communication between agents occurs at several levels of which we might mention, in particular:

1. The **Dialogue Management level** where agents undertake communicative activities including the construction of an utterance and management of turn taking.
2. The **Conceptual level** where agents transfer concepts, mental states and their related semantic nets and manage the various high-level elements of the conversation (topics, sequencing of utterances, social and cultural conventions).
3. The **Social level** where agents manage the elements that govern agent's relations within the multi-agent environment.

As we noted earlier, speech acts used in inter-agent interactions transfer concepts via structured objects. We call these objects speech act constructions. These speech act constructions form a conceptual network in each agent that facilitates the tracking of the conversation. Each conversational agent has a mental model composed of objects such as beliefs, desires and intentions with factual and ontological information, cultural and societal knowledge, and emotional information. We propose an approach to modelling conversations in a conversational agent framework based on structured speech act constructions considered as grammatical objects connected to the grammar of a language. This model can reflect various kinds of linguistic, ontological and cultural information that influences speech acts.

In this paper we have shown an outline of an integrated model of agents that employs constructions as grammatical objects to process speech act performatives as speech act constructions, with RRG as the underlying linguistic model. Our approach recognises that the prepositional content of some illocutionary force can actually be prepositional content plus some syntactic features encoding a construction pattern, and an utterance context.

We have situated this agent model within a framework for dialogue management for a language aware system supporting conversational software agents with speech acts central to the model. The model also has personality and emotion components. We have placed RRG within a central position in the kernel of the agent framework. Within the framework, we use a model of constructions as grammatical objects residing in a constructional repository to support formal representation of speech acts. We have indicated too points of synergy with the FunGramKB project which is also motivated by RRG. Work is ongoing realising this model in Java and it builds on previous computational research in RRG.

References

Butler, Christopher, S. 2009. Criteria of adequacy in functional linguistics. *Folia Linguistia: Acta Societatis Linguisticae Europaeae* 42(1): 1–66.

Butler, Christopher S. & Arista, Javier Martín (eds). 2009. *Deconstructing Constructions* [Studies in language Companion Series 107]. Amsterdam: John Benjamins.

Diedrichsen, Elke. 2010. Towards a reconsideration of Constructional Schemas in RRG: Are all constructions driven by "constructions"? In *Proceedings of the 10th International RRG Conference (RRG 2009)*, Wataru Nakamura (ed.), 52–79. <http://wings.buffalo.edu/linguistics//people/faculty/vanvalin/rrg/ProceedingsofRRG2009_02.pdf>

Diedrichsen, Elke. 2012. *The Theoretical Importance of Constructional Schemas in RRG*. In *New perspectives in Role and Reference Grammar,* Wataru Nakamura (ed.), 168–199. Newcastle upon Tyne: Cambridge Scholars.

Goldberg, Adele. 1995. *Constructions: A Construction Grammar Approach to Argument Structure*. Chicago Il: University of Chicago Press.

Goldberg, Adele. 2006. *Constructions at Work: The Nature of Generalization in Language*. Oxford: OUP.

Labrou, Yannis & Finin, Tim. 1994. A semantics approach to KQML – A general purpose communication language for software agents. In *CIKM '94 – Proceedings of the Third International Conference on Information and Knowledge Management,* 447–455. New York NY: ACM.

Mairal Usón, Ricardo & Ruiz de Mendoza, Francisco. 2009. Levels of description and explanation in meaning construction. In *Deconstructing Constructions* [Studies in Language Companion Series 107], Christopher S. Butler & J. Martín Arista (eds), 153–198. Amsterdam: John Benjamins.

Michaelis, Laura A. 2006. Construction Grammar. In *The Encyclopaedia of Language and Linguistics*, 2nd edn, Vol. 3, Keith Brown (ed.), 73–84. Oxford: Elsevier.

Michaelis, Laura A. 2010. Construction Grammar: The facts on the ground. In *The Oxford Handbook of Linguistic Analysis,* Bernd Heine & Heiko Narrog (eds). Oxford: OUP.

Murtagh, Irene. 2011. Towards an RRG-enabled Sign Language avatar. Paper presented at the International Conference on Role and Reference Grammar on "Functional Linguistics: Grammar, Communication & Cognition". Facultad de Letras, at the Pontificia Universidad Católica de Chile, in Santiago de Chile.

Nolan, Brian. 2011a. Characterising the effects of the referential hierarchy on Modern Irish ditransitive constructions. Paper presented at the International Workshop on Referential Hierarchies in three-participant constructions. The University of Lancaster, England.

Nolan, Brian. 2011b. Meaning Construction and Grammatical Inflection in the Layered Structure of the Irish Word: An RRG Account of Morphological Constructions. In *New perspectives in Role and Reference Grammar*, Wataru Nakamura (ed.), 64–103. Newcastle upon Tyne: Cambridge Scholars.

Nolan, Brian. 2011c. Constructions as grammatical objects. Paper presented at the International Conference on Role and Reference Grammar on "Functional Linguistics: Grammar, Communication & Cognition". Facultad de Letras, at the Pontificia Universidad Católica de Chile, in Santiago de Chile.

Nolan, Brian. 2011d. Constructional templates at the morphology-lexicon interface - meaning and the layered structure of the Irish word. Paper presented at the workshop on Meaning construction at the crossroads of grammar, cognition and communication. Societas Linguistica Europaea, University of La Rioja, Logroño, Spain.

Nolan, Brian. 2012a. *The Syntax of Irish: A Functional Account*. Sheffield: Equinox.

Nolan, Brian. 2012b. Constructions as grammatical objects: A new perspective on constructions in RRG. Paper presented at the 1st International Conference on Knowledge Representation and Meaning in FunGramKB and LCM. Facultad de Filología, at the Universidad Nacional de Educación a Distancia (UNED), in Madrid, Spain.

Nolan, Brian. 2013. Constructional polysemy and argument realisation with the Irish GET verb. In *Argument Structures in Flux: The Naples/Capri Papers* [Studies in Language Companion Series 131], Elly van Gelderen, Johanna Barðdal & Michaela Cennamo (eds), 87–113. Amsterdam: John Benjamins.

Nolan, Brian & Diedrichsen, Elke. 2013. *Linking Constructions into Functional Linguistics. The Role of Constructions in Grammar* [Studies in Language Companion Series 145]. Amsterdam: John Benjamins.

Nolan, Brian, Mairal-Uson, Ricardo & Periñán, Carlos. 2009. Natural language processing applications in an RRG Framework. In *Proceedings of the 10th International Role and Reference Grammar Conference. University of California, Berkeley USA*.

Nolan, Brian & Salem, Yasser. 2011. UniArab: RRG Arabic-to-English Machine Translation. In *New Perspectives in Role and Reference Grammar*, Wataru Nakamura (ed.), 312–346. Newcastle upon Tyne: Cambridge Scholars.

Periñán-Pascual, Carlos & Arcas Túnez, Francisco. 2007. Cognitive modules of an NLP knowledge base for language understanding. *Procesamiento del Lenguaje Natural* 39: 197–204.

Periñán-Pascual, Carlos & Arcas Túnez, Francisco. 2010. The architecture of FunGramKB. In *Proceedings of the Seventh International Conference on Language Resources and Evaluation*, European Language Resources Association (ELRA), 2667–2674.

Periñán-Pascual, Carlos & Mairal Usón, Ricardo. 2009. Bringing Role and Reference Grammar to natural language understanding. *Procesamiento del Lenguaje Natural* 43: 265–273.

Ruiz de Mendoza, Francisco & Mairal Uson, Ricardo. 2011. Levels of description and constraining factors in meaning construction: An introduction to the Lexical Constructional Model. *Folia Linguisticia* 42: 355–400.

Searle, John. 1969. *Speech Acts*. Cambridge: CUP.

Van Valin, Jr., Robert D. 2005. *Exploring the Syntax-Semantics Interface*. Cambridge: CUP.

The implementation of the CLS constructor in ARTEMIS

Carlos Periñán-Pascual and Francisco Arcas-Túnez
Universidad Politécnica de Valencia and Universidad Católica San Antonio

Most natural language processing researchers highlight the benefits of interlingua-based systems in multilingual settings. In this scenario, Role and Reference Grammar can contribute to build a cross-language semantic representation of the input text in terms of its logical structure. Our goal is to describe the various stages in the development of one of the first computational systems which employs a lexico-conceptual knowledge base to generate the logical structure of sentences. Our approach actually involved some changes in the standard functional model in order to convert the logical structure into an ontology-grounded representation of sentential meaning. In fact, we demonstrate that constructional schemata should become the cornerstone of the syntax-semantics interface in this computerized model of Role and Reference Grammar.

1. Introduction

In computational linguistics, lexical-semantic research is influenced by two mainstreams: syntax-driven and ontology-driven semantics (Nirenburg & Levin 1992). As has been the case in many lexicalist theories, syntax-driven semantics focuses on those meaning components which can predict the syntactic behavior of words. On the other hand, ontology-driven semantics tries to infer text meaning from some language-independent model of a world which is mapped to the lexicon of a given language. Although a single approach is not sufficiently effective, most of the knowledge-based natural language processing (NLP) systems are usually confined to one of these two models.

The goal of this chapter is to describe the design and development of an NLP system whose lexical-semantic model is not only oriented to the syntax of a given language but is also linked to a language-independent ontology-grounded representation of text meaning. As a result, we have implemented ARTEMIS (Automatically Representing TExt Meaning via an Interlingua-based System), a proof-of-concept prototype which is based on Role and Reference Grammar (RRG) as its linguistic model (Van Valin & LaPolla 1997; Van Valin 2005) and which exploits FunGramKB as its knowledge base (Periñán-Pascual & Arcas-Túnez 2004, 2005, 2007, 2008, 2010a, 2010b; Periñán-Pascual & Mairal-Usón 2009, 2010, 2011; Mairal-Usón & Periñán-Pascual 2009). We also intend to demonstrate that projectionist and constructivist approaches to sentential meaning can be conflated in a computer-tractable model of RRG.

This chapter is organised as follows: Sections 2 and 3 sketch out the FunGramKB and RRG models respectively, where in the latter we also introduce our major changes to the standard functional model; and Section 4 analyses the different processing stages involved in the CLS Constructor, which outputs a cross-language representation of the input text.

2. FunGramKB

ARTEMIS is a knowledge-based system, since it operates with a repository of knowledge (in our case, lexical, constructional and conceptual knowledge) which is clearly separated from the rest of the system and with an inference engine whose role is to apply relevant knowledge in problem resolution.[1] More particularly, ARTEMIS is provided with FunGramKB, a multipurpose lexico-conceptual knowledge base to be implemented in natural language understanding applications.[2] On the one hand, FunGramKB is multipurpose in the sense that it is both multifunctional and multilingual. Thus, FunGramKB has been designed to be potentially reused in many NLP tasks (e.g. information retrieval and extraction, machine translation, dialogue-based systems, etc) and with many natural languages.[3] On the other hand, our knowledge base comprises three major knowledge levels, consisting of several independent but interrelated modules:

a. Lexical level:
   a.1. The Lexicon stores morphosyntactic and collocational information about lexical units. The FunGramKB lexical model is not a literal implementation of the RRG lexicon, although some of the major linguistic assumptions of RRG are still preserved, e.g. the logical structure.
   a.2. The Morphicon helps our system to handle cases of inflectional morphology.

1. In the case of computational linguistics, one of these problems is word sense disambiguation.

2. We use the name "FunGramKB Suite" to refer to our knowledge-engineering tool (www.fungramkb.com) and "FunGramKB" to the resulting knowledge base. FunGramKB Suite was developed in C# using the ASP.NET platform and a MySQL database.

3. English and Spanish are fully supported in the current version of FunGramKB Suite, although we have just begun to work with other languages, such as German, French, Italian, Bulgarian and Catalan.

b. Grammatical level:
   b.1. The Grammaticon stores the constructional schemata which help RRG to construct the syntax-semantics linking algorithm. More particularly, the Grammaticon is composed of several Constructicon modules that are inspired in the four levels of the Lexical Constructional Model (LCM) (Ruiz de Mendoza & Mairal-Usón 2008; Mairal-Usón & Ruiz de Mendoza 2009), i.e. argumental, implicational, illocutionary and discursive.

c. Conceptual level:
   c.1. The Ontology is presented as a hierarchical catalogue of the concepts that a person has in mind, so here is where semantic knowledge is stored in the form of meaning postulates. The Ontology consists of a general-purpose module (i.e. Core Ontology) and several domain-specific terminological modules (i.e. Satellite Ontologies).
   c.2. The Cognicon stores procedural knowledge by means of scripts, i.e. schemata in which a sequence of stereotypical actions is organised on the basis of temporal continuity, and more particularly on Allen's temporal model (Allen 1983; Allen & Ferguson 1994).
   c.3. The Onomasticon stores information about instances of entities and events, such as Bill Gates or 9/11. This module stores two different types of schemata (i.e. snapshots and stories), since instances can be portrayed synchronically or diachronically.

In the FunGramKB architecture, every lexical or grammatical module is language-dependent, whereas every conceptual module is shared by all languages. In other words, linguists must develop one Lexicon, one Morphicon and one Grammaticon for English, one Lexicon, one Morphicon and one Grammaticon for Spanish and so on, but knowledge engineers build just one Ontology, one Cognicon and one Onomasticon to process any language input conceptually. In this scenario, FunGramKB adopts a conceptualist approach, since the Ontology becomes the pivotal module for the whole architecture.

FunGramKB is the product resulting from a knowledge-engineering project, where our major concern has always been its application in linguistically-aware and psychologically-plausible NLP systems. It is for this reason that the linguistic level in our knowledge base is grounded on the RRG theory, briefly described in the following section.

3. Role and Reference Grammar

3.1 The standard model

RRG is one of the most relevant functional models of language in current linguistics. RRG was not actually designed for NLP, but this linguistic theory presents three characteristics which make it a suitable model for NLP:

a. RRG is a model where morphosyntactic structures and grammatical rules are explained in relation to their semantic and communicative functions.
b. RRG is a monostratal theory, where the syntactic and semantic components are directly connected through a "linking algorithm".
c. RRG is a model which owns typological adequacy.

The features (a-c) are essential for a computational model which aims to provide the capability of natural language understanding. Firstly, a functional view of language allows us to capture syntactic-semantic generalizations which are fundamental to explain the semantic motivation of grammatical phenomena. Secondly, the system is more effectively designed if an algorithm is able to account for both the comprehension and the production of linguistic expressions. Thirdly, typological adequacy becomes an added value when working in a multilingual environment.

RRG is concerned with two fundamental aspects of language description: the relational structure, which deals with relations between a predicate and its argument(s), and the non-relational structure, which accounts for the hierarchical organization of phrases, clauses and sentences. Consequently, the notions of "logical structure" and "layered structure of the clause" (LSC) are fundamental in the analysis of language.

On the one hand, RRG rejects the standard formats for representing clause structure (e.g. grammatical relations), as can be seen in Figure 1 (Van Valin & LaPolla 1997: 38).[4]

This hierarchical structure is both semantically and pragmatically motivated, and not only syntactically based: whereas constituents such as the nucleus, core, periphery

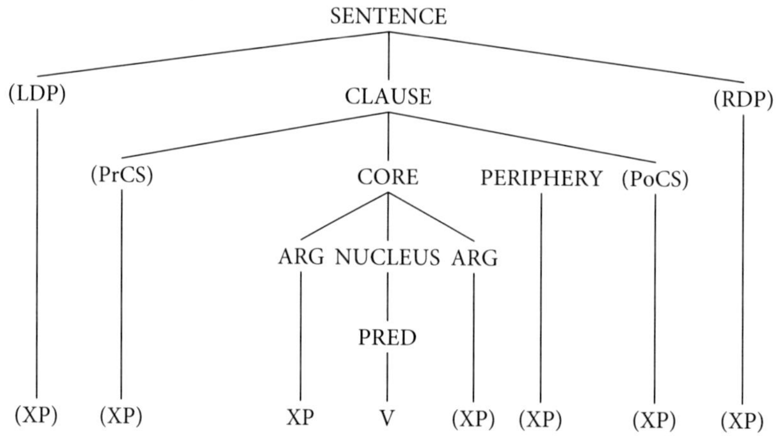

Figure 1. RRG layered structure of the clause

4. Abbreviations: LDP 'left-detached position', RDP 'right-detached position', PrCS 'precore slot', PoCS 'postcore slot', ARG 'argument', and PRED 'predicate'.

and clause are semantically motivated, the detached phrases and the extra-core slots seem to be pragmatically motivated (Van Valin 2005: 8). The LSC is universal; however, cross-linguistic variations are captured by means of the syntactic templates of each language, so syntactic representations are not built on phrase-structure rules.

On the other hand, the semantic representation of a sentence originates from the logical structure assigned to verbs and other predicates in the lexicon on the basis of its distribution in a typology of classes (i.e. state, activity, achievement, semelfactive, accomplishment, active accomplishment, and their corresponding causative forms). To illustrate, (1–3) show that each verb class is represented formally by means of a different logical structure, being composed of elements of a universal semantic metalanguage which consists of constants, variables and semantic operators.[5]

(1)	see: **see'** (x,y)	[state]
(2)	run: **do'** (x, [**run'** (x)])	[activity]
(3)	receive: BECOME **have'** (x,y)	[accomplishment]

Operators such as aspect, modality, tense or illocutionary force, among many others, are also represented in the logical structure of sentences. Thus, the sentence "Peter broke the glass", for example, is assigned the following semantic representation:

(4) $<_{IF}^{DEC} <_{TNS}^{PAST} <_{ASP}^{PERF}$ <[**do'** (Peter, Ø)] CAUSE [BECOME **broken'** (glass)]>>>>

In this model, the syntax-semantics linkage is divided into five steps, as shown in Figure 2:[6]

a. Determine the LSC.
b. Identify the macroroles (i.e. Actor and Undergoer)[7] of the core arguments in terms of the privileged syntactic argument selection hierarchy (Van Valin 2005: 100).
c. Retrieve from the lexicon the logical structure of the predicate in the nucleus of the clause.
d. Assign macroroles to the arguments in the logical structure according to the Actor-Undergoer hierarchy (Van Valin 2005: 126).
e. On the basis of their macroroles, link the arguments determined in step (a) with the arguments found in step (c) until all core arguments are linked.

5. The verb class adscription system is based on Vendler's (1967) Aktionsart distinctions, and the decompositional system is a variant of the one proposed by Dowty (1979).

6. The linkage algorithm has been hugely simplified and adapted from Van Valin (2005: 149–150).

7. The macroroles Actor and Undergoer can be regarded as the "logical subject" and the "logical object" respectively.

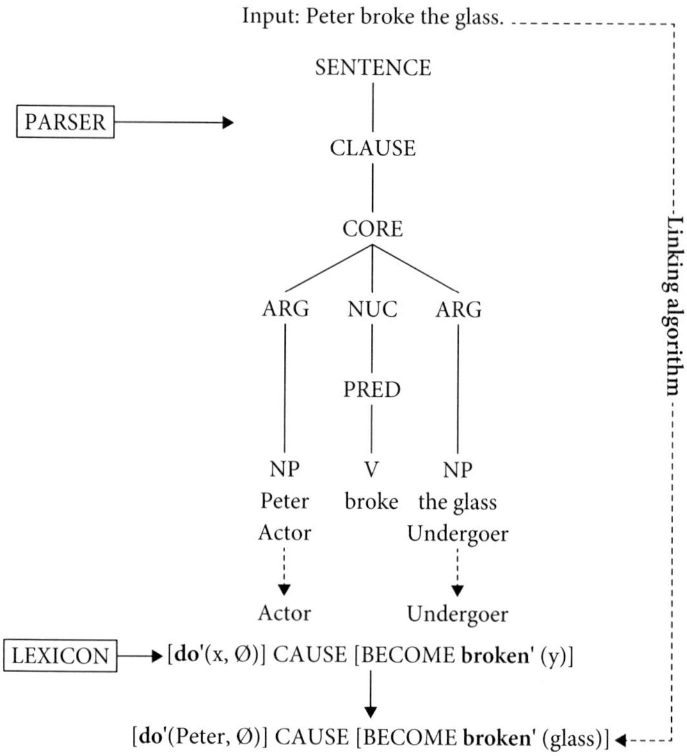

Figure 2. RRG syntax-semantics linkage[8]

Therefore, the macroroles Actor and Undergoer become a critical component in the syntax-semantics linkage. On the whole, the lexicon is the key module in the RRG framework, since the semantic representation of a sentence is built on the logical structure of the predicate. This is the reason why RRG is viewed as a projectionist model of language.

3.2 The computational model

Up to now, there have only been two serious attempts to implement some of the aspects of the RRG theory computationally. For instance, Guest (2009) developed a parser which is able to output the LSC of an English sentence. However, a more challenging research programme can be found in UniArab – Universal Arabic Machine

8. In the latest version of the RRG model, the label NP is now replaced by RP (Reference Phrase), which, unlike NP, is a non-endocentric construct: "The nucleus of an RP is neither restricted to nominals, nor is it restricted to lexical heads" (Van Valin 2009: 708).

Translator (Salem, Hensman & Nolan 2008), an interlingua-based machine translation prototype which is able to provide a working translation of Modern Standard Arabic to English. One of the primary strengths of UniArab is to build the logical structure of an Arabic sentence, but the project does not manage to provide a robust approach to the semantics of lexical units.

ARTEMIS comes into the scene as one of the first systems which employs a robust knowledge base to generate a full-fledged logical structure to be used in NLP applications requiring language comprehension capabilities. This new approach led us to make some changes to the RRG standard model, since an enhanced representation of the logical structure was required, as explained in the following section.

3.2.1 *The construction category*

Undoubtedly, constructional meaning improves the descriptive power of a semantic theory. Van Valin (2005: 3) recognised that "a theory of clause structure should capture all of the universal features of clauses", so we integrated the construction as a universal category into the LSC. Therefore, the clause is configured now as one or more argumental constructions (L1-CONSTRUCTION)[9] which are recursively arranged, as shown in Figure 3.

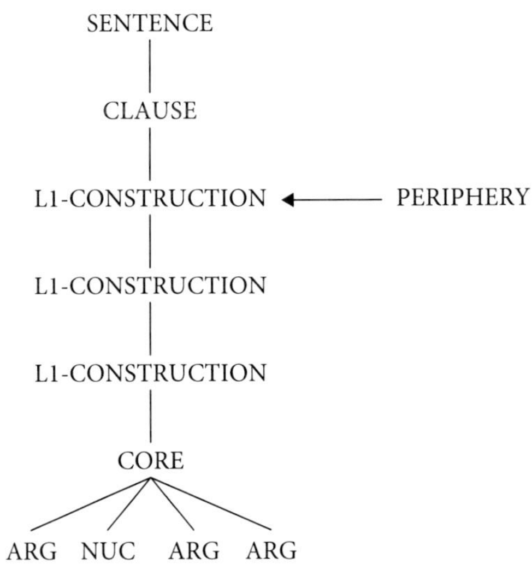

Figure 3. Enhanced model of the LSC

9. In fact, this type of construction belongs to the Level 1 of the LCM, i.e. the argumental layer which accounts for the core grammatical properties of lexical items.

It is clear that compositionality is one of the most distinctive features of sentential processing, but this is such an overused term that we want to focus on some nuances that will help us to provide a clear definition of "construction". Thus, following Pelletier's categorization (2012), FunGramKB adopts a compositional wholist model of computational semantics, which integrates the "functional compositionality" – as defined in (5) – of sentential semantics with the "ontological holism" – as defined in (6) – of constructional semantics.[10]

(5) The μ of a whole is a function of the μ's of its parts and the ways those parts are combined (Pelletier 2012: 153).[11]
(6) Some properties can only be attributed to entities that are not individuals (Pelletier 2012: 156).

In other words, functional compositionality allows a complex whole (e.g. the sentence) to have things (e.g. sentential meaning) which are not present in the parts (e.g. the words), providing that the function introduces this same material every time it is faced with the same parts and manner of combination (e.g. the construction). On the other hand, ontological holism allows a complex whole (e.g. the construction) to have properties (e.g. constructional meaning) which are not properties of any part (e.g. the words). In accordance with these complementary distinctions resulting from the view of compositionality and holism, our definition of "construction" is presented as follows:

(7) A construction is a pairing of form and meaning, serving as a building block in the compositionality of sentential semantics, whose meaning cannot be fully derived from the sum of the lexical meanings of the individual constructs taking part in the utterance.[12]

Thus, from the FunGramKB approach, the sentence "John pounded the nail flat into the wall" consists of three argumental constructions: Kernel-2, Transitive Resultative and Caused-Motion.[13]

(8) $[[[\text{John pounded the nail}]_{\text{Kernel-2}}\ \text{flat}]_{\text{Transitive-Resultative}}\ \text{into the wall}]_{\text{Caused-Motion}}$

The remaining components can only be perceived as constructs, whose meanings are directly derived from their meaning postulates. In terms of the FunGramKB model,

10. Unlike the computational meaning with which the word "ontology" is used throughout this chapter, the term "ontological holism" should be understood in its philosophical sense.

11. μ symbolizes the "meaning function", i.e. X = μ(A), where A is some syntactic item and X is the meaning of A.

12. Derivative morphemes are not considered to be linguistic objects in the current version of FunGramKB, so the minimal constructs in the processing of linguistic realizations take the form of lexical units.

13. Kernel Constructions correspond to basic intransitive (type 1), monotransitive (type 2) and ditransitive (type 3) constructions, where zero-argument verbs raise a Kernel-0 Construction.

lexical constructs get their meaning from the meaning postulates stored in the Ontology, whereas constructional meaning is shaped by the Core Grammar in the Lexicon and the constructional schemata in the Grammaticon.

The FunGramKB constructional schema, which serves as a machine-tractable representation of the construction, is defined in terms of constraints which license functional compositionality with other constructs or constructions. To illustrate, Figure 4 presents the attribute-value matrix (AVM) of the Caused-Motion Construction.

The constructional schema contains the properties common to all the instances of a given construction. Therefore, the Grammaticon stores types of constructions to which words in the Lexicon are linked. Up to now, these types of constructions are arranged in a flat organization, instead of relating them in terms of an inheritance hierarchy.[14] The properties which are defined in constructional schemata are rather independent from language so as to determine cross-linguistic generalizations. Indeed, phrase realizations of variables (e.g. NP, PP etc) and the typical prepositions heading prepositional phrases are the only two attributes in the AVM which are language-dependent (Figure 5).

L1-constr [Type CMOT]
CLS [Aktionsart CACC]
Variables [Type x]
[Type y]
[Type w
Role goal
Phrase PP
Syntax argument
Prefer +PLACE_00]
COREL scheme +(e1: +MOVE_00 (x1)Agent (x2: x)Theme (x3)Location (x4)Origin (x5: w)Goal (f1: (e2: <EVENT>))Manner)

Figure 4. The constructional schema of the Caused-Motion Construction[15]

14. For example, Goldberg (1995) suggested how to capture generalizations across constructions by means of an inheritance hierarchy of constructions, where the lower levels are specializations in form and function of the highest level. Whether this inheritance network is monotonic or non-monotonic is still a debatable issue.

15. Abbreviations: L1-constr 'L1-constructional schema' and Prefer 'Selectional preference'.

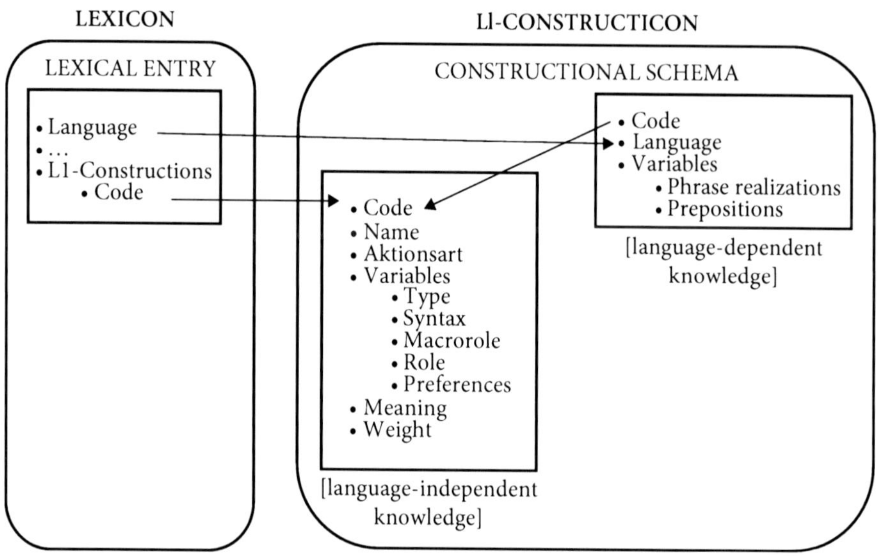

Figure 5. Attributes of the constructional schema

It is important to bear in mind that the universality of the category construction does not involve the claim that the whole inventory of constructional schemata should be shared by any language. In fact, a given construction can be licensed in a particular language if and only if there is at least one entry in the Lexicon which contains a pointer to that construction.[16] As a result, there was a need to create an L1-Constructicon module, whose interface is shown in Figure 6, for every language in FunGramKB Suite.

Although "(...) there has been a disagreement in the CxG literature about whether or not 'constructions must have meaning'" (Sag 2012: 87), FunGramKB constructions are essentially meaning-bearing devices, where their semantic burden lies in the Aktionsart (i.e. aspectual meaning) and/or the COREL scheme (i.e. conceptual meaning).[17] Indeed, we can infer from the definition (7) that the *raison d'être* of a construction is its semantic contribution to that part of the meaning of the sentence which cannot be derived from the lexical units.

In short, FunGramKB adopts a hybrid approach to constructional meaning, i.e. halfway between projectionism (e.g. Jackendoff 1990; Pustejovsly 1991; Rappaport Hovav & Levin 1998) and constructivism (e.g. Goldberg 1995; Croft 2001). On the one hand, our language model is much closer to projectionism in terms of how linguistic realizations of constructions are related to their semantic descriptions; in fact, Fun

16. As shown in Figure 5, construction-type codes in the lexical entry serve as pointers to constructional schemata.

17. COREL (COnceptual Representation Language) is an interface language to formalize conceptual knowledge in FunGramKB. Periñán-Pascual and Mairal-Usón (2010) described the grammar of this notational language.

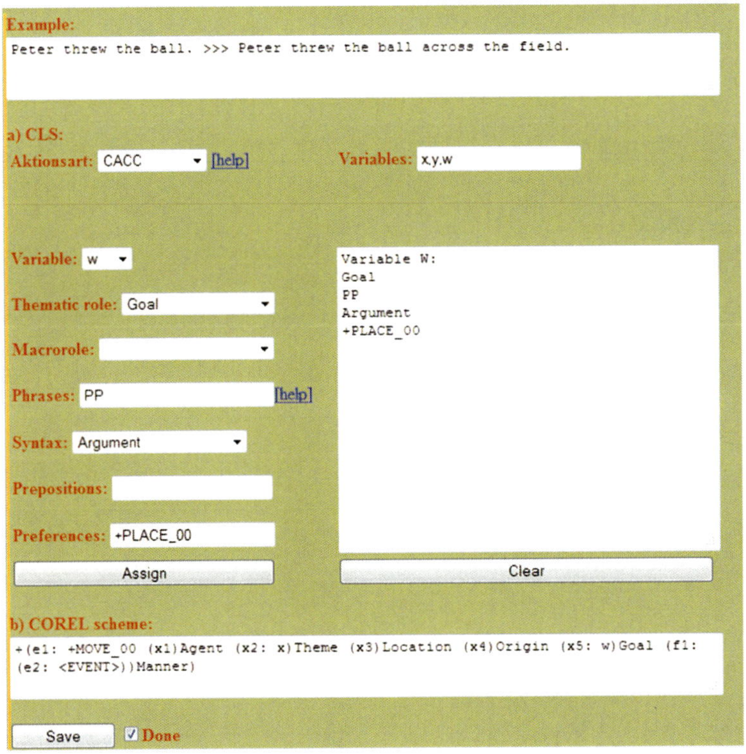

Figure 6. The L1-Constructicon interface

GramKB shows a clear-cut separation between the linguistic modules, i.e. the Lexicon and the Grammaticon, where the projection from syntax to semantics goes through the pointers in the lexical entries. On the other hand, our language model is much closer to constructivism in terms of how lexical units and constructions jointly affect sentential meaning.

3.2.2 *The conceptual logical structure*

Another key difference from the standard RRG model is the format of the logical structure, which now becomes a real cross-language representation to be used in multilingual NLP systems with FunGramKB as their knowledge base. As a result, there was a shift of the logical structure into the conceptual logical structure (CLS), which involved a number of changes as illustrated in (9).

(9) Peter broke the glass.
Logical structure:
$<_{IF}^{DEC} <_{TNS}^{PAST} <_{ASP}^{PERF}$ <[**do'** (Peter, Ø)] CAUSE [BECOME **broken'** (glass)]>>>>

CLS:
$<_{IF}^{DEC}<_{TNS}^{PAST}<_{ASP}^{PERF}<_{CONSTR\text{-}L1}^{KER2}<[_{AKT}^{CACC}$[**+BREAK_00(%PETER_00-** Theme, **$GLASS_00**-Referent)]]>>>>

Firstly, the instantiation of variables takes the form not of predicates but of ontological concepts (e.g. the terminal concept $GLASS_00 instead of the predicate *glass*). Secondly, every instantiated concept is assigned a thematic role from the thematic frame of the event to which the verb is linked (e.g. %PETER_00 is the Theme and $GLASS_00 is the Referent in the cognitive situation described by the event +BREAK_00). In contrast to RRG, thematic roles do play a paramount role in the CLS. Indeed, ARTEMIS is only able to perform the lexico-conceptual linkage once the constituents in the parse tree are tagged with the FunGramKB thematic roles. The NLP system can subsequently reach a deeper level of comprehension by deriving the extended COREL scheme (10) from the CLS in (9).

(10) +(e1: +DAMAGE_00 (x1: %PETER_00)$_{Theme}$ (x2: $GLASS_00)$_{Referent}$ (f1: (e2: +SPLIT_00 (x1)$_{Theme}$ (x2)$_{Referent}$))$_{Result}$)
'Peter damaged the glass into pieces'

We intend to enrich the extended COREL scheme not only with the knowledge from the meaning postulates in the Ontology but also with that from the scripts in the Cognicon and from the snapshots and stories in the Onomasticon.[18] Thirdly, every argumental construction is embodied in a constructional operator (i.e. CONSTR-L1) whose scope is the core of the clause. Finally, the Aktionsart operator (i.e. AKT) together with an "argument pattern"[19] headed by the event – as shown in (11) – replaces the semantic skeleton originated by the RRG decompositional system.

(11) [event (argument-role, argument-role...)]

These two new operators in the logical structure (i.e. CONSTR-L1 and AKT) play a joint role in shaping sentential meaning, since a given argumental construction not only contributes to the enrichment of the COREL scheme but also helps to determine the Aktionsart. In particular, and due to factors such as the linearity of processing, the concatenation of grammatical constituents and the functional compositionality described in the previous section, the right-most argumental construction which the processor finds in the input is the one which directly impacts on the aspectual value of the verb, as shown in (12–14).[20]

18. For example, a snapshot containing personal knowledge about Peter could reveal that he suffers from haemophilia, adding a potential risk to the state of affairs portrayed by the sentence.

19. Despite its name, an argument pattern can also introduce a further nucleus in the case of nuclear cosubordination, just as occurs with the Resultative Construction.

20. It should be noted that the right-most construction in the input is represented by the left-most CONSTR-L1 operator in the bracketed representation of the CLS.

(12) $<_{IF}^{DECL}<_{Tense}^{PAST}<_{CONSTR\text{-}L1}^{KER2}<_{AKT}^{ACT}$ [**$POUND_02** (**%JOHN_00**-Agent, +**NAIL_01**-Goal)]>>>>
'John pounded the nail'

(13) $<_{IF}^{DECL}<_{Tense}^{PAST}<_{CONSTR\text{-}L1}^{RESU}<_{CONSTR\text{-}L1}^{KER2}<_{AKT}^{CACC}$ [**$POUND_02** (**%JOHN_00**-Agent, +**NAIL_01**-Goal, +**FLAT_00**-Result)]>>>>>
'John pounded the nail flat'

(14) $<_{IF}^{DECL}<_{Tense}^{PAST}<_{CONSTR\text{-}L1}^{CMOT}<_{CONSTR\text{-}L1}^{KER2}<_{AKT}^{CACC}$ [**$POUND_02** (**%JOHN_00**-Agent, +**NAIL_01**-Goal, +**WALL_00**-Goal)]>>>>>
'John pounded the nail into the wall'

As occurs in (12), Kernel Constructions are the only type of constructions which are not formalised in the Constructicon, but are modeled within the lexical entry of the verb. On the other hand, in (13) the L1-Constructicon raises the Transitive-Resultative Construction (RESU) which makes the state of affairs become an a causative accomplishment (CACC), whereas in (14) the Caused-Motion Construction (CMOT) similarly brings forward a causative accomplishment. As shown in (13–14), constructional meaning ultimately determines aspectual meaning.[21] The following section describes how the whole CLS is automatically built.

4. The CLS constructor in ARTEMIS

To avoid being distracted from implementation details, Figure 7 shows the UML diagram[22] which serves to describe the logical activity which models the behaviour of the CLS Constructor.

In the following sections, we describe the main stages involved in the syntax-semantics linking algorithm with FunGramKB. To illustrate, we will use as an example the sentence (15), whose CLS is (16).

(15) John pounded the nail flat into the wall.

(16) $<_{IF}^{DECL}<_{Tense}^{PAST}<_{CONSTR\text{-}L1}^{CMOT}<_{CONSTR\text{-}L1}^{RESU}<_{CONSTR\text{-}L1}^{KER2}<_{AKT}^{CACC}$ [**$POUND_02** (**%JOHN_00**-Agent, +**NAIL_01**-Goal, +**FLAT_00**-Result, +**WALL_00**-Goal)]>>>>>>

21. Periñán-Pascual (2013) describes the interface between the Lexicon and the L1-Constructicon in sentential processing.

22. UML (Unified Modeling Language) is "a general-purpose visual modeling language that is used to specify, visualize, construct, and document the artifacts of a software system" (Rumbaugh, Jacobson & Booch 1999: 3).

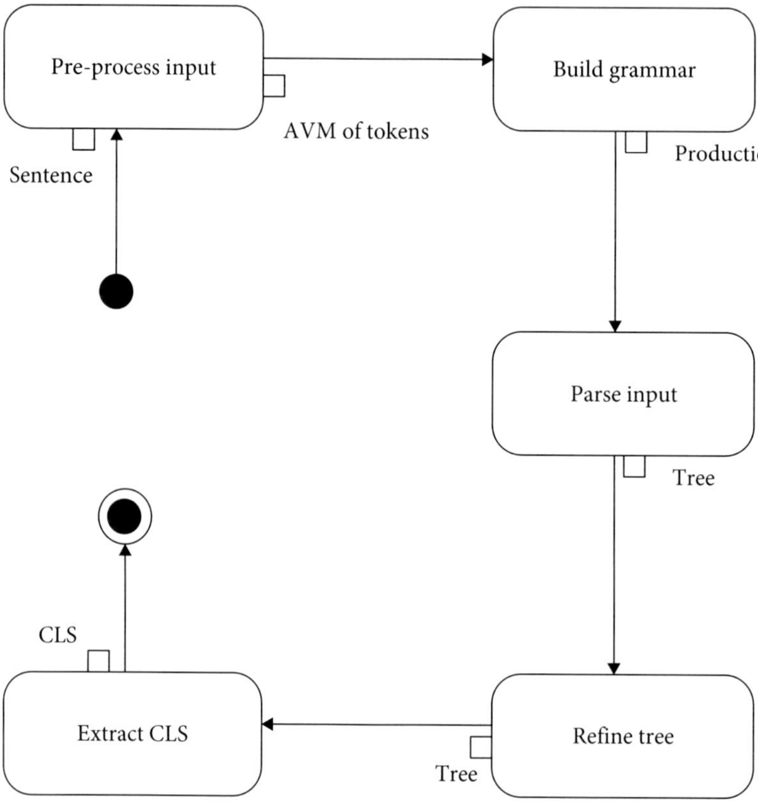

Figure 7. The ARTEMIS process (abridged version)

4.1 Pre-processing

First of all, the input is split into sentences, and then into word tokens. In other words, this task consists in segmenting the input into basic units of analysis. In the following task, the word tokens are lemmatised. Finally, every token is labeled with a unique part-of-speech tag. We employed the OpenNLP library (Baldridge, Morton & Bierner 2001) for tokenization and part-of-speech tagging, and the LemmaSharp library (Jursic, Mozetic, Erjavec & Lavrac 2010) for lemmatization. Following the object-oriented paradigm, we represent feature-based structures as AVMs which are computationally implemented in the form of user-defined objects in the programming language C#.[23] For example, this multi-task stage outputs the AVMs shown in Figure 8.

It is worth noting that part-of-speech tagging involves predicate conceptualization, bringing in the problem of word-sense disambiguation. Since lexical information in

23. Together with C++ and Java, C# (C-Sharp) is one of the most popular general-purpose object-oriented programming languages in modern computing.

Form	John
Lemma	John
POS	noun
Number	sing
Concept	%JOHN_00

Form	pounded
Lemma	pound
POS	verb
Tense	past
Concept	$POUND_02

Form	the
Lemma	the
POS	determiner

Form	nail
Lemma	nail
POS	noun
Number	singular
Concept	+NAIL_01

Form	flat
Lemma	flat
POS	adjective
Concept	+NAIL_01

Form	into
Lemma	into
POS	preposition

Form	wall
Lemma	wall
POS	noun
Number	singular
Concept	+WALL_00

Figure 8. AVMs of word tokens

FunGramKB is linked to the senses of words (i.e. sense-oriented approach), a word-sense disambiguator should firstly tag the lemmas with a single conceptual label from the Ontology, or, in the case of proper nouns, from the Onomasticon. This disambiguator is still work in progress, so now users must disambiguate polysemous words from the ARTEMIS interface before the parsing occurs.

4.2. Grammar building

ARTEMIS follows the well-known paradigm of constraint-based grammars, also known as unification grammars, which can encode grammatical knowledge irrespectively of the type of NLP algorithm.[24] The key component of constraint-based grammars can be found in the complex formal descriptions of grammatical units as AVMs, describing features which can be merged through the unification operation. Thus, parsing is not guided just by the sequence of phrase-structure rules but also by the satisfaction of a set of constraints,[25] which are intended to determine structural

24. Moreover, from the approach of computational linguistics, the time of grammar development with the formalisms of unification grammars is significantly shorter than with phrase-structure grammars (Uszkoreit & Zaenen 1995).

25. As Cooper (2002: 311) noted, parsing is reduced to a constraint satisfaction problem, i.e. "to ensure syntactic well-formedness of a word sequence it is necessary to ensure that all constraints are simultaneously satisfied by the sequence". For this reason, unification grammars are said to adopt a "constraint-satisfaction model".

preference and semantic plausibility, where no single type of constraint is able to resolve any type of local syntactic ambiguity.

Unlike an RRG syntactic analysis such as the one shown in Figure 2, which is based on an inventory of templates, i.e. syntactic trees which do not explicitly state the order of constituents but just their hierarchical organization, ARTEMIS relies on three types of feature-based production rules, i.e. syntactic, constructional and lexical rules. Firstly, syntactic rules are aimed to build the enhanced framework of the LSC (Figure 3). Secondly, constructional rules serve to embed the constructional schemata stored in the L1-Constructicon into the enhanced LSC. When constructional rules are built, some default values in constructional schemata are replaced by those values in the Core Grammar of the lexical entry of the verb; on the contrary, specific values in constructional schemata override those stated in the lexical entry, so non-monotonic inheritance takes place in the projection operation between the Lexicon and the L1-Constructicon. For instance, Figure 9 shows the Core Grammar of the verb *pound*.[26]

In this example, the verb is linked to the constructional schema of the Caused-Motion Construction, which was shown in Figure 4. Thus, the constructional CLS can inherit monotonically the AVMs of the X and Y variables from the lexical entry, whereas the AVM of the W variable is introduced and the Aktionsart value in the

```
[ [Headword      pound]                                                  ]
[ [Core grammar  [CLS  [Aktionsart  ACT]                              ]] ]
[ [              [     [Variables   [Type       x              ]      ]] ]
[ [              [     [            [Role       agent          ]      ]] ]
[ [              [     [            [Macrorole  agent          ]      ]] ]
[ [              [     [            [Phrase     NP             ]      ]] ]
[ [              [     [            [Syntax     argument       ]      ]] ]
[ [              [     [            [Prefer     +HUMAN_00      ]      ]] ]
[ [              [     [                                              ]] ]
[ [              [     [            [Type       y                   ] ]] ]
[ [              [     [            [Role       theme               ] ]] ]
[ [              [     [            [Macrorole  undergoer           ] ]] ]
[ [              [     [            [Phrase     NP                  ] ]] ]
[ [              [     [            [Syntax     argument            ] ]] ]
[ [              [     [            [Prefer     +CORPUSCULAR_00     ] ]] ]
[ [              [L1-constr [Type  CMOT]]                              ] ]
```

Figure 9. The Core Grammar of *pound*

26. It should be noted that, instead of letting lexical entries store the default macrorole, phrase realization and syntax of variable instantiations, these types of knowledge are actually retrieved from the RRG theoretical framework. Mairal-Usón and Periñán-Pascual (2009) presented the anatomy of the FunGramKB Lexicon by describing the different types of features which form part of a predicate's lexical entry.

lexical entry is overriden. Indeed, this is grounded on one of the basic tenets of constructivist grammars to resolve the conflict between lexical semantics and constructional semantics, i.e. the override principle (Michaelis 2003: 101):

> If lexical and structural meanings conflict, the semantic specifications of the lexical element conform to those of the grammatical structure with which that lexical item is combined.

Thirdly, lexical rules provide the tokens with morphosyntactic and semantic information from the Lexicon and the Ontology respectively. Unlike syntactic rules, which users can pre-define through the Grammar Development Environment, constructional and lexical rules are created dynamically at runtime. In other words, in order to make sentential processing faster and more effective, ARTEMIS will build only those constructional and lexical rules which can be directly derived from the constructional schemata and lexical entries being linked to the predicates in the input stream. Therefore, this stage finally outputs a single text file containing those constraint-based production rules which are required to parse a given input text. In this fashion, the system can gain efficiency by handling only those rules which are potentially relevant, thus minimizing the complexity of processing.

Before we begin to describe the ARTEMIS parser, we should note that Pickering and Van Gompel (2006) remind us that one of the main concerns in the language processing driven by a feature-based unification grammar is that the whole set of constraints which can be involved in the processing should be identified beforehand, as well as the precise way these constraints can affect that processing. As a result, this type of computational model requires a large-scale repository of fine-grained morphosyntactic, semantic and pragmatic knowledge on which NLP algorithms are based. Otherwise, the system would have to deal with a "lexico-constructional knowledge bottleneck". Indeed, this is the risk that comes when you fail to develop properly one of the key components in this type of applications, i.e. the knowledge base.

4.3 Syntactic parsing

Since ARTEMIS is currently a proof-of-concept NLP system, we chose to perform our syntactic analysis with the constraint-based chart parser in the NLTK library (Bird, Klein & Loper 2009: 327–356).[27] More particularly, the parser is based on Earley's algorithm (Earley 1970), which can be described as a bottom-up chart parser with

27. Since the FunGramKB Suite is developed in ASP.NET and C#, it was necessary to use IronPython to integrate the NLTK Python packages into the .NET framework. However, it is worth noting that Python is a script language, so the parser coding is in plain text files which are compiled at runtime and then interpreted. Therefore, as speed becomes a determining factor in any NLP system, we intend to implement a C# version of this chart parser when applied in a realistic scenario.

top-down prediction, thus improving the efficiency of parsing. Chart parsing uses dynamic programming to parse the text by iteratively adding edges to a chart. Each edge represents a hypothesis about the tree structure for a subsequence of the text. The chart parser incrementally adds new edges to the chart, where the chart rules specify the conditions under which new edges should be added to the chart. Parsing is complete when the chart reaches a stage where none of the chart rules adds any new edges. The psychologically-plausible behaviour of this parser lies in the fact that it is:

a. an incremental left-corner parser, where each successive word being encountered is incorporated into a larger structure by combining bottom-up processing with top-down predictions, and
b. a parallel parser, since multiple parse structures can be generated locally, so there is no need to re-analyse the input if one parse structure proves incorrect (i.e. no backtracking).

From a psycholinguistic approach, in contrast with the two-stage model of sentential processing,[28] the architecture of the constraint-based parser takes the form of an interactive processor which employs both syntactic and semantic information from the beginning of the analysis. In our case, ARTEMIS is based on an interactive model of language analysis which is built upon a database whose (non-)linguistic knowledge is stored in several rather independent modules.[29]

The second task in this stage consists in resolving global syntactic ambiguity, that is, the system should select a winner from among the multiple parse trees which can be generated from a given input sentence. A particularly common source of syntactic ambiguity is found in constructional co-occurrence, or the combination of several constructions within the same clause. Figure 10 illustrates the linguistic phenomenon of constructional co-occurrence, which is driven by the operation of constructional merger, and the impact on the syntax-semantics interface.

Each L1-CONSTRUCTION in the LSC (e.g. Kernel-2, Transitive-Resultative and Caused-Motion) typically involves the introduction of at least one argumental slot into the core of the clause (e.g. two, one and one for the previous three constructions respectively), so we could identify in the CLS a distinctive "argumental subpattern" for every instantiation of a given type of construction, where the first argumental subpattern (i.e. the bottom-most L1-CONSTRUCTION in the LSC) serves as the base of the argumental expansion. Consequently, any further L1-construction results from the merger of the new argumental slot(s) with the constructional base. For example, in Figure 10 the argumental pattern consists of three subpatterns, as shown in (17).

---

28. One of the best-known instances of the two-stage model is the Garden-Path (Frazier & Fodor 1978; Frazier 1979), in which a processor makes some initial decisions on the basis of strategies defined exclusively in terms of syntactic information and in a second phase semantic information is used to check whether the initial analysis is adequate.

29. See Section 2.

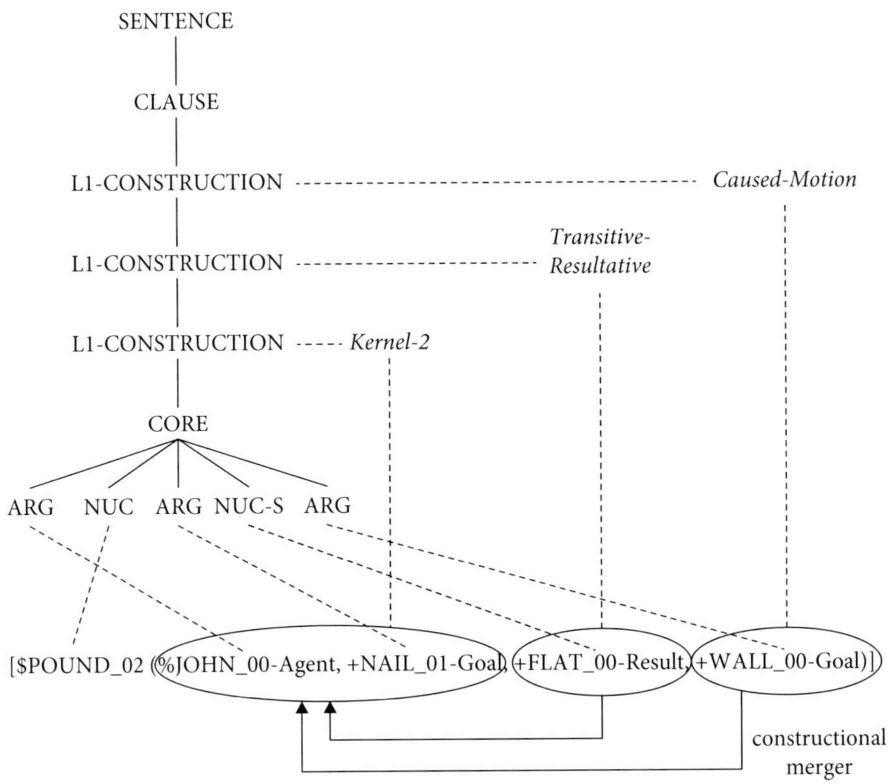

Figure 10. ARTEMIS syntax-semantics linkage

(17) Kernel-2, or constructional base: [**$POUND_02** (**%JOHN_00**-Agent, **+NAIL_01**-Goal)]
Resultative: [**$POUND_02** (**%JOHN_00**-Agent, **+NAIL_01**-Goal, **+FLAT_00**-Result)]
Caused-Motion: [**$POUND_02** (**%JOHN_00**-Agent, **+NAIL_01**-Goal, **+WALL_00**-Goal)]

Therefore, from the approach of the syntax-semantics linkage, we can conclude that:

a. the argumental pattern in the CLS is made up of one or more argumental slots, which are instantiated in constructs with the syntactic function of argument (ARG) or subordinated nucleus (NUC-S) in the core of the LSC, and
b. the semantic constraints determined by the constructional schema assigned to each type of construction in the LSC should also be validated for the corresponding argumental subpattern in the CLS.

Thus, since constructional co-occurrence is a specific instance of functional compositionality, we derive as a corollary the principle of argumental compositionality:

(18) The number of slots of the argumental pattern in the CLS must be equal to the sum of the number of slots in each constructional schema in the LSC.

When dealing with the resolution of the global syntactic ambiguity raised by constructional co-occurrence, we noted that argumental constructions cannot co-occur freely. For example, the Inchoative cannot co-occur with the Middle Construction in the same clause, or the Kernel-2 with the Intransitive Resultative, among many other impossible combinations. Therefore, we devised a weight-based distribution method to restrict constructional co-occurrence in the clause. Firstly, argumental constructions were distributed into groups on the basis of the number of arguments which are involved (i.e. one, two or three) and of the FunGramKB module from where the system retrieves most of the knowledge required to build the constructional rule (i.e. the Lexicon for Kernel Constructions and the L1-Constructicon for the remainder). Secondly, a weight was assigned to each constructional group resulting from the previous step. As shown in Table 1, the weight of the construction is fixed in proportion to the number of its argumental slots, and the weight is also greater if the constructional schema is derived from the L1-Constructicon rather than from the Lexicon.[30]

Table 1. Weight-based distribution of argumental constructions

Group	Description	Weight	Example
A.	An argument subpattern derived from a one-argument constructional schema in the L1-Constructicon	1	Inchoative Unexpressed object
B.	An argument subpattern derived from the one-argument constructional schema in the Lexicon Core Grammar	2	Kernel-1
C.	An argument subpattern derived from a two-argument constructional schema in the L1-Constructicon	3	Middle Instrument subject Intransitive resultative Location subject
D.	An argument subpattern derived from the two-argument constructional schema in the Lexicon Core Grammar	4	Kernel-2
E.	An argument subpattern derived from a three-argument constructional schema in the L1-Constructicon	5	Benefactive Caused motion Dative Transitive resultative
F.	An argument subpattern derived from the three-argument constructional schema in the Lexicon Core Grammar	6	Kernel-3

30. Although constructional merger needs further in-depth corpus-based research, our initial experiments have led us to define these two criteria as determining factors in the arrangement of constructional groups.

Thirdly, we determined the four principles which license constructional merger:

a. Principle of Constructional Anchorage: any L1-CONSTR node above the bottom-most one in the LSC should be argumentally anchored on the latter. In other words, the argumental slots in the constructional base should also be taken into account for the validation of the schemata linked to subsequent constructional types in the clause.
b. Principle of Argumental Expansion: the introduction of an L1-CONSTR node in the LSC typically involves the introduction of at least one argumental slot in the core. More particularly, in the case of those constructions serving as the constructional base, the number of arguments ranges from zero to three; on the other hand, any other further constructional type usually introduces one new argument.
c. Principle of Constructional Base Restriction: the constructional base can only be performed by Kernel Constructions or by one-argument constructional schemata (i.e. A, B, D and F group constructions). Indeed, these are the only types of constructions allowed to take this position in the LSC; otherwise, the compliance with the Principle of Constructional Anchorage would inevitably violate the Principle of Argumental Expansion.
d. Principle of Constructional Unicity: a given type of construction can occur only once in the same clause.

According to the above four principles, the operation of constructional merger can now be defined as the binary relation R^{Merger}, which is logically formalised in (19).

(19) $R^{Merger} \subsetneq \Phi \times \Omega \wedge ((\exists\varphi \in \Phi)\ (\exists\omega \in \Omega)\ (\langle\varphi, \omega\rangle \in R^{Merger})) \wedge ((\varphi' R^{Merger} \omega' \wedge \varphi'' R^{Merger} \omega'') \rightarrow (\varphi' \neq \varphi'') \wedge (\omega' = \omega''))$, where $\Phi = \{c, e\}$ and $\Omega = \{a, b, d, f\}$

where the variables [a-f] represent the argumental constructions belonging to the constructional groups [A-F] respectively. In particular, the above principles are applied to guide the mappings between constructional sets, since $\neg((\forall\varphi \in \Phi)\ (\forall\omega \in \Omega)\ (\langle\varphi, \omega\rangle \in R^{Merger}))$. For example, $\{\langle c, d\rangle, \langle e, f\rangle\} \not\subseteq R^{Merger}$, because two constructions which have the same number of argumental slots cannot co-occur; or for instance, $\langle c, f\rangle \not\subseteq R^{Merger}$, because the schema of any further construction added to the constructional base should have a higher number of argumental slots than those in the constructional base. In both examples, the Principles of Constructional Anchorage and Argumental Expansion could not be jointly complied with. In the end, the different possibilities of combining constructions are finally guided by the constructional merger relation, i.e. $R^{Merger} = \{\langle c, a\rangle, \langle c, b\rangle, \langle e, a\rangle, \langle e, b\rangle, \langle e, d\rangle\}$,[31] provided that constraints in constructional schemata are satisfied. To illustrate, the constructional merger taking place in Figure 10 is defined as $R^{Merger:\ John\ pounded\ the\ nail\ flat\ into\ the\ wall}$ = {‹Transitive-Resultative, Kernel-2›, ‹Caused-Motion, Kernel-2›}.

31. Strictly speaking, constructional merger is an asymmetric relation, since it is always the new argumental slot which is merged with the constructional base, and not the other way around.

However, although many incompatibilities in constructional co-occurrence are detected with the previous weight-based distribution method, global syntactic ambiguity can still persist, so there would be finally more than one parse tree. At this time, each tree would be provided with a weighted value as a result of the addition of all the weights corresponding to the constructions involved in the constructional merger operation.[32] Consequently, the winning parse tree is that which has the highest weighted value.

The idea of creating a weight-based scheme for argumental constructions was motivated primarily by the existence of psycholinguistic evidence showing that the human sentence parser can take into account the frequency of some constructions in order to resolve local ambiguity (cf. Pickering & Van Gompel 2006). In this regard, our current prototype can be improved in two key features. Firstly, it would be more effective to apply the "weight-based priority" from the beginning of the syntactic parsing with the purpose of minimizing global syntactic ambiguity. In fact, in line with the development of a psychologically-plausible interactive model of the sentence processor, we should not allow constraints to be satisfied in two stages, but we should consistently integrate the various constraint sources from the very beginning. Secondly, the relative frequency of constructions belonging to the same group can also be taken into consideration to resolve syntactic ambiguity, requiring us to perform a corpus-based research to obtain this probabilistic knowledge. In a nutshell, any improvement in the syntactic parser should be aimed at minimizing global syntactic ambiguity by resolving all instances of local structural ambiguity as they arise during the processing.

At the end of this stage, the winning parse tree is stored in an XML file. To illustrate, Appendix 1 shows the XML-formatted parse tree for the sentence "John pounded the nail into the wall", and Appendix 2 presents the XSD schema against which XML-formatted parse trees are validated to check well-formedness.

4.4 Parse tree refinement

This stage is aimed to structure the parse tree *à la RRG*, in such a way that we facilitate the building of the graphical representation of the tree[33] and the CLS. This stage consists of two basic tasks, i.e. relocating tree nodes and filtering out node attributes, whose XML-based procedures are actually very similar: both of them have as input the winning XML-formatted parse tree and support the refinement of that tree in accordance with the knowledge stored in other XML files. For example, when relocating tree nodes in the parse tree, (20) provides the system with the following instructions: any argument (ARG) or subordinated nucleus (NUC-S) introduced by L1-constructions

32. See Table 1.

33. More particularly, the XML file was mapped to the DOT language in GraphViz (www.graphviz.org) to draw the directed acyclic graph.

(CONSTR-L1) must be moved to the core in the clause, whereas all adjuncts must be placed under the same category of periphery (PER).

(20) <Nodes>
<Parent Node="CONSTR-L1">
<Child Target="CORE">ARG</Child>
<Child Target="CORE">NUC-S</Child>
<Child Target="PER">ADJUNCT</Child>
</Parent>
</Nodes>

For example, when filtering out attributes, (21) is used to identify the relevant attributes of the argument node (ARG). If the node is accompanied by non-relevant attributes, then they will be removed from the parse tree. On the contrary, if a required attribute does not go with the node, then the search will be performed among its subordinated nodes and, in the case of a failed attempt, among its superordinates. If the given attribute is finally not found, then it will be created with a null value.[34]

(21) <Node Type="ARG">
<Att>Type</Att>
<Att>Concept</Att>
<Att>Role</Att>
<Att>Macrorole</Att>
</Node>

XPath is the technology used for the search of elements such as nodes and attributes.

4.5 CLS extraction

At the final stage, the CLS results from the extraction of the most relevant semantic units together with their attributes from the XML-formatted refined tree in the previous stage. To accomplish this stage, we designed an XSLT[35] stylesheet which can define the pattern-matching rules for transforming the XML document into a bracketed representation of the CLS, resulting in tasks such as defining the style properties of elements,[36] changing the order in which elements appear in the CLS, and filtering some elements on the basis of a certain property. In other words, the syntax-driven

34. Since ARTEMIS is still a work-in-progress system, a grammatical feature provided with a null-value attribute should be understood as a grammatical gap in the computational implementation of the RRG theory. When ARTEMIS becomes a full-fledged system to process real-life texts, then null values will be non-existent.

35. XSLT stands for "Extensible Stylesheet Language Transformations".

36. For instance, the FunGramKB concepts are rendered in boldface, and the type and value of operators in sub- and superscript characters respectively.

semantics is so embedded in the parse tree itself, certainly much more than in the RRG model, that the system will do nothing but remove the morphosyntactic units of the LSC and relocate the operators according to their scope. For the formal description of the CLS notation, Appendix 3 presents the context-free grammar written in EBNF[37] as well as its graphical representation.

To summarize, Appendix 4 shows a fine-grained activity diagram for the whole process of CLS construction.

4.6 Final remark

At this point, we return to the issue of the linguistic models influencing our system and focus on the so-called "linking problem". In this respect, ARTEMIS adopts a monostratal model of language, but we do not fully agree with RRG that the relationship between semantic and syntactic relations should be conditioned by a hierarchy of semantic roles. It is true that macroroles in the enhanced LSC are identified according to the RRG privileged syntactic argument selection hierarchy, but these macroroles do not play a critical role in the syntax-semantics linkage. In fact, they become irrelevant, but they are still retrieved just in the case that they could play some role in the linguistic generation process.[38] As illustrated in Figure 10, constructional schemata actually become the cornerstone of the syntax-semantics interface, so a constructivist approach is adopted in this regard; indeed, some arguments are directly contributed by the L1-Constructicon. On the other hand, lexical entries should be provided with pointers to those types of constructions in which a given verb can occur, so a functional projectionist approach is adopted in this regard.

This position is much more in line with the LCM, which intends to build a bridge between constructivist and projectionist views of language comprehension. In this model of meaning construction, the notions of lexical template (i.e. low-level representation of the semantic and syntactic properties of a predicate) and constructional template (i.e. high-level representation of the semantic properties of a construction) are essential to explain the syntax-semantics interface. More particularly, the semantic interpretation results from a process of lexico-constructional subsumption, i.e. the unification between a lexical template and a constructional template. In ARTEMIS, the elaboration of constructional rules also involves a lexico-constructional subsumption. However, in contrast with the LCM, the lexico-constructional subsumption in ARTEMIS is not a projection process which is regulated by internal constraints – e.g. variable suppression or lexical blocking, among many others (cf. Mairal-Usón & Ruiz de Mendoza 2008), but it should be simply understood as a process of

37. EBNF (Extended Backus-Naur Form) is a standard notational language used to define context-free grammars formally.

38. Should this not be the case, macroroles would certainly end up disappearing in our computational model.

constructional activation within the framework of non-monotonic inheritance: that is, when constructional schemata are activated, in the case of attributes shared by the AVM of the constructional schema and that of the Core Grammar of the verb, specific values in the former override default values in the latter. Therefore, we prefer not to use the term "projection rules" but "constructional activation rules", where only some values are projected from the Lexicon to the Constructicon.

5. Conclusions

In this chapter, we have described ARTEMIS, a proof-of-concept NLP system which exploits FunGramKB as its knowledge base within the RRG framework to model the semantic representation of the input text in terms of a CLS. Although the RRG logical structure has been formally simplified for the sake of computational efficiency, we have finally achieved a cross-language semantically-enhanced representation by replacing predicates by ontological units and introducing the constructional operator, among some other changes. In fact, we regard constructions as meaning-bearing devices which play a paramount role in the LSC. Although we have focused this chapter on argumental constructions, we intend to progressively incorporate other types of constructional meanings into the CLS, such as implicational, illocutionary and discursive. Moreover, since ARTEMIS retrieves lexico-conceptual knowledge from FunGramKB, it will also be possible to exploit its reasoning engine to reach a deeper level of comprehension through the COREL scheme derived from the CLS. To conclude, we agree with Guest (2009) that RRG is a promising theory for extracting sentential meaning from a computational viewpoint, making this functional model a better alternative to Head-Phrase Structure Grammar and Dependency Grammar.

6. Acknowledgments

Financial support for this research has been provided by the DGI, Spanish Ministry of Education and Science, grants FFI2011-29798-C02-01, FFI2010-17610 and FFI2010-15983. We would like to thank Christopher Butler for detailed comments on the first draft. Any error is ours.

References

Allen, James F. 1983. Maintaining knowledge about temporal intervals. *Communications of the ACM* 26(11): 832–843.

Allen, James F. & Ferguson, George. 1994. Actions and events in interval temporal logic. *Journal of Logic and Computation* 4(5): 531–579.

Baldridge, Jason, Morton, Thomas & Bierner, Gann. 2001. The OpenNLP Toolkit. <http://sharpnlp.codeplex.com> (21 September 2012).

Bird, Steven, Klein, Ewan & Loper, Edward. 2009. *Natural Language Processing with Python*. Sebastopol CA: O'Reilly.

Cooper, Richard P. 2002. *Modelling High-Level Cognitive Processes*. Mahwah NJ: Lawrence Erlbaum Associates.

Croft, William. 2001. *Radical Construction Grammar*. Oxford: OUP.

Dowty, David. 1979. *Word Meaning and Montague Grammar*. Dordrecht: Reidel.

Earley, Jay. 1970. An efficient context-free parsing algorithm. *Communications of the ACM* 13(2): 94–102.

Frazier, Lyn. 1979. On Comprehending Sentences: Syntactic Parsing Strategies. PhD dissertation, University of Connecticut.

Frazier, Lyn & Fodor, Janet Dean. 1978. The sausage machine: A new two-stage parsing model. *Cognition* 6: 1–34.

Goldberg, Adele E. 1995. *Constructions: A Construction Grammar Approach to Argument Structure*. Chicago IL: University of Chicago Press.

Guest, Elizabeth. 2009. Parsing using the Role and Reference Grammar paradigm. <http://repository-intralibrary.leedsmet.ac.uk/open_virtual_file_path/i42n47491t/Parsing Using the Role and Reference Grammar Paradigm.pdf> (21 September 2012).

Jackendoff, Ray S. 1990. *Semantic Structures*. Cambridge MA: The MIT Press.

Jursic, Matjaz, Mozetic, Igor, Erjavec, Tomaz & Lavrac, Nada. 2010. LemmaGen: Multilingual lemmatisation with induced ripple-down rules. *Journal of Universal Computer Science* 16(9): 1190–1214.

Mairal-Usón, Ricardo & Periñán-Pascual, Carlos. 2009. The anatomy of the lexicon component within the framework of a conceptual knowledge base. *Revista Española de Lingüística Aplicada* 22: 217–244.

Mairal-Usón, Ricardo & Ruiz de Mendoza, Francisco José. 2008. Internal and external constraints in meaning construction: The lexicon grammar continuum. In *Estudios de Filología Inglesa: Homenaje a la Dra. Asunción Alba Pelayo*, Laura Alba Juez & María Teresa Gibert Maceda (eds), 219–237. Madrid: Universidad Nacional de Educación a Distancia.

Mairal-Usón, Ricardo & Ruiz de Mendoza, Francisco José. 2009. Levels of description and explanation in meaning construction. In *Deconstructing Constructions* [Studies in Laguage Compagnion Series 107], Christopher Butler & Javier Martín Arista (eds), 153–198. Amsterdam: John Benjamins.

Michaelis, Laura A. 2003. Word meaning, sentence meaning, and syntactic meaning. In *Cognitive Approaches to Lexical Semantics*, Hubert Cuykens, René Dirven & John R. Taylor (eds), 93–122. Berlin: Mouton de Gruyter.

Nirenburg, Sergei & Levin, Lori. 1992. Syntax-driven and ontology-driven lexical semantics. In *Lexical Semantics and Knowledge Representation: First SIGLEX Workshop*, James Pustejovsky & Sabine Bergler (eds), 5–20. Berlin: Springer.

Pelletier, Francis Jeffry. 2012. Holism and compositionality. In *The Oxford Handbook of Compositionality*, Markus Werning, Wolfram Hinzen & Edouard Machery (eds), 149–174. Oxford: OUP.

Periñán-Pascual, Carlos. 2013. Towards a model of constructional meaning for natural language understanding. In *Linking Constructions into Functional Linguistics: The Role of Constructions in RRG Grammars* [Studies in Language Companion Series 145], Brian Nolan & Elke Diedrichsen (eds), 205–230. Amsterdam: John Benjamins.

Periñán-Pascual, Carlos & Arcas-Túnez, Francisco. 2004. Meaning postulates in a lexico-conceptual knowledge base. In *Proceedings of the 15th International Workshop on Databases and Expert Systems Applications*, 38–42. Los Alamitos CA: IEEE Computer Society.

Periñán-Pascual, Carlos & Arcas-Túnez, Francisco. 2005. Microconceptual-knowledge spreading in FunGramKB. In *Proceedings of the 9th IASTED International Conference on Artificial Intelligence and Soft Computing*, 239–244. Anaheim CA: ACTA Press.

Periñán-Pascual, Carlos & Arcas-Túnez, Francisco. 2007. Cognitive modules of an NLP knowledge base for language understanding. *Procesamiento del Lenguaje Natural* 39: 197–204.

Periñán-Pascual, Carlos & Arcas-Túnez, Francisco. 2008. A cognitive approach to qualities for NLP. *Procesamiento del Lenguaje Natural* 41: 137–144.

Periñán-Pascual, Carlos & Arcas-Túnez, Francisco. 2010a. Ontological commitments in FunGramKB. *Procesamiento del Lenguaje Natural* 44: 27–34.

Periñán-Pascual, Carlos & Arcas-Túnez, Francisco. 2010b. The architecture of FunGramKB. In *Proceedings of the 7th International Conference on Language Resources and Evaluation*, 2667–2674. Malta: European Language Resources Association.

Periñán-Pascual, Carlos & Mairal-Usón, Ricardo. 2009. Bringing Role and Reference Grammar to natural language understanding. *Procesamiento del Lenguaje Natural* 43: 265–273.

Periñán-Pascual, Carlos & Mairal-Usón, Ricardo. 2010. La gramática de COREL: Un lenguaje de representación conceptual. *Onomázein* 21: 11–45.

Periñán-Pascual, Carlos & Mairal-Usón, Ricardo. 2011. The COHERENT methodology in FunGramKB. *Onomázein* 24: 13–33.

Pickering, Martin J. & Van Gompel, Roger P.G. 2006. Syntactic parsing. In *Handbook of Psycholinguistics*, Matthew J. Traxler & Morton A. Gernsbacher (eds), 455–503. Amsterdam: Elsevier.

Pustejovsky, James. 1991. The generative lexicon. *Computational Linguistics* 17(4): 409–441.

Rappaport Hovav, Malka & Levin, Beth. 1998. Building verb meanings. In *The Projection of Arguments: Lexical and Compositional Factors*, Miriam Butt & Wilhelm Geuder (eds), 97–134. Stanford CA: CSLI.

Ruiz de Mendoza, Francisco José & Mairal-Usón, Ricardo. 2008. Levels of description and constraining factors in meaning construction: An introduction to the Lexical Constructional Model. *Folia Linguistica* 42(2): 355–400.

Rumbaugh, James, Jacobson, Ivar & Booch, Grady. 1999. *The Unified Modeling Language Reference Manual*. Reading MA: Addison-Wesley.

Sag, Ivan A. 2012. Sign-based Construction Grammar: An informal synopsis. In *Sign-based Construction Grammar*, Hans C. Boas & Ivan Sag (eds.), 69–202. Stanford CA: CSLI.

Salem, Yasser, Hensman, Arnold & Nolan, Brian. 2008. Towards Arabic to English machine translation. *ITB Journal* 17: 20–31.

Uszkoreit, Hans & Zaenen, Annie. 1995. Grammar formalisms. In *Survey of the State of the Art in Human Language Technology*, Giovanni Varile & Antonio Zampolli (eds), 100–101. Cambridge: CUP.

Van Valin, Jr., Robert D. 2005. *Exploring the Syntax-Semantics Interface*. Cambridge: CUP.

Van Valin, Jr., Robert D. 2009. Role and Reference Grammar as a framework for linguistic analysis. In *The Oxford Handbook of Linguistic Analysis*, Bernd Heine & Heiko Narrog (eds), 703–738. Oxford: OUP.

Van Valin, Jr., Robert D. & LaPolla, Randy J. 1997. *Syntax, Structure, Meaning and Function*. Cambridge: CUP.

Vendler, Zeno. 1967. *Linguistics in Philosophy*. Ithaca CA: Cornell University Press.

Appendix 1. XML-formatted parse tree


```
  <?xml version="1.0"?>
- <Trees>
  - <S>
    - <CL Tense="past">
      - <CONSTR-L1 Weight="5" Template="CMOT">
        - <CONSTR-L1 Weight="4" Template="KER2">
          - <CORE Akt="CACC">
            - <ARG Concept="%JOHN_00" Type="x" Role="Agent" Macrorole="A">
              - <NP>
                  <n Num="sg">John</n>
                </NP>
              </ARG>
            - <NUC>
              - <PRED Concept="$POUND_02">
                  <v>pounded</v>
                </PRED>
              </NUC>
            - <ARG Concept="+NAIL_01" Type="y" Role="Goa" Macrorole="U">
              - <NP>
                - <det>the</det>
                  <n Num="sg">nail</n>
                </NP>
              </ARG>
            - <ARG Concept="+WALL_00" Type="W" Role="Goal" Macrorole="n">
              - <PP p="into">
                  <p>into</p>
                - <NP>
                    <det>the</det>
                    <n Num="sg">walk</n>
                  </NP>
                </PP>
              </ARG>
          </CORE>
        </CONSTER-L1>
      </CONSTER-L1>
    </CL>
  </S>
</Trees>
```

Appendix 2. XSD schema for the validation of XML-formatted parse trees

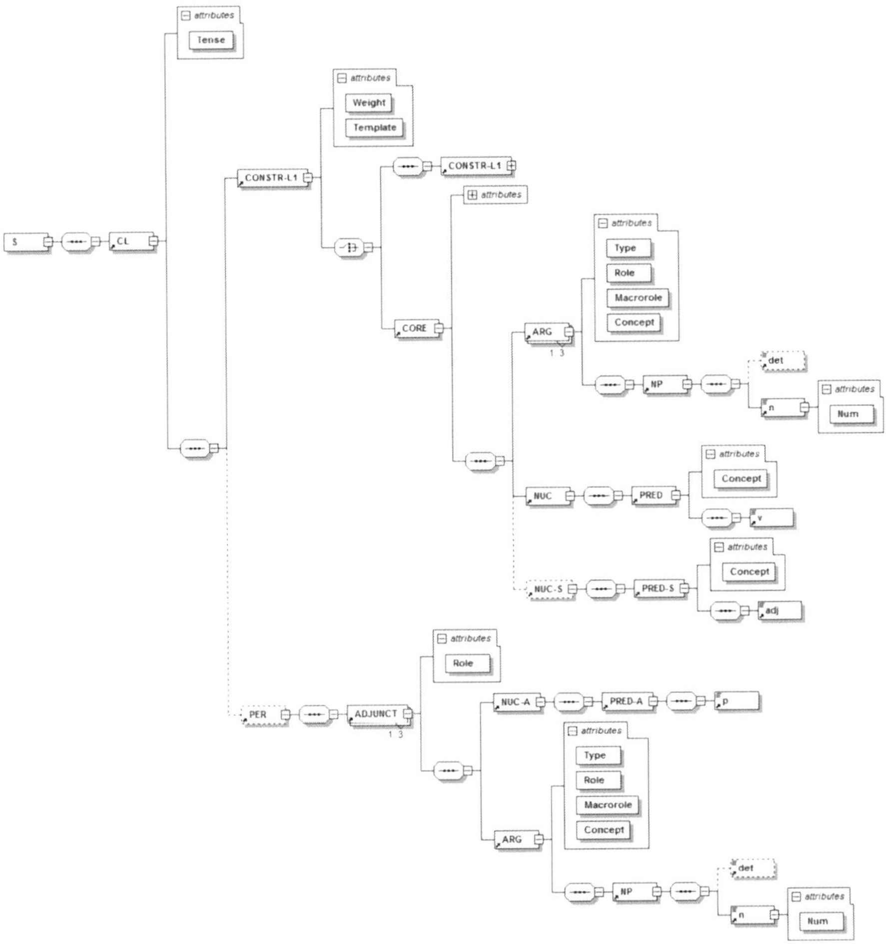

Appendix 3. Context-free grammar for the CLS (EBNF and graphical representation)

CLS ::='<' 'IF' 'DECL' '<' 'Tense' Tense CONSTR-L1 '>' '>'
Tense ::= 'rpast' | 'npast' | 'past' | 'pres' | 'nfut' | 'rfut' | 'fut'
CONSTR-L1 ::= '<' 'CONSTR-L1' Template CONSTR-L1* AKT '>
Template ::= 'BENE' | 'CMOT' | 'KER1' | 'KER2' | 'KER3' | 'INST' | 'LOCA' | 'MIDD' |'RESI' | 'RESU' | '... '
AKT ::= '<' 'AKT' Type CORE '>'

Type ::= 'STA' | 'ACT' | 'ACC' | 'ACH' | 'SEM' | 'ACA' | 'CSTA' | 'CACT' | 'CACC' | 'CACH' | 'CSEM' | 'CACA'
CORE ::= '[' 'Pred' '('('Arg '-' 'Role' ',') + 'NUC-S'')'']' ADJUNCT
ADJUNCT ::= '('Arg' '-' Role')'
Role ::= 'Agent' | 'Attribute' | 'Beneficiary' | 'Company' | 'Comparison' | 'Condition' | 'Duration' | 'Frequency' | 'Goal' | 'Instrument' | '...'

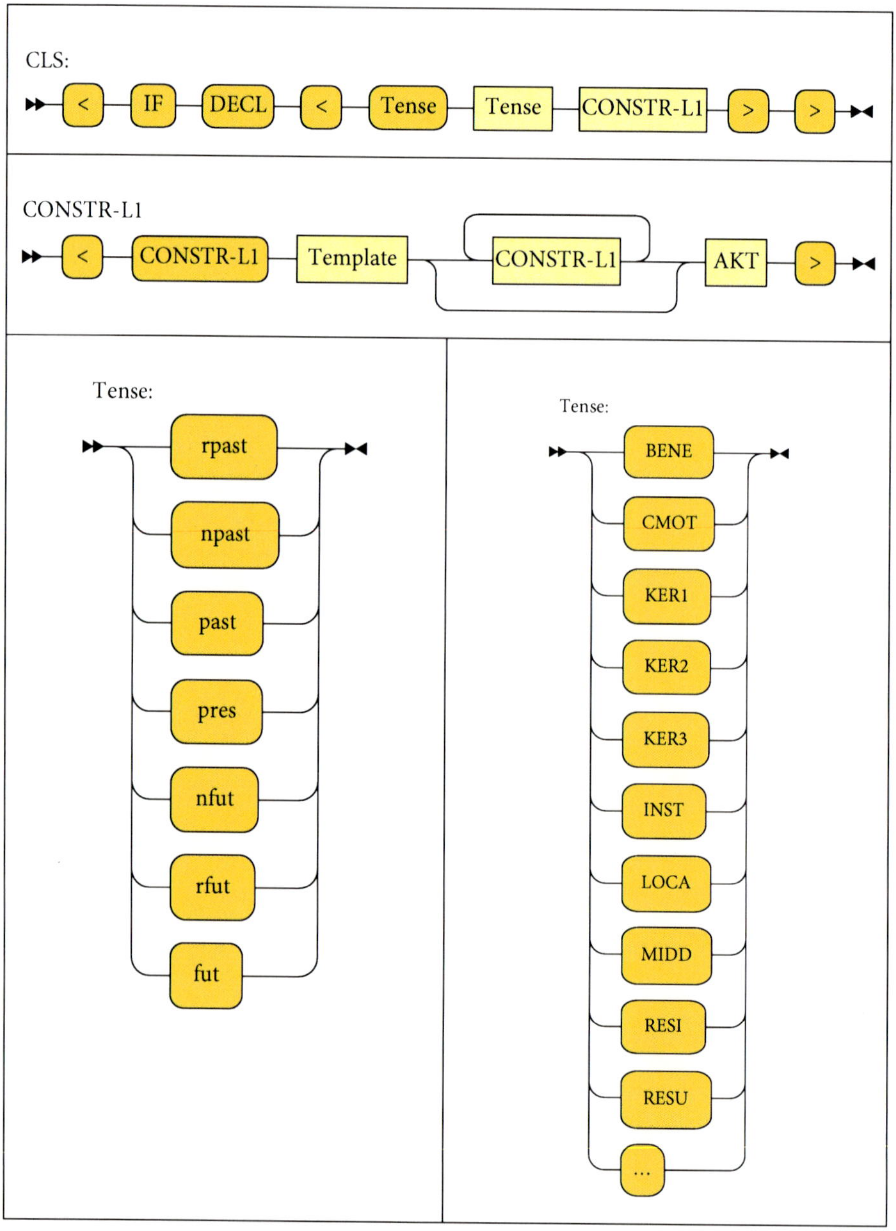

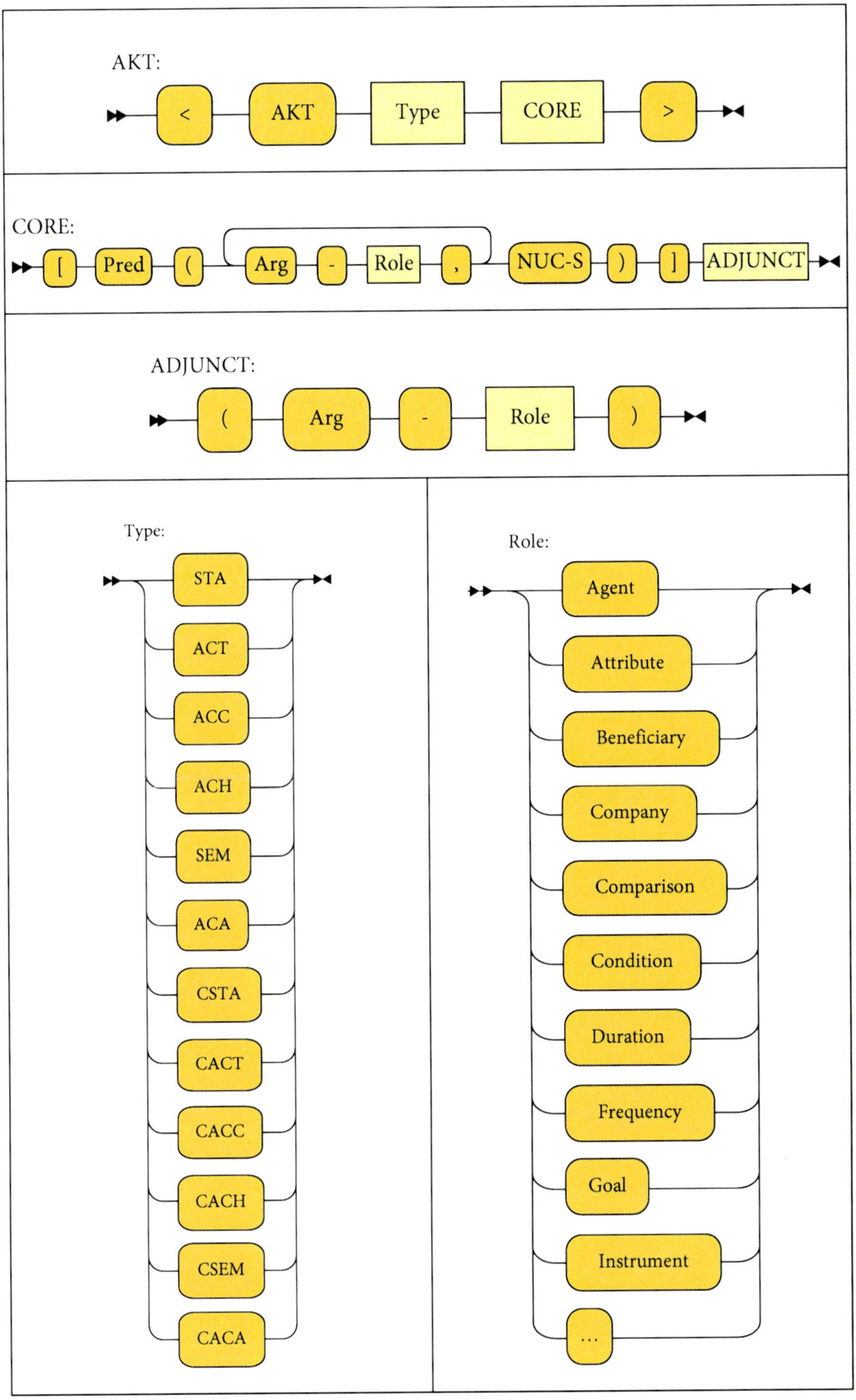
AKT:
<
AKT
Type
CORE
>
CORE:
[
Pred
(
Arg
-
Role
,
NUC-S
)
]
ADJUNCT
ADJUNCT:
(
Arg
-
Role
)
Type:
STA
ACT
ACC
ACH
SEM
ACA
CSTA
CACT
CACC
CACH
CSEM
CACA
Role:
Agent
Attribute
Beneficiary
Company
Comparison
Condition
Duration
Frequency
Goal
Instrument
…

Appendix 4. Activity diagram for the construction of the CLS in ARTEMIS

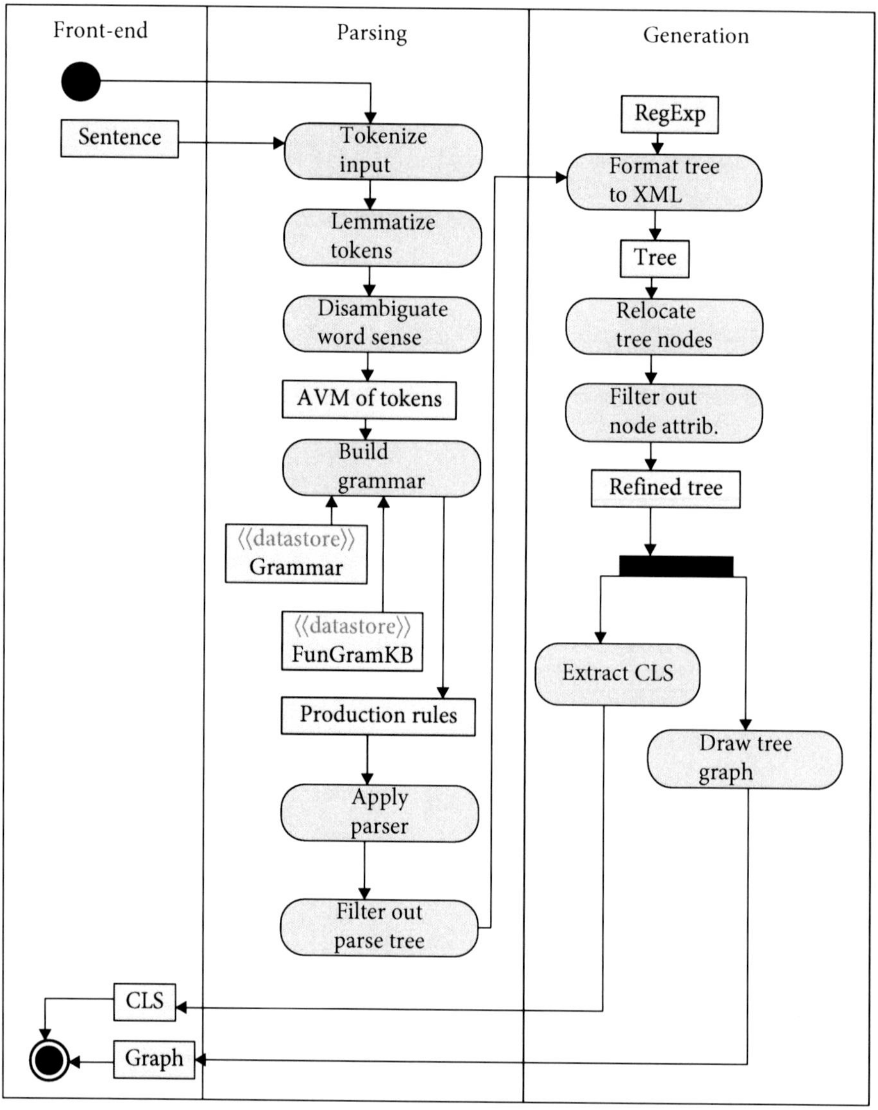

FrameNet and FunGramKB

A comparison of two computational resources for semantic knowledge representation*

Alba Luzondo-Oyón and Rocío Jiménez-Briones
Universidad de La Rioja and Universidad Autónoma de Madrid

This chapter presents a comparison between FunGramKB, a multipurpose lexico-conceptual base for Natural Language Processing (NLP) systems, and FrameNet, a lexical resource for English whose objective is to document the range of semantic and syntactic combinatory possibilities of each sense of a word. After providing the reader with an overview of the two resources under scrutiny, we address their similarities and differences by focusing on the following issues: (1) methodology; (2) information at the lexical and conceptual levels; (3) relations between frames and concepts; (4) information management; and (5) multilingualism. To illustrate this comparison, we analyze how the verb *dry* is represented in each project.

1. Introduction

Meaning representation has always been a major issue in the field of linguistics. More recently, with the development of natural language processing (NLP) systems, attention has also been paid to computational resources capable of handling this kind of information, since semantic knowledge plays a fundamental role in solving tasks that involve successful reasoning. As Periñán and Arcas (2007a: 197) point out, some NLP systems (e.g. information extraction or automatic indexing) do not really require representations that mirror the structure and organization of the cognitive system human beings are endowed with. By contrast, other tasks such as machine translation or text understanding call for the incorporation of reasoning. Although it is true that surface semantics (Velardi et al. 1991) may be sufficient for the former type of systems,

* The research on which this chapter is based has received financial support from the Spanish Ministry of Economy and Competitiveness, grants no. FFI 2010-17610/FILO and no. FFI2011-29798-C02-01.

the construction of a solid knowledge base grounded in deep semantics guarantees its use in most NLP task (cf. Periñán & Arcas 2007b: 279).

In this context, this chapter compares FunGramKB (Periñán & Arcas 2010a, 2010b; Mairal & Periñán 2010a, 2010b; Periñán & Mairal 2010), a multipurpose lexico-conceptual knowledge base for NLP systems, with FrameNet (FN; Petruck 1996; Baker et al. 1998; Fillmore et al. 2003a, 2003b; Boas 2005; Ruppenhofer et al. 2010), a lexical database that lately has also been involved in NLP applications (cf. Ovchinnikova et al. 2010: 3157). Consequently, by contrasting these two projects we aim to provide a detailed description of the ways in which a *deep* approach and a *shallow* approach to knowledge representation vary (Periñán 2013a). As will be shown, FunGramKB, which formally describes the conceptual content of lexical units, is an example of the former approach. By contrast, in a shallow account like the one adopted in FN, the cognitive content of a lexical item is characterized "by means of a simple feature value matrix of conceptual relations" (Periñán 2013a: 89). Thus, owing to the fact that FN and FunGramKB have been designed with different aims in mind, we should expect to find many aspects in which these resources differ. Nevertheless, FN and FunGramKB also share a similar view in other respects such as their treatment of polysemy, their use of organizational units larger than words, among others.

The reminder of this chapter is organized as follows. Section 2 provides the reader with a general overview of the two computational resources under examination. Section 3, which comprises the core of the study, details the similarities and differences between FN and FunGramKB with respect to the methodology employed (Subsection 3.1), the information stored at the lexical and conceptual levels (Subsection 3.2), the relations between frames and concepts that each computational resource posits (Subsection 3.3), how information is managed by these projects (Subsection 3.4), and their stances on the creation of multilingual resources (3.5). The case of *dry* will be used to illustrate this comparison. Finally, some concluding remarks are offered in Section 4.

2. Main tenets of FN and FunGramKB

2.1 FN

The FN project builds on *Frame Semantics* (cf. Fillmore 1976, 1982; Fillmore & Atkins 1992; see also Boas 2005, 2009a: 15 and references therein). As the following quote evidences, the main idea underlying this theory is that word meanings provide access to (or are described as belonging to) organized pieces of knowledge, i.e. *frames*:

> A word's meaning can be understood only with reference to a structured background of experience, beliefs, or practices, constituting a kind of conceptual prerequisite for understanding the meaning. [...] Within such an approach, words and word senses are not related to each other directly [...] but only by way of their links to common background frames and indications of the manner in which their meanings highlight particular elements of such frames (Fillmore & Atkins 1992: 76–77).

Frame Semantics has been applied to the construction of FN, an online lexical resource "that extracts information about the linked semantic and syntactic properties of English words" from electronic text corpora like the British National Corpus (BNC) (Fillmore et al. 2003a: 235). According to Fillmore et al. (2012), FN aims to account for the syntactic and semantic properties of lexical units, paying especial attention to their meanings, their syntactic and combinatorial affordances, as well as their relations to frames.

There are two main units of analysis in FN, namely, frames and lexical units (LU(s)). The former, as characterized by Fillmore et al. (2003b: 305), are schematic representations of a situation type (e.g. "going to the movies", "drying something", "buying", etc.), which can be defined in terms of participants and their functions. A frame is in turn *evoked* by a set of LUs (i.e. words taken in one of their senses), which involves that the separate senses of a polysemous word are connected to different semantic frames. For example, the verbal predicate *run* evokes, among others, the frames labeled "Leadership" and "Self motion" as exemplified in *It is she who runs that business* and *We ran into the house to get Mame*, respectively.

In FN, valence information is specified both semantically and syntactically via: (1) *frame elements* (FEs) or the entities taking part in the situation depicted by a given frame, and (2) phrase types (e.g. NP, PP, etc.) and their corresponding grammatical functions (Subject, Object, etc.) (cf. Fillmore et al. 2003a: 236–237). FEs, which are frame-specific instantiations of broader semantic roles (e.g. AGENT, PATIENT, EXPERIENCER, etc.; see Boas 2010: 61), may either be core (i.e. conceptually prominent components of the frame) or non-core/peripheral (i.e. elements that do not uniquely characterize a frame), as shown in (1a) and (1b):[1]

(1) Frame: "Becoming dry" ("An entity loses moisture with the outcome of being in a dry state").
  a. <u>Core FE:</u>
     Entity [Ent]: "The thing that loses moisture and becomes dry".
  b. <u>Some peripheral FEs:</u>
     Place [Pla]: "The location where the Entity becomes dry".
     Time [Tim]: "When the entity becomes dry".
     Manner [Man]: "The way in which the Entity becomes dry".

According to Boas (2005: 143), one of the primary goals of this project is to document all of the lexicographically relevant uses of a word as found in the corpus, in addition to the syntactic environments in which they occur. To illustrate this point, we now

1. According to Atkins et al. (2003: 268), there are two types of non-core FEs. The first kind includes adjuncts such as place, time, manner, purpose, etc. The second group comprises *extra-thematic* FEs (e.g. Iteration, Subregion, Frequency, etc.), i.e. those which do not conceptually belong to the frames they appear in, but which situate an event against a backdrop of another state of affairs (Ruppenhofer et al. 2010: 27–28).

Table 1. FEs for *dry* and their syntactic realizations

Frame element	Number annotated	Realization(s)
Entity	(11)	NP.Ext (11)
Manner	(4)	AVP.Dep (4)
Particular_iteration	(1)	AVP.Dep (1)
Place	(1)	PP[on].Dep (1)
Time	(1)	PP[in].Dep (1)

examine how the information that a given verb can display is formally handled in FN. Let us consider the case of *dry* one more time. The lexical entry for one of the senses of *dry* comprises the following elements: (1) the FN definition given to this specific verb sense (i.e. "to lose moisture"), (2) the larger frame it evokes, i.e. "Becoming dry", (3) a list of core (i.e. Entity) and non-core FEs (i.e. Manner, Place, etc.) and their syntactic realizations (see Table 1), as well as the valence patterns in which they may occur (see Table 2).

In the middle column in Table 1 we are provided with the number of corpus-based annotated instances for this word sense, in which, for example, the core FE labeled Entity is expressed eleven times as an NP, which grammatically works as a Subject (so-called External argument).[2] For reasons of space, only two examples are supplied here:

(2) a. [Her tears]$_{\text{ENTITY}}$ DRIED^{TARGET} as suddenly as they had appeared.
b. [The slab]$_{\text{ENTITY}}$ DRIES^{TARGET} [very quickly]$_{\text{MANNER}}$ and faces virtually due south (...).

In much the same vein, the Place FE is found once as a PP with *on*, grammatically functioning as a Dependent:

(3) (A)llow [the excess water]$_{\text{ENTITY}}$ to DRY^{TARGET} [on a flat surface between clean towels]$_{\text{PLACE}}$.

Finally, Table 2 itemizes the valence patterns of this verb, that is, the different combinations of FEs and their syntactic realizations which may appear in a particular sentence (cf. Fillmore et al. 2003b: 330).

But besides the information discussed thus far, FN includes frame-to-frame relations of different types (cf. Boas 2010: 61), which we will address in more detail in Section 3.3. Moreover, the role of "semantic types" (Ruppenhofer et al. 2010: 111–120) is that of recording those features that are not specified in their frames and frame element hierarchies. For instance, in the "Cause to be dry" frame, a semantic type labeled "sentient" delimits the nature of the Agent FE. This further clarifies that the Agent is

2. According to Ruppenhofer et al. (2010: 89–90), constituents occupying core syntactic slots fulfill the functions of Subject and Object. The rest of constituents accompanying a syntactic head are considered Dependents.

Table 2. Valence patterns for *dry* in "Becoming dry"

Number annotated	Patterns		
4 TOTAL	Entity		
(4)	NP Ext		
2 TOTAL	Entity	Entity	Manner
(2)	NP Ext	NP Ext	AVP Dep
2 TOTAL	Entity	Manner	
(2)	NP Ext	AVP Dep	
1 TOTAL	Entity	Particular_iteration	
(1)	NP Ext	AVP Dep	
1 TOTAL	Entity	Place	
(1)	NP Ext	PP[on] Dep	
1 TOTAL	Entity	Time	
(1)	NP Ext	PP[in] Dep	

necessarily a human entity (e.g. *Michael dehydrated the apples*), except for those examples in which the presence of the Cause FE (i.e. "the animate or inanimate entity, force or event that produces the state of dryness") excludes the Agent, as in *The wind dried the porch*.

Clearly, one of the main advantages of the FN project has to do with its manifest desire to offer a highly detailed account of phrase types and grammatical functions for each FE. For that matter, the linguist can benefit greatly from this lexicographic tool to indentify verb classes and to learn about the idiosyncratic semantic and syntactic behavior of an LU (see Boas 2011). Seemingly, the fact that the various FEs are highlighted in different colors in the list of annotated examples makes FN a user-friendly environment intended to facilitate the comparison of the often disparate syntactic behavior of verbs belonging to the same cognitive domain. However, although it is contended that, unlike commercial dictionaries, the set of examples displayed in the FN annotation reports "illustrate *all* of the combinatorial possibilities of "the lexical unit" (Ruppenhofer et al. 2010: 7, emphasis in the original), this is not always the case. At least for some frames, the sentences selected seem to instantiate the most typical combinatory affordances of an LU as attested in the corpus (cf. Fillmore et al. 2012), thus disregarding the occurrence of other, more or less frequent, configurations. Take some of the examples gathered from the annotation report of the predicate *drink*, respectively grouped under the labels *beer, bottle, coffee, cup*, etc.:[3]

(4) a. Jed DRANK two more beers.
b. They DRANK the whole bottle in perfect accord.
c. We DRANK coffee and talked some more.
d. He DRANK from the little blue-and-white cup.

Even though these sentences probably represent some of the most commonly employed collocations in which *drink* is embedded, this annotation report does not cover the occurrence of this predicate within, for example, the resultative construction. Surprisingly, the BNC retrieves realizations of the type *She drank herself to death* (BNC ABS), *She drank herself into stupidity* (BNC H7E), *They drank themselves blind* (BNC EUU), *You can drink yourself silly* (BNC KCT), *You have both drunk the barrel dry* (BNC HHC), etc. In principle, these realizations should have been incorporated into their annotation report, given that other instances of the resultative such as "freeze solid" or "push oneself free" can actually be found in other frames (i.e. "Change of Phase" and "Cause motion", respectively).[4] Consequently, if a construction grammarian wishes to study the ability of this lexical item to fuse with the resultative construction or the *way* construction (e.g. *I drank my way through the whole pot* (BNC FAP)), FN appears to fall short of this task. For this reason, the FN Constructicon is currently under development (Fillmore et al. 2012). Its explanation, however, goes beyond the scope of the present chapter.

2.2 FunGramKB

FunGramKB is a "user-friendly online environment for the semiautomatic construction of a multipurpose lexico-conceptual knowledge base for NLP systems" (Mairal & Periñán 2009: 219). FunGramKB is multipurpose in two ways. First, it has been designed to be reused in other NLP tasks, in particular in those that focus on language understanding (e.g. machine translation). Second, it faces the challenge of developing a multilingual tool that includes several western languages.[5] Most

3. The interested reader is referred to Newman and Rice (2005) for a corpus-based study of *drink* and *eat* in terms of preferred objects of consumption, degrees of affectedness of the Object, the most favored Subjects, etc.

4. The BNC offers a total of 8 examples for sentences containing "freeze solid", "freezes solid" or "froze solid". In turn, resultatives like "drank *(= someone) into" (e.g. *He drank himself into a stupor*), and "drink *(= someone) into" (e.g. *They drink themselves into a stupor on black PVC bar stools*) add up to a total of 12 instances. It thus comes as a surprise that in the annotation report of *drink* these examples are not considered.

5. Currently, English, Spanish and, to some extent, Italian, are fully supported. Work on the rest of languages (e.g. German, French, Catalan, etc.) is on its early stages.

importantly, this project is constructed on the basis of a deep semantics approach (cf. Periñán & Arcas 2007b), since it actually defines each concept individually through a machine-readable metalanguage called COREL (i.e. *Conceptual Representation Language*).

One of the central methodological assumptions sustained by FunGramKB is that there is a division of labor between the linguistic level (i.e. the various Lexica and the Grammaticon) and the conceptual component (namely, the Onomasticon, the Cognicon and the Ontology), which in Figure 1 is represented with a dashed line:[6]

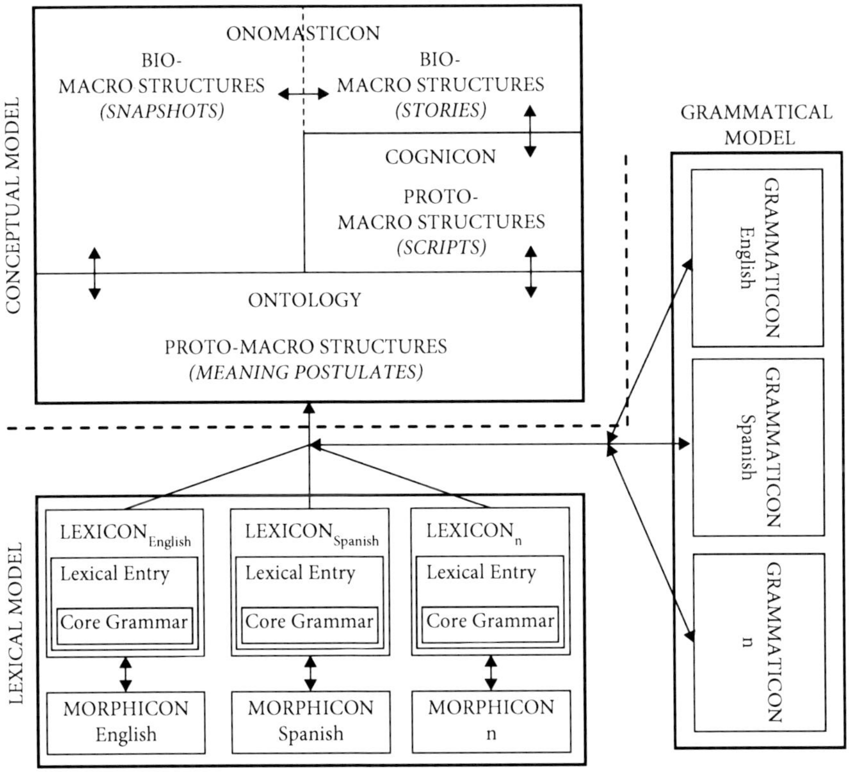

Figure 1. The architecture of FunGramKB and its different modules

6. In the Cognicon procedural knowledge in the form of conceptual macrostructures is stored (e.g. how to christen a baby). In turn, the Onomasticon stores information about instances of both events and entities (e.g. Johnny Cash, the Himalayas, or 9/11). In this chapter, only the Ontology will be discussed in detail.

As can be seen in Figure 1, FunGramKB comprises three knowledge levels consisting of several independent, albeit interrelated, modules:

1. The lexical level covers what is commonly referred to as linguistic knowledge, which thus becomes language-dependent. In this module, the various lexica store information regarding morphosyntactic and pragmatic factors, as well as any possible collocational preferences of a given lexical unit. Likewise, some of the basic assumptions of Role and Reference Grammar (RRG; Van Valin & LaPolla 1997; Van Valin 2005) are preserved (i.e. logical structures, macroroles and the linking algorithm). In turn, the role of the Morphicon is to handle cases of inflectional morphology.
2. The grammatical level, which is also language-specific, stores the constructional schemata helping RRG to build the syntax-to-semantics algorithm. In the Grammaticon, the four constructional layers of the Lexical Constructional Model (LCM; Ruiz de Mendoza & Mairal 2008, 2011; Mairal & Ruiz de Mendoza 2009; Ruiz de Mendoza.) are being implemented computationally.[7]
3. The conceptual level, which will be the focus of our attention, deals with non-linguistic (i.e. language independent) knowledge. Within this level, the Ontology, (i.e. a hierarchical structure of conceptual units), functions as the pivot around which the whole knowledge base revolves. For that matter, FunGramKB adopts a conceptualist approach which brings with it the acceptance of two major principles. Firstly, given that the conceptual level is the pillar that supports the different lexica, the semantic description of lexical items must rest upon the Ontology (Mairal & Periñán 2010b: 160). Consequently, FunGramKB is populated in a top-down fashion, since, in order for the description of a lexical item to be possible, there should previously exist a concept in the Ontology to which such lexical piece can be linked. Secondly, we cannot but stress that whereas the different lexica and the Grammaticon are idiosyncratic, the conceptual module, although being linguistically motivated, is nonetheless language independent. This entails that, while computational lexicographers will work on one Lexicon and one Morphicon for each of the languages currently supported, there is only one Ontology, one Onomasticon and one Cognicon to process any (culturally similar) language input.

There are three conceptual levels in the Ontology of FunGramKB, i.e. *metaconcepts, basic* concepts and *terminal* concepts (cf. Periñán 2013a for more details). Metaconcepts (e.g. #ABSTRACT, #MOTION, #COMMUNICATION, etc.), which represent

7. The four constructional layers or levels of the LCM are the following: level 1 deals with argument structure constructions; implicational constructions are part of level 2; level 3 is devoted to illocutionary constructions; and finally, level 4 is concerned with discourse analysis. The interested reader is referred to Periñán and Mairal (2009) for more information on the relation between FunGramKB and the LCM.

different cognitive dimensions, are the most abstract level in the hierarchy. In turn, basic concepts (e.g. +DIRTY_00, +DANCE_00, +BOOK_ 00, etc.) are the building blocks on the basis of which knowledge engineers define the meaning of a basic and/or terminal concept via Meaning Postulates (MPs). At last, the lowest level of the FunGramKB Ontology is made up of terminal concepts (e.g. $MOP_00, $GRASP_00, $SPORT_00, etc.), which contrast with basic concepts in that they cannot appear in MPs because they lack defining potential.[8] But essential to our discussion here is the fact that basic and terminal concepts are provided with semantic properties, namely, Thematic Frames (TFs) and MPs. In the Ontology, events (e.g. +DRY_01, +SWIM_00, +ANNOY_00), are assigned one TF, i.e. "a prototypical cognitive construct which states the number and type of participants involved in an event" (Periñán & Arcas 2007a: 200).[9] Partially inspired in Halliday's (1985) and Dixon's (1991) work, participants in FunGramKB, also called *thematic roles*, are expressed through indexed variables in the TF (i.e. (x1) (x2) (x3), etc.) and their nature is usually (although not compulsorily) delimited by basic concepts (e.g. +HUMAN_00, +ANIMAL_00, etc.) referred to as *selectional preferences*. For example, the TF of the basic concept +SWIM_00 (located within the metaconcept #MOTION), contains five cognitively necessary participants: (x1)Agent, (x2)Theme, (x3)Location, (x4)Origin and (x5) Goal. While Agent, Origin and Goal may be left unspecified, both the Theme and Location roles can be further spelled out by introducing the selectional preferences (x2: +HUMAN_00 ^ +ANIMAL_00)Referent and (x3: +WATER_00)Location.[10] As a result, the TF of +SWIM_00 describes a prototypical cognitive scenario in which a human or an animal moves in the water from an origin towards a destination. It is clear, however, that by merely stating the TF of a concept, we are not taking account of its meaning. Thus, the importance of MPs may now become apparent to the reader. According to Mairal and Periñán (2009: 224), MPs are sets of one or more logically connected predications (e_1, e_2, e_3, etc.), that is, conceptual constructs carrying the generic features of concepts. For instance, it is through the MP of +DRY_01 in Figure 2 that its conceptual meaning is represented in the Ontology. MPs are in turn lexicalized by various LUs in the languages currently supported, as shown in the boxes located at the bottom of Figure 2.

8. There is one exception to this general rule. As shown in (13), terminal concepts can appear in an MP when the event to be defined and the instrument used are the same (e.g. $TUMBLE_DRY_01).

9. Although this chapter revolves around the analysis of events (#EVENT), one of the Subontologies of FunGramKB, there are two additional subcomponents, namely, #ENTITIES (e.g. +BIRD_00, +SOUL_00, +FREEDOM) and #QUALITIES (e.g. +AFRAID_00, +HAPPY_00, +ALONE_00). While #ENTITIES and #QUALITIES correspond to nouns and adjectives respectively, #EVENTS account for verbs.

10. For an exhaustive account of the identification of selectional preferences in FunGramKB and its possible implications for the RRG logical structures, see Jiménez and Pérez (2011).

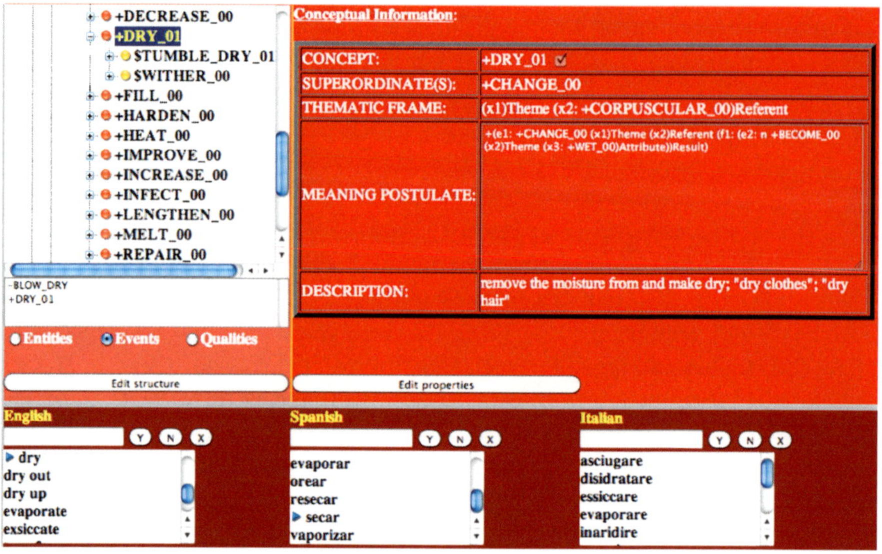

Figure 2. +DRY_01 and its related LUs

Let us explain the different components of Figure 2. We first observe that +DRY_01 is a subordinate of the parent concept or superordinate +CHANGE_00. Through inheritance – one of the reasoning mechanisms connecting concepts in FunGramKB (cf. Section 3.3)–, the subordinate concept +DRY_01 shares the MP of the superordinate one, i.e. +CHANGE_00. More concretely, +CHANGE_00 (i.e. the *genus*) must be specified in the first predication (e_1) of all of its subordinate concepts (cf. *e1: +CHANGE_00 (x1)Theme (x2)Referent*). Furthermore, the MPs of every subordinate concept need to contain a distinguishing feature (i.e. *differentia*) not present in the MP of the more generic or superordinate concept. In FunGramKB, such semantic distinctions or differentiae are codified through *satellites* (e.g. Manner, Purpose, Result, Instrument, etc.; see Periñán and Mairal 2010 for the complete list), such as *(f1: (e2: n +BECOME_00 (x2)Theme (x3: +WET_00)Attribute))Result*) in Figure 2 above. Hence, the final representation of this concept reads as follows: "an entity (x1) changes a three dimensional entity (x2: +CORPUSCULAR_00) and as a result (satellite f1), (x2) will not be wet". To conclude, words such as *dry, dehydrate*, Spanish *desecar*, or Italian *asciugare*, are some of the LUs lexicalizing this concept. The description of each of the LUs attached to the concept +DRY_01 is specified at the lexical level (cf. Section 3.2).

Having provided the reader with an overview of FN and FunGramKB, we are in a position to compare them in terms of the way in which each resource handles semantic knowledge. Likewise, we tangentially discuss the implications for the creation of NLP tasks.

3. Comparing a lexically-oriented and a conceptually-driven approach

In this section, we address the similarities and differences between FN and FunGramKB by paying attention to the following issues: (1) methodology; (2) information at the lexical and conceptual levels; (3) relations between frames and concepts; (4) information management; and (5) multilingualism. To illustrate this comparison, we concentrate on the representation of *dry*, which in FN would correspond to the frames "Becoming dry" and "Cause to be dry". As noted in (1), the former frame is defined as "an entity loses moisture with the outcome of being in a dry state". In such a scenario, the Entity FE is a core constituent, whereas the rest of FEs (i.e. Circumstance, Concessive, Degree, Manner, Particular iteration, Place and Time) are peripheral. This frame inherits from a frame labeled "Becoming" and is inchoative of "Being dry". "Becoming dry" is evoked by the following verb senses: *dehydrate, dry up, dry* and *exsiccate*. In turn, the causative counterpart of this frame, i.e. "Cause to be dry", is described as "an Agent causes a Dryee (either a surface or an entire entity, inside and out) to become dry". Here, Agent, Cause, and Dryee are core FEs, whereas notions such as Degree, Duration, Instrument, Manner, Means, Place, Purpose, Subregion, Temperature and Time are non-core. Moreover, this frame specifies two frame-to-frame relations: (1) it inherits from the "Transitive action" frame, and (2) it is causative of "Being dry". The verbal predicates *anhydrate, dehumidify, dehydrate, desiccate, dry, dry off, dry out, dry up*, and the nouns *desiccation* and *dehumidification* are defined against such a scenario.[11] As mentioned in Section 2.2, FunGramKB approaches the case of *dry* through the basic concept +DRY_01.

3.1 Methodology

We begin by pointing out two unquestionable similarities holding between FunGramKB and FN. First, both make use of organizational conceptual units that are larger than words, i.e. concepts and frames. Second, in both approaches the different senses of a word are assigned to different frames/concepts. For example, the "stop talking" sense of *dry up* in *Everyone became embarrassed and conversation dried up* (Longman dictionary) would not be part of the FunGramKB concept +DRY_01 examined herein.

FN and FunGramKB, however, seem to differ in other respects. When populating the FunGramKB Ontology, knowledge engineers invariably depart from a list of basic concepts, which is later on enriched through the addition of more specific terminal concepts and/or LUs from various languages. A thorough examination of dictionaries, thesauri, and corpora guides this process. In turn, FN begins by defining frame descriptions (based on corpus evidence) for the family of words to be analyzed (Boas

11. These frames are available at <https://framenet2.icsi.berkeley.edu/fnReports/data/frameIndex.xml?frame=Becoming_dry> and at <https://framenet2.icsi.berkeley.edu/fnReports/data/frameIndex.xml?frame=Cause_to_be_dry>

2009a: 16). The limited inventory of approximately 1,300 basic concepts in FunGramKB was identified by means of the defining vocabulary extracted from the *Longman Dictionary of Contemporary English* (Procter 1978). According to Periñán and Mairal (2011) and Boas (2009a), such a catalogue of basic vocabulary is a useful source for artificial language. Nevertheless, this reduced inventory has not been straightforwardly transformed into FunGramKB basic concepts. Instead, a deep revision was performed following the four-stepped COHERENT methodology, a label that stands for the phases termed COnceptualization, HIErarchization, REmodeling and refinemeNT (see Periñán & Mairal 2011 for more details). As such, a solid methodological approach supports the existing inventory of basic concepts on the grounds of which the subsequent creation of terminal concepts and analysis of related LUs will be carried out. By the same token, given that knowledge modeling is a fairly creative process, the population of the Ontology is guided by a protocol of seven ontological commitments, which work by preventing inconsistencies and reducing a number of common errors (Periñán & Arcas 2010a).

Going through the literature devoted to FN, we wonder about the strength of the methodology followed in FN. Drawing on Fillmore et al.'s (2003b) analysis of the "Attaching" frame, the following is a non-exhaustive summary of how the FN workflow unfolds (see also Atkins et al. 2003). The process begins with an informal description of the frame and an elaboration of a list of possible verbs that, according to the lexicographers' intuition, may evoke the frame. Dictionaries and thesauri are also consulted in this phase, along with the BNC, which is checked to extract sentences in which the central verb of the frame appears (e.g. *tie* in the "Attaching" frame) so that its syntax and semantics are fully accounted for. Once the initial analysis is completed, findings are compared with those of the *Concise Oxford Dictionary of the English Language* (COD). On the basis of examples and their informal characterization of the frame, the analyst can proceed to select and characterize the core and peripheral FEs of the frame. At last, with these FEs in mind, the lexicographer finally defines the frame under study. It should be emphasized that the steps described thus far are not rigid and modifications can be made at any given time, as much as it is possible to re-evaluate and readjust concepts in FunGramKB.

At this point, however, a basic methodological question arises: it is somewhat unclear how the FN lexicographer arrives at a new frame. That is, if it is the case – as may be deduced from the above explanation– that frame characterizations depart from one LU (e.g. *tie*), we may ask ourselves on what grounds that verb is deemed to be a central member. Likewise, we gather from Fillmore et al.'s (2003b) description that, although corpus sentences are examined, some of the work is, to a certain extent, based on intuitive assessments. Eventually, initial conclusions are later on checked against the COD. This may, nevertheless, be insufficient in that sometimes dictionaries vary in the number of senses acknowledged to exist for a given verb and/or the way they account for their definitions (cf. Boas 2009b: 61 for a similar perspective). A case in point is that of *wither*, one of the hyponyms of *dry*:

(5) Cobuild <http://dictionary.reverso.net/english-cobuild/>:
  a. If somebody or something withers, they become very weak: *Industries unable to modernize have been left to wither.*
  b. If a flower or plant withers, it dries up and dies: *The flowers in Isabel's room had withered.*

(6) Longman <http://www.ldoceonline.com/dictionary/>:
  a. If plants wither, they become drier and smaller and start to die.

(7) Oxford <http://oxforddictionaries.com/>:
  a. Of a plant, become dry and shriveled: *The grass had withered to an unappealing brown.*
  b. Fall into decay or decline: *It is not true that old myths either die or wither away.*
  c. Humiliate someone with a scornful look or manner: *She withered him with a glance.*

For instance, the Longman dictionary does not consider the figurative sense of *wither* expressed in (5a) or (7b). Likewise, neither the Longman nor the Cobuild provide an entry for the "humiliate" sense of this verb, which is, nonetheless, distinguished by the Oxford dictionary. These factors evidence the need to resort to more than one single dictionary in order to arrive at a more precise conclusion of the concept/frame to be described. For this reason, FunGramKB relies heavily on the use of dictionaries, thesauri and corpora. As such, more than three different English and Spanish dictionaries, together with the above-specified resources, are consulted in the process of creating terminal concepts and of assigning LUs to both basic and terminal concepts (see Jiménez & Luzondo 2011). It should be noted that, although we are by no means implying that the current frame classifications are inaccurate, there is a paucity of information as to how exactly the analyst arrives at a specific class of semantically related verbs (from which more general elements are abstracted away).

Nevertheless, in more recent work by Ruppenhofer et al. (2010), intuitive assessments appear to have been replaced by more explicit criteria:

> The core of the process has always been looking at corpus attestations of a group of words that we believe to have some semantic overlap, and dividing these attestations into groups. *In the past, the criteria for such grouping have been informal and intuitive, but recently, the criteria have become more explicit* (Ruppenhofer et al. 2010: 11, our emphasis).

Thus, according these authors, causatives and inchoatives should be split. Surprisingly enough, FN lexicographers do not appear to consistently apply this splitting approach to every LU. For example, *dry out* and *dry off* only evoke the "Cause to be dry" scenario, but not the inchoative one. Yet, online dictionaries provide users with both causative and non-causative definitions, as shown in (8) and (9):

(8) *Dry out*
  a. Longman: to become completely dry or to make something completely dry, especially after it has been very wet.
  b. Cobuild: if something dries out or is dried out, it loses all the moisture that was in it and becomes hard.
  c. Cambridge (http://dictionary.cambridge.org/dictionary/british/): to make something dry, or to become dry.

(9) *Dry off*
  a. Longman: to become dry or to make something dry, especially on the surface.
  b. Cobuild: if something dries off or if you dry it off, the moisture on its surface disappears or is removed.
  c. Cambridge: to make someone or something dry, or to become dry, especially on the surface.

In FunGramKB, instead of selecting more than one *Aktionsart* for *dry*, we treat it in its basic form, i.e. a causative accomplishment, while its inchoative counterpart is accounted for through the selection of the inchoative construction.[12]

3.2 Lexical and conceptual information

Both FN and FunGramKB share the aim of offering detailed semantic and syntactic characterizations for each LU. The basic difference, however, is the way in which each project deals with this information. As previously noted, for FN this mainly entails creating and describing frames and FEs, listing possible frame-evoking items, recording the range of semantic and syntactic combinatory possibilities of each word sense, providing corpus-attested examples, establishing connections between frames, etc. From our point of view, the lexical level of FunGramKB, which is divided into three subsections (i.e. "morphosyntax", "LCM core grammar" and "miscellaneous"), covers a broader spectrum of information (see Mairal & Periñán 2009 and Guerra & Sacramento 2011 for a full explanation):

1. In the morphosyntax subcomponent, we specify the following information for the headword:[13] (1) possible graphical variants (e.g. *favor/favour*), (2) abbreviations (e.g. *personal computer/PC*), (3) the head in a phrasal constituent or idiom (e.g. *dry*

12. As shown in 3.2, the lexical level contains a list of argument structure constructions. The lexicographer working on a given LU selects the grammatical configurations in which such an LU may be embedded, since these serve as pointers to the constructional information stored in the Grammaticon (see Periñán).

13. In this chapter, only information related to English verbs is supplied. It should be emphasized that other categories and languages will require the specification of different morphosyntactic data. To illustrate, English nouns must specify information about features such as their number and countability, and in the case of the Spanish lexicon, the gender of the noun needs to be recorded as well.

in the phrasal verbs *dry out* or *dry up*), (4) the particle(s) of a phrasal verb and whether they can be detached from the verb, in the sense of allowing the embedding of an object (e.g. *out* is the detachable particle in *dry out*), (5) category (e.g. verb), (6) verb paradigm, which records features regarding the regularity and irregularity of the verb, along with any possible constraints in voice or tense, and (7) pronominalization information (i.e. issues related to clitization and reciprocality, if applicable).

2. The LCM core grammar subsection is only available for verbs. Here, the RRG *Aktionsart* distinctions are adopted, which, suffice it to say, have been proved to be valid crosslinguistically in languages as typologically different as Italian, Tagalog, Lakota or Japanese. Thus, for each verbal predicate we select one *Aktionsart*. In order to build the lexical templates of the verbs included in the Lexicon, we shall begin by identifying the number of prototypical arguments or variables that they take. *See*, for example, would be a two-place state predicate (i.e. **see'** (x, y)), *run* is a monovalent activity (**do'** (x, [**run'** (x)]), while *dry*, which takes two arguments (x, y), is a causative accomplishment ([**do'** (x, ∅)] CAUSE [BECOME [**dried'** (y)]). We then state the idiosyncratic features or macroroles assigned to the verb, namely, actor and undergoer. In particular, we need to provide the number of macroroles that the verbal predicate selects (0, 1, or 2) and determine which variable will function as undergoer.[14] The next step consists in linking the variables of a predicate to one and only one participant in the TF of the concept to which such lexical item is connected. This is known as "thematic frame mapping" (Periñán & Mairal 2009: 268).[15] As for the bivalent predicate *dry*, the *x* variable maps onto the Theme, while *y* maps onto the Referent. At this point, it is necessary to note that all this linguistic information (i.e. *Aktionsart*, predicate variables, macroroles and the thematic frame mapping) serves as the input for the automatic generation of a computationally-tractable structure labeled "Conceptual Logical Structure" (CLS; Mairal, Periñán & Pérez 2012; Periñán), i.e. a lexically-oriented schema containing concepts through which the lexical, conceptual, and grammatical FunGramKB levels are connected.

   Lexical templates also need to accommodate information about the idiosyncratic prepositions a verb may require and the collocations with which it frequently co-occurs. Hence, computational lexicographers will record those prepositions that

14. In RRG macroroles are groups of semantic roles which function as umbrella semantic notions covering other more specific thematic relations (Van Valin 2005: 60). For example, the actor corresponds to the most agent-like argument, whereas the undergoer could be identified with the most patient-like participant. Basically, they could roughly be equated with what other theories label *logical subject* and *logical object*, respectively. The incorporation of macroroles into the FunGramKB Lexicon turns out to be crucial in the linkage between the lexical and the grammatical modules, which consists in binding the variables of the lexical template of a verb with those of the specific constructions into which it is integrated. Such constructions are stored in the Grammaticon.

15. It should be highlighted that not all the participants in the TF must be obligatorily mapped onto the variables of the LU.

obligatorily introduce the arguments of a verb (e.g. *on* for the *y* argument of the verb *depend*), as well as their more regular collocations (e.g. the verb *dry* typically collocates, to list just a few, with nouns such as *tears*, *hair*, *eyes* or *hands*).

Adding to this, another subdivision within the LCM core grammar contains a list of grammatical constructions which the linguist selects on the basis of corpus evidence. For example, *dry*, regardless of frequency, may be embedded into the following constructions: caused-motion (e.g. *Her blood has already dried into a brown crust* (COCA, 2001)); inchoative (e.g. *He dried the coat* >>*The coat dried*); middle (e.g. *Silverrood dries well* (COCA, 1994)); or what Levin (1993: 80) labels the natural force subject alternation (e.g. *I dried the clothes in the sun* >> *The sun dried the clothes*). These very same syntactic configurations are also listed in the FunGramKB Grammaticon, in particular, in the Level 1 Constructicon (i.e. one of the repositories in the four constructional layers of the LCM), where their syntactic, semantic, and categorial information is formalized. Although a more detailed examination of the Grammaticon is beyond the scope of this chapter, we would still like to briefly comment on the rather sketchy and unequal treatment of constructions in FN. To the best of our knowledge, FN makes no explicit claims on how argument structure constructions are to be dealt with. For instance, we can infer that the incorporation of the extra-thematic FEs Beneficiary and Recipient (cf. Ruppenhofer et al. 2010: 140), which are constituents not introduced by the main evoked frame but by an external one, capture the traditional benefactive and dative constructions. However, the unexpressed object construction (*John eats at noon*) is indeed treated in Atkins et al. (2003: 269) as a construction, in particular as a case of Indefinite Null Instantiation (INI). In FN, INI points to an unexpressed core FE that needs no extra information to be fully understood because it is inferred from its surrounding context or through the grammatical structure in which it appears. Finally, as mentioned in Section 2.1 in relation to the resultative construction, the same construction is recorded as a valence pattern for some lexical units (e.g. *freeze*) but not for others (e.g. *drink*). Thus, in the light of the erratic treatment given to constructions in FN, we argue in favor of the unified account provided in both the FunGramKB Lexica and Grammatical modules. The former list the argument structure constructions into which each LU is embedded, whereas the latter describe them formally as machine-readable representations.[16]

16. That constructions are not given a central role in FN is also supported by the fact that they do not count as a factor to sort out words into different frames. As Ruppenhofer et al. (2010: 15–16) claim: "At all times, we lump together those groups whose semantic differences are due to general constructions of the language: passive, middle, tense/aspect constructions, composition with extra-thematic frame elements". Ruppenhofer et al.'s (2010: 135–160) Appendix provides a detailed study of the independent status of extra-thematic FEs in FN along with their main types, functions, and the structures by which they are triggered.

3. At last, the "miscellaneous" subsection covers information regarding dialect, style (i.e. formal, informal, etc.), the knowledge domain in which a given LU may be located (e.g. architecture, medicine, anthropology, etc.), if any, and some representative examples extracted from dictionaries or corpora. Interestingly enough, FN is also recording these features by means of the use of semantic types, which can be equated to selectional preferences in FunGramKB but which, as Ruppenhofer et al. (2010: 111–112) stress, can function marking the types of fillers for FEs (e.g. Sentient, Degree, Manner, etc.), the types of frame (i.e. non-lexical), or the types of speech context differences of the LUs of a particular frame (e.g. Positive judgment, Negative judgment). Since an exhaustive list of these semantic types is not available and their annotation is not fully completed in all frames or LUs, we cannot venture to make an exact comparison between FN and FunGramKB in this respect. Suffice it to say that the semantic types employed in FN to classify the fillers of FEs could resemble FunGramKB's selectional preferences, with the proviso that the former had an ontological status and composed a closed class, as is the case of basic concepts. In fact, Ruppenhofer et al. (2010: 112) comment that "most of these [semantic] types correspond directly to synset nodes of WordNet, and can be mapped onto ontologies, e.g. Cyc." We wonder, however, how these semantic types (i.e. register, style, or evaluation of a particular LU) are going to be annotated in the lexical entry reports, since so far, apart from the dictionary definition, they only list the semantic and syntactic patterns of words (see Tables 1 and 2).

At this point, the reader may wonder how FunGramKB takes care of such vital issues as phrase types and grammatical functions, which as we have seen, is one of FN's strongest assets. Owing to the fact that FunGramKB is a knowledge base that has been developed with a view to creating NLP systems that demand language understanding, information related to phrases and syntactic functions is provided in the very first phases involved in text processing, namely, tokenization, morphological analysis, and syntax-semantics processing. As Periñán & Arcas (2011: 8–9) detail, the tokenizer divides the input text into sentences and orthographic words, whereas the morphological parser deprives words from their inflectional suffixes, which entails consulting the information stored in the Lexicon as well as in the Morphicon. Lastly, the syntax-semantics parser tags the parts of speech of the lemmas, assigning grammatical functions as well. At the end of this phase, the system outputs a structure where the lemmas have been replaced with concepts. Examples (10a)-(10d) illustrate the three phases responsible for text processing in FunGramKB (cf. Periñán & Arcas 2011: 9 for the rest of phases):

(10) a. Sally dried the shirts
b. Sally | dried | the | shirts
c. Sally | dry | the | shirt
d. S(NP(n(%SALLY_00)), VP(v(+DRY_00)), (NP(det(the), n(+SHIRT_00)))

In sum, FN and FunGramKB offer complementary types of information. FN exhibits a highly detailed account concerning the semantic and syntactic properties of lexical items. The thorough list of phrase types and grammatical functions, the variety of illustrative examples given, and the number of LUs recorded (12,715) are certainly FN's strongest points. In this respect, FN clearly surpasses FunGramKB. In FunGramKB the phases described in (10) are not visible for the user, nor is this conceptualist account concerned with offering a notable number of representative examples (see Table 3 below). Rather, its main focus is on processing any input text. Likewise, the number of LUs in FunGramKB, which amounts to a total of 3,707 in the English lexicon, is still scarce if compared to those already available in FN. We believe, however, that the FunGramKB Lexica provide the user with a broader spectrum of linguistic data than that furnished in FN, e.g. the morphological paradigm of a verb, its *Aktionsart*, macroroles, prepositions, collocations, and the associated grammatical constructions, apart from features related to dialect, style, etc. By way of example, Table 3 captures all the information that the FunGramKB user has access to for the LU *dry*:

Table 3. FunGramKB's lexical entry for *dry*

Headword	dry
Concept	+DRY_01
Thematic Fram	(x1) Theme (x2: +CORPUSCULAR_00)Referent
Meaning Postulate	+ (el: +CHANGE_00 (x1) Theme (x2) Referent (f1: (e2: n +BECOME_00 (x2) Theme (x3: +WET_00) Attribute)) Result)
POS	V
Paradigm	Regular
Tense Constraints	no
Reflexivity	Optional
Reciprocity	Never
Aktionsart	CACC
Lexical template: variables	X-Theme, Y-Referent
Lexical template: restrictions	MR2, U = Y
Collocations	Y = eyes, hair, hands, tears
Constructions	Caused-motion construction (transitive) Inchoative construction Middle construction Natural force subject construction
Dialect	Standard
Usage	Common
Topic	FACTOTUM
Examples	"Her mouth had dried." (GUE W_fict_prose) "She dried her hands on the kitchen towel, adding, "I worry about Ernest." (FPM W_fict_prose)

Adding to this, FunGramKB goes one step further in that all this linguistic information depends on the conceptual module, the pivot around which this knowledge base revolves, which explains why that is the very first piece of information that appears in an entry (see row 2 in Table 3). To illustrate this point, consider once again the two frames discussed throughout this chapter (i.e. "Becoming dry" and "Cause to be dry"). At the beginning of Section 3, we introduced the list of LUs evoking the aforementioned scenarios, here repeated for the reader's convenience. Verbs such as *dehydrate, dry up, dry* and *exsiccate* evoke the "Becoming dry" frame, whereas one of the senses of *anhydrate, dehumidify, dehumidification, dehydrate, desiccate, desiccation, dry, dry off, dry out* and *dry up* are connected to "Cause to be dry". At least in the case of the two frames under scrutiny, FunGramKB currently posits a more exhaustive list of the hyponyms of *dry*, with the added advantages brought about by the adoption of a purely conceptualist approach, namely: (1) although the Ontology is linguistically motivated as a result of its involvement with the semantics of the predicates, the knowledge stored is not language-specific, contrarily to what is the case in FN; (2) because meaning definitions are provided at the conceptual level, management of multilingual knowledge is facilitated; (3) since concepts are described through the metalanguage COREL, a reasoning engine will actually be capable of processing and understanding the information of all the modules included in the knowledge base.

With this in mind, consider now the complete organization of this conceptual subdomain. +DRY_01 in (11) functions as the basic concept within which two other terminal concepts are contained, i.e. $WITHER_00 and $TUMBLE_DRY_01. Their definitions in COREL, together with their translation into natural language, are given in (12a) and (13a). Note too that several LUs from English, Spanish and Italian depend on each of these conceptual units:

(11) a. MP of +DRY_01: +(e1: +CHANGE_00 (x1)Theme (x2: +CORPUSCULAR_00)Referent (f1: (e2: n +BECOME_00 (x2)Theme (x3: +WET_00) Attribute))Result) = 'An entity (x1) changes a three dimensional object (x2) so that as a result, (x2) will not be wet'.

b. Related LUs:
- English (En.): *air-dry, blow-dry, dehumidify, dehydrate, desiccate, drain, drip-dry, dry, dry off, dry out, dry up, exsiccate, torrefy.*
- Spanish (Sp.): *desecar, deshidratar, deshumedecer, disecar, enjugar, escurrir, orear, resecar, secar.*
- Italian (It.): *asciugare, disidratare, essiccare, inaridire, prosciugare, seccare.*

(12) a. MP of $WITHER_00: +(e1: +DRY_01 (x1)Theme (x2: +PLANT_00)Referent (f1: (e2: +BECOME_00 (x2)Theme (x3: +SMALL_00 | +WEAK_00) Attribute))Result (f2: (e3: ing +DIE_00 (x2)Theme))Result) = 'An entity (x1) dries a plant (x2) so that (x2) becomes small and weak and starts ('ing') to die'.

b. Related LUs:
   - En.: *wither, shrivel, scorch.*
   - Sp.: *agostar, ajar, marchitar, mustiar.*
   - It.: *appassire, avvizzire.*

(13) a. MP of $TUMBLE_DRY_01: +(e1: +DRY_01 (x1)Theme (x2: +CLOTHING_00)Referent (f1: $TUMBLE_DRY_00)Instrument) = 'An entity dries clothes using a tumble drier'.

b. Related LUs:
   - En.: *tumble dry.*[17]

As opposed to the way in which FN organizes the frames "Becoming dry" and "Cause to be dry", the basic concept +DRY_01 in FunGramKB is semantically decomposed into two terminal concepts (together with their related LUs). Thus, although FunGramKB has at its disposal a limited inventory of basic concepts to work with, the semantic knowledge stored in this resource is quite fine-grained. Besides, since such knowledge is formalized employing COREL, the descriptions are machine-readable, which means that the computer will have the capacity to discriminate between conceptually related events such as +DRY_01, $WITHER_00 or $TUMBLE_DRY_01. As for FN, the proliferation of frames and FEs is directly favored by the fact that the database focuses on the semantics and syntax of LUs instead of envisaging a limited repertoire of defining units.[18] On the contrary, in FunGramKB the division of labor between linguistic knowledge into the Grammaticon, Morphicon, and Lexicon, and of non-linguistic knowledge in the Ontology, Cognicon, and Onomasticon modules, supplies a well-balanced lexico-conceptual resource. This is so because in order to have lexical items in the lexicon of a particular language, there must previously exist a concept in the Ontology to which those lexical pieces can be associated.

17. As is clear from the case of $WITHER_00, the tendency sought in FunGramKB is to create terminal concepts to which several words in English, Spanish, Italian, etc. can be linked, so that the process of modeling conceptual meaning in the Ontology is not biased towards a particular language (Jiménez & Luzondo 2011: 21). However, lexical gaps among the different languages should not impede the creation of terminal concepts (e.g. $TUMBLE_DRY_01) "whenever there is at least one lexical unit whose meaning does not match any of the MPs stored in the knowledge base" (Mairal & Periñán 2009: 223).

18. Among others, an illustrative example of FN being semantically and syntactically driven is the case of *give*. This LU evokes the "Giving" frame but not the "Causation" frame, purely because of linguistic reasons, that is, because *give* is not always synonymous with *cause*. Consequently, they cannot appear in the same syntactic patterns (cf. Ruppenhofer et al. 2010:115–116). However, based on conceptual grounds, FunGramKB links *give* to the basic concept +GIVE_00, whose superordinate parents are +MOVE_00 >>> +TRANSFER_00; to put it simply, the event of giving "in the real world" implies causing something to move from one location to another.

3.3 Relations between frames and concepts

As advanced in 2.1, FN establishes frame-to-frame relations of various types, among which we will only focus on those that are useful for machine processing: Inheritance, Using, Perspective on, Subframe, Precedes, Inchoative of, and Causative of.

Inheritance covers those cases in which a child frame is a more specific elaboration of a superordinate or parent frame. For instance, the "Attaching" frame inherits information from its parent, i.e. the "Intentionally affect" frame (Fillmore et al. 2003b: 311). Inheritance in FN, which corresponds to the IS-A relationship employed in FunGramKB and other ontologies, is the most comprehensive, formally defined relation, since it not only organizes frames, but also FEs and semantic types (cf. Ruppenhofer et al. 2010: 104–105). The Using relation, however, makes reference to those situations in which the child frame employs the parent frame only as a background, that is, "when a part of the scene evoked by the subordinate frame refers to the parent frame" (Ruppenhofer et al. 2010: 110). For instance, the "Offering" frame utilizes the "Giving" frame, but the latter does not presuppose the former. As a further elaboration of the Using relation, the Perspective on relation has just been introduced in FN. Perspective on applies to those frames that express a different point of view of a given event (e.g. the "Get a job" and "Hiring" frames are perspectives of the "Begin employment" frame; see Ruppenhofer et al. 2010: 107). In turn, the Subframe relation allows FN lexicographers to characterize complex frames. Thus, Subframe is utilized to designate the different sequential parts of a complex event, such as the "Inchoative attaching" frame within the complex "Attaching" one (Fillmore et al. 2003b: 313). Similarly, the Precedes relationship organizes the occurrence of the component frames of a single complex one in terms of their precedence; that is to say, the "Criminal process" frame is preceded by the subframe "Criminal investigation" which, in turn, is preceded by the "Committing a crime" subframe (Ruppenhofer et al. 2010: 109).[19] Finally, the Causative of and Inchoative of relations capture the non-inheritance connection between, for example, the "Position on a scale", "Change position on a scale", and "Cause change of scalar position" frames (see Ruppenhofer et al. 2010: 110). It is interesting to note that all these frame-to-frame relations are shown in the frame reports and can be viewed through the FrameGrapher tool available on the main FN website. By way of illustration, Figure 3 portrays a partial snapshot of frame-to-frame relations:

19. Rosca (2012: 257) rightly points out that the FN Precedes relation parallels the before relation proposed in Allen's (1983) interval sequences, which FunGramKB employs in the Cognicon. Likewise, Rosca also establishes a connection between the Subframe relationship and the number of subscripts that make up a complex script in the Cognicon. The interested reader is referred to Periñán and Arcas (2010b) and Garrido and Ruiz de Mendoza (2011) for further details on the nature of the FunGramKB Cognicon.

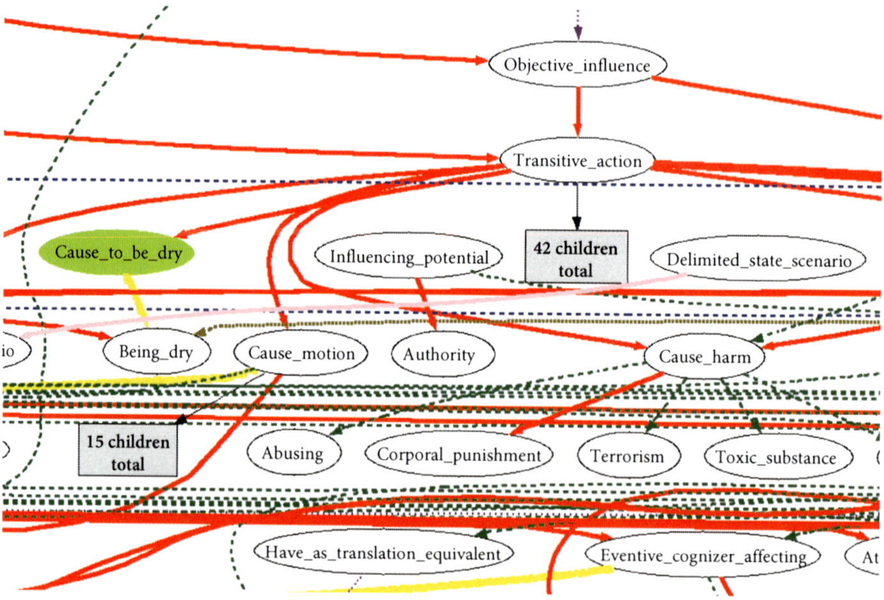

Figure 3. Frame-to-frame relations using FrameGrapher

Although FN was not originally designed for NLP tasks, this issue has lately gained ground in this project. Hence, Ruppenhofer et al. (2010: 16–18, 121–127) argue that the above-mentioned relations are extremely valuable for paraphrasing, inferencing, and the propagation of information.[20] Since FN does not directly tackle the near-paraphrasability between sentences or utterances but only between words, frame relations like Causative of or Using explicitly connect LUs that may, however, belong to different frames. To illustrate, examples like *The paste hardened due to hydration of the cement* and *The hydration of the cement hardened the paste* can be regarded as paraphrases of each other thanks to the Causative of relationship that links the two frames in which *harden* is stored (Ruppenhofer et al. 2010: 17). By the same token, frame relations, especially Inheritance, can explain some cases of (near) paraphrasability where inference is called upon. For example, *You needed my help so I got on the bus* and *You needed my help so I came* are considered near-paraphrases due to the fact that the LUs *bus* and *come* start off the inference process. As Ruppenhofer et al. (2010: 18) state, *bus* belongs to the "Vehicle" frame, which is associated to the "Motion" frame, this frame being employed by the "Arriving" frame, which is the one that lists the verb *come* among its LUs. Although we have tried to follow the conceptual path between *bus* and *come*, in the current "Vehicle" frame there is no link to the "Motion" frame but rather to the "Artifact" frame through Inheritance and, via the Is used by relation, to the

20. It is commonly agreed in the literature that a powerful NLP system should be able to (1) paraphrase an input text, (2) translate it into another language, (3) answer questions about its contents, and (4) draw inferences from it (cf. Liddy 2001).

"Convoy" and "Vehicle" subpart frames. We can venture here that inference may be triggered because the noun *bus* has in its lexical entry report the verb *come* as one of its governors, along with *catch, miss, leave,* etc., and thus *come* evokes the "Arriving" frame, among others. However, how the machine could arrive at such a connection is not made explicit in FN at this stage. Finally, Inheritance is also held responsible for the propagation of information both in terms of the semantic types and of the expected syntactical realization of the parent frame and its FEs down to the child frame and its FEs (see Ruppenhofer et al. 2010: 127–128).

Before moving on to FunGramKB, a number of issues need to be addressed here. As a glance at Figure 3 reveals, the baroque organization originated from the adoption of various types of frame-to-frame relations would most likely fail in an NLP environment as far as a reasoning engine is concerned. Furthermore, as Ruppenhofer et al. (2010: 121) contend, "more specific relationships between the words usually need to be ascertained to recognize or generate actual instances of paraphrases". Even though they claim that the wide range of relations proposed by WordNet could easily be mapped onto the FN LUs and vice versa, we are rather skeptical as to the efficiency of a reasoning engine that is required to handle not only the relations between frames but also between LUs and FEs, as "the relations of FEs and LUs to frames are intertwined with our Frame relations in various ways" (*ibid.* 126). We endorse here Ovchinnikova et al.'s (2010) proposal of improving these FN relations by employing an ontological analysis which, among other things, would entail connecting frames to categories in DOLCE (Masolo et al. 2003). As they rightly detail, such a methodological movement would solve issues such as FN's coverage poverty (i.e. the fact that semantically related frames that one would expect to be connected are, however, not captured that way in the FN taxonomy) which, as pointed out before in the *bus-come* example, hinder adequate inferences. Likewise, some of the conceptual discrepancies spotted in FN by Ovchinnikova et al. (2010) are claimed to stem from the fact that the FN Inheritance relation equally applies to frames, FEs, and semantic types. Consequently, serious reasoning problems can arise. Take, for instance, the example *Many [[parts]*^{PART}*]*$^{PART\ WHOLE}$ *[of tsunami-battered Aceh province]*^{WHOLE} *were not safe* (*ibid.*: 3158). Since in FN, the role WHOLE is connected to the "Substance" frame, which implies that its fillers will also be substances, the machine will wrongly process that the "Aceh province" is a substance. Therefore, Ovchinnikova et al. (2010: 3163) propose the axiomatization and restructuring of these FN relations, which will certainly improve the accuracy of natural language reasoning. In order to achieve this goal, an ontological analysis needs first to be applied to the current frames. In other words, frames are classified in terms of three of the categories employed by DOLCE, namely, perdurant, endurant, and quality, so that the relationships established between them can then be easily enriched, constrained, axiomatized, and cleaned up. As must be apparent to the reader, these DOLCE categories correspond to the three Subontologies already contemplated in FunGramKB (e.g. #EVENTS, #ENTITIES, and #QUALITIES), which highlights the benefits of an ontologically-driven approach to NLP systems vs. a lexically-oriented one.

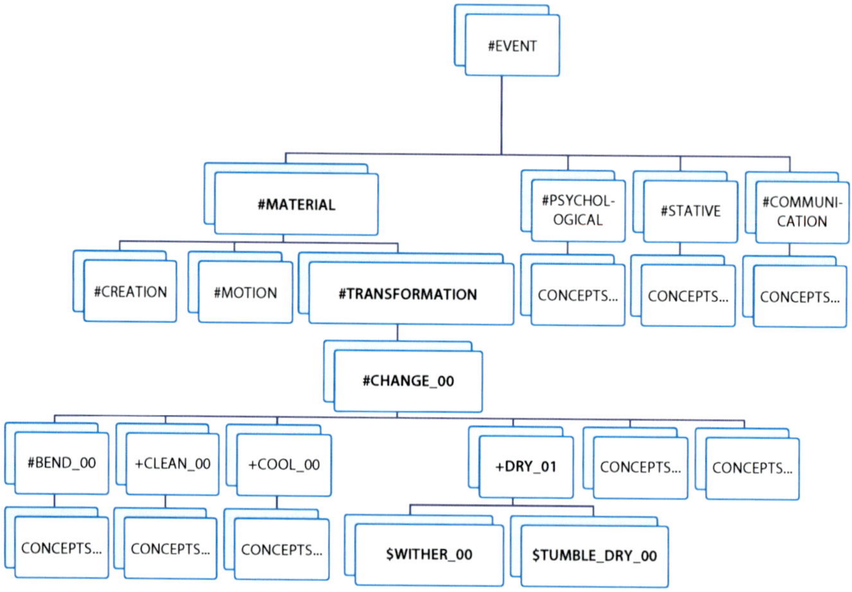

Figure 4. Conceptual path organization of +DRY_01 and its subordinates in FunGramKB

As for FunGramKB, IS-A is the only relation permitted. Figure 4 shows the hierarchical organization of the conceptual route of +DRY_01. Clearly, FunGramKB would benefit from a visual tool like FrameGrapher that could make explicit the inheritance flow of semantic knowledge in the taxonomy.

But the exhaustive use of IS-A in FunGramKB is not free from problems. For example, despite the application of the OntoClean methodology to the Subontology of entities (see Periñán & Mairal 2011: 25–27), instances of taxonomic misclassifications and redundancy are present. A case in point is that of +FUEL_00 and its subordinate concepts +COAL_00, +PETROLEUM_00, +PETROL_00 and +WOOD_00. Since this basic concept includes three conceptual parents in its MP (i.e. +LIQUID_00 ^ +GAS_00 ^ +SOLID_00), +FUEL_00 and all of its subordinates appear three times in the taxonomy, once under +LIQUID_00, once connected to +GAS_00, and once linked to +SOLID_00. Therefore, although the IS-A relation is claimed to minimize redundancy and maximize information, redundancy is still present at least in the case of entities. In our view, these hierarchical problems cannot be successfully tackled until the FunGramKB Ontology is completely populated and thoroughly revised for possible inconsistencies.

Regarding FN, the use of inheritance is merely descriptive. As already discussed, the "Cause to be dry" frame inherits from the "Transitive action" frame and it is also the causative counterpart of "Being dry" (see Figure 3 above). For practical purposes, however, there seems to be no real inheritance of information, since each actual frame is re-defined in its own terms. That is, although the "Cause to be dry" frame defined as

"An Agent causes a Dryee to become dry" is a subordinate of the "Transitive action" frame (i.e. "this frame characterizes, at a very abstract level, an Agent or Cause affecting a Patient"), such a specification is not fully incorporated into the definition of the causative frame itself, but rather, the connection between the two schemas is simply made explicit. A clearer example is that of the "Setting fire" frame, which also inherits from the "Transitive action" frame. Its definition is, however, the following: "this frame describes either the creation of Flame by a Kindler or the igniting of Flammables by a Kindler".

Besides inheritance, FunGramKB also envisages a second reasoning mechanism, i.e. inference, which is based on the semantic knowledge shared between concepts that do not form part of the same IS-A relation. Figure 5, taken from Periñán and Arcas (2005: 241), portrays both mechanisms as if they were applied to any MP within the conceptual route between the nuclear concept and its metaconcept:

We are fully aware that FN does not have NLP systems as one of its main goals. Therefore, we do not intend to criticize it for failing to provide what it was not designed to do. However, it is worth noting that FunGramKB already contemplates the existence of a reasoning engine that is able to work with the information and knowledge stored in the Ontology and in the Cognicon. Even though this reasoning engine is still being developed, there are two components that make it up: the Microconceptual-Knowledge Spreading or MicroKnowing and the Macroconceptual-Knowing Spreading or MacroKnowing. While the former runs on the Ontology, spreading the

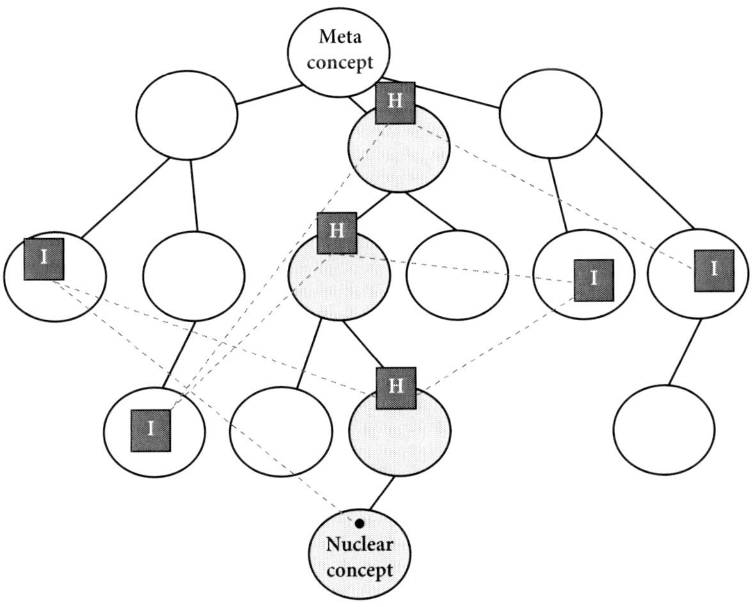

Figure 5. Inheritance (H) and Inference (I) mechanisms in FunGramKB

semantic knowledge contained in the MPs through the iterative application of inheritance and inference, the latter incorporates these MPs in the scripts stored in the Cognicon with a view to spreading the procedural knowledge recorded in FunGramKB.[21] Let us illustrate how the MicroKnowing process would expand the MP of + LIQUID_00 in (14) to include other concepts such as $BOTTLE_00, $GLASS_00, etc.

(14) MP of the entity +LIQUID_00: +(e1: +BE_00 (x1: +LIQUID_00)Theme (x2: +SUBSTANCE_00)Referent)

At the first spreading level, the inference mechanism is triggered, searching through the Ontology for any MP that contains the nuclear concept, that is, +LIQUID_00, as the selectional preference of the participants of a predication. For instance, the following predication from the MP of $BOTTLE_00 is inferred:

(15) *(e3: +CONTAIN_00 (x4: +LIQUID_00)Theme (x1)Location)

At the second spreading level, inheritance is applied so that those predications in the MP of the immediate superordinate concept of the nuclear concept are incorporated, namely, +SUBSTANCE_00:

(16) MP of the entity +SUBSTANCE_00: +(e1: +BE_00 (x1: +SUBSTANCE_00) Theme (x2: +ARTIFICIAL_OBJECT_00 ^ +NATURAL_OBJECT_00)Referent)

From this stage on, inference and inheritance are triggered iteratively, which results in the expansion of the conceptual meaning of +LIQUID_00 to incorporate the semantic knowledge from the predications of concepts such as +MELT_00, $GLASS_00, +WET_00, +TOUCH_01, +TASTE_01, +SPOON_00, etc.

This leads us to another crucial feature that distinguishes FN and FunGramKB, that is to say, how encyclopedic meaning is approached and dealt with by each resource. As far as frames describe types of situations, encyclopedic knowledge is accounted for in FN. However, the level of detail achieved is different from that attained in FunGramKB. As illustrated above with +LIQUID_00, the FunGramKB conceptual definitions are more comprehensive than frames, since, thanks to inference and inheritance, they can contain an ever-growing web of encyclopedic knowledge. Consequently, for the conceptual unit +LIQUID_00, apart from learning that it is a substance (cf. its MP in (14)), we also infer that it is typically contained in a bottle or a glass, that as a result of a melting process a solid entity turns into liquid, that it has the quality of being wet, that it can be touched, tasted or that a human entity can use a spoon to ingest it. By contrast, the "Substance" frame evoked by the noun *liquid* is redundantly characterized as: "This frame concerns internally undifferentiated Substances". The Substance is the core FE, described as

21. Periñán and Arcas (2005) provide the formal representation, the various spreading levels, and the resolution of incompatibilities of the MicroKnowing. The MacroKnowing does not as yet exist, but the interested reader can find a proper description in Periñán and Arcas (2007a).

"The undifferentiated entity which is presented as having a permanent existence". As for the "Substance by phase" frame to which the adjective *liquid* is linked, the definition is: "in this frame an Undergoer is in a phase brought about after a change of phase. This can be its inherent phase or indicate that it is returned to its inherent state". However, this definition does not seem to provide the fine-grained analysis and the amount of encyclopedic information supplied by FunGramKB, since FN does not envision the reasoning mechanisms described thus far which are, nevertheless, crucial in an NLP environment.

3.4 Information management

FunGramKB's thematic roles and satellites can be equated to FEs, although the way in which each project manages this information is different.

As previously stated, the "Cause to be dry" frame evoked by *dry* contains three core FEs: an Agent, the Cause, which excludes the Agent, and a Dryee.[22] Being non-causative, the only core FE in the semantic frame "Becoming dry" is the Agent. Each of these FEs needs to be defined with respect to the semantic frame to which they belong. As such, whereas in the former the Agent is "the person performing the intentional act causing the Dryee to become dry", in the latter the Agent is characterized as "the thing that loses moisture and becomes dry". In the case of *bend*, which evokes a frame labeled "Change posture", we find that the Core FE is a Protagonist, that is, "the individual whose posture changes". The "Cause change of phase" frame (evoked by one sense of *melt*) is composed by three core FEs: Agent (i.e. the entity that "causes the Undergoer to change phase"), Cause ("the non-Agent which brings about the change in the Undergoer") and Undergoer (the entity that "undergoes a change of phase brought about by the Agent"). Here, Cause also excludes the Agent.

From our point of view, the number of FEs in a given frame is rather unregulated, while it also seems that FEs are sometimes arbitrarily labeled. The nature of FN requires that each frame be provided with its own set of FE-types; some FEs usually occurring across frames (e.g. Manner, Place, Time, etc.), some largely varying from one frame to another, e.g. Importing area FE (frame "Importing"), Hot cold source FE ("Inchoative change of temperature" frame), Characteristic FE ("Path traveled" frame), Body part FE ("Grooming" frame), Food and Grower FEs ("Growing food" frame), Configuration FE ("Hair configuration" frame), etc. Except for the non-exhaustive list of extra-thematic FEs given in Appendix A of Ruppenhofer et al.'s (2010) book, there

22. In FunGramKB, instead of having an FE that excludes another FE, we would not specify a selectional preference in cases like this. Recall, by way of illustration, that in the MP of +DRY_01 in (11a), the (x1)Theme is left unspecified since different entities (e.g. a human being, the sun, etc.) can cause something to dry.

appears to be no clear policy that regulates the choice of one FE over another.[23] A case in point is that of the FEs "Dryee", "Patient" and "Item":

(17) "Cause to be dry" frame:
Core FEs: Agent, Cause, Dryee (i.e. "the entity which has the water removed from it", e.g. *Michael dehydrated* ***the apples***).

(18) "Cause to change strength" frame:
Core FEs: Agent, Patient (i.e. "entity that is being made stronger", e.g. *Weight training strengthens* ***the muscles***).
Core unexpressed FE: Cause

(19) "Cause temperature change" frame:
Core FE: Agent, Cause, Hot cold source, Item (i.e. "the Item undergoes the temperature change", e.g. *Ryan reheated* ***the pasta*** *in the microwave*).

While clearly Agent and Cause are applied consistently, we may ask ourselves on what grounds the more specific participants Dryee or Item are selected over that of the more inclusive notion of Patient in (18). Seemingly, the question arises as to where lexicographers draw the line when it comes to addressing the number of FEs that may be involved in each semantic frame. For instance, while we find a Result FE in the "Absorb heat" frame (e.g. *The lobster boiled to death*), the "Change phase" frame (e.g. *The lake froze solid*) or the "Emotion active" frame (e.g. *She was worrying herself sick about Biggles*), we have seen that this FE is not present in the "Ingestion" semantic frame to account for realizations of the type *They drank themselves blind* (BNC EUU), *The snake that ate itself to death* (BNC FBG), etc. Likewise, the "Ingestion" frame does not include the Iteration FE even though the BNC retrieves cases like *I fed her twice a day* (BNC C8U) or *She eats meat once a week* (BNC EG0).

In FunGramKB, thematic frames and satellites are managed in a significantly different fashion. First, the cognitive dimensions under which all concepts are organized amounts to a total of 15 metaconcepts in the Subontology of events (e.g. #MOTION, #COGNITION, #EXISTENCE, #EMOTION, etc., see Periñán and Mairal (2010) for the complete list). In turn, the catalogue of thematic roles is restricted to the following participants: Agent, Theme, Referent, Attribute, Location, Origin and Goal. Obviously, the number of thematic roles varies from one cognitive dimension to the other. #MOTION, for example, takes Agent, Theme, Location, Origin and Goal; #EXISTENCE only contains the Theme role, whereas Theme, Referent and Goal are the participants in the metaconcept #COMMUNICATION. Moreover, the characterization of this limited set of thematic roles is different depending on each dimension. For example, #CREATION, #TRANSFORMATION and #PERCEPTION include two thematic roles, i.e. a Theme (x1) and a Referent (x2). Their definitions, however, are the following:

23. Periñán (2013a: 89) argues that FN lexicographers probably "opted for this excessive granularity in semantic roles in order to compensate for the deficiencies" resulting from the adoption of a shallow approach to lexical meaning.

(20) #CREATION
 a. Theme: entity that creates another entity.
 b. Referent: entity that is created by another entity.

(21) #TRANSFORMATION
 a. Theme: entity that transforms another entity.
 b. Referent: entity that is transformed by another entity.

(22) #PERCEPTION
 a. Theme: entity that perceives another entity through any of the senses.
 b. Referent: entity that is perceived through any of the senses.

Take now the three LUs discussed at the beginning of this section (i.e. *dry*, *bend* and *melt*) and their corresponding basic concepts in FunGramKB (i.e. +DRY_01, +BEND_00 and +MELT_00). These conceptual units, together with others like +TRANSLATE_00, +SPLIT_00, +REPAIR_00, +CLEAN_01, etc., are located within the metaconcept #TRANSFORMATION. This entails that, despite the obvious meaning differences among these concepts, they and their subordinates must take an (x1) Theme and an (x2)Referent as participants in their TFs. However, the definition of these thematic roles (cf. example (21) above) is not altered so as to comply with the specifics of any of these concepts. The same rationale applies to #PERCEPTION in (22), since every single TF of any of the concepts situated under this metaconcept will only display two participant roles whose characterization is exactly the same throughout this entire portion of the Ontology.

Both FEs and the participants in the TF need to be defined against a given frame or metaconcept. Nonetheless, in FunGramKB the number and type of categories (i.e. 15 cognitive dimensions), and by extension the number of thematic roles and their definitions, is much more limited than in the case of FN. Additionally, it should be noted that in some cases, an FE can also take the form of a selectional preference in FunGramKB. For example, the TF of the terminal concept $FRY_00, a subordinate of +COOK_00, specifies two selectional preferences via two basic concepts: a human (i.e. (x1: +HUMAN_00)Theme) fries food (i.e. (x2: FOOD_00)Referent). In the "Apply heat" frame, the selectional preference (x2: +FOOD_00)Referent corresponds to the core FE Food of the verb *fry*. As was the case with metaconcepts and thematic roles, basic concepts also make up a limited inventory (cf. Section 3.1).

We have already explained that all subordinate concepts in the Ontology must specify a distinctive feature or *differentia*, which is not present in the MP of the superordinate. In the syntax of COREL, *differentiae* are expressed by employing satellites. FunGramKB thus posits a total of 16 satellites, namely, beneficiary, company, condition, duration, frequency, instrument, manner, means, position, purpose, quantity, reason, result, scene, speed and time. Some of these satellites are similar to the most widely occurring extra-thematic and peripheral FEs. However, as in the case of thematic roles, each of these satellites has one and only one definition independently of the peculiarities of any given concept. For comparative purposes, let us deal with one example. In FunGramKB, the manner satellite is described as the "entity or quality that describes the way in which the event occurs". By contrast, the Manner FE in FN may be defined as:

(23) "Abusing" frame:
Manner FE: Manner is used for any description of the abuse event which is not covered by more specific FEs, including secondary effects (*quietly, loudly*), and general descriptions comparing events (the same way). In addition, it may indicate salient characteristics of an Abuser that also affect the action (*presumptuously, coldly, deliberately, eagerly, carefully*), e.g. *It is fair to say that it was* ***malicious*** *abuse.*

(24) "Cause to make progress" frame:
Manner FE: A description of the progress, generally a description comparing events (the same way); in addition, it may describe characteristics and states of the Agent that also affect the development (no example is given).

(25) "Make noise" frame:
Manner FE: Manner expressions may be of lexicographic interest if they describe properties of a sound as such: *loudly, shrilly*, etc., e.g. *Jocelyn sobbed* ***loudly****.*

From this explanation it follows that FunGramKB opts for an economic, parsimonious organization of both thematic roles and satellites, which allows for the efficient management of information in an NLP environment.

3.5 Multilingualism

As rightly pointed out by Boas (2009b: 59), creating multilingual lexical databases (or knowledge bases, in the case of FunGramKB) that may be employed in a variety of (NLP) applications is a particularly challenging endeavor. Despite its indisputable difficulty, Boas (2009b: 59–60; see also Boas 2009a) contends that the English FN database facilitates the creation of multilingual lexical databases capable of overcoming linguistic problems concerning issues like diverging polysemy structures or differences in lexicalization patterns, among others. Thus, it is argued that semantic frames have been successfully utilized by a number of FN-type projects for both western languages (e.g. Spanish and German) and non-western languages like Japanese.

In building parallel non-English FNs various phases need to be followed, although only a simplified summary is included here (see Boas 2009b: 72–87 for more details). First, after downloading the English FN MySQL database, all language-specific information needs to be removed. Second, once only information not specific to English remains (i.e. conceptual information in the form of a frame relation table, frame elements table, etc.), the lexicographer can repopulate the database with lexical descriptions from another language. This step involves selecting a semantic frame from the stripped-down original database to which, with the help of dictionaries and parallel corpora, a set of LUs evoking that frame are added. Having completed these steps, corpus-attested sentences illustrating the use of each of the frame-evoking LUs are inserted. But the real labor-intensive process begins when parallel lexicon fragments are linked in order to map lexical information from one language to another. This entails that within a given semantic frame the lexicographer should find LUs in, for example, Spanish, which have corresponding semantic and syntactic combinatorial possibilities in English. Having identified comparable structures, the linking is performed via semantic frames, which work as *interlingual representations* (i.e. representations that combine aspects of true interlinguas and transfer-based systems). So far, only Spanish, German and Japanese FNs are associating their entries to entries from the English FN. Hence, the next step would require "linking lexical entries across languages in order to test the applicability of semantic frames as a cross-linguistic metalanguage" (Boas 2009b: 92).

The following conclusions may be gathered from the account given above. Even though individual FNs for various languages exist independently of one another, the approach adopted in the creation of frame-based multilingual databases is in line with the conceptualist account advocated by FunGramKB: both depart from linguistically motivated concepts (or semantic frames, in the case of FN), on the grounds of which LUs from various languages are interconnected. Two differences may be highlighted. First, unlike FN, FunGramKB was originally designed as an inherently multilingual knowledge base. Since the Ontology is the central component of the whole architecture and, therefore, semantic descriptions are provided at the conceptual level, the management of multilingual knowledge is facilitated. This avoids the removal of language-specific information and subsequent repopulation described by Boas (2009b). Instead, the process of defining language-independent concepts and that of inserting the set of related LUs lexicalizing them (in various languages) is carried out simultaneously. Second, because FunGramKB is a resource for NLP, the definition of concepts, in contrast to semantic frames, is formalized via the universal metalanguage, i.e. COREL, thanks to which the computer is able to understand and process knowledge. In spite of these advantages, it should be noted that so far FunGramKB has less monolingual and multilingual information than FN.

In closing, it is worth emphasizing that both projects appear to point in the same direction:

> At this early point, semantic frames do not serve as a true interlingua in which a concept is realized independently of a source language (...) *Once more languages are described, we may arrive at true universal semantic frames (e.g. communication, motion, etc.), which may then serve as a true interlingua*" (Boas 2009b: 87, our emphasis).

As previously mentioned, not only does FunGramKB already make use of the COREL metalanguage, but also its cognitive dimensions or metaconcepts, e.g. #COMMUNICATION, #MOTION, #POSSESSION, #PERCEPTION, #COGNITION, etc., appear to correspond to the future universal semantic frames pursued in FN.

4. Conclusion

This study has made an elaborate comparison between FN and FunGramKB by focusing on how each of these projects handles the representation of semantic knowledge. The implications for the creation of NLP tasks have also been peripherally touched upon, allowing us to make explicit the differences between a shallow approach and a deep approach to knowledge representation.

As detailed throughout the chapter, FunGramKB and FN have originally been created to fulfil different goals, which certainly speaks of their differences. On the one hand, FN is a lexical resource based on Frame Semantics whose aim is to document the semantic and syntactic combinatory possibilities of each word sense. FunGramKB, on the other hand, is a knowledge-base designed for its use in NLP. This does not mean, however, that these projects cannot be compared, since as we have seen, FN and FunGramKB are different in many respects but are also alike in others. To illustrate, we could list their common usage of organizational conceptual units larger than words, their equal treatment of polysemy, their account of semantic types, selectional preferences or encyclopedic knowledge, and their interest in developing multilingual resources.

In sum, FN and FunGramKB offer complementary types of information in many aspects, especially in the way they approach linguistic knowledge. However, at present, since FunGramKB assumes a division of labor between linguistic knowledge and conceptual knowledge in which the Ontology is the component that connects them, this knowledge base is more suitable for language processing. Additionally, given that text understanding implies the incorporation of a situation model so that the gestalt meaning of the text can be recovered by the machine from the words that make it up (Zwaan & Radvansky 1998, *apud* Periñán & Arcas 2007a), lexical knowledge *per se* is not sufficient. Thus, the fact that FunGramKB links each LU to a concept in the Ontology and the knowledge therein, a step that FN has not taken yet, assures the creation of more accurate NLP systems for language understanding.

References

Allen, James F. 1983. Maintaining knowledge about temporal intervals. *Communications of the ACM* 26(11): 832–843.

Atkins, Sue, Fillmore, Charles J. & Johnson, Christopher R. 2003. Lexicographic relevance: Selection information from corpus evidence. *International Journal of Lexicography* 16(3): 251–280.

Baker, Collin F., Fillmore, Charles J. & Lowe, John B. 1998. The Berkeley FrameNet project. In *COLING-ACL '98 Proceedings of the Conference*, 86–90. Montreal: Canada.

Boas, Hans C. 2005. From theory to practice: Frame Semantics and the design of FrameNet. In *Semantik im Lexikon*, Stefan Langer & Daniel Schnorbusch (eds), 129–160. Tübingen: Narr.

Boas, Hans C. 2009a. Recent trends in multilingual computational lexicography. In *Multilingual FrameNets in Computational Lexicography: Methods and Applications*, Hans C. Boas (ed.), 1–26. Berlin: De Gruyter.

Boas, Hans C. 2009b. Semantic frames as interlingual representations. In *Multilingual FrameNets in Computational Lexicography: Methods and Applications*, Hans C. Boas (ed.), 59–100. Berlin: De Gruyter.

Boas, Hans C. 2010. Linguistically relevant meaning elements of English communication verbs. *Belgian Journal of Linguistics* 24: 54–82.

Boas, Hans C. 2011. A frame semantic approach to syntactic alternations with build-verbs. In *Morphosyntactic Alternations in English*, Pilar Guerrero Medina (ed.), 207–234. London: Equinox.

Cambridge Advanced Learners Dictionary. <http://dictionary.cambridge.org/dictionary/british/> (September 2012).

Davies, Mark. *The British National Corpus* (BNC) <http://corpus.byu.edu/bnc/> (September 2012).

Davies, Mark. *The Corpus of Contemporary American English* (COCA) <http://www.americancorpus.org/> (September 2012).

Dixon, Robert M.W. 1991. *A New Approach to English Grammar on Semantic Principles.* Oxford: Clarendon Press.

English Cobuild Dictionary <http://dictionary.reverso.net/english-cobuild/> (September 2012).

Fillmore, Charles J. 1976. Frame Semantics and the nature of language. In *Origins and Evolution of Language and Speech*, Stevan R. Harnad, Horst D. Steklis & Jane Lancaster (eds), 20–32. New York NY: New York Academy of Sciences.

Fillmore, Charles J. 1982. Frame Semantics. In *Linguistics in the Morning Calm*, The Linguistic Society of Korea (ed.), 11–137. Seoul: Hanshin.

Fillmore, Charles J. & Atkins, Beryl T. 1992. Towards a frame-based organization of the lexicon: The semantics of RISK and its neighbors. In *Frames, Fields, and Contrasts: New Essays in Semantics and Lexical Organization*, Adrienne Lehrer & Eva Kittay (eds), 75–102. Hillsdale NJ: Lawrence Erlbaum Associates.

Fillmore, Charles J., Johnson, Christopher R. & Petruck, Miriam R.L. 2003a. Background to FrameNet. *International Journal of Lexicography* 16(3): 235–250.

Fillmore, Charles J., Lee-Goldman, Russell R. & Rhodes, Russell. 2012. The FrameNet construction. In *Sign-Based Construction Grammar*, Hans C. Boas & Ivan Sag (eds), 283–299. Stanford CA: CSLI.

Fillmore, Charles J., Petruck, Miriam R.L., Ruppenhofer, Josef & Wright, Abby. 2003b. FrameNet in action. The case of Attaching. *International Journal of Lexicography* 16(3): 297–332.

Garrido, Nazaret & Ruiz de Mendoza, Francisco J. 2011. La modelación de conocimiento procedimental en FunGramKB. *Anglogermánica Online* 8: 106–120.

Guerra, Fátima & Sacramento, Elena. 2011. El modulo léxico de FunGramKB. *Anglogermánica Online* 8: 52–65.

Halliday, Michael A.K. 1985. *An Introduction to Functional Grammar.* London: Edward Arnold.

Jiménez, Rocío & Luzondo, Alba. 2011. Building ontological meaning in a lexico-conceptual knowledge-base. *Onomázein* 23(1): 11–40.

Jiménez, Rocío & Pérez, María Beatriz. 2011. An account of selection restrictions in Role and Reference Grammar. *Revista Canaria de Estudios Ingleses* 62: 99–122.

Levin, Beth. 1993. *English Verb Classes and Alternations: A Preliminary Investigation.* Chicago IL: University of Chicago Press.

Liddy, Elizabeth D. 2001. Natural language processing. In *Encyclopedia of Library and Information Science,* 2nd edn, Miriam A. Drake (ed.). New York NY: Marcel Decker.

Longman Dictionary of Contemporary English. <http://www.ldoceonline.com/> (September 2012).

Mairal, Ricardo & Periñán, Carlos. 2009. The anatomy of the lexicon component within the framework of a conceptual knowledge base. *Revista Española de Lingüística Aplicada* 22: 217–244.

Mairal, Ricardo & Periñán, Carlos. 2010a. Role and Reference Grammar and ontological engineering. In *Los Caminos de la Lengua. Estudios en Homenaje a Enrique Alcaraz Varó*, José Luis Cifuentes, Adelina Gómez, Antonio Lillo, José Mateo & Francisco Yus (eds), 649–665. Alicante: Universidad de Alicante.

Mairal, Ricardo & Periñán, Carlos. 2010b. Teoría lingüística y representación del conocimiento: Una discusión preliminar. In *Tendencias en Lingüística General y Aplicada*, Dolores García Padrón & María del Carmen Fumero Pérez (eds), 155–168. Berlin: Peter Lang.

Mairal, Ricardo, Periñán, Carlos & Pérez, María Beatriz. 2012. La representación léxica. Hacia un enfoque ontológico. In *El Funcionalismo en la Teoría Lingüística. La Gramática del Papel y la Referencia. Introducción, Avances y Aplicaciones*, Ricardo Mairal, Lilián Guerrero & Carlos González (eds), 85–102. Akal: Madrid.

Mairal, Ricardo & Ruiz de Mendoza, Francisco J. 2009. Levels of description and explanation in meaning construction. In *Deconstructing Constructions* [Studies in Language Companion Series 107], Christopher Butler & Javier Martín Arista (eds), 153–198. Amsterdam: John Benjamins.

Masolo, Claudio, Borgo, Stefano, Gangemi, Aldo, Guarino, Nicola & Oltramari, Alessandro. 2003. WonderWeb Deliverable D18: Ontology library. Technical report. Laboratory for Applied Ontology, ISTC-CNR.

Newman, John & Rice, Sally. 2005. Transitivity schemas of English EAT and DRINK in the BNC. In *Corpora in Cognitive Linguistics: Corpus-based Approaches to Syntax and Lexis*, Stefan T. Gries & Anatol Stefanowitsch (eds), 225–260. Berlin: Mouton de Gruyter.

Ovchinnikova, Ekaterina, Vieu, Laure, Oltramari, Alessandro, Borgo, Stefano & Alexandrov, Theodore. 2010. Data-driven and ontological analysis of FrameNet for Natural Language Reasoning. In *Proceedings of the 7th Conference on International Language Resources and Evaluation (LREC'10)*, 3157–3164. Valletta, Malta.

Oxford Dictionaries. <http://oxforddictionaries.com/> (September 2012).

Periñán, Carlos. 2013a. A knowledge-engineering approach to the cognitive categorization of lexical meaning. *Vigo International Journal of Applied Linguistics* 10: 85–104.

Periñán, Carlos. 2013b. Towards a model of constructional meaning for natural language understanding. In *Linking Constructions into Functional Linguistics: The Role of Constructions in Grammars* [Studies in Language Companion Series 145], Brian Nolan & Elke Diedrichsen (eds). 205–230. Amsterdam: John Benjamins.

Periñán, Carlos & Arcas, Francisco. 2005. Microconceptual-Knowledge Spreading in FunGram-KB. In *Proceedings of the 9th IASTED International Conference on Artificial Intelligence and Soft Computing*, 239–244. Anaheim CA: ACTA Press.

Periñán, Carlos & Arcas, Francisco. 2007a. Cognitive modules of an NLP knowledge base for language understanding. *Procesamiento del Lenguaje Natural* 39: 197–204.

Periñán, Carlos & Arcas, Francisco. 2007b. Deep semantics in an NLP knowledge base. *Proceedings of the 12th Conference of the Spanish Association for Artificial Intelligence*, 279–288. Salamanca: Universidad de Salamanca.

Periñán, Carlos & Arcas, Francisco. 2010a. Ontological commitments in FunGramKB. *Procesamiento del Lenguaje Natural* 44: 27–34.

Periñán, Carlos & Arcas, Francisco. 2010b. The architecture of FunGramKB. In *Proceedings of the 7th International Conference on Language Resources and Evaluation*, 2667–2674. Malta: European Language Resources Association.

Periñán, Carlos & Arcas, Francisco. 2011. Introducción a FunGramKB. *Anglogermánica Online* 8: 1–15.

Periñán, Carlos & Mairal, Ricardo. 2009. Bringing Role and Reference Grammar to natural language understanding. *Procesamiento del Lenguaje Natural* 43: 265–273.

Periñán, Carlos & Mairal, Ricardo. 2010. La gramática de COREL: Un lenguaje de representación conceptual. *Onomázein* 21: 11–45.

Periñán, Carlos & Mairal, Ricardo. 2011. The COHERENT methodology in FunGramKB. *Onomázein* 24(2): 13–33.

Petruck, Miriam R. L. 1996. Frame Semantics. In *Handbook of Pragmatics*, Jef Verschueren, Jan-Ola Östman, Jan Blommaert & Chris Bulcaen (eds), 1–13. Amsterdam: John Benjamins.

Procter, Paul (ed). 1978. *Longman Dictionary of Contemporary English*. Harlow: Longman.

Rosca, Andreea. 2012. Bases for the Development of Ontological Semantics within the Conceptual Domains of Change and Possession. Implementations and Implications for the Lexico-Syntactic-Cognition Interface and the Development of Intelligent Agents. PhD dissertation, Universidad de La Rioja.

Ruiz de Mendoza, Francisco J. 2013. Meaning construction, meaning interpretation and formal expression in the Lexical Constructional Model. In *Linking Constructions into Functional Linguistics. The Role of Constructions in RRG Grammars* [Studies in Language Companion Series 145], Brian Nolan & Elke Diedrichsen (eds), 231–270. Amsterdam: John Benjamins.

Ruiz de Mendoza, Francisco J. & Mairal, Ricardo. 2008. Levels of description and constraining factors in meaning construction: An introduction to the Lexical Constructional Model. *Folia Linguistica* 42(2): 355–400.

Ruiz de Mendoza, Francisco J. & Mairal, Ricardo. 2011. Constraints on syntactic alternations: Lexical-constructional subsumption in the Lexical Constructional Model. In *Morphosyntacic Alternations in English*, Pilar Guerrero (ed.), 62–82. London: Equinox.

Ruppenhofer, Josef, Ellsworth, Michael, Petruck, Miriam R.L., Johnson, Christopher R. & Scheffczyk, Jan. 2010. *FrameNet II: Extended Theory and Practice*. <https://framenet2.icsi.berkeley.edu/docs/r1.5/book.pdf>

Van Valin, Jr., Robert D. 2005. *Exploring the Syntax-Semantics Interface*. Cambridge: CUP.

Van Valin, Jr., Robert D. & LaPolla, Randy J. 1997. *Syntax, Structure, Meaning and Function*. Cambridge: CUP.

Velardi, Paola, Fasolo, Michela & Pazienza, María T. 1991. How to encode semantic knowledge: A method for meaning representation and computer aided acquisition. *Computational Linguistics* 17(2): 153–170.

Zwaan, Rof A. & Radvansky, Gabriel A. 1998. Situation models in language comprehension and memory. *Psychological Bulletin* 123(2): 162–185.

Exploring the thematic-frame mapping in FunGramKB*

Fátima Guerra García and Elena Sacramento Lechado
Instituto de Lingüística Andrés Bello (Universidad de La Laguna)

FunGramKB (Functional Grammar Knowledge Base; Periñán and Arcas 2010a, 2010b; Periñán and Mairal 2010b) has three levels of knowledge representation (i.e. lexical, conceptual and grammatical). Conceptual modelling takes place within the Ontology, whereas the implementation of both the semantic and the constructional information of lexical units belongs to the lexical level. Both processes are designed to be completely independent within the knowledge base. Nevertheless, concept encoding and representation at the level of deep semantics and the semantic definitions of the predicates belonging to the lexicons of different languages are clearly intertwined. The objective of this paper is to analyse how the interaction of deep and shallow semantics takes place within this full-fledged knowledge base.

1. Introduction

FunGramKB Suite is a user-friendly online environment for the semiautomatic construction of a multipurpose lexico-conceptual knowledge base for natural language processing systems, and more particularly, for natural language understanding.[1] This knowledge base comprises three major levels, which are, in turn, subdivided into different modules:

---

* The work presented in this paper is part of the research project DESARROLLO DE PLANTILLAS LÉXICAS Y DE CONSTRUCCIONES GRAMATICALES EN INGLÉS Y ESPAÑOL APLICACIÓN EN LOS SISTEMAS DE RECUPERACIÓN DE LA INFORMACIÓN EN ENTORNOS MULTILINGÜES (reference no. FFI2011-29798-C02-02), and it has been possible thanks to the financial support of a research grant funded by the Spanish Ministry of Education, Culture and Sport (*Beca de Formación de Personal Investigador* BES-2009-017546, 2011) and a research grant funded jointly by the University of La Laguna and CajaCanarias (*Beca CajaCanarias de Investigación para Posgraduados*, 2011).

1. For an exhaustive explanation of the FunGramKB architecture and its modules, we refer the reader to the following sources: Periñán and Arcas 2004, 2005, 2007a, 2007b, 2008, 2010a, 2010b, 2011; Periñán and Mairal 2010a, 2010b, 2011.

- The *conceptual* (or cognitive) level, which includes the Ontology, the Cognicon and the Onomasticon, provides the non-linguistic knowledge, shared by all languages supported in the knowledge base. For that purpose, FunGramKB deploys an interlingua (i.e. COREL; Conceptual Representation Language).
- The *lexical* level, which consists of the Lexicon and the Morphicon, stores linguistic knowledge, so it is language-dependent.
- The *grammatical* level is also language-dependent and includes the Grammaticon, which stores the constructional schemata that help RRG (Role and Reference Grammar; Van Valin & LaPolla 1997; Van Valin 2005) to construct the semantics-to-syntax linking algorithm.

The architecture of FunGramKB pivots on the Ontology, one of the three modules of the conceptual level. It is the central component of the system, thus composing a model that is conceptually, instead of lexically, -oriented. The Ontology consists of the hierarchical catalogue of all the concepts that a person has in mind when talking about everyday situations. This module is hierarchically organized into metaconcepts, basic concepts and terminal concepts. Metaconcepts (preceded by #) represent cognitive dimensions such as #OBJECT, #ABSTRACT, #CREATION, #SPATIAL, #MOTION, among many others. They have not assigned meaning postulates since their meanings are very basic, not linked to a specific lexical unit.[2] Basic concepts (preceded by +) are defining units that enable us to construct meaning postulates, as well as taking part as selectional preferences in thematic frames (e.g. +NOSE_00, +LIMB_00). They were initially identified through the defining vocabulary of the *Longman Dictionary of Contemporary English* (Procter 1978). Terminal concepts (preceded by $) represent the final nodes in the hierarchical structuring because of their lack of definitory potential to take part in meaning postulates. They are the most specific concepts in the taxonomy and inherit characteristics of their superordinates (e.g. $BEAK_00, $TRUNK_00, $FLIPPER_00). Currently, the population of the Ontology is being carried out through the implementation of terminal concepts. All these concepts stored in the Ontology, which conceptualize our experience of the world, are lexicalized by different lexical units in each language, e.g. the concept +NOSE_00 is lexicalized by the lexical unit *nose* in the English language and by the lexical unit *nariz* in the Spanish language. Both lexical units, *nose* and *nariz*, are thus connected to the same concept in the Ontology. However, the individual analysis of each of them is completely out of the scope of the cognitive level. It is in their corresponding Lexicons, within the lexical level, where they will be analysed in detail by computational lexicographers.

One of the greatest advantages of this full-fledged knowledge base is that the implementation of its three different levels is independent, although they are clearly intertwined. In this way, conceptual information is enriched by the implementation of the different lexica, which are in turn completed and enhanced through the corresponding Grammaticon for the languages that take part in our knowledge base

2. Thematic frames and meaning postulates are fully explained in Section 3.

(i.e. English, Spanish, French, German or Italian). In this paper, we observe how conceptual information is reflected in the lexical level, through the analysis of the ontology-to-lexicon linkage, and we focus on the thematic-frame mapping (i.e. the connection between the participants of the cognitive situation described by an event and the variables taken by a verbal predicate at the lexical level).

This paper is organized as follows. Section 2 offers a brief account of the Lexicon editor. Section 3 describes the thematic-frame mapping in FunGramKB. In Section 4, we explore the thematic-frame mapping for some basic and terminal concepts belonging to the conceptual domains #CREATION and #MOTION in this knowledge base. Finally, some conclusions are drawn in Section 5.

2. The Lexicon editor

Within the lexical level, which is language-dependent, two modules can be found. On the one hand, in the Lexicon, knowledge engineers store morphosyntactic, pragmatic and collocational information about the lexical units of each of the languages which are part of the knowledge base.[3] On the other hand, the Morphicon deals with cases of inflectional morphology.

The Lexicon Editor allows knowledge engineers to develop large-scale lexica consistently, since the information included is precise, well-organized and linked to the Ontology (i.e. in order to construct lexical entries, a previous ontological modelling of the related concepts is required). FunGramKB lexical entries display the following information:

- Basic: headwork, index, and language.
- Morphosyntax: graphical variants, abbreviations, phrase constituents, category, number, gender, countability, degree, adjectival position, verb paradigm and constraints, and pronominalization.
- Core Grammar: *Aktionsart*, lexical template and constructions.
- Miscellaneous: dialect, style, domain, examples and translation.

In this paper we focus on Core Grammar and, more concretely, on one of the aspects that make up the lexical template of verbal predicates, namely, the thematic-frame mapping. Lexical templates include information such as *Aktionsart*, variables, macroroles, prepositions, collocations and thematic-frame mapping. The latter piece of information has proved to be of great value, providing us with interesting results about the interaction of deep semantics stored in the meaning postulates in the Ontology and shallow semantics of linguistic representations (see Figures 1 and 2 below).

3. See Mairal and Periñán (2009) for an exhaustive analysis of the Lexicon in FunGramKB.

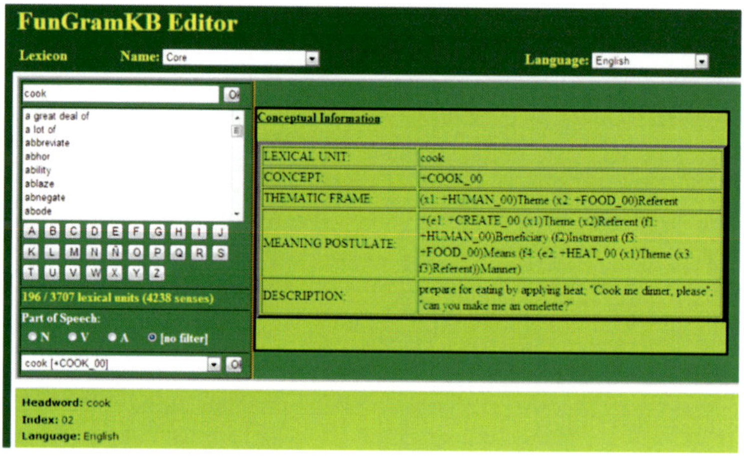

Figure 1. Partial view of the FunGramKB editor (lexical unit 'cook')

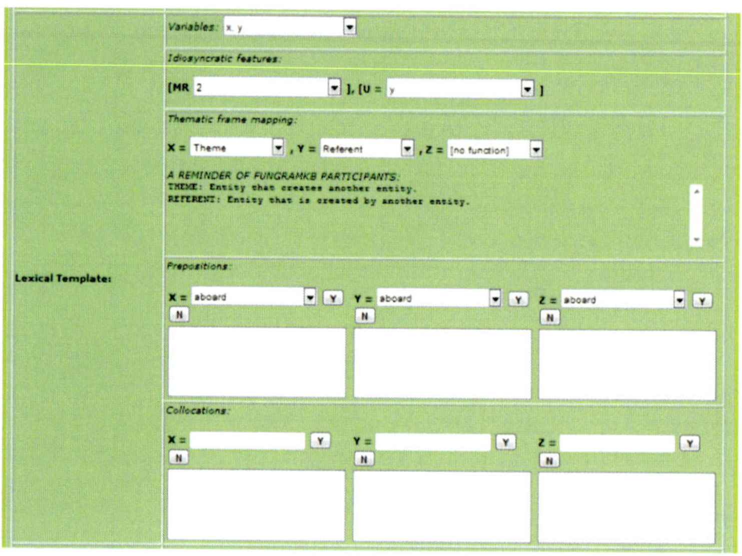

Figure 2. Information included within the editor for the lexical template of 'cook'

3. Thematic-frame mapping

The ontological concepts within our knowledge base have a rich internal structure due to the incorporation of the thematic frame and the meaning postulate. On the one hand, the *thematic frame* (hereafter TF) can be defined as a "prototypical cognitive construct which states the number and type of participants involved in the cognitive situation portrayed by an event". On the other hand, the *meaning postulate* (hereafter MP) refers to the "set of one or more logically connected predications (e_1, e_2...e_n), which are cognitive constructs carrying the generic features of the concept" (Periñán & Arcas 2007a: 200). In this way, the ontology-to-lexicon thematic-frame mapping deals with the link between conceptual information from the TF in the Ontology and more specific (i.e. lexical) information in the corresponding Lexicon. This link is created by assigning a thematic role from the TF of the concept in the Ontology to each of the variables of the predicate that lexicalize such a concept in the corresponding Lexicon.[4] For instance, the conceptual information stored in the Ontology for the concept +EXPLAIN_00 includes the following TF:

(1) (x1: +HUMAN_00)Theme (x2)Referent (x3: +HUMAN_00 ^ +ANIMAL_00) Goal

As can be seen, the TF of a concept in FunGramKB specifies the number of prototypical participants involved in the cognitive situation described by the event (i.e. x1, x2, x3...), their thematic roles (e.g. Theme, Referent, Goal, etc.) and their selectional preferences if required (e.g. +HUMAN_00, +ANIMAL_00, etc...).[5] This information is then mapped onto the Lexicon, where each of the variables taken by the verbal predicate *explain* in English corresponds to one of the participants making up the TF of the concept by sharing the same thematic role; see (2) and Figure 3 below:

(2) Participants in the TF → x1 = Theme, x2 = Referent, x3 = Goal
Variables taken by the verbal predicate → x = Theme, y = Referent, z = Goal

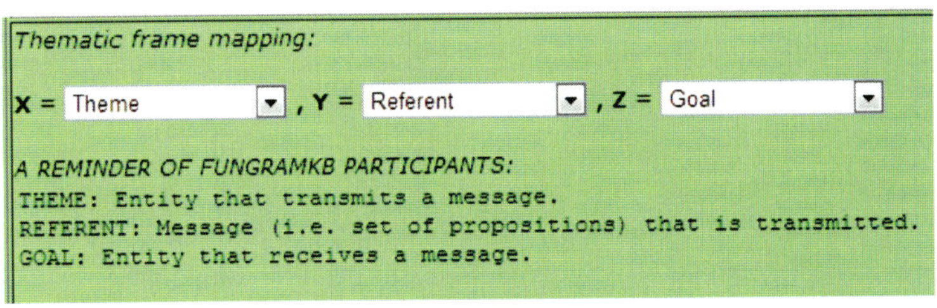

Figure 3. Thematic-frame mapping in FunGramKB

4. See Appendix 1 for the whole list of thematic roles that define each cognitive dimension.

5. Basic concepts in the Ontology are defining units which can be used as selectional preferences in TFs and MPs.

3.1 Thematic roles

In FunGramKB thematic roles of each metaconcept from the Ontology work as conceptual roles which describe the prototypical participants that take part in a cognitive dimension. It is worth mentioning that there are not different thematic roles for each cognitive dimension. Instead, there is a limited inventory of thematic roles and each of them acquires a different semantic interpretation in each metaconcept. The thematic roles used in FunGramKB are the following: *Agent*, *Theme*, *Referent*, *Attribute*, *Location*, *Origin* and *Goal*, where *Theme* is the central one that appears in all cognitive dimensions, although with a different meaning. For example, in the cognitive dimension #COGNITION, there are prototypically three participants with their corresponding thematic roles, i.e. [Agent],[6] Theme and Referent (see appendix 1), as illustrated through the basic concept +THINK_00 in (3):

(3) +THINK_00 [#COGNITION]
TF: (x1: +HUMAN_00)Theme (x2: +THOUGHT_00) Referent

The basic concept +THINK_00 takes just two of the three possible participants of the cognitive dimension, i.e. a first participant with the thematic role Theme and the selectional preference +HUMAN_00, and a second participant with the thematic role Referent and the selectional preference +THOUGHT_00.

As mentioned above, thematic roles acquire a different semantic interpretation in each metaconcept. Thus, in the cognitive dimension #CREATION, Theme and Referent are present again, but with a different meaning in this case. Whereas in #COGNITION the Theme is the entity that undergoes a cognitive process, in #CREATION the Theme is the entity that creates another entity.

The concepts in the Ontology and the lexical units and their CLSs (i.e. Conceptual Logical Structures)[7] in the lexical and grammatical levels share the same thematic roles, which guarantees the interchangeability of information among the different modules of the knowledge base. What is more, not only thematic roles but also the concepts from the Ontology and its interlingua (i.e. COREL) are common to all the modules, which permits the automated reasoner to combine and complete information from the three levels. This results in a robust knowledge base which allows us to discern the complex and intertwined mechanisms of natural language.

As a consequence of all these interrelations, it seems natural to start testing the level of impact of the deep semantics stored in the Ontology on the more shallow linguistic representations in the lexica, which naturally leads to posit the following questions: is there a parallel behaviour between the predicates stored under the same

6. Agent is an optional role in this cognitive dimension.

7. Conceptual Logical Structures (CLSs) are enriched representations of RRG logical structures. They represent an amalgam of RRG logical structures and concepts from the FunGramKB Ontology (Mairal & Periñán 2009).

concept in the Ontology? Do they have the same semantic structure or *Aktionsarten*? Is there an isomorphism between the TF of a concept and the predicate frames of the lexical units linked to it? Next, we analyse some examples to determine how the mapping seems to occur.

4. Cases of thematic-frame mapping

In the following subsections, several instances of verbal predicates belonging to different cognitive dimensions are analysed in order to describe how this phenomenon takes place in our knowledge base, observing what differences can be found throughout the concepts and lexical units making up each domain.

In the following subsections, several instances of verbal predicates belonging to different cognitive dimensions are analysed in order to show the reader how this ongoing research on the interaction between deep and shallow semantics or, in other words, non-linguistic and linguistic knowledge is being carried out.

4.1 Perfect mapping

It has been observed, for some verbal predicates, that there is a perfect mapping between the number of participants in the TF of the concept they belong to in the Ontology and the variables of the verbal predicate in the Lexicon. As an illustration, the verbal predicate *cook* can be considered. It belongs to the metaconcept #CREATION and, more concretely, to the basic concept +COOK_00, whose TF is composed of two participants, i.e. a Theme (the entity that creates another entity) and a Referent (the entity that is created by another entity).

In this case, the information stored in the Ontology maps perfectly onto the Lexicon, where the verbal predicate at hand takes two variables (x, y), each of them coinciding with the participants previously mentioned:

(4) During his stay <u>he</u> (x) cooked <u>*a five-course gala dinner*</u> (y) for 150. (BNC/A0C/W_misc)[8]

Another instance of perfect mapping is that of the English predicate *tell*. Three participants take part in the conceptual information of all concepts belonging to the cognitive domain #COMMUNICATION, i.e. a Theme (the entity that transmits a message), a Referent (the message that is transmitted) and a Goal (the entity that receives a message). All of them are mapped onto the variables x, y, z in their corresponding lexical templates, as shown by the following example:

8. The examples used in this paper have been taken from the BNC (British National Corpus) and the COCA (Corpus of Contemporary American English), available online at: <http://corpus.byu.edu/bnc/> and <http://corpus.byu.edu/coca/> respectively.

(5) I (x) haven't told you (z) *the whole story* (y)! (BNC/FR6/W_fict_prose)

4.2 Imperfect mapping

Thematic-frame mapping is not always a straightforward process, as might be observed for some basic concepts belonging to the conceptual domains #CREATION and #MOTION in the FunGramKB Ontology.

4.2.1 *#CREATION*

The conceptual domain #CREATION is composed of eleven basic concepts, among which the basic concept +SOUND_01 can be found.[9] Verbs belonging to this concept are associated to the creation of a sound, and their TF consists of a Theme (or entity creating another entity) and a Referent (the entity created by another entity, i.e. a sound). These verbs tend to present a semelfactive *Aktionsart*, such as *chatter*, *murmur*, *resonate* and *thunder* or semelfactive and causative semelfactive *Aktionsarten*, as in the case of *clang*, *clink*, *crack*, or *jingle*. The analysis of these verbs has provided us with some interesting results.

First of all, it has been observed that the type of *Aktionsart* expressed by a verbal predicate appears to be intrinsically linked to the number of variables mapped onto the predicate. Secondly, selectional preferences seem to indicate the number of arguments the verbal predicate will have in the Lexicon. Thus, for instance, in the case of the terminal concept $THUNDER_00, two participants can be observed, i.e. a Theme, the entity creating a sound (+THUNDER_00), and a Referent, the entity created (i.e. +SOUND_00).

However, the English verbal predicate *thunder* is semelfactive, it takes one macrorole and just one of the participants maps onto the Lexicon, i.e. the variable x. Therefore, when the concept is lexicalized in English, only this variable is part of the morphosyntax of the verb, and thus it is possible to find a sentence such as (6):

(6) The *sky* (x) thundered, followed quickly by a crack of lightning. (BNC/ CAB/W_fict_prose)

In the same way, in the terminal concept $TICK_00 (linked to the semelfactive *tick*), the two participants in the cognitive dimension, i.e. Theme (i.e. +CLOCK_00) and Referent (i.e. +SOUND_00) are reduced to only one variable in the Lexicon (x), which results in utterances such as (7) and which is illustrated in Figure 4 below:

(7) The *ormolu clock* (x) ticked on the mantelpiece. (BNC/ JY9/W_fict_prose)

---

9. The eleven basic concepts stored under #CREATION are the following (in alphabetical order): +BUILD_00, +COOK_00, +COUGH_00, +DIG_00, +LAY_00, +PLAY_01, +SHINE_00, +SOUND_01, +WEAVE_00, +WHISTLE_00 and +WRITE_00.

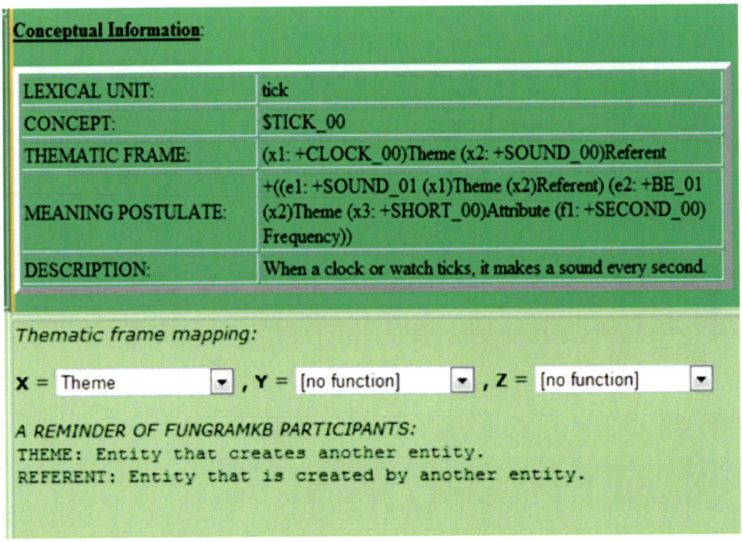

Figure 4. Thematic-frame mapping of the lexical unit 'tick'

Any lexical entry in the FunGramKB Lexicon displays the conceptual information of the ontological concept the lexical unit is associated to (i.e. concept, TF, MP and description). In Figure 4, the reader might take note of the fact that just the (x1: +CLOCK_00)Theme from the TF at the top of the figure is mapped onto the Lexicon, i.e. the Theme is linked to the variable x, as indicated at the bottom of the figure.

Interestingly, we have observed that participants in the cognitive dimension map onto the variables, influenced by the selectional preferences. Thus, for example, the presence of the human component (i.e. +HUMAN_00) in the TF seems to affect the causativity of verbal predicates. For instance, the TF of the terminal concept $TOLL_00 (i.e. "to ring slowly and repeatedly, especially to show that someone has died") is composed of a Theme (+HUMAN_00) and a Referent (+SOUND_00). The lexical unit *toll* associated with this concept may be both semelfactive and causative semelfactive, presenting two variables in the latter case, which allows an utterance such as (8), illustrated in Figure 5 below. We believe that this issue of how selectional preferences have an influence in the mapping is very interesting and we are currently doing more research on the matter.

(8) *He* (x) tolled *the bell* (y) once. (COCA/2008/MAG/AmericanSpectator)

Finally, the terminal concept $RESOUND_00, presenting a Theme and a Referent in the conceptual level, is represented in English by the verbal predicate *resound*, whose verb class is state and therefore, only one of the two participants is mapped onto the Lexicon, i.e. the variable x:

(9) *The crack of china* (x) resounded round the cafe as the saucer split in half. (BNC/G15/W_fict_prose)

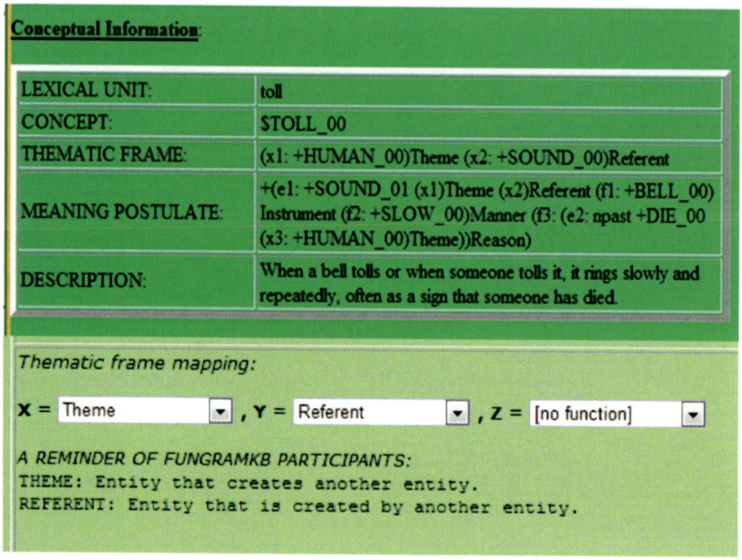

Figure 5. Thematic-frame mapping of the lexical unit 'toll'

However, the structure of this verbal predicate retakes two variables in the Grammaticon, since it is possible to find constructions such as the location-subject:

(10) *The locker room* (y) resounded with *laughter* (x).
(COCA/2011/FIC/Bk:Brotherhood)

4.2.2 *#MOTION*

The conceptual domain #MOTION is composed of two subordinates, the basic concept +MOVE_00 and the metaconcept #TRANSFER.[10] Our research focuses on the basic concept +MOVE_00 which is, at the same time, composed of twenty-four basic concepts and seven terminal concepts to date.[11] We have selected the basic concept +WALK_00 among them as an example of how the thematic-frame mapping operates between a motion concept and its related lexical units.

The verbs stored under this concept (including all its subordinates, e.g. $HIKE_00, $STROLL_00, +RUN_00, +WANDER_00, etc.) are associated with the meaning "a human or animal moving through the use of their legs as instrument". In the English Lexicon, the analysis of all the verbal predicates that lexicalize these concepts has

10. In FunGramKB, the metaconcept #TRANFER belongs to the broader metaconcept #MOTION but its study is out of the scope of this research.

11. Some concepts stored under +MOVE_00 are, for example, +ARRIVE_00, +CRAWL_00, +DANCE_00, +ENTER_00, +JUMP_00, +LEAVE_00 +PUT_00, +SHAKE_00, +SWIM_00, +TAKE_01, +VISIT_00 or +WALK_00, among others.

shown a predominance of activity and active accomplishment *Aktionsarten* (e.g. *limp, stroll, amble, wander, plod, prance* or *tiptoe*), some of them presenting a causative counterpart as well, as in the case of *walk* or *march*.

Perfect mapping is very uncommon among motion verbs. The basic concept +WALK_00, as well as all its subordinates, presents five participants in its TF, i.e. (x1) Agent, the entity that makes another entity move; (x2) Theme, the entity that changes its place or position (i.e. +HUMAN_00 or +ANIMAL_00); (x3) Location in which an entity moves (i.e. +GROUND_00); (x4) Origin from which an entity moves; and (x5) Goal to which an entity moves.

However, it is quite impossible to find these five participants mapped all together onto the Lexicon as argument variables of a verb. Thus, only one, two or three participants may turn into lexical arguments.[12] For example, for the English verbal predicate *limp*, associated to the concept $LIMP_00 in the Ontology, the *Aktionsarten* activity and active accomplishment have been selected. As a consequence, the verb takes a maximum of two variables, i.e. the variable x with the thematic role Theme and coinciding with the (x2)Theme of the TF, and the variable y (in the telic use of the verb) with the thematic role Goal, which corresponds to the conceptual participant (x5)Goal in the Ontology. See Figure 6 below as an illustration:

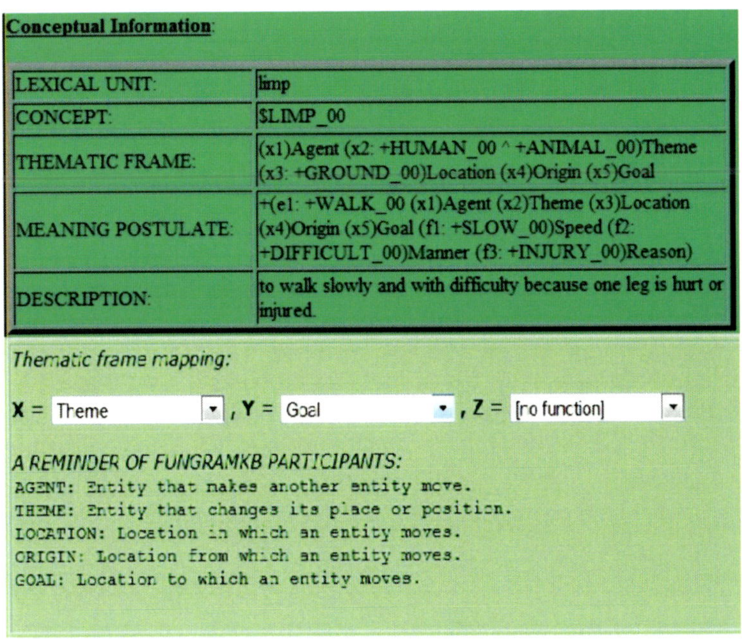

Figure 6. Thematic-frame mapping of the lexical unit 'limp'

12. Non-realized participants in lexical entries may be re-introduced periphrastically as adverbials in specific linguistic expressions.

This is also the case for other verbal predicates such as *hike*, *trek*, *tramp*, *trudge*, *prance*, *swagger*, *sidle*, *stroll* or *saunter*. Consider the following examples:

(11) Dolly (x) limped to the bed (y) and flung herself down on it. (BNC/CKE/W_fict_prose)

(12) There I (x) was strolling down the scrubby end of the Kings Road. (BNC/A6E/W_biography)

(13) When *the first Crusaders* (x) trudged *home* (y) for a rest from rape and pillage, they brought with them unknown spices. (BNC/CBC/W_newsp_other_social)

Meanwhile, other verbal predicates can be either intransitive or transitive, taking, in the latter case, the participant (x1)Agent from the TF of the concept as another variable in the case of behaving as causative activity or causative active accomplishments. Consider the following examples:

(14) *A solitary man* (x) walked *his dog* (y) *home* (z), up in the direction of the Windmill. (BNC/HR9/W_fict_prose)

(15) How many times a week would *you* (x) gallop *the horse* (y)? (BNC/HYC/S_interview_oral_history)

Something different seems to occur in the basic concept +JUMP_00. This concept shares the same five participants in the conceptual level. However, the verbal predicate *jump*, which lexicalizes the concept in the English Lexicon, is classified as semelfactive or active accomplishment. As a consequence, just a maximum of two participants are mapped into the verb's predicate frame, i.e. x = Theme and y = Goal, as illustrated in (16) and (17):

(16) I looked through the bedroom and *this chap* (x) was standing on this Mini, jumping up and down. (BNC/GY4/S_meeting)

(17) I had no idea whether *anyone* (x) else had jumped *the fence* (y) or not. (BNC/AD7/W_misc)

Nevertheless, a third variable, although not present in the *Aktionsarten*, can reappear in the Grammaticon when the verb incorporates into the Induced Action Construction (see (18) below). According to Levin (1993: 30), in this construction we find a causee that is typically an animate volitional entity, which is induced to act by the causer. Interestingly, she adds that the verb must be accompanied by a directional phrase and that such a phrase is understood even if it is not overtly expressed.

(18) The horse jumped over the fence → *Tom* (x) jumped *the horse* (y) over *the fence* (z). (Levin 1993: 266)

(19) If <u>*you*</u> (x) are planning on jumping, be sure to jump <u>*the horse*</u> (y) on several occasions. (WebCorp)[13]

(20) <u>*You*</u> (x) may even wish to jump <u>*the horse*</u> (y) a little from the long driving line (WebCorp)[14]

In other words, although just two of the five conceptual participants turned into lexical arguments in the thematic-frame mapping (see Figure 7 below), i.e. Theme and Goal, a third conceptual participant of the TF of the concept +JUMP_00, i.e. (x1)Agent, reappears when *jump* incorporates into the Induced Action Construction.

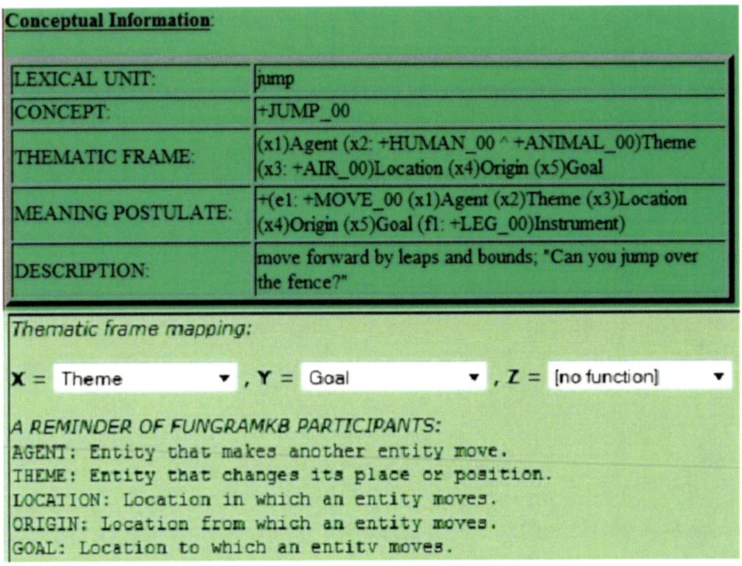

Figure 7. Thematic-frame mapping of the lexical unit 'jump'

13. We made use of WebCorp online corpus when the corpora BNC (British National Corpus) and COCA (Corpus of Contemporary American English) offered no hits. WebCorp is available online at: <http://www.webcorp.org.uk/live/index.jsp>. Example in (19) can be found in: <http://www.webcorp.org.uk/live/view.jsp?query=jump+the+horse&url=http%3A%2F%2Fwww.equusite.com%2Farticles%2Fbasics%2FbasicsLeasing.shtml> (24 May 2013).

14. Example in (20) can be found in: <http://www.webcorp.org.uk/live/view.jsp?query=jump+the+horse&url=http%3A%2F%2Fwww.horses-arizona.com%2Fpages%2Farticles%2Flinedriving.html> (24 May 2013).

5. Conclusions

This paper addresses the thematic-frame mapping, that is, the linkage between the participants in the cognitive situation described by an event and the variables taken by a verbal predicate at the lexical level within the FunGramKB knowledge base. This information offers an interesting line of research about how the deep semantics stored in the conceptual level are later on translated into more idiosyncratic features in the different lexica. We have observed that, in certain cases, this mapping process is straightforward (i.e. perfect mapping). However, this is not the general rule, and the linkage tends to be "imperfect" in the concepts belonging to the domains #CREATION and #MOTION that have been analysed. Moreover, we have observed that the cognitive participants which do not turn into lexical arguments can reappear later on when the verbal predicates incorporate into the different constructions, stored in the Grammaticons. Interestingly, there is a parallel behaviour between the predicates stored under the same concept in the Ontology, and they generally present the same *Aktionsart*. Research works on the thematic-frame mapping are still in progress and this paper aims to present the ongoing proceedings which are being carried out by the computer lexicographers working in FunGramKB. This paper offers the initial stage of this line of research. In order to provide an exhaustive analysis, the knowledge base needs to be further developed, especially the different lexica. Therefore, future research will continue to analyse this process in detail.

References

BNC (British National Corpus). <http://corpus.byu.edu/bnc/>

COCA (Corpus of Contemporary American English). <http://corpus.byu.edu/coca/>

Levin, Beth. 1993. *English Verb Classes and Alternations*. Chicago IL: The University of Chicago Press.

Mairal Usón, Ricardo & Periñán Pascual, Carlos. 2009. The anatomy of the lexicon component within the framework of a conceptual knowledge base. *Revista Española de Lingüística Aplicada* 22: 217–244.

Periñán Pascual, Carlos & Arcas Túnez, Francisco. 2004. Meaning postulates in a lexico-conceptual knowledge base. In *Proceedings of the 15th International Workshop on Databases and Expert Systems Applications*, 38–42. Los Alamitos CA: IEEE Computer Society.

Periñán Pascual, Carlos & Arcas Túnez, Francisco. 2005. Microconceptual-knowledge spreading in FunGramKB. In *Proceedings of the 9th IASTED International Conference on Artificial Intelligence and Soft Computing*, 239–244. Anaheim CA: ACTA Press.

Periñán Pascual, Carlos & Arcas Túnez, Francisco. 2007a. Cognitive modules of an NLP knowledge base for language understanding. *Procesamiento del Lenguaje Natural* 39: 197–204.

Periñán, Pascual Carlos & Arcas Túnez, Francisco. 2007b. Deep semantics in an NLP knowledge base. In *Proceedings of the 12th Conference of the Spanish Association for Artificial Intelligence*, 279–288. Salamanca: Universidad de Salamanca.

Periñán Pascual, Carlos & Arcas Túnez, Francisco. 2008. Modelling OLIF frame with EAGLES/ ISLE specifications: An interlingual approach. *Procesamiento del Lenguaje Natural* 40: 9–16.

Periñán Pascual, Carlos & Arcas Túnez, Francisco. 2010a. Ontological commitments in FunGramKB. *Procesamiento del Lenguaje Natural* 44: 27–34.

Periñán Pascual, Carlos & Arcas Túnez, Francisco. 2010b. The architecture of FunGramKB. In *Proceedings of the 7th International Conference on Language Resources and Evaluation*, 2667–2674. Malta: European Language Resources Association.

Periñán Pascual, Carlos & Arcas Túnez, Francisco. 2011. Introducción a FunGramKB. *Anglogermánica Online* 8: 1–15.

Periñán Pascual, Carlos & Mairal Usón, Ricardo. 2010a. La gramática de COREL: Un lenguaje de representación conceptual. *Onomázein* 21: 11–45.

Periñán Pascual, Carlos & Mairal Usón, Ricardo. 2010b. Tutorial de FunGramKB suite. <http://www.lexicom.es> and < http://www.fungramkb.com>

Periñán Pascual, Carlos & Mairal Usón, Ricardo. 2011. The COHERENT methodology in FunGramKB. *Onomazéin* 24(2): 13–33.

Procter, Paul (ed.). 1978. *Longman Dictionary of Contemporary English*. Harlow: Longman.

Van Valin, Jr., Robert D. 2005. *Exploring the Syntax-Semantics Interface*. Cambridge: CUP.

Van Valin, Jr., Robert D. & LaPolla, Randy J. 1997. *Syntax, Structure, Meaning and Function*. Cambridge: CUP.

WebCorp. <http://www.webcorp.org.uk/live/index.jsp>

Appendix 1. Semantic Interpretation of the Thematic Roles of Arguments

Metaconcept	Role	Definition
#COGNITION	[Agent]	Entity that makes another entity undergo a cognitive process.
	Theme	Entity that undergoes a cognitive process.
	Referent	Entity present in the consciousness of an entity that undergoes a cognitive process.
#COMMUNICATION	Theme	Entity that transmits a message.
	Referent	Message (i.e. set of propositions) that is transmitted.
	Goal	Entity that receives a message.
#CONSTITUTION	Theme	Entity that is made up of other entities.
	Referent	Entity that is part of another entity.
#CREATION	Theme	Entity that creates another entity.
	Referent	Entity that is created by another entity.
#EXISTENCE	Theme	Entity that exists.
#IDENTIFICATION	Theme	Entity that is identified by means of another entity.
	[Referent]	Entity that serves to define the identity of another entity.
	[Attribute]	Quality ascribed to an entity.
#INTENTION	Theme	Entity that pursues actively a determinate aim.
	Referent	Something which is actively pursued by an entity.
#LOCATION	Theme	Entity that stays in a location.
	Location	Location where an entity stays.
#MATERIAL	Theme	Entity that, volitionally or not, performs an event.
	[Referent]	Entity that is directly involved in the event caused by another entity.
#MOTION	Agent	Entity that makes another entity move.
	Theme	Entity that changes its place or position.
	[Location]	Location in which an entity moves.
	[Origin]	Location from which an entity moves.
	[Goal]	Location to which an entity moves.

Metaconcept	Role	Definition
#PERCEPTION	Theme	Entity that perceives another entity through any of the senses.
	Referent	Entity that is perceived through any of the senses.
#POSSESSION	Theme	Entity that owns another entity.
	Referent	Entity that is owned.
#TRANSFER	Agent	Entity that transfers another entity to a third entity.
	Theme	Entity that is transferred.
	Origin	Entity from which another entity is transferred.
	Goal	Entity to which another entity is transferred.
#TRANSFORMATION	Theme	Entity that transforms another entity.
	Referent	Entity that is transformed by another entity.

FunGramKB term extractor

A tool for building terminological ontologies from specialised corpora*

Ángel Felices-Lago and Pedro Ureña Gómez-Moreno
Universidad de Granada

Ontological engineering is a relatively young discipline that has nevertheless received considerable attention because of its great potential for application in a number of areas, including Machine Translation, Artificial Intelligence and the Semantic Web. A major field of research of the ontological endeavour concerns the building of specialised ontologies, i.e. concept hierarchies which formalise knowledge from expert areas of human activity such as medicine or law. This chapter focuses on the methodological aspects of the construction of specialised taxonomies in the framework of the FunGramKB knowledge base and in doing so it illustrates the FunGramKB Term Extractor, an innovative corpus-based tool for the semi-automatic extraction of terms.

1. Introduction

In the last few years there has been an attested growth in the development of ontologies that has been promoted by a renewed interest in their computational implementation for natural language processing and their applicability in a number of areas, including Data Mining, Machine Translation, Semantic Web technologies and Artificial Intelligence. Ontologies constitute representations of human knowledge which computers can use to process and mine information in a connected and efficient way (Gruber 1993). A distinction is commonly drawn at this point between top-level ontologies, which represent common-sense, and domain-level ontologies, i.e. taxonomies containing conceptual information specific to highly specialised areas of human knowledge

* This chapter is based on research currently being carried out within the framework of the project entitled "Development of a subontology in a multilingual context (English, Spanish and Italian): Using FunGramKB in the field of international cooperation in criminal matters: Terrorism and organised crime" funded by the Spanish Ministry of Economy and Competitiveness, code no. FFI2010-15983.

(for a recent discussion, see Lim et al. 2011). The importance of the latter lies in its potential for the automatic solving of reasoning tasks in which expertise is commonly required, as well as the design of artificial agents which can simulate human expert decisions. In the field of law, for example, Breuker et al. (2008) compiled a list of 33 legal ontologies, which is a considerable number and will be certainly increased in the next few years. However, in order to implement new domain ontologies it is essential to identify the specific concepts used by experts in their professional activity alongside the technical words that give a lexical shape to those concepts. In this context, therefore, terminological work plays a crucial role in domain-specific ontology engineering, providing the lexical substratum upon which conceptualisation is based.

This chapter is concerned with terminology extraction as a critical step in specialised taxonomy building within FunGramKB, a multi-purpose knowledge base for natural language processing, which has been designed to work with any human language (Periñán-Pascual & Arcas-Túnez 2004, 2005, 2010; Mairal-Usón & Periñán-Pascual 2009; Periñán-Pascual & Mairal-Usón 2009, 2010; Periñán-Pascual 2012). The architecture of FunGramKB encompasses three independent but interconnected models, namely the conceptual model, which in turn contains the Core Ontology, the Cognicon and the Onomasticon; the grammatical model – containing the Grammaticon – and the lexical model or Lexicon, which is responsible for storing morphosyntactic information. For that purpose, this chapter presents the FunGramKB Term Extractor (henceforth FGKBTE), a tool for the semi-automatic retrieval of terminology from domain-specific corpora, and the construction of domain ontologies (Periñán-Pascual 2011). The extractor is included in the FunGramKB Suite – an online platform for the edition of the knowledge base (Periñán-Pascual 2004). Domain ontologies, henceforth "Satellite Ontologies" in FunGramKB, are developed with a view to expanding the conceptual nucleus contained in the (Core) Ontology. The authors demonstrate the entire process of extraction from the initial preparatory corpus work to the final retrieval of terminological units (for an introduction to Corpus Linguistics, see Biber et al. 1998; Kennedy 1998 & Meyer 2002; for more details on building domain-specific corpora, see Bowker & Pearson 2002; Koester 2010 and Reppen 2010).

The remainder of this chapter is structured as follows. Section 2 outlines the basics of data collection and editing. Section 3 offers an overview of the main aspects of the terminological approach in FunGramKB, as well as a discussion of the methodological underpinnings for the retrieval of terminology. Section 4 highlights FGKBTE's utilities, and, for that purpose, it provides illustrative examples, mainly from a pilot study carried out with a text collection on criminal law (see Section 2). Finally, this chapter sums up the most outstanding issues within the proposed framework.

2. Corpus compilation

One of the main characteristics that defines *FunGramKB* is an effective combination of a conceptualist approach to reasoning and a solid grounding in natural language data. In fact, all conceptual units represented in the Core Ontology of the knowledge base must have at least one realisation in any of the existing human languages. This linguistic commitment is especially remarkable in the implementation of Satellite Ontologies, since one of the main requirements of terminological retrieval is precisely a repository of texts relevant to the knowledge domain under conceptualisation. This section examines the main aspects involved in the compilation of *ad hoc* textual repositories for use as corpora in FGKBTE. During this analysis, we refer to the Global Crime Term Corpus (GCTC) – a text collection which is currently being compiled for the creation of the Satellite Ontology on terrorism and organised crime.

The first step in the compilation lies in the selection of sources, i.e. academic and professional repositories containing specialised documents on the topic(s) of interest. This step is of paramount importance, since it will determine to a great extent whether the corpus is optimal, both qualitatively and quantitatively, for the purpose of term extraction. The selected sources must therefore meet high scientific standards or be highly regarded by the professional community. For example, the GCTC contains a selection of more than 10 sources, such as the European Union, the Council of Europe or the International Criminal Court, which offer reliable information concerning co-operation against criminal and terrorist activities. In addition to the data sources, another important decision is the representativeness of the corpus (Biber 1993). In this regard, the English component of the GCTC consists of approximately 5,600,000 tokens from a wide variety of text types, including international treaties, fact sheets, rules, resolutions, conventions and acts, among others. The corpus is also reasonably balanced with respect to the number of texts on the domains under study, i.e. 49% are focused on terrorism, while 35% deal with organised crime and 16% account for texts on both types of subject areas.

The second step in the compilation of the corpus is the editing of the texts. Essentially, it is necessary to convert original files into plain text in order to minimise the occurrence of irrelevant elements (e.g. images and special characters) and to correct spelling mistakes emerging as a result of the reformatting. There are many potential spelling and typographical errors that may occur during formatting and which consequently require editing. Below are some of the most common editing tasks (1–8):

1. The redesigning of 2-column texts. Text is converted into a single column;
2. The correction of spelling errors. These are frequently found for instance with the strings "f", "fl", or "fi";
3. The correction of erroneous interleaves between the body of the text and the headers, letterheads or titles;
4. The correction of interleaved footnotes and the body of the text;

5. The correction of syllables or letters separated by spaces (e.g. "f i e l d");
6. The correction of syllables or letters mistakenly separated and joined together with others words (e.g. "criminal alactivity" instead of "criminal activity");
7. The correction of words that are hyphenated at line-break;
8. The deletion of web links and e-mail addresses.

Many of these editing tasks are significantly time-consuming and therefore it is highly recommended at this stage that a team of coordinated editors be organised in order to reduce the impact of intensive editing. The team must work manually, while also trying to automate specific subtasks through the application of computer commands. These commands must be capable of repairing errors efficiently by means of either individual or batch processing.

Besides the compilation, formatting and editing of the corpus, the third step lies in creating a database which includes a record of all the relevant data of the documents in the collection such as the title, a brief description, the date in which the document was accessed and stored, as well as the original source name. Figure 1 shows the database created in the compilation of the GCTC.

The first field, "ID", assigns a unique numeric code to each text. The field "Language" contains information about the language in which the text is written. "Brief description" offers very succinct information about the contents of the text. "Title" provides a title that summarises the specific topic of the document. The "Topic" field, on the other hand, records the subdomain the text belongs to; in the case of GCTC, a distinction is drawn between "Organised crime", "Terrorism" or "Both". Finally, the field "Type of document" contains information about the text type (e.g. joint action, agreement, green paper, proceedings, etc.), while "Source" adds a reference on the source from which the original document was extracted. The data gathered in the database has three main objectives. First, it serves as a guide to monitor criteria such as corpus balance and representativeness. Second, some of the data registered in the database will be used during the uploading of texts onto the extractor and must therefore be conveniently stored. Finally, the database also provides the documentary basis for the calculation of simple descriptive statistics about the corpus.

ID	Language	Brief description	Title	Topic	Type of document	Source
1	English	Fight aganist organised crime	EOAct (joint) law enforcement cooperation	Organised crime	Joint action	Eur-Lex
2	Spanish	Fight aganist organised crime	SOAct (joint) law enforcement cooperation	Organised crime	Joint action	Eur-Lex

Figure 1. Corpus database

Before moving on to the discussion of terminological extraction proper, it is necessary to say a word about the identification label to be assigned to each of the files collected. With regards to the GCTC, two main nominalisation criteria were considered. First, file names had to be distinctive enough to minimise the risks of overlapping among files. Second, the name assigned to a file had to conveniently match the name assigned to the same file in the database, so that any modification in either of the two had to be changed accordingly. It is necessary to highlight that both the nomenclature and the data recorded in the database must use English, regardless of the language of the documents themselves. Examples 1, 2 and 3 illustrate three different documents in the GCTC alongside a comment on each of the parts that compose the file-labels:

(1) "ETDeci combating terrorism";
(2) "SORes persons traffic suppression";
(3) "IBRep anti money laundering".

where:

1. The first letter indicates the language in which the text is written. In this case, "E" (English), "S" (Spanish) and "I" (Italian);
2. The second letter indicates the subdomain which the text belongs to. In this case, "T" (terrorism), "O" (organised crime) or "B" (both);
3. The last three letters of the first word refer to the document type. In this case, "Res" (resolution), "Deci" (decision) and "Rep" (report);

The rest of the file name can be seen after a blank space and contains a short title describing the contents of the document. In this case, "combating terrorism", "persons traffic suppression" and "anti money laundering", respectively. In cases where multiple files contain the same subtitle, a numerical index may be added to differentiate them, e.g. "combating terrorism1" and "combating terrorism2". In any case, the title for each file will not exceed a maximum of 40 characters (including spaces), since the extractor does not support a larger number of characters per title.

3. FunGramKB term extractor

FGKBTE is the cornerstone in the process of creating Satellite Ontologies. The main function of this tool is to retrieve terms, here roughly defined as specialised lexical units within a domain of knowledge and despite the fact that they do not have clear boundaries. This definition should not ignore the distinction between technical terms, semi-technical terms and general vocabulary (Gómez González-Jover 2007) and the necessary exhaustive scrutiny of the selected units to decide their inclusion or not in a specific domain (for a more detailed discussion, see Cabré 1999; Temmerman 2000; Temmerman & Kerremans 2003; and L`homme 2004). There are currently a large number of extractors available online, some of them with radically different approaches to terminology acquisition. In this regard, a general distinction can be drawn between statistically-based extractors, which rely on the calculation of the semantic weight of corpus tokens, and linguistically-based extractors, which are oriented towards the identification of relevant morphosyntactic patterns in which terminology is theoretically found in a recursive way. FunGramKB, and more precisely FunGramKB Suite, which constitutes a user-friendly environment for the semiautomatic construction of the knowledge base, has recently released the above-mentioned extractor, which belongs to the former type. The statistical approach has two advantages. First, it is not necessary to carry out a previous elicitation of the linguistic structures in which terminological units can potentially occur in a language. Second, it is not necessary to use taggers or to establish which grammatical class each token belongs to (Bowker & Pearson 2002: 168). FGKBTE is designed to retrieve sets of candidate terms, that is, lexical units which are identified as terminological by automatic means. In addition, the extractor serves as the linking interface between the Core Ontology, and one or more Satellite Ontologies, and the Lexicon. The terms identified during the extraction process are integrated into the Lexicon, while conceptualised for inclusion in the corresponding Satellite Ontologies.

As mentioned above, terminological extraction in FGKBTE is based on corpus data, since this can contribute to finding the relevant terminology used by professionals and practitioners within a domain. Once the textual repository is set up, it enters the process of extraction, which comprises two stages, namely an automatic phase and a manual phase (Figure 2).

In the automatic stage the extractor performs preparatory clean-up tasks on the input corpus through a number of filters, mainly the tokenising and the removal of non-alphabetical characters (e.g. numbers, non-ASCII symbols), as well as removal of punctuation marks, as none of these elements are relevant for terminological purposes.

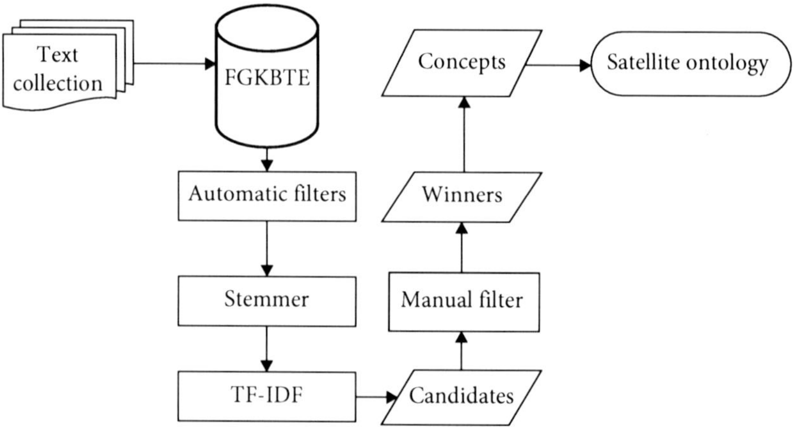

Figure 2. Flowchart of semi-automatic term extraction in FGKBTE

The filtered sample then passes on to the in-built stemmer, which is based on the algorithm first proposed by Porter (1980), and whose function is to truncate the lexical items in the corpus and to group them under a set of common linguistic forms. For example, the group "com" may serve as the truncated host form for different words such as "community", "compensation" or "communist". A major advantage of truncation is that it presents candidate units in a more compact view, facilitating manual filtering at later stages. Finally, the extractor applies statistics on the pre-processed data and generates a list of term candidates classified according to three types of n-grams – unigrams, bigrams and trigrams, that is, strings of one, two, or three units, respectively. Statistical analysis in FGKBTE is based on the calculation of the term-frequency inverse document frequency (TF-IDF) for each token in the corpus. This statistical method belongs to a family of information retrieval measures aimed at determining the statistical relevance, also referred to as the "weight" (w), of a token in a document collection (Spärck-Jones 1972, Salton 1989). Figure 3 shows the TF-IDF formula.

where the relative term frequency (*tf*) shows the number of occurrences of a token i in a document j, while the inverse document frequency (*idf*), in the formula represented by the second multiplier, refers to the relative occurrence of the same token in the entire document collection. The *idf* is obtained by dividing the total number of documents in a corpus (N) by the number of documents containing i (*df*). The terminological relevance of a candidate – and the likelihood that it is in fact a term – increases or decreases proportionally with the TF-IDF value. The TF-IDF prioritises terms showing high absolute frequency and low *idf*, while it relegates or discards terms that occur in many (or most) of the documents in the corpus. The higher the index, the more significant and terminological a given unit is. Units ranking below 3 are automatically excluded from the candidate set during the automatic phase and, therefore, the statistical phase works as another filtering mechanism before the candidate set is finally obtained.

Automatic extraction simplifies the process of ontological creation considerably. However, it is essential to complement it with manual editing. As L`Homme (2006: 182) states: "Terminologists [...] should make more use of evidence found in corpora as a basis for making decisions about terms". Consequently, the manual phase in FGKBTE involves discarding the candidate terms identified in the automatic extraction which either show low statistical significance or are semantically irrelevant for a target Satellite Ontology. The role of the terminologist is crucial at this stage, since he/she is responsible for evaluating the suitability of candidates and deciding upon a closed set of terms. In every field, at least two or three members of the team of researchers who

$$w_{i,j} = tf_{i,j} \times \log \left(\frac{N}{df_i}\right)$$

Figure 3. TF-IDF formula

are involved in the semi-automatic extraction of winning terms are specialists or have investigated various aspects of the knowledge domain. The manual filtering of term candidates in the GCTC was carried out by researchers trained in the following topics: international criminal law, cognitive semantics, terminology and specialised translation in various languages, corpus and computational linguistics, knowledge engineering, axiological semantics and onomasiological lexicography. This diverse and complementary expertise contributes, on the whole, to a better foundation of the links between conceptual and lexical levels in the process of creating a terminological subontology in a multilingual context and, eventually, to an adequate population of the concepts.

Manual inspection must adhere to pre-established lexical and conceptual criteria, notably two. First, terminologists must check candidates against concepts in the Core Ontology and the lexical units in the Lexicon. They must ascertain whether a certain unit is already included in any of these models. Second, they should work with specialised dictionaries and expert sources to account for the inclusion or exclusion of candidates (Felices-Lago & Ureña Gómez-Moreno 2012). The extractor offers an additional automatic filter that eliminates irrelevant unigrams at three linguistic levels. First, stopwords, i.e. functional words such as pronouns, conjunctions and connectors; second, basic vocabulary, including common words such as *man*, *study* or *flower*; and finally, advanced vocabulary such as *promise*, *forecast* or *pour*, which show relatively lower frequency of appearance within the core vocabulary but are rarely found in technical contexts. Lexical filtering across the three levels is only available for unigrams, on the assumption that functional, basic and advanced units can enter the formation of complex units but are not likely to form terms by themselves. The lexical filter, moreover, is specifically designed as an optional tool which can be either activated or deactivated when required (see the left-hand panel in Figure 7).

4. FGKBTE's main functions

The two phases of the semi-automatic term extraction are carried out through the options available in the extractor's interface, consisting of six tabs which in turn contain the tools both for corpus management, and the extraction and editing of terminological units. The extractor is based on permission policies so that the tabs are only available at certain stages of the process and only for users who are previously granted access to them. Figure 4 captures the main menu:

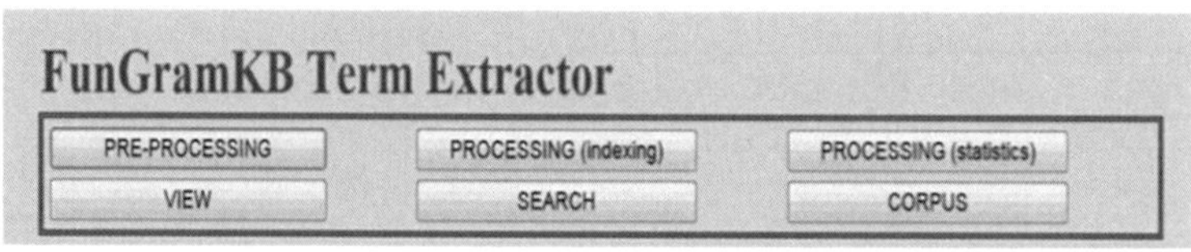

Figure 4. FGKBTE main menu

"Pre-processing" is designed as an area for testing and evaluating new applications for future implementation. This is a restricted-access area that is not directly involved in extraction and therefore requires no further comment.

The "Processing (indexing)" tab is intended for the uploading of the batch onto the extractor of corpus files alongside basic documentary information, specifically a representative title, a field tag and a brief description of the main contents of the texts. This information is stored online and is available for consultation, even after the extraction is completed. In this tab the user can pack and send up to ten files from a single loading screen, which has the advantage of reducing the time that he/she must employ in this mechanical task. It is also necessary to note that the uploading of texts is not a reversible process, that is, once included in the extractor, a text cannot be removed, nor can its information be corrected. This characteristic therefore makes it necessary for terminologists working at this stage to follow the proposed methodology in a meticulous way. Introducing the corpus onto the extractor is divided into two phases: preload and load proper. In the former, the user is requested to enter four parameters: (1) the file to be loaded, (2) the title of the text, (3) a description of the contents of the text, and (4) a label identifying the subdomain. Figure 5 illustrates these parameters.

In the "load" phase the terminologist must check the information entered and either validate it permanently or, on the contrary, make the necessary corrections by punctually accessing the preload stage again. To facilitate corroboration of data, the load screen displays a summary with the preloaded text title and its corresponding

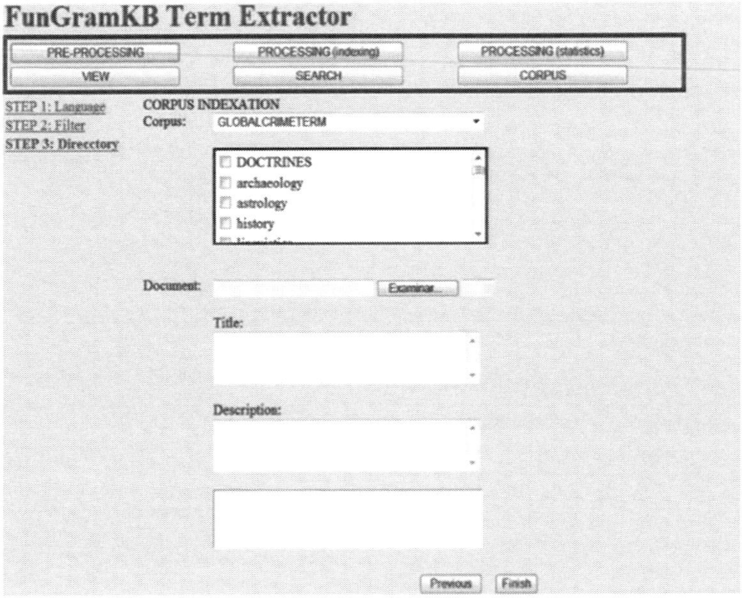

Figure 5. FGKBTE "Processing (indexing)" panel: preload screen

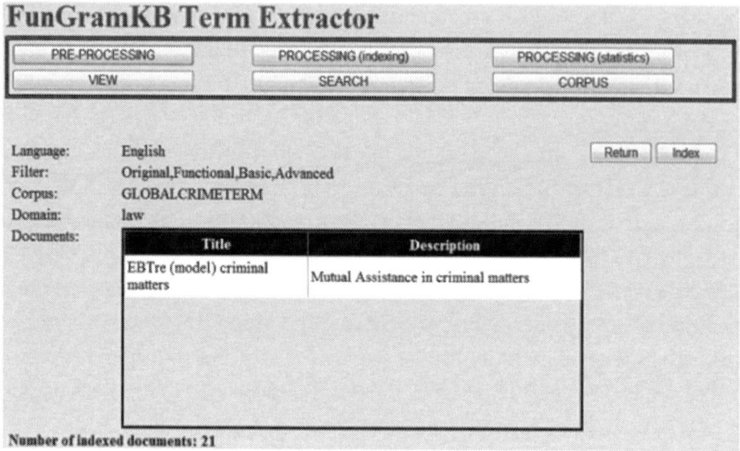

Figure 6. FGKBTE "Processing (indexing)" panel: Load screen

description (Figure 6). If the information is correct, the terminologist can then validate it and the text is finally recorded. Additionally, if this final step is successful, the texts show on the "Corpus" tab instantly (see Figure 11 below).

The "Processing (statistics)" tab is responsible for the acquisition of terminology from the corpus. At this stage, the extractor applies each of the filters described above and displays the results.

The "View" tab is concerned with the editing, definition and validation of terminological units (Figure 7). At this tab the terminologist decides upon the *termhood* of the candidate terms obtained during the automatic extraction.

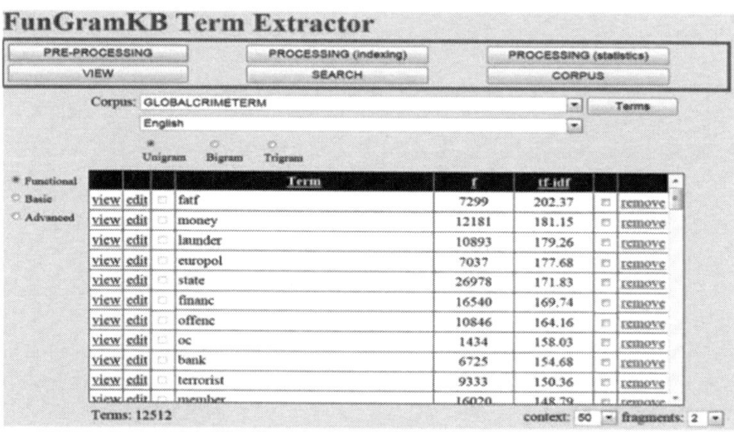

Figure 7. FGKBTE "View" panel

There are two options for deleting false candidates from FGKBTE: simple and nested removal. Simple removal allows the terminologist to delete a single candidate, irrespective of its formal complexity. For example, if there is a false term such as "triangle" which the terminologist does not consider pertinent, this option deletes "triangle" from the list of unigram candidates. Likewise, applying simple removal to the bigram "red triangle" and the trigram "strange red triangle" deletes the strings "red triangle" and "strange red triangle", respectively. It is important to notice that simple unigram removal does not function over the bigramatic and trigramatic sets but is limited to the list of unigrams. In other words, operating removal on "triangle" deletes this word from the list of unigrams, while it does not drop "triangle" from the sequences "red triangle" or "strange red triangle", which remain unaltered in their corresponding candidate lists.

In contrast, nested removal allows the deletion of individual bigrams and trigrams, alongside their component parts and the combinations that take place among them. For instance, in a bigram such as "football player" and a trigram such as "government colonial literature" that the terminologist considers irrelevant, nested removal deletes these two sequences from their corresponding candidate lists as well as "football", "player" and "football player" in the first case, and "government", "colonial", "literature", "government colonial" and "colonial literature" in the second case. The type of multiple-removal carried out by nesting across the three lists of n-grams posits this as a suitable option prior to the application of simple removal, since the former has a much wider scope, thus contributing to the reduction of manual filtering dramatically. A caveat must be considered here: nested removal performs differently depending on whether the unit to which it is applied contains lexical or functional words, or a combination of both. More specifically, nesting has been designed to remove lexical units from the list of unigrams, bigrams and trigrams – however, it cannot eliminate functional words from any candidate list. For example, applying nesting to the trigram "renting on car" rules out the combination "renting on car" from the list of trigrams, and it also eliminates "renting" and "car" from unigrams. However, "on" is preserved as a standalone form in the unigram set (if that is the case) and it is not dropped from other combinations in the remaining lists of n-grams. Table 1 summarises the functioning of both simple and nested removal regarding the formal patterns of n-grams. The first column shows the formal distribution of n-grams as they are identified in the automatic phase, the second column indicates the result of applying both removal and nesting on each pattern in the first column, and the third column illustrates each case with real corpus examples (for ease of exposition, words are shown below in their expanded instead of their truncated form).

On the other hand, "Edit" also provides the necessary tools for working with candidates that are eventually considered terms. To understand each subsection included in the "Edit" option better, they are described below starting with "Senses" and showing the other subsections in a clockwise fashion (Figure 8).

Table 1. Formal patterns and removal types in FGKBTE

Formal realisation	Result of removal and nesting	Instantiation
Trigram "XYZ" (lexical + lexical + lexical)	Remove = *XYZ Nesting = *XYZ | *X | *Y | *Z | *XY | *YZ	Trigram: "international global crime" Remove = *international global crime Nesting = *international global crime | *international | *global | *crime | *international global | *global crime
Trigram "XYZ" (lexical + functional + lexical)	Remove = *XYZ Nesting = *XYZ | *X | *Z	Trigram: "criminal or terrorist" Remove = *criminal or terrorist Nesting = *criminal or terrorist | *criminal | *terrorist
Trigram "XYZ" (lexical + lexical + functional)	Remove = *XYZ Nesting = *XYZ | *X | *Z	Trigram: "access to such" Remove = *access to such Nesting = *access to such | *access | *such
Trigram "XYZ" (functional + lexical + lexical)	N/A	N/A
Bigram "XY" (lexical + lexical)	Remove = *XY Nesting = *XY | *X | *Z	Bigram: "avoid transactions" Remove = *avoid transactions Nesting = *avoid transactions | *avoid | *transactions
Bigram "XY" (lexical + functional) or (functional + lexical)	N/A	N/A
Bigram "XY" (functional + functional)	N/A	N/A
Unigram "X" (lexical)	Remove = *X	Unigram: "combat" Remove = *combat
Unigram "X" (functional)	N/A	N/A

Note: Letters "X", "Y" and "Z" represent variables, here lexical units. Two parallel lines (=) represent the equal sign. An asterisk (*) before an element indicates "deleted", while the pipe (|) stands for "and".

"Senses" stores the different senses of homonymous and polysemous terms. Each sense shall carry a distinctive numerical index (e.g. +FRAUD_00, +FRAUD_01 and so on). The information displayed in this box is generated automatically after the information in the other fields has been provided. The "Delete" and "Rename" options allow the terminologist to make corrections before eventually validating the term at work toname that serves as a host cognitive category of the terminological unit. "Description", as the name suggests, is a space set aside for entering a description in natural language gether

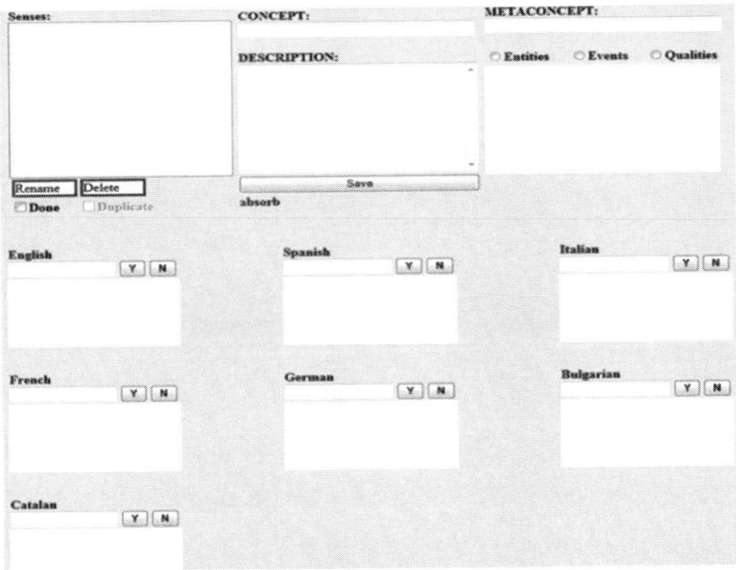

Figure 8. Lexical-conceptual FunGramKB Term Extractor editing interface

with its lexical-conceptual information. "Concept" is the label or the COREL[1] that captures the meaning of the concept. It is worth recalling that FGKBTE uses English as an interlingua for this purpose. "Metaconcept" is completed automatically with the ontological data selected among "entities", "events" or "qualities". This option is a first contribution to the hierarchical organization of concepts in the domain. "Save" stores the information online automatically and "Duplicate" serves the purpose of creating mirror concepts. If the concept to be introduced into the Satellite Ontology is already included in the Core Ontology, a note appears prompting the user to rename the concept or otherwise to create a mirror concept. The last element in the "Edit" menu is the Lexicon, which gathers the different terminological units instantiating specialised concepts. FGKBTE is currently designed to hold lexical data in seven languages: English, Spanish, Italian, French, German, Bulgarian and Catalan. The dialog boxes in the Lexicon allow the assignment of one or more terms for each concept. Once the data mentioned above have been introduced, the user can finally click on the tab "Done" and all the information is validated. Nevertheless, this process can be reversed in case further changes are needed. The importance of the tab "Done" is that, on final validation, only the terms marked thus in this option are included in the Satellite Ontology, while the rest are discarded.

In order to illustrate the editing function further, Figure 9 captures a screen with the dialog boxes shown above but now filled in with information relative to the term "counterterrorism":

1. COREL (Conceptual Representation Language) is the notation language used to represent knowledge in FunGramKB.

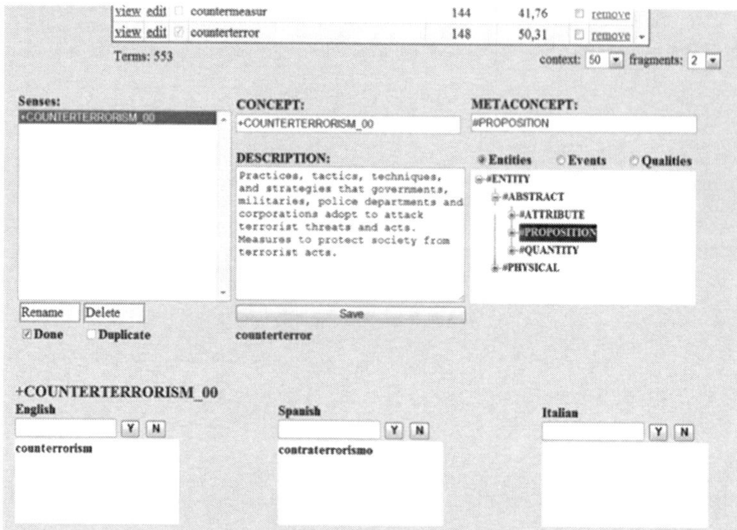

Figure 9. Lexical-conceptual FunGramKB Term Extractor editing interface: A case study

"Description" needs further attention and clarification, since it must meet some basic characteristics. In general, this option must include a comprehensive semantic definition of the concepts encompassing the main information found in a number of relevant dictionaries. Another factor to be taken into account concerns universality. Although much referential information in the legal domain can be considered universal (or shared knowledge), terminology also retains a great deal of culture-specific information which is only relevant (or true) in a particular legal apparatus. In order to meet universality criteria, while also including cultural knowledge, FGKBTE allows the terminologist to introduce pivots with information about the context of a given proposition. For example, legislations vary considerably as to the penalties or sanctions imposed on perpetrators, and therefore it is necessary in this case to introduce labels such as [*UK] or [*SP] depending on whether a certain penalty is only relevant to the British or the Spanish legal system, respectively.

Identifying terms is not a straightforward task; indeed, it raises a number of theoretical problems. To facilitate term identification, we propose below a four-criterion methodology to be considered by terminologists during the manual filtering process. These four criteria are presented in a sequential order (see 1–4).

1. *Statistical criterion*: the first and primary criterion for deciding about units' *termhood* is their statistical significance. As seen in Section 2, FGKBTE obtains a list of candidate terms after ruling out false terms whose TF-IDF index is equal to or less than three. In the manual filtering, on the one hand, it is the terminologist who must filter the candidate list by analysing units above TF-IDF 3. In doing so, he/she must rank candidates from higher to lower scores, and then consider units

with the highest value as likely terms. All in all, TF-IDF scores are often difficult to interpret, with almost insignificant TF-IDF variations among many of the candidate terms. Therefore, the statistical factor is complemented with the remaining criteria shown below.

2. *Ontological criterion*: To decide whether a candidate is a specialised unit, the speaker's mere introspection is sometimes a valid criterion. However, while it is easy to discern the *non-termhood* of units such as *table*, *rain* or *dream*, there are terms that are semantically more complex which laypeople are not familiar with. Within the framework of *FunGramKB*, introspection is carried out at the level of the Core Ontology, so that the question of whether a candidate is actually a term can be answered by means of another more specific question: does the Core Ontology contain a concept that could include this candidate as a possible lexical realisation? Thus, whenever a lexical unit under scrutiny (or a specific semantic sense) has been previously conceptualised in the Core Ontology, it must be discarded as a term, even though there are exceptions in the case of the so called "mirror concepts". Taking *judge* as an example, one can observe that concepts like this are used in specialised communication, but they also pertain to the *general language* of laypeople. This difference of knowledge is in turn represented by the diverse density of content (or granularity) between general information (the meaning postulate including the common sense information in the Core Ontology) and specialised information (additional meaning postulate predications related to the domain-specific information in the Satellite Ontology). On the other hand, the absence of a conceptual unit in the Core Ontology must not unmistakably be considered to indicate that it is a term; instead, the terminologist must consider additional criteria.
3. *Lexicological criterion*: A third criterion relates to the lexicological features of the candidate terms. Terms were traditionally characterised by a univocal, unambiguous monosemic meaning. This misconception has been successfully overcome in the last 50 years and new tendencies generally concentrate on one of the two following alternative theoretical enquiries: should the term be viewed as a component of a conceptual (sociocognitive) system or as a lexical unit with a given meaning that occurs in corpora? However, aspects such as meaning banalisation, that is, the use of terms by non-specialist speakers often leads to terms acquiring new or additional nuances. On other occasions, it is science that borrows expressions from the general language to produce, through processes such as metaphorical and metonymic mapping, new terms or specialised senses, occasionally inheriting nuances from the original meaning. This bi-directional process is even more evident in the soft sciences such as law or history. Due to their purely humanistic and social scope of application in everyday life, terms belonging to these disciplines often transcend the scope of academic and professional praxis to be used in different contexts of human life. Given this double nature as both technical and non-technical units, in some cases it is more appropriate to refer to

"specialised senses" rather than "specialised lexical units". For example, although the word *sentence* appears in a general-purpose dictionary with several senses, only one really stands out as technical within the legal domain. Therefore, taking all these factors into consideration the third criterion must be interpreted in the following terms: the terminologist must check whether a candidate is polysemous or homonymous and, if so, decide which sense is technical and discard common knowledge meanings. On the other hand, if the candidate is monosemic and the previous two criteria are fulfilled, the terminologist must finally consider the candidate unit for the fourth criterion in the methodology.

4. *Lexicographical criterion*: The criteria suggested above have not only served to analyse whether a lexical unit is a term but also to avoid including redundant information in the Ontological module. The most important criterion, nevertheless, is the consultation of specialised dictionaries, since they reflect the necessary knowledge for the understanding of expert knowledge. It is necessary to note that trained terminologists and lexicographers (with the advice and support of domain-specific experts and practitioners) are the best placed to determine and define terms, since they know how to concisely formulate a definition in a systematic way. However, it is a common problem that expert counselling is not always available due to issues related to accessibility and time. For this reason, terminological dictionaries can work as inanimate experts to which knowledge engineers can address their enquiries. In the case of legal Satellite Ontologies, law dictionaries and technical volumes on law, as well as online glossaries are good starting points. The fact that a candidate term appears listed in any of these sources will be the fundamental criterion to conclude that a candidate is a specialised unit. On the contrary, if a candidate cannot be found in a terminological dictionary the terminologist must judge whether the corpus shows a wider coverage than the consulted dictionaries, or, eventually, whether the candidate is not a term.

Finally, there are two secondary tools in FGKBTE that are worth mentioning, namely the "Search" and the "Corpus" tools. Within the "Search" engine, the terminologist can run queries to retrieve specific examples and contexts in which a word or phrase is used in any of the stored corpora. Examples obtained in this way are available even when the query string is not in the candidate list or has otherwise been removed from it (Figure 10).

The tab "Corpus" has the basic function of providing the terminologist with an overview of the text collections included in FGKBTE as well as displaying descriptive statistics, in particular the number of tokens of each corpora (Figure 11).

In addition to this informative role, this tab holds a list of false candidates which were deleted during the removal stage and it includes an option for the recovery of terms that could have been accidentally discarded during manual filtering. In such case, the button "Recover a term" restores a selected element to the original candidate list from which it was deleted (Figure 12).

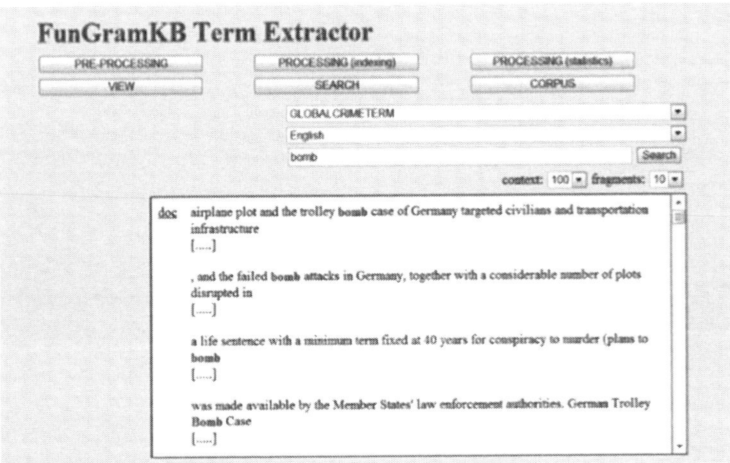

Figure 10. FGKBTE "Search" panel

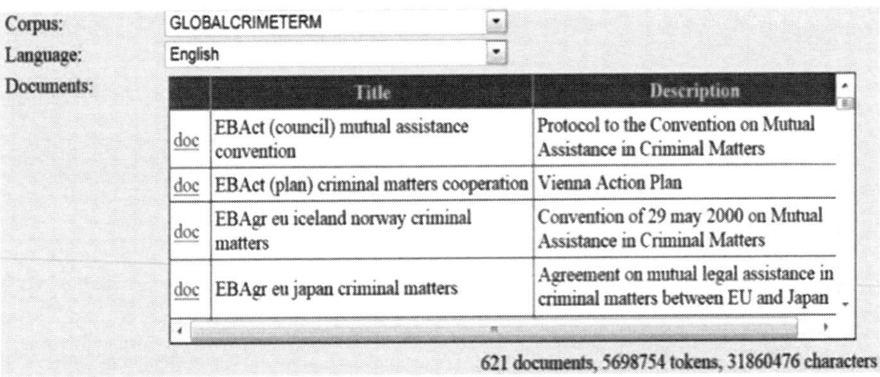

Figure 11. FGKBTE "Corpus" panel

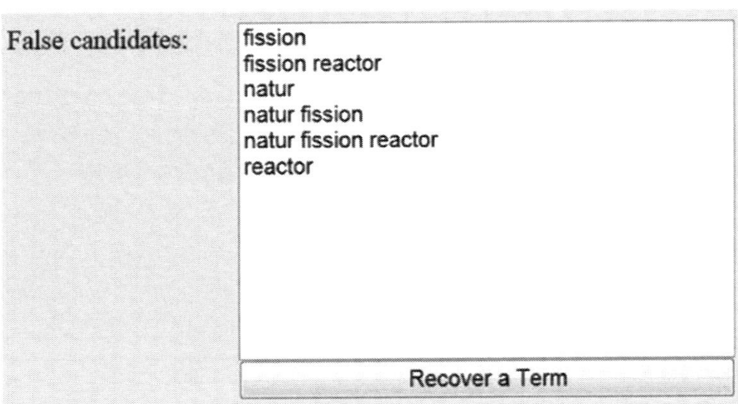

Figure 12. FGKBTE "Corpus" panel: Recovery of false candidates

5. Conclusions

Terminological extraction is a key aspect in the modelling and population of Satellite Ontologies, which are defined as terminologically-driven conceptual taxonomies representing specialised knowledge from technical areas of human knowledge. This chapter has presented *FunGramKB Term Extractor*, an innovative online tool for the semi-automatic extraction and management of terminology from corpus data which relies on statistics. It thus serves the purpose of enhancing the FunGramKB knowledge base with specialised knowledge, as the knowledge base has been so far implemented to work with elementary common-sense concepts of human cognition. The main two advantages of FGKBTE are the cost-effective managing of otherwise extremely time-consuming extraction tasks, as well as its suitability for operating with any language. The extractor, additionally, acts as an interface module connecting the Satellite Ontologies, the Core Ontology and the different terminological Lexica.

References

Biber, Douglas. 1993. Representativeness in corpus design. *Literary and Linguistic Computing* 8(4): 243–257.

Biber, Douglas, Conrad, Susan & Reppen, Randi. 1998. *Corpus Linguistics. Investigating Language Structure and Use*. Cambridge: CUP.

Bowker, Lynne & Pearson, Jennifer. 2002. *Working with Specialized Language. A Practical Guide to Using Corpora*. London: Routledge.

Breuker Joost, Casanovas, Pompeu, Klein, Michel C.A. & Francesconi, Enrico. 2008. *Law, Ontologies and the Semantic Web*. Amsterdam: IOS Press.

Cabré Castellvi, María Teresa. 1999. *Terminology. Theory, Methods and Applications*. [Terminology and Lexicography Research in Practice 1]. Amsterdam: John Benjamins.

Felices-Lago, Ángel & Ureña Gómez-Moreno, Pedro. 2012. Fundamentos metodológicos de la creación subontológica en FunGramKB. *Onomázein* 26(2).

Gómez González-Jover, Adelina. 2007. Léxico especializado y traducción. In *Las lenguas profesionales y académicas*, Enrique Alcaraz Varó, José Mateo Martínez & Francisco Yus Ramos (eds), 27–40. Barcelona: Ariel.

Gruber, Thomas R. 1993. A translation approach to portable ontology specifications. *Knowledge Acquisition* 5(2): 199–220.

Kennedy, Graeme. 1998. *An Introduction to Corpus Linguistics*. London: Longman.

Koester, Almut. 2010. Building small specialised corpora. In *The Routledge Handbook of Corpus Linguistics*, Anne O' Keeffe & Michael McCarthy (eds), 66–79. London: Routledge.

Lim, Edward H.Y., Liu, James N.K. & Lee, Raymond S.T. 2011. *Knowledge Seeker -Ontology Modelling for Information Search and Management. A Compendium*. Berlin: Springer.

L'Homme, Marie-Claude. 2004. *La terminologie: Principes et techniques*. Montréal: Les Presses del'Université de Montréal.

L'Homme, Marie-Claude. 2006. *Processing of Terms in Specialized Dictionaries: New Models and Technique*. Special issue of *Terminology* 12(2).

Mairal-Usón, Ricardo & Periñán-Pascual, Carlos. 2009. The anatomy of the lexicon component within the framework of a conceptual knowledge base. *Revista Española de Lingüística Aplicada* 22: 217–244.

Meyer, Charles F. 2002. *English Corpus Linguistics. An Introduction*. Cambridge: CUP.

Periñán-Pascual, Carlos. 2004. *FunGramKB Suite*. <http://www.fungramkb.com/> (September 2012).

Periñán-Pascual, Carlos. 2011. *FunGramKB Term Extractor*. <http://www.fungramkb.com/> (September 2012).

Periñán-Pascual, Carlos. 2012. The situated common-sense knowledge in FunGramKB. *Review of Cognitive Linguistics* 10(1): 184–214.

Periñán-Pascual, Carlos & Arcas-Túnez, Francisco. 2004. Meaning postulates in a lexico-conceptual knowledge base. In *Proceedings of the 15th International Workshop on Databases and Expert Systems Applications*, 38–42. Los Alamitos CA: IEEE.

Periñán-Pascual, Carlos & Arcas-Túnez, Francisco. 2005. Microconceptual-knowledge spreading in FunGramKB. In *Proceedings of the 9th IASTED International Conference on Artificial Intelligence and Soft Computing*, 239–244. Anaheim CA: ACTA Press.

Periñán-Pascual, Carlos & Arcas-Túnez, Francisco. 2010. The architecture of FunGramKB. In *Proceedings of the 7th International Conference on Language Resources and Evaluation, European Language Resources Association (ELRA)*, 2667–2674.

Periñán-Pascual, Carlos & Mairal-Usón, Ricardo. 2009. Bringing Role and Reference Grammar to natural language understanding. *Procesamiento del Lenguaje Natural* 43: 265–273.

Periñán-Pascual, Carlos & Mairal-Usón, Ricardo. 2010. La gramática de COREL. Un lenguaje de representación conceptual. *Onomázein* 21: 11–45.

Porter, Martin F. 1980. An algorithm for suffix stripping. *Program* 14(3): 130–137.

Reppen, Randi. 2010. Building a corpus. What are the key considerations? In *The Routledge Handbook of Corpus Linguistics*, Anne O' Keeffe & Michael McCarthy (eds), 31–37. London: Routledge.

Salton, Gerard. 1989. *Automatic Text Processing. The Transformation, Analysis and Retrieval of Information by Computer*. Boston MA: Addison-Wesley.

Spärck-Jones, Karen. 1972. A statistical interpretation of term specificity and its application in retrieval. *Journal of Documentation* 28(1): 11–21.

Temmerman, Rita. 2000. *Towards New Ways of Terminology Description. The Sociocognitive-Approach* [Terminology and Lexicography Research in Practice 3]. Amsterdam: John Benjamins.

Temmerman, Rita & Kerremans, Koen. 2003. Termontography. Ontology building and the sociocognitive approach to terminology description. In *Prague CIL17*–conference. <http://www.hf.uib.no/forskerskole/temmerman_art_prague03.pdf>

Deep semantic representation in a domain-specific ontology

Linking EcoLexicon to FunGramKB

Antonio San Martín and Pamela Faber
Universidad de Granada

EcoLexicon is a frame-based visual thesaurus on the Environment that is gradually evolving towards the status of a formal ontology. For this purpose, the information in its relational database is in the process of being linked to the ontological system of FunGramKB, a multipurpose knowledge base. This enables the explicitation of specialized knowledge as an extension of general knowledge through its representation in the domain-specific satellite ontology of a main general ontology. This paper describes the linking process and more specifically, how the general concepts in FunGramKB can be extended and reused in deep semantic representations in a domain-specific ontology.

1. Introduction

Although specialized knowledge in the human mind is built on general knowledge, domain-specific knowledge bases are normally created as standalone products with a very limited reference to general knowledge. Not making reference to general concepts or leaving them undefined in a specialized knowledge base may cause its upper-level structure to be incoherent and/or incomplete, and lead to ambiguity.

EcoLexicon[1] (Faber et al. 2006, 2007, 2009; Faber 2012) is a frame-based visual thesaurus on the Environment that is gradually evolving towards the status of a formal ontology (León and Magaña 2010). For this purpose, the information in its relational database is in the process of being linked to the ontological system of FunGramKB, a multipurpose knowledge base that has been specifically designed for natural language understanding with modules for lexical, grammatical, and conceptual knowledge (Mairal & Periñán 2009; Periñán & Arcas 2010). This enables the explicitation of

1. EcoLexicon is publicly available at <http://ecolexicon.ugr.es>.

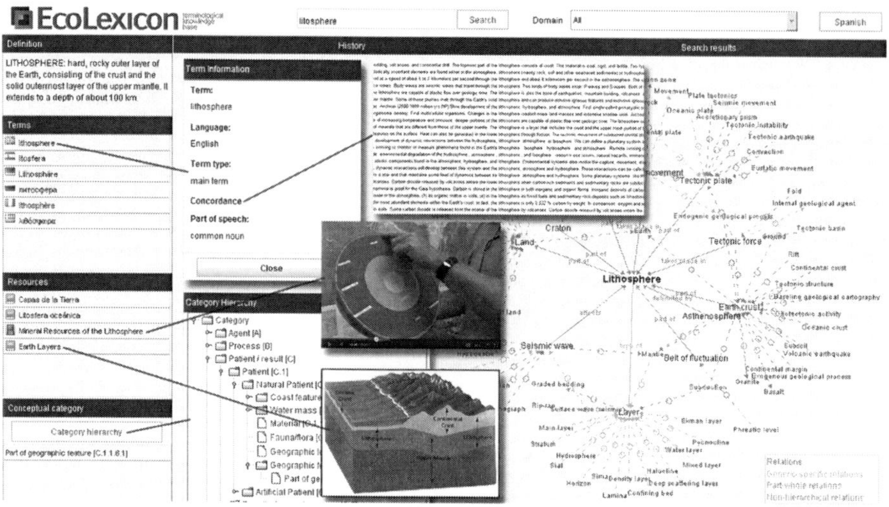

Figure 1. Entry for LITHOSPHERE in EcoLexicon

specialized knowledge as an extension of general knowledge through its representation in the domain-specific satellite ontology of a main general ontology.

Each entry in EcoLexicon provides a wide range of interrelated information. Figure 1 shows the entry for LITHOSPHERE.[2] Users are not obliged to view all this information at the same time, but can browse through the interface depending on their needs.

The concept definition is shown in the box *Definition* (upper-left corner of the window). The terminological units, under the tag *Terms* show the designations of the concept in English, Spanish, German, Russian, French and Modern Greek. Contexts and concordances also appear when the terms are clicked on, and users are thus provided with both conceptual and linguistic information. Graphical resources are displayed when clicking on the links in the box *Resources* (in the left-hand margin towards the middle). Under the tag *Conceptual category*, an ontological structure shows the exact position of the concept in the class hierarchy. LITHOSPHERE, for example, is PART OF GEOGRAPHIC FEATURE (bottom-left corner of the window). At a more fine-grained level, conceptual relations are displayed in a dynamic network of related concepts (right-hand side of the window). Users can click on any of these concepts and thus further expand their knowledge of the specialized domain.

Data in EcoLexicon are primarily hosted in a relational database. Nevertheless, relational modelling has certain limitations, such as its limited capacity to represent real-world entities since implicit knowledge cannot be inferred. Relational models organize data structure and ensure integrity, whereas ontologies specify the underlying conceptualization (Barrasa 2007). In EcoLexicon, semantic information is stored in

2. Throughout this article, EcoLexicon concepts are written in small capitals.

the ontology and the rest is stored in the relational database. However, this semantic information regarding specialized knowledge categories will be enriched when its general knowledge links are made explicit.

2. Linking EcoLexicon to FunGramKB

When linking two ontologies, there are generally three options: (1) merging, which involves the creation of a new ontology by fusing two source ontologies; (2) integration, which also results in the creation of a new ontology though only some parts of the ontologies are merged; (3) alignment, which consists of making the ontologies mutually consistent and coherent though they are kept separate (Hameed et al. 2004). Other authors such as Bouquet et al. (2004: 5) propose the term *ontology coordination* and consider alignment as a set of correspondences between two or more ontologies (a process also present in merging and integration).

We have chosen the alignment or coordination approach for the linking of FunGramKB and EcoLexicon. This means that EcoLexicon will eventually be a satellite ontology of the FunGramKB core ontology though each resource will continue to be independent. This involves a process of ontology reconciliation so that they can become interoperable.

The alignment of EcoLexicon with FunGramKB is naturally based on the use and extension of FunGramKB's basic and terminal concepts[3] in the deep semantic representation of concepts in EcoLexicon. More specifically, a crucial aspect of this linking is the mapping of *overlapping concepts*, or concepts that are represented in both FunGramKB and EcoLexicon. They are part of basic knowledge,[4] but in the environmental domain they also acquire specialized meaning. Although these shared concepts have the same core meaning and referent (in the case of real-world entities), their non-core meaning is different. In EcoLexicon, general concepts (i.e. those in FunGramKB) are a scaffold from which the specialized meaning can be extended (Faber & San Martín 2011: 58).

For example, RAIN in the EcoLexicon satellite ontology needs to be extended from its general meaning ("falling of water from the sky") to include specialized information such as the fact that rain generally falls from nimbostrati. However, this is not an easy task for many reasons. Most of the difficulties that arise in the alignment of two ontologies stem from heterogeneity, which can take several forms. Although there are many classifications of ontological heterogeneities (e.g. Bouquet et al. 2004; Euzenat &

3. Note that in FunGramKB, core ontology terminal concepts are never used in the meaning postulates of other concepts. However, when formalizing EcoLexicon concepts in COREL (FunGramKB's conceptual representation language) this restriction will not be applied.

4. In FunGramKB a concept is considered to pertain to commonsense knowledge if it appears in language-learning dictionaries (Mairal et al. 2011: 8).

Shvaiko 2007: 40–42, *inter alia*), the most important types are syntactic, terminological, conceptual, and pragmatic.

In the following subsections, we analyze some of these types that were detected in relation to the alignment of FunGramKB and EcoLexicon. In this case, we have unified conceptual and pragmatic heterogeneity because the pragmatic mismatches caused by divergences in the interpretation of the concepts or the intended use of the ontology have implications at the conceptual level.

2.1 Syntactic heterogeneity

Syntactic heterogeneity occurs when two ontologies are not expressed in the same representation format (Bouquet et al. 2004: 6). This is the case of FunGramKB and EcoLexicon. FunGramKB uses meaning postulates, in other words, logically-connected predications written in COREL, to formalize meaning (Periñán & Arcas 2005), whereas EcoLexicon is hosted in a relational database (León et al. 2009: 17) in which meaning is represented by relations between concepts, and natural-language definitions.

This mismatch is resolved by the addition of a COREL deep semantic representation of EcoLexicon concepts. When the linking process is finally completed, there will be three interrelated levels of concept representation in EcoLexicon:

- Level 1: the deep semantic representation of concepts in terms of meaning postulates. These meaning postulates are encoded in the conceptual representation language COREL. Users will be able to access these representations as natural language translations (Level 3).
- Level 2: a surface semantic representation, which the user can consult and interact with via ThinkMap visualization software. This is the current knowledge representation approach in EcoLexicon. The information encoded in meaning postulates will be mainly based on surface semantic conceptual propositions.
- Level 3: meaning definitions, encoded as the natural-language translation of meaning postulates written in COREL. In all likelihood, this translation will need to be adapted since certain features in the meaning postulates will have to be added, omitted, or modified for the sake of explanatory adequacy.

2.2 Terminological heterogeneity

When the same concept in different ontologies is named differently, there is terminological heterogeneity (Bouquet et al. 2004: 7). This usually stems from the use of different natural languages (RAIN vs. LLUVIA) or from terminological variation: different levels of specificity (WATER CYCLE vs. HYDROLOGIC CYCLE), synonymy (WEATHER FORECASTING vs. WEATHER PREDICTION), geographical variants (AUTUMN vs. FALL), etc. This kind of problem is an obstacle to automatic matching by means of a computer application. Even though a human agent can spot and solve most of these mismatches quite easily, it can be tedious and time-consuming.

In our alignment process, the most frequent problems concerning terminological mismatching will, in all likelihood, be due to terminological variation. However, EcoLexicon concepts are always associated with their designations in English (and other languages). There is one main entry term, whereas the other terms referring to the same concept are labeled as some type of variant. This, along with FunGramKB's lexical module, should help to solve the problems derived from terminological heterogeneity.

2.3 Conceptual heterogeneity

Conceptual heterogeneity stems from divergences in conceptual modeling. This occurs at a metaphysical level when the concepts represented are not the same or when they are categorized and arranged differently. It occurs at an epistemic level when these concepts are not described in the same fashion as far as semantic content is concerned (Bouquet et al. 2004:7). According to Bouquet et al. (2004), there are three types of conceptual modeling difference that lead to conceptual heterogeneity: (1) difference in coverage (or *partiality* in Benerecetti et al. [2000]); (2) difference in granularity (or *approximation*); (3) difference in perspective.

Difference in coverage. This kind of conceptual heterogeneity occurs when two ontologies focus on different (sometimes overlapping) portions of knowledge (Euzenat & Shvaiko 2007: 41). The case of FunGramKB and EcoLexicon is an excellent example. On the one hand, the objective of FunGramKB is to store all the concepts that a person has in mind when talking about everyday situations (Periñán & Arcas 2007: 198). In contrast, EcoLexicon is a domain-specific knowledge base about the Environment. Some of the areas of coverage in both resources overlap since many concepts related to the Environment are part of everyday life and EcoLexicon has an informally arranged upper-level set of concepts that are part of commonsense knowledge.

Difference in granularity. This kind of conceptual heterogeneity occurs when two ontologies describe knowledge at different levels of detail (Euzenat and Shvaiko 2007: 41). FunGramKB not only describes knowledge from many different spheres of life but is also limited to the knowledge of the world generally possessed by a prototypical well-educated speaker (Jiménez & Luzondo 2011: 23). Unlike EcoLexicon, it does not aspire to represent in-depth expert knowledge. In this respect, FunGramKB and EcoLexicon complement each other since EcoLexicon represents specialized information with a high degree of detail, accuracy, and precision, while the FunGramKB core ontology offers a uniform representation of upper-level concepts (Speranza & Magnini 2010: 230).

Difference in perspective. This kind of conceptual heterogeneity occurs when two ontologies describe knowledge from different perspectives (Euzenat & Shvaiko 2007: 41). Pragmatic factors have an important influence here. The perspective from which FunGramKB depicts reality is that of a normal person interacting with his/her surroundings. In contrast, EcoLexicon represents knowledge from the perspective of Environmental Science and related fields. Nevertheless, as the Environment is such a vast interdisciplinary domain, it has been divided into various subdomains. Concepts are thus represented from the perspective of the subdomains in which they appear and within the global context of a unifying general environmental representation (León & San Martín 2011, 2012).

The description of basic scientific concepts for the general public is often at odds with their description for scientists and engineers. Definitions of the same concept can be rather different, depending on the knowledge level of the targeted user group to the extent that they sometimes appear to have little or no relation with each other. For example, Lipschultz & Litman (2010) found that many entities that are defined as forces in WordNet are really not forces according to Physics. Consequently, an ontology reconciliation process will have to be carried out during the alignment of EcoLexicon and the FunGramKB core ontology.

2.4 Phases of the process

The process of linking EcoLexicon and FunGramKB involves three phases:

1. Identification of overlapping concepts.
2. Hierarchical rearrangement.
3. Conceptual modeling and mapping.

2.4.1 *Identification of overlapping concepts*

Especially for the linking process, EcoLexicon is divided in three sections. Concepts will receive a different treatment in the alignment, depending on their respective section. In Figure 2, EcoLexicon (the pyramid on the left[5]) is represented before the linking process and the sections are labeled 1E, 2E, and 3E:

1E: Upper-level concepts of EcoLexicon. Concepts in this section have such a low degree of specificity that a general description of the type provided in FunGramKB is sufficient. They are normally basic superordinate concepts that do not have a mental image associated with them (Rosch 1978).

2E: Mid-level concepts of EcoLexicon. Most of these concepts can be considered part of commonsense knowledge and appear in language-learning dictionaries (Mairal et al. 2011: 8). Nevertheless, mid-level concepts can acquire specialized meaning in an environmental context. The distinction between upper-level concepts and mid-level concepts, however, is fuzzy, and the decision to assign concepts to one group or the other is ultimately a subjective one.

5. The pyramid representation of the alignment of a general knowledge ontology and a domain-specific one has been taken from Speranza & Magnini (2010).

3E: Lower-level concepts of EcoLexicon. These are highly specialized environmental concepts.

As for the FunGramKB core ontology (the pyramid on the right in Figure 2), it is also divided in three sections corresponding to its three conceptual levels: 1F are metaconcepts; 2F, basic concepts; 3F, terminal concepts.

As can be observed in Figure 3, the upper-level (1E) and mid-level (2E) concepts in EcoLexicon, and the basic (2F) and terminal concepts (3F) in the FunGramKB ontology overlap. EcoLexicon upper-level concepts will always correspond to FunGramKB basic concepts, while mid-level concepts can overlap with either basic or terminal concepts.

As shown in Figure 4, the upper-level concepts of EcoLexicon are eliminated, and thus FunGramKB becomes the upper-level ontology of EcoLexicon. The only section

Figure 2. EcoLexicon and the FunGramKB core ontology prior to alignment

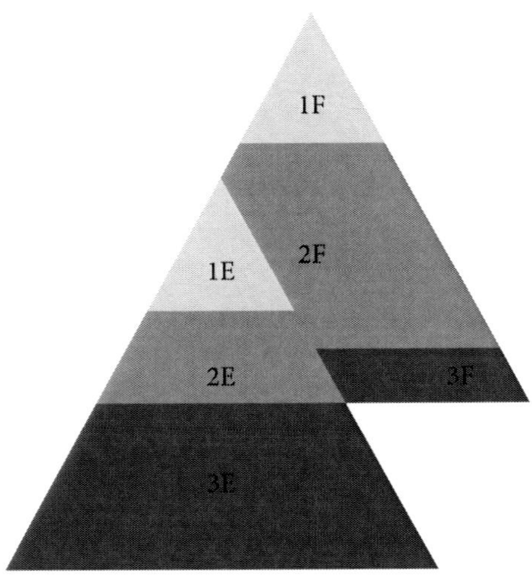

Figure 3. EcoLexicon and the FunGramKB core ontology prior to alignment superposed

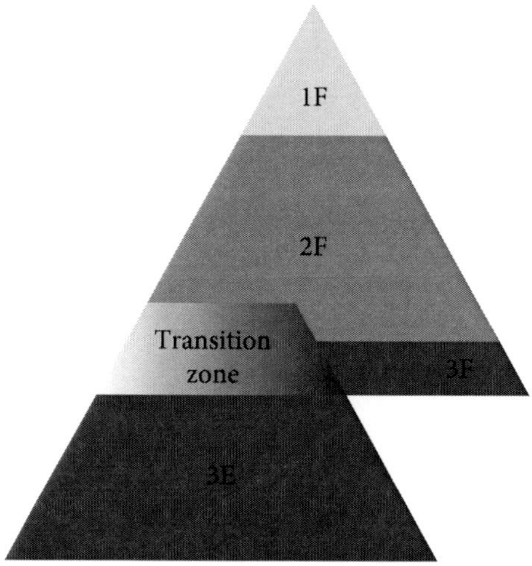

Figure 4. EcoLexicon and the FunGramKB core ontology during the alignment process

that needs to be aligned is the transition zone, where EcoLexicon and FunGramKB overlap once 1E has been suppressed. However, certain concepts near the transition zone may also require adjustment, especially since the FunGramKB core ontology is in its early stages of development and, as a consequence, many areas of the ontology still have many conceptual gaps. In addition, EcoLexicon's hierarchical structure needs refining, especially since its upper-level limit was never clearly defined.

2.4.2 *Hierarchical rearrangement*

Prior to the modeling of overlapping concepts and the specification of mappings, the hierarchies need to be arranged to render them parallel. As stated in the introduction of this paper, EcoLexicon is in the process of being recontextualized, which means that conceptual propositions are currently being linked to different contextual subdomains (León 2009). This recontextualization process is guided by feature relevance and also by facet incompatibility (León et al. 2013). This approach is compatible with defeasible logic, which is the type of non-monotonic inheritance used in FunGramKB (Periñán & Arcas 2010: 33).

As a result of the recontextualization process in EcoLexicon, there are several hierarchical structures solely based on *is-a* relations (León & San Martín 2012), like the hierarchy in the FunGramKB core ontology. On the one hand, there is an explicit general environmental hierarchy which is being developed by choosing the most representative and encompassing categorization compatible for all contextual subdomains. On the other hand, other hierarchies can be inferred for each contextual subdomain by following the path of the *is-a* relations. These subhierarchies are automatically revised so that they are not incompatible with the general environmental hierarchy and its alignment with the FunGramKB core ontology.

The general environmental hierarchy is the one that is to be connected to the FunGramKB hierarchy. That does not mean that the other subsumption relations will not be formalized. They will be represented in the meaning postulates along with the many other conceptual features. Furthermore, all of the features will be correspondingly labeled in order to mark their recontextualization in a certain contextual subdomain or their application to the whole environmental domain.

2.4.3 *Conceptual modeling and mapping*

Once the hierarchies are parallel, prior to mapping overlapping concepts, it is necessary to apply conceptual modeling techniques that tailor commonsense knowledge so that it can be seamlessly extended to encompass and encode specialized knowledge representations of the same concept (Faber & San Martín 2011: 48). Only in this way can potential inconsistencies be eliminated.

In Figure 5, we can see the result of the ontology reconciliation. EcoLexicon overlapping concepts in the mid-level/transition zone (TZ-2E) will have been completely mapped onto the FunGramKB basic and terminal concepts in the transition zone (TZ-2F and TZ-3F, respectively). Overlapping concepts are mapped by means of a subsumption relation formalized in the meaning postulate of the EcoLexicon concept. For example, the first predication of =RAIN_00[6,7] would be:

+(e1: +BE_00 (x1: =RAIN_00)Theme (x2: +RAIN_00)Referent)

Thus, the EcoLexicon concept would inherit all the data linked to the FunGramKB concept and the specialized concept can be built on commonsense knowledge to include the specialized meaning.

Finally, after the alignment, EcoLexicon and FunGramKB, though still independent, will be linked and interoperable.

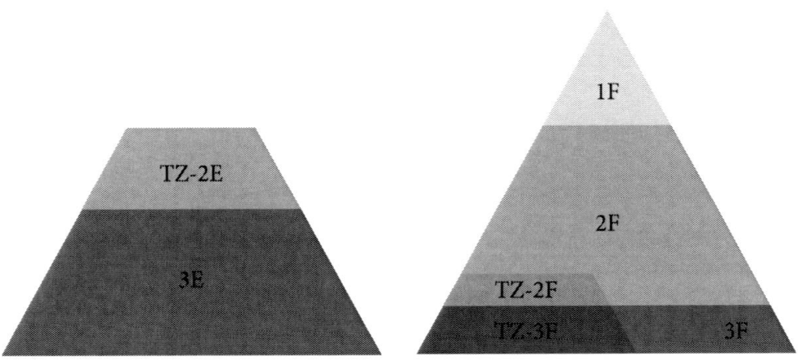

Figure 5. EcoLexicon and FunGramKB after the alignment process

6. In contrast to EcoLexicon concepts, concepts in COREL are written in capital letters.

7. The use of the sign = to precede EcoLexicon concepts in COREL is not definitive.

3. The case of RAIN

3.1 +RAIN_00 in FunGramKB

+RAIN_00 is a basic concept in FunGramKB. According to its position in the core ontology, it is a subordinate concept of +WEATHER_00 and +WATER_00. Nevertheless, its meaning postulate only reflects the subsumption relation with +WATER_00:

+(e1: +BE_00 (x1: +RAIN_00)Theme (x2: +WATER_00)Referent)

As reflected in this meaning postulate, this concept has not as yet been modeled, but only roughly sketched.

In FunGramKB, there is a non-monotonic inheritance mechanism that transfers strict and non-blocked defeasible predications from superordinate concepts to their subordinate ones in the ontology (Periñán & Arcas 2005). It is thus important to take the meaning postulates of the superordinate concepts into account so as to avoid inconsistencies and redundancies. In this paper, we only focus on overlapping concepts, since other concepts are outside the scope of the alignment process being described.

Figure 6 shows a concept map of +RAIN_00 and its superordinate and subordinate concepts along with their meaning postulates.

As shown in Figure 6, +RAIN_00 is categorized as a type of +WEATHER_00 or +WATER_00. In the +WATER_00 hierarchy there are two superordinate concepts (+NATURAL_OBJECT_00 and +BEVERAGE_00), as reflected in the meaning postulates. Although +WATER_00 is categorized as +LIQUID_00 in the core ontology hierarchy, this means that there are two *is-a* paths that determine the predications to be inherited by it and by +RAIN_00 as well (Figure 7).

Although the explicit formalization of +WATER_00 as a type of +NATURAL_OBJECT_00 in the meaning postulate may seem redundant, this indicates that +WATER_00 is not an +ARTIFICIAL_OBJECT, since +SUBSTANCE_00 is subsumed under both types of object mentioned. This is the way that FunGramKB manages multiple inheritance (Periñán & Arcas 2010: 32).

While the first *is-a* path is applicable to +RAIN_00, the second one is not. Although +RAIN_00 could be drunk in extreme conditions of thirst and deprivation, it certainly is not a beverage, since it is fairly unusual for a person (or another type of animal) to quench his/her thirst with water falling from the sky.

This inconsistency can be solved by stating that +WATER_00 is always a +NATURAL_OBJECT, but in most cases, it is not a +BEVERAGE_00. This means that subordinate concepts can take either the first path or both paths in Figure 7, but not the second path exclusively. The first predication of +WATER_00 would be as follows:

+(e1: +BE_00 (x1: +WATER_00)Theme (x2: (+LIQUID_00 & +NATURAL_OBJECT_00) | (+BEVERAGE_00 & +NATURAL_OBJECT_00))Referent

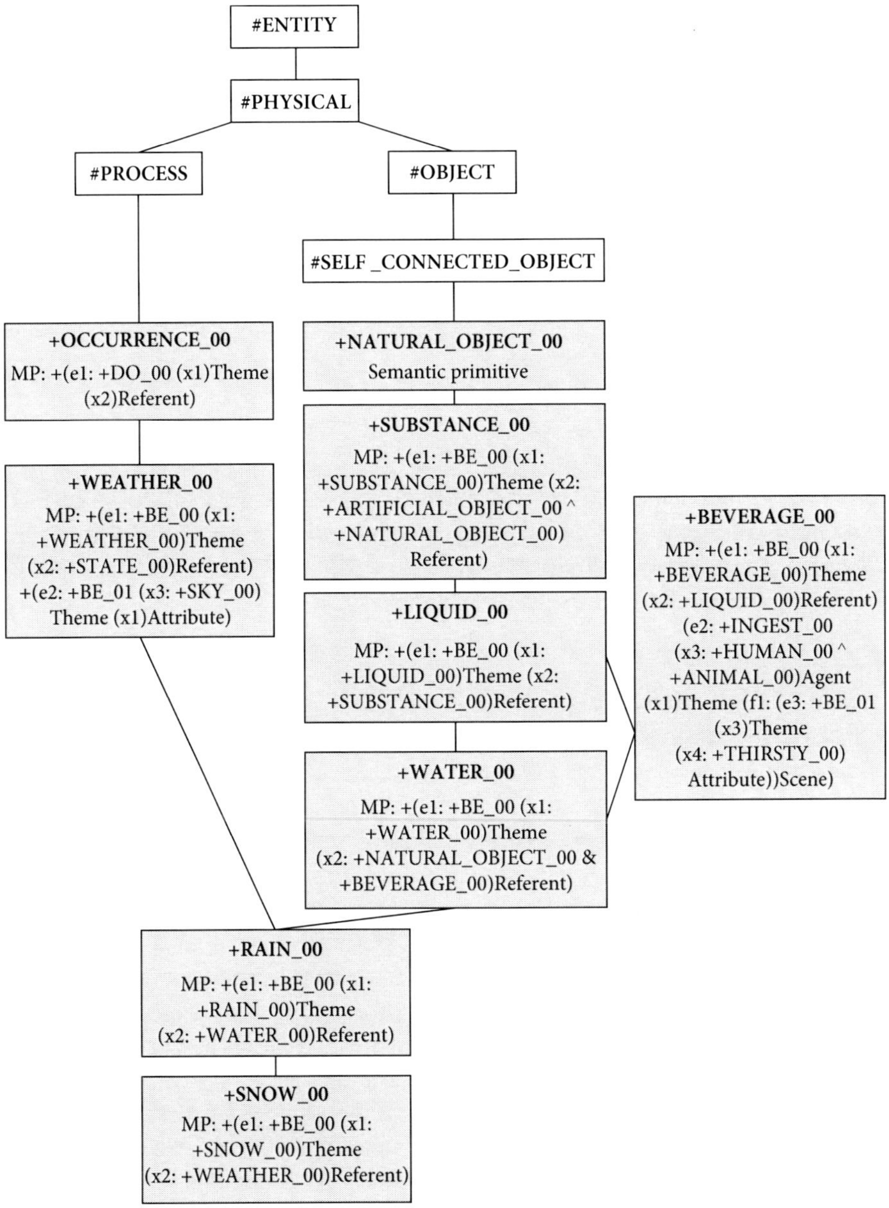

Figure 6. +RAIN_00 and its superordinate and subordinate concepts

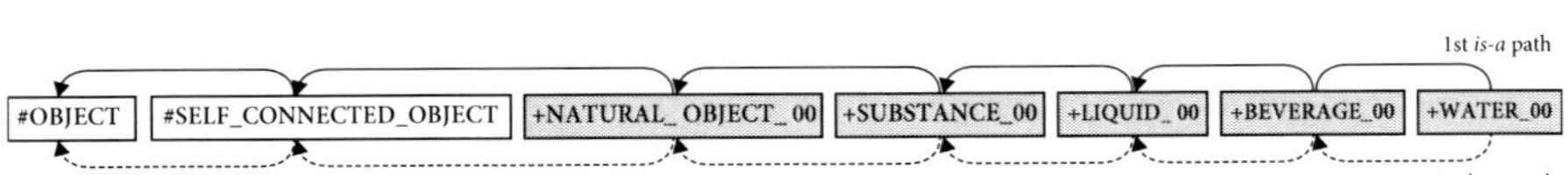

Figure 7. Is-a paths determined by the meaning postulates of +WATER_00

On the other hand, when +RAIN_00 is a subordinate of +WEATHER_00, this entails that +RAIN_00 is a #PROCESS as well as "a state of the sky" (i.e. what the meaning postulate of +WEATHER_00 represents). Despite the fact that +RAIN_00 is a type of #PROCESS, in our opinion, it should not be subsumed to +WEATHER_00. Furthermore, the fact that +RAIN_00 is categorized as both #OBJECT and #PROCESS brings up the question of the polysemy of this concept. According to Pustejovsky (2005), RAIN would be a dot object because it is inherently polysemic and its senses are connected in a regular and well-defined way (Rumshisky, Grinberg & Pustejovsky 2007). RAIN is an example of the dot type PROCESS · RESULT. This is dealt with in EcoLexicon by representing RAIN as two separate entities and connecting them by the conceptual relation *result-of*.

3.2 RAIN in EcoLexicon

As previously mentioned, RAIN in EcoLexicon is represented as two different entities: RAIN and RAINWATER. RAIN is categorized, in the general environmental hierarchy, under PRECIPITATION, ATMOSPHERIC PROCESS, NATURAL PROCESS, and PROCESS. In certain contextual subdomains, such as Hydrology or Meteorology, it is also subsumed to concepts such as HYDROLOGICAL PROCESS or METEOROLOGICAL ELEMENT, respectively. Moreover, RAIN belongs to the NATURAL PROCESS category in the Environmental Event (Faber et al. 2009: 8).

All the superordinate concepts of RAIN are connected by means of non-hierarchical relations to other concepts in EcoLexicon. Many of these conceptual propositions are inherited by RAIN[8] and, along with RAIN's own propositions, make up its surface-semantic representation. Figure 8 shows the conceptual network of RAIN in the user interface of EcoLexicon as a ThinkMap representation.

RAIN's most direct superordinate concept is PRECIPITATION. It has has three subordinate concepts, namely FREEZING RAIN, ACID RAIN, and RESIDUAL RAIN. There are also three non-hierarchical relations which are "RAINWATER *result-of* RAIN", and "RAIN *takes-place-in* NIMBOSTRATUS" and "RAIN *takes-place-in* ALTOSTRATUS".

These conceptual propositions are present in the natural language definition: "Precipitation [RAIN *type-of* PRECIPITATION] of liquid water in the form of drops with a diameter greater than 0.5 mm [RAINWATER *result-of* RAIN]. It generally falls from nimbostrati and rarely from altostrati [RAIN *takes-place-in* NIMBOSTRATUS/ALTOSTRATUS]". This "translation" from surface-semantic conceptual propositions to a natural-language definition reflects potential problems of this process, which will have to be dealt with.

In EcoLexicon, the inventory of conceptual relations is extended very cautiously in order to guarantee the consistency of the resource. The drawback to this, however,

8. Currently, EcoLexicon does not have a formal inheritance system since its conversion into an ontology has not been completed yet.

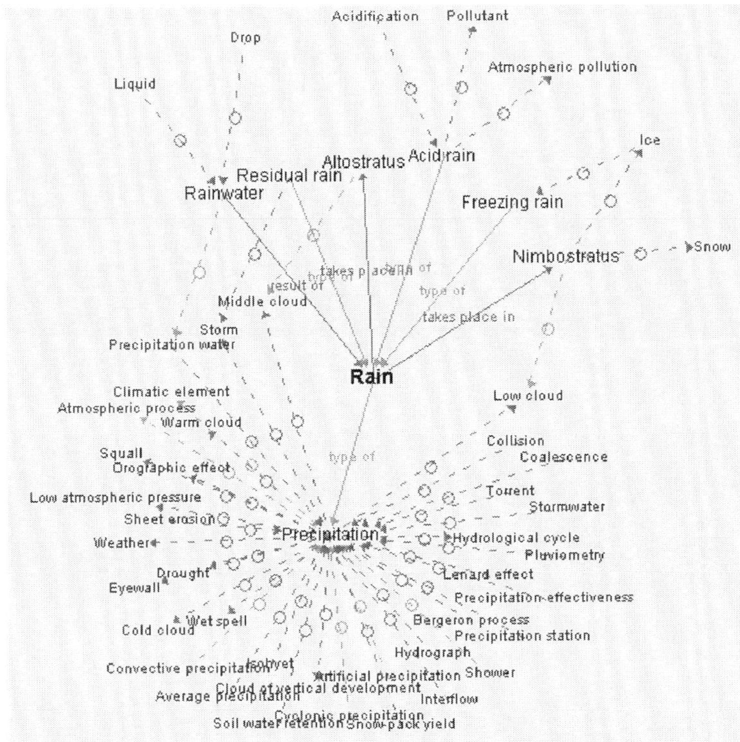

Figure 8. Conceptual network of RAIN in EcoLexicon

is that relations are occasionally not sufficiently expressive. For instance, it is still not possible to formalize the fact that RAIN starts in nimbostrati and altostrati. Instead, the relation *takes-place-in*, which is considerably less precise, needs to be used. It is also not feasible to express the variation in frequency with respect to the origin of the rain (*generally* or *rarely*). Furthermore, for the moment, in EcoLexicon no integer values are allowed. All these deficiencies have been compensated so far with the natural language definitions, which allow the terminologist to qualify what has been formalized in the conceptual propositions (San Martín 2012). However, such definitions are not machine-readable. In this context, a deep semantic representation in COREL has the advantages of being machine-readable as well as having a greater power of expression that will help to overcome the drawbacks of surface-semantic representations.

This translation process also has certain particularities. For example, the proposition "RAINWATER *result-of* RAIN" is not expressed as such, but is extended from the information related to RAINWATER. The reason for this is that in the definitions of dot objects, the tendency in EcoLexicon is to concentrate most information in the definition of only one of the dot-object concepts. Nonetheless, given that definitions are the natural language translation of the conceptual structure of a domain (Faber 2002), it is not sufficient to only represent direct conceptual propositions in the case of knowledge systems based on Surface Semantics, or only represent the information contained in the meaning postulate because a concept is associated with a wider range of knowledge (Periñán & Arcas 2005). Originally devised as the base of the FunGramKB reasoner, the MicroKnowing process can be especially useful in the formulation of definitions, since terminologists could be provided with relevant information to be represented in the definition or conceptual description automatically extracted from meaning postulates of other concepts. Otherwise, this process would have to be performed manually, which would be extremely time-consuming.

As for RAINWATER, it is categorized as a type of PRECIPITATION WATER, WATER, and SUBSTANCE. Furthermore, it belongs to the RESULT category in the Environmental Event. Figure 9 shows its ThinkMap conceptual network.

This concept only establishes four direct conceptual relations with other concepts:

- RAINWATER *type-of* PRECIPITATION WATER
- RAINWATER *result-of* RAIN
- DROP *part-of* RAINWATER
- LIQUID *attribute-of* RAINWATER

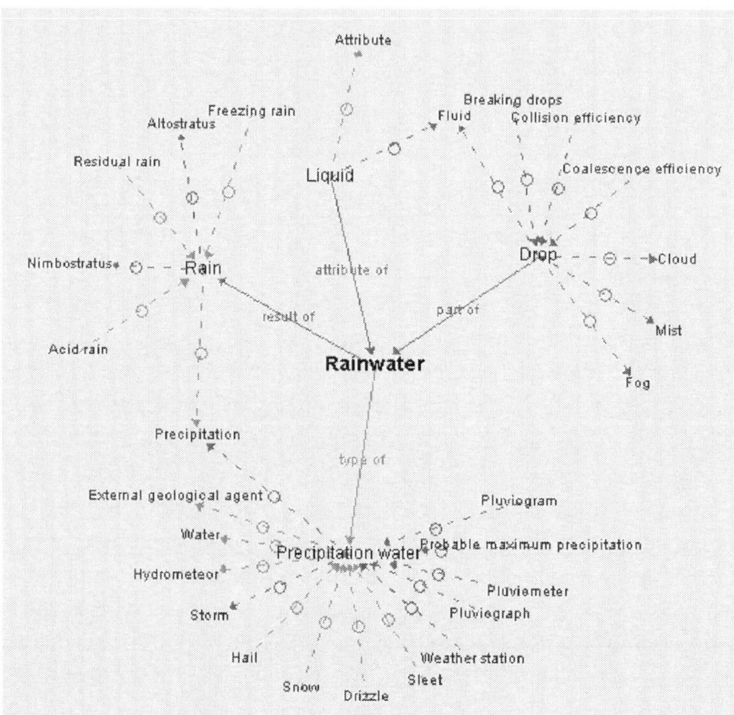

Figure 9. Conceptual network of RAINWATER in EcoLexicon

Given that, as previously mentioned, most of the information has been concentrated in the definition of the process, the natural language definition of RAINWATER is more succinct: "Liquid [LIQUID *attribute-of* RAINWATER] precipitation [RAINWATER *type-of* PRECIPITATION WATER] result of the process of rain [RAINWATER *result-of* RAIN]".

3.3 Identification of overlapping concepts and hierarchical rearrangement

Firstly, the corresponding part of the EcoLexicon general environmental hierarchy is divided into the three levels outlined in Section 2.4.1 (Figure 10).

Upper-level concepts (1E) are always deleted from EcoLexicon during the alignment and substituted with the corresponding basic concept in FunGramKB.

In the case of mid-level concepts (2E), if there is a corresponding concept in FunGramKB, they are then overlapping concepts. If there is no corresponding concept, there are two options:

1. If the concept is suitable for a commonsense ontology, the FunGramKB equivalent is created, and then both become overlapping concepts.
2. If the concept is too specialized for FunGramKB, no FunGramKB equivalent is created and then the FunGramKB core ontology will bypass it.

As for lower-level concepts (3E),[9] FunGramKB equivalents are never created. However, as any other EcoLexicon concept, their deep semantic representation may include FunGramKB basic or terminal concepts.

Consequently, apart from the naming of EcoLexicon concepts following COREL rules, certain changes are applied. This article outlines the changes to the RAIN hierarchy and the RAINWATER hierarchy separately for the sake of simplicity. This study only

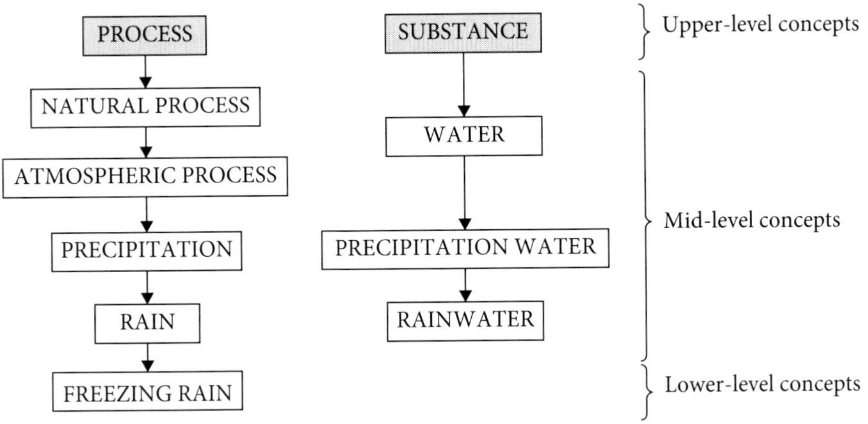

Figure 10. EcoLexicon concepts subdivided in three levels before alignment

9. In this paper, the only subordinate concept of RAIN considered is FREEZING RAIN.

focuses on RAIN and its superordinate concepts as an illustration of the alignment process. However, it goes without saying that this task should ultimately involve a larger number of concepts that would be simultaneously aligned.

The changes to be applied to the RAIN (process) FunGramKB and EcoLexicon hiearchies are the following:

- PROCESS, since it is an upper-level concept (E1) is substituted for +OCCURRENCE_00.
- +NATURAL_PROCESS_00 and +ARTIFICIAL_PROCESS_00 are created in FunGramKB, which results in two overlapping concepts: +ARTIFICIAL_PROCESS_00/=ARTIFICIAL_PROCESS_00 and +NATURAL_PROCESS_00/=NATURAL_PROCESS_00.
- +PRECIPITATION_00 is created, resulting in the overlapping concept +PRECIPITATION_00/=PRECIPITATION_00. The concept =ATMOSPHERIC_PROCESS is bypassed in the FunGramKB core ontology and thus, the direct subordinate concept of +PRECIPITATION_00 is +NATURAL_PROCESS_00, whereas =PRECIPITATION_00 will have =ATMOSPHERIC_PROCESS_00 as its direct superordinate concept. Of course, this signifies that in the meaning postulate of =PRECIPITATION_00, its *is-a* path will have to be made explicit since an =ATMOSPHERIC_PROCESS_00 can be either a =NATURAL_PROCESS_00 or an =ARTIFICIAL_PROCESS_00. In addition, as a result, +WEATHER_00 is no longer a superordinate concept of +RAIN_00.
- The scope of the concept +RAIN_00 is limited to the process and will form an overlapping concept with =RAIN_00.

The hierarchies resulting from these changes are shown in Figure 11.

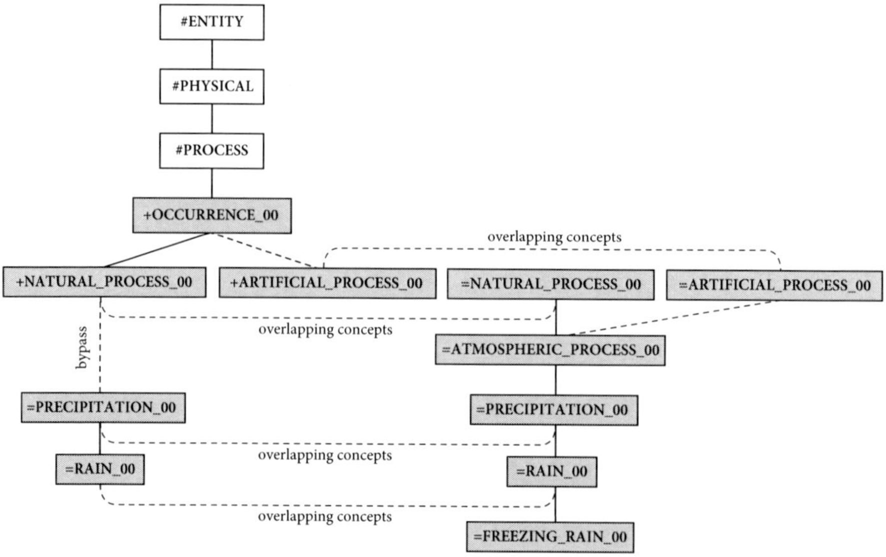

Figure 11. FunGramKB and EcoLexicon RAIN (process) hierarchies after rearrangement

As for RAIN (water) in the FunGramKB and EcoLexicon hierarchies, the changes to be applied are the following:

- SUBTANCE, since it is an upper-level concept (E1), is substituted for +SUBSTANCE_00.
- +WATER_00 and =WATER_00 become overlapping concepts. We also propose that +WATER_00/=WATER_00 have +SOLID_00, +LIQUID_00, +GAS_00 as superordinate concepts because water can be found in any of these three states and sometimes the term *water* designates this substance regardless of the state (even though the liquid state is the most prototyipical). An example of this is when PRECIPITATION is categorized as a type of WATER, since PRECIPITATION may be either solid water or liquid water (unlike RAIN, which is always liquid). This is all formalized by well-defined *is-a* paths in the corresponding meaning postulates.
- +PRECIPITATION_01 and +RAIN_01 are created, resulting in the overlapping concepts +PRECIPITATION_01/=PRECIPITATION_01 and +RAIN_01/=RAIN_01.

The resulting hierarchies are shown in Figure 12.

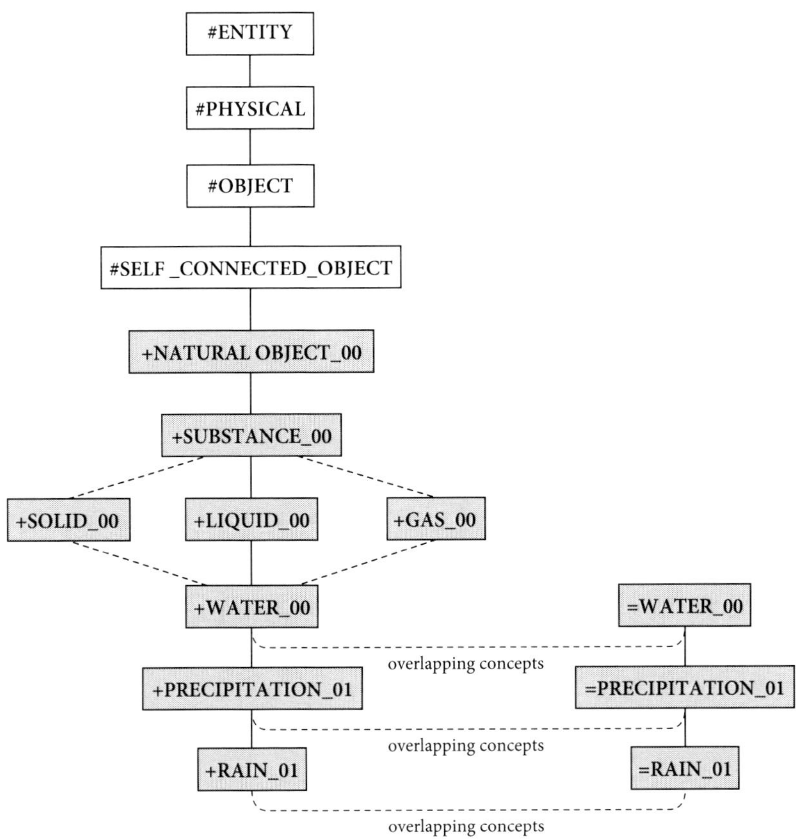

Figure 12. FunGramKB and EcoLexicon RAIN (WATER) hierarchies after rearrangement

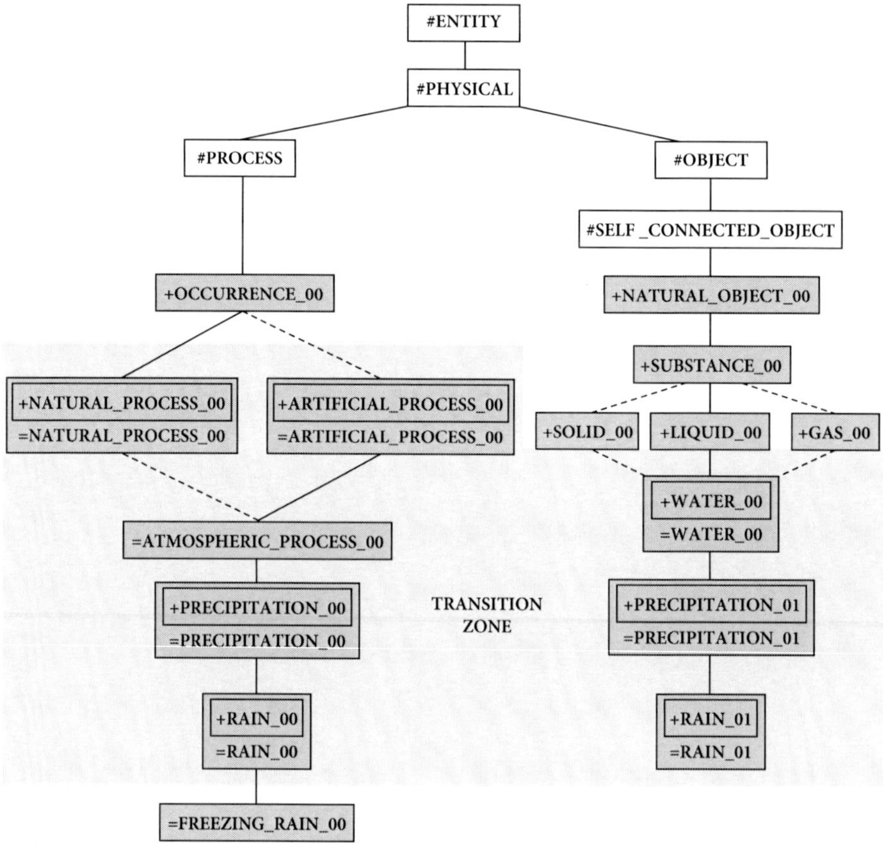

Figure 13. Superposed RAIN hierarchies

Finally, once the hierarchies are reconciled, they can be superposed (Figure 13) and the conceptual modeling and mapping stage can begin.

3.4 Conceptual modeling and mapping: Deep semantic representation in EcoLexicon

This section primarily focuses on the overlapping concepts +PRECIPITATION_00/= PRECIPITATION_00, +RAIN_00/=RAIN_00, +PRECIPITATION_01/=PRECIPITA TION_01, and +RAIN_01/=RAIN_01. Nevertheless, where necessary, the deep semantic representation of other closely related concepts is also discussed.

3.4.1 +PRECIPITATION_00/=PRECIPITATION_00, and +RAIN_00/=RAIN_00

+PRECIPITATION_00		
Meaning postulate		*Translation*
P1	+(e1: +BE_00 (x1: +PRECIPITATION_00) Theme (x2: +NATURAL_PROCESS_00 ^ +ARTIFICIAL_PROCESS_00)Referent)	Precipitation is a type of natural process or an artificial process.
P2	+(e2: +DESCEND_00 (x3)Agent(x4: +PRECIPITATION_01)Theme (x5) Location (x6: +CLOUD_00)Origin (x7) Goal (f1:x1)Scene)	Precipitation water falls from the clouds during precipitation.
P3	+(e3: +DO_00 (x1)Theme (x8)Referent (f2: +ATMOSPHERE_00)Location)	Precipitation takes place in the atmopshere.

P1 specifies that +PRECIPITATION_00 can be either a natural or an artificial process because, even though all of its hyponyms in the FunGramKB core ontology are natural processes, there is a specialized type of precipitation that is caused by human intervention: =ARTIFICIAL_PRECIPITATION_00. Thus, for the sake of consistency,[10] this distinction will be made for hyponyms of +PRECIPITATION_00 and =PRECIPITATION_00.

In P3, since a non-existent +ATMOSPHERIC_PROCESS_00 is bypassed, the information that would have been inherited from such concept is represented there.

=PRECIPITATION_00		
Meaning postulate		*Translation*
P4	+(e1: +BE_00 (x1: =PRECIPITATION_00) Theme (x2: +PRECIPITATION_00 & =ATMOSPHERIC_PROCESS_00) Referent)	Precipitation (EcoLexicon) is a type of precipitation (FunGramKB) and an atmospheric process.
P5	+(e2: +DESCEND_00 (x3)Agent(x4: =PRECIPITATION_01)Theme (x5) Location (x6: =MIDDLE_CLOUD_00 ^ =LOW_CLOUD_00 ^ =CLOUD_WITH_VERTICAL_DEVELOPMENT_00)Origin (x7)Goal (f1:x1)Scene)	Precipitation water falls from middle clouds, low clouds or clouds with vertical development during precipitation.

10. Since =PRECIPITATION_00 is mapped onto +PRECIPITATION_00, it inherits all the predications of +PRECIPITATION_00.

P6	+(e3: +DO_00 (x5: =COLLISION_00 & =COALESCENCE_00)Theme (x1) Referent) (f2: +BE_00 (x6)Theme (x8: =WARM_CLOUD_00)Referent)Condition)	Precipitation is caused by collision and coalescence if the cloud from which precipitation water falls is a warm cloud.
P7	+(e4: +DO_00 (x9: =BERGERON_PROCESS_00)Theme (x1)Referent) (f3: +BE_00 (x6)Theme (x10: =COLD_CLOUD_00) Referent)Condition)	Precipitation is caused by the Bergeron process if the cloud from which precipitation water falls is a cold cloud.

P4 maps =PRECIPITATION_00 onto +PRECIPITATION_00. As for P5, it is simply an extension of P2, and thus, certain concepts are substituted for a more specialized and fine-grained representation.

=RAIN_00		
Meaning postulate		*Translation*
P8	+(e1: +BE_00 (x1: +RAIN_00)Theme (x2: +PRECIPITATION_00)Referent)	Rain is a type of precipitation.
P9	+(e2: +DESCEND_00 (x3)Agent (x4: +RAIN_01)Theme (x5)Location (x6: +CLOUD_00)Origin (x7)Goal (f1:x1)Scene)	Rainwater falls from the clouds during rain.

The only difference between P9 and P2 is that the water that falls is rainwater instead of precipitation water. As shall be seen, rainwater has its specificities (namely, it is liquid water and its drops have a certain diameter) compared to precipitation water.

=RAIN_00		
Meaning postulate		*Translation*
P10	+(e1: +BE_00 (x1: =RAIN_00)Theme (x2: +RAIN_00 & =PRECIPITATION_00) Referent)	Rain (EcoLexicon) is a type of rain (FunGramKB) and precipitation (EcoLexicon)
P11	+(e2: +DESCEND_00 (x3)Agent (x4: =RAIN_01)Theme (x5)Location (x6: =NIMBOSTRATUS_00)Origin (x7)Goal (f1:x1)Scene (f2: +OFTEN_00)Frequency)	Rainwater often falls from nimbostrati during rain.

P12	+(e3: +DESCEND_00 (x3)Agent (x4) Theme (x5)Location (x8: =ALTOSTRATUS_00)Origin (f3:x1)Scene (f4: $OFTEN_N_00)Frequency)	Rainwater rarely falls from altostrati during rain.

In P12, a FunGramKB terminal concept is employed ($OFTEN_N_00). As previously shown, the deep semantic representation in EcoLexicon is not restricted to basic concepts, unlike the one in FunGramKB.

3.4.2 *+PRECIPITATION_01/=PRECIPITATION_01, and +RAIN_01/=RAIN_01*

+PRECIPITATION_01		
Meaning postulate		*Translation*
P13	+(e1: +BE_00 (x1: +PRECIPITATION_01) Theme (x2: +WATER_00 & (+SOLID_00 ^ +LIQUID_00))Referent)	Precipitation water is a type of water and a type of solid or liquid.

P13 defines the *is-a* path of +PRECIPITATION_01 which can be either "+WATER_00>+SOLID_00>+SUBSTANCE_00>..." or "+WATER_00>+LIQUID_00>+SUBSTANCE_00>...". This is the only predication of +PRECIPITATION_01 because other information related to the concept is to be retrieved by inference.

=PRECIPITATION_01		
Meaning postulate		*Translation*
P14	+(e1: +BE_00 (x1: =PRECIPITATION_01) Theme (x2: +PRECIPITATION_00 & =WATER_00)Referent)	Precipitation water (EcoLexicon) is a type of precipitation (FunGramKB) and a type of water (EcoLexicon).

In P14, =PRECIPITATION_01 is subsumed to +PRECIPITATION_00 in order to map them, and also to =WATER_00, which is its most immediate superordinate. It is not necessary to state that =PRECIPITATION_01 can be either a +SOLID_00 or a +LIQUID_00 because that is inherited from +PRECIPITATION_00.

+RAIN_01		
Meaning postulate		*Translation*
P15	+(e1: +BE_00 (x1: +RAIN_01)Theme (x2: +PRECIPITATION_00 & +LIQUID_00) Referent)	Rain is a type of precipitation and a type of liquid.

For commonsense knowledge, the only difference between precipitation water and rainwater is that the latter is liquid. Thus, +RAIN_01 only has one possible *is-a* path as defined in P15.

=RAIN_01		
Meaning postulate		*Translation*
P16	+(e1: +BE_00 (x1: =RAIN_01)Theme (x2: +RAIN_01 & =PRECIPITATION_01) Referent)	Rainwater (EcoLexicon) is a type of rainwater (FunGram-KB), and a type of precipitation water(EcoLexicon).
P17	+((e2: +COMPRISE_00 (x1)Theme (x3: m +DROP_00)Referent) ((e3: +MEASURE_00 (x3)Theme (x4: >0.5 =MILIMETER_00)Attribute) (e4: +BE_00 (x4)Theme (x5: =DIAMETER_00)Referent)))	Rainwater is formed by many drops whose diameter is greater than 0.5 mm.

In a specialized representation of precipitation water and rainwater, rainwater has more *differentiae* than in a more general representation of the concept. Firstly, in P16, since =RAIN_01 and +RAIN_01 are mapped, the *is-a* path involving the subsumption to +LIQUID_00 is inherited.

Then, in P17, the diameter of a drop of rainwater is formalized. For this purpose, we have employed the sign ">" (more than), which we propose to include, along with "<" (less than), as additions to the set of COREL quantity operators. Furthermore, no decimal integers have been used in the FunGramKB core ontology so far. This is understandable since they are probably not needed in the representation of commonsense knowledge. However, decimals are indispensable in specialized deep semantic representations.

4. Conclusions

In this paper, we have given a broad outline of a possible methodology for the linking of EcoLexicon to FunGramKB. Nevertheless, there are still many points that need to be researched and clarified. For instance, even though our goal is the semi-automatic conversion of EcoLexicon propositions into COREL predications, there are still significant obstacles.

Conversion rules would have to be implemented, depending on the types of concept involved and their location in the Environmental Event. Moreover, since natural language definitions enrich propositions with a low level of expressivity, the conversion proposed by the machine would require human revision. Nevertheless, even if the machine conversion process turned out to be totally accurate, human intervention throughout the ontology alignment process would be necessary for the reasons given in this paper. Consequently, the first step in the alignment process would be a semi-automatic proposition conversion into COREL.

Furthermore, in the future, the possibility of replicating the basic/terminal concept structure in EcoLexicon will be considered by testing its usefulness for specialized knowledge representation.[11]

The recontextualization process that EcoLexicon is currently undergoing (León et al. 2013) is another challenge to linking the two ontologies. This means that the FunGramKB reasoner will be required for processing subdomain-specific predications inside meaning postulates. A set of rules will thus need to be developed so that recontextualization can be encoded in COREL.

Finally, the integration of EcoLexicon in FunGramKB at the conceptual level signifies that EcoLexicon will need to develop its own Cognicon[12] and Onomasticon, which will be associated with those in FunGramKB. For NLP purposes, the creation of associated FunGramKB Lexicons in different languages will also be necessary.

Acknowledgements

This research was funded by the Spanish Ministry of Economy and Competitiveness (Project FFI 2011-22397) and the Spanish Ministry of Education, Culture, and Sports (FPU Program AP2009-4519).

References

Barrasa, Jesús 2007. Modelo para la definición automática de correspondencias semánticas entre ontologías y modelos relaciones. PhD dissertation, Universidad Politécnica de Madrid.

11. As a matter of fact, a FunGramKB satellite ontology on organized crime and terrorism is being developed from scratch and the basic/terminal concept structure is used (Felices et al. 2011).

12. León & Reimerink (2011) describe how Cognicon scripts can be developed to formalize procedural information stored in EcoLexicon.

Benerecetti, Massimo, Bouquet, Paolo & Ghidini, Chiara. 2000. Contextual reasoning distilled. *Journal of Experimental & Theoretical Artificial Intelligence* 12(3): 279–305.

Bouquet, Paolo, Euzenat, Jérôme, Franconi, Enrico, Serafini, Luciano Stamou, Giorgos & Tessaris, Sergio. 2004. *D2.2.1 Specification of a Common Framework for Characterizing Alignment.* <http://eprints.biblio.unitn.it/archive/00000653/01/090.pdf> (17 September 2012).

Euzenat, Jérôme & Shvaiko, Pavel. 2007. *Ontology Matching.* Berlin: Springer.

Faber, Pamela. 2002. Terminographic definition and concept representation. In *Training the Language Services Provider for the New Millennium*, Belinda Maia, Johann Haller & Margherita Ulyrich (eds), 343–354. Porto: Universidade do Porto.

Faber, Pamela (ed.). 2012. *A Cognitive Linguistics View of Terminology and Specialized Language.* Berlin: De Gruyter Mouton.

Faber, Pamela, León Araúz, Pilar & Prieto Velasco, Juan Antonio. 2009. Semantic relations, dynamicity, and terminological knowledge bases. *Current Issues in Language Studies* 1:1–23.

Faber, Pamela, León Araúz, Pilar, Prieto Velasco, Juan Antonio & Reimerink, Arianne. 2007. Linking images and words: The description of specialized concepts. *International Journal of Lexicography* 20(1): 39–65.

Faber, Pamela, Montero Martínez, Silvia, Castro Prieto, María Rosa, Senso Ruiz, José, Prieto Velasco, Juan Antonio, León Araúz, Pilar, Márquez Linares, Carlos & Vega Expósito, Miguel. 2006. Process-oriented terminology management in the domain of Coastal Engineering. *Terminology* 12(2): 189–213.

Faber, Pamela & San Martín, Antonio. 2011. Linking specialized knowledge and general knowledge in EcoLexicon. In *TOTh 2011. International Conference on Terminology & Ontology: Theories and Applications*, 47–61. Annecy: Institut Porphyre.

Felices Lago, Ángel, Ureña Gómez-Moreno, Pedro & Alameda Hernández, Ángela. 2011. FunGramKB y la adquisición terminológica. *Anglogermanica Online*: 66–86.

Hameed, Adil, Preece, Alun & Sleeman, Derek. 2004. Ontology reconciliation. In *Handbook on Ontologies*, Steffen Staab & Rudi Studer (eds), 231–250. Berlin: Springer.

Jiménez Briones, Rocío & Luzondo, Alba. 2011. Building ontological meaning in a lexico-conceptual knowledge base. *Onomázein* 23(1): 11–40.

León Araúz, Pilar. 2009. Representación multidimensional del conocimiento especializado: El uso de marcos desde la macroestructura hasta la microestructura. PhD dissertation, Universidad de Granada.

León Araúz, Pilar & Magaña, Pedro Javier. 2010. EcoLexicon: Contextualizing an environmental ontology. In *Proceedings of the Terminology and Knowledge Engineering (TKE) Conference 2010*, Dublin.

León Araúz, Pilar, Magaña, Pedro Javier & Faber, Pamela. 2009. Building the SISE: An environmental ontology. In *European conference of the Czech Presidency of the Council of the EU TOWARDS eENVIRONMENT Opportunities of SEIS and SISE: Integrating Environmental Knowledge in Europe*, Jiří Hřebíček, Jiří Hradec, Emil Pelikán, Ondřej Mirovský, Werner Pillmann, Ivan Holoubek, & Thomas Bandholtz (eds), 16–23. Brno: Masaryk University.

León Araúz, Pilar & Reimerink, Arianne. 2011. EcoLexicon and FunGramKB: Applying COREL to domain-specific knowledge. In *Proceedings of the Twenty-Fourth International Florida Artificial Intelligence Research Society Conference*, Murray, Charles & McCarthy, Philip M. (eds.), 138–143. Menlo Park CA: AAAI Press.

León Araúz, Pilar, Reimerink Arianne & García Aragón, Alejandro. 2013. Dynamism and context in specialized knowledge. *Terminology* 19(1): 31–61.

León Araúz, Pilar & San Martín, Antonio. 2011. Distinguishing polysemy from contextual variation in terminological definitions. In *Actas del X Congreso de la Asociación Europea de Lenguas para Fines Específicos: La investigación y la enseñanza aplicadas a las lenguas de especialidad y a la tecnología*, María Luisa Carrió, Josefa Contreras, Françoise Olmo, Hanna Skorczynska, Inmaculada Tamarit & Debra Westall (eds), 173–186. Valencia: Universitat Politècnica de València.

León Araúz, Pilar & San Martín, Antonio. 2012. Multidimensional categorization in terminological definitions. In *Proceedings of the 15th EURALEX International Congress*, Ruth Vatvedt Fjeld & Julie Matilde Torjusen (eds), 578–584. Oslo: Euralex.

Lipschultz, Michael & Litman, Diane. 2010. Correcting scientific knowledge in a general-purpose ontology. In *Intelligent Tutoring Systems (ITS)*, Part II: *LNCS*, Vol. 6095, Vincent Aleven, Judy Kay & Jack Mostow (eds), 374–376. Berlin: Springer.

Mairal Usón, Ricardo & Periñán Pascual, Carlos. 2009. The anatomy of the lexicon within the framework of an NLP knowledge base. *RESLA* 22: 217–244.

Mairal Usón, Ricardo, Periñán Pascual, Carlos & Samaniego Fernández, Eva. 2011. Using ontologies for terminological knowledge representation: A preliminary discussion. In *Technological Innovation in the Teaching and Processing of LSPs: Proceedings of TISLID'10*, Noa Talaván, Francisco Palazón & Elena Martín Monje (eds). Madrid: UNED.

Periñán Pascual, Carlos & Arcas Túnez, Francisco. 2005. Microconceptual-knowledge spreading in FunGramKB. In *9th IASTED International Conference on Artificial Intelligence and Soft Computing*, 239–244. Anaheim CA: ACTA Press.

Periñán Pascual, Carlos & Arcas Túnez, Francisco. 2007. Cognitive modules of an NLP knowledge base for language understanding. *Procesamiento del Lenguaje Natural* 39: 197–204.

Periñán Pascual, Carlos & Arcas Túnez, Francisco. 2010. Ontological commitments in FunGramKB. *Procesamiento del Lenguaje Natural* 44: 27–34.

Pustejovsky, James. 2005. *A Survey of Dot Objects*. Technical report, Brandeis University.

Rosch, Eleanor. 1978. Principles of categorization. In *Cognition and Categorization*, Rosch, Eleanor & Barbara B. Lloyd (eds), 27–48. Hillsdale NJ: Lawrence Erlbaum Associates.

Rumshisky, Anna, Grinberg, Victor A. & Pustejovsky, James. 2007. Detecting selectional behavior of complex types in text. In *4th International Workshop on Generative Lexicon*. Paris.

San Martín, Antonio. 2012. Hacia la flexibilización de la definición terminológica. In *Empiricism and Analytical Tools for 21st Century Applied Linguistics. Selected Papers from the XXIX International Conference of the Spanish Association of Applied Linguistics (AESLA)*, Izaskun Elorza, Ovidi Carbonell, Reyes Albarrán, Blanca García Riaza & Miriam Pérez-Veneros (eds), 739–756. Salamanca: Ediciones Universidad de Salamanca.

Speranza, Manuela & Magnini, Bernardo. 2010. Merging global and specialized linguistic ontologies. In *Ontology and the Lexicon*, Chu-Ren Huang, Nicoletta Calzolari, Aldo Gangemi, Alessandro Lenci, Alessandro Oltramari & Laurent Prévot (eds), 224–238. Cambridge: CUP.

A functional and constructional approach for specialized knowledge resources

Beatriz Sánchez-Cárdenas and Pamela Faber
University of Granada

This paper describes how verbs are represented in EcoLexicon (ecolexicon.ugr.es), a specialized knowledge resource in environmental science. Based on the hypothesis that human cognition organizes concepts in semantic categories (Tranel et al. 2001; H. Damasio et al. 2004), verbs are conceptually structured in lexical domains (Mingorance 1985, 1900, 1995; Faber & Mairal 1999). These domains are based on the premises of the Lexical Grammar Model (Faber & Mairal 1999). Once the members of a lexical domain are specified, the conceptual structure of the domain is mapped out. Semantic categories are thus organized in a tangled hierarchy. The semantic relation of troponymy (Fellbaum 1990; Miller & Fellbaum 1991) determines the hierarchical structure of verbal lexical domains. The third step consists in the design of a lexical template based on the principles of the Lexical Constructional Model (Ruiz de Mendoza & Mairal 2008, Mairal & Ruiz de Mendoza 2009). Each lexical template consists of the following: (a) an Aktionsart module according to Role and Reference Grammar (Van Valin 1993, 2005, Van Valin & LaPolla 1997) in which the actantial structure of verbs is established; (b) a semantic module that specifies the thematic relations (Van Valin 2005), macroroles and types of noun selected by each verb. The French and English verbs of MOVEMENT in the field of Volcanology are analyzed as an illustration of this method.

1. Terminological knowledge bases and linguistic theory

A terminological database is a repository containing a more or less detailed description of a set of specialized knowledge units or terms, which are used by experts in a given domain to communicate with each other in different situational contexts. These terms are the linguistic designations of the concepts that represent the knowledge in a given field. Given the connection between specialized language and domain-specific knowledge, a well-designed terminological knowledge resource is of great value. In fact, when such a resource is coherently structured, it can constitute an access point to domain knowledge and facilitate knowledge acquisition. Consequently, the design decisions for a terminological knowledge base (TKB) should not be made randomly. Rather, they should be firmly grounded in a coherent set of premises derived from linguistic theory and knowledge organization (Faber 2012).

It is no accident that many of the terminology resources developed in recent years are based on linguistic models, such as the Generative Lexicon (Pustejovsky 1995), Frame Semantics (Fillmore 1982, 2003), and Explanatory Combinatorial Lexicology (Mel'čuk et al. 1995)[1]. These linguistic models have been used to implement new research methodologies, to create models of multidimensional macrostructures, and to include relevant semantic and syntactic information in terminological entries[2].

This research highlights the value of linguistic models for the design of new terminological tools for translators. It presents the premises underlying a dictionary prototype for the description of verbs in specialized knowledge fields. Potential users include Spanish-French technical writers as well as translators who must consult a lexicographic resource for text generation and encoding purposes. This prototype is based on Stepwise Lexical Decomposition (Dik 1978ab), the Lexical Grammar Model (Faber & Mairal 1999), and Role and Reference Grammar (Van Valin 1993, 2005). These models are used to do the following:

a. classify verbs in lexical domains.
b. specify the actantial structure of the verbs through aspectual analysis.
c. configure the hierarchical structure of lexical domains.

2. Verbs in terminology

Because of their frequency and role in sentence structure, verbs are crucial for the production of any kind of text, specialized or otherwise. Verbs set the scene for the rest of the elements in a sentence, and determine the roles taken by their arguments. However, until now, terminological resources have paid little attention to the description of verbs. Possible reasons for this neglect include the inherent difficulty involved in describing such a complex unit (Faber & Mairal 1999) as well as the belief that the verbs in specialized texts are not terms. It is generally claimed that noun phrases carry most of the semantic load in specialized texts and are thus ultimately responsible for their meaning. However, this is extremely debatable for two reasons.

The first reason is the key role that verbs play in specialized communication. They are used in specialized texts to express the relations between entities as well as to

1. See L'Homme (2006: 183) for further details on linguistic theoretical frameworks to describe terms.

2. Bergenholtz and Tarp (2010: 33) underline the necessity to include more grammatical and syntactic information concerning terms in the target language.

designate activities and processes. For example, in Volcanology texts, the noun phrase, *tectonic plates,* frequently has the semantic role of agent in conjunction with verbs such as *diverge, collide, subduct,* and *submerge.* These verbs express the movement events that *tectonic* plates actively engage in. As is well known, the characteristics of a specialized domain constrain the choice of verbs in the specialized texts that describe its prototypical activities (Busch-Lauer 1995). Not surprisingly, each specialized domain has preferences for certain verbs, which give rise to a lexico-grammar typical of each subject area. This is especially true in scientific writing, where conventions are deeply ingrained (Gledhill 2000, Frath & Gledhill 2005).

Secondly, the brain links entities and events. Since meaning is not based on a set of objective external criteria, but rather on bodily interaction (Johnson 1987, Lakoff 1987), nouns cannot be understood, stored in the brain, or retrieved without picturing the actions prototypically associated with these nouns. Evidence of this type of conceptual knowledge can be found in neuroscientific research. As shown in the work of H. Damasio et al. (2004) and A. Damasio (1989), related entities are bound together by convergence zones. For example, we are able to recognize a *tree* when we perceive its different parts (*leave, branch* and *fruit*) because all these entities are localized in groups of neurons that fire together. This is also true of events (Chatterjee et al. 1999), which are linguistically represented by verbs. Entities and the events associated with them are also connected by convergence zones in the brain (A. Damasio 1989, Patterson et al. 2007). Thus, it is not possible to fully understand terms, such as *magma, tectonic plate,* or *oceanic crust* without thinking of the prototypical events associated with them. Consequently, from a terminological perspective, it is neither useful nor accurate to describe a term without reference to the verbs to which the entity is prototypically linked.

3. Lexical domains in terminology

Despite the fact that the majority of linguistic tools are organized semasiologically, human cognition processes knowledge through categorization (Lakoff 1987) and meaning. This is also true for the linguistic forms that designate concepts (Tranel et al. 2001, H. Damasio et al. 2004). It would thus seem that if lexicographical and terminological resources indeed strive for psychological adequacy, they should be organized onomasiologically or in areas of conceptual meaning.

The lexical database, FrameNet, of the International Computer Science Institute at the University of California at Berkeley is an example of a conceptually organized tool (Fillmore 1982, 1985, 2006; Fillmore et al. 2003). Lexical items are defined in terms of their *frames,* which are "schematic representations of situation types (eating, spying, removing, classifying, etc.), together with lists of the kinds of participants, props, and other conceptual roles that are seen as components of such situations"[3]. For example, in

3. FAQs of FrameNet <http://framenet2.icsi.berkeley.edu>

the sentence, "At convergent boundaries, tectonic plates collide with each other" the verb *collide* belongs to the Impact Frame, describing an action in which "an Impactor makes sudden, forcible contact with the Impactee, or two Impactors both move, mutually making forcible contact". This frame means that when users look up a certain verb, they have immediate access to verbs in the same subdomain with the same or similar meaning.

The knowledge resource, EcoLexicon <http://ecolexicon.ugr.es>, created by of the LexiCon research group (Faber et al. 2006, 2007; Faber 2012) is based on premises from Frame Semantics[4] (Fillmore 1982, 1985, 2006, Fillmore et al. 2003). Its organization can be described as onomasiological, multidimensional, and multimodal. To this end, concepts are represented in accordance to the hierarchical and non-hierarchical relations that they maintain with other members of their domain (López Rodríguez et al. 2010; Faber 2012). Verbs are currently being incorporated in this resource. For this purpose, the premises underlying Frame Semantics are being used to define the number and type of semantic role that each verb selects.

This paper describes the methodology for verb description in EcoLexicon. The following sections explain the process followed to classify verbs into lexical domains, determine their actantial structure, and establish the semantic dependency links between the verbs of each subdomain.

4. Lexical domains through semantic deconstruction

The Lexical Grammar Model (Faber & Mairal 1999), based on Martín Mingorance (1990, 1995) integrates Dik's (1978a) Functional Grammar and Coseriu's (1977) Lexematic Theory. According to this model, the membership of a verb in a lexical domain is meaningful in regards to its semantic configuration. Thus, it is possible to predict the argument structure of a verb once its lexical domain is known. Van Valin (1993) also endorses the idea that the semantic affiliation of a verb has a syntactic projection. One method of ascertaining the lexical domain of a verb is by means of semantic decomposition.

Based on Dik (1978b), verbs can be defined in terms of more general verbs by semantic factorization. This semantic decomposition is based on data in lexicographical resources. When the verb can no longer be decomposed in terms of a more general verb, this verb is the semantic primitive underlying the definition of all the other verbs in the lexical domain, similarly to the semantic primitives in the Natural Semantic Metalanguage (NSM) of Wierbizcka (1995). It is claimed that this set of primitives corresponds to innate and general ideas that all human beings share. One postulate that reinforces the existence of these semantic primitives is that if it is possible to translate texts in different languages, there must be a group of minimal units of meaning common to all humankind.

4. EcoLexicon is also based on the Lexical Grammar of Martín Mingorance (1984, 1990) as explained in Faber and Mairal (1999).

After analyzing 12000 English verbs in a set of various monolingual dictionaries[5], Faber & Mairal (1999) found that the generic terms in verb definitions were the following: *be/happen, become, have, say, feel, do/make, know/think, move (go/come), see/hear/taste/smell/touch, use*. These terms correspond to the lexical domains of EXISTENCE, CHANGE, POSSESION, SPEECH, EMOTION, ACTION, COGNITION, MOVEMENT, PHYSICAL PERCEPTION, and MANIPULATION (Mairal & Faber 2007: 7).

As an example of how semantic decomposition works, we have extracted this sentence from the French corpus of EcoLexicon:

1. Le volcan a craché un panache de cendres atteignant 20 km de hauteur.
   [The volcano has ejected ashes 20 km up into the sky].

The verb *cracher* is defined by the *Trésor de la Langue Française Informatisé* as "rejeter hors de la bouche" (to spit out of one's mouth). *Rejeter* can be redefined in terms of its immediate hypernym, which is in turn defined by a more general verb until arriving at the most generic term of the lexical domain, *aller* (to go):

cracher → rejeter → jeter → envoyer → faire aller → aller
(spit → eject → throw away → send → make go → go)

The generic term, *aller* (go), belongs to the lexical domain of MOVEMENT. This is meaningful for two reasons. First of all, it helps to classify all the verbs that belong to this lexical domain in the field of Volcanology. As a result, *cracher* can be related to other verbs that are defined by the same generic term (e.g. *rejeter, émettre, échapper, ejecter, dégager,* etc.), all of which encode movement out or away from a source, though from different perspectives.

2. Le volcan de l'Eyjafjallajokull rejette des cendres (The volcano Eyjafjallajokull ejects ashes).
3. Le volcan de l'île de Vulcano, en sommeil depuis 1890, émet des fumerolles (The volcano of Vulcano Island, asleep since 1890, is ejecting steam).
4. Le volcan laisse échapper des gaz (The volcano spews gas).
5. Le volcan a éjecté d'énormes masses de laves et de cendres (The volcano has ejected a big amount of lava and ashes).
6. Les volcans dégagent du souffre (Volcanos release sulphur).

Moreover, the lexical domain of a verb constrains its argument structure. The verbs in examples (2–6) belong to the lexical domain of MOVEMENT. Boons (1987) defines a verb of motion as "a verb of movement which implies that a body moves from one place to another without any modification of its form or of its substance during the

5. *Collins Cobuild, The American Heritage Dictionary, Longman Lexicon of Contemporary English, Oxford Advanced Learner's Dictionary, Longman Dictionary of Contemporary English, Webster's New World Dictionary for Young Readers, The Random House Dictionary of the English Language.*

process". In these examples, it is a question of causative movement, which is characterized by two semantic roles: (i) an agent; (ii) the goal. In this lexical domain, path is also an important element though in French and English, it is generally encoded by means of a prepositional phrase. In this case, the energy of the volcano (a natural force) causes another entity (smoke, ash, gas, lava) to move out of a container entity (the volcano landform). Thus, the force or energy of the volcano appears, from an actantial point of view, as the agent causing the movement.

The domain of MOVEMENT verbs has a very complex structure and multiple subdomains. This is not surprising since movements are characterized by a wide range of temporal and spatial patterns that are highly salient (Faber & Mairal 1999: 234). Thus, the actantial structure derived from the lexical domain is very general and needs to be further specified.

To this end, the final step of the analysis involves the enrichment of general information with FrameNet database descriptions[6]. The verbs, *cracher* (spit), *rejeter* (eject), *émettre* (emit), and *laisser échapper* (let escape), belong to the Removing Frame, which is regarded as a lexical subdomain of MOVEMENT. In this frame, "an Agent causes a Theme to move away from a location, the Source". However, in the field of Volcanology, the Agent and the Source tend to coincide. Interestingly enough, this is due to the fact that a volcano is conceptualized as an anthropomorphic entity. The linguistic evidence for this is that the Agent *volcan* [volcano] is often associated with verbs that describe actions that only humans and other animals perform, such as *cracher* [spit] or *exhaler* [exhale].

7. Le volcan crache de la lave/des cendres/des fumerolles/des gaz [The volcano emits lava/ashes/steam/gas].
8. Le volcan a exhalé 20 millions de tonnes de CO_2 et d'énormes quantités d'anhydride sulfureux [The volcano has spewed 20 million tons of CO_2 and large quantities of sulphur dioxide].

It is also common to find event nouns (e.g. *éruption*) as the Agent in these contexts:

9. Les éruptions du volcan islandais Eyjafjöll ont généré un nuage de cendres perturbant [The eruptions of the Icelandic volcano Eyjafjöll have generated a disturbing ash].

Finally, the verb can have a third argument role of Path or Location, expressing the direction of movement or the place where the Goal or Theme is relocated:

10. Le volcan chilien sème ses cendres **dans le ciel Australien** [The Chilean volcano has filled the Australian sky with ashes].

6. Because French FrameNet has not been developed yet, it is necessary to translate the verb into English before searching for it in the database.

Consequently, in Volcanology, the verbs, *cracher, rejeter, émettre, échapper,* and *ejecter,* belong to the domain of MOVEMENT and the Removing Frame. As a result, they share the same actantial structure: Agent, Verb, Theme, and Location.

5. Hierarchical organization through semantic dependency properties

The preceding sections described the methodology to organize the lexical units of our resource in lexical domains and subdomains. They also demonstrated how these results could be used to extract the actantial structure of verbs. However, it is not only necessary to classify verbs in domains and subdomains, but also to specify the internal organization of each subdomain.

Linguistic research has generally focused on the semantic relationships between lexical units. However, in such studies, nouns often seem to have received more attention than verbs. Evidently, verb entailment is quite different from noun dependency links (Fellbaum 1990: 285). Accordingly, verbs cannot be analyzed with the hyponym/hypernym relationship tests that have been described by authors such as Lyon (1990) and Kleiber and Tamba (1990). Hyponymy is not applicable to the verbal lexicon since verbs are not referentially independent (Sánchez Cárdenas 2010). Consequently, verbs need arguments to anchor and further specify their meaning. Because verbs can have a wide range of nouns and complements, dependence structures are quite complex. For the sake of simplicity, the description of dependency relationships is restricted to ±troponomy, which applies to the lexical domain of MOVEMENT.

According to Miller and Fellbaum (1991: 217), troponymy is the most common relationship between verbs of any language. Troponymy describes temporal inclusion between verbs such as *limp-walk* or *snore-sleep* (Fellbaum 1990). The more specific verb (i.e. *limp, snore*) entails the more general verb (*walk, sleep*). When troponymy is positive, [+troponymy], the dependent verb (*limp*) must temporally co-occur with the more general verb (*walk*). When troponymy is negative, [–troponymy], it is not obligatory for the dependent verb (*snore)* to occur every time the general verb (*sleep*) does[7]. In verbs with a +troponomy relation, the more specific verb describes a particular way of doing the more general verb. MOVEMENT verbs typically related to volcano, participate in this kind of relationship; "éjecter de la lave" is "rejeter de la lave" [to eject lava is to throw lava out].

The verbs that most frequently appear in the field of Volcanology generally have the +troponymy relation. Regarding types of dependence, we use Talmy's (1985) semantic patterns: MANNER, INTENTION, FIGURE, GROUND, CAUSE, SOURCE, GOAL, PATH, and DIRECTION. Amaro (2005: 2) proposes a method of isolating these patterns, which involves a series of linguistic tests.

7. A person that snores does not inevitably do so during the whole night but a person that limps cannot avoid doing so every time he/she walks.

Table 1. Amaro (2005) tests

	Description	**Test**[8]	**Example**
MANNER	how the event develops	to V2 is to V1 how?	to crawl is to move with the body close to the ground
INTENTION	purpose/intended goal of the event /	to V2 is to V1 for what with what intention?	to promenade is to move for pleasure or recreation
FIGURE	object that undergoes the event	to V2 is to V1 who/ what?	to bury is to put a dead body in the earth
GROUND	object with respect to which the FIGURE undergoes the event	to V2 is to V1 with respect to what?	to overtake is to move forward with respect to something in motion
CAUSE	what brings about the event	to V2 is to V1 because/ due to what?	to tremble is to shake due to fear or cold
SOURCE	FIGURE initial location	to V2 is to V1 from where?	to defenestrate is to jump from a window
GOAL	FIGURE final location	to V2 is to V1 to where?	to closet is to lock in a storage place
PATH	medium location(s) between the SOURCE and the GOAL	to V2 is to V1 through where	to backtrack is to move back through the same path
DIRECTION	way in which the motion event occurs	to V2 is to V1 in which direction?	to rise is to move upwards

In order to apply these tests to the verbs, *cracher, dégager, émettre, éjecter, laisser échapper, exhaler, rejeter*, it is necessary to extract the semantic patterns in Table 1 from their lexical entries. To this end, we used *the Trésor de la Langue Française Informatisé* and *Le Petit Robert* to obtain these definitions:

- *Cracher*: éjecter hors de la bouche [to eject something from the mouth].
- *Dégager*: faire sortir une émanation (de la chaleur, une odeur, un parfum) [to cause something to come out, such as heat, an odor, or a scent].
- *Échapper*: laisser d'être pris ou retenu [to let go of something that was held or retained].
- *Ejecter*: rejeter hors de soi quelque chose avec force [to cause something to come out forcefully].
- *Émettre*: faire sortir de soi [to cause something to come out of oneself].
- *Exhaler*: émettre, dégager des odeurs ou des vapeurs [to emit, to give off smells or vapors].
- *Rejeter*: repousser, renvoyer à quelque distance (puissamment) [to forcefully send something far away].

8. V1 is the more general verb, whereas V2 is the more specific one.

Table 2. The Amaro tests applied to outward MOVEMENT (verbs in French)

	V1	V2	Test	EN
	émettre	exhaler	Exhaler c'est émettre quoi? Exhaler c'est émettre **des substances gazeuses.**	Exhaling is emitting what? Exhaling is emitting **gaseous substances.**
FIGURE	émettre	laisser échapper	Laisser échapper c'est émettre quoi? Laisser échapper c'est émettre **ce qui était retenu.**	Letting something escape is emitting what? Letting something escape is emitting something **that was trapped.**
GOAL	exhaler	rejeter	Rejeter c'est exhaler où? Rejeter c'est exhaler **hors de soi.**	Throwing something out is exhaling it to where? Throwing something out is exhaling it **outside of sth.**
	dégager	émettre	Emettre c'est dégager d'où? Ëmettre c'est dégager **de soi.**	Emitting something is letting it out from where? Emitting something is releasing it **from somewhere.**
SOURCE	rejeter	cracher	Cracher c'est rejeter d'où? Cracher c'est rejeter **de la bouche.**	Spitting something is throwing it out of where? Spitting is throwing something **out of something's/somebody's mouth.**
MANNER	rejeter	éjecter	Éjecter c'est rejeter comment? Éjecter c'est rejeter **puissament.**	Ejecting something is throwing it out how? Ejecting is throwing something out **with great force.**

The Amaro (2005) tests were applied to these verbs, and the results are shown in Table 2.

This final step establishes the dependency links between the verbs. The hierarchical entailment is shown in Figure 1.

6. Towards a lexical entry

Although this paper mainly deals with the macrostructure of the resource, we briefly describe the methodology and frame used for the design of lexical entries. The design of lexical entries, based on the Lexical Constructional Model (Mairal & Ruiz de Mendoza 2008), accounts for the semantic and syntactic features of verbs.

1. **dégager**: libérer une substance
Les volcans dégagent du souffre.
+ SOURCE (initial location)
1.1. **émettre**: dégager quelque chose (de soi).
Le volcan de l'île de Vulcano émet des fumerolles.
+ FIGURE (object that undergoes the event)
1.1.1. **laisser échapper**: émettre ce qui était retenu.
Le volcan laisse échapper des gaz.
1.1.2. **exhaler**: émettre des substances gazeuses.
Le volcan a exhalé 20 millions de tonnes de CO2 .
+ GOAL (final location)
1.1.2.1. **rejeter**: exhaler hors de soi.
Le volcan de l'Eyjafjallajokull rejette des cendres.
+ SOURCE (initial location)
1.1.2.1.1. **cracher**: rejeter hors de la bouche.
Le volcan a craché un panache de cendres.
+ MANNER (how the event develops)
1.1.2.1.2. **éjecter**: rejeter avec force.
Le volcan a éjecté d´énormes masses de laves et de cendres.

Figure 1. Lexical hierarchical domain of MOVEMENT verbs in the field of Volcanology

6.1 Aktionsart classes

Firstly, the relevant grammatical features are represented with Role and Reference Grammar logical structures (Van Valin 2005), based on Vendler's (1967) aspectual classes. To this end, predicates are classified in one of the following classes: *state, activity, achievement, semelfactive, accomplishment, active accomplishment* and *causative accomplishment*. Each class is based on four aspectual properties, each of which can be either positive or negative: (i) *staticity* (the state consists of uninterrupted uniform phases); (ii) *dynamicity* (the event involves an action); (iii) *telicity* (the event culminates); (iv) *punctuality* (the event takes place instantaneously). As an example, the *state* class has positive staticity and punctuality and negative *dynamicity* and *telicity*: *state* [+staticity], [+punctuality], [–dynamicity], and [–telicity].

Each of these features is specified with a set of semantic tests (Sánchez Cárdenas 2010). For instance, two of the characteristics of positive dynamicity are the impossibility of causing the event to become progressive or to admit any place complement:

(1) Volcanoes are monuments to Earth's origin.
(2) *Volcanoes **are being** monuments to Earth's origin.
(3) ?Volcanoes are monuments to Earth's origin **in Europe**.

The verbs in Figure 1 have the following set of features: *achievement*: [– staticity], [–dynamicity], [+telicity], and [+punctuality].

As a matter of fact, the events linked to these verbs are non-static (because the action does not imply a movement); dynamic (since there is an action happening in time); non-telic (since action eventually ends even though volcanoes can erupt for years); and punctual (given that it is not possible to divide the event into phases).

6.2 Semantic roles and macroroles

Once the actantial structure of verbs is determined, thematic relations and macroroles (Van Valin 1993, 2005) are used in order to account for the semantic behaviour of arguments. Thematic relations are generalisations over semantic roles. The fact that they are not specific to any particular verb makes them useful for capturing semantic regularities across different verbs. In the case of verb arguments in the field of Volcanology, the thematic role of Agent describes the entity performing the action (*volcano*) and Theme, the entity undergoing the process (*ashes, lava, gas,* etc.).

Verb arguments are also described in terms of RRG macroroles, which are overgeneralizations of thematic relations. Thematic relations and macroroles make it possible to distinguish between the semantic and syntactic behaviour of arguments. This is especially relevant in Lexicography since one argument can change its syntactic position and maintain its thematic role and macrorole:

14. Le volcan crache des cendres [The volcano spits out ashes].

	Macrorole	Thematic role	Syntax
Le volcan [The volcano]	ACTOR	Agent	Subject
des cendres [ashes]	UNDERGOER	Theme	Direct object

15. Les cendres ont été crachées à des milliers de kilomètres [The ashes were spit out over thousands of kilometers].

	Macrorole	Thematic role	Syntax
Les cendres [The ashes]	ACTOR	Theme	Subject
à des milliers de kilomètres [over thousands of kilometers]	(none)	Location	Circumstantial complement

As shown in the previous examples, *les cendres* [the ashes] can appear as a direct object or subject without changing its macrorole and thematic role configuration.

6.3 Lexical restrictions in verbs arguments

Apart from the semantic and syntactic nature of verb arguments, another important piece of information that users need for encoding purposes is the set of semantic restrictions that verbs impose on their arguments. In this respect, corpus analysis makes it possible to profile the semantic classes that most frequently appear in the argument slots of verbs. This is important because in certain syntactic positions, different nouns can have different meanings, and thus, different translations (16–18):

16. I **count** on you for my party.
    → Je **compte** sur toi pour ma soirée.
17. This weekend will be sunny, I count on the Weather Channel.
    → Ce weekend sera ensoleillé, je **fais confiance** au Weather Channel.
18. You can **count** on the sausage at Lokal in Sonoma
    → La saucisse de Loka, à Sonoma, ne vous **décevra** pas.

Consequently, the most frequent noun phrases that appear as the arguments of each verb should be extracted from the corpus and classified in semantic domains. Table 3 lists examples of the NPs in the Agent and Theme semantic roles of the verbs *éjecter* and *cracher* in our French Volcanology corpus.

Since specialized domain knowledge constrains the meanings and combinatorial patterns of lexical units, the nouns in each verb's argument positions are restricted. For example, *volcan* was the entity that most frequently appeared in the Agent role of *éjecter* and *cracher*. Even though all the MOVEMENT verbs in Volcanology can have a natural geological entity in their Theme position, the semantic range of these entities varies, depending on the verb. As shown in Table 3, *éjecter* accepts a wide range of nouns, whereas the semantic profile of those associated with *cracher* is more restricted.

Based on these results, more precise analytical methods are required to establish the semantic classes of each argument. To this end, further research will explore whether Pustejovsky's (1995) Qualia structure and Gross's (1994) "classes d'objets" can provide viable ways of representing specialized knowledge units. Finally, the design of each lexical entry will be enriched with information concerning the syntactic patterns of each verb.

Table 3. Most frequent NPs occupying the Theme slot of *éjecter* and *cracher* in the domain of Volcanology

Agent	Verb	Theme
Volcan	*éjecter*	*des poussières en fusion, des cendres, des lambeaux de lave incandescente, bombes volcaniques, panache de cendres, tephra, éjecta, pyroclastes, tuf volcanique, lapilli, clastes, blocs, ignimbrite, gouttes de lave, gaz volcaniques, volumes de magma, matériaux*
	cracher	*des cendres, de la lave, des pierres, des météorites, des bombes, des scories*

7. Conclusion

Verbs have long been neglected in Terminology since they have not been regarded as terms. This paper has shown how linguistic theories can effectively be used in Terminology research to analyze verbs in specialized fields. This was demonstrated by analyzing the verbs related to the French term *volcan* in a specialized corpus of Volcanology texts. More specifically, the MOVEMENT verbs most typically used in this field were hierarchically classified in lexical domains, based on the genus of their dictionary definitions. The semantic entailment relationships between the verbs of each group were found to be based on troponymy and analyzed with sets of semantic tests that highlighted their conceptual meaning profile. Regarding the verb entry itself, *Aktionsart* classes and Role and Reference Grammar were used to ascertain actantial structure and describe arguments from a semantic perspective.

Such information should be included in monolingual or multilingual terminographic databases since it helps user groups, such as technical writers and translators, who consult such resources for text generation and encoding processes

Acknowledgements

This research has been carried out within the framework of the project RECORD: *Representación del Conocimiento en Redes Dinámicas* [Knowledge Representation in Dynamic Networks, FFI2011-22397], funded by the Spanish Ministry of Science and Innovation.

References

Amaro, Raquel. 2005. Semantic incorporation in a Portuguese WordNet of verbs of movement: On aktionsart shifting. In *Proceedings of the Third International Workshop on Generative Approaches to the Lexicon*, 1–9. Genève: University of Genève.

Bergenholtz, Henning & Tarp, Sven. 2010. LSP Lexicography or Terminography? The lexicographer's point of view. In *Specialised Dictionaries for Learners* [Lexicographica Series Maior], Pedro A. Fuertes-Olivera (ed.), 26–37. Berlin: Walter de Gruyter.

Boons, Jean-Paul. 1987. La notion sémantique de déplacement dans une classification syntaxique des verbes locatifs. *Langue Française* 76: 5–40.

Busch-Lauer, Ines-Andrea. 1995. Textual organization in English and German medical abstracts. In *Organization in Discourse. Proceedings from the Turku Conference* [Anglicana Turkuensia 14], Brita Warvik, Sanna-Kaisa Tanskanen & Risto Hiltunen (eds), 175–185. Turku: University of Turku.

Chatterjee, Anjan, Southwood, M. Helen & Basilico, David. 1999. Verbs, events and spatial representations. *Neuropsychologia* 37: 395–402.

Coseriu, Eugenio. 1977. *Principios de semántica estructural.* Madrid: Gredos.

Damasio, Antonio. 1989. The brain binds entities and events by multiregional activation from convergence zones. *Neural Computation* 1: 123–132.
Damasio, Hanna, Tranel, Daniel, Grabowski, Tomas, Adolphs, Ralph & Damasio, Antonio. 2004. Neural systems behind word and concept retrieval. *Cognition* 92(1–2): 179–229.
Dik, Simon. 1978a. *Functional Grammar*, Dordrecht: Foris.
Dik, Simon. 1978b. *Stepwise Lexical Decomposition*. Lisse: Peter de Ridder.
Faber, Pamela & Mairal, Ricardo. 1999. *Constructing a Lexicon of English Verbs*. Berlin: Mouton de Gruyter.
Faber, Pamela (ed.). 2012. *A Cognitive Linguistics View of Terminology and Specialized Language*. Berlin: Mouton de Gruyter.
Faber, Pamela, León, Pilar, Prieto, Juan Antonio & Reimerink, Arianne. 2007. Linking images and words: The description of specialized concepts. *International Journal of Lexicography* 20: 39–65.
Faber, Pamela, Montero, Silvia, Castro, Rosa, Senso, José, Prieto, Juan Antonio, León, Pilar, Márquez, Carlos & Vega, Miguel. 2006. Process-oriented terminology management in the domain of coastal engineering. *Terminology* 12: 189–213.
Fellbaum, Christiane. 1990. English verbs as a semantic net. *International Journal of Lexicography* 3: 278–301.
Fillmore, Charles, Johnson, Christopher R. & Petruck, Miriam R.L. 2003. Background to Framenet. *International Journal of Lexicography* 16: 235–250.
Fillmore, Charles. 1982. Frame Semantics. In *Linguistics in the Morning Calm*, Linguistic Society of Korea (ed.),111–37. Seoul: Hanshin.
Fillmore, Charles. 1985. Frames and the semantics of understanding. *Quaderni di Semantica* VI(2): 222–254.
Fillmore, Charles. 2003. Background to FrameNet. *International Journal of Lexicography* 16: 235–250
Fillmore, Charles. 2006. Frame Semantics. In *Cognitive Linguistics: Basic Readings*, Dirk Geeraerts (ed.), 373–400. Berlin: Mouton de Gruyter.
Frath Pierre & Gledhill, Christopher. 2005. Qu'est-ce qu'une unité phraséologique? *Cahiers de l'Institut de Linguistique de Louvain* 31(2–4):11–25.
Gledhill, Christopher. 2000. *Collocations in Science Writing*. Tübingen: Gunter Narr.
Gross Gaston. 1994. Classes d'objets et description des verbes. *Langages* 115: 15–30.
Johnson, M. 1987. *The Body in the Mind*. Chicago IL: University of Chicago Press.
Kleiber, Georges & Tamba, Irene. 1990. L'hyponymie revisitée: Inclusion et hiérarchie. *Langages* 25(98): 7–32.
L'Homme, Marie-Claude. 2006. The processing of terms in dictionaries: New models and techniques. A state of the art. *Terminology* 12: 181–188.
Lakoff, G. 1987. *Women, Fire, and Dangerous Things: What Categories Reveal about the Mind*. Chicago IL: University of Chicago Press.
López Rodríguez, Clara Inés, Faber, Pamela, León, Pilar, Prieto, Juan Antonio, & Tercedor, Maribel. 2010. La Terminología basada en marcos y su aplicación a las Ciencias Ambientales: Los proyectos Marcocosta y Ecosistema. *Arena Romanistica* 7: 52–74.
Mairal, Ricardo & Faber, Pamela. 2007. Lexical templates within a functional cognitive theory of meaning. *Annual Review of Cognitive Linguistics* 5: 137–172
Mairal, Ricardo & Ruiz de Mendoza, Francisco José. 2008. New challenges for lexical representations within the Lexical-Constructional Model (LCM). *Revista Canaria de Estudios Ingleses* 57: 137–158.

Mairal, Ricardo & Ruiz de Mendoza, Francisco José. 2009. Levels of description and explanation in meaning construction. In *Deconstruction Constructions* [Studies in Language Companion Series 107], Christopher S. Butler & J. Martín Arista (eds), 153–198. Amsterdam: John Benjamins.
Martín Mingorance, Leocadio. 1998 [1985]. Bases metodológicas para un estudio contrastivo del léxico derivado. In *El Modelo Lexemático Funcional*, Amalia Martín Rubiales (ed.), 61–82. Granada: Universidad de Granada.
Martín Mingorance, Leocadio. 1984. Lexical fields and stepwise lexical deconstruction in a contrastive English-Spanish verb valency dictionary. In *LEXeter 83: Proceedings of the International Conference on Lexicography*, Reinhart Hartmann (ed.), 226–236. Tübingen: Niemeyer.
Martín Mingorance, Leocadio. 1990. Functional grammar and lexematics. In *Meaning and Lexicography* [Linguistic and Literary Studies in Eastern Europe 28], Jerzy Tomaszczyk & Barbara Lewandowska-Tomaszczyk, 227–253. Amsterdam: John Benjamins.
Martín Mingorance, Leocadio. 1995. Lexical logic and structural semantics: Methodological underpinnings in the structuring of a lexical database for natural language processing. In *Panorama der Lexikalischen Semantik,* Ulrich Hoinkes (ed.), 461–474. Tübingen: Gunter Narr.
Mel'čuk, Igor 1996. Lexical functions: A tool for the description of lexical relations in the lexicon. In *Lexical Functions in Lexicography and Natural Language Processing* [Studies in Language Companion Series 31], Leo Wanner (ed.), 37–71. Amsterdam: John Benjamins.
Mel'čuk, Igor, Clas, André & Polguère, Alain. 1995. *Introduction à la lexicologie explicative et combinatoire.* Louvain-la-Neuve: Duculot.
Miller George & Fellbaum, Christiane. 1991. Semantic networks of English. *Cognition* 41: 197–229.
Patterson Karalyn, Nestor, Peter J. & Rogers, Timothy T. 2007. Where do you know what you know? The representation of semantic knowledge in the human brain. *Nature Reviews. Neuroscience* 8: 975–987.
Pustejovsky, James. 1995. *The Generative Lexicon.* Cambridge MA: The MIT Press.
Ruiz de Mendoza Ibáñez, Francisco J. & Mairal Usón, Ricardo. 2008. Levels of description and constraining factors in meaning construction: an introduction to the Lexical Constructional Model. *Folia Linguistica* 42: 355–400.
Sánchez Cárdenas, Beatriz. 2010. *Paramètres linguistiques pour la constitution d'un dictionnaire électronique bilingue (français/espagnol) destiné à la traduction. Le cas des verbes de comptage.* Granada: University of Granada.
Talmy, Leonard. 1985. Lexicalization patterns: Semantic structure in lexical forms. Language typology and lexical descriptions. In *Grammatical Categories and the Lexicon,* Vol. 3, Timothy Shopen, 36–149. Cambridge: CUP.
Tranel, Daniel, Adolphs, Ralph, Damasio, Hanna, & Damasio, Antonio R. 2001. A neural basis for the retrieval of words for actions. *Cognitive Neuropsychology* 18: 655–674.
Van Valin, Jr., Robert D. (ed.). 1992. A synopsis of Role and Reference Grammar. In *Advances in Role and Reference Grammar* [Current Issues in Linguistic Theory 82]. Amsterdam: John Benjamins.
Van Valin, Jr., Robert D. 2005. *Exploring the Syntax-Semantics Interface.* Cambridge: CUP.
Van Valin, Jr., Robert D. & LaPolla, Randy. 1997 *Syntax: Structure, Meaning & Function.* Cambridge: CUP.
Vendler, Zeno. 1967. *Linguistics in Philosophy.* Ithaca NY: Cornell University Press.
Wierzbicka, Anna. 1995. Universal semantic primitives as a basis for lexical semantics. *Folia Lingüística* 29(1–2): 149–169.

Applying the lexical constructional model to ontology building

Elena Montiel-Ponsoda and Guadalupe Aguado de Cea
Universidad Politécnica de Madrid

Knowledge acquisition strategies based on lexico-syntactic patterns have shown to significantly contribute to the automatic identification of concepts and relations from texts, but have not investigated how to represent that information in ontologies. Since this is one of the most critical steps in ontology building, we propose to establish a correspondence between lexico-syntactic patterns, specifically verbal patterns representing taxonomic and meronymic relations, and their corresponding ontological structures represented by Ontology Design Patterns. In this way, the transformation of linguistic expressions into ontological structures could be automated and it would support domain experts in the development of ontologies. In order to reliably establish this correspondence, we need to dissect the meaning of predicates. For this aim, we rely on the Lexical Constructional Model, as a comprehensive theory of meaning construction. In this contribution we demonstrate how such a model permits to identify the ontological structure(s) that better capture the meaning of predicates in an ontological resource.

1. Introduction

In order to facilitate and speed up the construction of terminological and ontological resources, many efforts have been devoted to investigate different *knowledge acquisition* strategies aimed to reduce the time and efforts involved in these activities. Both in Terminology and Ontology Engineering, the knowledge acquisition process has been mainly applied to "learning the terms or concepts relevant for a given domain, as well as the relations holding between them, also known as conceptual relations" (Meyer 2001: 280). As such, concepts and conceptual relations together with their linguistic realizations, i.e. the terminological units, are the basic research objects in Terminology, and also the starting point in ontology development.

For the aim of automatically learning terms or concepts, we can basically distinguish three main trends: (a) methods relying on statistical measures about co-occurrence of terms (see Agirre et al. 2000) (b) the application of machine learning algorithms to the extraction of conceptual relations (Maedche & Staab 2000), and (c) approaches based on regular linguistic expressions or patterns previously identified in a manual process. Within the latter ones, we are interested in *pattern-based approaches that specifically rely on verbs to automatically extract information from texts.* Here we can make a distinction between patterns focusing on taxonomic or meronymic relationships – the most researched ones- and others that put the emphasis on the identification of non-taxonomic relations, aka *ad-hoc* relations, which are generally domain specific. In Section 2, we will refer to some approaches that have focused on verbal predicates for knowledge acquisition.

As explained below, these approaches present some drawbacks, being the most important one the fact that once concepts and relations have been identified, they do not investigate how that knowledge is to be represented in ontologies (Aguado de Cea et al. 2008). To overcome this issue, we propose to establish a correspondence between linguistic patterns and ontological structures. We take as a starting point *Ontology Design Patterns* (Gangemi 2005), broadly defined as design solutions for certain ontological representations that follow best practices in ontology modelling (see Section 3). In this sense, by establishing a correspondence between linguistic patterns and Ontology Design Patterns, we achieve a twofold objective: the (semi-) automatic acquisition of knowledge, on the one hand, and the transformation of that knowledge into an ontological representation, providing support to non-ontology engineers in the modelling process, on the other.

To reach this target, it is necessary to systematically analyze the *deep semantics* of verbal patterns to find out all their possible meaning realizations in different contexts, and establish a reliable mapping with the most appropriate ontological constructs. We contend that a comprehensive theory of meaning construction like the Lexical Constructional Model or LCM (Mairal & Ruiz de Mendoza 2006, 2008), briefly described in Section 4, can provide the clues to capture semantics at different levels. By relying on the LCM lexical templates (Ruiz de Mendoza & Mairal 2006), in Section 5 we analyze the semantics of some of the most common verbal predicates that represent hypernymy-hyponynmy and meronymy relations in English. Such an analysis will allow us to spell out the specific features to be considered in these relations when modelling them in ontologies in order to guarantee an accurate processing by computers. Establishing a reliable correspondence between verbal predicates and ontology design patterns opens a range of possibilities for methods and tools that support novice users in modelling ontologies in a user-friendly way. Finally, conclusions are presented in Section 6.

2. Pattern-based approaches for knowledge acquisition

The idea of applying linguistic patterns to the discovery of semantic relations was introduced in Computation by Marti Hearst in the early 1990s (Hearst 1992). Her research goal was the automatic acquisition of hypernym-hyponym relations from corpora to enrich lexical resources such as WordNet (Fellbaum 1998). Hearst defined *lexico-syntactic patterns* as linguistic structures that are "easily recognizable, that occur frequently and across text genre boundaries, and that indisputably indicate the lexical relation of interest."

An example of Hearst's patterns is: NP_0 such as {NP_1, NP_2... (and | or) NP_n, where NP stands for Noun Phrase followed by the conjunction *such as*, and then a list of Noun Phrases linked by the conjunctions *and* or *or*. An example of a sentence containing that kind of construction is "The bow lute, such as the Bambara ndang, is plucked and has an individual curved neck for each string" (from Hearst's work).

Researchers in the terminology and ontology fields recognized the role of verbs "as a central connecting element between concepts" (Schutz & Buitelaar 2005), and its importance for the automatic acquisition of terms or concepts. In the next section we give an overview of knowledge acquisition approaches that rely on verb-centred patterns to extract conceptual relations from texts.

2.1 Verb-centred patterns for knowledge acquisition

Although most of the approaches dealt with in this section have their roots in the Terminology domain for different languages, most follow Hearst's legacy and have been used to automatically enrich ontologies with new relations, concepts and instances.

In the first group, we find the CAMÉLÉON pattern repository and extraction tool (Aussenac-Gilles et al. 2000, Aussenac-Gilles 2005). This pattern repository includes more than 100 patterns in French, identified manually or with the help of corpora processing tools. Most of them convey the relations of hypernymy-hyponymy and meronymy, and a small group suggests function relations. The resulting set of patterns is used by the CAMÉLÉON tool for the automatic extraction of relations from texts. Examples of these patterns are: *définir, être-un, inclure, partie de, situé dans, c-à-dire* (Aussenac-Gilles & Jacques 2006).

Marshman et al. (2002), also in the field of Terminology, rely on inventories of manually identified linguistic patterns with the same idea of automatically extracting conceptual relations from texts. Their work is based on the notion of *knowledge-rich contexts*, "a context indicating at least one item of domain knowledge that could be useful for conceptual analysis" (Meyer 2001). In this first work, the authors focus on patterns indicating hypernymy, meronymy and function, identified in French corpora about computers and genetics. In subsequent studies, Marshman (2007) investigates so-called *ad hoc* relations in the medical domain, specifically relations of association and cause-effect in English and French. For instance, as cause-effect patterns, she mentions: *implicating, relevant to, induces*, etc; as association relations: *associés à, predict, participate in, involved in*, or *contribute to*.

A similar approach is followed by Feliu and Cabré (2002) and Feliu (2004), with the aim of supporting the process of terminology extraction as well. The authors focus on specialized corpora and identify patterns in Catalan for the relations of similarity (*assemblar-se a, diferenciar-se de*), hypernymy-hyponymy (*considerar-se, ser com*), sequentiality (*iniciar-se, propagar-se a través de, arribar a*), causality (*deure's a, implicar*), instrument (*servir com a*), meronymy (*constar de, tenir, mostrar*), and association (*correspondre a, reflectir*).

As for Spanish, Alarcón Martínez and Sierra Martínez (2003) and Sierra et al. (2008) focus on the analysis of what they refer to as *definitional verbal patterns*. Based on the manual extraction of patterns from both machine readable dictionaries and scientific and technical corpora, they establish a typology of definitions that consists of four types: analytical definition (*referir, significar, comprender*), synonymical definition (*equivaler, llamar, ser similar*), functional definition (*emplearse, funcionar, servir*), and meronymical definition (*consistir, constar, contener*).

Also centred on Spanish, Soler and Alcina (2008) focus on meronymy relations, and extract linguistic structures that relate *wholes* and their *parts* from a corpus of texts about ceramics. Their classification follows Winston et al.'s classification (Winston et al. 1987) of partitive relations, namely, component-object, member-collection, mass-count, material-object, characteristic-activity, and place-area. Some of the most productive verbal patterns in this domain were: *constituido por, provisto de, confeccionado con, rico en, compuesto de/por, consta de, a base de*, or *formado por*.

Regarding those research works that investigate verb-centred patterns for the task of learning ontology concepts and relations, we can mention Aguado de Cea and Álvarez de Mon (2006) for Spanish, and Cimiano and Wenderoth (2007) and Sánchez Ruenes (2007) for English. Aguado de Cea and Álvarez de Mon (2006) extract a set of verbs of classification from an *ad hoc* corpus of textbook documents related to the following subjects: histology, biology and zoology. Examples of these patterns are: *clasificar en, clasificar según/de acuerdo con, clasificar como, (entre otros/el/la/los/las que) figurar*.

Finally, Cimiano and Wenderoth (2007) investigate the impact of some verbs that convey Pustejovsky's qualia structures (Pustejovsky 1995). The authors propose patterns for learning formal (*is a kind of*), constitutive (*is made up of*), telic (*is used to*), and agentive (*to create, produce, build a new*) relations. Regarding the work of Sánchez Ruenes (2007) and Sánchez and Moreno (2008), the authors aim at discovering *ad hoc* relations of the medical domain (mainly cause-effect relations) in an automatic fashion. The set of patterns identified in this case is: *suffer from, is associated with, is treated with, is caused by, accelerates, is inherited, affects, causes, reduces, increases, develops*.

2.2 Main Limitations of pattern-based approaches for knowledge acquisition

Despite the quantity and quality of the patterns above mentioned, most of the authors are in favor of a supervised approach in which the user (terminologist or ontology engineer) validates the knowledge-rich contexts identified by the patterns before including terms and relations in the final resource (terminology or ontology). One of the principal reasons for this is the *noise* or *invalid* knowledge-rich contexts that some of these patterns generate, which sometimes exceed the number of good matches. In Marshman (2008), the author offers a comprehensive analysis of the features that invalidate knowledge-rich contexts for direct reuse. The lexical elements are:

1. indicators of quantification (E.g., *some* X are classified into...)
2. hedging (E.g., X is *basically* classified into...)
3. use of modal verbs (E.g., X groups of Y *may* be distinguished...)
4. use of negation (E.g., one *cannot* distinguish X from Y...)

Soler & Alcina (2008) refer to the problems of polysemy, anaphora, morpho-syntactic variety, and domain dependence when extracting patterns. A further challenge posed by patterns is that they may need to be adapted or tuned for each new domain; otherwise they may miss concepts and relations relevant for that domain. For this reason, most of the authors agree on the importance of a careful and wise selection of the corpus to be used for pattern extraction (see Condamines & Rebeyrolle 2000).

Finally, apart from the disadvantages mentioned, none of the presented approaches provides support in the representation of the acquired knowledge in an ontology. And, in fact, this is far from being a straightforward task, as the representation formalisms used in ontology building are based on logics and require specific training on the side of ontology practitioners (Rector et al. 2004).

In this contribution we also aim at identifying recursive patterns in domain descriptions following a manual process. Indeed, we claim that verb-centred patterns have the advantage of reliably conveying a semantic relation between concepts. However, there are two central aspects that differentiate our proposal from the ones previously analyzed:

a. We do not pursue the automatic extraction of concepts and relations directly from domain corpora, but from statements made by domain experts when developing an ontology, i.e., domain experts express linguistically the knowledge to be represented in the ontology.
b. We lay particular emphasis on modelling; in other words, on the formal representation of the obtained knowledge in the ontology, focusing on newcomers to ontology engineering as the target users of our approach.

Additionally, we assert that relying on linguistic models is necessary to analyze the deep semantics of the identified linguistic constructs. To this end, we draw on the LCM. Our approach focuses on processing the utterances formulated by users and offering them the most appropriate ontological construct to model the knowledge expressed in the user statement. These ontological constructs or ontology modelling components correspond to Ontology Design Patterns, which are the starting point in our research, as indicated in the introduction.

3. Ontology design patterns

Ontology Design Patterns (henceforth ODPs) are defined as "archetypal solutions to design problems" (Gangemi 2005). In other words, ODPs can be considered "small ontologies", a small set of concepts and relations representing a particular meaning, that do not have a straightforward representation in the most common ontology formalisms. As such, ODPs offer modelling solutions that have proven appropriate to solve a certain modelling problem and that can be reused whenever a similar problem appears. ODPs provide the following benefits in the modelling task: a) they allow less experienced users to produce a better design; b) they encourage the reuse of best practices; and c) they improve communication between designers by defining a common design terminology (Prechelt 1997).

In Ontology Engineering, several ODP types have been defined, from which we will focus on the so-called *Logical* and *Content ODPs*. Logical ODPs are content-independent and solve structural problems, i.e., they can solve design problems where primitives of ontology languages usually cannot. Some examples of Logical ODPs are: subclass-of, equivalence relation, or disjoint classes. Content ODPs can solve design problems of specific domains, i.e., though general enough and reusable in ontologies of several domains, these patterns already contain certain domain information. Examples of Content ODPs are: participation pattern (modelling the participation of objects or people in events), collection-entity pattern (modelling the relation between collections and the entities that are members of that collection), agent-role pattern, etc.[1] From the set of Logical and Content ODPs defined in the state of the art, in this chapter we concentrate on the following ODPs:

Logical ODPs

The *Logical ODP for modelling "Subclass of" Relations*: This pattern expresses that the elements belonging to a certain group or set also belong to a more general set. For instance, when one wants to model business tasks as subclasses of tasks.[2]

The *Logical ODP for modelling Disjoint Classes*: It indicates that elements belonging to a certain group or set cannot belong to another group or set, i.e., the two sets are disjoint and do not share instances. For example, one wants to represent that plans and tasks are disjoint.

The *Logical ODP for modelling Exhaustive Classes*: It expresses that a general group or set is the union of several more specific groups or sets, which in its turn are mutually disjoint. For instance, someone wants to express that the types into which a control task can be divided into can only be a begin task, an end task and a sequential task.

1. For a detailed description of all these patterns, see Suárez-Figueroa *et al.* (2007) and Presutti *et al.* (2008). ODPs can also be accessed online in the Ontology Design Patterns Portal (www.ontologydesignpatterns.org).

2. Examples extracted from Suárez-Figueroa et al. 2007.

Content ODPs

The *Content ODP for modelling Simple Part-Whole Relations*: This pattern models general relations between wholes and their parts in a transitive manner, i.e., the part of an object is also part of the whole that contains the object. E.g., someone wants to represent that the brain is part of the human body, and that the *substantia nigra* is part of the brain.

The *Content ODP for modelling Constituency*. This pattern represents the constituents of a layered structure. E.g., someone models a table constituted of different types of wood.

The *Content ODP for modelling Componency*. This pattern represents that objects are either proper parts of other objects, or have proper parts. This relation is understood in a non-transitive way, i.e., the part of an object is not part of the whole that contains the object. Suppose that someone wants to model that a turbine is a part of the engine; this does not mean that the parts of the turbine are also parts of the engine.

The *Content ODP for modelling Collection-Entity*. It models the relation between collections or groups and its members. For instance, someone wants to model that the Louvre has a collection of Egyptian objects.

Quite often, the Logical ODP for "subclass of" relation is used in combination with the ones for modelling disjoint and exhaustive classes, because providing this information is considered good practice in ontologies. Moreover, automatic reasoning in ontologies will certainly obtain better results if we state that subclasses are disjoint, and the set of subclasses represented in the ontology are the only ones into which the more general one can be divided. As for the Content ODPs for modelling Constituency, Componency or Collection-Entity, they can be understood as more specific types of those for modelling Simple Part-Whole Relations.

Therefore, once we had identified the ODPs we wanted to deal with, we searched for and extracted *candidate verbal patterns* in domain corpora following different manual and semi-automatic strategies.[3] By candidate verbal patterns we understand those patterns which "at first sight" seem to convey a certain relation of interest. These patterns included the verb *classify* for the Subclass of relation, Disjoint Classes and Exhaustive Classes, and the verbs *include* and *contain* for the Simple Part-Whole Relation. Then, we examined the *deep semantics* of those verbal patterns in the framework of the LCM theory.

4. The lexical constructional model

As explained in greater detail in this book, the LCM is a "model for the investigation of meaning construction at all levels of linguistic description, including pragmatics and discourse" (Mairal & Ruiz de Mendoza 2009: 153). In full agreement with these

3. We refer the interested reader to Montiel-Ponsoda and Aguado de Cea (2011)

authors, we contend that this model provides the strands to systematically explain the semantics of the verbal predicates considered in this work, by combining ideas from a variety of approaches, specifically, Van Valin's Role and Reference Grammar, Wierzbicka's Semantic Primes, and Pustejovsky's Generative Lexicon.

The LCM was primarily influenced by the tenets of Dik's Functional Grammar (1997), which put the lexicon in a prominent position. In this theory, terms were described by predicate frames that *projected* their underlying structures. A further model influencing the LCM was the Functional Lexematic Model (FLM) (Martín Mingorance 1990, 1998). This model shared the onomasiological approach to the lexicon, and proposed structuring the lexicon in terms of lexical fields or domains. The primary task of the FLM was to investigate the paradigmatic structure of the lexicon, i.e., the hierarchical structure of lexemes, and only afterwards the syntagmatic potential could be investigated, namely, the combinatorial properties of lexical items (Butler 2009: 121). However, this model failed to provide a systematic account of the mapping between semantics and syntax.

With the aim of filling this gap, the LCM turned to another functional theory, the Role and Reference Grammar (henceforth RRG) (Van Valin & La Polla 1997; Van Valin 2004, 2005), which attempts to provide a clear linkage of semantic representation to syntactic structures. The RRG model relies on the lexical decomposition of verbs in order to establish relations among semantically related verbs and their arguments. An example of verb decomposition is illustrated by the verb *to kill*, which is decomposed into an activity (to do) carried out by an actor or doer (x) that causes that someone (y, the undergoer) is dead (example extracted from Van Valin 2005).

kill [do' (x, Ø)] CAUSE [BECOME dead' (y)]

The principles of this decomposition are adopted with some modifications by the LCM in the form of lexical templates, as will be spelled out below. This lack of systematicity on how this lexical decomposition had to be carried out made the authors of the LCM search for other theories that could give account of a systematic decomposition of predicates to arrive at indefinable elements. The LCM introduced then a set of primitives that, to a greater extent, correspond to Wierzbicka's semantic primitives or primes, and which have been proposed in the framework of the Natural Semantic Metalanguage (NSM) theory. Semantic primitives are defined as "elements which can be used to define the meaning of words and cannot be defined themselves; rather, they must be accepted as indefinibilia" (Wierzbicka 1996: 10). Examples of semantic primes are: DO, HAPPEN, MOVE, and TOUCH for the grammatical categories such as actions, events, movement, and contact, respectively. As such, these semantic primitives represent one of the main innovations with respect to the original RRG proposal.

The last step in the configuration of the LCM has been the inclusion of Pustejovsky's Generative Lexicon (1995, 2002, 2006), specifically, *qualia* structures. These elements permit to establish a more straightforward relation between the semantic module and the logical module, i.e., the event and argument structures provided in the RRG's logical structures.

Next, for a deeper understanding of the lexical templates used in this work following the LCM, we review the main principles of the Generative Lexicon.

4.1 The Generative Lexicon

The Generative Lexicon (Pustejovsky 1995) provides some guidelines on how to interpret the semantics of lexical items, and at the same time it also provides the mechanisms to represent that semantics. One of the main objectives of the theory of the Generative Lexicon is to account for polysemy in natural language. Pustejovsky believes that lexical items have a semantic representation conventionally assumed, that can be modified due to certain constraints (one sense is activated against other potential senses). In Pustejovsky's words (1995: 58): "A generative lexicon is a system that involves four levels of semantic representations, namely argument structure, event structure, *qualia* structure and Lexical Inheritance Structure". In the following we describe the first three levels with some detail as they will be considered in our lexical templates.

Argument structure, which specifies the number and type of arguments that a lexical item carries. The number of arguments has a correspondence with syntactic constituents. Pustejovsky distinguishes three types of arguments (Pustejovsky 1995: 63–64):

1. True arguments (ARG): syntactically realized parameters of the lexical item (e.g., *John* arrived late)
2. Default arguments (D-ARG): parameters which participate in the logical expressions in the *qualia*, but which are not necessarily expressed syntactically (e.g., John built the house *out of bricks*)
3. Shadow arguments (S-ARG): parameters which are semantically incorporated into the lexical item. They can be expressed only by operations of subtyping or discourse specification (e.g., Mary buttered her toast *with an expensive butter*)

Pustejovsky's view on the argument structure coincides with the consideration of arguments in RRG's logical structures.

Event structure, which characterizes not only the basic event type of a lexical item, but also the internal, sub-eventual structures. Events can be classified into three types: states, processes and transitions. Pustejovsky (1995: 68) argues that in a verb several events take place which are intertwined, and that it is necessary to identify those events (or sub-events) because each of them may be given prominence in different contexts. This is referred to as *event headedness*, i.e., the property of events of being ordered not only temporally, but also according to their prominence.

For example, the verb *build* contains two sub-events e_1 and e_2. e_1 represents the activity or process of building a house, whereas e_2 represents the state or result of building a house. This justifies the construction of sentences like *He is building a house* vs. *He built a house.*

The ordering restriction (RESTR) that takes place on events can be of three types:

a. *exhaustive ordered part of* (e<∞), one sub-event preceding the other. For example, *build, arrive* (when building a house, the action of building precedes the result)
b. *exhaustive overlap part of* (eo∞), two sub-events occurring simultaneously. For example, *accompany* (going with someone and being with him or her occur at the same time)
c. *exhaustive ordered overlap* (e<o∞), two simultaneous sub-events, where one starts before the other. For example, *walk, begin* (the action of starting walking and the walking action are simultaneous, but the one has happened before the other)

Related to this, there is the generative mechanism of co-composition.[4] Co-composition is defined as an operation in which verbal complements carry information that acts on the verb, taking the verb as argument and shifting its event type. This is a further mechanism to capture polysemy and obviate the need for listing multiple senses. To put it in simple words, co-compositionality is a form of coercion or selection mechanism that picks out knowledge from the verbal complement (as stored in its *qualia* structure) and influences the verbal semantics by also selecting one of its senses.

Let us illustrate this operation by means of the verb *float*, whose reading can change from an activity to an active accomplishment. According to Van Valin (2004) *float* would be defined as a process verb in which something is moving as in *The bottle is floating in the river*. If the verb is combined or composed with a prepositional phrase of the sort *into the cave*, as in *The bottle floated into the cave*, the result is an event change in which the verb has become an active accomplishment, because a final result has been achieved.

***Qualia* structure.** According to the Generative Lexicon, lexical items encode semantic information in the *qualia*, i.e., by stating the *qualia* structure of a certain lexical item we are able to define the essential aspects of a word's meaning. These are the four essential aspects of the *qualia* structure (Pustejovsky 1995: 76):

a. FORMAL: that which distinguishes a lexical item within a larger domain (hyponymy)
b. CONSTITUTIVE: the relation between an object and its constituent parts (meronymy)
c. TELIC: its purpose and function (function)
d. AGENTIVE: factors involved in its origin or "bringing about" (causality)

Since we are interested in the semantic description of verbs, in the following we present the representation of the event (EVENTSTR), argument (ARGSTR) and

4. The other two generative devices are type coercion and selective binding. For more information on this we refer the interested reader to Pustejovsky (1995), Chapter 7 on Generative Mechanisms in Semantics.

qualia structure (QUALIASTR) of the verb *build* in Table 1, adapted from Pustejovsky (1995: 103).

To *build* is an accomplishment verb that involves a process and a resulting state ordered by the exhaustive ordered part of (<∞) restriction. The sub-event headed is the process one, which means that the activity of building a house is headed against the final result. Then, the argument structure is represented by three arguments, two syntactically realized arguments (the animate individual that builds the house and the resulting artefact, i.e., the house), and one default argument (the material of which the house is made of), which is not syntactically realized. The semantic properties of the arguments involved in the event are specified by means of the *qualia* structure. Three *qualia* structures are present in this verb. The formal *quale* indicates the final result of the building activity, and involves ARG_2. The agentive *quale* describes the process and involves ARG_1, the person carrying out the activity, and the default argument (*D-ARG*), which describes the material used in the building of the artefact.

Mairal and Ruiz de Mendoza (2008) saw in this formalism some similarities with the configuration of the lexical templates proposed so far in the LCM model, mainly, that both representations included an event structure description, which to a large extent coincides with the Aktionsart module of the RRG, and a semantic module or *qualia* structure that permits to account for the semantic properties of arguments and events. For this reason, in a latter version of their lexical templates, they combined the logical structures of the RRG with Pustejovsky *qualia* structures, because this representation has the advantage of explicitly assigning semantic descriptions to the event and argument structures of the predicate.

5. Analyzing LSPs with the LCM lexical templates

The template we propose to analyze candidate verbal patterns is slightly different from the one proposed by Mairal and Ruiz de Mendoza (2008) in that event and argument

Table 1. Event, argument and *qualia* structure of the verb *build*

build	
EVENTSTR:	$E_1 = e_1$: [process]
	$E_2 = e_2$: [state]
	$Restr$ = [<∞]
	$HEAD = [e_1]$
ARGSTR:	ARG_1 = [x: animate individual]
	ARG_2 = [y: artifact]
	$D\text{-}ARG$ = [z: material]
QUALIASTR:	Q_F = [exist (e_2, y)]
	Q_A = [build_act (e_1, x, z)]

structures are separately specified according to the mechanisms provided by Pustejovsky (1995: 104 ff), as can be seen in Table 2. We believe that by keeping event, argument and *qualia* structures independent from each other, we can account for each of these structures in more detail. However, we adopt Mairal and Ruiz de Mendoza's event structure based on the *Aktionsart* module and Wierzbicka's semantic primitives, because this formalism allows us to encode those meaning elements that differentiate one predicate from others in the same domain, according to the lexicon philosophy.

LCM EVENTSTR stands for the *Aktionsart* module as understood by Mairal and Ruiz de Mendoza (2008) in the LCM. GT stands for Generative Lexicon and indicates that event (EVENTSTR), argument (ARGSTR) and *qualia* (QUALIASTR) structures are represented according to the formalisms defined by Pustejovsky.

We have selected the following verbal patterns: *classify* (with its variants), *include* and *contain*. We shall proceed to describe the lexical templates in the following manner: First, we describe GT EVENTSTR, GT ARGSTR and GT QUALIASTR, and then we look into the LCM EVENTSTR. This order reproduces the steps taken for the semantic description of the verbal predicates. We first identify the type of event or (sub) events involved in the verbal structure. Then, we identify the number and the type of arguments that participate in the structure. In the third step, we define the *qualia* structure, whose purpose is to specify the semantic properties of each of the arguments and (sub)events. As a corollary, the LCM EVENTSTR brings together the descriptions provided by the rest of structures.

So, by analyzing the meaning of the verbal predicates that we have previously identified in domain documents, we can reliably predict the meaning of linguistic structures and establish a link or correspondence to the ODPs that better represent the

Table 2. Proposed lexical template

Lexical Template	
verbal pattern	**infinitive form**
LCM EVENTSTR	*Aktionsart* module
GT EVENTSTR:	$E_1 = e_1$: [state, activity, achievement, etc.]
	$E_2 = e_2$: [state, activity, achievement, etc.]
	$Restr = [<\infty, o\infty, <o\infty]$
	$HEAD = [e_1\ e_2]$
GT ARGSTR:	ARG_1 = [human, artifact, class, etc.]
	ARG_2 = [human, artifact, class, etc.]
	D-ARG = [human, artifact, class, etc.]
	S-ARG = [human, artifact, class, etc.]
GT QUALIASTR:	Q_F = [hypernymy-hyponymy]
	Q_C = [meronymy]
	Q_T = [function]
	Q_A = [origin, cause]

meaning conveyed by those predicates. We argue that this decomposition of verbal templates in their semantic and pragmatic properties is a critical issue when using these patterns in a system that will perform the automatic transformation of natural language inputs into ontological constructs.

5.1 Lexical template for *classify*

In Table 3 we represent the lexical template for the verb *classify*. *Classify* represents an activity as in *I am classifying the books*. However, it can also become a telic predicate when the result is headed: *I have classified the books*. In this respect, we have decided to treat this verb as an active accomplishment, considering that the definitional contexts we are interested in for ontology building conveyed this meaning.

The event structure (LCM EVENTSTR) encodes two sub-events: an activity or process (e1) and a final resulting state (e2). The relation between the activity and the result involves an exhaustive ordered part of restriction, as signalized by the symbol <μ. Each sub-event maps onto one quale: the agent quale (QA) specifies the nature of the activity sub-event, and the formal quale (QF) maps onto the result of the activity.

Depending on which event is headed, we would have a non-telic interpretation (e1) or a telic interpretation (e2), in which the final result would be foregrounded. In the present template, we head the activity, as indicated by the HEAD property (HEAD=e1). The telic interpretation, however, would ask for into which classes are books classified. The explicit mention of the classes into which something is classified is additional information that complements or composes the semantics of the verb *classify*. This could be analyzed in the same template, but we have decided to create a new one for the *classify into* pattern for the sake of clarity (see Table 4).

Table 3. Lexical template for *classify*

Lexical Template	
verbal pattern	**classify**
LCM EVENTSTR	[do' (x, move to (other) place' (x, y)]e_1 & [BECOME be in (new) place (y)]e_2 $<_\infty E_2$
GT EVENTSTR:	$E_1 = e_1$: [process]
	$E_2 = e_2$: [state]
	$Restr = [<_\infty]$
	$HEAD = [e_1]$
GT ARGSTR:	ARG_1 = x [human]
	ARG_2 = y [class]
	D-ARG = w [criteria]
GT QUALIASTR:	Q_F = [classified (e_2, y)]
	Q_C = [classify_act (e_1, x, y, w)]

Regarding the argument structure of the non-telic interpretation of *classify*, there are two true arguments and one default argument. In the LCM EVENTSTR we try to combine event, argument and *qualia* structure by making use of the semantic primitives MOVE and PLACE. This structure should be rendered as a movement action that results in the object being in a new place or position. The movement activity precedes the state represented by the new position, which is modified by the telic operator (BECOME).

5.2 Lexical template for *classify into*

When the subclasses of a classification are explicitly mentioned, the lexical template is extended in order to account for the new position of the classes, which was unknown in the previous structure. This additional meaning is introduced by the preposition *into*, as represented in Table 4. The new derived sense is generated on the basis of the co-composition method (Pustejovsky 1995), in which the meaning of the verb and the meaning of the preposition are combined. The event structure in this case is quite complex. It consists of four sub-events: two activities or processes and two states. The first process and state (e_1 and e_2) coincide with the previous template of the verb *classify*, and correspond to the first part of the formal and agentive *qualia*, respectively. The agent *quale* corresponds to the classify act or process, according to certain criteria, and the formal *quale*, to the result of the classification (I am classifying -have classified- the books according to the topic).

Table 4. Lexical template for *classify into*

Lexical Template	
verbal pattern	**classify into**
LCM EVENTSTR	[do' (x, move to (other) place' (x, y) & place in (x, y, v)]e_1 e_3 & [BECOME be in (new) place (y) & have types (y, v)]e_2 e_4 <∞ (E_1, E_2), <∞ (E_3, E_4)
GT EVENTSTR:	$E_1 = e_1$: [process]
	$E_2 = e_2$: [state]
	$E_3 = e_3$: [process]
	$E_4 = e_4$: [state]
	Restr = [<∞ (E_1, E_2), <∞ (E_3, E_4)]
	HEAD = [e_4]
GT ARGSTR:	ARG_1 = x [human]
	ARG_2 = y [superclass]
	ARG_3 = y [subclasses (subclass ≠ subclass ≠ subclass...)]
	D-ARG = w [criteria]
GT QUALIASTR:	Q_F = [classified (e_2 y), exist in a relation of kind of to (e_4 y, v)]
	Q_C = [be only types (e_4, y), be disjoint (e_4, y)]
	Q_A = [classify_act (e_1, x, y, w), move into new class (e_3, y, v)]

However, if we want to spell out the (sub)classes that result from the classification, we create a set of disjoint classes (disjoint in the sense that if one item is classified under one of the subclasses, it cannot belong to any other subclass). For instance, I have classified the books into Natural Science books and Literature books. Moreover, the new set of subclasses is assumed to make up the superclass, which means that all subclasses have been accounted for, and no subclass is missing (although this does not need to be true for a different classification). This characteristic of exhaustiveness is represented by the constitutive *quale*. The second part of the agentive *quale* describes the change of position. The items that belong to the superclass are now distributed into the different subclasses. The second part of the formal *quale* indicates the existence of a set of subclasses that are in a relation of "kind of" with respect to the superclass.

The final state (e_4) is headed, which corresponds to the set of subclasses that now exist and into which the items of the superclass have been divided. This representation matches sentences in which the result of the classification is foregrounded as in the following example:

(1) *Membrane proteins are classified into integral proteins and peripheral proteins.*

As previously mentioned, the argument structure accounts for four arguments: three true arguments and one default argument. ARG3 is represented by the subclasses, which have the property of being disjoint among them, so that the items of the superclass can be indisputably placed under the right subclass. The temporal sequence between sub-events is encoded by means of the relation $<\propto$ (E1, E2), $<\propto$ (E3, E4), which means that the first pair process-state (E1, E2) precedes the second pair process-state (E3, E4).

The LCM EVENTSTR represents an active accomplishment involving an activity and a final resulting state modified by the telic operator BECOME. The activity event maps onto the agentive *quale* and describes the placement action. The final result indicates that the subclasses have been classified or are in a new place, and that the result of the classification consists of the superclass staying in a relation of "have types" to the subclasses.

It is also important to note that sometimes a further argument is included with the aim of determining the number and type of classes into which a class is divided. Let us slightly modify example (1):

(2) *Membrane proteins are classified into* **two categories:** *integral proteins and peripheral proteins.*

In this sentence, the generic class name "category" has been included, together with the number of categories into which membrane proteins are classified. It could be stated that this argument has a referential (cataphoric) nature, because it introduces the number of categories that are going to be spelled out after the colon. This can be redundant in the case of *classify into*, but other verbal patterns may need it for disambiguation (see example (6) in Section 5.3).

5.3 Lexical template for *classify as*

Next, we deal with a further co-compositionally derived sense of the verb *classify*, in which its original meaning is constrained by the use of the prepositional phrase introduced by *as*. Once again, the event structure depicts four sub-events and four arguments (see Table 5).

What is relevant here is that the order of the second and third argument has been inverted, so that subclasses come first in the order, and then the superclass to which they belong is mentioned. This is also reflected in the formal *quale* related to the fourth sub-event (e_4) that establishes a relation of "subclass of" or "kind of" between arguments. Note also that the constitutive *quale* present in the previous template for *classify into* has disappeared, and, therefore, exhaustiveness cannot be assured for the second argument (y) in this construction.

Finally, we will refer to a verb that can participate in the three senses and alternations analyzed here for the verb *classify*: categorize. This is illustrated by the examples below:

(3) *Cigars are categorized by the country where they were made.*
(4) *These novels are categorized into beginner, intermediate, and advanced levels.*
(5) *Historical research is categorized as a qualitative research method.*

Table 5. Lexical template for *classify as*

Lexical Template	
verbal pattern	**classify as**
LCM EVENTSTR	[do' (x, move to (other) place' (x, y) & place in (x, y, v)]e_1 e_3 & [BECOME be in (new) place (y) & be kind of (y, v)]e_2 e_4 $<\infty$ (E_3, E_4), $<\infty$ (E_1, E_2)
GT EVENTSTR:	$E_1 = e_1$: [process] $E_2 = e_2$: [state] $E_3 = e_3$: [process] $E_4 = e_4$: [state] *Restr* = [$<\infty$ (E_3, E_4), $<\infty$ (E_1, E_2)] *HEAD* = [e_4]
GT ARGSTR:	ARG_1 = x [human] ARG_2 = y [subclasses (subclass ≠ subclass ≠ subclass...)] ARG_3 = v [superclass] *D-ARG* = w [criteria]
GT QUALIASTR:	Q_F = [classified (e_2 y), exist in a relation of kind of to (e_4 y, v)] Q_A = [classify_act (e_1, x, y, w), move into (super)class (e_3, y, v)]

A further example in which the co-composition generative mechanism is clearly manifested is represented by the verb fall and its phrasal structure fall into. Originally, to fall denotes a change of position, and would typically involve an activity followed by a resulting state. However, when combined with the preposition into, and specifically within a construction of the type fall into the group/class/category..., it acquires the meaning of the *classify into* verbal phrase. See an example below:

(6) *The psalms fall into different categories, such as hymns, thanksgivings, laments, royal psalms, pilgrimage songs, etc.*

5.4 Lexical template for *include*

This verb exhibits an erratic behaviour. Faber and Mairal (1999: 291) consider it a possession verb and define it as "to have something within as a part". The same definition applies also to *contain*. Sentences that comply with this definition are listed below:

(7) *Members of the committee include Mrs Milton Bernet, Mrs J. Clinton Bowman, Mrs Rollie W. Bradford, etc.*
(8) *Miscellaneous soils include sticky substances and colorless liquids.*
(9) *Some new cars include iPod cables in the dash.*
(10) *Industrial constructions include warehouse and factory units.*

In sentence (7) the verb *include* is used with the sense of people belonging to a group. In sentence (8), we find a relation between an object and the materials or substances it is made up of. And finally, in sentences (9) and (10), we identify a relation between a whole and its parts. However, in the corpora analyzed in this work, we also came across sentences in which the relation existing between the two arguments of the sentence is from a superclass to its subclasses. Consider the following sentences:

(11) *Single-seeded dry fruits used for flavoring include cumin, dill, fennel, and angelica.*
(12) *Products of crude oil refineries include gasoline, diesel fuel, heating oil, kerosene, jet fuel, bunker fuel oil, and liquified petroleum.*

According to sentences (11) and (12), we would regard the verb *include* as an activity belonging to the general lexical domain of "movement", in which someone places something in a class or group, as in the case of the *classify* verb. Actually, these two senses of the verb *include* are to be found in the *Oxford Shorter Dictionary* (OSD) (Brown 1993), which reads:

include *(...)* 2. *Contain as part of a whole or as a subordinate element (...) 3. Place in a class or category; treat or regard as part of a whole (...)*

Definition number 3 would be more in line with the definition of the verb *classify into*. Similarly, the result of the movement and placement activities is foregrounded. For this reason, we would propose the same template for the verb *include* (see Table 7).

Nevertheless, contrary to the *classify into* lexical template, the human actor would become a default argument, since it is not syntactically realized in the sentences. In addition to that, the second argument (y) cannot be said to be composed of all the subclasses that make up the superclass, i.e., exhaustiveness is not a feature of the *y* argument defined by the constitutive *quale*. Despite all these differences, this sense of the verb *include* would allow the so-called container subject alternation (Levin 1993: 82), in which the whole or superclass is expressed in a prepositional phrase, as in the case of *classify into*. This means that the sentences above introduced could be also formulated as:

(13) *Cumin, dill, fennel, and angelica are included in single-seeded dry fruits used for flavoring.*

(14) *Gasoline, diesel fuel, heating oil, kerosene, jet fuel, bunker fuel oil, and liquified petroleum are included in (the class of) products of crude oil refineries.*

However, this alternation would not be possible in the case of sentences conveying the part-whole relation, because the parts, members or substances are part of the wholes, and the latter cannot exist without them. Consider the sentences below (the asterisk symbol indicates that the sentence is grammatically incorrect)

Table 6. Lexical template for *include*

Lexical Template	
verbal pattern	**include**
LCM EVENTSTR	[do' (x, move to (other) place' (x, y) & place in (x, y, v)]e_1 e_3 & [BECOME be in (new) place (y) & have types (y, v)]e_2 e_4 $<\infty$ (E_1, E_2), $<\infty$ (E_3, E_4)
GT EVENTSTR:	$E_1 = e_1$: [process] $E_2 = e_2$: [state] $E_3 = e_3$: [process] $E_4 = e_4$: [state] *Restr* = [$<\infty$ (E_1, E_2), $<\infty$ (E_3, E_4)] *HEAD* = [e_4]
GT ARGSTR:	*D-ARG* = x [human] ARG_2 = y [superclass] ARG_3 = v [subclasses (subclass ≠ subclass ≠ subclass...)] *D-ARG* = w [criteria]
GT QUALIASTR:	Q_F = [classified (e_2 y), exist in a relation of kind of to (e_4 y, v)] Q_C = be disjoint (e_4, y) Q_A = [classify_act (e_1, x, y, w), move into (super)class (e_3, y, v)]

(15) *Mrs Milton Bernet, Mrs J. Clinton Bowman, Mrs Rollie W. Bradford are included in members of the committee.
(16) *Sticky substances and colorless liquids are included in miscellaneous soils.
(17) *Warehouse and factory units are included in industrial constructions.

In this respect, we regard the 'subclass of' meaning of *include* as being composed of the primary sense of *include*, plus the meaning of the prepositional phrase introduced by *in/into*, although the latter is not usually lexicalized. Conversely, the *part-whole* relation expressed by the verb *include* would rely on the primary sense of *include*, as described in Table 7 for the verb *contain*. In this sense, it can be said that we have moved from a co-compositionally formed sense to its primary sense. Accordingly, *include* in the sense of part-whole relation would only participate in the latter alternation.

5.5 Lexical template for *contain*

As in the case of *include*, Faber and Mairal (1999: 291) consider it a "possession" verb defined as "to have something within as a part". The OSD provides the following definition:

> ***contain*** *1. Include as a part or the whole of its substance or content; comprise.*

Apart from the recursiveness of the definitions provided for *include* and *contain* in the OSD, this definition indicates that the verb does not share the sense of "subclass of" conveyed by the active accomplishment in the case of *include*.

The formal *quale* describes that there is a meronymy relation between the arguments. Depending on the nature of the arguments, the relation would be further specified as a relation between a whole and its parts, a group and its members, or an object and its constituents (material or substance). The LCM EVENTSTR makes use of the primitives HAVE and PART to define a relation of possession between the first and the second argument.

Table 7. Lexical template for *contain*

Lexical Template	
verbal pattern	**contain**
LCM EVENTSTR	have parts (x, y)
GT EVENTSTR:	$E_1 = e_1$: [state]
	$HEAD = [e_1]$
GT ARGSTR:	ARG_1 = x [human, object, animate-individual, artifact, etc.]
	ARG_2 = y [superclass]
GT QUALIASTR:	Q_F = [classified (e_2 y), exist in a relation of kind of to (e_4 y, v)]

Although the relation of meronymy is not a simple one, we will restrict here to three types of relation: part-whole, group-member, and object-constituent, which according to Climent Roca (2000) are the three basic mereologic schemas.

Other verbs that follow the same template as *contain* are the following: *comprise, make up, compose, constitute, be part of,* and *form part of. Contain, comprise* and *consist* are normally used in the active voice, whereas *make up, compose* and *constitute* are more usual in the passive voice. Interestingly enough, in the corpora analyzed we find all these verbs conveying the different types of meronymical relations mentioned above.

(18) *Foam machines (...) stock consist of two or more pumping units.* (part-whole)
(19) *This board consists of two of the trustees of the college, the director, and two members of the board of freeholders.* (group-member)
(20) *Crude oil consists of hydrocarbons.* (object-constituent)
(21) *All organisms are made up of one or more cells.* (part-whole)
(22) *The Working Group is made up of Administrative Office staff, Federal Defender Organization attorneys, a private criminal defense attorney representative, and Department of Justice representatives.* (group-member)
(23) *Bones are made up of calcium, phosphorous, sodium, and other minerals, as well as the protein collagen.* (object-constituent)

However, these polysemous uses will have to be disambiguated to be appropriately modeled in the ontology, since each type of meronymical relation is represented by a different Ontology Design Pattern.

6. From linguistic patterns to ontological constructs: A user-centred approach

Once such a deep semantic analysis has been performed, we are in the position to establish a reliable correspondence to ODPs (see Section 3). This correspondence is not always a one-to-one correspondence, but more often than not, a verbal pattern conveys the semantics encoded in various ODPs. Even more, it is often the case that the same linguistic structure can have various modelling possibilities that are not compatible. This happens when dealing with polysemous verbal patterns, as is the case of some of the verbs analyzed in the previous section. Therefore, we can establish three types of correspondence links, namely:

a. 1 linguistic pattern corresponds to 1 ODP
b. 1 linguistic pattern corresponds to a combination of 2 or more ODPs
c. 1 linguistic pattern corresponds to 2 or more disjoint ODPs

In the verbal patterns dealt with in Section 5 we find examples of these three types. As for the first type, it is exemplified by the verb *classify as*. This verb can be said to straightforwardly convey a relation of "subclass of" between the arguments of the predicates. Neither disjointness nor exhaustiveness can be assured.

The verbal pattern represented by *classify into* would be a nice exponent of the second type of correspondence, 1 linguistic pattern corresponding to a combination of several ODPs. As evidenced by the lexical template for this verb, such a linguistic structure requires the combination of three Logical ODPs, i.e., subclass-of, disjoint classes, and exhaustive classes.

A further example of this correspondence is represented by the verb *include* in the sense of *place in a class or category*. This linguistic structure would convey the meaning expressed by the Logical ODP for modelling subclass-of relations and the one for modelling disjoint classes. The feature of exhaustiveness, however, could not be derived from the analysis of its deep semantics, as evidenced by the lexical template illustrated in Table 6. Nevertheless, *include* would also belong to those patterns that correspond to 2 or more disjoint ODPs, as it is a polysemous verb. Specifically, *include* can convey the meaning represented by the Logical ODP for modelling subclass-of relations and the Content ODP for modelling simple part-whole relations. Only the nature of the arguments can help in the disambiguation process.

Regarding the verb *contain* (as well as *include* in the sense of *contain as part of a whole*), it is worth mentioning that, although in a first stage we would classify this verb as belonging to bullet point a) 1 linguistic pattern corresponds to 1 ODP, we realized that in fact, it can also be included in bullet point b) 1 linguistic pattern corresponding to 2 or more disjoint ODPs. This means that once a correspondence to the Content ODPs has been established, for modelling simple part-whole relations, we need to disambiguate among the more specific types of meronymy, i.e., part-whole, group-member and object-constituent, represented by the Content ODPs for modelling constituency, componency and collection-entity respectively.

7. Conclusions

Our research is targeted at applying a comprehensive theory of meaning construction, like the LCM, to the analysis of the verbal predicates that realize linguistic structures used in classification and that correspond to some ontological constructs, the so-called Ontology Design Patterns. The complexity and subtlety of these ontological structures called for a model that could cater for its semantic complexity. The analysis performed also permits to represent verbal polysemy in a systematic way. In this chapter, we have shown how the LCM allows for rich semantic representations of these classification verbal predicates, and how these representations can be mapped to ODPs. By connecting these verbal patterns to ODPs in a univocal way, we aim at modestly contributing in several aspects: first, to the approaches focused on (semi-) automatically acquiring knowledge from experts, thus helping domain experts to model ontologies. Second, although verbal constructions representing conceptual relations have called researchers' attention from different fields, classification structures had not been previously analyzed by the LCM researchers, neither had they been applied to ontology construction.

Acknowledgements

The research described in this paper was supported by the European Union under Grant No. 248458 for the Monnet project, *Multilingual Ontologies for Networked Knowledge*, and by the Spanish Ministry of Science and Innovation under Grant No. TIN2010-17550, for the *BabeLData* project.

References

Agirre, Eneko, Ansa, Olatz, Hovy, Eduard H. & Martínez, David. 2000. Enriching very large ontologies using the WWW. In *Proceedings of the Workshop on Ontology Learning at ECAI00*, CEUR Vol. 31, Steffen Staab, Alexander Maedche, Claire Nedllec & Peter M. Wiemer-Hastings (eds), 25–30. Berlin: Springer.

Aguado de Cea, Guadalupe & Álvarez de Mon, Immaculada. 2006. Estructuras de clasificación en español. Terminología y adquisición de conocimiento explícito para la web semántica. In *Proceedings of the 5th Internacional AELFE Conference*, 492–498. Zaragoza: Universidad de Zaragoza.

Aguado de Cea, Guadalupe, Gómez-Pérez, Asunción, Montiel-Ponsoda, Elena & Suárez-Figueroa, Mari Carmen. 2008. Natural language-based approach for helping in the reuse of ontology design patterns. In *Knowledge Engineering: Practice and Patterns, Proceedings of the Knowledge Engineering Conf. (EKAW)*, 32–47. Springer: Heidelberg.

Alarcón Martínez, Rodrigo & Sierra Martínez, Gerardo. 2003. The role of verbal predications for definitional contexts extraction. In *Proceedings of the on Terminology and Artificial Intelligence Conference (TIA03)*, 11–20.

Aussenac-Gilles, Nathalie, Biébow, Brigitte & Szulman, Sylvie. 2000. Revisiting ontology design: A method based on corpus analysis. In *Knowledge Engineering and Knowledge Management: Methods, Models and Tools*, Rose Dieng & Olivier Corby (eds), 172–188. Berlin: Springer.

Aussenac-Gilles, Nathalie 2005. Supervised text analysis for ontology and terminology engineering. In *Proceedings of the Dagstuhl Seminar on Machine Learning for the Semantic Web*, 35–46.

Aussenac-Gilles, Nathalie & Jacques, Marie-Paule. 2006. Designing and evaluating patterns for ontology enrichment from texts. In *Managing Knowledge in a World of Networks, Proceedings of the 15th International Conference EKAW06*, Vol. 4248, Steffen Staab & Vojtech Svatek (eds). Berlin: Springer.

Butler, Christopher S. 2009. The Lexical Constructional Model. Genesis, strengths and challenges. In *Deconstructing Constructions* [Studies in Language Companion Series 107], Christopher S. Butler & Javier Martín-Arista (eds), 117–152. Amsterdam: John Benjamins.

Brown, Lesley (ed.). 1993[1933]. *The New Shorter Oxford English Dictionary On Historical Principles*. Oxford: Clarendon Press.

Cimiano, Philipp & Wenderoth, Johanna. 2007. Automatic acquisition of ranked qualia structures from the web. In *Proceedings of the Annual Meeting of the Association for Computational Linguistics,* 888–895.

Climent Roca, S. 2000. Individuación e información parte-todo. Representación para el procesamiento computacional del lenguaje. PhD dissertation, Universitat de Barcelona. <http://elies.rediris.es/elies8/>

Condamines, Anne & Rebeyrolle, Josette. 2000. Construction d'une base de connaissances terminologiques à partir de textes: Expérimentation et définition d'une méthode. In Jean Charlet, Manuel Zacklad, Gilles Kassel & Didier Bourigault (eds), *Ingénierie des connaissances, évolutions récentes et nouveaux défis,* 225–242. Paris: Eyrolles.

Dik, Simon C. 1997. *The Theory of Functional Grammar.* Berlin: Mouton de Gruyter.

Faber, Pamela B. & Mairal Usón, Ricardo. 1999. *Constructing a Lexicon of English Verbs.* Berlin: De Gruyter.

Feliu, Judit & Cabré, Maria Teresa. 2002. Conceptual relations in specialized texts: new typology and an extraction system proposal. In *Proceedings of the Terminology and Knowledge Engineering conference (TKE2002),* 45–49.

Feliu, Judit. 2004. Relacions conceptuals i terminologia: anàlisi i proposta de detecció semiautomàtica. PhD dissertation, Institut Universitari de Lingüística Aplicada. Universitat Pompeu Fabra.

Fellbaum, Christiane. 1998. *WordNet. An Electronic Lexical Database.* Cambridge MA: The MIT Press.

Gangemi, Aldo. 2005. Ontology design patterns for semantic web content. In *Proceedings of the 4th ISWC,* Yolanda Gil, Enrico Motta, V. Richard Benjamins & Mark Musen (eds), 262–276. Berlin: Springer.

Hearst, Marti A. 1992. Automatic acquisition of hyponyms from large text corpora. In *14th International Conference on Computational Linguistics,* 539–545.

Levin, Beth. 1993. *English Verb Classes and Alternations: A Preliminary Investigation.* Chicago IL: University of Chicago Press.

Maedche, Alexander & Staab, Steffen. 2000. Discovering conceptual relations from text. In *Proceedings of the 14th European Conference on Artificial Intelligence (ECAI00),* 321–325. Amsterdam: IOS Press.

Mairal, Ricardo & Ruiz de Mendoza, Francisco José. 2006. Internal and external constraints in meaning construction: The lexicon-grammar continuum. In *Estudios de filología inglesa: Homenaje a la Dra. Asunción Alba Pelayo.* Madrid: UNED.

Mairal, Ricardo & Ruiz de Mendoza, Francisco José. 2008. New challenges for lexical representation within the Lexical-Constructional Model (LCM). In *Revista Canaria de Estudios Ingleses. Grammar, Construction and Interfaces* (57): 137–158.

Mairal, Ricardo & Ruiz de Mendoza, Francisco José. 2009. Levels of description and explanation in meaning construction. In *Deconstructing Constructions* [Studies in Language Companion Series 107], Christopher S. Butler & Javier Martín-Arista (eds) 153–198. Amsterdam: John Benjamins.

Marshman, Elizabeth, Morgan, Tricia & Meyer, Ingrid. 2002. French patterns for expressing concept relations. *Terminology* 8(1): 1–29.

Marshman, Elizabeth. 2007. Towards strategies for processing relationships between multiple relation participants in knowledge patterns. An analysis in English and French. *Terminology* 13: 1–34.

Marshman, Elizabeth. 2008. Expressions of uncertainty in candidate knowledge-rich contexts. *Terminology* 14: 124–151.

Martín Mingorance, Leocadio. 1990. Functional grammar and lexematics in lexicography. In *Meaning and Lexicography* [Linguistic and Literary Studies in Eastern Europe 28], Jerzy Tomaszczyk & Barbara Lewandowska-Tomaszczyk (eds), 227–253. Amsterdam: John Benjamins.

Martín Mingorance, Leocadio. 1998. El modelo lexemático-funcional: El legado lingüístico de Leocadio Martín Mingorance. In *El modelo lexemático-funcional,* Amalia Marín Rubiales (ed.). Granada: Universidad de Granada.

Meyer, Ingrid. 2001. Extracting knowledge-rich contexts for terminography. a conceptual and methodological framework. In *Recent Advances in Computational Terminology* [Natural Language Processing 2], Didier Bourigault, Christian Jacquemin & Marie-Claude L'Homme (eds), 279–302. Amsterdam: John Benjamins.

Montiel-Ponsoda, Elena & Aguado de Cea, Guadalupe. 2011. Using natural language patterns for the development of ontologies. In *Researching Specialized Languages* [Studies in Corpus Linguistics 47], Vijay Bhatia, Purificacion Sánchez Hernández & Pascual Pérez-Paredes (eds), 211–229. Amsterdam: John Benjamins.

Prechelt, Lutz. 1997. An experiment on the usefulness of design patterns: Detailed description and evaluation. Technical Report. University of Karlsruhe.

Presutti, Valentina, Gangemi, Aldo, David, Stefano, Aguado de Cea, Guadalupe, Suárez-Figueroa, Mari Carmen & Montiel-Ponsoda, Elena. 2008. D2.5.1: A Library of Ontology Design Patterns: Reusable solutions for collaborative design of networked ontologies (Tech. Rep.). NeOn Project Deliverable.

Pustejovsky, James. 1995. *The Generative Lexicon*. Cambridge MA: The MIT Press.

Pustejovsky, James. 2002. Polysemy and underspecification. In *The Lexicon in Focus. Competition and Convergence in Current Lexicology*, Leila Behrens & Dietmar Zaefferer (eds), 187–208. Frankfurt: Peter Lang.

Pustejovsky, James. 2006. Type theory and lexical decomposition. *Journal of Cognitive Science* 6: 39–76.

Rector, Alan L., Drummond, Nick, Horridge, Matthew, Rogers, Jeremy, Knublauch, Holger, Stevens, Roger, Wang, Hai & Wroe, Chris. 2004. OWL pizzas: Practical experience of teaching OWL-DL: Common errors and common patterns. In *European Conference on Knowledge Acquisition*, Enrico Motta & Nigel Shadbolt (eds), 63–81. Berlin: Springer.

Ruiz de Mendoza, Francisco José & Mairal, Ricardo. 2006. How to design lexical and constructional templates: A step by step guide. <http://www.lexicom.es/drupal/files/templateDesign.pdf>

Sánchez Ruenes, D. 2007. Domain Ontology Learning from the Web. PhD dissertation, Universitat Politècnica de Catalunya.

Sánchez, David & Moreno, Antonio. 2008. Learning non-taxonomic relationships from web documents for domain ontology construction. *Data Knowledge Engineering* 64: 600–623.

Schutz, Alexander & Buitelaar, Paul. 2005. RelExt: A tool for relation extraction from text in ontology extension. In *Proceedings of the 4th International Semantic Web Conference (ISWC05).*

Sierra Alarcón, Gerardo, Rodrigo Aguilar, César & Bach, Carme. 2008. Definitional verbal patterns for semantic relation extraction. *Terminology* 14(1): 74–98.

Soler, Victoria & Alcina, Amparo. 2008. Patrones léxicos para la extracción de conceptos vinculados por la relación parte-todo en español. *Terminology* 14(1): 99–123.

Suárez-Figueroa, Mari del Carmen, Brockmans, Saartje, Gangemi, Aldo, Gómez-Pérez, Asunción, Lehmann, Jos, Lewen, Holger, Presutti, Valentina & Sabou, Marta. 2007. NeOn D5.1.1. *NeOn Modelling Components*. NeOn Project.

Van Valin, Jr., Robert & LaPolla, Randy. 1997. *Syntax. Structure, Meaning and Function*. Cambridge: CUP.

Van Valin, Jr., Robert. 2004. Lexical representation, co-composition, and linking syntax and semantics.<http://linguistics.buffalo.edu/people/faculty/vanvalin/rrg/vanvalin_papers/LexRepCoCompLnkgRRG.pdf>

Van Valin, Jr., Robert. 2005. An overview of Role and Reference Grammar. <http://linguistics.buffalo.edu/people/faculty/vanvalin/rrg/RRG_overview.pdf>

Wierzbicka, Anna. 1996. *Semantics. Primes and Universals*. Oxford: OUP.

Winston, Morton E., Chaffin, Roger & Herrmann, Douglas. 1987. A taxonomy of part-whole relations. *Cognitive Science* 11(4): 417–444.

The interaction of non-linguistic and linguistic knowledge in FunGramKB*

Fátima Guerra García
Universidad de La Laguna

This chapter investigates how the non-linguistic knowledge stored in the conceptual level of FunGramKB interacts with the idiosyncratic linguistic knowledge stored in the other two levels, i.e. the lexical and the grammatical levels. It will be argued that the pivotal module of this knowledge base, the Ontology, and the conceptual information stored for the concepts building its taxonomy may be a good source to predict certain aspects of the different lexicalization patterns of the lexical units that lexicalize those concepts and the constructions in which they are subsumed. Consequently, the nature of this work is that of a cross-level analysis. At the same time, this work also analyzes how a verb-framed language like Spanish and a satellite-framed language like English draw different information from the same conceptual base.

1. Introduction

Within the framework of FunGramKB (which stands for Functional Grammar Knowledge Base, FGKB henceforth) (Periñán & Arcas 2010), the non-linguistic conceptual knowledge stored in the pivotal level of this knowledge base, the Ontology, has proved to have an impact beyond the cognitive module itself, reaching the lexical and the grammatical levels – where idiosyncratic linguistic knowledge is stored. The Ontology is a hierarchical system of semantic representation of concepts designed to be universally shared. Here, "universal" means:

a. Every existing concept, as long as it is expressed by a linguistic unit, can have a place in the Ontology.
b. The conceptual information which is introduced in order to describe a concept, i.e. the Thematic Frame (TF henceforth) and the Meaning Postulate (MP henceforth), contains features which are common to the various languages comprising

* The research on which this paper is based has received financial support from the Spanish Ministry of Education and Science (BES-2009-017546) and is part of the research projects No. FFI2008-05035-C02-02 and FFI2011-29798-C02-02.

> the knowledge base.[1] Consider, for example, the case of the concept +WALK_00. The universally shared conceptual information is encoded in its five conceptual participants (i.e. agent, theme, location, origin and goal), the presence of the selectional preferences "human or animal" for the entity that changes location (that is, the theme), and the fact that the motion is achieved through the use of the legs.

Cross-linguistic differences in lexical and syntactic behavior are stored in the linguistically-oriented modules of the knowledge base, i.e. the lexical and the grammatical levels. Nevertheless, despite the methodological independence of these three levels in the knowledge base, the cognitive non-linguistic information assigned to a concept (e.g. +WALK_00) in the conceptual level has proved to have an influence on the behavior of the predicates that lexicalize that concept in the linguistic modules (as is the case of *walk* or *wade* in the English Lexicon or *andar* 'walk', *caminar* 'walk' in the Spanish Lexicon). Thus, for example, we can expect some verbal predicate(s) linked to +WALK_00 to have a causative *Aktionsart*, as is the case of *walk* or *march*, since this concept has a conceptual participant with the thematic role Agent which can be lexicalized by the lexical units. Likewise, we can foresee that the verbal predicate *jog* can be incorporated into a resultative construction while *go* or *ir* (in Spanish) cannot, the reason lies in the Ontology: the MP of the concept +WALK_00, to which *go* and *ir* are linked to, includes a predication to describe the path of motion, more specifically the goal within the path, whereas the MPs of the concepts +RUN_00 and $TROT_00, to which *trot* and *jog* are linked to, contain a satellite describing manner of motion, which turns out to be a crucial piece of information in those cases. In accordance with Talmy´s (1985, 2000) lexicalization patterns, *jog* lexicalizes the event of motion together with the manner in which it takes place. Thus, it is hardly surprising that *jog* is able to fuse with a resultative construction (following Goldberg's (1995) terminology), as in *They jogged the pavement thin,* since this construction adds information, more precisely the result of the motion event, which is not lexicalized in the verb.[2]

A preliminary study of the connection between the ontological deep semantics and the semantic definitions of the predicates belonging to the Lexicons is carried out in Guerra García and Sacramento Lechado (this volume). Nevertheless, although in that work the interrelation between the three levels of the knowledge base – an issue frequently attested in the FGKB literature– was verified, further research beyond the limits of a concept's TF and its mapping into verbs' argument structures is still needed,

1. TFs and MPs are explained in Section 3.1.

2. Following Ruiz de Mendoza Ibañez and Mairal-Usón (2007), the process of subsumption is, in very general terms, the incorporation of lower-level structures (or Lexical Templates) into higher-level structures (or Constructional Templates). Lexical Templates are thus absorbed by higher-level characterizations such as the caused-motion, the resultative or the benefactive constructions. This absorption is a straightforward process constrained by a number of principles that determine their scope of application.

as the range of influence may be broader than was first estimated. The present study advances this line of research.

The primary goal of this chapter is to trace the location of a group of motion verbs (in English and Spanish) within FGKB in order to elucidate what precise features from the conceptual information stored in the ontological module conflate as components in the possible lexicalization patterns of the predicates and which other components are part of the configuration of the constructions they participate in. In line with the usage-based approach (cf. Gonzálvez-García & Butler 2006: 42–45) all the examples used in this paper have been taken from: BNC (British National Corpus), COCA (Corpus of Contemporary American English), Corpus del Español de Mark Davies (CEMD) and WebCorp.

It is almost impossible to think of motion-event descriptions without bearing in mind Talmy's (1985/2000) seminal work; in fact, it is interesting to observe how his theory of lexicalization patterns and his typology of languages are in many ways confirmed along this study. Consequently, building upon Talmy's study, we will analyze how a verb-framed language like Spanish and a satellite-framed language like English draw information from the same conceptual base.

To prevent this work from getting cumbersome, the motion verbs under scrutiny here are just translational motion verbs, in other words, verbs where the figure (in Talmy's terminology) or moving object's basic location shifts from one point to another in space; self-contained motion verbs (i.e. the object moves its body by changing its posture or orientation but not its location) being out of the purview of this work. More precisely, we have analyzed:

a. Path verbs (or inherently directed motion verbs in Levin's (1993) terminology) such as *entrar* 'enter', *salir* 'exit', *ir* 'go', *venir* 'come', *enter, exit, go* or *come*.
b. Manner verbs pertaining to human and animal locomotion, especially ways of walking and ways of running (*run* verbs for Levin), such as *andar/caminar* 'walk', *correr* 'run', *trotar* 'trot', *tambalearse* 'stagger', *walk, run, trot, trudge, plod, stumble, stagger, jog*. Other manner of motion verbs like change of posture, motion using vehicles, motion of non-volitional entities (*roll* verbs following Levin (1993)), motion while dancing (*waltz* verbs following Levin (1993)), etc. are out of the purview of this study.

The remainder of this chapter is structured into six sections. Section 2 contains an overview of the three levels of knowledge which make up the architecture of FGKB. Section 3 focuses on the Ontology, presenting a detailed description of a concept's conceptual information. Section 4 and 5 present the lexical and grammatical levels of the knowledge base respectively. Section 6 contains a brief account of Talmy's theory of lexicalization patterns and his two-way typology of languages. Finally, Section 7 concentrates on the cross-level analysis of motion concepts. Section 8 offers some conclusions.

2. An overview of FGKB

FGKB is a multipurpose lexical-conceptual knowledge base for natural language understanding whose main objective is to become a useful application for Natural Language Processing (NLP) systems. It is multipurpose because it is multifunctional and multilingual. In other words, FGKB has been designed to be reused for various NLP tasks such as information retrieval and extraction, machine translation, dialogue-based systems, etc.,[3] and to work with and cover several natural languages.[4]

The knowledge base comprises three major levels of information: a lexical level, a grammatical level and a conceptual or cognitive level. All these levels are made up of independent but interrelated modules, as can be seen in Figure 1 below:

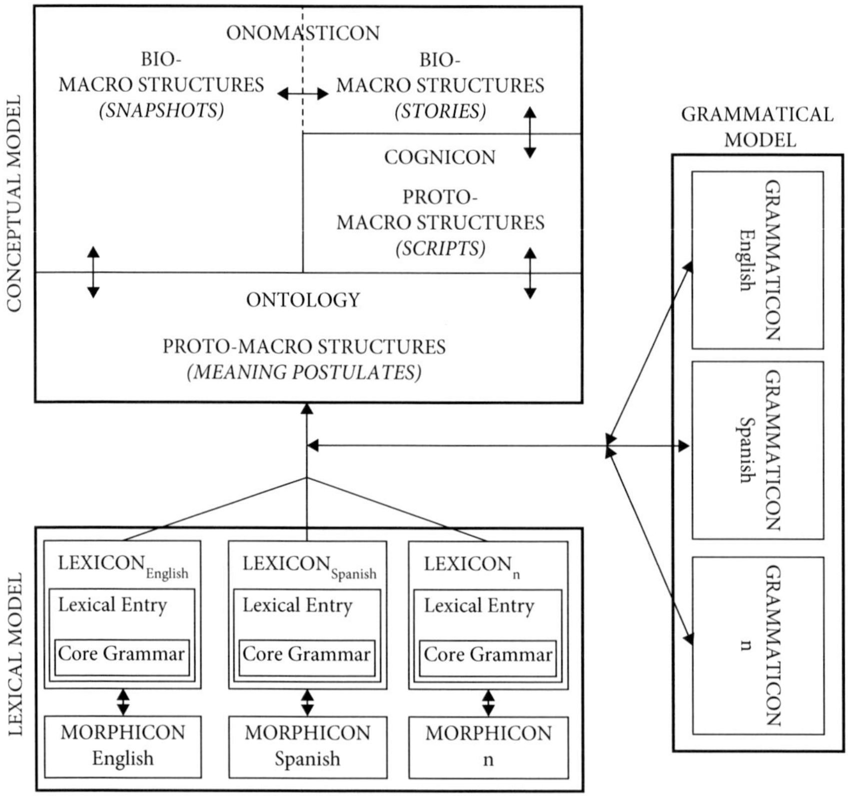

Figure 1. General architecture of FGKB.

3. Periñán and Mairal-Usón (2010b) describe the integration of FGKB to the machine translator UniArab.

4. In the current version of FGKB Suite English and Spanish are fully supported and work has begun to implement it with other languages, such as German, French, Italian, Bulgarian and Catalan.

- The lexical level includes the Lexicon and the Morphicon. The Lexicon stores morphosyntactic, pragmatic and collocational information about lexical units, preserving the major linguistic assumptions of Role and Reference Grammar (RRG) (Van Valin & LaPolla, 1997; Van Valin, 2005), although with some important contributions. In turn, the Morphicon helps the system to handle cases of inflectional morphology.
- The grammatical level or Grammaticon stores the constructional schemata corresponding to the four layers identified in the Lexical Constructional Model (LCM) (Ruiz de Mendoza & Mairal-Usón 2007, 2008; Mairal-Usón & Ruiz de Mendoza, 2008), which helps RRG to construct the semantics-to-syntax linkage. The LCM, being partially grounded on the RRG framework, becomes thus the main linguistic model behind FGKB.
- We turn now to the conceptual level, which comprises the *Onomasticon*, the *Cognicon* and the *Ontology*.
    - The *Onomasticon* stores information about instances of entities and events, such as *Bill Gates, New York City, Taj Mahal,* or *9/11*. This module stores two different types of schemata (i.e. snapshots and stories) because instances can be portrayed synchronically or diachronically.
    - The *Cognicon* stores procedural knowledge in the form of script-like conceptual schemata in which a sequence of stereotypical actions is organized on the basis of temporal continuity, more particularly on the basis of Allen's (1983) temporal model; for example, "eating in a restaurant" or "how to fry an egg" are conceptual schemata made out of different temporarily-ordered predications or events.
    - Finally, the *Ontology* is a hierarchical catalogue of the concepts that a person has in mind describing everyday reality, so here is where semantic knowledge is stored. The meaning of concepts such as *ostrich, hand, jealous, ready, run* or *cook,* is described in the Ontology through MPs. The Ontology consists of a general-purpose module (i.e. Core Ontology), where concepts regarding basic human knowledge are stored, and several domain-specific terminological modules (i.e. Satellite Ontologies or Sub-Ontologies) for concepts from specialized fields of knowledge such as law, science or engineering.

In this knowledge base every lexical or grammatical module is language dependent (covering linguistic knowledge) while cognitive modules are shared by all languages included in the knowledge base (covering non-linguistic knowledge). This means that computational lexicographers must develop one Lexicon, one Morphicon and one Grammaticon for each language stored, but knowledge engineers working at the cognitive level build just one Ontology, one Cognicon and one Onomasticon to capture any language input cognitively.

3. FGKB's Ontology

FGKB's Core Ontology, called simply the Ontology, stores semantic knowledge or cognitive information about concepts we have in mind to describe everyday situations, something similar to a mental thesaurus of concepts. This semantic knowledge is stored in the form of proto-microstructures called MPs: *proto* because the knowledge represented is prototypical and *micro* because it is represented atemporally (i.e. meaning postulates contain just atemporal features).

These "universal" concepts (cf. Section 1) about the world are hierarchically structured in a taxonomy. What is more, in this IS-A taxonomy multiple inheritance is allowed, what means that a subordinate concept can inherit properties from more than one superordinate.

A second reasoning mechanism of inference allows the system to connect information shared between conceptual units from different subsumption relations within the Ontology. For example, the concept $ROBIN_00 in FunGramKB – to which lexical units like English *robin* and Spanish *petirrojo* are linked – inherits features belonging to its superordinate in the ontological structure, as can be seen in Figure 2 below. At the same time, through inference mechanism, the system is able to associate $ROBIN_00 with other concepts such as +NEST_00, +SING_00 or $FLOCK_00 (see Figure 3 below), thus enriching the concept's meaning. The fact that all the concepts in the hierarchy are linked through non-monotonic relations endows the model with defining brevity and expressive power.

The Ontology is subdivided into three Sub-Ontologies, *entities, qualities* and *events* in order to make the Ontology more easily accessible and for organizational purposes. There are three types of conceptual units in the Ontology, which can be observed in Figure 2 below.

#ENTITY
- → #PHYSICAL
  - → #OBJECT
    - → #SELF_CONNECTED_OBJECT
      - → #NATURAL_OBJECT
        - → #CORPUSCULAR_00
          - → #SOLID_00
            - → #ORGANISM_00
              - → #ANIMAL_00
                - → #VERTEBRATE_00
                  - → #BIRD_00
                    - → **$ROBIN_00**

Figure 2. Ontological taxonomy of the concept $ROBIN_00 in FGKB[5]

5. Figure taken from Sacramento Lechado and Guerra García (2012)

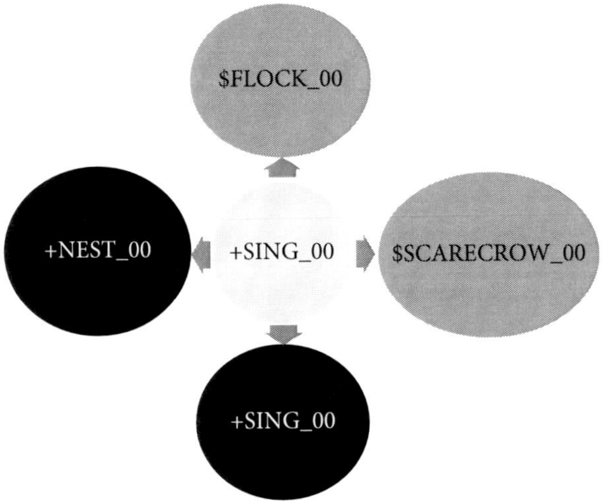

Figure 3. Inference mechanisms in the Ontology[6]

- Metaconcepts are cognitive dimensions such as #TRANSFORMATION, #MOTION, #MATERIAL or #ABSTRACT. They are the upper level in the taxonomy and they are always preceded by the symbol #.
- Basic concepts (e.g. +BOOK_00, +WALK_00, +THIN_00) were originally identified following the defining vocabulary of the *Longman Dictionary of Contemporary English* (Procter, 1978). However, as shown in Periñán and Mairal-Usón 2011, they were subject to deep revision. In FunGramKB, basic concepts are always preceded by the symbol + and they used as defining units in the construction of MPs for basic concepts and terminal concepts. As will be shown later on, basic concepts are also employed as selectional preferences in TFs.
- Terminal concepts (e.g. $DICTIONARY_00, $STROLL_00, $FRAIL_00, etc.) are the final and lower levels in the conceptual hierarchy. They are semantic specifications of basic concepts and are preceded by the symbol $.

Although it could sound paradoxical, FGKB's Ontology is linguistically motivated but not language-dependent. As Periñán and Arcas (2010: 2668) explain "the Ontology is involved with the semantics of lexical units, but the knowledge stored is not specific to any particular language". On the practical front, this means that for the creation of a concept's meaning postulate, knowledge engineers carry out a long and not devoid of difficulties work with lexicographic sources, such as dictionaries, thesaurus and other ontologies, in order to elucidate what features of the semantics of lexical units belonging to different languages go beyond the linguistic level. The final concept is therefore not specific to any particular language. This is the reason why it is said to be a universal

6. Figure taken from Sacramento Lechado and Guerra García (2011)

taxonomy since any concept can have a place in the Ontology as long as it is lexicalized through a lexical unit(s) in a language.

The knowledge base is populated from top to bottom levels, which means that the existence of a lexical entry in any of the Lexicons will "involve the previous ontological modeling of their corresponding concepts" (Mairal-Usón & Periñán 2009: 221). Thus, providing that some knowledge engineer has introduced the concept +WALK_00, then linguists are able to type in information concerning the lexical units *walk* or *caminar.* This is the reason why the authors maintain "that this model is conceptually rather than lexically-drive" (Mairal-Usón & Periñán 2009: 221), since the Ontology becomes the pivotal module for the whole architecture. In this scenario, consider Figure 4 below:

Figure 4 illustrates not only the centrality of the Ontology in the architecture of the model but also the methodological independence of the conceptual, the lexical and the grammatical level. In the cognitive level, a concept of what a dog is would be stored

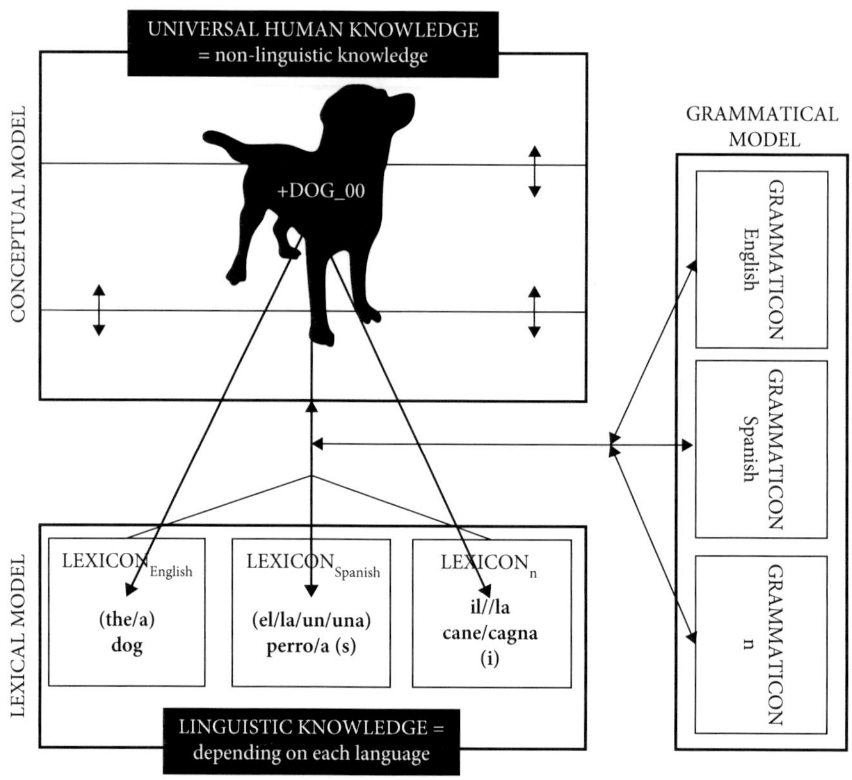

Figure 4. Linguistic and non-linguistic knowledge in FGKB

with the name +DOG_00.[7] The concept's MP would contain features such as being an animal, having four legs, one head, a tail, etc., features which are shared by the definitions of *dog* in many monolingual dictionaries and encyclopedia and represent speaker's common-sense knowledge about the world. Meanwhile, it is in the lexical level where the different lexical units that lexicalize the concept in different languages (e.g. *dog* in the English language, *perro* in the Spanish language or *cane* in the Italian language) are stored together with morphosyntactic, core grammar information, etc.

Finally, all this knowledge stored in the form of a MP is represented through a conceptual representation metalanguage called COREL (*Conceptual Representation Language*). All conceptual schemata in the knowledge base (i.e. meaning postulates, snapshots and stories and scripts) are represented with the same metalanguage, which endows the system with a great inferential power to combine information from the three modules. This notational system is machine readable and conceptually oriented.[8]

3.1 Ontological conceptual information

A concept's entry in FGKB's Ontology contains four basic semantic properties: its superordinate (or hypernym), a TF, a MP and a final description in natural language.[9] The entry is completed with a list of the lexical units that lexicalize the concept in different languages.[10] Below, (1) shows the information found in the entry of the concept +WALK_00:

(1) +WALK_00
SUPERORDINATE: +MOVE_00
THEMATIC FRAME (TF): (x1)Agent (x2: +HUMAN_00^+ANIMAL_00) Theme (x3: +GROUND_00)Location (x4)Origin (x5)Goal
MEANING POSTULATE (MP): +(e1: +MOVE_00 (x1)Agent (x2)Theme (x3)Location (x4)Origin (x5)Goal (f1: +LEG_00)Instrument)
DEFINITION: Use one's feet to advance; advance by steps
LEXICAL UNITS:
English: Go on foot, hoof, pace, toodle, wade, walk.
Spanish: andar, caminar, campear, pasear.

Indicating a concept's superordinate in its entry is fundamental in order to trace back the cognitive domain or metaconcept it belongs to. As consequence of the IS-A

7. Basic concepts in the Ontology are preceded by a + symbol and followed by underscore (_) and a numbering (00, 01, etc.) which are conventions of the representation metalanguage called COREL used to represent knowledge in the cognitive level.

8. For more information about deep semantics in FGKB and the metalanguage COREL we refer the readers to Periñán and Mairal-Usón (2010a) and Periñán and Arcas (2007a, 2007b, 2010).

9. It is important to notice that conceptual information is introduced manually from lexicographic sources and the introspection of the knowledge engineers.

10. In this work, we will focus on Spanish and English.

taxonomic organization, a concept would inherit great part of its TF and the genus of its MP from its superordinate.

The TF specifies the number of conceptual participants involved in the cognitive situation portrayed by the event. In FGKB each cognitive dimension (e.g. #COGNITION, #MOTION, etc.) is represented by a number of participants with given thematic roles.[11] For example, the cognitive dimension #MOTION has the prototypical TF seen in (2), where Agent and Theme are compulsory participants that must appear in all concepts within the domain while Location, Origin and Goal are optional. As a result, any concept subordinated to #MOTION (e.g. +WALK_00, $LIMP_00, $ACCOMPANY_00, +WANDER_00, etc.) will inherit the same TF; this can be seen in the previous example (1) which shows the TF of the basic concept +WALK_00. The natural language equivalent of (1) would be "an agent causes a theme, human or animal, to move through the ground from an origin to a goal".

(2) #MOTION → (x1)Agent (x2)Theme (x3)Location (x4)Origin (x5)Goal
Agent = entity that makes another entity move.
Theme = entity that changes its place or position.
[Location] = location in which the entity moves.
[Origin] = Location from which an entity moves.
[Goal] = Location to which an entity moves.

Common-sense knowledge about the world tells us: i) that only people and animals are able to walk; and ii) that the process of walking necessarily takes place on ground. This knowledge is captured through selectional preferences, which in FGKB are saturated by basic concepts from the Ontology: +HUMAN_00, +ANIMAL_00 and +GROUND_00 in (2b) above. As we can see, selectional preferences provide non-linguistic information, since:

> "the information expressed through features like 'human', 'animal', etc., has no relation whatsoever with our knowledge of languages like English, Spanish or Japanese, but with 'the real world' and our experiences there" (Jiménez-Briones and Pérez-Cabello de Alba (2011: 106).[12]

Syntactic behavior of predicates varies depending on the different senses they may have. Thus, the predicate frame or argument structure of the predicate *walk* changes if we are dealing with the intransitive or transitive sense, as in (3).

11. FGKB has a limited inventory of thematic roles and each of them acquires a different semantic interpretation depending on which metaconcept the concept we are dealing with is integrated in. The thematic roles we work with are: *Agent, Theme, Referent, Attribute, Location, Origin,* and *Goal* out of which *Theme* is the central one that appears in all cognitive dimensions.

12. For a more detailed treatment of selectional preferences of participants in FGKB, see Jiménez-Briones and Pérez-Cabello de Alba (2011).

(3) a. walk[1]: {(agent, x)} = to move or go somewhere by putting one foot in front of the other on the ground
b. walk[2]: {(agent, x) (theme, y)} = to make an animal walk somewhere.

From a conceptual point of view, the concept +WALK_00 must be broad (even "abstract") enough to capture all the different idiosyncratic behaviors of the predicates that lexicalize the concept. The knowledge engineer has to abstract himself/herself from the linguistic level in order to capture the cognitive scenario. In other words, all the different lexical units and their syntactic behavior should be included and easily represented with the concept's semantic properties, being that the reason why TFs should present always the highest number of participants.

MPs must be equally versatile. They represent a concept's meaning, in other words, the semantic content of the concept. MPs consist of "one or more logically connected predications (e_1, e_2...e_n), i.e. conceptual constructs carrying the generic features of concepts" (Periñán & Mairal-Usón 2009: 267). The first predication of a concept is always its *genus,* which places it within a broader category – identifying its hypernym. Following the *genus* we find the *differentia,* which contains the distinctive features that set the concept apart from the other concepts of the taxonomy. In COREL, *differentiae* features are represented through *satellites* and are introduced by the symbol *f* plus a numbering.[13] As an illustration, the MP of the concepts +WALK_00 and +RUN_00 can be seen in (4) and (5):

(4) MP of +WALK_00:
+(e1: +MOVE_00 (x1)Agent (x2)Theme (x3)Location (x4)Origin (x5)Goal (f1: +LEG_00)Instrument)

(5) MP of +RUN_00:
+(e1: +WALK_00 (x1)Agent (x2)Theme (x3(Location (x4)Origin (x5)Goal (f1: +FAST_00)Speed)

The natural language equivalent of (4) would be "an agent causes a theme, human or animal, to move through the ground from an origin to a goal using +LEG_00 as instrument". "Using legs as instrument" is the *differentiae* and is represented in COREL with the satellite (f1: +LEG_00)Instrument. As can be seen in the examples, basic concepts from the Ontology (+CONCEPT_00) are not only used as selectional preferences in the TFs, as in (1) above, but also as predicating features in the MPs, as in (4) and (5). Similarly, in the definition of the concept +RUN_00 in (5), meaning "walking fast", we represented its distinctive feature, i.e. fast, through the satellite (f1: +FAST_00)Speed.

13. Knowledge engineers working on FGKB's Ontology have a limited list of satellites to choose from, namely *beneficiary, company, condition, duration, frequency, instrument, manner, means, position, purpose, quantity, reason, result, scene, speed* and *time.*

Finally, a concept's entry closes with a dictionary definition of the concept and a list of lexical units that lexicalize the concept in different languages.

4. The FGKB lexicon

In the lexical level we find a Lexicon for each of the languages included in the knowledge base. Since "lexical units are heavily influenced by the Ontology" (Mairal-Usón & Periñán 2009: 219), the first thing that can be observed in the entry of a lexical unit in FGKB is the conceptual information of their corresponding concept. Next, more morphosyntactic, core grammar and semantic features are assigned to each lexical unit which we now proceed to explain in greater detail below:

a.. Basic information includes: (1) a headword, which helps to differentiate the different senses of a lexical unit,[14] (2) an index, a numerical string to arrange the different senses of a lexical unit, and (3) the language to which the lexical unit belongs.

b. Morphosyntactic information: FGKB stores all graphical variants and abbreviations (if the lexical unit consists of a single orthographic word or a head and a particle in the cases of complex ones), category (FGKB stores information about open-class words, i.e. verbs, nouns and adjectives), number (i.e. dual: regular, dual: irregular, singular, plural or common), gender (i.e. dual: regular, dual: irregular, masculine, feminine, common or ambiguous), countability (i.e. countable, uncountable or dual), degree (i.e. if the comparative and superlative forms of adjectives are built in an inflectional or periphrastic way), adjectival position (the standard position of the adjective within the phrase, i.e. attributive, predicative or dual), verb paradigm and constraints (if the verb is regular or irregular and if it has constraints in the paradigm), and, finally, pronominalization (i.e. reflexivity and reciprocity).

c. The LCM Core Grammar section contains crucial aspects in the verb's lexical templates such as:[15] (1) *Aktionsart* (drawing on Vendler's *Aktionsart* distinctions (cf. Vendler 1967), RRG divides verb classes into *states, activities, achievements, semelfactives, accomplishments* and their causative), (2) the number of variables assigned to the *Aktionsart*; (3) "M(acrorole)-Transitivity, which refers to the

14. FGKB's lexical entries are word-sense-oriented, thus "an entry is defined as a collection of features linked to a particular sense of the lexical unit". Therefore $march_{\text{month}}$ and $march_{\text{motion}}$ have two different lexical entries, each one linked to a different concept: +MARCH_00 and +MARCH_01 respectively (Mairal-Usón & Periñán 2009: 227).

15. The notion of lexical template in LCM "is originally a development of the LOGICAL STRUCTURES (LS) postulated in ROLE AND REFERENCE GRAMMAR (RRG) (cf. Van Valin & LaPolla 1997, Van Valin 2005) which uses a decompositional system to represent the semantic structure and argument structure of verbs and other predicates" (Ruiz de Mendoza Ibañez & Mairal-Usón 2008: 360).

number of macroroles that the verb allows, and the assignment of the value of Undergoer (if there is one),[16] (4) thematic frame mapping, which is the link between conceptual information from the TF in the Ontology and more specific (i.e. lexical) information in the corresponding Lexicon. This link is created by assigning a thematic role from the concept's TF in the Ontology to each of the variables of the predicates lexicalizing such concept in the corresponding Lexicon (Guerra Garcia and Sacramento Lechado in this volume), (5) prototypical prepositions and collocations of the verb's arguments are also indicated, (6) finally, constructions in which the verbal predicate fuses are specified (here, the computational lexicographers have to select the appropriate constructions from a given list), e.g. the verb *walk* can fuse in the following constructions: resultative construction (*Cathy walked herself to exhaustion*), induced action alternation (*Claire walked the dog down the street/The dog walked down the street*) and preposition drop alternation (*She walked across the town/She walked the town*).

d. Miscellaneous information such as: (1) dialect, (2) style or different types of lexical registers, which "is a potential source of variation between cognitive synonyms" (Mairal-Usón & Periñán 2009: 236), (3) domain, containing a subset of forty-eight domains such as architecture, sport, medicine, etc. in which the lexical units are topically clustered, (4) examples from the *Corpus de Referencia del Español Actual* and the BNC help to illustrate the meaning of the lexical units for Spanish and English respectively, (5) finally, default translation equivalents into other languages are provided.

5. The FGKB grammaticon

As we said in advance in Section 2, FGKB's grammatical level stores the constructional schemata corresponding to the four layers identified in the Lexical Constructional Model (LCM) (Ruiz de Mendoza and Mairal-Usón 2007, 2008; Mairal-Usón and Ruiz de Mendoza, 2008), which helps RRG to construct the semantics-to-syntax linkage (the LCM being partially grounded on the RRG framework).

The LCM is a multidimensional model that incorporates all aspects of language as meaning dimensions, not only grammar but also pragmatic implicature, illocution and discourse coherence. All these aspects of language affect one another and are the

16. RRG distinguishes two types of transitivity, the S(yntactic)-Transitivity, which refers to the number of direct core arguments, and M(acrorole)-Transitivity, which refers to the number of macroroles that a verb allows. Accordingly, there are atransitive (0 macroroles), intransitive (1 macrorole) and transitive (2 macroroles). There are two macroroles distinguished in RRG, the Actor, i.e. the generalized agent-like participant or "logical subject", and the Undergoer, i.e. the generalized patient-like participant or "logical object". Their assignment is predicted in terms of the argument's position in Logical Structures according to a scale called the Actor-Undergoer Hierarchy (cf. Van Valin 2005: 58)

reason why the model has four levels of representation: a core grammar level, an implicative level, an illocutionary level and a discourse level.

The grammatical level in FGKB is formed by several Grammaticon modules (one for each language implemented in the knowledge base) and "captures the properties that are specific to the most relevant constructional families in the languages under consideration on the basis of corpus data" (Jiménez-Briones & Luzondo Oyón 2011: 14). Thus, for the English language, for example, each of the constructional levels of the LCM is computationally implemented into a Constructicon (L1-Constructicon, L2-Constructicon, L3-Constructicon and L4-Constructicon). LCM Level 1 constructional representations will be stored in the L1-Constructicon, LCM Level 2 constructional representations will be stored in the L2-Constructicon, etc.

Following Periñán and Mairal-Usón (2009: 265) robust NLP systems require a solid linguistic model since, although it is "much easier to build NLP systems when linguistic theories are neglected, but those systems will unavoidable fail [...] since they don´t allow natural language understanding". For this reason, FunGramKB lexical and grammatical levels are "grounded in sound linguistic theories [i.e. RRG and the LCM], allowing the system to capture syntactic-semantic generalizations which are able to provide both explanations and predications of language phenomena." (Periñán & Arcas 2010: 2671). RRG and the LCM share two features which are essential for a computational model of language: (1) their functional view of language, which allows capturing syntactic-semantic generalizations, (2) their strong commitment to typological adequacy, which implies that universal distinctions are introduced as part of the linguistic framework (Periñán & Mairal-Usón 2009: 266).

6. Talmy's theory of lexicalization patterns

A vast amount of research on the linguistic expression of motion events in English and Spanish has been produced over the last two decades inspired by Talmy's typological work. In the following sections we will analyze how a verb-framed like Spanish and a satellite-framed language like English draw different information from the same conceptual base. In this context, this section introduces very briefly some basic concepts of Talmy's lexicalization patterns and typology of languages. To this end, we have followed the works of Talmy (1985, 2000), Cifuentes-Férez (2009) and Mora (2001).[17]

According to Talmy, complex events are made up of a main event or framing event and a subordinate event or co-event, both of which are "conceptualized as unitary events" (Cifuentes-Férez 2009: 20). The framing motion event consists of the following internal components: figure (moving object), ground (reference points such as source/origin, goal or milestone), path (trajectory with respect to the ground) and motion (motion per se). In addition to this, a motion event can be related to an external

17. We refer readers to these works for a more detailed explanation of these issues.

co-event reflecting Manner of movement or Cause of movement. From looking at which of these components are lexicalized in verb roots, in addition to the fact of motion, he developed his theory of lexicalization patterns. Thus, Talmy distinguished three principal lexicalization types: (1) verb roots expressing the co-event (manner or cause), English being a prototypical example (e.g. *I slid/rolled the keg into the storeroom*), (2) verb roots encoding the path, Spanish being an example (e.g. *Metí el barril a la bodega rodándolo*), and finally, (3) verb roots expressing the figure, a northern Hokan polysynthetic languages of northern California called Atsugewi being a representative examples of this type (e.g. *-lup-* is a verb in the Atsugewi language which means "for a small shiny spherical object (e.g. a round candy, an eyeball, a hailstone) to move/ be-located"; thus, these type of languages have whole groups of verbs expressing the movement of objects or materials) (Mora 2001).

The two-way typology of verb-framed languages and satellite-framed languages resulted from looking at the morphosyntactic constituents that characteristically encoded the path components (main/framing event for Talmy):

a. In verb-framed languages, like Spanish, the path appears verb roots and the co-event (manner or cause) as an independent element like adverbials or gerunds (what Talmy calls satellites),[18] for example *Entró al sótano corriendo ('(the man) went into the cellar running')*
b. In satellite-framed languages, like English, verb roots usually encode motion plus co-event and the path is lexicalized in the satellite (from here satellite-framed), for example *I ran my way down the stairs.*[19]

7. Beyond ontological postulates

In this section, we will carry out a cross-level analysis of the data stored in FGKB. Taking into account Talmy's theory of lexicalization patterns, we study what features of the MPs and TFs from the ontological module conflate as components in the possible lexicalization patterns of the predicates and which other components are part of the configuration of the constructions they participate in.

7.1 Concepts with path specifications in the MPs

In this section, the concepts +ENTER_00, +ARRIVE_00 and +LEAVE_00 are analyzed as examples of concepts whose MPs contain path components. The concept

18. Taken from Mora (2001) quoting Talmy, a satellite is "the grammatical category of any constituent other than a nominal complement that is in a sister relation to the verb root. [...], which can be either a bound affix or a free word".

19. All examples in Section 4 are taken from Mora (2001).

+ENTER_00 has the same five conceptual participants in its TF as the rest of concepts within the cognitive domain of #MOTION (seen in (2a)). Both the MP and the TF of the concept can be seen in (6) below:

(6) +ENTER_00
TF: (x1)Agent (x2)Theme (x3)Location (x4)Origin (x5)Goal
MP:
+(e1: +MOVE_00 (x1)Agent (x2)Theme (x3)Location (x4)Origin (x5)Goal **(f1: (e2: +BE_02 (x4)Theme (x5)Location (f2: +OUT_00)Position))Condition (f3: (e3: +BE_02 (x2)Theme (x5)Location (f4: +IN_00)Position)) Result)**[20]

The natural language equivalent of the MP in (6) would be something like "a moving entity moves from an origin that is located in an outside position and as result of the motion event it happens to be located in a goal that is located in an inside position", or in a simpler dictionary definition "to come or go into".

The lexical units *enter* and *entrar* associated to this concept in the English and Spanish Lexicon are *active accomplishments* following the *aktionsart* distinctions by Van Valin and LaPolla (1997) and Van Valin (2005). Therefore, just two of the five conceptual participants are mapped into the verb's Logical Structure (LS henceforth) in Van Valin's theory, i.e. the theme and the goal. As a way of illustration, (7) shows the link between the conceptual participants and the verb's LS:

(7) (x1)Agent (x2)Theme (x3)Location (x4)Origin (x5)Goal
↙ ↓
do' (x2 [**+ENTER_00** (x2)]) & INGR **+BE_02** (x5, x2])[21] [22]

Cifuentes-Férez (2009) classifies these two predicates as path verbs which specify the path detail "into ground". According to Talmy (2000), the path component of motion present in *enter* is that of Conformation, related to the geometry of grounds, which can

20. Emphases in boldface in the MPs throughout the paper are mine and are used in order to highlight aspects under study.

21. The semantics of the concept +BE_02 corresponds to **be_LOC.**

22. As can be seen, Van Valin's LSs are subject to some modifications in this work. Lexical functions and semantic primitives are replaced with concepts (+CONCEPT_00) from the Ontology and instead of the common (x, y, z) for the verb's variables we use x_1, x_2, x_n imitating the cognitive level. In this way, the thematic frame mapping from the Ontology to the Lexicon is more easily observed. What is more, each time a concept is introduced in the verb's LS all its conceptual information can be retrieved from the Ontology, thus enriching the LS.

be conceptualized as containers.[23] Levin (1993: 263) lists *enter* as a verb of inherently directed motion even in the absence of the directional phrase. Going back to (6), in the MP of the concept +ENTER_00, we have highlighted in boldface the satellites where this path of motion component can be seen as an important part of the core meaning of the concept at the ontological level.

Regarding the syntactic behavior of *enter*, Levin (1993: 267) points out that inherently directed motion verbs fuse in the locative preposition drop alternation, e.g. *Martha slowly descended down the stairs/Martha slowly descended the stairs* (Levin 1993: 43). This author explains that these verbs can be found intransitively with a directional phrase complement or transitively with a path, goal or source as direct object. However, she does not include *enter* in the small group of inherently directed motion verbs which do participate in the alternation.[24] In accordance with this, our search in different corpora returned an overwhelming majority of examples with the verb's argument structure, i.e. x = theme and y = goal (as direct object), as the example in (8a). However, although few in number, the American Corpus (COCA) returned some hits of the verb *enter* with a directional phrase complement, see (8b) and (8c). Finally, in the Spanish language the verbal predicate *entrar* 'enter' only allows the intransitive use with a directional phrase complement as the example in (8d) (the transitive use implying a change in the sense of the verb).

(8) a. *I entered the room where Taswell lay (COCA/2011/FIC/Bk:KateVaiden)*
b. *You enter into the hotel lobby that's whiter than Donny Osmond's teeth (COCA/2012/NEWS/SanFranChron)*
c. *We enter into the drawing room of M. Durand-Ruel (COCA/1991/ACAD/ArtBulletin)*
d. *Todo lo que puedo decir es que entró en la habitación rápidamente (CEMD/19-OR/Entrevista (ABC))*

Levin does not suggest any other possible alternation or construction in which these verbs may participate.

The case of the concept +ARRIVE_00 is slightly similar although some differences can be observed. Its meaning is "to reach a destination" and its MP, in (9), contains a path component in the satellite *Result* which expresses the reaching of a goal (x5) by the theme (x2):

23. According to Talmy, the three main components of path are the Vector (refers to the direction of the motion of the figure with respect to the ground, thus Vector can denote motion from a source, past or along a milestone and to or towards a goal), the Conformation (related to the geometry of grounds, which can be conceptualized as containers, surfaces, points, etc.) and the Deictic (motion towards the speaker and in direction other than the speaker).

24. Levin groups *ascend, depart, descend, escape, flee* and *leave* as verbs which participate in this alternation and adds that *arrive, come, go* and *return* do not do so (Levin 1993: 43). Interestingly, *enter* is not mentioned in this list.

(9) **MP**
+(e1: +MOVE_00 (x1)Agent (x2)Theme (x3)Location (x4)Origin (x5)Goal
(f1: (e2: +BE_02 (x2)Theme (x5)Location))Result)

From all the lexical units that lexicalize this concept in the English and Spanish lexica, we have concentrated on Spanish *llegar* and *venir* and English *arrive* and *come* (just the sense of the verbs related to the concept's meaning). Following Cifuentes-Férez (2009), the path component of motion present in these lexical units are Vector (related to the direction towards a goal) and the Deictic component (motion towards the speaker) instead of Conformation as was the case of *enter/entrar.* Levin (1993: 263) lists them as verbs of inherently directed motion even in the absence of the directional phrase.

In the Lexica, *llegar, venir, arrive* and *come* are classed as *accomplishment*. Being accomplishments, they are two-placed predicates; the entities theme and goal mapped from the Ontology (see (10) below) as also happened with *enter/entrar* in (7).

(10) (x1)Agent (x2)Theme (x3)Location (x4)Origin (x5)Goal

BECOME +**BE_02** (x5, x2)

However, if we compare (10) here with (7) above, we will see that the LS of the verbal predicates *enter* and *entrar* presented an aspect of dynamicity in the first part of the LS, i.e. **do'** (x2 [**+ENTER_00** (x2)]), which is absent now in (10).

As Levin (1993: 43, 263) suggests, the search in corpora retrieves no hit of the verbs *arrive* and *come* participating neither in the Locative Preposition-Drop alternation, nor the causative or resultative alternations. We only found examples as the one in (11a) and (11b) below. Other examples showed the addition of more details of the path. In the example in (11c), these additional details coincide with a forth component of path proposed by Slobin called the Earth-grid component, which is related to the direction of motion to earth-based components such as north-south-east-west, up-down, etc. (Cifuentes-Férez 2009: 88). In (11d) and (11e) another component of the path, the origin, which is not present in the verb's LS is expressed; a cognitive participant (x4) Origin in the Ontology being therefore recovered:

(11) a. *A police car finally arrived at the scene and officers spoke to the motorist (BNC/K6D/S_brdcast_news)*
b. *En medio de estas encidencias llegó a España el obispo de Chiapa (CEMD/18/ Vidas de los españoles célebres)*
c. *Would you like to come up to the top of the house, to my office? (BNC/CH1/W_newsp_tabloid)*
d. *my husband arrived home from the war in nineteen forty eight (BNC/J8G/S_interview_oral_history)*
e. *El médico, que vino desde la ciudad a ver a la enferma, (CEMD/18/Amistad funesta)*

The third concept analyzed in this section is +LEAVE_00. Its meaning is "to go away from a place or person" and its MP in COREL is the following:

(12) +(e1: +MOVE_00 (x1)Agent (x2)Theme (x3)Location (x4)Origin (x5)Goal **(f1: (e2: +BE_02 (x2)Theme (x4)Location (f2: +IN_00)Position))Condition (f3: (e3: +BE_02 (x5)Theme (x4)Location (f4: +OUT_00)Position))Condition)**

As in the previous two cases, the MP of +LEAVE_00 presents path components in the satellites highlighted in boldface. The English lexical units *leave* and the Spanish verbs *salir* and *dejar* specify the path component Vector, as happened with *enter/entrar*, although this time it is the departure from an origin what is lexicalized in the verbs (in Talmy's terms, following Cifuentes-Férez words, "away from Ground"). In the Lexica, *leave, salir* and *dejar* are listed as *active accomplishments*, therefore, the two entities mapped from the Ontology are theme and origin.

(13) (x1)Agent (x2)Theme (x3)Location (x4)Origin (x5)Goal

do' (x2 [**+LEAVE_00** (x2)]) & INGR NOT **+BE_02** (x4, x2])

Levin (1993: 264) does not mention any possible construction in which the verb *leave* may be subsumed, just a brief mention to the fact that the direct object of the verbs is the location that has been left. This seems to be supported by the corpora consulted, since the majority of the examples found only showed the verb's argument structure being semantically fulfilled, as in (14a) and (14b) below:

(14) a. *I left the house at quarter to seven (BNC/K5J/W_newsp_other_social)*
b. *Lidia salió de la habitación y se encerró en el cuarto de baño (CEMD/19-F/Para toda la vida)*

7.2 Concepts with manner semantics in the MPs

The following concepts were analyzed as examples of concepts with manner semantics in the MPs: +WALK_00, $MARCH_01, $PLOD_00, $STAGGER_00, $STROLL_00, +RUN_00, $TROT_00 and +WANDER_. Their MPs (written in COREL) are presented from (15) to (21):

(15) MP of $MARCH_01: +(e1: +WALK_00 (x1)Agent (x2)Theme (x3)Location (x4) Origin (x5)Goal **(f1: ((e2: +DO_00 (x2)Theme (x6: m +STEP_00)Referent) (e3: +BE_01 (x6)Theme (x7: +SIMILAR_00 & +LONG_00)Attribute)))Manner)**

(16) MP of $PLOD_00: +(e1: +WALK_00 (x1)Agent (x2)Theme (x3)Location (x4) Origin (x5)Goal **(f1: ((e2: +DO_00 (x2)Theme (x6: +STEP_00)Referent) (e3: +BE_01 (x6)Theme (x7: +SLOW_00 & +HEAVY_00)Attribute)))Manner** (f2: (e4: +BE_01 (x2)Theme (x8: +TIRED_00)Attribute))Reason)

(17) MP of $STAGGER_00: +(e1: +WALK_00 (x1)Agent (x2)Theme (x3)Location (x4)Origin (x5)Goal **(f1:((e2:n+CONTROL_00(x2)Theme (x6: +MOTION_00)Referent) (e3: +BE_01 (x6)Theme (x7: +DIFFICULT_00)Attribute)))Manner** | (f2: (e4: prob +DESCEND_00 (x6)Agent (x2)Theme (x3) Location (x8: +UP_00)Origin (x9: +DOWN_00)Goal))Result)

(18) MP of $STROLL_00: +(e1: +WALK_00 (x1)Agent (x2)Theme (x3)Location (x4)Origin (x5)Goal **(f1: +SLOW_00 & +CALM_00)Manner** (f2: +PLEASURE_00)Purpose)

(19) MP of +RUN_00: +(e1: +WALK_00 (x1)Agent (x2)Theme (x3)Location (x4) Origin (x5)Goal **(f1: +FAST_00)Speed)**

(20) MP of $TROT_00: +(e1: +RUN_00 (x1)Agent (x2)Theme (x3)Location (x4) Origin (x5)Goal **(f1: +SLOW_00)Speed (f2: ((e2: +DO_00 (x2)Theme (x6:+STEP_00)Referent) (e3: +BE_01 (x6)Theme (x7: +SHORT_00 & +SIMILAR_00)Attribute)))Manner)**

(21) MP of +WANDER_00: +(e1: +WALK_00 (x1)Agent (x2)Theme (x3)Location (x4)Origin (x5)Goal **(f1: (e2: n +KNOW_00 (x2)Theme (x5)Referent)) Manner)**

In all the MPs above, the manner of walking or running is central to the meaning of the concepts as the satellites highlighted in boldface show. The satellites used are mainly *Manner* and *Speed,* which have to do with the manner in which the movement is achieved or carried out. The TFs of all these concepts have the same five conceptual participants shared by all concepts within the cognitive domain of #MOTION (seen in (2a)), we repeat them in (22) below for clarity of exposition. The selectional preferences, on the other hand, are specific to this sub-domain of concepts pertaining to the human and animal locomotion.

(22) TF: (x1)Agent (x2: +HUMAN_00 ^ +ANIMAL_00)Theme (x3: +GROUND_00)Location (x4)Origin (x5)Goal

If we move to the lexical level, all the lexical units that lexicalize these concepts in the English and the Spanish Lexica (in (23) below) are classified as *activities* in Van Valin and LaPolla (1997) and Van Valin (2005) classification, therefore they are one-place predicates with the LS shown in (24) below. As a result, just one conceptual participant from the TF is being mapped onto the lexical level, namely, the theme (i.e. entity that changes its place or location):

(23) List of lexical units under study (corresponding to concepts found from (15) to (21)):
English verbs: *walk, stroll, ramble, amble, plod, trudge, stagger, stumble, run, trot, jog, wander,* and *roam.*
Spanish verbs: *caminar, andar, pasear, tambalear(se), correr, trotar* and *vagar.*[25]

25. The fact that there are thirteen English verbs and just seven Spanish verbs in our list of lexical units under study is due to the following reasons: (1) The Spanish language has only one

(24) (x1)Agent (x2)Theme (x3)Location (x4)Origin (x5)Goal

do' (x2 [+WALK_00 (x2)])[26]

Levin (1993: 265) put all these verbs in (23) in a group called run verbs. Cifuentes-Férez (2009) classifies all these verbs in (23) as manner of motion verbs making a thorough classification with fine-grained manner details such as ways of walking, ways of running, speed of motion (rate-fast/slow), energy-high/low, unbalanced motion, gradual steps, steps-heavy, etc. In FGKB, many of these details are present at the conceptual level as features in the MPs, being this the reason why we have used LSs from RRG instead of the more semantically complete LTs from the LCM.[27]

If we move to the Grammaticon, manner concepts and their corresponding lexical units present important differences with respect to the cases of "path concepts" in Section 5.1. Following Levin (1993), manner verbs pertaining to human/animal locomotion do subsume into some constructions which affect the verb's transitivity by introducing a new entity, or participant, not present in the verbs' LSs. In so doing, we focus on three constructions: the directional phrase with non-directed motion verbs (e.g. *Audrey tiptoed/Audrey tiptoed to the floor* (Levin 1993: 105)), the induced action alternation (e.g. *The scientist ran the rats through the maze/The rats ran through the maze* (Levin 1993: 31, 266)) and the resultative phrase (e.g. *Tom ran the soles off his shoes* (Levin 1993: 266)).

First of all, the directional phrase with non-directed motion verbs is of obvious interest for us because different verbs of manner participate of it including run verbs. In the following examples we find verbs that are not inherently verbs of displacement in a particular direction (so, no path or ground is lexicalized in the verb root, following Talmy's terminology) but they take this meaning when they are found with a directional or goal prepositional phrase (Levin 1993: 106). Therefore, they introduce the path through

lexical unit which lexicalizes $STROLL_00, i.e. *pasear*, while the English language has three, i.e. *stroll, ramble* and *amble;* (2) In the same way, the concept $STAGGER_00 is lexicalized in the Spanish language with just one lexical unit, i.e. *tambalear(se),* while in the English language we can find two, i.e. *stagger* and *stumble;* (3) Similarly, +WANDER_00 has two lexical units annotated in the English Lexicon, i.e. *wander* and *roam,* and just one in the Spanish Lexicon, i.e. *vagar;* (4) The concept $PLOD_00 is lexicalized in English through two lexical units, i.e. *plod* and *trudge,* while in Spanish this concept is paraphrased in the absence of lexical units.

26. In this LS, +WALK_00 can be substituted by the corresponding concept from (15) to (21) but since they are hyponyms of +WALK_00 in the ontological taxonomy this LS embraces them all.

27. For example, the LT of *plod* in LCM would be something like [LOC_{IN}(land) INSTR(feet)] Manner(heavily, difficult) Propt(feeling_type: tiredness)] [**do** (x, [**plod** (x)])], consisting of two modules: (1) a semantic module, and (2) a logical representation or *Aktionsart* module (Mairal-Usón and Ruiz de Mendoza 2008: 165). The semantic module of the LT enriches the LS with pragmatic and semantic parameters, but in FGKB many of those semantic details are present in the TF and MP of the concept.

satellites (again is Talmy's terminology) supporting Talmy's classification of English as a satellite-framed language. The following corpus examples illustrate the point:

(25) a. *Stroll into town and you'll find a great choice of restaurants... (BNC/3/AMO/W_advert)*
b. *He and Doyle trotted across the cracked patio and into the house through the back door (BNC/CES/W_fict_prose)*
c. *Marguerite marched to the front door of the shop and flung it open (COCA/2011/FIC/Bk:RoyalLikeness)*
d. *Just at that moment a man staggered out of the door of the bank (BNC/A77/W_non_ac_soc_science)*

Corpus searching returned hits for all English verbs in (23) above, although we have only included here some examples. As we stated before, they are *activity* verbs turning into *accomplishments* with the presence of the directional phrase therefore the construction is turning atelic verbs into telic and recovering from the Ontology the argument goal. Figure 5 illustrates this three-level inter-relation:

Very few hits were retrieved in the case of the Spanish verbs under study with a directional phrase like those in (26a) and (26b). Examples such as (26c) and (26d), in which the verb root lexicalizes the path and manner is introduced through satellites, were much more frequent what is basically supporting Talmy's classification of the Spanish language as a verb-framed language:

(26) a. *[...] hizo una reverencia y trotó hacia una camioneta (CEMD/19-F/Los hombres de a caballo)* ([...] made a bow and trotted towards a truck).
b. *Paseé hasta un pequeño mirador (CEMD/18-F/Manzanos)* (I walked to a small "viewpoint"/ *mirador*).
c. *Zan y Don Pedro Luis se fueron paseando hacia la ermita (CEMD/18/Jarrapellejos)* (Zan and Mr. Pedro Luis departed/left strolling towards the chapel).
d. *Los dormidos vinieron trotando donde estaban los demás (CEMD/18/La edad de Oro: publicación mensual... dedicada a los niños)* (The asleep came trotting to where the rest were)[28]

CONCEPTUAL LEVEL = TF:(xl)Agent (x2)Theme (x3)Location (x4)Origin (x5)Goal

LEXICAL LEVEL = **do**' (x2 [+**WALK_00** (x2)])

GRAMMATICAL LEVEL= **do**' (x2, [+**WALK_00** (x2)]) & INGR (NOT) +**BE_02** (x5, x2)

Figure 5. Directional phrase with non-directed motion verbs

28. Our translations. They are literal and may be ungrammatical.

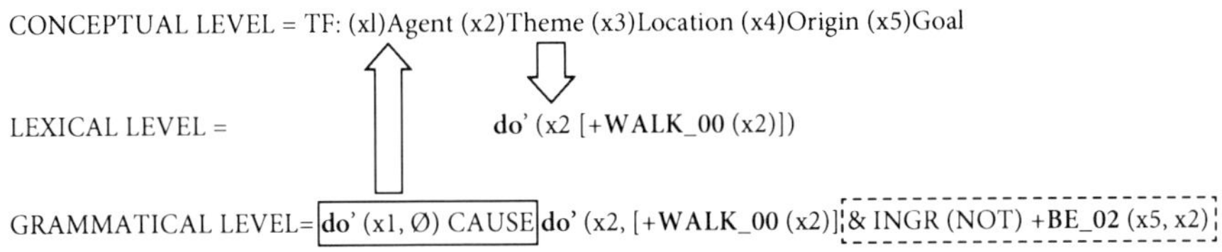

Figure 6. Causative path resultative/induced action alternation

The induced action alternation in Levin's terms or the causative path resultative, a subtype of the caused-motion construction, in Goldberg & Jackendoff (2004) demands the presence of an Agent causer (animate volitional entity) which induces a causee (the theme) to act or move. Hence, the (x1)Agent from the Ontology is recovered in the construction. Figure 6 above illustrates this point:

As Levin herself notices, in the transitive causative use, verbs are usually accompanied by a directional phrase which adds information about path. Examples (27b)-(27e) below illustrate this point and are the reason why we have added the & INGR +BE_02 (x5, x2) as an addition at the end of the constructional template. In examples such as (27b), the element of the path specified is that of goal or end-point (*back home)* in which cases the event turns telic.[29]

(27) a. *He'd walked his dog in the town square in the early morning (COCA/2011/FIC/BK:Scotched)*

b. *I walked the grandkids back home (COCA/2011/FIC/Analog)*

c. *He marched the heavily armored Crusaders across a treeless plain (COCA/2008/MAG/MilitaryHist)*

d. *The scientist ran the rats through the maze* (example taken from Levin 1993: 31)

e. *They waited while Crane trotted his horse across to the Tower. (BNC/31/BMX/W_fict_prose)*

Not all the English verbs under study work with this construction. The corpora used only retrieved examples for *walk, run, march, trot* and *jog,* respectively connected to the concepts +WALK_00, +RUN_00, $MARCH_01 and $TROT_00. The lexical units belonging to $PLOD_00, $STAGGER_00, $STROLL and +WANDER_00 returned no hits.

In the CEMD, we only found examples of this construction with the verb *pasear* 'stroll' and *marchar* 'march'. What is more, in those examples, these two verbs appeared with very restricted collocations (the direct object having usually the selectional restriction of being dogs or horses) and very low-frequency. Examples such as (28a) and (28b), where verb roots express the co-event, i.e. manner of motion, were very few. Meanwhile, cases such as (28c) and (28d), where verb roots encode the path and the

29. However, this turning from atelic to telic is a consequence of the directional phrase not of the recovery of the Agent causer of the causative path resultative.

manner of motion is introduced through an infinite in a verbal periphrasis, had a higher frequency:

(28) a. *La vecina del cuarto «A» paseaba a su perro por la vereda (CEMD/19-F/El Nombre Prestado)* (* the neighbour from the fourth floor strolled her dog through the path)
b. *El marqués ordenó a Clindor que pasease su caballo durante un cuarto de hora alrededor del patio (CEMD/18/Los caballeros de Bois-Doré)* (* the marquis ordered Clindor to stroll his horse for a quarter of an hour around the patio)
c. *Me levanté temprano para sacar a pasear al perro hasta la Avenida 9 de Julio (WebCorp/http://resisteunarchivo.blogspot.com/2009/07/hace-20-anos-el-primer-dia-de-la-tv.html)* (I woke up early to take out the dog to stroll up to 9 de Julio Avenue)
d. *Guardaos de hacer marchar vuestras tropas contra él, repuso el conde. (CEMD/18/Don Juan I de Castilla ó La...)* (Beware of making your troops march against him, said the Count)

Finally, the resultative construction or, in Goldberg & Jackendoff's (2004) terms, causative property resultative, describes the state achieved by the referent of a completely new noun phrase (x6) as a result of the action named by the verb; see Figure 7 below.

The following examples are used by Levin (1993: 100, 266,) and Levin and Rappaport (1999: 199) respectively:

(29) a. *Belinda walked the soles off her shoes.*
b. *Tom ran the soles off his shoes.*
c. *The joggers ran the pavement thin.*

Following Cortés (2007) the verbal subevent -here the manner of motion verb *walk*- describes the means by which the constructional subevent (i.e. the soles of the shoes being off) takes place. Therefore, if we adapt the constructional template from Figure 7 to (29a), for example, we would obtain the following: **do'** (Belinda [**+WALK_00** (x2)]) CAUSE BECOME/INGR **+OFF_00** (the soles of the shoes).[30] Something very

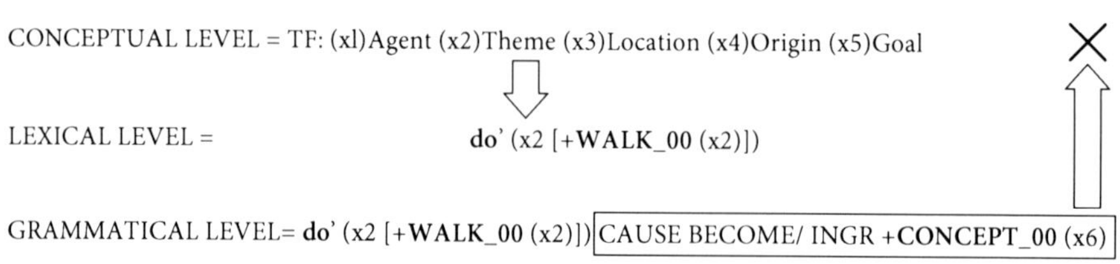

Figure 7. Causative property resultative

30. As can be observed, +CONCEPT_00 can be substituted by any concept from the Ontology that better suits the new resultant state of x6.

interesting of the resultative construction is that this new x6 participant is intrinsically linked to the +CONCEPT_00 (being it +OFF_00, +THIN_00, +FLAT_00, etc.) and is not mapped from the conceptual level. It is a new argument completely idiosyncratic of the construction.

Subsumption of our manner of motion verbs with this construction is of very low frequency at least that is what the corpora suggest. The examples in (29) above are found in the work of Levin (1993), in the case of examples (29a and 29b), and Levin and Rappaport Hovav (1999). However, BNC and COCA offered no hits at all for any of the verbs under study. On the contrary, some examples were retrieved by WebCorp for *walk* and *run*, especially from running web-pages:

(30) a. *6 weeks to save up to get a pair for 20£ that I walk the soles out of in a couple of month* <WebCorp/http://www.guardian.co.uk/commentisfree/2009/sep/30/welfare-public-spending-pensions>

b. *Now every time I get the blues I walk the soles right off my shoes* <WebCorp/http://www.stlyrics.com/songs/f/flattandscruggs16927/downtheroad464971.htm>

c. *The man who ran the soles of his feet off* <http://www.webcorp.org.uk/live/view.jsp?query=ran+the+soles&url=http%3A%2F%2Fwww.amazon.ca%2FInsi de-Delta-Force-Americas-Counterterrorist%2Fdp%2F0385336039>

Following Pérez Hernández and Peña Cervel (2009: 59), although web-based corpora search tools have obvious disadvantages, as the impossibility to replicate an experiment in an exact way at a later time due to updates of web-pages or the lack of liability of some of the services provided by the engine, "where the BNC retrieved no hits, WebCorp provided us with a small, but extremely valuable set of real use examples of the verbs under consideration." Accordingly, our examples in (30), even with low-frequency and being taken from web-based corpora, show the construction is being used with manner of walking/running verbs.

Interestingly enough, the construction is used only with lexical units belonging to +WALK_00 and +RUN_00, which are high in the hierarchical structure and show less manner details in their MPs. Meanwhile, none of the lexical units of the rest of terminal concepts analyzed, which are lower in the taxonomic structure and present more fine-grained manner details ($STROLL_00, $STAGGER_00, $PLOD_00, $TROT_00, etc.) seem to be able to fuse with the causative property resultative.

In the Spanish Grammaticon this construction is incompatible with Spanish manner of walking and running verbs and consequently no examples were found in the different Spanish corpora consulted.

8. Conclusions

The aim of this work has been to trace a group of verbs of motion (in English and Spanish)- such as *walk, caminar, andar, trudge, plod, stumble, run, correr, trot, trotar* or *jog* – from top to bottom and vice versa in FGKB, that is, from the Ontology to the Grammaticon passing through the Lexicon, in order to ascertain how the conceptual non-linguistic knowledge and the linguistic knowledge interact. At the same time, attention has been paid to the manner and path/result components present in the MPs of concepts in the Ontology in order to observe how Talmy's lexicalization patterns and typology of languages work in a practical setting such as FGKB.

Thus, building on the data obtained, we can state some very brief concluding observations. Concepts with path or result specifications in their MPs (i.e. +ARRIVE_00, +ENTER_00 and +LEAVE_00) do not have a big impact in the third level of the knowledge base, i.e. the Grammaticon, as concepts with manner components do (+WALK_00, $STAGGER_00, $TROT_00, etc.). On the contrary, concepts pertaining to human and animal locomotion with manner specifications in the MPs do fuse with some constructions that affect the verb's transitivity. Thus, for example, some lexical unit(s) linked to +WALK_00, +RUN_00, $MARCH_01 and $TROT_00 change from non-causative to causative *Aktionsarten* when fusing in the causative path resultative, recovering from the conceptual base an agent that had not been lexicalized in the verb. Likewise, verbal predicates such as *walk* and *run* fuse in the causative property resultative, incorporating a direct object completely idiosyncratic to the construction. In accordance with Talmy´s lexicalization patterns, *walk* and *run* lexicalize the event of motion together with the manner in which it takes place, i.e. the co-event. The fact that there is not a result feature present anywhere in the conceptual base makes possible for the verbs to fuse with constructions that add a resultant state, e.g. *the joggers ran the pavement thin*. Hence, the construction would be adding information that is not conceptualized in the concept nor lexicalized in the verb. In contrast, verbs such as *enter, arrive* and *leave* do have a result component lexicalized in the verb root and that is why their fusion with a resultative construction is never activated in the Grammaticon. Finally, the directional phrase with non-directed motion verbs has proved to be very prolific with English manner verbs and less frequent with the Spanish ones, which supports Talmy's typology of languages. At the same time, it confirms that, in English, information about the manner of motion is usually given in the verb root (in other words, in the background) and path information foregrounded through satellites (e.g. directional phrases). This may be the reason why the English corpora consulted retrieved hundreds of examples like the ones in (25). In the Spanish corpus, on the other hand, examples of verb roots encoding manner with path in the satellites, like *trotó hacia una camioneta ('trotted towards a truck')*, were very few while examples with verb roots encoding path and manner of motion being introduced through satellites (e.g. gerund) abounded.

References

Allen, James F. 1983. Maintaining knowledge about temporal intervals. *Communications of the ACM* 26(11): 832–843.

BYU-BNC: British National Corpus. <http://corpus2.byu.edu/bnc/> (15 July 2012).

Cifuentes-Férez, Paula. 2009. *A Crosslinguistic Study on the Semantics of Motion Verbs in English and Spanish*. Munich: Lincom.

Corpus of Contemporary American English. <http://corpus2.byu.edu/coca/> (15 July 2012).

Corpus del Español de Mark Davies. <http://www.corpusdelespanol.org/> (15 July 2012).

Cortés Rodríguez, Francisco J. 2007. Building a onstructicon: Templates, constraints and unification. Ms, Universidad de La Laguna.

Gonzálvez-García, Francisco & Butler, Christopher S. 2006. Mapping functional-cognitive space. *Annual Review of Cognitive Linguistics* 4: 39–96.

Goldberg, Adele E. 1995. *Constructions: A Construction Grammar Approach to Argument Structure*. Chicago IL: University of Chicago Press.

Goldberg, Adele E. & Jackendoff, Ray. 2004. The English resultative as a family of constructions. *Language* 80: 532–568.

Jiménez-Briones, Rocío & Pérez-Cabello de Alba, Beatriz. 2011. An account of selection restrictions in Role and Reference Grammar. *Revista Canaria de Estudios Ingleses* 62: 99–122.

Jiménez-Briones, Rocío & Luzondo Oyón, Alba. 2011. Building ontological meaning in a lexico-conceptual knowledge base. *Onomazein* 23: 11–40.

Levin, Beth. 1993. *English Verb Classes and Alternations: A Preliminary Investigation*. Chicago IL: The University of Chicago Press.

Levin, Beth & Rappaport Hovav, Malka. 1999. Two structures for compositionally derived events. In *Proceedings of SALT 9* [Cornell Linguistics Circle Publications], 199–223. Ithaca NY: Cornell University.

Mairal-Usón, Ricardo & Periñán Pascual, Carlos. 2009. The anatomy of the lexicon component within the framework of a conceptual knowledge base. *Revista Española de Lingüística Aplicada* 22: 217–244.

Mairal-Usón, Ricardo & Ruiz de Mendoza Ibáñez, Francisco José. 2008. Levels of description and explanation in meaning construction. In *Deconstructing Constructions* [Studies in Language Companion Series 107], Chrisopher S. Butler & Juan Martín Arista (eds), 153–198. Amsterdam: John Benjamins.

Mora Gutiérrez, Juan Pablo. 2001. Directed motion in English and Spanish. In *Estudios de Lingüística del Español* 11. <http://elies.rediris.es/elies.html>.

Pérez Hernández, Lorena & Peña Cervel, María Sandra. 2009. Pragmatic and cognitive constraints on lexical-constructional subsumption. *Atlantis. Journal of the Spanish Association of Anglo-American Studies* 31(2): 57–73.

Periñán Pascual, Carlos & Arcas Túnez, Francisco. 2007a. Cognitive modules of an NLP knowledge base for language understanding. *Procesamiento del Lenguaje Natural* 39: 197–204.

Periñán Pascual, Carlos & Arcas Túnez, Francisco. 2007b. Deep semantics in an NLP knowledge base. In *12th Conference of the Spanish Association for Artificial Intelligence*, 279–288. Salamanca: Universidad de Salamanca.

Periñán Pascual, Carlos & Arcas Túnez, Francisco. 2010. The architecture of FunGramKB. In *7th International Conference on Language Resources and Evaluation, Proceedings of the Seventh International Conference on Language Resources and Evaluation, European Language Resources Association (ELRA)*, 2667–2674. Valeta, Malta.

Periñán Pascual, Carlos & Mairal-Usón, Ricardo. 2009. Bringing Role and Reference Grammar to natural language understanding. *Procesamiento del Lenguaje Natural* 43: 265–273.

Periñán Pascual, Carlos & Mairal-Usón, Ricardo. 2010a. La gramática de COREL: Un lenguaje de representación conceptual. *Onomázein* 21 (1): 11–45.

Periñán Pascual, Carlos & Mairal-Usón, Ricardo. 2010b. Enhancing UniArab with FunGramKB. *Procesamiento del Lenguaje Natural* 44: 19–26.

Periñán Pascual, Carlos & Mairal-Usón, Ricardo. 2011. The coherent methodology in FunGramKB. *Onomázein* 24: 13–33.

Procter, Paul (ed.). 1978. *Longman Dictionary of Contemporary English*. Harlow: Longman.

Real Academia Española: Banco de datos (CREA). *Corpus de referencia del español actual.* <http://www.rae.es> (10 August 2012).

Ruiz de Mendoza Ibáñez, Francisco José & Mairal-Usón, Ricardo. 2007. High-level metaphor and metonymy in meaning construction. In *Aspects of Meaning Construction in Lexicon and Grammar,* Günter Radden, Klaus-Michael Köpcke, Thomas Berg & Peter Siemund (eds), 33–49. Amsterdam: John Benjamins.

Ruiz de Mendoza Ibáñez, Francisco José & Mairal-Usón, Ricardo. 2008. Levels of description and constraining factors in meaning construction: An introduction to the Lexical Constructional Model. *Folia Linguistica* 42(2): 355–400.

Sacramento Lechado, Elena & Guerra García, Fátima. 2011. Ontología de la base de conocimiento FunGramKB: Desarrollo y creación de conceptos, III Coloquio de Lingüística Andrés Bello, Universidad de La Laguna, Tenerife.

Sacramento Lechado, Elena & Guerra García, Fátima. 2012. Ontología de la base de conocimiento FunGramKB: Desarrollo y creación de conceptos. En *Estudios sobre lengua, cultura y cognición,* Gerd Wotjak, Dolores García Padrón & María del Carmen Fumero Pérez (eds), 215–226. Frankfurt: Peter Lang.

Talmy, Leonard. 1985. Lexicalization patterns: Semantic structure in lexical forms. In *Language Typology and Syntactic Description,* Vol. III: *Grammatical Categories and the Lexicon,* Timothy Shopen (ed.), 57–149. Cambridge: CUP.

Talmy, Leonard. 2000. *Towards a Cognitive Semantics.* Cambridge MA: The MIT Press.

Van Valin, Jr., Robert D. 2005. *Exploring the Syntax-Semantics Interface.* Cambridge: CUP.

Van Valin, Jr., Robert D. & LaPolla, Randy. 1997. *Syntax, Structure, Meaning and Function.* Cambridge: CUP.

Vendler, Zeno. 1967. *Linguistics in Philosophy.* Ithaca NY: Cornell University Press.

WebCorp Live. *Concordance the Web in Real-time.* <http://www.webcorp.org.uk/live/> (15 July 2012).

Low-level situational cognitive models within the Lexical Constructional Model and their computational implementation in FunGramKB*

Francisco José Ruiz de Mendoza Ibáñez
University of La Rioja

This paper investigates the notion of low-level situational cognitive model, its role in linguistic description and its possible computational treatment in the knowledge base FunGramKB. Low-level situational models are exploited metonymically to produce situation-based implicatures. When such inferences become stably associated with a formal pattern, they give rise to implicational constructions. Other kinds of construction make use of different kinds of cognitive model. For example, argument-structure constructions are based on high-level non-situational cognitive models. The paper then provides a typology of low-level situational cognitive models, which can be roughly equated with Schank and Abelson's now classical notion of script. Schank and Abelson's classification into *situational, personal* and *instrumental* scripts is revised and refined to make it include a further division into *simple*, *complex* and *composite* scripts. Simple scripts capture sequences of actions, while complex scripts consist of chained sequences of subscripts and composite scripts are combinations of independent subscripts. Since scripts are cases of procedural knowledge, which is included in the so-called *cognicon* of FunGramKB, the paper explores the incorporation of this typology into the architecture of this part of the knowledge base. This incorporation is argued to endow the cognicon with greater descriptive parsimony, which results in a more efficient computational implementation. Finally, the paper uses the FunGramKB representation metalanguage COREL as an adequate way of supplying precise descriptions in terms of event structure variables and their sequencing, which turns out to be useful to enhance descriptive adequacy in the linguistic model itself.

* Financial support for this research has been provided by the Spanish Ministry of Economy and Competitiveness, grant FFI 2010-17610/FILO.

1. Introduction

The assumption that word meaning cannot be understood independently of the vast repository of encyclopedic knowledge to which it is linked has not gone unnoticed in two different related fields of research: artificial intelligence (AI) and theoretical linguistics. From the 1970s to the mid 1980s, AI theorists proposed the notions of *frames* (Minsky 1975), *schemata* or *schemas* (Rumelhart 1975), *scripts* (Schank & Abelson 1977), and *scenarios* (Sanford & Garrod 1981). For example, according to Minsky, a *frame* is a memory structure that people select when faced with a new situation (or when making a substantial change in their view of a present problem). Minsky defines a frame as a data-structure for representing a stereotyped situation, like being in a certain kind of living room, or going to a child's birthday party. Connected to each frame, it is possible to find several kinds of information. Some of this information is about how to use the frame, some about what one can expect to happen next and some about what to do if these expectations are not confirmed.

In the early 1980s, these constructs, which were originally created in order to organize and encapsulate world knowledge into a computer-readable format, went beyond the domain of AI and Natural Language Processing (NLP) into linguistics through discourse studies (e.g. Beaugrande & Dressler 1981; Graesser 1981; Van Dijk & Kintsch 1983; Kintsch 1988) and Frame Semantics (Fillmore 1982; Fillmore & Atkins 1992). Moreover, linguistic models, especially Cognitive Linguistics, began to work in this direction and several proposals were developed in order to account for the nature of encyclopedic knowledge, namely, *frames* (Fillmore 1975, 1977, 1982, 1985; Fillmore & Atkins 1992)[1], *domains* (Langacker 1987) and *Idealized Cognitive Models* (ICMs) (Lakoff 1987). The notion of frame and its implications for linguistic description and explanation has been the object of an impressive amount of study; interested readers may be referred to Atkins, Fillmore & Johnson (2003), Fillmore, Johnson & Petruck (2003), Ruppenhofer et al. (2010), and Baker & Ruppenhofer (2002) for developments of Frame Semantics into the FrameNet Project, and to Boas (2005) for in-depth linguistics exploitation.

Within this context, the present paper has two aims. The first aim is to revise the notion of ICM by drawing on the explanatory potential of the Lexical Constructional Model (LCM). As will be shown below, the LCM is a meaning construction model with a functional-cognitive grounding (Ruiz de Mendoza & Mairal 2008, 2011; Mairal & Ruiz de Mendoza, 2009; Ruiz de Mendoza 2013; cf. Butler 2009, 2013 for two overviews of its origins and an assessment of its strengths and challenges). The LCM provides a far-reaching typology of cognitive models (or coherent schematizations of our experience) based on two basic taxonomic criteria: (i) the situational versus non-situational nature of knowledge; and (ii) the degree of genericity of their elements. The

1. Frame Semantics has resulted in the FrameNet Project <https://framenet.icsi.berkeley.edu/fndrupal/>, a multilingual lexical database.

combination of these two criteria gives rise to the following cognitive model types: *low-level non-situational models, low-level situational models, high-level situational models, high-level non-situational models.* We anticipate that the LCM low-level situational models correspond to a large extent with the classical notion of *script*, first postulated by Schank and Abelson (1977). The second aim is to show how low-level situational cognitive models are represented in a knowledge engineering project like FunGramKB <www.fungramkb.com>.

In order to meet our two aims we have organized this paper as follows: Section 2 provides a classification of the typology of cognitive models within the framework of the LCM. Section 3 deals with the formal nature of low-level situational cognitive models (LLSC) and offers three different parameters that enrich former descriptions like Schank and Abelson's scripts. Section 4 is concerned with the representation of LLSC in the FunGramKB *cognicon*. Finally, Section 4 provides some concluding remarks.

2. Cognitive modeling in the LCM

Drawing on Lakoff's (1987) typology of ICMs, Ruiz de Mendoza (1996) proposed to classify ICMs into two broad types: *operational* and *non-operational*. The latter cover propositional (i.e. frames) and image-schematic constructs, while the former refer to metaphoric and metonymic processes. *Frames* (cf. Fillmore 1985; Fillmore & Atkins 1992) are coherent schematizations of our experience capturing relations among entities and their properties; for example, skydiving requires people jumping out of a flying aircraft and falling freely for a given amount of time and using their parachutes to slow down during the final part of the fall. The skydiver, the aircraft and the parachute are essential frame entities that relate as described on the basis of world knowledge. *Image schemas* (Johnson 1987; Peña 2008) are topological constructs that abstract structural relations away from the space and time properties of objects in the world. To give an example, consider the notion of container, which generalizes over the structural properties of man-made objects such as bottles, cartons, cans, and jars, and either artificial or naturally-occurring three-dimensional spaces and other bounded regions in space, such as caves, pools, ponds, gardens, etc. As a refinement of Lakoff's proposal, Ruiz de Mendoza and Pérez (2003) and Ruiz de Mendoza (2011) have given linguistic evidence that both metaphor and metonymy are cognitive operations (rather than cognitive models) acting on non-operational cognitive models. This is not unreasonable if we consider what Lakoff's (1993) definition of metaphor as a cross-domain conceptual mapping involves. In Lakoff's now broadly accepted proposal metaphor is constructed by mapping selected structure from a conceptual domain, called the source, to another domain called the target. The function of the mapping is to help us talk and reason about the target domain on the basis of the meaning implications of the source (which Lakoff refers to as the "logic" of the domain). Now, metaphorical source and target domains are made up of either frame structure or image-schematic structure. Mappings involving frame-like structure take place when speakers feel the need to highlight one or more properties or structural elements of an entity or a state of affairs in the target in terms of corresponding source properties and elements of objects and states of affairs in the source. For example, *Your teeth are pearls* maps the smoothness and whitish brightness of the outermost mineral layer of pearls onto corresponding attributes of teeth enamel. Often, we can use either a conventional or a constructed scenario as the source of a metaphor, as in *She feels tossed in a rowboat in a hurricane*, used to talk about a situation of unwanted conflict where the protagonist is at the mercy of other people's violent behavior. Mappings of this kind do not involve abstract structure. By contrast, mappings involving image schemas have abstract targets, such as emotions, states, processes, and actions. For example, states can be seen as locations (*I'm in pain*), changes of state as changes of location (*She went from bad to worse*), processes as motion (*He went into a depression*), actions as transfers (*He gave me a kick*), and so on.

This preliminary classification into operational and non-operational cognitive models was later completed in Ruiz de Mendoza (2007) with a more sophisticated one that takes into account levels of abstraction in cognitive modeling. Thus, Ruiz de Mendoza (2007) makes a further distinction between low-level, primary-level, and high-level ICMs:

- ***Low level:*** non-generic level of conceptual representation created by making well-entrenched, coherent links among elements of our encyclopedic knowledge store. Knowledge of physical (e.g. people, plants, animals, objects) and non-physical entities (e.g. emotions, thoughts) and their relations is part of this level.
- ***Primary level:*** generic level of conceptual representation directly grounded in bodily experience. This level includes not only image schemas, but also our knowledge of motor programs and our visual, auditory, tactile, gustatory and olfactory experience.
- ***High level:*** generic level of conceptual representation created by deriving structure common to multiple low-level models. A set of low-level models, such as specific actions, can give rise to more than one high-level representation. For example, 'hit', 'kick', 'push' are contact-by-impact verbs that can cause motion; they thus underlie, together with other low-level concepts, cause-effect relations; but they can also underlie (controlled and dynamic) action-result relations. These are different from process-result ones, which, although dynamic, are uncontrolled. In combination with cause-effect ones, action-result relations structure high-level actional-causal cognitive models.

Moreover, it is important to consider still one more refinement, according to which propositional cognitive models at any level of abstraction can be divided into *situational* and *non-situational* propositional models. In fact, the LCM has made use of this distinction in order to further distinguish between three kinds of meaning construction levels that go beyond argument structure specifications, i.e. the implicational, the illocutionary, and the discourse levels. Below we introduce this new parameter to identify the nature of concepts at the various descriptive levels of the LCM:

a. **Low-level non-situational models**: house, chair, stone, man, kiss, hit, die, etc. These lie at the basis of the lexical component of the argument-structure level (or level 1) of the LCM.
b. **Low-level situational models**: taking a taxi, playing chess, reading a book, etc. These form part of the implicational level (level 2) in the LCM. They lie at the basis of some constructions. Consider the expression *Who do you think you're talking to?*, which carries the heavily conventionalized implication that the addressee has acted in a way that upsets the speaker. The strength of the conventional implication depends to a large extent on the *do you think* element (cf. *Who are you talking to?*), which thus acquires a fairly stable status within the construction. But the meaning implications can go beyond those obtained on the basis of this constructional mechanism. The *Who Do You Think You're X?* configuration is typically associated with every-day situations where the speaker gets upset when the addressee has behaved in socially inappropriate ways that directly affect the speaker negatively. In this situation the speaker may feel that he has a right to challenge the addressee's behavior.
c. **High-level non-situational models**: such notions as action, process, instrument, etc. are the result of abstracting away properties that low-level non-situational models have in common (e.g. killing, hitting, breaking are actions; burning, growing, dying are processes, etc.). They thus underlie level-1 argument structure constructions, which take in low-level verbal structure. Think, for example, of the resultative expression *She painted the wall green*. The verb *paint* is an action verb that matches the conditions for its use with a resultative construction. Other verbs fit naturally into the construction: *hammer* (*The blacksmith hammered the metal flat*), *wipe* (*They wiped the table clean*), *eat* (*He ate himself sick*), etc. (cf. Ruiz de Mendoza & Luzondo, forthcoming). When they come in pairs (e.g. condition-consequence, evidence-conclusion, time precedence, etc.) they create coherence conditions at the discourse level or level 4 of the LCM; for example, *You should invite her; after all she's your boss* makes use of the conclusion-evidence discourse relation, while *She's your boss, so you should invite her* is based on the converse evidence-conclusion relation (cf. Ruiz de Mendoza & Mairal 2008).
d. **High-level situational models**: This distinction underlies the work carried out by Ruiz de Mendoza and Baicchi (2007) on illocutionary scenarios. Such scenarios, which are constructed by deriving conceptual structure common to multiple low-level situational models, underlie illocutionary constructions. For example, advising is a complex concept that contains generalizations on the speaker trying to make the hearer aware that engaging himself in a given course of action is better for him than pursuing a different one or doing nothing. This scenario is a

high-level situational model constructed on the basis of more specific (i.e. low-level) scenarios where people are actually faced with everyday choices as to whether to buy or sell property, to read one book or another, or where to go on holidays, to give just a few examples. There are constructions that exploit this high-level situational model: *If I Were You, I'd X, Consider/Think About X, You Must/Have To/Need to X, X Is A Good Idea, Why Not X?* (*If I were you, I'd buy that house*; *Consider/think about investing in this company*; *You must/have to/need to go ahead with your project*; *Starting a new business is a good idea*; *Why not take the chance?*) (see Del Campo 2012)

The importance of this approach for our object of analysis in the present paper is based on the still programmatic proposals made for level 2, where low-level situational models are integrated. Such situational models within level 2 of the LCM will provide the linguistic basis for our analysis of script-like structures in a knowledge engineering project.

3. Towards a typology of low-level situational schemata

The LCM low-level situation schemata are closely related to Schank & Abelson's (1977) notion of script, which, as commented above, was formulated within the framework of AI. In what follows, drawing on Schank and Abelson's pioneering work we argue that their initial classification can be enriched by looking at the formal nature of scripts.

Schank & Abelson (1977) proposed the notion of *script*, which is a structure that describes appropriate sequences of events in a particular context or a predetermined and stereotyped sequence of actions that defines a well-known situation. These authors affirmed that not all scripts are of the same kind and distinguished three different

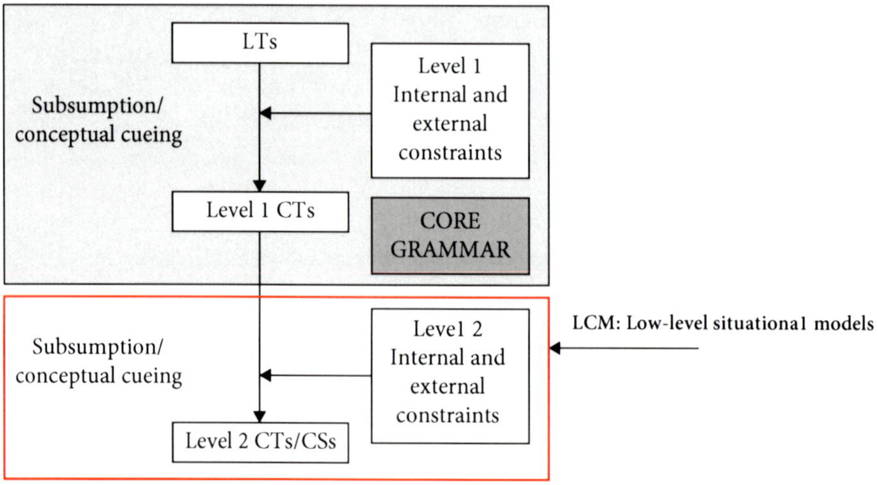

Figure 1.

types. The first type is *situational scripts*, in which (i) a situation is specified, (ii) there are several participants that have interlocking roles to follow, and (iii) the participants share an understanding of what is expected to happen, e.g. "eating in a restaurant". Then, the second type is *personal scripts*, which consist in sequences of possible actions that lead to a desired goal. Personal scripts do not behave in the stylized fashion of situational scripts. All the participants in the personal scripts are not necessarily aware of their participants. A personal script exists solely in the mind of its main actor. Finally, the third type is *instrumental scripts*, which are quite like situational scripts in structure. They describe prescribed sequences of actions, for example "starting a car" or "lighting a cigar" etc. The order of events is very rigid, and each and every one of the events in the script must take place. The main difference between instrumental and situational scripts is found in the number of actors and the overall intention. Instrumental scripts have only one participant. The three types of scripts can occur together in juxtaposition.

In connection with this, we claim that this classification, though basically correct, misses some generalizations regarding the formal nature of scripts. Not all scripts have the same structure: for example, some are more complex than others, a distinction that has important consequences in their representation in a knowledge base. For example, it may be the case that within a given situational script, "going to the theatre", we may find other scripts, for example "pay cash" or "pay by credit card", etc., a feature which shows that the internal structure of a given script may consist of several layers of complexity depending on the formal nature of the script involved[2]. Hence, we thus propose to divide scripts up into *simple*, *complex* and *composite*.

Simple scripts are those that are made of a sequence of actions, each of which is constitutive, i.e. a necessary part of the script. For example, if we consider the script class "having leisure time", we can think of a number of simple scripts that have their own status, that is, they consist of a number of actions, each of which provides a description of the whole script, i.e. "watching TV", "listening to the radio", "reading a book", etc.). If we were asked to identify the number of actions that form part of the simple script "reading", the following would be in order. Note that each action is an integral part of the script and the absence of any of those would not provide a complete description:

– Someone takes a book, a magazine or a newspaper in order to read one of them. Maybe the person who is going to read wants to sit on a chair. Then he or she opens the book, the magazine or the newspaper to start reading. While he is reading, he turns the pages to continue reading. When s/he finishes reading, s/he closes the book, the magazine or the newspaper.

2. For example, as discussed below, the very same notions of "host" and "guest" scripts makes sense within a complex script.

Other examples of simple scripts are the following: "making a phone call", "reading a newspaper", "listening to the news on the radio", "listening to the news on TV", all of which would be grouped under the class script "making use of communication services". A similar case is the group of simple scripts that belong to the script class "attending ceremonies", which groups the following simple scripts: "attending a funeral", "attending a marriage ceremony", "attending a christening ceremony", "attending an inaugural ceremony", "attending a military decoration ceremony: awarding a medal/ distinction", "attending a civil decoration ceremony: awarding a diploma (university/ school)", "awarding a civil merit distinction".

Complex scripts are those that consist of chained sequences of subscripts. The chain is usually non-modifiable both in terms of its constitutive elements and their sequencing. For example, the complex script "going to the airport to take a flight", consists of a number of obligatory subscripts, which occur in a pre-established order. In the case that concerns us here, the following chain of subscripts would provide a complete description of the complex script "going to the airport to take a flight": "buy tickets", "take transportation to the airport", "check in", "get on the plane", "fly to destination", "get off the plane", "reclaim luggage". This chain of subscripts is subjected to a rigid time sequence since each of the previous subevents is a condition for the occurrence of the next. Moreover, if one of them were left out, the resulting description would be incomplete. A similar case is that of the script "going to school to take classes", which consists of the following chain of subscripts: "taking transportation to school", "getting into the building and finding the classroom", "taking the classes", "going to a tutorial", "going to the canteen", "taking transportation back home".

It is interesting to observe, as commented below, that the very nature of complex scripts allows for the possibility to build a whole script into another script: for example, within the script "eating in a restaurant", the "pay cash" script can be activated. Hence, within the same script we may find the presence of one or more scripts that will here be called *guest scripts* in contrast to *host scripts* (cf. below). This interaction possibility gives knowledge engineers the opportunity to introduce culturally-biased knowledge into the cognicon. As shown in Periñán and Mairal (forthcoming), every script is assigned a geographical feature determining the continent, country, etc., where the knowledge is typically true or widely accepted. Thus, FunGramKB is sensitive to "cultural distinctiveness", which is a recurrent feature in procedural knowledge.

Composite scripts consist of a main script, which is, in turn, made up of a number of different scripts called *independent subscripts*. Unlike complex subscripts, none of these independent subscripts is a necessary part of the main script and the order in which they are organized is completely irrelevant. For example, if we consider the composite script "doing the housework", the following independent subscripts are relevant: "washing dishes", "doing the laundry", "making beds", "cleaning the carpets", "vacuum cleaning the floors/ upholstery". None of these is dependent on the other but rather each has its own independent status. In this way, the main script "going out" may consist of the following independent subscripts, among others: "going to the restaurant", "going to the cinema", "going to a thematic park", "going to the disco", "going to have a coffee", "going to the library", etc.

This typology is provisional and it can be refined in future work as the cognicon becomes populated. A further step now is to see how these distinctions can be represented in a knowledge engineering project like FunGramKB.

4. The framework: FunGramKB

Over the past four years, the LCM has gone well beyond the linguistic realm into AI concerns thanks to the implementation of a knowledge base called FunGramKB. FunGramKB is a multipurpose lexico-conceptual knowledge base for natural language processing systems, and more particularly for natural language understanding (Periñán & Arcas 2004, 2005, 2006, 2007, 2010a,b; Periñán & Mairal 2009, 2010, 2012; Mairal & Periñán 2009ab, 2010, etc.). The main advantage of this knowledge base over NLP systems based on scripts and/or schemas in the 1970s and 1980s is that it takes into account a wider variety of constructs or knowledge schemata. As shown in Figure 2, FunGramKB includes two modules, both of which are synergetically interconnected:

a. The *conceptual module* consists of (i) a universal *ontology*, which is linked to language-specific lexica; (ii) a *cognicon*, which captures procedural knowledge (e.g. going to the cinema, climbing mountains, buying and selling, etc.) of the kind that was postulated by Schank and Abelson in their work on scripts; (iii) an *onomasticon*, which stores information about instances of entities and events (e.g. Merkel, Moscow, the Taj Mahal, etc.).[3]
b. The *linguistic module* is language specific and includes a lexical level (a lexicon and a morphicon) and a grammaticon that stores the linguistic properties of constructional schemata.

Firstly, the typology of low-level situation schemata and their classification into simple, complex and composite reside in the cognicon, that is, that part of the ontology that deals with procedural knowledge. The following notational device is used to mark each script: @. Moreover, it is important to note for the purposes of this paper that the three levels of the conceptual module are represented in COREL (*Conceptual Representation Language*), a machine-readable metalanguage that serves as input to a reasoning engine. This means that the formal representation of the inventory of low-level situational schemata will take place in the FunGramKB cognicon and will be represented using COREL. As shown in Periñán and Mairal (2010), COREL is the conceptual language used to describe the properties of the three modules in the cognitive level, i.e. the ontology, the cognicon, and the onomasticon. Hence, the conceptual

3. For reasons of space, it is impossible to provide a detailed description of FunGramKB. Hence, we refer the reader to the project website: <www.fungramkb.com>.

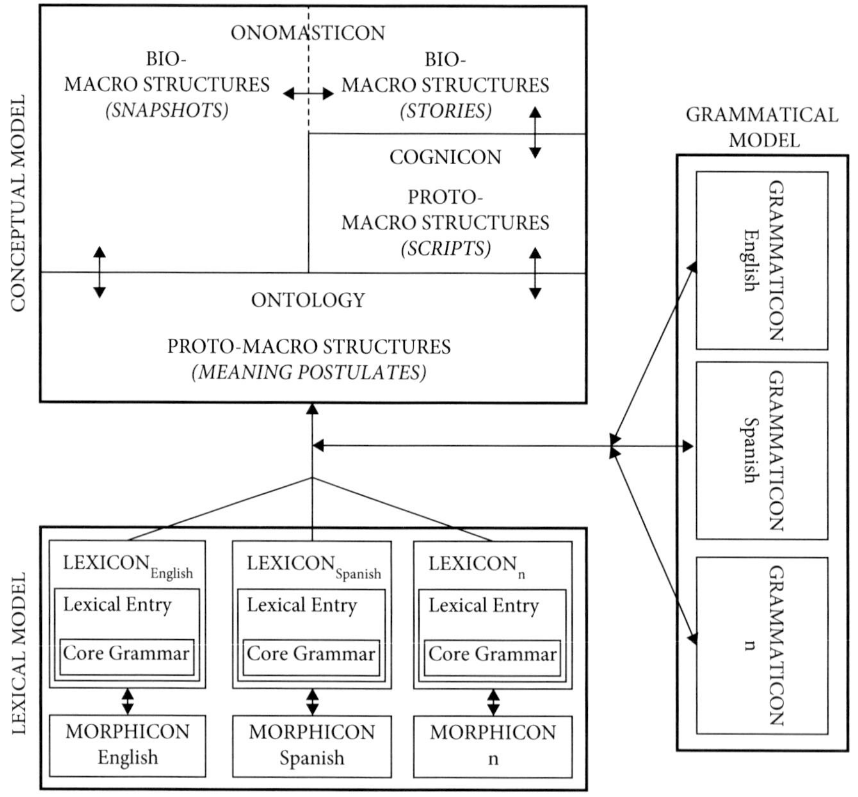

Figure 2.

properties of the cognitive level are expressed in a COREL scheme. A COREL scheme consists of a number of predications expressed by the letters (e_1, e_2, e_n), each expressing a semantic feature of whatever is being described and modified by a number of operators: logical operators (&, ^), reasoning operators (+, *), temporal and aspectual operators, etc. Moreover, basic conceptual units from the ontology, which are symbolized with a +NAMEOFCONCEPT_00 format, are used as defining elements. The following example provides a COREL scheme of the entity "ostrich", which is linked to the terminal conceptual entity $OSTRICH_00 in the ontology[4]:

4. The FunGramKB ontological module consists of three types of conceptual units: (i) metaconcepts, which are symbolized by #, represent cognitive dimensions that are similar to those in other ontological projects; e.g. #COMMUNICATION, #MOTION, # PSYCHOLOGICAL, #STATIVE, etc.; (ii) basic concepts, which are represented by a + and a suffix numerical code of the type 00 or 01, serve to define terminal concepts; +WALK_00, +TRAFFIC_00, +WRITE_00, +SWEET_00, etc. are examples of basic concepts; (iii) terminal concepts, which are expressed by the symbol $, are the last step in the decompositional chain; e.g. $GRASP, $BOW_00, $SUBTITLE_00, etc. This, however, does not mean that these are conceived as primitives but instead what is meant is that these are not used to define other concepts.

(1) +(e1: +BE_00 (x1: $OSTRICH_00)Theme (x2: +BIRD_00)Referent)
*(e2: +BE_01 (x1)Theme (x3: +BIG_00)Attribute)
*((e3: +COMPRISE_00 (x1)Theme (x4: 2 +LEG_00 & 1 +NECK_00) Referent) (e4: +BE_01 (x4)Theme (x5: +LONG_00)Attribute))
*((e5: +COMPRISE_00 (x1)Theme (x6: +FEATHER_00)Referent) (e6: +BE_01 (x6)Theme (x7: +BIG_00 & +SOFT_00)Attribute))
*((e7: +LIVE_01 (x1)Theme (x8)Location) (e8: +BE_01 (x8)Theme (x9: +HOT_00)Attribute))
+(e9: n +FLY_00 (x1)Agent (x1)Theme (x10)Origin (x11)Goal)
*(e10: +RUN_00 (x1)Agent (x1)Theme (x12)Location (x13)Origin (x14)Goal (f1: +FAST_00)Speed)

This representation includes ten different predications, each introducing a different semantic feature. Each predication is preceded by a reasoning operator, either +, if the predication is strict, that is, if it is true in every possible world, or *, which indicates defeasible, i.e. cancellable under certain circumstances. Moreover, basic conceptual units are used as defining elements and a range of different operators is also present: quantifiers (1, 2 4 etc.), negation operators (n in predication e9), logic operators (& in predication e5).

As advanced above, the same metalanguage is used in the two other cognitive modules, the cognicon – as shall be shown in the remainder of this paper– and the onomasticon, as illustrated with the representation of the entity Tah Mahal in COREL:

(2) +(e1: +BE_02 (x1: %TAH_MAHAL_00)Theme (x2: %INDIA_00)Location)
*(e2: +BE_01 (x1)Theme (x3: +WHITE_00 & $MARBLE_00)Attribute)
*(e3: +COMPRISE_00 (x1)Theme (x4: I $DOME_00 & 4 +TOWER_00) Referent)
+(e4: past +BUILD_00 (x1)Theme (x2: %TAH_MAHAL_00)Referent (f1: 1633)Time)
+(e5: past +BE_00 (x2)Theme (x3: %WORLD_HERITAGE_SITE)Referent (f2: 1983)Time)

This representation consists of a number of predications (e1...e5), some of which are strict (+e1, +e4, and +e5) while the other two (*e2 and *e3) are defeasible. Moreover, basic and terminal conceptual units are used as defining elements (+BE_02, +BUILD_00, &MARBEL_00 etc.). Then, the following operators are present: time operators (past in e5), the logical disjunctive operator | in f2, the quantifiers 1 and 4 in e3, etc. This short introduction to the basics of COREL is sufficient to understand the representation of low-level schemata in a knowledge engineering project like FunGramKB, an issue that is the central concern of the following section.

4.1 The representation of low-level situational schemata in the cognicon

Before we discuss how the three types of low-level situational schemata are actually represented, a methodological note is in order. As Periñán (2012) notes, the FunGramKB cognicon follows Allen's (1989) model of time relation. This model is mainly based on the representation of time as a partially-ordered graph where nodes represent events and where arcs are labelled with one or more relations of temporal ordering. According to Allen (1989), every predication that is included in a script represents an event E which is treated as an interval consisting of a pair of time points (i, t), i.e. the starting point (i) and the end time-point (t). The next table shows the interval relations and constraints that are going to be applied in the cognicon.

In order to illustrate how the previous table applies in the case of a description based on procedural knowledge, we have chosen the first nine predications of the @ GOING_TO_A_RESTAURANT script, whose resulting graph is presented later in Figure 3.

Table 1. Interval Relations in the Cognicon

	Interval relations	Constraints
1	Before(E1, E2)	(t1 < i2)
2	Meets(E1, E2)	(i2 = t1)
3	Overlaps(E1, E2)	(i1 < i2) & (i2 < t1) & (t1 < t2)
4	Starts(E1, E2)	(i1 = i2) & (t1 < t2)
5	During(E1, E2)	(i2 < i1) & (t1 < t2)
6	Finishes(E1, E2)	(i2 < i1) & (t1 = t2)
7	Equals(E1, E2)	(i1 = i2) & (t1 = t2)

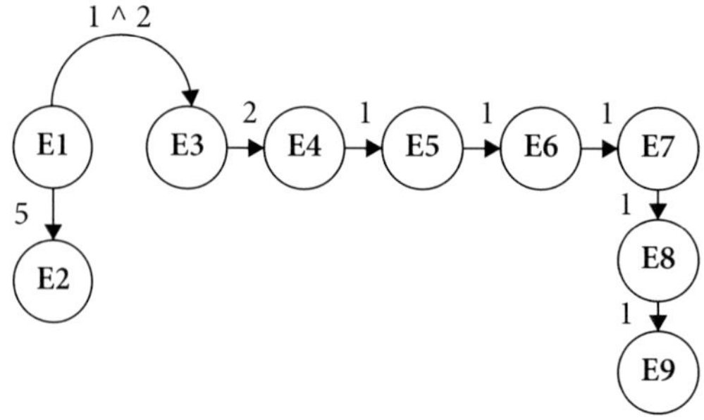

Figure 3.

(3) *(e1: +ENTER_00 (x1)Agent (x2: +CUSTOMER_00)Theme (x3)Location (x4)Origin (x5: +RESTAURANT_00)Goal (f1: (e2: +BE_01 (x2)Theme (x6: +HUNGRY_00)Attribute))Reason)
*(e3: +TAKE_01 (x7:+WAITER_00)Agent (x2)Theme (x5)Location (x8)Origin (x9: +TABLE_00)Goal)
*((e4: +SIT_00 (x2)Theme (x10: +CHAIR_00)Location) (e5: +BE_02 (x10) Theme (x9)Location (f2:m +NEAR_00)Position))
*(e6: +TAKE_01 (x7)Agent (x11: $MENU_00 | $WINE_LIST_00)Theme (x5) Location (x12)Origin (x9)Goal)
*(e7: +GIVE_00 (x7)Agent (x11) Theme (x13)Origin (X2)Goal)
*(e8: +SEE_00 (X2)Theme (x11)Referent)
*((e9: +CHOOSE_00 (x2)Theme (x14: +MEAL_00 & +WINE_00)Referent (e10: +BE_02 (x14)Theme (x11)Location (f3: (x15) +IN_00)Position))

As stated above, simple scripts are those that capture a non-composite situation, i.e. one where there is only a sequence of events that does not need further scripts to be comprehended perfectly. It is true that every single script could be understood as a single one, but there are many scripts that need more than one script to describe all the events that take place in it. In order to show an example of a single script, we have chosen @ READING_00, which has been included within the script class "having leisure time" as is the case of @WATCHING_TELEVISION_00. This script can be perfectly comprehended by itself, that is, we do not need the presence of another script. The first thing we have to do is to describe this case of procedural knowledge in our natural language, so as to facilitate its translation into COREL, which we did before in Section 3 for the case of the present script. We repeat the description here for convenience:

- **@READING_00**: Someone takes a book, a magazine or a newspaper in order to read one of them. Maybe the person who is going to read wants to sit on a chair. Then he or she opens the book, the magazine or the newspaper to start reading. While he is reading, he turns the pages to continue reading. When s/he finishes reading, s/he closes the book, the magazine or the newspaper.

The sequence of events that can take place in @READING_00 are then annotated in COREL as follows:

(4) +(e1:+TAKE_00(x1:+HUMAN_00)Theme(x2:+BOOK_00 ^ +MAGAZINE_00 ^ +NEWSPAPER_00)Referent)
*(e2: +SIT_00 (x1)Theme (x3: +CHAIR_00)Location)
+(e3: +OPEN_01 (x1)Agent (x2)Theme (x4)Location (x5)Origin (x6)Goal (f1:(e4: +COMPRISE_00 (x2)Theme (x7: s +PAGE_00)Referent))Condition)
+(e5: +READ_00 (x1)Theme (x2)Referent)
*(e6: +CHANGE_00 (x1)Theme (x7)Referent)
+(e7: +CLOSE_00 (x1)Agent (x2)Theme (x6)Location (x5)Origin (x4)Goal)

Note that some predications are defeasible while others are strict, depending on whether the event described needs to compulsorily occur. For example, in order to read, it is necessary to actually take a book, a magazine, a newspaper, etc. Hence, the following strict predication would be preceded by the symbol [+]:

(5) +(e1:+TAKE_00 (x1:+HUMAN_00) Theme (x2:+BOOK_00^ +MAGAZINE_00 ^ +NEWSPAPER_00) Referent)

By contrast, one does not have to sit on a chair in order to read something; therefore, this predication becomes defeasible:

(6) *(e2: +SIT_00)

A further step is to delimit the temporal relation between predications according to Allen's temporal relation (cf. below). We have considered that in order to read, one follows a series of temporally ordered events, although, at the same time, a given event may occur more than once, as is the case of predications *e5* and *e6,* which indicate that the subject is reading as s/he turns the page. The following schema represents the @READING_00 temporal relation:

(7) e1 → e2 [Before ^ Equals]
e2 → e3 [Before ^ Equals]
e3 → e5 [Before]
e5 → e6 [Before ^Equals]
e6 → e7 [Before]

Another example of simple script that we have mentioned above is that of @WATCHING_TELEVISION_00. Once again, the first thing we have to do is to write it in natural language.

- **@WATCHING_TELEVISION_00**: Someone sits on a chair and takes the remote control to switch on the television. Then s/he uses the remote control and switches on the TV. S/he watches TV and maybe, while s/he is watching TV, s/he wants to change the channel. S/He takes the remote control again and changes the channel. Then s/he switches off the TV.

Once we have written all the possible sequences of events that can occur in 'watching TV', we proceed to describe @WATCHING_TELEVISION_00 in COREL:

(8) *(e1: +SIT_00 (x1: +HUMAN_00)Theme (x2: +CHAIR_00)Location)
*(e2: +TAKE_00 (x1)Theme (x3: $REMOTE_CONTROL_00)Referent)
*(e3: +USE_00 (x1)Theme (x3)Referent)
+(e4: +OPERATE_00 (x3)Theme (x4: +TELEVISION_00)Referent)
*(e5: +SEE_00 (x1)Theme (x4)Referent)
*(e6: +TAKE_00 (x1)Theme (x3)Referent)
*(e7: +USE_00 (x1)Theme (x3)Referent)
*(e8: +CHANGE_00 (x3)Theme (x5: $CHANNEL_00)Referent)
*(e9: +TAKE_00 (x1)Theme (x3)Referent)
*(e10: +USE_00 (x1)Theme (x3)Referent)
*(e11: $SWITCH_OFF_00 (x3)Theme (x4)Referent)

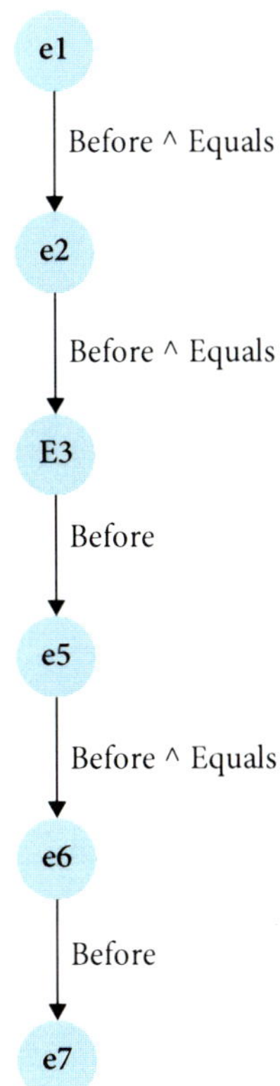

Figure 4.

As was the case with the 'reading' event, we can see that some of the predications are defeasible and/or strict. For instance, in order to watch TV it is necessary to switch it on, so this predication is preceded by [+]:

(9) +(e4: +OPERATE_00)

By contrast, you do not have to sit on a chair in order to watch TV; therefore, this predication is defeasible, as specified in

(10) *(e1: +SIT_00)

Allen's temporal relation shows that in order to watch TV, people follow a series of temporally ordered events, even if at the same time a given event may occur more than once, as is the case of predications *e5* and *e6,* where one is able to watch TV *while* one takes the remote control to change channels. The following schema represents the @WATCHING_TELEVISION_00 temporal relation:

(11) e2 → e3 [Before]
e3 → e4 [Before]
e4 → e5 [Before]
e5 → e6 [Equals]
e6 → e7 [Before]
e7 → e8 [Before]
e8 → e9 [Before]
e9 → e10 [Before]
e10 → e11 [Before]

Complex scripts incorporate others that consist of sequences of subscripts. That is, in the representation of a typical scenario, more than one script can be found and thus the amalgamation of scripts gives rise to a complex script. At this point, it is essential to discuss the notions of host and guest scripts. The former include in their predications guest scripts; as a result, the latter are to be incorporated into a host script. Following Periñán (2012), the following convention has been used to indicate a script activator:

(12) <script ID> (<outcoming mapping>; <incoming mapping>)

For the purposes of illustrating this convention, consider that we are defining the script "going to the restaurant". At one point of this description, we will propose a predication (e22), which will call for a guest script, "pay cash":

(13) @GOING_TO_RESTAURANTS
*(e22: @PAY_CASH_00 (x1: x2, x2: f1))

The representation in (13) shows that the participants x1 and x2 in the host script are mapped onto the x2 and f1 participants of the guest script. We can even go further and find cases where more than one guest script is activated:

(14) *(e22: @PAY_CASH_00 (x1: x2, x2: f1)) ^ @PAY_CARD_00 (x1: x1, x2:x2)

In this case, we use a disjunctive logical operator (^) to represent the two, as is shown in (14). Let us consider @GOING_TO_THE_DISCO_00[5], which is part of the generic script "having leisure time". Since this particular script contains @PAY_CASH_00 as a guest script, we will begin working on this host script. As a consequence, we first have to create the whole sequence of events of @PAY_CASH_00 in natural language:

- **@PAY_CASH_00:** A customer gives a shop assistant/salesman/waiter, etc. money for a service or for something s/he has bought. Then, the shop assistant takes the money and s/he opens the cashbox or till. S/He puts the money into the till. Maybe

5. At the same time, this script is included inside a composite script, since it consists of a set of subscripts, none of which is a necessary part of the main script, so they can be understood on their own.

the customer has paid for something with more money than the item costs, so the shop assistant gives the customer the change and the bill. The shop assistant closes the till and finally the customer keeps the change and the bill.
A prototypical description of @PAY_CASH_00 could be the following:

(15) +(e1: +PAY_00 (x1: +CUSTOMER_00)Agent (x2: +MONEY_00)Theme (x1) Origin (x3: +HUMAN_00)Goal)
*(e2: +OPEN_01 (x3)Agent (x4: $TILL_00)Theme (x5)Location (x6)Origin (x7)Goal)
*(e3: +ENTER_00 (x3)Agent (x2)Theme (x8)Location (x3)Origin (x4) Goal(f1:+IN_00)Position)
*(e4: +STORE_00 (x4)Theme (x2)Referent)
*(e5: +TAKE_01 (x3)Agent (x9: $CHANGE_01 & +INVOICE_00)Theme (x10)Location (x11)Origin (x1)Goal)
*(e6: +GIVE_00 (x3)Agent (x9)Theme (x12)Origin (x1)Goal)
*(e7: +CLOSE_00 (x3)Agent (x4)Theme (x13)Location (x14)Origin (x15) Goal)
*(e8: +STORE_00 (x1)Theme (x9)Referent)

In the script @PAY_CASH_00, the vast majority of predications are defeasible, since they may or may not occur. For instance, when people pay for something that they have bought, consumed, etc., they can give the seller the exact amount of money, so they do not have to receive the change. Similarly, not everybody stores the money in a till. However, all the knowledge we include in the cognicon comes from our own introspection about everyday situations.

In the following temporal relation graph, we can see how preceding predications usually take place before the next predication, i.e. the end of *e1* comes before the beginning of *e2*, and so on. There is one case, however, which is that of predications *e6* and *e7* and *e7* and *e8*, in which such predications may begin and finish at the same time (*Equals* interval) or they may start together but then the preceding predication has to finish before.

(16) e1 → e2 [Before]
e2 → e3 [Before]
e3 → e4 [Before]
e4 → e5 [Before]
e5 → e6 [Before]
e6 → e7 [Starts ^ Equals]
e7 → e8 [Starts ^ Equals]

Once the guest script @PAY_CASH_00 has been created, we now proceed to write in natural language the prototypical sequence of events that occur in @GOING_TO_THE_DISCO_00.

– **@GOING_TO_THE_DISCO_00**: Someone goes into a disco because s/he wants to dance or have a drink. Then s/he goes to the box office to buy a ticket to get into the disco. S/He asks the shop assistant for the tickets. The shop assistant gives the person the ticket and then s/he pays it. S/He goes into the disco and maybe s/he dances to the music. While s/he is dancing, s/he may want to have a drink, so s/he goes to the bar in order to ask for a drink. S/He asks the waiter for a drink. Then the waiter takes a glass and a bottle. The waiter fills in the glass with the drink and then gives it to him/her. The person who is at the disco pays the waiter. Maybe s/he drinks at the same time s/he is dancing. Finally, s/he leaves the disco.

We have described @GOING_TO_THE_DISCO_00 by introducing a guest script @ PAY_CASH_00 (in bold):

(17) *(e1: +ENTER_00 (x1: +HUMAN_00)Agent (x1)Theme (x2)Location (x3) Origin (x4: +BUILDING_00)Goal (f1: (e2: +DANCE_00 (x1)Agent (x1) Theme (x5)Location (x6)Origin (x7)Goal))Reason &(f2:(e3: +INGEST_00 (x1)Agent (x8: +LIQUID_00)Theme (x9)Location (x10)Origin (x11: +STOMACH_00)Goal))Reason)
*(e4: +MOVE_00 (x1)Agent (x1)Theme (x12)Location (x13)Origin (x14: $BOX_OFFICE_00)Goal)
+(e5: +REQUEST_01 (x1)Theme (x15: +TICKET_00)Referent (x16: +WORKER_00)Goal)
+(e6: +GIVE_00 (x16)Agent (x15)Theme (x17)Origin (x1)Goal)
+(e7: +TAKE_00 (x1)Theme (x15)Referent)
+(e8: **@PAY_CASH_00 (x1: x16, x1: x3)**)
+(e9: +MOVE_00 (x1)Agent (x2)Theme (x17)Location (x18)Origin (x19: $DISCO_00)Goal)
*(e10: +DANCE_00 (x1)Agent (x2)Theme (x20)Location (x21)Origin (x22) Goal (f3: (e11: +SOUND_01 (x23: +HUMAN_00 ^ +MACHINE_00)Theme (x24: +MUSIC_00)Referent))Condition)
*(e12: +MOVE_00 (x1)Agent (x1)Theme (x25)Location (x26)Origin (x27: $BAR_00)Goal)
*(e13: +REQUEST_01 (x1)Theme (x28: s +BEVERAGE_00)Referent (x29: +WAITER_00)Goal)
*(e14: +TAKE_00 (x29)Theme (x30: $GLASS_00)Referent (f4: (e15: +BE_01 (x30)Theme (x31: $FULL_N_00)Attribute))Condition)
*(e16: +TAKE_00 (x29)Theme (x32: +BOTTLE_00)Referent (f5:(e17: +BE_01 (x32)Theme (x33: +FULL_00)Attribute))Condition)
*(e18: +FILL_00 (x29)Theme (x30)Referent (f6: (e19: +BE_01 (x30)Theme (x34: +FULL_00)Attribute))Result)
*(e20: +GIVE_00 (x29)Agent (x30)Theme (x35)Origin (x1)Goal)
*(e21: +TAKE_00 (x1)Theme (x30)Theme)
+(e22: **@PAY_CASH_00 (x1: x29, x1: x3)**)

*((e23: +INGEST_00 (x1)Agent (x28)Theme (x30)Location (x36)Origin (x5) Goal) (e24: +BE_02 (x28)Theme (x30)Location (f7:+IN_00)Position))
*(e25: +DANCE_00 (x1)Agent (x1)Theme (x20)Location (x21)Origin (x22) Goal)
*(e26: +LEAVE_00 (x1)Agent (x1)Theme (x19)Location (x37)Origin (x38: +STREET_00)Goal)

We must bear in mind that in predications *e8* and *e22,* @PAY_CASH _00 has been inserted into the whole script. Whereas the participants in *e8* x1 and x16 belong to the host script, participants x1 and x3 are part of the guest script. The same happens with predication *e22.* Besides defeasible or strict predications, *free* and *bound* predications or quantifiers can take part in the script, as is illustrated in predication e1, where *e2* and *e3* depend on *e1* (a) and quantifier *s* appears in x28 (b).

(18) a. *(**e1**: +ENTER_00 (x1: +HUMAN_00)Agent (x1)Theme (x2)Location (x3)Origin (x4: +BUILDING_00)Goal (f1: (**e2**: +DANCE_00 (x1)Agent (x1)Theme (x5)Location (x6)Origin (x7)Goal))Reason &(f2:(**e3**: +INGEST_00 (x1)Agent (x8: +LIQUID_00)Theme (x9)Location (x10)Origin (x11: +STOMACH_00)Goal))Reason)
b. *(e13: +REQUEST_01 (x1)Theme (x28: s +BEVERAGE_00)Referent (x29: +WAITER_00)Goal)

The temporal relation between predications shows what we have seen in previous examples. That is, normally, preceding predications happen before their next predication, but within @GOING_TO_THE_DISCO_00 we find alternations in their temporal relation. For instance, the temporal relation among predications *e10* and *e12* can be of various kinds. Thus, the dancing subevent may occur before, at the same time, or after going to the bar to ask for a drink. The same happens when one is drinking, since one can dance at the same time as one drinks, or one can drink after one finishes dancing, and both predications can start and finish at the same time.

(19) e1 → e4 [Before]
e4 → e5 [Before]
e5 → e6 [Before]
e6 → e7 [Before]
e7 → e8 [Before]
e8 → e9 [Before]
e9 → e10 [Before]
e10 → e12 [Before ^ Meets ^ Overlaps ^ Starts ^ During ^ Equals]
e12 → e13 [Before]
e13 → e14 [Before]
e14 → e16 [Before ^ Meets]
e16 → e18 [Before]
e18 → e20 [Before]

e20 → e21 [Before]
e21 → e22 [Before ^ Meets]
e22 → e23 [Before]
e23 → e25 [Before ^ Meets ^ Overlaps ^ Starts ^ During ^ Equals]
e25 → e26 [Before]

@GOING_TO_THE_DISCO_00 can also be included in the last group of scripts, i.e. composite scripts, given that it introduces a set of subscripts, none of which is a necessary part of the main script. Remember that composite scripts can be understood without making reference to more than one script. In plain words, this group comprises generic scripts that include specifications as script members. As we have seen in the previous @GOING_TO_THE_DISCO_00 example, these scripts can be complex ones, since composite groups can gather the rest of scenarios described above, as is the case of "going out", which is a generic script in which we can find subscripts like "going to a restaurant", "going to the disco", "going to the thematic park", etc. All those scripts belong to a generic one and can be perfectly understood on their own.

5. Conclusion

In this paper we have looked into the notion of low-level situational cognitive model, which lies at the base of level-2 inferential activity in the LCM, and have provided a typology of cognitive models at this level. We have proposed that this typology has to be incorporated into the architecture of the cognicon in FunGramKB, with a view to endowing this part of the knowledge base with greater descriptive parsimony, which will make the system more efficient computationally (cf. Veale, 2006). Second, we have made use of the tools developed in FunGramKB for the computational implementation of so-called procedural knowledge or scripts. We have found that the FunGramKB representation metalanguage COREL goes a long way to supplying the analyst with precise descriptions in terms of event structure variables and their sequencing.

As we have made abundantly clear, the overall architecture of FunGramKB has large areas of correspondence with the structure of the LCM, particularly with level 2, to such an extent that the classification of low-level situational models within level 2 of the LCM provides the linguistic basis for our analysis of scripts in the FunGramKB cognicon. Low-level situational models in the LCM are claimed to be the linguistic counterpart of the scripts that are stored in the cognicon. In using COREL, low-level situational schemata, or natural language scripts, are to be converted into a machine-readable formal language.

It goes without saying that the research presented herein is preliminary. Future developments and refinements will have to work on the identification of more scripts and their classification and their incorporation into the cognicon within the knowledge base. This may require the partial modification of the classification that we have offered. In addition, in order to include a larger amount of scripts, the description should be further objectified for any script. This is due to the fact that scripts are built into our common understanding of everyday-life situations together with the insights obtained from searches into dictionaries, encyclopedias, thesauri, etc.

References

Allen, James F. 1989. Maintaining knowledge about temporal intervals. In *Readings in Qualitative Reasoning About Physical Systems,* Daniel S. Weld & Johan de Kleer (eds), 361–372. San Francisco CA: Morgan Kaufmann.

Atkins, Sue, Fillmore, Charles J. & Johnson, Christopher R. 2003. Lexicographic relevance: Selecting information from corpus evidence. *International Journal of Lexicography* 16(3):251–280.

Baker, Colin F. & Ruppenhoffer, Josef. 2002. FrameNet's frames vs. Levin's verb classes. In *Proceedings of the 28th Annual Meeting of the Berkeley Linguistics Society,* Julie Larson & Mary Paster (eds), 27–38.

de Beaugrande, Robert & Dressler, Wolfgang U. 1981. *Introduction to Text Linguistics.* London: Longman.

Boas, Hans C. 2005. From theory to practice: Frame semantics and the design of FrameNet. In *Semantik im Lexikon,* Stefan Langer & Daniel Schnorbusch (eds), 129–160. Tübingen: Narr.

Butler, Christpher S. 2009. The Lexical Constructional Model: Genesis, strengths and challenges. In *Deconstructing Constructions* [Studies in Language Companion Series 107], Christopher S. Butler & Javier Martín Arista (eds), 117–151. Amsterdam: John Benjamins.

Butler, Christopher S. 2013. Constructions in the Lexical Constructional Model. In *Linking Constructions into Functional Linguistics: The Role of Constructions in a Functional Grammar* [Studies in Language Companion Series 145], Brian Nolan & Elke Diedrichsen (eds), 271–294. Amsterdam: John Benjamins.

Del Campo Martínez, Nuria. 2012. A constructional account of advising: Construal operations and social conventions. *Atlantis: Revista de la Asociación Española de Estudios Anglo-Norteamericanos* 33: 115–132.

Fillmore, Charles J. 1975. An alternative to checklist theories of meaning. In *Proceedings of the First Annual Meeting of the Berkeley Linguistics Society,* 123–131. Amsterdam: North Holland.

Fillmore, Charles J. 1977. Scenes-and-frames semantics. In *Linguistic Structures Processing,* Antonio Zampolli (ed.), 55–82. Amsterdam: North Holland.

Fillmore, Charles J. 1982. Frame Semantics. In *Linguistics in the Morning Calm,* Linguistic Society of Korea (ed.), 111–138. Seoul: Hanshin.

Fillmore, Charles J. 1985. Frames and the semantic understanding. *Quaderni di Semantica* VI(2): 222–254.

Fillmore, Charles J. & Atkins, B.T. Sue. 1992. Towards a frame-based lexicon: The semantics of RISK and its neighbors. In *Frames, Fields, and Contrast: New Essays in Semantics and Lexical Organization,* Adrienne Lehrer & Eva Kittay (eds), 75–102. Hillsdale NJ: Lawrence Erlbaum Associates.

Fillmore, Charles J., Johnson, Christopher R. & Petruck, Miriam R.L. 2003. Background to Framenet. *International Journal of Lexicography* 16(3): 235–250.

Graesser, C. 1981. *Prose Comprehension Beyond the Word.* New York: Springer-Verlag.

Johnson, Mark. 1987. *The Body in the Mind: The Bodily Basis of Meaning, Imagination, and Reason*. Chicago IL: University of Chicago Press.

Kintsch, Walter. 1988. The use of knowledge in discourse processing: A construction-integration model. *Psychological Review* 95: 163–182.

Lakoff, George. 1987. *Wome, Fire, and Dangerous Things: What Categories Reveal About the Mind*. Chicago IL: University Press.

Lakoff, George. 1993. The contemporary theory of metaphor. In *Metaphor and Thought*, 2nd. edn, Andrew Ortony (ed.), 202–251. Cambridge MA: CUP.

Langacker, Ronald W. 1987. *Foundations of Cognitive Grammar*, Vol 1: *Theoretical Prerequisites*. Stanford CA: Stanford University Press.

Mairal Usón, Ricardo & Periñán-Pascual, Carlos. 2009a. Teoría lingüística y representación del conocimiento: Una discusión preliminar. In *Tendencias en lingüística general y aplicada*, Dolores García Padrón & Maria del Carmen Fumero Pérez (eds), 155–168. Berlín: Peter Lang.

Mairal Usón, Ricardo & Periñán-Pascual, Carlos. 2009b. The anatomy of the lexicon within the framework of an NLP knowledge base. *Revista Española de Lingüística Aplicada* 22: 217–244.

Mairal Usón, Ricardo & Periñán-Pascual, Carlos. 2010. Teoría lingüística y representación del conocimiento: Una discusión preliminar. In *Tendencias en lingüística general y aplicada*, Dolores García Padrón & Maria del Carmen Fumero Pérez (eds), 155–168. Berlin: Peter Lang.

Mairal Usón, Ricardo & Ruiz de Mendoza, Francisco José. 2009. Levels of description and explanation in meaning construction. In *Deconstructing Constructions* [Studies in Language Companion Series 107], Christopher S. Butler & Javier Martín Arista (eds),153–198. Amsterdam: John Benjamins.

Minsky, Marvin. 1975. A Framework for Representing Knowledge. MIT-AI Laboratory Memo 306.

Peña Cervel, Sandra. 2008. Dependency systems for image-schematic patterns in a usage-based approach to language. *Journal of Pragmatics* 40(6): 1041–1066.

Periñán-Pascual, Carlos. 2012. The situated common-sense knowledge in FunGramKB. *Review of Cognitive Linguistics* 10(1): 184–214.

Periñán-Pascual, Carlos & Arcas Túnez, Francisco. 2004. Meaning postulates in a lexico-conceptual knowledge base. In *15th International Workshop on Databases and Expert Systems Applications*, 38–42. Los Alamitos CA: IEEE.

Periñán-Pascual, Carlos & Arcas Túnez, Francisco. 2005. Microconceptual-knowledge spreading in FunGramKB. In *Proceedings on the 9th IASTED International Conference on Artificial Intelligence and Soft Computing*, 239–244. Anaheim CA: ACTA Press.

Periñán-Pascual, Carlos & Arcas Túnez, Francisco. 2006. Reusing computer-oriented lexica as foreign-language electronic dictionaries. *Anglogermánica Online* 4: 69–93.

Periñán-Pascual, Carlos & Arcas Túnez, Francisco. 2007. Cognitive modules of an NLP knowledge base for language understanding. *Procesamiento del Lenguaje Natural* 39: 197–204.

Periñán-Pascual, Carlos & Arcas Túnez, Francisco. 2010a. Ontological commitments in FunGramKB. *Procesamiento del Lenguaje Natural* 44: 27–34.

Periñán-Pascual, Carlos & Arcas Túnez, Francisco. 2010b. The Architecture of FunGramKB. In *Proceedings of the Seventh International Conference on Language Resources and Evaluation*, 2667–2674. Malta, ELRA.

Periñán-Pascual, Carlos & Mairal Usón, Ricardo. 2009. Bringing Role and Reference Grammar to natural language understanding *Procesamiento del Lenguaje Natural* 43: 265–273.

Periñán-Pascual, Carlos & Mairal Usón, Ricardo. 2010. La gramática de COREL: Un lenguaje de representación conceptual. *Onomázein* 21: 11–45.

Periñán-Pascual, Carlos & Mairal Usón, Ricardo. 2012. La dimensión computacional de la Gramática del Papel y la Referencia: La estructura lógica conceptual y su aplicación en el procesamiento del lenguaje natural. In *El funcionalismo en la teoría lingüística. La Gramática del Papel y la Referencia. Introducción, avances y aplicaciones,* Ricardo Mairal Usón, Lilián Guerrero & Carlos González (eds), 333–348. Madrid: Akal.

Periñán-Pascual, Carlos & Mairal Usón, Ricardo. In preparation. Cultural distinctiveness in a knowledge engineering project. Ms.

Ruiz de Mendoza, Francisco José. 1996. Semantic networks in conceptual structure. *Epos. Revista de Filología* XII: 339–356.

Ruiz de Mendoza, Francisco José. 2007. High-level cognitive models: In search of a unified framework for inferential and grammatical behavior. In *Perspectives on Metonymy,* Krzysztof Kosecki (ed.), 11–30. Frankfurt: Peter Lang.

Ruiz de Mendoza, Francisco José. 2011. Metonymy and cognitive operations. In *Defining Metonymy in Cognitive Linguistics. Towards a Consensus View* [Human Cognitive Processing 28], Reka Benczes, Antonio Barcelona & Francisco José Ruiz de Mendoza (eds), 103–123. Amsterdam: John Benjamins.

Ruiz de Mendoza, Francisco José. 2013. Meaning construction, meaning interpretation and formal expression in the Lexical Constructional Model. In *Linking Constructions into Functional Linguistics: The Role of Constructions in a Functional Grammar* [Studies in Language Companion Series 145], Brian Nolan & Elke Diedrichsen (eds), 231–270. Amsterdam: John Benjamins.

Ruiz de Mendoza, Francisco José & Baicchi, Annalisa. 2007. Illocutionary constructions: Cognitive motivation and linguistic realization. In *Explorations in Pragmatics: Linguistic, Cognitive, and Intercultural Aspects,* Istvan Kecskes & Laurence Horn (eds), 95–128. Berlin: Mouton de Gruyter.

Ruiz de Mendoza, Francisco José & Luzondo Oyón, Alba. In preparation. Figurative and non-figurative motion in the expression of result in English. Ms.

Ruiz de Mendoza, Francisco José & Mairal Usón, Ricardo. 2008. Levels of description and constraining factors in meaning construction: An introduction to the Lexical Constructional Model. *Folia Linguistica* 42(2): 355–400.

Ruiz de Mendoza, Francisco José & Mairal Usón, Ricardo. 2011. Constraints on syntactic alternation: Lexical-constructional subsumption in the Lexical-Constructional Model. In *Morphosyntactic Alternations in English,* Pilar Guerrero Medino (ed.), 62–82. London: Equinox.

Ruiz de Mendoza, Francisco José & Pérez Hernández, Lorena. 2003. Cognitive operations and pragmatic implication. In *Metonymy and Pragmatic Inferencing,* Klaus-Uwe Panther & Linda Thornburg (eds), 23–50. Amsterdam: John Benjamins.

Rumelhart, David E. 1975. Notes on a schema for stories. In *Representation and Understanding: Studies on Cognitive Science,* Daniel Gureasko Bobrow & Allan M. Collins (eds). New York NY: Academic Press.

Ruppenhofer, Josef, Ellsworth, Michael, Petruck, Miriam R.L., Johnson, Christopher R. & Scheffczyk, Jan. 2010. FrameNet II: Extended theory and practice. Technical Report, International Computer Science Institute, Berkeley. <http://framenet.icsi.berkeley.edu/>

Sanford, Anthony J. & Garrod, Simon C. 1981. *Understanding Written Language.* Chichester: John Wiley & Sons.

Schank, Roger C. & Abelson, Robert P. 1977. *Scripts, Plans, Goals, and Understanding*. Hillsdale NJ: Lawrence Erlbaum Associates.

Van Dijk, Teun A. & Kintsch, Walter. 1983. *Strategies of Discourse Comprehension*. New York NY: Academic Press.

Veale, Tony. 2006. Computability as a test on linguistic theories. In *Cognitive Linguistics. Current Applications and Future Perspectives,* Gitte Kristiansen, Michel, Achard, René Dirven & Francisco José Ruiz de Mendoza (eds),461–484. Berlin: Mouton De Gruyter.

Index

Symbols
(West) Germanic 27

A
Abau 30, 31, 37
actantial structure 297, 298, 300, 302, 303, 307, 309
actions 145, 152, 154, 155, 167, 189, 299, 302, 311, 320, 343, 367, 370–373
actor 5, 82–86, 97, 99, 146, 147, 153, 158, 159, 169, 170, 211, 307, 320, 330, 351, 373
actor-undergoer hierarchy 83, 86, 146, 147, 169, 351
adequacy 1, 3, 6, 7, 10, 81, 143–145, 159, 162, 168, 274, 299, 352, 367
Afrikaans 23, 27–29, 36
agent architecture 145
agent-embedded speech acts 143, 144, 159
agent's internal beliefs, desires, and intentions 7, 143, 145
agents plans 160
Aktionsart 107, 169, 174, 176, 180, 210, 211, 214, 235, 240, 246, 297, 306, 309, 323, 324, 340, 350, 354, 359
algorithmic typology 16, 38
Ama 31, 32
Arabic 4, 11, 60, 81, 104, 151, 163, 170, 171, 191
areal information 7, 13, 15, 21, 23–26, 34
Argumental construction 176
argument structure 51, 89, 142, 162, 190, 204, 210, 212, 300, 301, 321, 323, 325, 327, 348, 350, 355, 357, 365, 371
argument structure constructions 204, 210, 212, 371
ARTEMIS 81, 165, 166, 171, 176–183, 187–189
aspect 30, 31, 43, 70, 80, 105, 110, 115, 169, 212, 268, 273, 356
attribute value matrix 90
Austronesian 28–30, 32
auxiliary 48, 106, 107, 109, 111–116, 127, 128, 142
avatars 2, 145
AVM 90, 91, 94, 173, 180, 189

B
Basic concept 205, 207, 215, 216, 220, 238–240, 242–244, 280, 285, 348
BDI states 7, 143
Belief, Desire and Intention (BDI) state 154
beliefs 7, 42, 143, 145, 160, 161, 198
Bigram 261, 262
bracket structure 7, 105–109, 112, 115

C
candidate term 266
case marking 18, 27, 30, 32, 33
categorization 14, 36, 71, 72, 172, 230, 278, 295, 299
Chimbu 30
Cifuentes-Férez 352, 354, 356, 357, 359, 365
Clause 1, 4, 5, 7, 8, 18, 33, 80, 81, 85, 86, 91, 97, 99, 105–110, 114, 115, 129, 130, 140, 141, 149, 153, 158, 160, 168, 169, 171, 176, 182, 184, 185, 187
CLS constructor 81, 165, 166, 177
cognicon 10, 152, 167, 176, 203, 204, 216, 217, 221, 222, 234, 252, 293, 343, 367, 369, 374, 375, 377, 378, 383, 386
commonsense knowledge 273, 275, 276, 279, 292
complex scripts 367, 374, 382
composite scripts 367, 374, 386
computational adequacy 1, 3, 7, 81, 144, 159
computational framework 7, 143, 149
computational framework for agents 149
Computational resource 198
computation of form and function 150
computation of meaning 150
Concept 1, 3, 4, 6–8, 41, 43–46, 54, 63, 68, 72, 74, 84, 91, 141, 142, 144, 157, 165, 176, 181, 187, 189, 203–207, 209, 211, 214–216, 220–222, 225, 227, 228, 233, 234, 237–246, 251, 263, 265, 272–276, 279, 280, 282, 284–287, 289, 291–294, 310, 335, 339–341, 344–351, 353–357, 359, 362–364, 371
concept-semantics-syntax interfaces 144
conceptual heterogeneity 275
conceptualisation 252, 253
Conceptual level 9, 152, 161, 167, 204, 215, 227, 234, 241, 244, 246, 274, 293, 339, 340, 343, 359, 363
conceptual mapping 369
conceptual modeling 275, 276, 279, 288
conceptual network 161, 282–284
Conceptual participant 243, 245, 340, 358
conceptual relation 282
Conceptual Representation Language (COREL) 174, 203, 234, 263, 273, 274, 347, 375
conceptual structure 9, 283, 297, 371, 389
constituent projection 107, 113–115
constraint 90, 91, 109, 157, 179–182, 186

construct 149, 152, 167, 170, 177, 205, 234, 235, 237, 317, 343, 351
Construction 1, 2, 6–8, 10, 11, 28, 56, 60, 65, 70, 74, 83, 84, 87, 94, 97–104, 106, 107, 109, 111–114, 132–140, 142, 144, 146–150, 152, 153, 156–163, 171–174, 176, 177, 180, 182–185, 188, 190, 191, 196, 198, 199, 202, 210, 212, 214, 229–231, 233, 244, 245, 251, 252, 256, 311, 313–315, 319, 322, 328, 329, 333–336, 340, 345, 351, 355, 357, 360–368, 370, 371, 388, 389
Constructional merger 182, 184–186
constructional schema 91, 94, 97, 99, 100, 102, 107, 146, 150, 173, 174, 180, 183, 184, 189
construction body 99, 100, 148, 149, 158
Construction Grammar 162, 190, 191, 229, 365
construction repository 94, 100, 102, 103, 148, 150, 157
constructions 2, 6, 9–11, 63, 64, 68, 80, 83–85, 96, 97, 99, 103, 104, 107, 110, 115, 131, 140–144, 146–149, 152, 153, 161–163, 171–175, 177, 182, 184–186, 188–190, 204, 210–212, 214, 230, 231, 235, 242, 246, 311, 329, 331, 333–335, 339–341, 351, 353, 359, 364, 365, 367, 371, 372, 387–389
Constructions as grammatical objects 2, 104, 144, 146–149, 161–163
Constructivism 174, 175
conversational actors 145, 155
conversational agents 2, 7, 143–146, 149, 152–155, 157–161
Conversational Partner Model 153, 155
conversational software agents 143, 162
conversation tracking 145
Core 22, 34, 83, 106–108, 110–115, 140, 144, 167–169, 171, 173, 176, 180, 182–185, 187, 189, 193, 194, 198–200, 207–212, 222–225, 235, 252, 253, 256, 258, 263, 265, 268, 273, 275–278, 280, 285, 286, 289, 292, 343, 344, 347, 350–352, 355
Core FE 199, 200, 212, 222–225
COREL 174, 176, 189, 191, 203, 215, 216, 225, 227, 231, 234, 238, 247, 263, 269, 273, 274, 279, 283, 285, 292–294, 347, 349, 357, 366, 367, 375–377, 379, 380, 386, 389
core ontology 167, 252, 253, 256, 258, 263, 265, 268, 273, 275–278, 280, 285, 286, 289, 292, 343, 344
corpus 8, 10, 33, 36, 43, 184, 186, 199–202, 207–210, 212, 227–230, 239, 245, 246, 251–254, 256–261, 266–269, 301, 308, 309, 316, 317, 334, 336, 341, 351, 352, 355, 360, 364–366, 387
corpus linguistics 252, 268, 269, 336
coverage 85, 141, 219, 266, 275
cultural norms 145, 160

D
database 9, 14, 21, 25, 26, 33, 38, 41, 72, 73, 81, 101, 166, 182, 198, 216, 226, 227, 254, 255, 271–274, 297, 299, 302, 311, 335, 368
data reduction 14, 18, 19, 38
dative shift 87
Deaf Sign Language 145
deep semantic representation 271, 273, 274, 283, 285, 288, 291
Deep semantics 8, 198, 203, 231, 233, 235, 238, 246, 314, 317, 319, 333, 340, 347, 365
defeasible predications 280
degree of synthesis 16, 30
descriptive adequacy 367
dialogue management 146, 153, 154, 161, 162
Dialogue Manager 153, 154
Diedrichsen 4, 7, 11, 84, 91, 103, 105–107, 109, 112, 113, 141, 142, 144, 146, 147, 162, 163, 190, 230, 231, 387, 389
Differentia 206, 225, 349
discourse interaction 145, 155
discourse level 103, 352, 371
discourse representation theory 95
ditransitive 83–85, 87, 88, 90, 91, 96, 103, 104, 150, 163, 172
ditransitive construction 83, 87, 150
domains 2, 4, 6, 9, 10, 15, 18, 36, 231, 235, 240, 246, 253, 297–301, 303, 308, 309, 318, 320, 351, 368, 370
domain-specific corpora 252
domain-specific ontology 9, 252, 271
dot object 282
DRT See discourse representation theory

E
Earley's algorithm 181
East Papuan 30
EcoLexicon 8, 9, 271–279, 282–294, 297, 300, 301
emotion 145, 153, 154, 156, 159, 162, 224, 301
Encyclopedic meaning 222
English 4, 7–9, 11, 17–19, 40, 49, 65, 68, 75, 76, 79, 80, 82–84, 87, 94, 95, 97, 99, 103, 104, 114, 141, 151, 155, 157, 163, 166, 167, 170, 171, 191, 197, 199, 202, 208–210, 214–216, 226, 227, 229–231, 234, 235, 237, 239–247, 251, 253, 255, 263, 269, 272, 275, 297, 301, 302, 309–311, 314–316, 334, 335, 339–342, 344, 345, 347, 348, 351–354, 356–361, 364–366, 389
environmental event 282, 284, 293
environment information 145
Evoke 41, 208, 209, 215
explanatory adequacy 81, 144, 274
Explanatory Combinatorial Lexicology 298
external model of the agent 7, 143, 145
Extra-thematic FEs 199, 212, 223

F
feature 7, 15, 18, 21–24, 26–35, 47, 48, 50, 55, 56, 58, 63, 64, 72, 84, 87, 89–91, 93, 94, 100, 103, 105, 110, 111, 116–130, 178, 180, 181, 187, 198, 206, 222, 225, 272, 278, 330, 333, 349, 364, 373, 374, 376, 377
feature extraction 34

feature rings 15, 23, 27, 29, 31, 34
focus 8, 16, 20, 22, 24, 26, 37, 81, 85, 90, 95–97, 99–103, 109, 115, 172, 188, 202, 204, 214, 217, 235, 275, 280, 315, 316, 318, 336, 347, 359
Formalism 54, 71, 72, 74, 323, 324
Frame 5, 8–10, 42, 108, 129, 176, 198–200, 207–213, 215–229, 231, 233, 235–237, 239–247, 271, 298, 300, 302, 303, 305, 310, 339, 347, 348, 351, 354, 368–370, 387
FrameNet 8, 42, 75, 197, 198, 228–231, 299, 302, 310, 368, 387, 389
frames 8, 42, 197–202, 205, 207, 210, 212, 213, 215–219, 222–224, 226, 227, 229, 234, 239, 299, 310, 320, 368, 369, 387
Frame Element (FEs) 199
Frame Semantics 10, 42, 198, 199, 228, 229, 231, 298, 300, 310, 368, 387
frame structure 370
Frame-to-frame relations 200, 207, 217–219
functional domain 15, 33
Functional Grammar 3, 5, 6, 8, 71, 143, 229, 233, 300, 310, 311, 320, 335, 336, 339, 387, 389
FunGramKB 8–10, 81, 104, 144, 147, 149, 151, 152, 157, 162, 163, 166, 167, 172–177, 179–181, 184, 187, 189, 191, 197, 198, 202–217, 219–231, 233–238, 240–242, 246, 247, 251–253, 255, 256, 263–265, 268, 269, 271, 273–280, 284–287, 289–295, 339, 344, 345, 352, 365–367, 369, 374–378, 386, 388
FunGramKB core ontology 273, 275–278, 285, 286, 289, 292
FunGramKB Suite 166, 174, 181, 233, 247, 252, 256, 269

G
Gender 30, 56, 64, 70, 105, 106, 111, 116–129, 210, 235, 350
Generalised Semantic Roles 107
general logical structure 88
Generative Lexicon 191, 295, 298, 311, 320–322, 324, 336
German 7, 28, 36, 45, 103, 105–110, 112–115, 130, 131, 140–142, 166, 202, 226, 227, 235, 263, 272, 309, 342
gesture 161
GLS 88, 91, 94
goals 20, 42, 145, 160, 199, 221, 228, 390
Grammar Development Environment 181
grammar-lexicon-construction continuum 144, 152, 158
Grammatical level 152, 167, 204, 234, 342, 343, 346, 351, 352
grammatical object 97, 99, 148–150
Grammaticon 152, 167, 173, 175, 203, 204, 210–212, 216, 234, 242, 244, 252, 343, 351, 352, 359, 363, 364, 375
granularity 144, 159, 224, 265, 275
graph 37, 90, 186, 378, 383
graphical user interface 7, 105, 110, 130, 140, 141
guest scripts 374, 382

H
hierarchical rearrangement 276, 278, 285
high-level ICMs 370
high-level non-situational models 369, 371
high-level situational models 369, 371
host scripts 374
Hungarian 17, 18
Huon-Finisterre 29

I
Idealized Cognitive Models (ICMs) 10, 368
illocutionary constructions 204, 371, 389
illocutionary force 109, 155–157, 161, 169
Indo-European 26, 27
Inference 166, 218, 219, 221, 222, 291, 344, 345
information structure 7, 79, 84, 88, 91, 95, 97, 100, 103–106, 150
inheritance 22, 87–91, 93, 94, 103, 173, 180, 189, 206, 217–222, 278, 280, 282, 321, 344
Inheritance 22, 87–91, 93, 94, 103, 173, 180, 189, 206, 217–222, 278, 280, 282, 321, 344
inheritance network 87–91, 93, 94, 173
instrumental scripts 367, 373
intelligent conversational agents (ICA) 144, 159
intelligent conversational agents paradigm 7, 143, 144, 159
interfaces 1–3, 6, 21, 144, 151, 335
Interlingua 2, 8, 144, 151, 165, 171, 227, 234, 238, 263
internal model of the agent 7, 143, 145
Internet 2, 145
intransitive 88, 89, 109, 110, 112, 115, 172, 184, 244, 348, 351, 355
IS-A relation 220, 221
IS-A taxonomy 344

J
Java 7, 10, 22, 105, 110, 130, 131, 141, 142, 162, 178

K
Karkar-Yuri 31, 32
Knowledge acquisition strategies 9, 313
Knowledge base 8, 9, 81, 151, 163, 165–167, 171, 175, 181, 189–191, 198, 202, 204, 213, 215, 216, 227, 228, 230, 231, 233–236, 238, 239, 246, 251–253, 256, 268, 269, 271, 275, 294, 295, 298, 339–343, 346, 347, 350, 352, 364, 365, 367, 373, 375, 386, 388
knowledge engineering 2, 258, 294, 334–336, 369, 372, 375, 377, 389
knowledge organization 298
Knowledge representation 8, 163, 190, 197, 198, 228, 233, 274, 293, 295, 309
Koine Greek 17–19

L
Labrou and Finin 155, 156
language genealogy/language hierarchy
Layered Structure of the Clause 1, 80, 81, 86, 110, 115, 129, 141, 168
LCM Lexical templates 314, 323

legal ontologies 252
Levin 165, 174, 190, 191, 212, 230, 244, 246, 330, 335, 341, 355–357, 359, 361–363, 365, 387
Lexematic Theory 300
Lexical Constructional Model (LCM) 10, 167, 343, 351, 368
lexical domain 9, 18, 88, 297, 300–303, 329
lexical entry 62, 86, 94, 105, 116–129, 160, 174, 177, 180, 181, 200, 213, 214, 219, 241, 305, 308, 346
Lexical Grammar Model 297, 298, 300
Lexicalization patterns 9, 226, 311, 339–341, 352, 353, 364, 366
Lexical level 8, 43, 152, 166, 204, 206, 210, 233–235, 246, 342, 343, 347, 350, 358, 375
lexical template 188, 211, 214, 235, 236, 297, 324–326, 328–331, 333, 350
Lexical units 8, 9, 40–44, 47, 50, 57, 60, 68, 69, 71, 74, 152, 166, 171, 172, 174, 175, 198, 199, 212, 233–235, 238, 239, 242, 255, 256, 258, 261, 262, 266, 303, 308, 339, 340, 343–347, 349–351, 354, 356–359, 361, 363
Lexicography 42, 45, 75, 228, 229, 258, 268, 269, 294, 307, 309–311, 336, 387
Lexicology 42, 298, 336
lexicon 1–3, 5–8, 40, 41, 43–45, 47, 48, 60, 61, 65, 66, 68, 69, 73, 74, 79, 81, 86–89, 91, 97, 99–103, 105, 110, 115, 116, 119, 122, 126–128, 130, 140, 141, 144, 148–153, 158–160, 163, 165–167, 169, 170, 173–175, 177, 180, 181, 184, 189–191, 204, 210, 211, 213, 214, 216, 227, 229, 230, 234, 235, 237, 239–244, 246, 252, 256, 258, 263, 269, 295, 298, 300, 301, 303, 309–311, 320–322, 324, 335, 336, 340, 343, 350, 351, 354, 359, 364–366, 375, 387, 388
linguistic complexity 37, 144
Linguistic knowledge 9, 103, 107, 160, 182, 204, 216, 228, 234, 239, 339, 343, 346, 364
linguistic typology 14, 16, 36–38
linking algorithm 5–7, 79, 80, 84–87, 99–103, 146, 151, 152, 167, 168, 177, 204, 234
linking system 1, 7, 105, 143, 145, 151, 152, 158–160
logical structure 4, 8, 81, 83, 86, 88, 99–103, 105, 107, 116–129, 146, 150, 151, 157, 165, 166, 168–171, 175, 176, 189, 211, 354
low-level non-situational models 369, 371
low-level situational models 367, 369, 371, 372, 386

M
machine translation 2, 8, 11, 81, 104, 141, 144, 151, 163, 166, 171, 191, 197, 202, 251, 342
macro areas 21, 23–25, 27
macrorole 83, 85–87, 89, 180, 187, 240, 307, 351
Mangga Buang 32, 33, 37
Manner of motion verb 362
manual filtering 257, 258, 261, 264, 266
Maori 17, 18
massive open distributed systems 145
Meaning Postulate (MP) 347
Meronymic relations 9, 313
Metaconcept 205, 221, 224, 225, 238, 239, 242, 248, 263, 347, 348
metonymic processes 369
MicroKnowing 221, 222, 284
mirror concept 263
modelling of human language in software 143, 144, 159
Multilingualism 8, 197, 207, 226
multi-word expressions 7, 39–41, 43, 44
Murtagh 4, 10, 11, 81, 104, 145, 162

N
narrow focus 95, 96, 99–101
natural language definition 282, 285
Natural Language Processing (NLP) 8, 10, 41, 66, 165, 197, 342, 368
Natural Semantic Metalanguage 300, 320
negation 16, 19, 29–33, 37, 317, 377
nesting 261, 262
NLP 5, 8, 10, 41, 66, 163, 165–167, 171, 175, 176, 179, 181, 189, 191, 197, 198, 202, 206, 213, 218, 219, 221, 223, 226–228, 230, 231, 246, 293, 295, 342, 352, 365, 368, 375, 388
Nolan 1, 3, 4, 7, 10, 11, 79, 81, 82, 91, 94, 97, 99, 103–105, 107, 142–144, 146–148, 151, 163, 171, 190, 191, 230, 231, 387, 389
Non-linguistic knowledge 9, 216, 234, 339, 343, 346, 364
non-macrorole 83
non-monotonic inheritance 180, 189, 278, 280
non-operational cognitive models 369, 370
Nucleus 58–60, 65–68, 70, 72, 74, 107, 110–115, 140, 168–170, 176, 183, 186, 252

O
onomasticon 152, 167, 176, 179, 203, 204, 216, 234, 252, 293, 343, 375, 377
Ontological constructs 314, 317, 325, 332, 333
ontological heterogeneities 273
ontological semantics modelling 143
Ontology 8, 9, 94, 152, 157, 158, 165, 167, 172, 173, 176, 179, 181, 190, 203–205, 207, 208, 215, 216, 220–222, 225, 227, 228, 230, 233–235, 237–240, 243, 246, 252, 253, 256–258, 263, 265, 268, 269, 271–280, 282, 285, 286, 289, 292–295, 313–319, 325, 332–336, 339–341, 343–351, 354, 356, 357, 360–362, 364, 375, 376
ontology alignment 293
Ontology building 9, 269, 313, 317, 325
Ontology concepts 316
ontology coordination 273
Ontology learning 334, 336
ontology linking 271
ontology reconciliation 273, 276, 279, 294
operational cognitive models 369, 370
operator projection 111, 113, 115

operators 91, 101, 102, 105, 110, 111, 115, 157, 169, 176, 187, 188, 292, 376, 377
overlapping concept 286

P
Papua New Guinea 28, 29, 37
Papuan Tip 30
parallel texts 13–17, 19, 33, 34, 36
parser 7, 41, 43, 77, 80, 81, 105, 106, 110, 114–116, 119, 122, 126–128, 130, 131, 140, 141, 170, 181, 182, 186, 213
passive 40, 52, 106, 110, 114, 115, 212, 332
Path verbs 341, 354
perfect 28, 105, 106, 112–115, 142, 202, 239, 243, 246
performative 155, 157, 158
Performative verbs 155
Peripheral FEs 199, 208, 225
periphrastic construction 106, 107, 113
personality 145, 153, 154, 159, 162
personality model 154
personal scripts 373
perspective 3–6, 8, 13, 22, 36, 37, 41, 43, 79, 86, 89, 104, 148, 149, 163, 208, 217, 275, 276, 299, 309
Phraseology 72, 74
polysemy 11, 163, 198, 226, 228, 282, 295, 317, 321, 322, 333, 336
population 208, 234, 258, 268
pragmatic heterogeneity 274
PreCore slot 106, 110–114, 140, 141, 168
predications 82, 205, 222, 237, 265, 274, 280, 289, 293, 334, 343, 349, 352, 376–383, 385
prefixation 18, 27–31
prepositional phrase 112, 114, 302, 322, 328, 330, 331, 359
Principle of Argumental Expansion 185
Principle of Constructional Anchorage 185
Principle of Constructional Base Restriction 185
Principle of Constructional Unicity 185
procedural knowledge 152, 167, 203, 222, 343, 367, 374, 375, 378, 379, 386
Projectionism 174
PSA selection rules 107
pseudo-code 79, 80, 86, 87, 100, 101
psychological adequacy 145, 299

Q
Qualia structures 316, 320, 323, 324, 335
quantity operators 292

R
recontextualization 278, 279, 293
repository 9, 94, 100, 102, 103, 148, 150, 157, 162, 166, 181, 190, 253, 256, 297, 315, 368
resultative construction 176, 177, 202, 212, 340, 351, 362–364, 371
Role and Reference Grammar (RRG). 105, 143
RRG 1, 4–8, 11, 79–82, 84–87, 89–91, 97, 99, 102–108, 110–114, 130, 131, 140–155, 157–159, 161–163, 166–168, 170, 171, 175, 176, 180, 186–190, 204, 205, 211, 231, 234, 238, 307, 320, 321, 323, 337, 343, 350–352, 359

S
Salem 3, 4, 11, 81, 104, 144, 151, 163, 171, 191
Satellite 9, 167, 206, 226, 252, 253, 255–257, 263, 265, 266, 268, 271–273, 293, 339–341, 343, 349, 352, 353, 355, 360
Satellite-framed language 9, 339, 341, 352, 360
satellite ontology 9, 253, 257, 263, 265, 271–273, 293
scientific writing 299
scripts 9, 10, 152, 167, 176, 222, 293, 347, 367–369, 372–375, 379, 382, 386, 387, 390
Searle 156, 163
Selectional preferences 205, 213, 225, 228, 234, 237, 240, 241, 340, 345, 348, 349, 358
Semantic knowledge 111, 152, 167, 197, 206, 216, 220–222, 228, 231, 311, 343, 344
semantic primitive 300
Semantic type 200
Sentence 4, 5, 7, 40, 43, 44, 48–50, 56, 67–70, 83, 84, 87, 95–97, 99, 100, 104–108, 110–115, 129, 132–142, 146, 151, 153, 158, 169–172, 174, 176, 177, 182, 186, 190, 200, 240, 266, 298, 300, 301, 315, 327, 329, 330
Sepik 30, 31
Shallow semantics 8, 233, 235, 239
signature 91, 94, 97, 98, 100, 102, 109, 148, 149, 153, 157–159
simple scripts 367, 373, 374, 379
Siroi 33
situational scripts 373
Social Context Model 155
Social interactions 160
social relationship 145, 155
software agent 7, 145, 158
software specifications 144
Spanish 4, 9, 39–42, 49, 51–53, 57, 58, 60–64, 67, 68, 74, 141, 166, 167, 189, 197, 202, 206, 209, 210, 215, 216, 226, 227, 231, 233–235, 246, 251, 255, 263, 264, 272, 293, 295, 298, 309, 311, 316, 334, 339–342, 344, 347, 348, 351–360, 363–365, 367
specialised ontologies 8, 251
specialized communication 298
specialized knowledge 9, 271–273, 279, 293, 294, 297, 298, 308
speech acts 1, 7, 8, 143–145, 149, 152, 153, 155, 156, 158–163
stepwise lexical decomposition 298, 310
strict predications 385
Subordinate concept 206, 280, 285, 286, 344
suffixation 18, 27–31
sunburst visualization 6, 13, 15, 22, 30
Superordinate concept 206, 222, 282, 286
surface semantic representation 274
Swahili 18
syntactic heterogeneity 274

T
Talmy 36, 103, 303, 311, 341, 352–355, 357, 359, 360, 364, 366
Taxonomic relations 314

Taxonomy 9, 219, 220, 234, 252, 318, 339, 344–346, 349, 359
Tepehuan Norte 18
term extractor 251, 252, 255, 263, 264, 268, 269
term-frequency inverse document frequency (TF-IDF) 257
Terminal concept 176, 205, 225, 240, 241, 291, 293
terminological heterogeneity 274, 275
terminological knowledge base 298
terminology 73, 252, 256, 258, 260, 264, 268, 269, 294, 298, 299, 309, 310, 313, 315, 317, 318, 334–336, 340, 341, 359, 360
terminology extraction 252, 315
text collection 252, 253
Thematic-frame mapping 233, 235–237, 239–243, 245, 246
Thematic Frame (TF) 347
thematic relation 90, 91, 94
Thematic role 176, 237, 238, 243, 307, 340, 351
ThinkMap 274, 282, 284
three-place predicates 7, 79, 82–85, 87, 95, 97, 99, 102–104
token 7, 17, 27, 29, 31, 91, 97, 99, 100, 105, 110, 130, 178, 208, 218, 256, 257
topic 4, 8, 37, 54, 59, 100–103, 108, 109, 214, 253, 254, 326
transitive 52, 85, 86, 88, 90, 91, 110–112, 114, 115, 130, 172, 177, 182, 184, 185, 207, 214, 220, 221, 244, 319, 348, 351, 355, 361
translation 2, 8, 10, 11, 17, 40, 43, 68, 74, 80, 81, 104, 112, 114, 131, 141, 144, 151, 163, 166, 171, 191, 197, 202, 215, 235, 251, 258, 268, 274, 282, 283, 289–292, 342, 351, 379
trigram 261, 262
troponymy 9, 297, 303, 309
turn taking 105, 106, 109, 153, 161
typological adequacy 3, 6, 168, 352

U
undergoer 5, 7, 79, 80, 82–87, 89, 91, 95, 97, 103, 146, 147, 169, 170, 211, 223, 307, 320, 351
UniArab 11, 81, 104, 151, 152, 163, 170, 171, 342, 366
Unification grammar 181
unigram 261, 262
universals 13, 16, 36, 337
user interaction 24

V
Valence pattern 212
Van Valin 4, 6, 11, 79, 80, 82–91, 95, 96, 99, 101, 103–105, 107, 109, 141, 142, 146, 147, 152, 163, 166, 168–171, 191, 204, 211, 231, 234, 247, 297, 298, 300, 306, 307, 311, 320, 322, 337, 343, 350, 351, 354, 358, 366
Variable 7, 17, 18, 23, 79, 82, 84, 87–89, 91, 94, 95, 97, 99, 100, 103, 180, 188, 211, 240, 241, 243, 244
variable undergoer linking 7, 79, 82, 84, 87, 89, 91, 95, 97, 103
Verbal patterns 9, 313, 314, 316, 319, 323, 324, 327, 332, 333, 336
Verb-framed language 9, 339, 341, 360
Verbs of classification 316
visual analytics 6, 13, 14, 16, 19–24, 35, 37
visualization 6, 13, 15, 16, 19–31, 33–38, 274
visual variables 15, 20, 23, 34
volcanology 9, 297, 299, 301–303, 306–309

W
workspace 99, 109, 148–150, 157–160
world map 22–29, 31, 33, 35

X
Xhosa 28
XML-based metadata 151

Y
Yau 33

Z
Zoque (Francisco León) 18
Zulu 17, 18, 28